# Preparing Students From the Academic World to Career Paths:
## A Comprehensive Guide

Cassandra Sligh Conway
*South Carolina State University, USA*

Andy Jiahao Liu
*University of Arizona, USA*

A volume in the Advances in Higher Education and Professional Development (AHEPD) Book Series

Published in the United States of America by
IGI Global
Information Science Reference (an imprint of IGI Global)
701 E. Chocolate Avenue
Hershey PA, USA 17033
Tel: 717-533-8845
Fax: 717-533-8661
E-mail: cust@igi-global.com
Web site: http://www.igi-global.com

Copyright © 2024 by IGI Global. All rights reserved. No part of this publication may be reproduced, stored or distributed in any form or by any means, electronic or mechanical, including photocopying, without written permission from the publisher. Product or company names used in this set are for identification purposes only. Inclusion of the names of the products or companies does not indicate a claim of ownership by IGI Global of the trademark or registered trademark.

       Library of Congress Cataloging-in-Publication Data

CIP Pending

Preparing Students From the Academic World to Career Paths
Cassandra Sligh Conway, Andy Jiahao Liu
Information Science Reference 2024

ISBN: 978-1-7998-7999-2
eISBN: 978-1-6684-8317-6

This book is published in the IGI Global book series Advances in Higher Education and Professional Development (AHEPD) (ISSN: 2327-6983; eISSN: 2327-6991)

British Cataloguing in Publication Data
A Cataloguing in Publication record for this book is available from the British Library.

All work contributed to this book is new, previously-unpublished material. The views expressed in this book are those of the authors, but not necessarily of the publisher.

For electronic access to this publication, please contact: eresources@igi-global.com.

# Advances in Higher Education and Professional Development (AHEPD) Book Series

Jared Keengwe
University of North Dakota, USA

ISSN:2327-6983
EISSN:2327-6991

## Mission

As world economies continue to shift and change in response to global financial situations, job markets have begun to demand a more highly-skilled workforce. In many industries a college degree is the minimum requirement and further educational development is expected to advance. With these current trends in mind, the **Advances in Higher Education & Professional Development (AHEPD) Book Series** provides an outlet for researchers and academics to publish their research in these areas and to distribute these works to practitioners and other researchers.

**AHEPD** encompasses all research dealing with higher education pedagogy, development, and curriculum design, as well as all areas of professional development, regardless of focus.

## Coverage

- Adult Education
- Assessment in Higher Education
- Career Training
- Coaching and Mentoring
- Continuing Professional Development
- Governance in Higher Education
- Higher Education Policy
- Pedagogy of Teaching Higher Education
- Vocational Education

> IGI Global is currently accepting manuscripts for publication within this series. To submit a proposal for a volume in this series, please contact our Acquisition Editors at Acquisitions@igi-global.com or visit: http://www.igi-global.com/publish/.

The Advances in Higher Education and Professional Development (AHEPD) Book Series (ISSN 2327-6983) is published by IGI Global, 701 E. Chocolate Avenue, Hershey, PA 17033-1240, USA, www.igi-global.com. This series is composed of titles available for purchase individually; each title is edited to be contextually exclusive from any other title within the series. For pricing and ordering information please visit http://www.igi-global.com/book-series/advances-higher-education-professional-development/73681. Postmaster: Send all address changes to above address. Copyright © 2024 IGI Global. All rights, including translation in other languages reserved by the publisher. No part of this series may be reproduced or used in any form or by any means – graphics, electronic, or mechanical, including photocopying, recording, taping, or information and retrieval systems – without written permission from the publisher, except for non commercial, educational use, including classroom teaching purposes. The views expressed in this series are those of the authors, but not necessarily of IGI Global.

# Titles in this Series

*For a list of additional titles in this series, please visit: http://www.igi-global.com/book-series/advances-higher-education-professional-development/73681*

*Incorporating the Human Element in Online Teaching and Learning*
Laura E. Gray (South College, USA) and Shernette D. Dunn (Florida Atlantic University, USA)
Information Science Reference • copyright 2024 • 346pp • H/C (ISBN: 9798369341315) • US $255.00 (our price)

*Applications of Service Learning in Higher Education*
Sandy White Watson (University of Louisiana at Monroe, USA)
Information Science Reference • copyright 2024 • 341pp • H/C (ISBN: 9798369321331) • US $235.00 (our price)

*Global Perspectives on Micro-Learning and Micro-Credentials in Higher Education*
Kizito Omona (Uganda Martyrs University, Uganda) and Modest Kayi O'dama (Uganda Martyrs University, Uganda)
Information Science Reference • copyright 2024 • 360pp • H/C (ISBN: 9798369303436) • US $240.00 (our price)

*Prioritizing Skills Development for Student Employability*
Bryan Christiansen (Southern New Hampshire University, USA) and Angela M. Even (Purdue University, USA)
Information Science Reference • copyright 2024 • 340pp • H/C (ISBN: 9798369335710) • US $245.00 (our price)

*Promoting Intercultural Agility and Leadership Development at Home and Abroad for First-Year Students*
Jon Stauff (South Dakota State University, USA) and Jill E. Blondin (Virginia Commonwealth University, USA)
Information Science Reference • copyright 2024 • 292pp • H/C (ISBN: 9781668488324) • US $245.00 (our price)

*Advancing Student Employability Through Higher Education*
Bryan Christiansen (Southern New Hampshire University, USA) and Angela M. Even (Purdue University, USA)
Information Science Reference • copyright 2024 • 429pp • H/C (ISBN: 9798369305171) • US $215.00 (our price)

*Perspectives on Transforming Higher Education and the LGBTQIA Student Experience*
Andrew Herridge (The University of Southern Mississippi, USA) and Kaity Prieto (The University of Southern Mississippi, USA)
Information Science Reference • copyright 2024 • 322pp • H/C (ISBN: 9781668499146) • US $280.00 (our price)

*Reshaping Entrepreneurial Education Within an Industry 4.0 Context*
Vannie Naidoo (University of KwaZulu-Natal, South Africa) and Rahul Verma (Delhi University, India)
Business Science Reference • copyright 2024 • 351pp • H/C (ISBN: 9798369304099) • US $265.00 (our price)

*LGBTQIA Students in Higher Education Approaches to Student Identity and Policy*

701 East Chocolate Avenue, Hershey, PA 17033, USA
Tel: 717-533-8845 x100 • Fax: 717-533-8661
E-Mail: cust@igi-global.com • www.igi-global.com

# Table of Contents

**Foreword** .................................................................................................................................. xii

**Preface** .................................................................................................................................... xiii

**Acknowledgment** .................................................................................................................... xix

**Chapter 1**
Countering Soloist Impostor Syndrome Among African American Male First-Year Students at Historically Black Colleges and Universities: Preventative Solutions for Future Post-Graduate Career Preparation and Professional Success ............................................................................... 1
    *Patrick L. Stearns, Claflin University, USA*

**Chapter 2**
Demystifying the Process of Attending, Presenting at, and Reviewing for Academic Conferences: Considerations for Graduate Students ........................................................................................ 12
    *Andy Jiahao Liu, University of Arizona, USA*

**Chapter 3**
Engaging International Students as Curriculum Co-Creators ................................................... 29
    *Chi Maher, University of Greenwich, London, UK*
    *Catherine Bedwei-Majdoub, Ravensbourne University, London, UK*

**Chapter 4**
Interdisciplinary Curriculum for Engineering Graduates: A Constructive Alignment With Career Competency ................................................................................................................................ 53
    *Swati Gupta, Universal AI University, India*

**Chapter 5**
The Interplay Between Career Adaptability and Foreign Language Skills in an Unstable Labor Market ......................................................................................................................................... 86
    *Maria-Anca Maican, Transilvania University of Brașov, Romania*
    *Elena Cocoradă, Transilvania University of Brașov, Romania*
    *Felicia Constantin, University of Oradea, Romania*

**Chapter 6**
Reflecting on Empowering Students in Museum Work Through Federal Work-Study Positions: A USA Case Study .................................................................................................................................. 117
    *Kathryn Medill, Rocky Mountain College of Art and Design, USA*

**Chapter 7**
Student Challenges During COVID-19: Can Experiential Learning Be Effective Online? ............... 163
    *Erika Galindo-Bello, Universidad de las Américas, Puebla, Mexico*

**Chapter 8**
From University to the Labour Market: Assisting Students Through Personal Career Maps ............ 186
    *Elena Ramona Richiteanu-Nastase, Bucharest University of Economic Studies, Romania*
    *Monica Elisabeta Paduraru, Bucharest University of Economics Studies, Romania*

**Chapter 9**
The Undergraduate Career Compass: A Seven-Step Plan for Navigating the Transition From Academia to the World of Work ........................................................................................................ 206
    *Randika Perera, Gampaha Wickramarachchi University of Indigenous Medicince, Sri Lanka*

**Chapter 10**
From Classroom to Career: A Holistic Approach to Student Preparedness ....................................... 232
    *Ruby Jindal, Department of Physics, School of Basic and Applied Sciences, K.R. Mangalam University, Gurugram, India*

**Chapter 11**
The Intersection of Academics and Career Readiness ....................................................................... 246
    *Ranjit Singha, Christ University, India*
    *Surjit Singha, Kristu Jayanti College (Autonomous), India*
    *Elizabeth Jasmine, Indian Institute of Psychology and Research, India*

**Chapter 12**
Impact of Frequency and Consistency in Preparing Students for Career Paths ................................. 267
    *Saptarshi Kumar Sarkar, Brainware University, India*
    *Piyal Roy, Brainware University, India*
    *Shivnath Ghosh, Brainware University, India*
    *Amitava Podder, Brainware University, India*
    *Subrata Paul, Brainware University, India*

**Compilation of References** ......................................................................................................... 293

**About the Contributors** .............................................................................................................. 327

**Index** ............................................................................................................................................. 332

# Detailed Table of Contents

**Foreword** .................................................................................................................................... xii

**Preface** ......................................................................................................................................... xiii

**Acknowledgment** ........................................................................................................................ xix

**Chapter 1**
Countering Soloist Impostor Syndrome Among African American Male First-Year Students at
Historically Black Colleges and Universities: Preventative Solutions for Future Post-Graduate
Career Preparation and Professional Success ..................................................................................... 1
    *Patrick L. Stearns, Claflin University, USA*

Impostor syndrome details the occurrence of individuals who have a tendency to doubt their achievements and the skills that accompany them, despite the feedback that they are receiving from others. People who exhibit the behavior of the soloist function of impostor syndrome believe that they must solve any setbacks in their life on their own, without any outside help. This chapter focuses on soloist imposter syndrome (SIS) in first-year African American male students in the Historically Black Colleges and Universities or HBCU environment. The chapter's goal is to help the student overcome SIS by fostering workable curriculum, advising, mentoring and counseling, and career preparatory-based solutions for their success. Additionally, the chapter also stresses the student's ability to access spirituality by using their relationship with the higher power of their understanding to assist in adapting to the new environment.

**Chapter 2**
Demystifying the Process of Attending, Presenting at, and Reviewing for Academic Conferences:
Considerations for Graduate Students................................................................................................ 12
    *Andy Jiahao Liu, University of Arizona, USA*

The "publish or perish" culture has put graduate students and faculty worldwide under increasing pressure to demonstrate their research productivity (i.e., producing and disseminating knowledge). Academic conferences, as a typical way of knowledge dissemination, offer chances for graduate students to socialize in the academic community and receive timely feedback from peers. However, those new to the conference experience may feel confused or even daunted. Drawing on the personal experience of an early career faculty in the field of applied linguistics, this chapter demystifies the whole process related to attending, presenting at, and reviewing for academic conferences. Mapping out the author's experiential trajectory as an active graduate student at academic conferences, the author details how the author has transitioned from a graduate attendee to an experienced presenter and a junior gatekeeper for academic conferences. Besides, the author offers a set of dos and don'ts to potential attendees, presenters, and reviewers at academic conferences.

### Chapter 3
Engaging International Students as Curriculum Co-Creators ............................................................. 29
*Chi Maher, University of Greenwich, London, UK*
*Catherine Bedwei-Majdoub, Ravensbourne University, London, UK*

The chapter examines the process of engaging post-graduate students in co-creation of the curriculum. Despite extensive research in curriculum design, there remains more to discover about how engaging postgraduate students in co-creation of the curricular impacts their awareness of the link between their learning and their career chosen paths. The research employed qualitative data collected from 54 post-graduate international business management students studying in UK higher education institutions. The findings suggest encouraging students to co-design the curricular empowers, motivates them as active participants in their learning and prepares them for the world of work. The research contributes to the literature by demonstrating that providing opportunities for students to co-create the curriculum should be embedded from the start of the curriculum development process.

### Chapter 4
Interdisciplinary Curriculum for Engineering Graduates: A Constructive Alignment With Career Competency ....................................................................................................................................... 53
*Swati Gupta, Universal AI University, India*

Interdisciplinary teaching combines multiple subjects. Business, communication, and sustainability may be part of an interdisciplinary engineering curriculum. An interdisciplinary curriculum can help engineering students learn more. Students can prepare for more careers by combining engineering with other subjects. Employers value interdisciplinary skills and competencies. Interdisciplinary coursework helps students develop critical thinking, problem-solving, communication, and collaboration skills. Effective interdisciplinary engineering curricula align. This means the curriculum should match employers' career competencies so students can succeed. Interdisciplinary education helps engineering graduates develop career-ready skills. An interdisciplinary curriculum aligns with employer needs to prepare students for engineering careers.

### Chapter 5
The Interplay Between Career Adaptability and Foreign Language Skills in an Unstable Labor Market ............................................................................................................................................. 86
*Maria-Anca Maican, Transilvania University of Brașov, Romania*
*Elena Cocoradă, Transilvania University of Brașov, Romania*
*Felicia Constantin, University of Oradea, Romania*

Career adaptability is a soft skill that allows people to cope with professional tasks in an unpredictable labor market. Today's global labor market also requires language skills to facilitate employees' collaboration across linguistic boundaries. The chapter is built around a quantitative study with participants from a large public university in the south-eastern part of Central Europe, and it aims to analyze the connection between career adaptability, foreign languages, and personal traits. The results show significant gender differences regarding adaptability and the perceived role of foreign languages for employability and in one's career development, all in favor of girls. Concerning students' status as employed/unemployed, the tendencies regard only unemployed students' stronger confidence in and lower concern with the future. Career adaptability is predicted by foreign language anxiety, conscientiousness, openness to experience, and self-perceived FL proficiency. Some implications for teachers are presented at the end of the chapter.

**Chapter 6**
Reflecting on Empowering Students in Museum Work Through Federal Work-Study Positions: A USA Case Study.................................................................................................................................... 117
*Kathryn Medill, Rocky Mountain College of Art and Design, USA*

This chapter serves as a reflective case study, in which ex-colleagues, who held different institutional roles—federal work study student worker and manager—discuss their experiences as part of the visitor engagement team at a university art museum in relation to their transition from academia to their professional fields. These conversations serve as anecdotes other professionals can reference when building student work study positions for universities. The conversation is a unique opportunity to unpack the impact a student work study program had from the perspective of its participants. Specific themes explored are 1) the expectations of participants' regarding their role at the museum, 2) reflections from participants about their lived experiences as museum employees, 3) the transferable skills participants feel they developed as a result of their role, 4) if/how they utilize those transferable skills in their current professional practice, and 5) suggestions for institutions who have or would like to build similar roles.

**Chapter 7**
Student Challenges During COVID-19: Can Experiential Learning Be Effective Online? ............... 163
*Erika Galindo-Bello, Universidad de las Américas, Puebla, Mexico*

During the COVID-19 pandemic, internships were translated into home office modality; organizations, universities, and students faced significant challenges to which they had to adapt in a short period of time. This chapter describes the effects of COVID-19 in the experiential learning activities, specifically the case of internship programs for marketing students at an emerging market university, in order to learn about their experiences during the pandemic and incorporate the lessons in post pandemic experiences. Students and organizations were surveyed to know about their internship experiences and perceptions. Results indicate that under certain conditions, online internship experiences can be successful.

**Chapter 8**
From University to the Labour Market: Assisting Students Through Personal Career Maps ............ 186
*Elena Ramona Richiteanu-Nastase, Bucharest University of Economic Studies, Romania*
*Monica Elisabeta Paduraru, Bucharest University of Economics Studies, Romania*

Adjusting to university life is a challenge for many students, who find it difficult to cope with academic demands and complete their studies. Preparing for a career can generate anxiety, stress, maladjustment, vulnerability. At university level, students` counselling can be a solution to help students adapt to the demands of this environment and their future career. This chapter clarifies concepts such as academic adjustment, career counselling strategy, and institutional support. Furthermore, the authors will present the Personal Career Map as a specific theory and instrument that can be used in counselling students. The structure of the career map, the career profiling questionnaire, the benefits, and limitations of this approach will be highlighted. Personal Career Map offers suggestions for student`s counselling plan, detailing concrete steps that can be taken at personal and university level to enhance students' academic and professional insertion. Discussions and recommendations on the use of this approach at university level will be addressed.

## Chapter 9
The Undergraduate Career Compass: A Seven-Step Plan for Navigating the Transition From Academia to the World of Work ................................................................................................................ 206
*Randika Perera, Gampaha Wickramarachchi University of Indigenous Medicince, Sri Lanka*

Higher education's ultimate achievement is to position the undergraduate towards professionalism successfully. Recently, higher education institutes have recognized this need and offered various services to realistically place students in the world of work. Throughout the academic journey, undergraduates acquire the hard and soft skills to meet the demands of the work world. Nevertheless, properly positioning undergraduates in the world of work is a self-responsibility and exploration journey. Therefore, this chapter introduces a self-directed mechanism under the title of career compass and elaborates on seven steps that undergraduates need to follow for success in their career or professional development. These seven steps positively contribute to lifelong personal and professional development.

## Chapter 10
From Classroom to Career: A Holistic Approach to Student Preparedness ........................................ 232
*Ruby Jindal, Department of Physics, School of Basic and Applied Sciences, K.R. Mangalam University, Gurugram, India*

Within this chapter, the exploration focuses on the varied journey students undertake when transitioning from their academic endeavors to the professional sphere. The emphasis lies in acknowledging the importance of embracing a holistic perspective that incorporates their academic foundation, skill development, practical experiences, mentorship, and fostering a growth-oriented mindset. Practical real-world examples and strategies are provided to aid students in effectively navigating this transitional phase. This chapter serves as an invaluable resource for educators, career advisors, and students navigating the dynamic and ever-evolving job market.

## Chapter 11
The Intersection of Academics and Career Readiness ......................................................................... 246
*Ranjit Singha, Christ University, India*
*Surjit Singha, Kristu Jayanti College (Autonomous), India*
*Elizabeth Jasmine, Indian Institute of Psychology and Research, India*

This chapter emphasizes the significant correlation between vocation readiness and academic achievement, highlighting the thoughtful consequences for students' triumphs. This highlights the significance of effectively integrating theoretical knowledge with hands-on vocational training, cultivating aptitudes for analysis, resolution of challenges, and flexibility. Case studies that have achieved success serve as illustrations of successful integration, highlighting the cooperative nature of academic departments and career services. Exploration of early career options, practical experience, and transferable skills are crucial components. Collaborative platforms, curricular redesign, and technology integration are all reasonable solutions. Notwithstanding the obstacles encountered, educators are motivated to maintain their commitment to this incorporation as a top priority, guaranteeing that students are adequately equipped to confront the workforce's ever-changing demands and facilitate a smooth transition into the professional realm.

**Chapter 12**
Impact of Frequency and Consistency in Preparing Students for Career Paths ................................... 267
    *Saptarshi Kumar Sarkar, Brainware University, India*
    *Piyal Roy, Brainware University, India*
    *Shivnath Ghosh, Brainware University, India*
    *Amitava Podder, Brainware University, India*
    *Subrata Paul, Brainware University, India*

The modern labor market is constantly evolving, making it challenging to prepare students for rewarding career paths. This chapter emphasizes the importance of consistency and regularity in career preparation, highlighting the impact on educators, career counselors, and students. It explores how frequency and consistency shape students' preparedness for the changing world of work, drawing on research and real-world experiences. Consistency in learning and skill development leads to greater proficiency and adaptability and is crucial in setting objectives, habit formation, and time management. This understanding can help educators, career advisors, and students navigate the intricacies of the modern labor market with greater resilience and confidence. The chapter also lays the groundwork for future research and real-world implementations, providing a strong foundation for improving job readiness in a time of innovation and transition.

**Compilation of References** ............................................................................................................. 293

**About the Contributors** .................................................................................................................. 327

**Index** ................................................................................................................................................. 332

# Foreword

As many of us attend different institutions of learning and acquire knowledge through internships or externships, there comes a time when it is a moment to actually start working. Once in this process, I learned words like soft skills, hard skills, networking, mentoring, and marketing myself. The key to success can be a combination of different opportunities. What makes a successful journey from academia to careers is that we learn from the mountain and valley experiences.

The editors, Dr. Sligh Conway and Prof. Andy Liu, have provided robust chapters that embrace the importance of promoting students from academia to the world of work. The chapters discussed the academic to career transition of students from Historically Black universities, technical colleges, international and global academic experiences.

We are now in a world that embraces education in and outside of the classroom. Both worlds are essential in students receiving a quality and well-rounded education. Many authors in the book state that we must embrace the whole student when educating them. What a phenomenal way to view education!

Based on the latest research in the area of academics and transitions to career paths, this book delivers on how faculty and staff must provide students with a well-rounded education with many experiences.

In my experiences as Provost at a Historically Black University, I can conclude that relevant research is included in the book, "Preparing Students from the Academic World to Career Paths: A Comprehensive Guide." This book provides educators, academicians, and practitioners with a torchlight of information and a comprehensive review of what works well with diverse populations. From a background in this area and being in the trenches where the decisions we make as educators can affect those we provide services to, I am in agreement with the chapters that do an astounding job of relaying the global needs of students. For instance, one chapter touched on teaching students soft skills along the journey in acquiring an education. Once the soft skills are taught and role played in the classroom environment, it can then be a force to be reckoned with as students transitions in the world of work. This, by far, is an example of how this guide serves as a transformational piece adding to the quality of life of the learner. Several chapters in the book also discussed the relevance of motivating, mentoring, and encouraging students in many different disciplines. This allows many students to feel like their needs are a priority and that faculty and staff are concerned about their career transitions and successful outcomes.

Overall, the mission of the book is definitely an eye-opening topic. From this mission, educators and students are educated beyond the classroom. This book is one that penetrates the hearts of many who care about the lives of the students in and beyond the classroom.

*Frederick Evans*
*South Carolina State University, USA*

# Preface

## BACKGROUND: WHY THIS BOOK?

Embracing a career path can be a stressful and significant decision for many new to the job market. For some people, choosing to pursue an advanced degree in their interests will ease their anxiety temporarily and increase their employability through the protected time in graduate school. In contrast, many others will opt to seek a job and start their careers after their undergraduate studies due to personal or professional development concerns (e.g., family financial support issues, practitioner-oriented mindset, and unpredictability of the job market). Regardless of which group you will find resonance with, we think it is reasonable to state that your ultimate goal after attending universities/colleges is to prepare yourself for transitions from the academic world to career paths, whether in academia or industry.

The hidden message, however, is that the job market is never a "level-playing-the-field" game. The unexpected COVID-19 pandemic worldwide has even worsened the situation with shrinking job positions in an everlasting manner. Notably, securing a desired job offer has been ever tough and challenging in this post-pandemic era, particularly for first-generation and minority students. In fact, we agree that the university/college career centers (or something similar with different wordings) are meaningful and helpful in providing consultation services and offering workshops to clarify students' confusion. And yes, they often provide feedback or guidance on developing a competitive job market application package (e.g., curriculum vitae or resume, cover letter, and letters of recommendation) for students. A quick search with keywords, such as "curriculum vitae writing tips," "cover letter guidelines," and "strategies to ace a job interview" on the Internet will easily generate thousands of information entries for reference and additional readings. Today's classrooms also increasingly include relevant content to help students shift from the academic world to career paths. Unfortunately, the explosive information can sometimes lead to adverse emotional outcomes, such as stress and overwhelmingness.

The existing literature also documented a number of books that have been published to focus on different aspects of career readiness and planning. These books can generally be categorized into two types. One primary category is to introduce and list suggestions and practices to help students achieve successful shifts from graduate school to academic career paths. For example, Kelsky's (2015) *The professor is in: The essential guide to turning your Ph.D. into a job* offers a compendium of practical advice with dos and don'ts to help Ph.D. students land the job market in a successful manner. Plonsky (2020) and Kessler and Casal (2024) provide suggestions for professional development and tips for thriving as a graduate student in the field of applied linguistics in particular. Another common type is to develop and hone job-seeker's skills in preparing for a compelling profile or seminal events in job-seeking. Wallwork (2019), for instance, specifically outlines common writing tips and frequently asked questions in creating academic curricula vitae, resumes, and online profiles. Albakry and Bryan (2024) present and introduce necessary considerations for writing recommendation letters, though the target readers are mostly graduate students, junior career researchers, and faculty.

Yet few books talk candidly about necessary support and workable practices for first-generation graduate and minority students to transition seamlessly from academia to their chosen career paths, especially in their undergraduate periods. That's why we edited this book. Specifically, this collection, with considerations of diversity, equity, and justice, begins to fill this gap by offering practical guides across disciplines and countries to facilitate post-secondary educators and student-supporting staff to integrate necessary transferrable skills into curriculum design and advising practices. Combining practical tips and empirical research in an interdisciplinary manner, *Preparing Students From the Academic World to Career Paths: A Comprehensive Guide* thus doubles as a professional book for educators and a resource book for students (particularly undergraduates) to reference for holistic developments and whole cultivation of life competencies while embarking on career practices or paths.

An important point to bear in mind is that this collection is edited with particular interest to engage and empower students from underrepresented groups and backgrounds, including those attending Historically Black Colleges and Universities (HBCUs), minority-serving institutions, and other marginalized student groups, to thrive in their academic pursuits and beyond. However, the diversified voices and perspectives presented in this reference, we believe, will enable this collection to reach a broader audience for inspiration, thoughts, and tips. It will also speak to a broad number of topics and issues that other student groups may face in their transition to career paths. With all these in mind, let's have a look at the organization of this edited volume.

## KEY ISSUES IN THIS BOOK

The book approaches the preparation for and transition of students to the career world with inclusive coverage. Across 12 chapters, this edited volume addresses topics from emotional readiness to combat impostor syndrome to students' learning challenges during the pandemic. These chapters also range from those that are more personal in nature (e.g., student preparedness and step-by-step workable plans) to those that are more specific and discipline-related (e.g., cocreators of curriculum and foreign language skills). Below follows a synopsis of each chapter.

In Chapter 1, Patrick Stearns explores the soloist behavior of the impostor syndrome of first-generation African American male students in the Historically Black Colleges and Universities. Drawing on personal experiences of working as a faculty in the HBCU environment for 16 years, Stearns challenges the existing mindset—seeking external help is a sign of weakness—among African American male students, highlights the difficulties those HBCU students experienced, and shares counter-strategies from the institutional level (e.g., finding a balance between career counseling and career preparatory courses). An important message brought to the fore by Stearns is that HBCUs are critical nurturing "villages" for African American male students. To prepare students for academic and professional success, HBCUs should retain a structure intersected with academic, social, psychological, and spiritual sources.

Andy Jiahao Liu, one of the volume editors, visions conference presentations as a bridge for graduate students to socialize into the academic community for career preparedness in Chapter 2. Aiming to demystify the near-mythical dynamic trajectories from the peripheral participation (i.e., conference

*Preface*

attendees) to its full participation (i.e., conference gatekeepers), Liu uses personal experience to outline the necessary *dos and don'ts* from attending, presenting at, to reviewing for academic conferences. Through the different engagement levels of academic conferences, Liu also shows identity formation and transformation (i.e., attendees, presenters, and reviewers) in the community of practice. Particularly, Liu picks up on the particular functions of the desire for development and imagined identities in the socializing process for career networks and preparedness.

Writing from the United Kingdom, Chi Maher and Catherine Bedwei-Majdoub, in Chapter 3, focus on the engagement of graduate students as curriculum co-creators in an International Business Management course. Though explorative in nature, Maher and Bedwei-Majdoub showcase the feasibility and importance of welcoming students as co-producers and partners in curriculum development rather than subordinates to course instructors. With face-to-face semi-structured interviews with 54 students, they report multiple ways to engage students as co-creators and present the impact of engagement as co-creators in curriculum development on career paths and learning. This explorative engagement, according to Maher and Bedwei-Majdoub, not only enables underrepresented groups to have a say in their academic world, but further empowers them to hone critical thinking skills and cultivate the know-why, know-whom, and know-how competencies for career paths.

Continuing the same line of discussions on graduate students, Swati Gupta emphasizes, in Chapter 4, the essentials of interdisciplinary education and awareness in preparing engineering graduate students to succeed in the Accounting for Managers course. Reflecting on personal experiences in developing the course with a comprehensive blend of theoretical, design, technical, and communication contexts, Gupta provides insights into how the analytical and problem-solving activities of engineering graduates can be used in the accounting course to cultivate competent professionals and pioneering thinker at the nexus of engineering and finance. The chapter also offers a situated portrayal of the implementation of holistic curriculum design, the application of experiential learning, the necessity of offering development feedback, and the alignment between course objectives and goals.

In Chapter 5, Maria-Anca Maican, Elena Cocoradă, and Felicia Constantin, discuss the important yet underrepresented topic of soft skills (specifically career adaptability) and its intersection of foreign language skills in the current tough and unstable job market. Romania-based, they report on findings from the involvement of 328 Bachelor's degree students in multiple scale instruments. The statistical analysis shows a significant gender difference (with girls favored) in the perceived role of foreign language for employability and professional tasks. Interestingly, Maican and colleagues also note that unemployed students tend to be more confident in the future, but employed students are more concerned with the future. Besides, results reveal that career adaptability correlates with foreign language anxiety, positive behaviors during the class, and foreign language learning motivation.

Shifting to the autobiographical approach with reflective insights, Kathryn Medill, in Chapter 6, presents a reflective account of being a student manager in a Federal Work-Study program—a financial aid initiative in the United States—within an art museum. Following the book theme, Medill introduces the lack of diversity among museum staff to call for the recruitment of more minority and/or first-generation students within museums. The collaborative reflection also suggests the importance of internship and experiential learning in preparing students to embark on the career world. In addition to offering strategies for improving the current Federal Work-Study Program, Medill underscores three key elements to support students' transitions from academia to professional practice—growing students' options, building support, and promoting work satisfaction.

Similarly, Erika Galindo-Bello, in Chapter 7, uncovers a compulsory internship course in a Mexican private university. Particularly, Galindo-Bello presents the issues, controversies, and problems in translating the said internship courses into the online context during the pandemic. Though interview results suggest limited opportunities from organizations and companies due to unpreparedness for the work-from-home modality and disappointment among students, Galindo-Bello advocates that experiential learning is of critical importance to prepare students for career paths and can be successfully implemented under certain conditions in online contexts. Additionally, Galindo-Bello welcomes the transitional role of internship in bridging students from the academic world to career paths.

Pursuing the same theme of career planning and readiness, the following chapters seek to present and introduce multiple strategies for the smooth transition from the academic world to the career equivalent. In Chapter 8, Elena Richiteanu-Nastase and Monica Paduraru analyze the difficulties students face when seeking counseling services and offer the Personal Career Map as a specific strategy that university and student career counseling specialists should use to meet students' needs. In detail, Richiteanu-Nastase and Paduraru explain the four functions—informational, diagnostic, remedial, and forecasting—and the six career factors—motivations, values, career plans, decision-making aspects, expectations, and training needs—of personal career maps. Stage-by-stage strategies and suggestions are also proposed to support students in better adapting to their academic and career preparation pathways.

Along similar lines, yet from a different perspective, Randika Perera, in Chapter 9, introduces a seven-step plan for undergraduate students to successfully navigate the transition from academia to the world of work. Critical to the discussion, Perera offers an in-depth analysis of the nature of the world of work, concluding that students in this era are increasingly embracing jobs interplaying with technological innovations and multiple skills. To aid students in addressing the said needs, Perera recommends the seven realistic steps: a) Self-evaluation and self-understanding, b) acquiring knowledge of the world of work, c) recognizing the most suitable career options, d) networking, e) deciding on a specific industry and career, f) creating a professional development plan, and e) planning for the management of personal and professional life.

In Chapter 10, Ruby Jindal presents a holistic approach to detail how students can better prepare themselves for the professional world. Concurring with Maria-Anca Maican and co-authors, Jindal argues that, beyond academic excellence in the classroom, soft skills and practical competencies are critical in preparing students for successful careers. In particular, Jindal highlights and delves deeper into the following important skills and competencies: interdisciplinary competence, problem-solving and critical thinking, adaptability and resilience, practical experiences and internships, as well as mentorship and networking. Throughout this chapter, Jindal discloses that the journey from the academic world to a successful career is multifaceted and dynamic.

In Chapter 11, Ranjit Singha, Surjit Singha, and Elizabeth Jasmine, discuss the intersection of academic achievement and career readiness. With particular interests, R. Singha and colleagues promote an all-encompassing educational methodology and underscore the reciprocal relationship between academic achievement and professional success. Like Jindal, they advocate for cultivating skills and abilities, such as critical thinking, problem-solving, and adaptability, to equip students to join the dynamic career world. Additionally, R. Singha and colleagues suggest that combining early career exploration, real-world examples, and transferable skills is necessary to enhance students' foundations for success in the ever-changing professional world.

*Preface*

Saptarshi Kumar Sarkar, Piyal Roy, Shivnath Ghosh, Amitava Podder, and Subrata Paul end this collection with a thorough discussion on the impact of frequency and consistency in preparing students for career paths in Chapter 12. Framing frequency and consistency as two critical elements in the challenging career preparation cycle, Sarkar and colleagues further expand them into possible matters related to continued skills development, memory retention, flexibility, and self-confidence. In line with the features of the world of work highlighted by Perera, this chapter also pays particular attention to the use of digital tools for career preparations. Through detailed explanations of sub-elements and their potential impacts, Sarkar and colleagues call for the involvement of teachers and career counselors to help equip students with the necessary tools for overcoming the problems in the job market.

## CLOSING REMARKS

Across the chapters, *Preparing Students From the Academic World to Career Paths: A Comprehensive Guide* conveys the shared message that the successful transition from the academic world to career paths is never a one-person business. In fact, this process will inevitably engage different degrees of participation from surrounding stakeholders, such as course instructors, university career counselors, or even formal and informal mentors. With this in mind, we hope you will start considering how to collaborate with relevant stakeholders to better achieve a smooth transition to join the career community of practice while reading this volume featuring international voices.

Like many other books, this book is not without limitations. Although we have attempted to be inclusive and diverse in our coverage, some topics (e.g., HBCUs) are less well represented. Also, voices from Australia and New Zealand are unexpectedly absent to present a well-rounded picture. We hope, nevertheless, that the volume will inspire you, whether a student, career counselor, graduate or undergraduate instructor, university administrator, or post-secondary admission officer, to find innovative practices and strategies to participate in the transition from the academic world to career paths. We also hope you will try many things mentioned in this book in your own context. However, you may want to make necessary modifications to fit your particular context or needs.

We realize that the book will not answer *all* questions or concerns you may have, but we hope you at least will share the following consensus with us. The global reality is that in discussions about academia to career transitions, a focus must include persons with disabilities, diverse populations, and international students. Without including these populations and the challenges they face in the academic to career world, the focus is not on inclusion but on making these populations invisible.

*Andy Jiahao Liu*
*University of Arizona, USA*

*Cassandra Sligh Conway*
*South Carolina State University, USA*

*March 30, 2024*

## REFERENCES

Albakry, M., & Bryan, C. (2024). *Writing recommendation letters: The discourse of evaluation in academic settings.* University of Michigan Press ELT. doi:10.3998/mpub.12792982

Kelsky, K. (2015). *The professor is in: The essential guide to turning your Ph.D. into a job.* Crown.

Kessler, M., & Casal, J. E. (2024). *Making the most of graduate school: A practical guidebook for students in applied linguistics, education, and TESOL.* Applied Linguistics Press.

Plonsky, L. (Ed.). (2020). *Professional development in applied linguistics: A guide to success for graduate students and early career faculty.* John Benjamins. doi:10.1075/z.229

Wallwork, A. (2019). *English for academic CVs, resumes, and online profiles.* Springer. doi:10.1007/978-3-030-11090-1

# Acknowledgment

This project, in fact, was launched around four years ago. There are numerous individuals to whom we are grateful while progressing this project despite pandemic-related issues. We are grateful to Dr. Tiffanie Turner-Henderson and Dr. Elaine Eskew for serving as temporary editors in the early stages of this book project. Their meaningful engagement has kept this book project on track and made it possible for us to progress it with wonderful contributions across disciplines and countries. We are also very thankful to our chapter authors for their contribution, cooperation, and patience, as some chapter manuscripts have been with us for around two years.

We would also like to thank Dr. Frederick M. G. Evans for his generous foreword. A big thank you to Elizabeth Barrantes, Jocelynn Hessler, and other staff at IGI Global, who have continued to support this project.

This collaborative project would not have come to fruition without their involvement. We hope you will enjoy reading it.

# Chapter 1
# Countering Soloist Impostor Syndrome Among African American Male First-Year Students at Historically Black Colleges and Universities:
## Preventative Solutions for Future Post-Graduate Career Preparation and Professional Success

**Patrick L. Stearns**
*Claflin University, USA*

## ABSTRACT

*Impostor syndrome details the occurrence of individuals who have a tendency to doubt their achievements and the skills that accompany them, despite the feedback that they are receiving from others. People who exhibit the behavior of the soloist function of impostor syndrome believe that they must solve any setbacks in their life on their own, without any outside help. This chapter focuses on soloist imposter syndrome (SIS) in first-year African American male students in the Historically Black Colleges and Universities or HBCU environment. The chapter's goal is to help the student overcome SIS by fostering workable curriculum, advising, mentoring and counseling, and career preparatory-based solutions for their success. Additionally, the chapter also stresses the student's ability to access spirituality by using their relationship with the higher power of their understanding to assist in adapting to the new environment.*

As faculty in the Historically Black College and University (HBCU) system for 16 years, the author of the chapter has noticed a hypothetical trend of many first-generation African American male students who engage in what is known as the soloist behavior of the Impostor Syndrome (Clance, 1985; Young,

DOI: 10.4018/978-1-7998-7999-2.ch001

2011). There have been students who, upon experiencing a personal traumatic experience such as the death of a loved one, financial difficulties that may have their academic career in jeopardy, or personal mental challenges, and instead of notifying the faculty member in private early on in the semester, may many times, wait until Midterm Exam time halfway through the term, or worse yet, near the end of the term to notify the instructor. The Impostor Syndrome "describes a psychological experience of intellectual and professional fraudulence" (Clance and Imes, 1978; Matthews and Clance, 1985). This fraudulence can manifest itself in five different behavioral patterns; the perfectionist, the natural genius, the soloist, the expert, and the superhero (Raypole, 2021). This essay's focus is based on the goal of eliminating in first-year African American male students, the soloist behavioral function, in order to prepare them for future post-graduate professional workplace success. When Soloist Imposter Syndrome (SIS) is present in African American co-cultural circles, it can discourage African American males from seeking help when needed for fear of being seen among other male peer group members as being weak or "soft" for not keeping the issues to themselves and somehow figuring out and solving the problems on their own. This essay also seeks to identify the point in which many African American male students who are struggling on the HBCU higher education level, experience cultural pressure from their family or peer group's belief that men aren't supposed to show weakness of any kind especially when dealing with a racist society, means that they must be "soloists," who can only rely on themselves to climb out of their academic rut, while believing that reaching out for help is a sign of weakness, instead of a proactive act of strength. The goal is to empower first-year African American male students to eliminate SIS by giving them instructional tools that will empower them to overcome it, therefore paving the way for their unhindered professional workplace-oriented development. Kunjufu (1997) suggests that many African American males learn this mindset through interaction with their childhood peer groups; planted social seeds that surface in their elementary school years, and continues to be cultivated through middle and high school as well. Majors and Billson (1993) argue that many of these deep-rooted beliefs are still present when the African American male reaches adulthood. The reality of being a first-generation university student, the process of figuring out how to be a successful man in the midst of many not having their biological father in the home growing up, and being exposed to limited positive male role models, and emerging from an elementary and secondary educational environment that did not adequately prepare them for the university setting are believed to be contributing factors of feelings of SIS that the researcher seeks to successfully provide solutions to counter it. Additionally, the essay will especially emphasize the role of the Historically Black Colleges and Universities-HBCUs in providing counter strategies to this problem through effective early detection, faculty-to-student mentorship, and weekly communication with the student as a way of checking overall wellness academically and otherwise. HBCUs have shown proven success in helping African American male students successfully overcome issues that hinder student success (Shorette & Palmer, 2015; Palmer, Davis & Maramba, 2010). Additionally, this essay also seeks to emphasize the strategy of the reliance on positive coping strategies that Black males taken on during their undergraduate years to equip themselves to overcome SIS through spirituality, in the form of ascribing to a power higher than oneself for strength to deal with the academic setting as well as everyday life, as well as taking on other positive coping techniques such as undergoing strategies to reduce stress (Norman, 2008; Riggins, McNeal & Herndon, 2008). The essay's ultimate purpose is to provide a structure in which HBCU faculty can help African American men dealing with to identify and break the behavior patterns associated with SIS and replace those patterns with positive habits designed for African American male student success. To understand how to eliminate SIS among African American first-year HBCU students and prepare them for academic and professional success, one must know and understand the background from which many African American male students who are entering HBCU's come from. By the time a significant group of African American men arrive to the HBCU campus, they have had to deal with what the essayist has found to be the key factors that have influenced the presence of SIS in their lives: fatherlessness, a significant absence of many positive adult role models, especially male ones, lack of preparation for college-level classes due to poorly equipped high schools, and a community that frowns upon mental health assistance in the form of counseling (Taylor et al., 2010). The present generation of African American male college students attending HBCUs are of the generation in which 2006 statistics showed that 63% of African American children live in homes in which their father was not present (U.S. Census Bureau, 2006). Studies have also shown that African American children whose fathers are not present have are prone to have more psychological disorders than their counterparts who do have their father and mother in the household (Murry, Bynum, Brody, Willert, & Stephens, 2001).An additional component of the Soloist Imposter Syndrome also reveals itself in the form of the African American male student whose financial situation limits their access to purchasing food or accessing a university meal plan that fits their needs, while not telling class instructors of this issue that may affect their performance in the class. A recent study also concluded that African American students were more likely to experience some form of food insecurity while on an HBCU campus moreso than those on Predominantly White Universities (PWIs) (Duke et al., 2021). The solution for the African American male's emancipation from SIS is based on the HBCU having a structure that alleviates the Soloist Imposter Syndrome through a focused educator-to-student mentorship and a curriculum of compassion and clarity, regarding understanding how to equip African American male students with the skills and tools to eliminate the Soloist Imposter Syndrome and learn how to prepare for post-graduate professional life. HBCUs have a long, significant history of preparing African Americans for professional life (Cooper & Hawkins, 2016; Franklin, Younge & Jensen, 2023). The same HBCUs have accomplished this task by infusing the importance of communicative people skills, cultural pride, and positive behavioral change necessary for competing and becoming successful in a competitive and still racist society. African American men who lack the academic preparatory background for the university experience come to HBCUs desperately needing the interpersonal communicative skills, discipline and focus to succeed in college. Many begin their collegiate experience without these skills and don't get off to a good start, due to SIS, will suffer in silence, and not inform faculty, academic advisors, or administrators of the personal difficulties they may be facing due to the aforementioned skills deficit due to an unfavorable high school experience, personal family issues, mental disorders or challenges or other situations, and feel that they must "push through" and solve their own problems. It is the task of faculty members, who are on the front lines of working to solve this problem, to somehow get through to the African American male student struggling in their classes, and be successful in doing so as early in the semester as possible. This essay's goal is to argue that early detection, administration of countermeasures, counseling, mentoring, intervention by faculty and administrators, and college life preparatory courses are integral to combating African American male SIS and retaining and seeing that student graduate and become a productive post-graduate professional. These techniques must especially be administered to first-year students in the 100-level university experience classes, and all other classes the student is taking. The countermeasures are the importance of learning and applying coping strategies in the collegiate environment (Norman, 2008), seeking immediate counseling for personal mental disorders and challenges that affect overall well-being (Bernard et. al, 2017), alerting the "chain of command," from faculty member to counselor, to academic advisor, and administrators such as the dean of students, when applicable, and doing it early on (Bernard & Lowe,

2019), and identifying root causes of SIS that the particular student is acting out, and seeking to gain the student's trust to provide solutions to alleviate and eliminate the behavior. Also, first-year 100-level courses that introduce the student to the do's and don'ts of collegiate life and the recipes for academic success, retention and an overall, effective student life balance must be a part of the solution as well. One of the first lines of defense must be to take head on the student who may be susceptible to SIS by intercepting the symptoms first by emphasizing the discipline and time management necessary to student success. Here, the academic advisor's role is key to ensuring that the student enroll in courses such as these right away, so that they can immediately indoctrinate the student into understanding the positive habits and strategic measures that not only constitute the student achieving a life balance during their first-year, but establishing a positive framework of habits that will remain throughout the student's collegiate experience and their future professional lives as well. Additionally, faculty must always be aware of the fact that a significant number of these students could possibly be first-generation college students who have not been briefed by family members as to what to expect upon arriving to campus, much less understanding how to adjust to and prepare for the experience. Also, the impact of fatherlessness in many African American households, and the limited amount of mentorship once many students arrive to campus is another factor. Studies such as those conducted by Earl and Lohmann (1978) have found that fatherlessness in the African American community has affected children of the same community in the form of interfering with their intellectual and emotional development. Finally, the essay will provide emphasis on the importance of either introducing the student to, or reminding them of, the importance of incorporating spirituality in their daily lives, in the form of ascribing to and relying on a power greater than themselves, a higher power that provides guidance and life-balance leadership for every aspect of their lives (Riggins, McNeal & Herndon, 2008). The resulting goal is to apply the preventative measures early on to African American male students to immediately give them the tools to unlearn the non-useful, negative, destructive behavior of the mindset associated with acting out SIS. The ultimate goal is to get the African American male to not only change the way he thinks regarding SIS, but to change his behavior and initiate positive habits, strategies and techniques designed to change his way of proactively and daily, engaging in the countermeasures that will eliminate SIS altogether. The goal is to replace the SIS mindset with positive habits and thinking processes that immediately result in future academic and professional success. The first line of defense in detecting and rooting out SIS in first-year African American HBCU students takes place with faculty. The faculty member who is the student's class instructor spends significant time with the student during the course of the semester. The faculty members challenge is being observant, regarding detecting any behavioral changes of the student in the classroom that may indicate a personal crisis. The faculty member, upon noticing a behavioral change could approach the student after class and ask how he is doing, since the instructor had noticed behavior not detected before in class, such as aloofness, distracting behavior, sleeping in class, not paying attention to the in-class materials, etc. A key first goal should be the instructor doing their best to form what could be the beginnings of a mentorship relationship with the African American male student, if that student is open to it. This is the first part of a strategy that, in the HBCU environment, has been key and has been documented as one of the most important things an HBCU offers African American male students (Toldson, 2014). A faculty member, especially an African American male faculty member should have the openness of wanting to be a mentor to the student, with the understanding that he may be a part of the over half of young African American men who don't regularly see positive role models that look like them. The African American male faculty member might be one of the few positive role models that look like him, that he has ever met. Studies show that only 3% of full-time university faculty in the United States are African American men, with 6% being of the Black Diaspora as a whole (National Center for Education Statistics, 2020). Therefore, faculty members must educate themselves as to how to effectively communicate with the first-year African American male HBCU student, by understanding the culture in which they were raised and nurtured. Harper and Wood (2016) point out that there has been leadership in the university setting of whom has made the mistake of placing all African American undergraduate men into one homogenous group, without any regard to the various groupings of these same men. They state that the groups of African American men in the university setting are as follows: Black gay and bisexual men, Black men in historically Black fraternities, Black male student athletes, Black undergraduate men at historically Black colleges and universities, Black underprepared, disengaged low performers, and Black males college achievers and student leaders (p.102). Being involved in the HBCU environment as an educator for 16 years, the essayist has observed all of the above African American male student categories in the HBCU setting. Thus, the goal of the educator in the HBCU environment must understand all of the aforementioned co-cultures to understand the African American HBCU male first-year student. However, for that first-year student, membership in historically Black fraternities would not apply, since these organizations usually do not allow them to pursue the membership process until after their first-year on campus. The HBCU structure and historical foundation in which the African American male first-year student must have is learning the necessary foundational people skills that they must carry into professional, post-graduate life. Studies show people skills, also known as soft skills, such as mutual respect of co-workers and etiquette, are just as important for balancing with hard skills, or knowing how to do the job (Administrative Professional Today, 2022). Because of the background many African American males come from, many may not have been taught basic people skills first, in the form of manners and etiquette, and must have that foundation, followed by understanding the do's and don'ts of the professional work environment. First-year experience courses that stress this are a must. The 100-level course is the foundation in which the first-year African American male student is introduced to the basic, beginning recipes for success, regarding HBCU on-campus life. At the same time, in order for the first-year and especially the first generation HBCU student to make a successful transition from the post-secondary educational environment to the collegiate one, he must have access to and immediately be encouraged by faculty to take advantage of institutionally offered services such as academic advising, career counseling, personal counseling, and educational planning resources (Shumaker & Wood, 2016). This is a preventative measure that must happen sooner, rather than later. This action is the first line of defense for early detection of SIS in the first-year African American HBCU student. The moment the instructor notices any alarming behavior in the student, such as tardiness or absenteeism, lack of paying attention in class, disruptive behavior, or lack of completing class assignments, the aforementioned HBCU campus resources must converge together to work to be the academic village that nurtures and corrects the student's collegiate experiential vessel, and keep it from sinking. Bernard and Lowe (2019) state that when left untreated and unaddressed, SIS contains "a wide range of negative mental health consequences associated with internalized beliefs of being a fraud," and when detected in students of color, scholars "have predicted a wide range of negative mental health outcomes, including symptoms of depression, anxiety and interpersonal sensitivity (p. 40). Thus, the First-year Experience courses lay down student expectations, the personal and career counseling, advising and educational planning resources must be administered to the student with such effectiveness, that it sows the seeds for combatting SIS before it can achieve firm footing within the HBCU African American male first-year student. Additionally, Riggins, McNeal and Herndon (2008) also found that African American male HBCU students who have a religious background have a tendency to access their spirituality in the form of prayer as a tool for guidance and coping, spirituality used in a social context, and the support from religious institutions; all three thematic elements being additional resources that the African American male student can access for retention and academic success, as well as coping with the HBCU environment (p.70). HBCUs continue to be a key nurturing environment for African American male students. Wood and Palmer (2015) state that research has shown that Black students at HBCUs have stronger academic self-concepts, are more satisfied with their college experience, and are engaged at higher levels than their same race counterparts at PWI (Predominately White Institutions). Despite this truth, Shorette and Palmer (2015) found that although the positive, nurturing environment is the most favorable one for the African American male student, even in this uplifting atmosphere HBCU leadership have identified "revealed challenges to the retention and persistence for Black men at an HBCU that many researchers would characterize as predictors of attrition." and further found that "poor help-seeking behavior, lack of financial aid, and problems at home were each identified as salient challenges in the lives and experiences of the participants" (p.20). The aforementioned challenges to African American male retention are some of the key examples of SIS among African American HBCU students. The structures that are standing by to help deal with the aforementioned issues are not activated due to the student believing that if they divulge any of these problems to anyone on campus, they will be viewed as "soft" or weak, and are unable to take care of their problems on their own. Many view the process of reaching out for help when experiencing these issues are seeing the process of seeking help as being an act of weakness in itself, and not what it really is; an act of strength. The student may be immersing himself in the "cool pose," which is the masking of problems and issues over issues he may be experiencing, with the exterior mindset of "I'm good," when in reality, he's not "good" or in a favorable set of circumstances at the time. One beginning red flag that could be an indicator of a problem shows itself in chronic tardiness and absenteeism. Although this occurrence could very well be an example of lack of self-discipline, it also could be an indicator of maladjustment to the collegiate environment. Asking the student to come to office hours and succeeding in his arrival can be a challenge in that many students associate this as having to go to the principal's office back in elementary, middle or high school, with the mindset that they are in trouble. When this does not work, the faculty's dependence on an effective Early Alert system at the HBCU may end up being by default, the first breakthrough). Faculty involvement in Early Alert Systems (EAS) must be a top priority. These systems are "mechanisms that allow faculty and professional staff to notify students and advisors that academic progress is being jeopardized by their behavior or performance" and "have been identified as a successful retention program practice" (Delmas & Childs, 2021). The system will help the instructor explain that the referral is not a reprimand, but rather, a reaching out to the student who is in need of assistance, regarding adjusting to the rigors of academic life. Additionally, there must also be a structure of retention with rigor for a proper foundation, even if the student has to go back and take remedial courses for that aforementioned Foundation the first year African American male student who is struggling you must have that firm Foundation in order to successfully build their academic house professionally and educationally. That has to be there. HBCUs as well as PWIs are always concerned with graduation rates and retention rates, however it cannot be at the expense of not properly preparing the students, and it starts at the first year level. Students must have that remedial structure if needed and must have foundational courses that educate their head heart and hands. Also, there has to be in place along with the aforementioned information and structure one where there has to be proper academic advising, as early identification as possible career interest for that preparation, even if hypothetically, due to the fact that an 18 year old may not have a total commitment as to his career path. However, there must be some indication as to what multiple streams of income-type career aspirations the student has to make sure that the structure is molding and shaping a strategic curriculum that suits their career interest but also prepares them for a well-balanced successful work-life balance.

Thus, the curricular structure and its rigor, along with proper nurture, career preparation and guidance through early identification of specific student major and minor-related concentrations that have the best potential for multiple streams of income could be an important motivator for increased student success and performance. The faculty member must ask the African American male student about their concentration-related interests that motivate them daily; the thing that they're excited about once they wake up in the morning, for example. Also, for their post-graduate life, the faculty member must strive to offer the best guidance and, if allowed by the student, mentorship possible. This must come from the course instructors, Early Alert program leadership for course correction and success, academic advisors, and the leaders and arrangers of campus motivational and achievement-based programs that inspire and encourage African American male students. Also, the HBCU environment's encouraging of the student to engage in continuous cultivation of their relationship with a higher power that helps them to cope with the academic world and ultimately, life in general, for the goal of ensuring a well-balanced, well-adjusted first-year African American male student in the HBCU environment, should also be encourage. The first line of defense, soft skills, begins in the classroom. Whether it's the first year experience 100-level classes, which specifically focus on these issues, or any other class, all HBCU faculty must be the village that raises the student's level of soft skills. Key basic examples are proper eye contact speaking up and raising their voice to an acceptable, professional level, teaching basic personal finance, proper resume'-writing training, interview etiquette and skills of the like must be top priority (Points of View Reference Center 2019. The first two systems must be highly-functional ones with faculty involvement through helping monitor the student's progress especially during the course of the African American male student's first year. The third element involves the process of all faculty, staff and administration, but faculty especially in a classroom or academic advising capacity, to look for opportunities to be mentors to the students, if they will allow it. Kunjufu (2007) states that when it comes to relating to African American males in the classroom, it is impossible to teach them if you don't love them. He was referring to the fatherly, *agape* love that a faculty member must somehow convey to them through showing them by example, with the establishment of mentoring relationships being a case and point. The full disclosure of a faculty member expressing through voice and action, their *agape* love for their students can, at times, elicit responses that may signal possible mentorship breakthrough opportunities between faculty and African American first-year students. This breakthrough may manifest itself in the little things that may be signs of a student-faculty mentorship connection; the student having conversations with the faculty member after class about life issues other than academic ones, taking place in an empty classroom, a happenstance meeting on the campus "yard," or a conversation during office hours. Also, the next breakthrough can actually take place through encouraging a struggling student to work on their vertical alignment through a more meaningful relationship with the higher power of their understanding, improved relationships with their loved ones, and being their best academically, while also doing so to properly prepare one's self for the professional workplace. The essayist has had conversations of this nature with first-year African American male students who have admitted to struggles at home in the classroom. Ultimately, the goal is to achieve this level of trust as soon as possible early on in the semester as a part of the strategy for the student to confidentially disclose what is really going on in their lives, combating the secrecy and the damage caused by undetected SIS. Once the African American student tells the faculty member of the situation causing lack of academic and career preparatory success in the classroom, the faculty member's goal is to detect the problem early enough in the semester to actually have enough time to help the student strategize as to the necessary steps to solve the problem before the semester's end. The essayist has found that too many times, the student will wait until the Midterm or Final Exam time periods late in the semester for partial or full disclosure of the problems hindering their academic performance. The goal for the faculty member is to always "strike while to iron is hot" through early observance and detection of a problem, and address it as soon as possible with the student, preferably early in the semester. The faculty member's success in early detection is crucial, in that she or he, the academic advisor, the career center personnel a trusted positive on or off-campus role model and mentor, a counselor or therapist, can work together to help the African American male first-year student overcome the aforementioned obstacles associated with SIS.

## THE PROPOSED IN-CLASS AND POST-CLASS SOLUTION: THE COUNSELING-CAREER GUIDANCE BALANCE

The key challenge to assist the African American male first-year HBCU student in overcoming SIS is to have in place 100-level first year experience courses that right away, teach the habits of post-graduate professionalism expected in that workplace atmosphere, coupled with career counseling (Canadian Press, 2019; Shumaker and Wood, 2016; Palmer, Davis & Marimba, 2011; Owens, Lacey, Rawls & Holbert-Quince, 2010). This class structure is an important precursor to their future practicum and internship classes that will be the next crucial steps in preparing the students. Although the latter courses usually take place during their junior and senior years, the former ones that take place during their freshman year are necessary to emphasizing the habits of timeliness, proper workplace attire and etiquette, and the ethical behavior expected as well. Instructors in the aforementioned first-year experience classes must introduce and emphasize the soft skills and discipline needed to succeed in the workplace early on. This action sets the tone for the students' necessary, required advance practice of professional habits that constitute post-graduate success. At the same time, the first-year African American male student must make a decision. He must decide right away in these professional development classes whether or not he is going to incorporate the necessary discipline to learn and practice these habits. This grasping of the recipe for success is crucial to the first-year African American male student in the HBCU environment. Mykerizi and Mills (2008) found that African American males who attend and graduate from most HBCUs gain on the average, higher professional workplace studies than their counterparts who are majority institution graduates. Still, the HBCU environment must be one comprised of a series of career preparatory structures that understand from whence they came, regarding their adjusting to the collegiate environment as a whole, and their need to adjust to the new environment while preparing for their future careers.

The career-counseling element that must be in lock-step with the career preparatory courses cannot be overstated. There must be a structure in which the first-year African American HBCU student must have a balance of the career counseling and the career preparatory courses classroom experience Owens, et. al (2010) state that "first-generation African American male students who are entering colleges and universities across the country may also need extensive support in the development and implementation of their career plans because of their lack of information about and exposure to college environments," and that student affairs personnel, being aware of the challenges that these students have experienced just to make it to the collegiate level and their worldviews, must draw upon these previous experiences to "provide first-generation African American male college students with career education and counseling that will enable them to choose a personally satisfying career that fits both their abilities and their interests" (p. 294). HBCU career counselors, understanding the societal barriers that African American male first-year college students have and will continue to face if they chose to pursue careers in the United States are primary concerns that HBCU career counselors must prepare to deal with, providing coping mechanisms and long-term strategic measures for the students' career preparation and success (Shumaker and Wood, 2016).

Finally, it must be understood that the aforementioned career preparatory structure designed to eliminate SIS from the mindset of the first-year African American male first-year HBCU student will only be successfully executed if HBCU administrators incorporate and encourage private, anonymous spaced on the university setting, such as counseling centers and new, future career-enhancing experiences. Bernard and Lowe (2019) state that "left unchecked, impostor syndrome can lead to a myriad of negative consequences, including social isolation, increased burnout and inappropriate career choices" they suggest the remedy of administrators addressing the negative mental health consequences associated with SIS, addressing the fact that SIS decreases self-esteem among students to the point of negatively affecting their academic performance, and establishing programs in which faculty can be liaisons to encourage students to seek professional counseling, join groups that foster support, and realize that it is a mark of strength, and not weakness, to engage in therapy-related experiences to improve one's mental health. Therefore, the key is the exposure of mental health counseling, career development courses, and career counseling that must be the workable triumvirate to combat SIS amongst first-year African American male HBCU students, and seek to eliminate the challenge before the student reaches the remaining on-campus years.

## CONCLUSION

The HBCU environment is a village for the African American male first-year student. That village must have the workable, effective resources and structures to encourage and assist the student to be the best academically and professionally-prepared individual possible. Academic, social, psychological and spiritual structures must be in place for the student's overall, well-rounded preparatory future academic and professional success. The HBCU that forges and retains this structure while never losing the rigor of the academic and professional preparatory areas, while showing care via the psychological, social and spiritual ones with the inclusion of sincere mentorship, are the environments that have obtained the blueprint for the student's ongoing, future success.

## REFERENCES

*Ways to Fix Education to Make Students Job Ready*. (2019). Canadian Press.

Bernard, D., & Lowe, T. (2019). Impostor Syndrome, Black College Students and How Administrators Can Help. *Diverse Issues in Higher Education*, *36*(14), 40.

Bernard, D. L., Hoggard, L. S., Neblett, E. W. Jr, & Neblett, E. W. (2018). Racial discrimination, racial identity, and impostor phenomenon: A profile approach. *Cultural Diversity & Ethnic Minority Psychology*, *24*(1), 51–61. doi:10.1037/cdp0000161 PMID:28414495

Bernard, D. L., Lige, Q. M., Willis, H. A., Sosoo, E. E., & Neblett, E. W. (2017). Impostor Phenomenon and Mental Health: The Influence of Racial Discrimination and Gender. *Journal of Counseling Psychology*, *64*(2), 155–156. doi:10.1037/cou0000197 PMID:28182493

Bernard, N. S., Dollinger, S. J., & Ramaniah, N. V. (2002). Applying the Big Five Personality Factors to the Impostor Phenomenon. *Journal of Personality Assessment*, *78*(2), 321–333. doi:10.1207/S15327752JPA7802_07 PMID:12067196

Clance, P. R. (1985). *The Impostor Phenomenon*. Peachtree.

Clance, P. R., & Imes, S. A. (1978). The imposter phenomenon in high achieving women: Dynamics and therapeutic intervention. *Psychotherapy (Chicago, Ill.)*, *15*(3), 241–247. doi:10.1037/h0086006

Cooper, J. N., & Hawkins, B. (2016). An anti-deficit perspective on black male student athletes' educational experiences at a historically black college/university. *Race, Ethnicity and Education*, *19*(5), 950–979. doi:10.1080/13613324.2014.946491

Duke, N. N., Campbell, S. D., Sauls, D. L., Stout, R., Story, M. T., Austin, T., Bosworth, H. B., Skinner, A. C., & Vilme, H. (2021). Prevalence of food insecurity among students attending four Historically Black Colleges and Universities. *Journal of American College Health*, 1–7.

Franklin, R., Younge, S., & Jensen, K. (2023). The role of historically Black colleges and universities (HBCUs) in cultivating the next generation of social justice and public service-oriented moral leaders during the racial reckoning and COVID-19 pandemics. *American Journal of Community Psychology*, *71*(1-2), 1. doi:10.1002/ajcp.12648 PMID:36661445

Haskins, N. H., Hughes, K. L., Crumb, L., Smith, A. R., Brown, S. S., & Pignato, L. (2019). Postmodern Womanism: Dismantling the Imposter Phenomenon for Black American College Students. *Negro Educational Review*, *70*(1–4), 5–25.

Kunjufu, J. (1997). *To Be Popular or Smart: The Black Peer Group*. African American Images.

Kunjufu, J. (2007). *Raising Black Boys*. Academic Press.

Mak, K. K. L., Kleitman, S., & Abbott, M. J. (2019). Impostor Phenomenon Measurement Scales: A Systematic Review. *Frontiers in Psychology*, *10*, 671. doi:10.3389/fpsyg.2019.00671 PMID:31024375

McElwee, R. O., & Yurak, T. J. (2010). The Phenomenology of the Impostor Phenomenon. *Individual Differences Research*, *8*(3), 184–197.

McGowan, B. L., Palmer, R. T., Wood, J. L., & Hibbler, D. F. (2016). *Black Men in the Academy: Narratives of Resiliency, Achievement, and Success*. Palgrave Macmillan. doi:10.1057/9781137567284

Murry, V. M., Bynum, M. S., Brody, G. H., Willert, A., & Stephens, D. (2001). African American single mothers and children in context: A review of studies on risk and resilience. *Clinical Child and Family Psychology Review*, *4*(2), 133–155. doi:10.1023/A:1011381114782 PMID:11771793

Mykerezi, E., & Milis, B. F. (2008). The Wage Earnings Impact of Historically Black Colleges andUniversities. (cover story). *Southern Economic Journal*, *75*(1), 173–187. doi:10.1002/j.2325-8012.2008.tb00897.x

National Center for Education Statistics. (2020). *Race/Ethnicity of College Faculty*. Author.

Norman, M. V. (2008). Coping Strategies: A Case Study of an African-American Male. *Annals of the American Psychotherapy Association*, *11*(3), 15–19.

Owens, D., Lacey, K., Rawls, G., & Holbert-Quince, J. A. (2010). First-Generation African American Male College Students: Implications for Career Counselors. *The Career Development Quarterly*, *58*(4), 291–300. doi:10.1002/j.2161-0045.2010.tb00179.x

Palmer, R. T., Davis, R. J., & Maramba, D. C. (2010). Role of an HBCU in Supporting Academic Success for Underprepared Black Males. *Negro Educational Review*, *61*(1–4), 85–106.

Peteet, B. J., Montgomery, L., & Weekes, J. C. (2015). Predictors of Imposter Phenomenon among Talented Ethnic Minority Undergraduate Students. *The Journal of Negro Education*, *84*(2), 175–186. doi:10.7709/jnegroeducation.84.2.0175

Rosenberger, A. (2021). The Impostor Phenomenon. *ITA Journal*, *49*(2), 24–26.

Shorette, C. R. II, & Palmer, R. T. (2015). Historically Black Colleges and Universities (HBCUs): Critical Facilitators of Non-Cognitive Skills for Black Males. *The Western Journal of Black Studies*, *39*(1), 18–29.

Shumaker, R., & Wood, J. L. (2016). *Understanding First- Generation Community College*. Academic Press.

Soft vs. hard skills: Know the difference. (2022). *Administrative Professional Today, 48*(2), 4.

Students: An Analysis of Covariance Examining Use of, Access to, and Efficacy Regarding Institutionally Offered Services. (n.d.). *Community College Enterprise, 22*(2), 9–17.

Taylor, Z. E., Larsen-Rife, D., Conger, R. D., Widaman, K. F., & Cutrona, C. E. (2010). Life stress, maternal optimism, and adolescent competence in single mother, African American families. *Journal of Family Psychology, 24*(4), 468–477.

Toldson, I. A. (2014). Myths Versus Realities. *Crisis, 121*(4), 12–17.

U.S. Census Bureau. (2006). *Current population survey: America's families and living arrangements*. Retrieved from www.census.gov/ population/www/socdemo/hh-fam/cps2006.html

Whitley, D. M., & Fuller-Thomson, E. (2017). African-American Solo Grandparents Raising Grandchildren: A Representative Profile of Their Health Status. *Journal of Community Health, 42*(2), 312–323. doi:10.1007/s10900-016-0257-8 PMID:27651164

Wood, J. L., Harrison, J. D., & Jones, T. K. (2016). Black Males' Perceptions of the Work–College Balance. *Journal of Men's Studies, 24*(3), 326–343. doi:10.1177/1060826515624378

# Chapter 2
# Demystifying the Process of Attending, Presenting at, and Reviewing for Academic Conferences:
## Considerations for Graduate Students

**Andy Jiahao Liu**
https://orcid.org/0000-0002-4586-0640
*University of Arizona, USA*

## ABSTRACT

*The "publish or perish" culture has put graduate students and faculty worldwide under increasing pressure to demonstrate their research productivity (i.e., producing and disseminating knowledge). Academic conferences, as a typical way of knowledge dissemination, offer chances for graduate students to socialize in the academic community and receive timely feedback from peers. However, those new to the conference experience may feel confused or even daunted. Drawing on the personal experience of an early career faculty in the field of applied linguistics, this chapter demystifies the whole process related to attending, presenting at, and reviewing for academic conferences. Mapping out the author's experiential trajectory as an active graduate student at academic conferences, the author details how the author has transitioned from a graduate attendee to an experienced presenter and a junior gatekeeper for academic conferences. Besides, the author offers a set of dos and don'ts to potential attendees, presenters, and reviewers at academic conferences.*

## INTRODUCTION: SETTING THE SCENE

The trending marketization of universities across the globe has brought the front graduate students and academic staff to publish in high-status international journals. In some countries (e.g., China), the international publication emerges as an increasing graduation requirement for doctoral and Master's students (Flowerdew, 2013). Consequently, graduate students are under pressure to "disseminate their research findings in English" (Flowerdew & Habibie, 2022, p.13). The publication of research articles, however, is in concert with other genres. For example, research articles may be preceded by conference presentations (Flowerdew & Habibie, 2022); in a similar vein, Swales (2004) pointed out that conference presentations maintain an *intermediate* status between research work and the accepted manuscript.

As an integral part of research communities (Rowley-Jolivet, 2002), the conference presentation deals with research work across levels of completion, varying from work-in-progress to publication dissemination and promotion. More often, conference presentations showcase preliminary findings and offer only "provisional claims and explanations" (Swales, 2004, p.202). Though researchers have already emphasized that conference presentation is a critical skill for academic researchers (Rowley-Jolivet & Carter-Thomas, 2005), graduate students and early career faculty would still find it challenging, confusing, or even daunting, especially for those new to the conference experience. Such an emotional burden may be intensified by public speaking anxiety, time pressure, and/or intensive real-time information processing during the *Question-and-Answer* section. What is worse, presenters also represent their programs and universities.

Besides the said high-stake and high-pressure characteristics, conference presentations popularize nowadays with their unique advantages. They provide venues for graduate students and early career faculty to socialize into the academic community of their field; offer chances for presenters to receive timely feedback on their research from peers; keep attendees informed of peer research preferences, the latest trend within the field, and future research directions. As Ventola (1999) artfully put it, "the conference situation creates a momentary feeling of intellectual companionship and sense of common understanding and experience, but unfortunately its effects may remain very *short-lived and local* (p.122).

To make the most of those *short-lived and local* conference experiences, prospective attendees, presenters, or even reviewers should familiarize themselves with the conventions or 'behind the scenes' information of academic conferences. Applied linguists, as Rowley-Jolivet and Cater-Thomas (2005) advocated, should shoulder their responsibilities to help scientific researchers play the conference game with essential discourse practices knowledge. Discussions about such discourse practices knowledge are well-documented in the literature (e.g., Hood & Forey, 2005; Hyland, 2004, 2012, 2015; Ventola et al., 2002; Wulff et al., 2009). Hood and Forey (2005), for example, analyzed ways of building interpersonal relationships with audiences at the *set-up* stage during conference presentations. In addition, there are also published experience-sharing manuscripts (e.g., De Costa, 2020; Galer-Unti & Tappe, 2009) detailing considerations and recommended actions before, during, and after the conference. Drawing on his extensive experience in attending the annual conference of the American Association for Applied Linguistics (AAAL), De Costa (2020) proposed various ways of navigating the AAAL conferences from the perspectives of presenters, concluding that attending conferences does "raise your visibility within the field" (p.48) either as graduate students or tenure-track faculty.

However, very little is known about the near-mythical dynamic trajectories from the peripheral participation (i.e., attendee) to its full participation (i.e., gatekeeper) at academic conferences as far as ERPP (English for Research Publication Purposes) is concerned. Also informing this study is De Costa's (2022) advocation that established scholars and emerging applied linguistics should spend strenuous efforts to "foster greater diversity, equity, inclusion and access" (p.96) for the next generations of scholars within the field. As a matter of fact, thriving in academic conferences is a long and uncertain process, and developing presenting and reviewing skills is a journey of endless trial and error for most scholars. This chapter therefore aims to address the said research gap and advocation, demystifying the whole process from attending, presenting at, to reviewing for academic conferences by drawing on the lived experience of an early career faculty (see more details in *My Personal Notes*) in the field of applied linguistics. Employing an autoethnographic approach, I detail how I transitioned from a graduate attendee to an experienced presenter and a junior reviewer for academic conferences within my field. Besides, I offer a set of *dos and don'ts* for potential attendees, presenters, and reviewers at academic conferences.

It is worth mentioning that this chapter does not intend to generalize its recommendation or present a particular position but to provide a critical view or considerations for graduate students and novice scholars. And even though I write with an applied linguistics background and use examples within the broad TESOL field, I feel that the practice and suggestions proposed here will hold true of any other conferences across disciplines. In the meantime, this autoethnography may serve as a starting point to encourage researchers from other disciplines to share the disciplinary-specific "behind-the-scene" information on academic conferences with wider audiences.

By scaffolding the socialization of newcomers into the conference community, this chapter will offer practical advice for graduate students to make the most of academic conferences and embrace the new normal of their academic careers. This chapter will also be of particular interest to researchers within the field of ERPP in particular and practitioners of EAP (English for Academic Purposes) and academic writing tutors in general.

## THEORETICAL AND METHODOLOGICAL LENS

As a particular communicative event, the conference presentation is featured with sociocultural and disciplinary characteristics. The understanding of and proficiency in conference presentations, sometimes a hidden curriculum for graduate education, thus is "an acquired, or learned skill" (Rowley-Jolivet & Carter-Thomas, 2005, p.45) within the community of practice (Lave & Wenger, 1991). Such a skill is usually acquired through *legitimate peripheral participation* (Lave & Wenger, 1991) or *learning in doing* within the context (i.e., conference venues in this case). As highlighted in the notion of legitimate peripheral participation, Lave and Wenger, from a sociocultural perspective, viewed learning as "a process of participation in communities of practice, participation that is at first legitimately peripheral but that increases gradually in engagement and complexity" (cover page).

*Legitimate,* because newcomers are given access to participate in social activities through membership or credited apprenticeship-like relationships with established members within the community. *Peripheral,* because participants come to the community of practice with a novice status. Through the interactions with old-timers, participants gain access to "sources for understanding through growing involvement" (Lave & Wenger, 1991, p.37) in a gradual manner. *Participation,* because participants acquired the skills via actual engagement during the process. In other words, the newcomers play various roles within the community of practice to develop the same knowledge as old-timers. Together, legitimate peripheral participation "provides a way to speak about the relations between newcomers and old-timers, and about activities, identities, artifacts, and communities of knowledge and practice" (Lave & Wenger, 1991, p.29).

Of particular interest to this chapter is the move from peripheral participation to full participation in the community of practice. In this chapter, the mastery of knowledge and skills related to conference presentation is situated and interrelated with the status change from *the attendee* to *the presenter* to *the reviewer* (see Figure 1). That is, the newcomers usually come to the conference as an attendee (i.e., audience) and/or a presenter to learn as much through various peripheral participation opportunities, such as listening to the keynote or plenary speeches, sitting in different parallel sessions, communicating with other attendees or presenters, and transferring the acquired-information into personal strategies or skills. After numerous presentations at conferences, newcomers will gradually gain acquittance with the old-timers or organizing committees. Such interactions will raise the visibility of newcomers and help presenters enter the review board to serve as gatekeepers via invitation or recommendation. Possibly, experienced presenters can also self-nominate themselves as reviewers for academic conferences; I will return to this point in the section titled *Being and becoming a conference reviewer*.

Methodologically, I adopt the autoethnography approach to recount my personal transition from a graduate attendee to an experienced conference presenter and a junior reviewer. As an often-used naturalistic approach within the field of ERPP, autoethnography builds on the researcher's lived personal experiences to connect with other like-minded scholars (Habibie et al., 2021) and enhance the understanding of "similar social phenomena in other sociocultural landscapes" (Yu, 2022, p.4). Through exploring hidden aspects of complex sociocultural contexts (Anderson, 2006), autoethnography also allows individuals to reflect on the socialization into various communities – in this case, academic conferences (Austin & Hickey, 2007).

With these methodological considerations, I then draw on personal memory (Canagarajah, 2012) to better map out the memorable moments marking my identity formation and transformation within the academic conference community of my field. To enhance trustworthiness, I revisited dozens of emails received from the conference organizing committees, dividing them into three categories: conference program book sharing, abstract acceptance/rejection status informing, and reviewer status alerting. Reflecting back, my transition resonates with the learning in doing as suggested by Lave and Wenger (1991), though I learned and grew up through trials and errors. Thus, the autoethnography approach adopted here also provides me with "an open and malleable frame in which a person *struggles* to come to terms with an ever-changing, ever-reconstructed, and reconstituted reality ... and the *struggle towards self-understanding* (Bochner, 2007, p.207).

## MY PERSONAL NOTES

*Thank you for your submission to the International Conference on xxx, which will be held virtually on xxx. After a rigorous review has been taken place, we are pleased to inform you that your abstract entitled xxx has been accepted for presentation at the conference. Congratulations on your acceptance. We look forward to meeting you at the conference. (Abridged from one of the abstract acceptance emails to the author of the present chapter)*

Researchers with conference abstract/proposal submission experiences should not be unfamiliar with the above email except for announcing the review result, either acceptance or rejection. Usually, academic conferences undergo four essential stages, initiated from the *call for papers (CFP)* to *abstract review and result announcement*, followed by *real-time conference presentations* happening months later, and perhaps concluded by *conference proceedings or similar publication opportunities in journals*.

In February 2021, I received the said email when I was hanging out with my friend in the street. I now can still recall how excited I was at the moment. The email exploded with joy in my heart, and a violent wave of happiness and relief washed over me. Similar to what scholars share on Twitter recently, I soon edited a Moment on WeChat (a Chinese counterpart to WhatsApp), spreading the news to my

*Figure 1. Academic conference: From peripheral participation to full participation*
Note. The size of the circle indicates the participation proportion within the community.

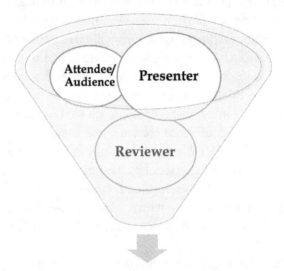

world. As my first attempt to socialize into the academic conference community, this email undoubtedly boosted my confidence and marked the beginning of my conference presenter identity. At that time, I was a first-year graduate student who had finished the first-semester coursework.

However, it should be acknowledged that not all (first) attempts will end with acceptance. Though I had a charming opening to attending conferences, I, several months later, began to receive rejection emails from stellar conferences (e.g., LTRC [Language Testing Research Colloquium]) in my field. The rejection emails, like those with congratulations, bring emotional influences to me and similar researchers worldwide. This time, I felt frustrated and disappointed.

I am not saying that first-timer should then give up due to the potential emotional burden. Instead, I am saying that graduate students should bravely reach out to seize potential opportunities to contribute to academic conferences, as rejection is a recurrent theme within academia. As a rule of thumb, graduate students can always start with their course papers or research projects with classmates, consulting professors for prospective conference information.

Following numerous national, regional, and international conference presentations, I then served as a graduate student reviewer for academic conferences of my field. In June 2022, I started my first review assignments for the incoming *TESOL 2023 International Convention & English Language Expo*. Unlike those with recommendations from or connections with established members, I self-nominated and competed for the reviewer position after I read the *Call for Reviewer* information on the conference website. In a similar vein, I earned two other reviewer appointments.

In total, during my MA (Master of Arts) period (i.e., 2020–2022), I disseminated my research findings at 17 conferences (including 1 offline conference and 16 online ones) and reviewed 22 proposals/abstracts for two high-ranking conferences in my community. I now work as an early career faculty with appointments in the English Language and Literature Studies Programme at my current affiliation. As

*Demystifying the Process of Attending, Presenting at, and Reviewing for Academic Conferences*

a continuum of my conference participation as a graduate student, I am still contributing abstracts to major conferences *(N=5, as of March 2023)* and soliciting reviewer opportunities.

Through sharing my personal story, I attempt to "evoke readers a feeling that the experience described is lifelike, believable, and possible" (Ellis, 2014, p.124). My identity trajectory from graduate student audience to presenter and reviewer is presented below in Figure 2. It is worth noting that I sometimes register as an audience only, though I often serve dual roles (i.e., audience and presenter) in conferences.

In the remainder of this chapter, I will detail how being a graduate student audience, graduate student presenter, and graduate student reviewer laid my growth from peripheral participation to the full circle of the academic conference community. In the meantime, I will introduce *dos and don'ts* at academic conferences from the perspectives of audience, presenter, and reviewer.

## AUDIENCE: EXPLORING SESSIONS BEFORE AND DURING THE CONFERENCE

This section presents graduate students with two core considerations in attending the academic conference as audiences. I first showcase how graduate students can secure the legitimate status of being an audience through appropriate access and registration fee. Following this, I elaborated on the strategies for audiences to maximize their participation through different conference sessions to make the most of the conferences before and during the conference.

### Access and Registration Fee

Being a conference audience provides graduate students with the least peripheral participation, as the audience primarily acts as knowledge consumers during the conference. Even though technological innovations have enabled a few conferences to offer free access to interested participants, conferences usually require all participants to pay a registration fee. Typically, graduate students can pay the said fee at a low cost, either with special offerings or a discount (e.g., *early bird price*). In my case, I primarily self-financed myself to pay the registration fee during the MA period. However, I encourage the reader to check the institution's policies before making the payment, as some institutions do offer travel funding to graduate students (especially Ph.D. students/candidates) to offset the cost.

But where could I get the conference information? How could I be an audience if funding is sufficient? All these questions may need to be clarified for novice graduate students. First and foremost, I

*Figure 2. Memorable moments in my identity transition*

| Audience | Presenter | Reviewer |
|---|---|---|
| December 2020 | February 2021 | June 2022 |

often pay attention to the emails sent within the institution, because faculty and departments will have internal activity promotions for webinars, workshops, and conferences. In the meantime, I sometimes would approach my course instructors for information, as professors, with full participation within the community, are happy to support and guide postgraduate students into the community. More importantly, the invisible connections among professors will make them an ideal source bank for calls for conference abstracts/proposals, manuscripts, or book chapters.

Besides those internal resources and activities, I also learn conference information by being a student member of professional organizations in my field. The discounted student membership identity grants me access to the resources and information shared within the community of practice. In that community, old-timers, in a frequent manner, would post the *calls for papers* announcements in *email listservs* for conferences, books, and special issues for journals. I would then seize the opportunities to increase my participation within the conference community. Readers within the applied linguistics field, for instance, could consider joining the BAAL (British Association of Applied Linguistics) and subscribe to the mailing list for prospective information. However, as the discussion of a professional organization is beyond the scope of this chapter, interested readers are recommended to read Byrnes (2020) for a full discussion related to engaging with professional organizations.

In addition, social networking applications, in this technological era, play an essential role in promoting incoming conference information. As one belonging to Generation Z, I rely on academic tweets from established members to keep up with conferences or the latest publication information. I also read conference advertisements from academic groups on Facebook and daily push notifications from scholarly official accounts on WeChat, where volunteers summarize the newest conference information worldwide. Put unsurprisingly, my sharp information literacy has facilitated or even sped up my growth into full participation in the conference community.

Though numerous information channels are discussed above, graduate students should keep away from those predatory conferences. Similar to predatory journals, these conference counterparts are organized by unknown conferencing organizing committees, claiming fake conference reputations and invited speakers. Meanwhile, predatory conferences only care about the profits they can make; to them, quantity is always over quality. I, therefore, suggest that graduate students double-check the information with peers and course instructors to avoid such unpleasant conference experiences. As presented below, the organizing committee of a predatory conference often attempts to seduce researchers with attractive benefits (i.e., Keynote Speaker).

*Greetings from XXX conferences! With great pleasure, we invite you to join us as* <u>a keynote speaker</u> *at our prestigious event "4th World Conference on XXX", which is all set to take place on XXX in XXX. (Abridged from one of the spam emails I received from the organizing committee of a predatory conference)*

## Time-Planning and Follow Your Interest

After obtaining access to conference information and settling down the registration fee, graduate students can prepare for the traveling. I encourage potential attendees to book a room in advance, particularly those near the conference venue, as wasting hours on transportation during the conference days is exhausting and will "make you miss social events ... that often take place in the evening" (De Costa, 2020, p.44). It is also worth noting that conference organizing committees often negotiate with nearby hotels for discount coupons. Graduate students can keep an eye out for potential information on conference websites or emails from the organizing committee.

Closer to the conference, the organizing committee will post the conference program book on its official website or via email for the audience's and presenter's reference. On the reception day, attendees can also find a physical copy of the program book in their reception packages. As the most important *Holy Bible* during the conference, the program book provides detailed information on presenter information, conference sessions (with time and venue information), and accepted abstracts. Readers can consult the *Key Terms and Definition* section for more details about the conference sessions.

On the audience side, graduate students should read through the program book in advance, circulating or marking out those sessions that interest them. As paid knowledge consumers, graduate students have the right to attend only those engaging sessions and leave early during the sessions they attend in a polite manner. Nevertheless, graduate students new to the conference experience should attend the designed *New Comer Sessions* to familiarize themselves with the conference in a relatively systematic and quick manner. In addition, the audience can write emails to interested presenters for a short meeting during the reserved conference networking session (De Costa, 2020) or have a personalized social event or coffee break.

On the main conference days, graduate students can go to the corresponding venue, immerse themselves in learning for hour(s), and take notes. After all, the attended sessions may inspire audiences with new research ideas or offer audiences support for their ongoing studies. Of note is that graduate students can bravely raise their hands during the *Question-and-Answer* section to ask for clarifications or link the presentation with their research. It should always bear in mind that, however, the audience should ask questions in a polite manner, as the interaction is a sort of scholarly communication rather than debate or quarrel. Besides, graduate students can later email the presenter to start a new conversation or continue the existing one.

Together, planning ahead of time, selecting a series of interesting sessions, and communicating with presenters in a critical but friendly manner enable graduate students to maximize their participation as audiences during the conference. Drawing on the lessons learned from audience experiences, graduate students can consider contributing abstracts/proposals to conferences and becoming a presenter.

## REVISITING CONFERENCE PRESENTATION: YOUR RESEARCH TALK(S)

The graduate student does not become a presenter at academic conferences overnight. Following the *Call for Papers* announcement, potential graduate student presenters will get involved in the presentation process with a tailored abstract relevant to the conference theme and topics. (Un)being recognized as a presenter is then subject to the acceptance/rejection status released by the conference organizing committee. To improve the acceptance rate, graduate students must impress reviewers with their abstracts. This section thus introduces skills in composing high-quality abstracts, followed by considerations before, during, and after the presentation.

### Abstract Matters: Status and Strategies

A conference abstract is different from its counterpart in journal articles or book chapters, because the conference abstract is composed with reference to and evaluated by varying criteria across conferences.

For example, the abstract should be themed to that particular conference for the sake of fitness and meet the word requirement as stipulated in the *Call for Papers* announcement. Although some authors, for post-publication dissemination, would use the same abstract that appeared in the publication, they would still need to revise or even rewrite that abstract to keep it in line with the conference requirements. To grant a presenter status, graduate students therefore are highly recommended to tailor their conference abstracts for each conference with minor or major editing.

Besides granting the presenter identity status, conference abstracts also serve as the basis for award selection. Graduate students can usually compete for the *Student Travel Award* and *Best Student Paper Award*; however, the evaluation criteria depend on the conference organizing committee. In the meantime, some conferences would assess the presentation quality of student presenters and nominate them for *Best Student Presenter Award*. Limited by words, this chapter will not disclose details; interested readers can find more details about such award information on each conference website or in email communications with the organizing committee. One rule of thumb is that never hesitate to compete for these awards.

Being the gatekeeper of presenter identity and prospective student awards, conference abstracts thus pose challenges to graduate students with extending meaning and impression within limited wordings. Writing a high-quality conference abstract thus requires graduate students to get familiar with the conventions. Below, I illustrate abstract writing skills with the 'behind the scenes' information from the perspective of a junior reviewer.

Briefly, the conference abstract, according to its original research characteristics, falls into two major categories: empirical and theoretical. In an empirical-oriented abstract, graduate students should save space for describing the rigorous research design/methodology and presenting the novel findings. In contrast, the theoretical-oriented ones lure graduate students to showcase the theoretical basis (i.e., where does this theory/framework from?) and potential contributions to the field. Though these two types of abstracts are organized around different emphasis, graduate students still could follow the basic writing strategies:

a) compose a catchy title for the abstract;
b) state the background in a succinct manner with reference to real-life situations or the available literature;
c) identify the existing problem against the mentioned backdrop and illustrate a strong justification for the urgent need to solve the identified problem (i.e., the research gap and research significance);
d) present responses to the existing problem in the present study (i.e., research questions, research design);
e) highlight the contributions and implications to the field.

After composing the draft abstract, graduate students can attempt to read those previously award-winning abstracts or existing accepted abstracts to identify the potential room for improvement. If inaccessible to the said abstracts, graduate students can read the evaluation criteria of each component, inviting peers or instructors to offer a mock review for the abstract or scheduling a writing consultation with the university writing center. With rounds of revision, the abstract should be uploaded to the submission system with other required personal information.

Following months of reviewing, the conference organizing committee would send separate emails to alert submitters of their abstracts being accepted or rejected. The acceptance marks a new cycle of preparations for the incoming presentations. However, the rejection doesn't mean anything related to the academic potential, and graduate students should not take feedback personally; in fact, only limited slots would be offered at each conference, and being rejected is expected within the academic community. If the conference organizing committee offers reviewer feedback, graduate students should then read critically to revise the abstract, address some outstanding concerns mentioned by the reviewers, and resubmit the abstract to other conferences. After all, every abstract will finally find a home to present.

## Before the Presentation

*Congratulations on being accepted for the presentation!* Graduate students surely can feel happy about and proud of their achievements so far. However, graduate students should calm down and make preparations for the presentation. Abstract only admits graduate students into the presenter cycle, and the presentation to happen months later establishes graduate students' identity as qualified presenters or research disseminators for scholarly communication within that community of practice.

To get started, graduate students need to condense their page(s)-length manuscripts into 15-minute/25-minute research talks with real-time discussion sections, depending on the conference arrangements. In this reorganizing process, graduate students transfer essential information into Slides as visual supports during the presentation. To make it engaging, graduate students could add some animations or GIFs (Graphic Interchange Format); however, the animations and GIFs undoubtedly will distract the audience's attention. Figures within the Slides should also be planned carefully, as a figure speaks more than thousands of words. In addition to those visual considerations, the chunk of text in each slide should be manageable for both the presenter and the audience; the audience would not expect a presenter to read word-by-word within each slide. Personally, I would limit the text on each page to a maximum of 130 words. In the meantime, the majority of the presentation time should be reserved for the methodology and results/findings section (*the most exciting part*), where researchers explain their strategies for handling the research gap and showcase their contributions to the field.

After finishing the presentation slides, graduate students could proofread the slides after three or five days to identify typos. Meanwhile, they could hold a pre-presentation rehearsal among peers for feedback on slide design and mode of delivery. When the conference venue information is confirmed, the graduate student presenter should mark down the exact time schedule and location information. If possible, the student presenter could arrive 30 minutes before the session to check the device compatibility (e.g., light and sound). Though technical issues infrequently happen, identifying potential problems will rescue graduate students from possible embarrassing situations. Besides, following the dress code will present audiences with a professional attitude.

## During the Presentation

On the reserved presentation timeslot, the graduate student presenter stands in front of numerous audience (including experts within the field and peers eager to know the research), feeling anxious or pressured. However, the presenter should be clear that the audience comes with interest and curiosity. They are not coming to judge the research; instead, they come to learn and keep informed of the research design and findings. So, dear graduate student presenter, take a deep breath and greet the audience with a smile.

Following that, the presenter can start the slide presentation and deliver it at a comfortable pace as what they have done in the pre-presentation rehearsal. Refrain from feeling anxious about the accent; the audience does not assess the presenter as speaking test examiners. They only care about the research;

presenters, especially non-native English speakers, thus should emphasize presenting the research in a clear manner.

## After the Presentation

Graduate students typically take relief after the presentation, as they no longer need to worry about the presentation delivery. However, the most challenging part – the real-time *Question & Answer* section – comes subsequently after the thank-you message. During the following five to ten minutes, graduate students are questioned by audiences for clarification on different research aspects and even challenged by audiences in research design and research findings. This, of course, is not an easy task.

However, being cognizant of the hidden rules will ease the anxiety and improve the situation. First, the audience uses questions as a channel for scholarly communication; they are not criticizing the presenter or the research. Thus, graduate students should not feel frustrated with questions. Second, the presenter is always the Master of that presentation; no one in this world will ever be more familiar with this research than the presenter. In other words, the presenter owns the final say in whether accept or reject the suggestion from the audience. But the presenter should and must make the rebuttal or reply in a polite manner; we are not coming to conferences for debate and quarrels.

Furthermore, some audience may send follow-up emails to the student presenter with questions or requests for slides. To enhance identity formation, graduate students are encouraged to make timely responses in their spare time during the conference days. Sometimes, such connections may turn into collaboration and friendship. Another potential venue is that the conference organizing committee may edit so-called conference proceedings to collect presented papers. If this is the case, the presenter should revise the slides and reorganize the written manuscript with feedback from the audience to improve the quality and tailor the length and structure for the proceeding contributions.

## BEING AND BECOMING A CONFERENCE REVIEWER

Being and becoming a conference reviewer presents graduate students with chances to fully understand the review mechanism behind the scenes. Such information will help potential reviewers improve their abstracts according to the evaluation criteria. Besides functioning as gatekeepers in screening out qualified abstracts/proposals, reviewers also work as facilitators in helping submitters/authors improve their submissions with detailed feedback and comments. However, being and becoming a reviewer does not happen overnight. Typically, reviewers are expected to have expertise in relevant topics in particular and knowledge of the field in general. As noted above, an experienced conference presenter grows into a conference reviewer through the invitation from the conference organizing committee, the recommendation from established members within the community of practice, or the self-nomination in public recruitment announcements. The present chapter, drawing on my lived experience, only focuses on self-nomination in public recruitment announcements.

Self-nomination in public recruitment announcements, in fact, is a response to the global "ongoing peer-review crisis" (Habibie & Starfield, 2022). The said crisis and the pandemic worldwide have posed challenges for editors or conference organizing committees to seek qualified reviewers for the voluntary but time-exhausting review job. The self-nominated peer reviewer thus can back up the rigorous review process. Nevertheless, not all self-nominated peer reviewers are accepted. As a measure of quality assurance and management, the conference committee would screen the interested party's previous experience in presenting at and reviewing for academic conferences. Though challenging, graduate students, with sufficient presentation experience, are encouraged to submit their applications when they notice such a *Call for Reviewer* notice on the conference website.

Once informed of the reviewer application status, graduate students will receive information related to the review system, the evaluation criteria (or rubrics), review assignments, and potential reviewer training videos. As novice reviewers, graduate students should read through the shared documents or information to familiarize themselves with the review process; some conferences may even offer one or two previous abstracts for training purposes.

After skimming through the assigned abstracts, reviewers would make evaluations of the quality of the abstract. The evaluation normally comprises three parts: scale evaluation, review recommendation, and feedback/comments. The scale evaluations require student reviewers to indicate a score (e.g., 1-5) for different criteria (e.g., appropriateness to the conference theme and quality of research design) as stipulated in the *Call for Papers*. The review recommendation asks reviewers to indicate their overall impression of the abstract, choosing from accept, accept on the waitlist, or reject. Together, the given score and the review recommendation serve as the main indicators for the conference organizing committee to include or exclude an abstract in the conference program book. The *optional* feedback/comments section provides sources for authors to improve the abstract. To level the playing field, each abstract is usually reviewed by two or three reviewers.

However, composing high-quality and constructive reviews is challenging. Graduate students often learn to write such comments through imitation or recommendations in the reviewer training documents. As reviewers, graduate students should write in a professional, friendly, and collegial manner, using that review to communicate with the author(s). *Professional*, because the reviewer shows their understanding of the abstract and offers suggestions for improvement. *Friendly and collegial*, because the reviewer is making suggestions and will recognize the author once the program book is available. In the meantime, graduate students should focus on the content rather than the language dimension, as academic English is an additional language for all researchers (Flowerdew & Habibie, 2022). Of particular note is that graduate students should rescue themselves from the situation where they recognize the abstract submitter from acquittanced peers or colleagues. A review comment is presented below for graduate students' reference and consideration:

*Thank you for submitting your proposal to XXX. Materials development, especially localized materials with adherence to the existing curriculum, is one area with increased attention. Developing and creating a mini-book by students, for sure, will improve their engagement with language learning and will develop their competencies. While I feel this topic will interest audiences to some extent, the information revealed from the proposal has prevented me from accepting it for presentation. For one thing, your title is not formatted in a scholarly manner. At the current stage, I can only get a general sense, but not the specific areas you want to address in the presentation. For another, your writing in the Summary, especially the cohesion and coherence, is broken. I have no idea how the first paragraph is suddenly changed to 'First' concerning the development procedures in your context. In the meantime, the missing reference within the text and the strange reference that appeared at the end suggest that the academic convention is not followed. You should and must cite literature to support your claims and your argumentation. Again, thanks for your submission. (Abridged from one of the abstract review comments I wrote)*

## CONCLUDING REMARKS

Collectively, this autobiographical reflective account details my progress from graduate attendee to conference gatekeeper and my peripheral participation to full participation within the academic conferences. As noted throughout the chapter, the identity integration among the audience, presenter, and reviewer has shaped my current socialization into the community of practice. For example, my reviewer identity has also undoubtedly further improved my performance as a presenter and audience in future academic conferences. In other words, my desire for development and my existing experience accumulated throughout the engagement with academic conferences have collaboratively facilitated my socialization process and helped me achieve initial success in my academic career during the MA (Master of Arts) period. While I don't mention it in an explicit manner, the hidden support and encouragement from peers and mentors (i.e., course instructors and supervisors) have moved me forward toward this gatekeeper identity.

This chapter will also bring implications, albeit small, for other graduate students worldwide. While each of us may experience different trajectories throughout the progress, the above-mentioned considerations for conference presentations in general and the following recommendations in particular may still be useful even though they are not generalizable. First, graduate students worldwide should make use of technology to get them informed of the latest research trend and research opportunities. For example, keeping an eye on academic social networking applications (ResearchGate, Twitter, Academia.edu) would offer graduate students to get updated knowledge and promote their research for a broad impact. Second, graduate students should take the initiatives to join and embrace the community of practice. Academia would not offer chances to those who are waiting but only to those who could seize the opportunity. Third, the hidden curriculum within academia can only be learned through trial and error if graduate students do not own the resources and access to supportive mentors. Though challenging, the stories experienced and the marks left during that trajectory would undoubtedly make graduate students well-prepared to embrace the incoming ups and downs.

In the meantime, this chapter will assist educators, especially EAP (English for Academic Purposes) or academic writing tutors, in better preparing graduate students for academic conferences. For example, academic writing tutors could provide explicit instructions on composing high-quality abstracts based on the tips showcased within the present chapter. Besides, EAP faculty, with reference to this chapter, may consider developing a specialized course detailing the considerations before, during, and after the academic conference; the teachers could organize a small-scale mock conference to enhance the presentation skills of graduate students. Alternatively, EAP faculty can convert ideas expressed within the chapter into workshop series. With explicit instructions, graduate students will gradually get accustomed to academic conferences, contributing well-written abstracts and delivering impressive conference presentations.

With these considerations in mind, I hope potential readers, especially graduate students, can make the most of conference experiences to enjoy "a momentary feeling of intellectual companionship and sense of common understanding and experience" (Ventola, 1999, p.122).

## ACKNOWLEDGMENT

This study received no specific funding from any funding agency in the public, commercial, or not-for-profit sectors. As a reflection of my academic conference experiences during the MA (Master of Arts) period, this book chapter is dedicated to the generous support and trust from those who mentored and encouraged me. In the meantime, I value and appreciate the editors' and anonymous reviewers' feedback and comments on the earlier drafts of this book chapter. However, the remaining errors are entirely my responsibility.

## REFERENCES

Anderson, L. (2006). Analytic autoethnography. *Journal of Contemporary Ethnography*, *35*(4), 373–395. doi:10.1177/0891241605280449

Austin, J., & Hickey, A. (2007). Autoethnography and teacher development. *The International Journal of Interdisciplinary Social Sciences: Annual Review*, *2*(2), 369–378. doi:10.18848/1833-1882/CGP/v02i02/52189

Bochner, A. P. (2007). Notes toward an ethics of memory in autoethnographic inquiry. In N. K. Denzin & M. D. Giardina (Eds.), *Ethical futures in qualitative research: Decolonizing the politics of knowledge* (pp. 197–208). Routledge.

Byrnes, H. (2020). Engaging with professional organizations. In L. Plonsky (Ed.), *Professional development in applied linguistics* (pp. 139–152). John Benjamins. doi:10.1075/z.229.10byr

Canagarajah, A. S. (2012). Teacher development in a global profession: An autoethnography. *TESOL Quarterly*, *46*(2), 258–279. doi:10.1002/tesq.18

De Costa, P. I. (2020). Making the most of your applied linguistic conference experience: Things to do before, during, and after the event. In L. Plonsky (Ed.), *Professional development in applied linguistics* (pp. 41–48). John Benjamins. doi:10.1075/z.229.04dec

De Costa, P. I. (2022). Opening the gates for the next generation of scholars. In P. Habibie & A. K. Hultgren (Eds.), *The Inner World of Gatekeeping in Scholarly Publication* (pp. 83–98). Springer Nature. doi:10.1007/978-3-031-06519-4_6

Ellis, C. (2004). *The ethnographic I: A methodological novel about autoethnography*. Altamira Press.

Flowerdew, J. (2013). English for research publication purposes. In B. Paltridge & S. Starfield (Eds.), *The handbook of English for specific purposes* (pp. 301–321). Wiley.

Flowerdew, J., & Habibie, P. (2022). *Introducing English for research publication purposes*. Routledge.

Galer-Unti, R. A., & Tappe, M. K. (2009). Demystifying the abstract submission and conference presentation process. *Health Educator : Journal of Eta Sigma Gamma*, *41*(2), 64–67.

Habibie, P., Sawyer, R. D., & Norris, J. (2021). Thinking beyond ourselves: Career reflections on the Trojan Horse of Hegemonic Discourses. In P. Hibibie & S. Burgess (Eds.), *Scholarly publication trajectories of early-career scholars: insider perspectives* (pp. 299–320). Springer. doi:10.1007/978-3-030-85784-4_17

Habibie, P., & Starfield, S. (2022). English for research publication purposes: Two significant exigencies. *Journal of English for Research Publication Purposes*, *3*(2), 165–168. doi:10.1075/jerpp.00012.edi

Hood, S., & Forey, G. (2005). Introducing a conference paper: Getting interpersonal with your audience. *Journal of English for Academic Purposes, 4*(4), 291–306. doi:10.1016/j.jeap.2005.07.003

Hyland, K. (2004). *Disciplinary discourses: Social interactions in academic writing*. University of Michigan Press.

Hyland, K. (2012). *Disciplinary identities: Individuality and community in academic discourse*. Cambridge University Press. doi:10.1017/9781009406512

Hyland, K. (2015). *Academic publishing: Issues and challenges in the construction of knowledge*. Oxford University Press.

Lave, J., & Wenger, E. (1991). *Situated learning: Legitimate peripheral participation*. Cambridge University Press. doi:10.1017/CBO9780511815355

Rowley-Jolivet, E. (2002). Science in the making: Scientific conference presentations and the construction of facts. In E. Ventola, C. Shalom, & S. Thompson (Eds.), *The language of conferencing* (pp. 95–125). Peter Lang.

Rowley-Jolivet, E., & Carter-Thomas, S. (2005). The rhetoric of conference presentation introductions: Context, argument, and interaction. *International Journal of Applied Linguistics, 15*(1), 45–70. doi:10.1111/j.1473-4192.2005.00080.x

Swales, J. M. (2004). *Research genres: Exploration and applications*. Cambridge University Press. doi:10.1017/CBO9781139524827

Ventola, E. (1999). Semiotic spanning at conferences: Cohesion and coherence in and across conference papers and their discussions. In W. Bublitz, U. Lenk, & E. Ventola (Eds.), *Coherence in spoken and written discourse* (pp. 101–123). John Benjamins. doi:10.1075/pbns.63.09ven

Ventola, E., Shalom, C., & Thompson, S. (2002). *The language of conferencing*. Peter Lang.

Wulff, S., Swales, J. M., & Keller, K. (2009). "We have about seven minutes for questions": The discussion section from a specialized conference. *English for Specific Purposes, 28*(2), 79–92. doi:10.1016/j.esp.2008.11.002

Yu, C. (2022). An autoethnography of an international English language teaching assistant's identity paradoxes in an EFL context. *International Journal of Qualitative Studies in Education*. doi:10.1080/09518398.2022.2061624

## ADDITIONAL READINGS

Becker, L. (2014). *Presenting your research: Conferences, symposiums, poster presentations and beyond*. SAGE Publications. doi:10.4135/9781473919815

Burford, J., & Henderson, E. F. (2023). *Making sense of academic conferences: presenting, participating and organizing* (1st ed.). Routledge. doi:10.4324/9781003144885

Coleman, J. A. (2014). How to get published in English: Advice from the outgoing Editor-in-Chief. *System*, *42*, 404–411. doi:10.1016/j.system.2014.01.004

De Costa, P. I. (2020). Making the most of your applied linguistic conference experience: Things to do before, during, and after the event. In L. Plonsky (Ed.), *Professional development in applied linguistics* (pp. 41–48). John Benjamins. doi:10.1075/z.229.04dec

Hood, S., & Forey, G. (2005). Introducing a conference paper: Getting interpersonal with your audience. *Journal of English for Academic Purposes*, *4*(4), 291–306. doi:10.1016/j.jeap.2005.07.003

Konzett, C., Jessner, U., & Kramsch, C. J. (2012). *Any questions?: Identity construction in academic conference discussions*. De Gruyter. doi:10.1515/9781614510246

Madden, C. G., & Rohlck, T. N. (1997). *Discussions and interaction in the academic community*. University of Michigan Press.

Mair, J. (2014). *Conferences and conventions: A research perspective*. Routledge. doi:10.4324/9780203121740

Rowley-Jolivet, E., & Carter-Thomas, S. (2005). The rhetoric of conference presentation introductions: Context, argument, and interaction. *International Journal of Applied Linguistics*, *15*(1), 45–70. doi:10.1111/j.1473-4192.2005.00080.x

Swales, J. M. (2004). *Research genres: Exploration and applications*. Cambridge University Press. doi:10.1017/CBO9781139524827

Ventola, E., Shalom, C., & Thompson, S. (2002). *The language of conferencing*. Peter Lang.

## KEY TERMS AND DEFINITIONS

**Keynote/Plenary Presentation:** Invited speeches from big names/rising scholars within the relevant field. Often, presenters will introduce and showcase the whole field/topic in detail and recommend future research agendas.

**Networking Event:** It is usually arranged by the conference organizing committee to make presenters or audience get acquittance with each other, if only. Sometimes, the organizing committee will make special arrangements, such as "Meeting the Editors" or "the graduate students networking session."

**Paper Presentation:** Oral research showcase lasting for specific times (e.g., 30 minutes) with(out) Question and Answer section. The length and format vary across conferences.

**Parallel/Concurrent Session:** Papers or posters are presented at the same time but in different locations. Usually, the conference organizing committee will arrange a series of concurrent sessions throughout the conference.

**Poster Presentation:** Visual research showcase happening at a fixed time during the conference. Most often, the conference organizing committee will ask presenters to stand in front of their posters to answer questions from interested audiences.

**Pre-Conference Workshop:** Invited speakers offer hours of learning chances reserved for particular topics, including but not limited to, statistical analysis, addressing peer review, and innovative pedagogies. It usually happens before the main conference days and requires separate registration at a low cost.

**Predatory Conference:** Conference with fake reputations or high similarity to the high-ranking/stellar conferences within the field. Normally, predatory conferences will charge high registration fees for profit.

**Symposium/Colloquium:** It usually includes three or four presentations on specific topics/themes. Following the presentation, a discussant or facilitator will summarize key points and invite discussions among speakers.

# Chapter 3
# Engaging International Students as Curriculum Co-Creators

**Chi Maher**
*University of Greenwich, London, UK*

**Catherine Bedwei-Majdoub**
https://orcid.org/0009-0007-5735-305X
*Ravensbourne University, London, UK*

## ABSTRACT

*The chapter examines the process of engaging post-graduate students in co-creation of the curriculum. Despite extensive research in curriculum design, there remains more to discover about how engaging postgraduate students in co-creation of the curricular impacts their awareness of the link between their learning and their career chosen paths. The research employed qualitative data collected from 54 post-graduate international business management students studying in UK higher education institutions. The findings suggest encouraging students to co-design the curricular empowers, motivates them as active participants in their learning and prepares them for the world of work. The research contributes to the literature by demonstrating that providing opportunities for students to co-create the curriculum should be embedded from the start of the curriculum development process.*

## 1. INTRODUCTION

This chapter is an exploration of the link between business management student's participation in co-curriculum design and their chosen career paths. It approaches this exploration via the recent conceptual shift in higher education in the perceived place of students – from subordinates to their lecturers and professors (traditionally seen as purveyors and creators of knowledge) to their co-producers and partners in imparting knowledge and stimulating learning. This conceptual shift is, in this chapter, encapsulated by the phrase 'curriculum co-creation,' and specifically the idea of students as co-creators of the curriculum *alongside* academics in the higher education sector. Furthermore, the chapter explains how international students on postgraduate business management courses have been involved in curricula

DOI: 10.4018/978-1-7998-7999-2.ch003

co-creation and how their involvement connects them to their chosen career paths. In the 21st Century how individuals plan their career paths may be related to their profession, qualifications or simply moving around to maximize progression.

Students' participation in Higher Education curricula co-creation dates to Dewey (1916; William, 2017), who argued that education is a social contract facilitated by educators who, Dewey thought, could move individuals towards national identity, citizenship, and authentic democracy. These democratic ideals persist and endure within the contemporary higher education environment. In the UK, the base for those who participated in the research used for this chapter, international students arriving for postgraduate study are finding themselves positioned as important stakeholders whose experiences and unique perspectives are as equally valid as the academic staff tasked to teach them. They were encouraged to engage in their studies as co-producers of knowledge. That is, as active participants with their peers' learning and development. In short, once in the UK, international students discover that they are studying at non-traditional, pragmatic, and increasingly Deweynian learning environments (Bacon & Sloam, 2010) that prioritize autonomous thinking over the deference to lecturers and professors expected of them in their home countries. In the UK's pervading liberality (Kings College, 2023), increasingly higher education staff are involving students in curriculum co-creation and celebrating it as a late recognition of their equal validity.

But what is curriculum co-creation? According to Cook-Sather et al., (2014, pp. 6-7) it is "a collaborative, reciprocal process through which all participants have the opportunity to contribute equally, although not necessarily in the same ways, to curricular or pedagogical conceptualization, decision making, implementation, investigation, or analysis". Thus, they urge academics not to speak frivolously about partnering with students to improve learning and teaching. They ask them to establish curriculum co-creation on strong working relationships that foster respect, reciprocity, and shared responsibility: and their emphasis are supported by literature. For example, Kolb (1984) and Tomlinson (2023) provided a range of rationales for involving students in the development and design of the curriculum, with the key among them being that learning deepens with engaged activity and through experience, i.e., that it is shared between the instructor (enabling conceptualization) and the student (reflecting from ontic experiences and actions). Bovrill et al., (2011) and Gironella (2023) have found that students' participation in curriculum co-creation emboldens them to take more responsibility for their own learning and commitment.

Moreover, Senior et al., (2014) and Kahn and Anderson (2019) have noticed that participating students have enhanced levels of confidence, satisfaction, and critical thinking, i.e., skills that are much-sought after by public, private and third sector organizations. Additionally, Finn and Zimmer (2012) established links between curriculum co-creation and student engagement, while Shafaei and Nejati (2012) connected co-creation to empowerment, and Senior et al. (2014) to employability. Furthermore, Borge et al., (2020) and Vulperhorst et al., (2020) found positive links between student's involvement in curriculum co-creation and improved grades, learning, collaboration, confidence, and motivation.

Despite the variousness of the above research, there is still limited exploration of *how* international students studying in the UK are being involved and whether their involvement helps them to better understand the progression from academic context to world of work.

The chapter attempts to redress this knowledge gap, and thus represents an important contribution to what is known about the importance and practice of curriculum co-creation within higher education environments. Its value emerges from the fact that the business environment and the world of work rapidly change. The recent Covid-19 pandemic confirmed this. Following the slowdown and even standstill of whole industries, work-from-home, and furloughs brought on by the national lockdowns in 2019, individuals have been searching for alternative modes of work and income streams.

Organizations in industries and sectors that had already downsized, and/or delayed their workforce, were finding that employees wanted even greater freedom, more flexibility. In short, the coronavirus revealed that career paths based on a hierarchical, vertical progression from one role "up-the-ladder" to the better next one above, need not be the only model for progression for individuals or organizations. In other words, career path choices are no longer determined by how the organization does business (Steup & Neta, 2020), but by how individual employees see themselves in them; creating and recreating their identities by self-directing and managing their careers to achieve their ambitions.

The last two decades have confirmed that graduates often chose lateral and cross-functional career moves, as Arthur (2017) intelligent career model suggests. This model (discussed in section 2.2 below) proposes three ways of knowing: knowing-why (motivation to work), knowing-how (acquiring job related skills and knowledge so by implication learning), and knowing-whom (developing work related relationships and networks). Thus, it is a useful framework for this chapter's exploration of how the academic environment can prepare students for their career paths because it implies that the individual's career motives, motivation, networking work-based learning, values, and career needs shape the trajectory of their progression from academic to their chosen career paths.

Most Higher Education Institution students (of any discipline) are concerned with how their studies can bring them closer to their ideal career. For international students embarking on postgraduate education in a time of high student fees – at an average cost of £11,000 per year at UK universities – access to a career is the critical factor when choosing a university course. Therefore, it is reasonable to assume that students of business management are particularly invested in how their courses can support their pursuit of a career.

This assumption is predicated on the popularity of business management courses across the UK and beyond. According to the British Academy (2021) business related courses attracted 16.3% of the UK's 2.5 million University students in 2019/2020 opting for this subject ahead of medicine (which attracted just 11.7% of the total student population). Their report notes that the majority percentage represents 1 in 5 postgraduates. These larger numbers of students choosing to study business management - and this popularity is visible globally rather than a phenomenon of only the UK higher education institutions - highlights the importance of smoothing students' path from their academic learning into performing well at work.

Accordingly, in the following sections, the academic-student co-creation of the curriculum will be discussed as the ideal substantive situation for postgraduate international business management students wanting to establish their business careers by a prior or contemporaneous close academic study of business and management. In this context of using their academic programs to prepare students for the world of work, this chapter facilitates discourse on the value and meaning of co-creation by evaluating how international students on postgraduate business programs are being engaged in curriculum co-creation in Higher Education Institutions in the UK. The chapter identifies different activities in which students participated in the process and discusses learning and career benefits for students, and thus bridges the knowledge gap in this area. The chapter is putting forward student involvement in curriculum co-creation as an exemplar for career preparation to support their chosen career path. Consequently, the research informing this chapter had the following aim, objectives, and questions.

## 1.1 Research Aim

To understand how students are engaged in curriculum co-creation and if their participation influences their chosen career paths.

## 1.2 Research Objectives

In view of the above research aim, the research objectives are to:

a.  identify how students are being involved in curriculum co-creation at Higher Education Institutions in the UK.
b.  investigate how students' participation in co-creation of the curriculum influences their chosen career paths.
c.  understand the learning and career benefits of encouraging students to participate in co-creation of the curriculum.

Considering these research objectives and the research aim, the study sought to address the following research questions:

1.  What are the different ways in which students are being actively involved in curriculum co-creation?
2.  Does students' participation in co-creation of curriculum influence their chosen career paths?
3.  Are there learning and career benefits of encouraging students to participate in curriculum co-creation?

In relation to the aim, objectives, and research questions, the following review of literature has the dual purpose of offering a background to international students on postgraduate business management courses at UK higher education institutions. It then discusses the concept of curriculum co-creation, the boundaryless career model's usefulness as a framework for exploring how and whether involving students as co-creators of the curriculum helps them to prepare for the world of work.

## 2. LITERATURE REVIEW

The review of literature has two key aims. The first is that it traces out the possible connections between co-creation (when educators work collaboratively with others, including students, to create components of the curricula) and students' career paths (a series of job roles and work experiences that enables an individual to achieve their chosen career path goals). It endorses co-creation as an effective teaching approach, a creative pedagogy, that also helps academics to learn more about international students' perspectives and experiences of UK Higher Education institutions. The second is that it draws on an existing career framework from which international students' progression from the academic setting to work can be discussed.

Research scholars (Lomer & Mittelmeier, 2021; Valiente-Riedl et al., 2021) have noted that, due to how teaching and learning is approached in international student's home countries, these students are often reluctant recipients of creative pedagogies. Their desire to uphold the status quo and their unfamiliarity with the level of critical thinking required in postgraduate learning sessions, coupled with their limited range of UK standard academic skills, and sometimes, fragile grasp of the English language proficiency, limits their engagement and contributions to curriculum co-creation, especially with regards to the loftier goals Higher Education Institutions have for curriculum co-creation.

As an example of how Higher Education Institutions tend to view the process, University College London, ranked among the world's Top 10 universities for the past twelve years, describe their understanding and use of co-creation as that which 'informs curriculum and assessment design;' what 'happens within the curriculum;' and an 'equity-seeking practice,' that 'disrupts more traditional staff/student relationships, asking both students and educators to occupy new roles within the process of learning that may seem unfamiliar,' (University College London, 2023).

For the purposes of this chapter, this type of disruption of hierarchy, promoted on the basis that it gives access to otherwise under-represented groups, is an exploration of the insights from international students on their input into co-creation sessions. Such insights *should* confirm, as Wood and Louw (2018) and Collins and Callaghan (2018) have already indicated, that being involved in curriculum co-creation improves students' 'cognitive development, their socialization and cross-cultural understanding' (Bedwei-Majdoub, 2023, pp. 2). However, as the next section indicates, the matter is not that straightforward. Indeed (in section 2.2 below), it becomes apparent that students are not often aware of the important connections between co-creation and knowledge acquisition, cognitive success, and career paths.

## 2.1 Co-Creation and the Business Management Curriculum

Co-creation is a constructivist view of knowledge as something that is socially constructed rather than being passed from academics to students (Bovill, 2020; Doyle et al., 2021). The social constructivist conceives learning as collaborative, and knowledge as emerging from an individual's interaction with culture, society, and its members. In Higher Education Institutions context, the inference for student curriculum co-creators is that they are likely to develop a deeper "heavyweight" knowledge about their chosen subjects and career paths. The theoretical exploration of curriculum content and the process of considering its practical, relevance and facilitating student's acquisition of both active and propositional knowledge. Thus, student co-creators would gain knowledge from Higher Education Institutions which would satisfy the epistemic conditions for substantial knowledge (i.e., comprising aspects that are factual, procedural, conceptual, and metacognitive (Krathwohl, 2002, & Bloom1956) as justified true belief (Ichikawa & Steup, 2017) about the subject of business management programs and its place at in the workplace.

However, from the perspective of international students and how they have experienced education prior to arriving in the UK, co-creation could destabilize how they conceive what is 'true' and 'knowledge.' This is because involving such students in the creation of their curricula implies that the academic (who the student would hitherto see as the expert, the one to tell them what is true knowledge) needs their assistance. Moreover, they are ambivalence about how they should learn and develop the knowledge they need for the careers they would like to pursue, succeed in and which they have paid tuition fees to learn from qualified and experienced experts is equally valid and worth participating in. In other words, while student co-creators are given the opportunity to appreciate the relevance of their studies to their careers, this opportunity should be carefully presented to students as a valid teaching and learning context before its inherent collaborative and participative characteristics are emphasized. Most international students want to be guided by a knowledgeable expert even if the liberal pedagogies of UK higher education institutions (Bacon & Sloam, 2010) want them to know that there are no experts, only learners.

Nevertheless, the idea of co-creation is precisely that: it is the rejection of hierarchy and the strong emphasis on equality that is at the heart of liberalism. Co-creation holds the dimension of working with others (collaboration) in the production or creation of something new, a curriculum, and of taking part or sharing in matters that comes to exist (participation). With collaboration, students brings what they know about learning, from the workplace or industry and the teaching they have experienced to the process of curriculum co-creation Lubicz-Nawrocka & Bovill, 2023). Hence the equal access it gives to under-represented groups and international students potential to co-created curriculum for inclusivity. Whereas participation is the space where theories and concepts become more tangibly identified and there is a cerebral progression of an idea to its reality. The student contributes to and becomes involved in and participates in what they have collaboratively co-created with educators. The co-created curriculum in action should give students their identities as business management graduates and future leaders. Moreover, as Cook-Sather (2018) points out, belonging to the co-creating group enhances students' sense of agency and of the freedom to seek and establish connections and meaning.

This aspect of meaning-making through belonging to the collaborative and participatory co-creating group is especially relevant to the context of international business management students being explored here. The relevance emerges because the culturally diverse cohorts so prevalent in the UK Higher Education Institution impacts on the levels of participations students wants to be involved in. UK domicile students tend to see international students as passive, disinclined, 'cash cows' for Higher Education Institutions (Lomer & Mittelmeier, 2021) argue that often lack the ability to take part in group discussions and participate in group projects (Valiente-Riedl et al., 2021). In short, unequal in terms of learning and participatory ability. International students are often aware that they are perceived as unequal (Maher, 2023) and, consequently, tend to feel unwanted and excluded, i.e., as not belonging. However, through curriculum co-creation, which encourages students to intellectually contemplate meaning and uses of subject content, could enable UK domicile students and international students to gain a deeper sense of motivations, commitment, and value of their counterparts. Both sets students, can in the more global contexts created by the inclusion of international students in co-creating groups, and empowered to offer their insights and to use their experiences and unique perspectives to shape the curriculum (Nasri et al, 2023). Also, to prepare students for the business world which is itself characterized by collaborative, inclusive and diverse working groups, and teams. The co-creation of curricula can bring equality into learning sessions.

Co-creation draws attention to the value-adding aspect of stakeholder involvement in design processes (Hsu et al., 2023) It also anticipates the destabilization of the expert-neophyte binary that business students are likely to discover in several industries, which international business students may be unfamiliar with until their studies in the UK. Nonetheless, to effectively prepare students for their career paths, co-creation is what they should be encouraged to be involved in. It will help them develop skills required in the marketplaces that they are hoping to enter either to start their own business or as an employee. Consequently, co-creation is itself, and should be endorsed as, a student-centered pedagogy suitable for business management postgraduate degrees, because these degrees gain their authenticity from their simulation and exploration of workplace or industry contexts and activities.

Students' participation in curricula co-creation should not remove the need for the expertise of academic staff. This latter is enhanced when it embodies and incarnates industry workplace priorities and concerns, and this embodiment and incarnation can be achieved by academics embracing co-creation as a pedagogy. One that encourages and empowers international students to collaborate and participate, at first in small groups with the academics, then as their confidence grows, more boldly with their peers in learning sessions. Thus, the involvement, within Higher Education Institutions, of students in curriculum co-creation, is made possible and depends on the knowledge and pedagogical expertise of academic staff. Particularly in terms of how academic staff draw-out the culturally diverse perspectives of international students (Nasr et al., 2023) to produce a unique way of working that, while disrupting the more traditional academic staff/student relationship, empowers and emboldens them to contribute and participate, on an equal footing, with the UK domicile students that they share learning sessions with and would help them in developing skills for their future career paths.

## 2.2 Knowledge and the Link Between Co-Creation and Career Paths

According to literature (DeFillippi & Arthur;1994; Maher, 2018), the 'traditional' career paths developed during the Industrial Revolution in the late 19th century and early 20th century. During this period of growth within large industrial organizations, individuals worked for one or two organizations for all or most of their working life. However, improvements in the global economy and technological advancements towards the end of the 20$^{th}$ Century and the beginning of the 21$^{st}$ Century impacted attitudes to work; and thus, on organization structures and career paths. Today fewer people are employed to carry out work inside of a workplace or organizational space due to the invention of computers and the internet. Furthermore, several researchers (DeFillippi & Arthur, 1994; Biemann et al., 2012) suggest that with downsizing and de-layering, organizations offer limited opportunities for vertical career path progression. They contend that career paths should be viewed within the context of changes taking place in the employment market. Therefore, organizations should consider career paths that are relevant to the employment market, and to diverse individual needs: and this consideration of the relevance and appropriateness of career paths is facilitated by the boundaryless career model.

The boundaryless model is useful for exploring how engaging students in curricula co-creation prepares them for their career paths. It conceptualizes a career path as the vertical and non-vertical moves an individual makes in relation to their values and needs within their personal and professional lives (Arthur & Rousseau, 1996; Wiernik & Kostal, 2019; Maher, 2020). From this perspective the individual's career motives influence their selection and choice of career path (DeFillippi & Arthur, 1994; Arthur & Rousseau, 1996; Arthur, 2014). Van Burren (2003) echoes DeFillippi and Arthur (1994) and Arthur and Rousseau's (1996) perennial arguments that, for individuals to determine their career paths, they must accumulate and develop marketable skills and competencies; and to do this more so during unsettled economies and competitive labor markets.

These scholars also confirm that downsizing and de-layering have reduced the number of hierarchical tiers within organizational structures; that in advances information technology have precipitated flexible forms of working; that with the aging population of developed markets, individuals are staying on at work past the state retirement age; and that this latter reality is changing the pace and shape of the labor market. Therefore, DeFillippi and Arthur's (1994) suggestion that an individual should pursue a boundaryless career path, *remains relevant and current*. More so because, they describe that pursuit in terms of a *timeless* skill and knowledge acquisition, viz. coming to know-why, know-whom, and know-how. These three dimensions of knowledge are, they say, vital for the choice and development of successful careers (Bredin & Söderlund, 2013; Quinlan & Renninger, 2022). DeFillipi and Arthur (1994) employed the phrase "intelligent career model" (pp. 309) to describe the knowledge and skills required for an individual to pursue their chosen career path.

In this regard, the attainment of knowledge and (employability) skills are especially essential for individuals seeking job opportunities in the wider labor market. The three ways of knowing in the intelligent career model are described as follows:

1. **"Knowing-why" competencies**: these relate to an individual's personal values and motivation, and provide the individual with a sense of purpose, career clarity, and identification with the world of work. Knowing-why reflects an individual's response to the question, "why do you work?" and incorporates an individual's self-concept and the interests that are invested in pursuing a career. A core concept is the individual self: that is, being a person who has a distinctive social world and lived experiences (Sultana & Malik, 2019).
2. **"Knowing-whom" competencies:** these are network relationships that individuals have inside and outside the organization. They are used to develop opportunities and a reputation which can assist them to progress their career.
3. **"Knowing-how" competencies:** these encompass the skills and knowledge individuals accumulate over time through learning and work, which are transferable across organisational and occupational boundaries. Knowing-how reflects an individual's response to the question "how do you work?" and enables the individual to combine explicit knowledge, such as those learned from a course or self-directed reading, and tacit knowledge (Nonaka & Takeuchi, 1995; Jo et al., 2023). Tacit knowledge is what an individual knows "but cannot tell" (Polanyi, 1962; Jo et al., 2023). This type of knowledge would occur mostly in occupations where individuals learn on-the-job.

These three ways of knowing are employed in a range of research projects, for example to examine the skills and knowledge graduates accumulate from their MBA program (Sturges et al., 2003), or to explore what executives gain from global business assignments (Carr et al., 2005). They continue to be popular in career and employability literature (Sultana & Malik, 2019; Jo et al., 2023). Each way of knowing is connected to the other: they are not mutually exclusive. For example, an individual takes a job because the person is attracted to the job (knowing-why to knowing-how), enjoys the experience of the job itself (knowing-how to knowing-why), makes new acquaintances through the job (knowing-how to knowing-whom), learns on the job from co-workers (knowing-whom to knowing-how), and through it, finds encouragement and validation from others (knowing-whom to knowing-why).

Researchers have criticized the boundaryless career model perspectives on career paths (Lazarova & Taylor, 2009: Gunz & Mayrhofer, 2010; Kost et al., 2020). These scholars argue that there is limited evidence to support the view that individuals are self-directing and managing their career paths across organizations and boundaries, especially given the challenges of securing permanent employment in the current economic climate. They suggest that, given its *employee*-centricity, the boundaryless career model has underestimated how contextual factors and social structures impact career path choices of individuals.

Despite these criticisms of the boundaryless career model, holds true to career patterns in the 21st century. For instance, an individual undergoing insecurity and uncertainty whilst completing a higher education course would be obliged to develop careers through their networks, collaborations, and to become involved in the type of self-directed activities which, Arthur and Rousseau's (1994) model, posit as the active effective mode for removing career boundaries (Kost et al., 2020). Beyond the stated literature, epistemologists, who are careful about what they call 'knowledge,' also consider these three ways of knowing, as examples of cognitive success (Steup & Neta, 2020). They have yet to settle on the importance of how to identify – for example, between awareness and acquaintance - impacts on any knowledge success claim. However, for the more pragmatic social science disciplines, the foremost being business management, employer-employee lived experiences seem to settle the argument that knowing a few facts about a person is not the same as being acquainted with the person, but that this latter state, acquaintance, is enough for knowing whom in a business context.

Employees can be sufficiently "acquainted' with their CEO without knowing very much about that CEO. Moreover, knowing the differences between the benefits of unique styles of leadership is quite different from knowing *how* to lead well. Nevertheless, those facts about business leadership can still be called 'knowledge;' because in the real world of learning and work, knowing *what* often precipitates knowing *how*, and knowing *whom* facilitates both (Guan, et al., 2019). Therefore, developing these competencies through curriculum co-creation which might involve introducing participating students to industry collaborators and to have them find their own (knowing-whom) and concerns (knowing-why) could prepare students for efficacious self-management (knowing-how) of their career paths (Arthur, 1994). Supporting this view, Sodergen (2002), Purohit and Jayswal (2022) confirm that individuals interested in accumulating knowledge apropos their chosen careers enthusiastically seek and welcome substantive opportunities to do so. In the findings and discussion section, the three ways of knowing – know-why, know-who, and know-how – will be applied as the decisive model of cognitive success (referred to here as the tripart model of cognitive success, or the TCS-model) that will assist the evaluation of student responses on how they have been involved in curriculum co-creation, their impressions of that involvement and that how the process supports their chosen careers.

## 3. METHODOLOGY

The research methodology was designed to allow for the collection and analysis of data on whether students' participation in co-creation of the curriculum influences their chosen career paths. The intent for this process is to answer the study research questions and to further inform the body of knowledge on the connection between students as active participants in curriculum design and the world of work. Consequently, in-depth qualitative data was collected from participants via face-to-face semi-structured interviews with 54 International Business Management students (from countries such as, India, Nepal, Pakistan, Nigeria, Kenya, Ghana, and China) studying postgraduate courses in four UK Higher Education Institutions, of which twenty-seven were female, twenty-five male and two non-binary. Interviews ranged from 45 to 64 minutes with an average of 54 minutes. Participants were asked to comment on their experiences as co-creators of the curriculum, and how they understood the idea of co-creation.

The qualitative research involved asking participants about their experiences of participation in curriculum co-creation. Miles and Huberman (1994, pp. 28) explain that qualitative data "are a source of well-grounded, rich descriptions and explanations of processes in identifiable local contexts. With qualitative data, one can preserve chronological flow, see precisely which events lead to which consequences, and derive fruitful explanations." This view of qualitative research is supported by many contemporary qualitative researchers about the benefits of employing qualitative data in a research project (Hennink et al., 2020; Bell et al., 2022).

The researchers used the semi-structured interview to allow for a degree of flexibility, i.e., for the participants to expand on their responses (Bell et al., 2022). This method also enabled the researchers to explore the range of feelings, attitudes and motivations expressed by each participant (Köhler et al.,

2022) and to arrive at a deeper understanding of each individual account of participation in co-creation of the curriculum.

At the end of each interview, participants were given the opportunity to indicate any additional information that they considered relevant to the research. All interviews were digitally audio-recorded with the permission of each participant to record the interview. The use of acronyms by participants were written in full of […] to demonstrate when the authors have done so. Non-verbal communication that could not be captured on the digital recordings were manually noted by the researchers. Participants were invited to report on or revise the transcripts (and none did).

To satisfy the research goal, the researchers followed Myers' (2020) process of data analysis. This approach requires the researchers to reflexively explore the data for emerging thematic. The process involved, the authors transcribed each interview, then manually checked the data for accuracy. They employed computer-assisted qualitative data analysis software (CAQDAS) package NVivo 11 to facilitate the data coding and clustering of themes.

To maintain anonymity, the authors did not name the participants or include the names of students' institutions. The authors identify each participant by a number to ensure that readers of the research cannot identify the views of specific participants. Ensuring that participants did not restrict their disclosure was an important consideration for the research and involved the assurance of confidentiality (Bryman and Bell, 2011; Hennink, et al., 2020). The information verification process employed by the authors during the data collection can be regarded as contributing to the methodological rigour of the research. The next section discusses data ascertained from the research participants.

## 4. FINDINGS

In this section, participants responses will be highlighted and reported on under headings of the three research questions. The key objective is to guide program directors, module convenors and academics more broadly in reflective attempts to improve curriculum design, and to foster awareness of how international business management students can be encouraged to become more invested in their own learning and co-creation of the curriculum as they progress through the academic environment, in preparation for work and developing successful career paths

### 4.1 What Are the Different Ways in Which Students Are Being Actively Involved in Curriculum Co-Creation?

Responses in Appendix 1 represent types of activities participants participated in within the curriculum co-creation process. It shows that overall, students were more often involved as co-designers of resources, and in revalidations and program reviews. Appendix 1 also shows that international students (and by extension their educators) were not fully aware of the scope of curriculum co-creation and seemed to limit it to the basic activities relevant to validating or inputting on already decided teaching content. While their responses are useful for understanding what participants value from being involved in co-creation of the curriculum, they also reveal that fewer educators are facilitating students' participation on the deeper and more fundamental co-creation activities, such as course design prior to the start of a program.

No participant stated that they were asked to input course structures, types of modules on offer, or to suggest assessment tasks and methods. This lack may be due to lack of experience of academic staff on how to encourage students to participate in curriculum co-creation. However, it may also be down to other factors such as that some professional bodies require academic staff to cover specific content. Nonetheless, over half of the participants reported that they have participated in program meetings where they suggested activities to be include in the curriculum. Some suggestions included fieldwork, visits to companies and student projects involving collaboration with external agencies. Examples of typical student statements are:

a. "I want to work in HRM [Human Resources Management] so I said to my lecturer if we can meet HRM managers to get an insight into what HRM managers actually do … this was arranged … I'm going to shadow a HR manager in a few weeks' time" (Participant: 8).
b. "I've chosen the work placement module … we were told to find a company … a placement in the field we would want to work in … my placement was in a charity at XXX. I enjoyed working there. The experience will look good on my CV when the time comes to look for work" (Participant: 7).
c. "We are given the freedom to make decisions and come up with ideas about our research project. Most of us have chosen a topic to research that links with the areas where we want to develop our future careers" (Participant: 9).

Participants 8, 7, and 9 indicate that students' participation included offering suggestions for workplace and industry participation. Moreover, these students valued the fact that their suggestions were heard and acted upon. Nevertheless - and specifically because their ideas and proposals are essentially pedestrian and somewhat expected activities and offerings found in most business courses (see Appendix 1 for a fuller set of activities that students were involved in) - there is a sense that the quality of their participation is mirrored by their desire to have what they say be approved by academics. That is, students' belonging aspirations that Cook-Sather (2020) highlighted as a benefit of co-creation is prioritized by the participating student.

In general participants were proposing what they are likely to expect on business management courses. They are not seeking any fundamental structural or content changes: and there is little evidence of innovative "out of the box" thinking but much proof that supports the literature that, given the chance, international students seek approval from the status quo (Lomer & Mittelmeier, 2021; Valiente-Riedl et al., 2021). Even when, as Participant 9 implies, they are urged to disrupt it. Therefore, any worry that student-tutor co-creation, especially when it involves international students, could lower standards seems misplaced.

Participants' responses seem to suggest that co-creation is a channel for reinforcing usual practice within business management courses, and to have students approve that reinforcement (see Appendix 1). Accordingly, it would benefit from input that gives students access to the *modus operandi* of disciplines other than their own, and from examples of alternative content or structures. In short, while Higher Education Institutions may want curriculum co-creation to completely destabilize the traditional academic/student relationship, the evidence suggests that its success will *depend on* the traditional roles at least in the initial stages of the process.

Student responses also reveal a desire to align themselves with what employers are after. For instance, one respondent stated that:

d. "A management role is like being Jack of all trades… being flexible with your job role … I like to have a say in what is included in the curriculum … so that I'm prepared when I graduate … don't get me wrong our tutors are great … but it's my career on the line here … I've done my research… I know what skills the companies want out there" (Participant: 11).

While this statement highlights the student's understanding of what management is and shows their appreciation of the opportunity to connect the curriculum more to industry, to even exhibit what they know, it also reveals a fundamental misunderstanding of the co-creation process. The student appears to think that their own research of business somehow supersedes that of the academics and that the co-creation process is in fact an acknowledgement of this possibility. If so, then there is a need for a more careful explanation of curriculum co-creation to students.

Nonetheless, participants' responses confirm that being involved in co-creating the curriculum, which they saw as being consulted on topics to be included, helps them to gain the knowledge that might be relevant for their careers. Thus, the evidence supports Defilippi and Arthur's (1994) and Gerli et al., (2015) view that individuals are acquiring knowledge and skills essential to seeking employment opportunities and pursuing their chosen career paths. With reference to the TCS-model, participants responses reveal that the know-how in cognitive success is lacking in students' awareness and understanding of the co-creation process and its facilitation of moving them across discipline and career path boundaries, i.e., moving them effective through the academic world into the world of work.

## 4.2 Does Student Participation in Co-Creation of Curriculum Influence Their Chosen Career Paths?

Several participants reported that academic staff had encouraged them to participate in program re-validations, selecting case studies for class discussions, designing module questionnaire feedback, consulting in new module development, and choosing the topic for their research project. This was supported by statements such as:

a. "I was asked to help with designing a feedback questionnaire for a module… we worked in groups and said what we think. We gave our views and made suggestions …. I enjoyed it" (Participant: 2).
b. "At the end of each term, I complete a module evaluation form for each module … I said how the lectures and module contents can be improved to help us with finding a job and building our career" (Participant: 5).
c. "It has been great participating in co-creating the curriculum … I have enjoyed it. I will always remember this experience … when I'm in work I'll tell my colleagues about this experience" (Participant: 52).

These statements, indicative of those from the other participants and including those mentioned earlier with the first research question, which suggest that students have been encouraged to participate what can be described as pedagogic consultants: advising on resources, teaching experienced, and course and module content. Overall, international students held a positive view of how they had been involved. Their comments support Cook-Sather, (2008) and Bovril et al., (2011) views that involving students in the co-creation of the curriculum enhances students' understanding of the learning process.

However, and with reference to the TCS-model, while respondents were cognizant of why and what they were doing, they did not seem to overtly link the co-creation event to the process of choosing careers, i.e., to knowing how. From the above, they could see the benefits to their studies and work of the activities they had been engaged in, and their participation gave them a deeper appreciation of the link between what they learn in the academic world and what they do in the world of work. While the participants did not communicate any awareness of the long-term influences on their interest in their careers, they do reveal an appreciation for the opportunity of their viewpoints to be heard. Nonetheless, there is little evidence of their recognition of how collaborating with tutors and peers (with diverse opinions, experiences, expertise) impacts their contemplation of the different dimensions of their discipline or opens them up to those dimensions. Participants appears to be finding meaning in just taking part: but their taking part has been permitted also for the choice of meaning they are seeking and could find beyond the Higher Education Institution.

## 4.3 Are There Learning and Career Benefits of Encouraging Students to Participate in Curriculum Co-Creation?

Participants pinpointed activities that they would like to see as a part of co-creating the curriculum. These activities pertained to how they saw themselves developing the skills and knowledge required for their chosen career paths. Other participants reported that they wished to contribute more to discussions about course content and learning opportunities. Representative statements were:

a. "I would like tutors to consult with us [students] before the scheme of work is put into the handbook. We know what we want to do … I want to be a marketer … some marketing options will be nice (Participant: 22).
b. "I'd like module convenors at the end of semester to discuss more of what we are going to learn next semester… how our leaning will help us to develop skills for personal development and industry. Employers are looking for us to have certain skills when we go for interviews … it all helps" (Participant: 28).
c. "Having to have a say … within my own learning and my future situation is really motivating" (Participant: 42).

These participants wish to be encouraged to contribute more to discussions about course content and described the chance to do so as motivating and relevant. They were clearly interested in participating in co-creation of the curriculum and see it as supporting the chosen career paths. Thus, their response supports Coetzee and Roythorne-Jacobs's (2007) view that individuals are consciously accumulating competencies for entry into the workplace. This attitude seems standard as, anecdotally, Higher Education Institution academics are very aware that the more they align their teaching sessions and assessments with industry requirements or employability skills, the more student participation increases.

Additionally, as with Participant 28 who already had an eye on the next semester, other participants were also forward looking through the co-creation process. They were more concerned about academics forward planning and felt that their input would be relevant for tutors' schemes of work. However, their responses show a lack of trust in academics capacity to know what students might need to learn, and less an appreciation of co-creation as a tutor/student partnership. In the TCS-model, while their comments might seem promising, they are in fact symptomatic of what practitioners wanting to incorporate co-creation opportunities into their curriculums need to guard against clearly defined roles and co-creating contexts. That is, that students consider their opinions and inputs (know-why) more valuable than those predicated on tutors' expertise and research (know-what and know-how).

Contrary views were expressed by some participants. The basic comments were either about being excluded from co-creation or seeing it as another task that they were being asked to do. Such statements were:

d. "No one asked me about curriculum design ... I completed module evaluation forms to say what I think of the module ... that's all (Participant: 34)
e. "Curriculum design .... Isn't that the role of the teacher ... yes ... it's for them, the teachers, to do ... I wasn't asked to help in curriculum design" (Participant: 30)

These participants appear disinterested in curriculum design, seeing it as the academic's job. Indeed, this much is in line with perspectives on international students' attitudes towards contemporary or creative pedagogies mentioned earlier (e.g., Lomer & Mittelmeier, 2021). Whilst Participant 5 recognized the module evaluation as a route into co-creation, Participant 34 does not. However, although these participants reported being unfamiliar with co-creation of curriculum, they expressed an interest in becoming more involved when the process and benefits were explained to them. Hence, students attend Higher Education Institutions precisely for the stated benefits of curriculum co-creation, cognitive and intellectual development, employability, belonging, and a sense of agency (Cook-Sather, 2018). Therefore, the challenge of curriculum co-creation is not in getting students to participate. On the contrary, it is to ensure that their participation is meaningful, in terms of their future career path needs and ambitions, and readiness for the world of work.

Consequently then, co-creation of the curriculum is not straightforward. On one hand, the process is important because it promotes student's autonomy and fosters learner agency. Additionally, there is a clear sense that being involved in the activities mentioned above enhances students' awareness of the link between their academic learning and work. On the other hand, there is no straightforward evidence that students' participation in the process influences their choice of careers. Moreover, the data shows that curriculum co-creation is limited in the form that it is currently practiced in the UK Higher Education Institutions. Nonetheless, the research should help students to better recognize their motivations and values (knowing-why), and educators to see that student and academic roles and input contexts must be more clearly delineated for effective partnerships and relationships (knowing-whom) and increased boundaryless careers (knowing-how).

Overall, the research findings provide insights into how students´ have been encouraged to participate in co-creation of the curriculum. It shows that the Higher Education Institutions should do more to embed the practice of co-creation into the development and design of programs and modules. It validates the academic context as the preparation setting for developing students as co-creators of the curriculum to support their career path needs. Particularly, as the world of work has been changing because of the COVID-19 pandemic and an increasingly competitive jobs market, acquiring new career skills, knowledge adapting to changes in industries, are important prerequisite for developing career paths.

## 5. RECOMMENDATIONS

The findings are based on data from fifty-four postgraduate international business management students in four higher education institutions in the UK. However, they are likely to be generalizable beyond these students and institutions, to others within the UK, and even globally to other countries such as the USA, Canada, Australia, and others within the European Union countries, which attract international students with similar profiles as those who choose to study in the UK.

Participant responses imply that they feel better prepared for work; this being often characterized by different lenses and perspectives. The findings also suggest that participants seemed aware of the competencies (Arthur & Rousseau, 1994; Coetzee & Roythorne Jacobs, 2007) they need for their careers. Moreover, encouraging students to participate in curriculum co-creation could help them to take more responsibility for their own learning and preparation for professional life. Accordingly, based on the research findings outlined above, it is recommended that:

1. Co-creation activities should, early in the process, be defined by academic staff and should demonstrate how they are listening to and responding to student views and acting on the ideas they generate.
2. While student contributions and ideas can invigorate teaching, learning experiences and students career opportunities; Higher Education Institutions should ensure that the destabilising of the tutor-student relationship does not undermine academics, but that it promotes their creativity and inventiveness.
3. Higher Education Institutions leadership should actively support student-staff curriculum co-creation throughout all year levels and should provide additional support for activities that may already take place within these institutions and that could constitute co-creation, such as inputting on the structure and content of work-based learning, work placement projects, peer mentoring, and using students as teaching assistants. Such activities could be embedded within module schemes of work or used as assessment tasks.
4. If Higher Education Institutions want students to participate in curriculum design, programme directors, lecturers, student union officials and support services staff should inform and prepare students during induction week of the process. They should help students to understand the career benefits of participating in co-creating the curriculum d. Such an approach might enhance students' metacognition regarding the relevance of their learning and development to their chosen career paths. In addition, curriculum designers might want to ask the following questions at the start of curriculum development:
   A. What type of career path are students going on to?
   B. What should be included in the curriculum to prepare students for future careers?
   C. Have we built-in opportunities for flexibility in the curriculum to support students to gain the skills and knowledge required by changes in industry?
   D. How can we involve students as curriculum co-creators from the grassroots?

## 6. FUTURE RESEARCH

It is anticipated that future research will include data from a larger cohort and should be designed as a longitudinal study. Further studies could evaluate the experiences of academic staff participating in the co-creation of the curriculum, especially with regards to how they respond when their teaching methods and approaches are influenced or determined by students involved in the design of courses prior to teaching.

Further research should also facilitate the development of guidelines and recommend practical steps and policies that will promote and support international students to actively participate in co-creation of the curriculum by way of a closer look at the import of culture and cultural dimensions on how international students respond to co-creation opportunities. Such research should explore ways in which academics and students have co-created curricula in different disciplines within national and international contexts, as this type of expansive consideration would assist those wanting to implement collaborative curriculum co-creation. Moreover, it would provide a deeper insight into how to engage students from diverse cultural backgrounds in their academic environments to better prepare them for work. This deeper insight and discourse would be better served by additional research via alumni from international cohorts that were not involved in curricula co-creation opportunities so there can be a comparative study of how they chose and established themselves in their respective careers after their postgraduate studies.

## 7. CONCLUSION

This chapter has presented curriculum co-creation as a pedagogical approach that develops students' critical thinking skills and engages them more deeply in both the subject content and its application in the world of work. The research offered here identifies several activities that some students saw as curriculum co-creation. These activities include module evaluations, inputting on work placements, research topics, schemes of work, and semester planning and preparation. Although these activities are valid examples of curriculum co-creation, it was suggested above via the TCS-model - the know-why, know-whom, know-how tripartite model of cognitive success - that they are limited examples that, on one hand, are more representative of students' desire to validate the status quo. But on the other hand, that also reveal tutor/student tensions emerging from the co-creation process, with some students potentially seeing their input and own opinions on what might be right for them and their career paths, as more legitimate than those established on tutors' expertise and research. Or as not what they should be expected to contribute, being students do not tutor. Subsequently, that international business management students should be given access to co-creation activities on other disciplines to encourage innovations and enhanced creativity, and that co-creating contexts and roles should be very carefully set out and more carefully introduced.

Through a review of pertinent literature, this chapter has also suggested that involving students in co-creation of the curriculum empowers under-represented groups to have a say in what is taught., but also empowering international students' participation by using the smaller more intimate environments for curriculum co-creation to get them on a more equal footing as the UK domicile students they join in the larger learning sessions. The implication of this is that the curriculum would become a more inclusive and equal place that examines multiple perspectives and experiences rather than privileges certain viewpoints and forms of knowledge.

The chapter has shown that inviting students to participate in co-creation of the curriculum has not been fully embedded in all levels of curriculum development and creation. If Higher Education Institution wants the process to be meaningful and value-adding for students preparing for business careers, more should be done to ensure those students better understand what co-creation entails and what full-range of activities students can be involved in while learning from academics about business management. The findings indicate that Higher Education Institutions should delineate curriculum co-creating scope students have, whilst also reaffirm the legitimacy of academic's expertise and research to help students to identify and understand how the process supports future their career path needs.

# REFERENCES

Arthur, M. B. (2014). The Boundaryless Career At 20: Where Do We Stand, and Where Can We Go? *Career Development International*, *19*(6), 627–640. doi:10.1108/CDI-05-2014-0068

Arthur, M. B., & Rousseau, D. M. (1996). *The Boundaryless Career: A New Employment Principle for a New Organizational Era*. OUP. doi:10.1093/oso/9780195100143.001.0001

Bacon, M., & Sloam, J. (2010). John Dewey and the Democratic Rose of Higher Education in England. *Journal of Political Science Education*, *6*(4), 336–352. doi:10.1080/15512169.2010.518087

Bedwei-Majdoub, C. (2023). *An Aquinian Virtue Ethics Approach to Action Learning Sets on Postgraduate Business Programmes Attracting International Students* [Paper Presentation]. *International Action Learning Conference. Action Learning Research and Practice.*

Bell, E., Bryman, A., & Harley, B. (2022). *Business Research Methods*. OUP. doi:10.1093/hebz/9780198869443.001.0001

Borge, M., Toprani, D., Yan, S., & Xia, Y. (2020). Embedded Design: Engaging Students as Active Participants in the Learning of Human-Centered Design Practices. *Computer Science Education*, *30*(1), 47–71. doi:10.1080/08993408.2019.1688592

Bovill, C. (2020). Co-Creation in Learning and Teaching: The Case for Whole Class Approach in Higher Education. *Higher Education*, *79*(6), 1023–1037. doi:10.1007/s10734-019-00453-w

Bovill, C., Cook-Sather, A., & Felten, P. (2011). Students as Co-Creators of Teaching Approaches, Course Design, and Curricula: Implications for Academic Developers. *The International Journal for Academic Development*, *16*(2), 133–145. doi:10.1080/1360144X.2011.568690

Bovill, C., Cook-Sather, A., Felten, P., Millard, L., & Moore-Cherry, N. (2016). Addressing Potential Challenges in Co-creating Learning and Teaching: Overcoming Resistance, Navigating Institutional Norms, and Ensuring Inclusivity in Student–Staff Partnerships. *Higher Education*, *71*(2), 195–208. doi:10.1007/s10734-015-9896-4

Bredin, K., & Söderlund, J. (2013). Project Managers and Career Models: An Exploratory Comparative Study. *International Journal of Project Management*, *31*(6), 889–902. doi:10.1016/j.ijproman.2012.11.010

British Academy. (2021). Business and Management Provision in UK Higher Education. *The British Academy.* https://www.thebritishacademy.ac.uk/publications/business-and-management-provision-in-uk-higher-education/

Bron, J., & Veugelers, W. (2014). Why We Need to Involve Our Students in Curriculum Design: Five Arguments for Student Voice. *Curriculum and Teaching Dialogue, 16*(1/2), 125.

Chuang, N. K., Lee, P. C., & Kwok, L. (2020). Assisting students with career decision-making difficulties: Can career decision-making self-efficacy and career decision-making profile help? *Journal of Hospitality, Leisure, Sport and Tourism Education, 26*(4), 1–15. doi:10.1016/j.jhlste.2019.100235

Collins, H., & Callaghan, D. (2018). The Role of Action Learning in Supporting Cross-Cultural Adaptation of International Students. *Action Learning, 15*(3), 267–275. doi:10.1080/14767333.2018.1510633

Cook-Sather, A. (2018). Listening to Equity-Seeking Perspectives: How Students' Experiences of pedagogical Partnership Can Inform Wider Discussions of Student Success. *Higher Education Research & Development, 37*(5), 923–936. doi:10.1080/07294360.2018.1457629

Cook-Sather, A., Bovill, C., & Felten, P. (2014). *Engaging Students as Partners in Learning and Teaching: A Guide for Faculty*. Jossey-Bass.

DeFillippi, R. J., & Arthur, M. B. (1994). The Boundaryless Career: A Competency-Based Perspective. *Journal of Organizational Behavior, 15*(4), 307–324. doi:10.1002/job.4030150403

Doyle, E., Buckley, P., & McCarthy, B. (2021). The Impact of Content Co-creation on Academic Achievement. *Assessment & Evaluation in Higher Education, 46*(3), 494–507. doi:10.1080/02602938.2020.1782832

Gerli, F., Bonesso, S., & Pizzi, C. (2015). Boundaryless Career and Career Success: The Impact of Emotional and Social Competencies. *Frontiers in Psychology, 6*. Advance online publication. doi:10.3389/fpsyg.2015.01304 PMID:26388809

Gironella, F. (2023). Gamification Pedagogy: A Motivational Approach to Student-Centric Course Design in Higher Education. *Journal of University Teaching & Learning Practice, 20*(3), 4.

Guan, Y., Arthur, M. B., Karpova, S. N., Hall, R. J., & Lord, R. G. (2019). Career boundarylessness and career success: A review, integration, and guide to future research. *Journal of Vocational Behavior, 110*, 390–402. doi:10.1016/j.jvb.2018.05.013

Hennink, M., Hutter, I., & Bailey, A. (2020). *Qualitative Research Methods*. Sage.

Hsu, J., Lin, L. C., & Stern, M. (2023). Curriculum Co-Creation: Knowledge Co-Creation in an Educational Context. *International Journal of Knowledge-Based Organizations, 13*(1), 1–24. doi:10.4018/IJKBO.317116

Ichikawa, J. J., & Steup, M. (2017). The Analysis of Knowledge. *Stanford Encyclopedia of Philosophy.* https://plato.stanford.edu/entries/knowledge-analysis/#LighKnow

Jackson, D., & Tomlinson, M. (2019). Career Values and Proactive Career Behavior Among Contemporary Higher Education Students. *Journal of Education and Work*, *32*(5), 449–464. doi:10.1080/13639080.2019.1679730

Jo, H., Park, M., & Song, J.H. (2023). Career Competencies: An Integrated Review of Literature. *European Journal of Training and Development*. . doi:10.1108/EJTD-04-2023-0052

Kahn, P., & Anderson, L. (2019). *Developing Your Teaching Towards Excellence*. Routledge. doi:10.4324/9780429490583

Kim, N. R., & Lee, K. H. (2018). The Effect of Internal locus of Control on Career Adaptability: The Mediating Role of Career Decision-making Self-efficacy and Occupational Engagement. *Journal of Employment Counseling*, *55*(1), 2–15. doi:10.1002/joec.12069

Kings College. (2023). UK Now Among Most Socially Liberal of Countries. *Kings College London*. https://www.kcl.ac.uk/news/uk-now-among-most-socially-liberal-of-countries#:~:text=The%20UK%20now%20ranks%20among,divorce%2C%20according%20to%20new%20data

Köhler, T., Smith, A., & Bhakoo, V. (2022). Templates in qualitative research methods: Origins, limitations, and new directions. *Organizational Research Methods*, *25*(2), 183–210. doi:10.1177/10944281211060710

Kost, D., Fieseler, C., & Wong, S. (2020). Boundaryless Careers in a Gig Economy: An Oxymoron? *Human Resource Management Journal*, *30*(1), 100–113. doi:10.1111/1748-8583.12265

Krathwohl, D. R. (2002). A Revision of Bloom's Taxonomy: An Overview. *Theory into Practice*, *41*(4), 212–218. doi:10.1207/s15430421tip4104_2

Kulcsár, V., Dobrean, A., & Gati, I. (2020). Challenges and Difficulties in Career Decision Making: Their Causes, and Their Effects on the Process and the Decision. *Journal of Vocational Behavior*, *116*, 103346. doi:10.1016/j.jvb.2019.103346

Lee, M. C. Y., McMahon, M., & Watson, M. (2018). Career Decisions of International Chinese Doctoral Students: The Influence of the Self in the Environment. *Australian Journal of Career Development*, *27*(1), 29–39. doi:10.1177/1038416217743023

Liu, Z. Q., Dorozhkin, E. M., Davydova, N. N., & Sadovnikova, N. O. (2020). Co-Learning as a New Model of Learning in a Digital Environment: Learning Effectiveness and Collaboration. *International Journal of Emerging Technologies in Learning*, *15*(13), 34–48. doi:10.3991/ijet.v15i13.14667

Lomer, S., & Mittelmeier, J. (2021). Mapping the Research on Pedagogies with International Students in the UK: A Systematic Literature Review. *Teaching in Higher Education*. https://www.tandfonline.com/doi/full/10.1080/13562517.2021.1872532

Lubicz-Nawrocka, T. (2018). Students as Partners in Learning and Teaching: The Benefits of Co-creation of the Curriculum. *International Journal for Students as Partners, 2*(1). doi:.v2i1.3207 doi:10.15173/ijsap

Lubicz-Nawrocka, T., & Bovill, C. (2023). Do students experience transformation through co-creating curriculum in higher education? *Teaching in Higher Education*, *28*(7), 1744–1760. doi:10.1080/13562517.2021.1928060

Maher, C. (2018). *Understanding Managerial Career Anchors and Career Path Preferences: A Case Study of Third Sector Social Enterprise Managers*. Scholar's Press.

Maher, C. (2020). *Career Needs and Career Values: The Mediating Role of Organisational Culture. In Recent Advances in the Roles of Cultural and Personal Values in Organizational Behaviour. 240-260.* IGI Global. doi:10.4018/978-1-7998-1013-1.ch012

Maher, C. (2023). *Understanding Stressors for International Students.* Sharing Pedagogic Research and Practice in Greenwich University Business School. https://blogs.gre.ac.uk/sebe/2023/10/19/understanding-stressors-for-international-students/

Mello, R., Suutari, V., & Dickmann, M. (2022). Taking Stock of Expatriates' Career Success After International Assignments: A Review and Future Research Agenda. *Human Resource Management Review*, 100913.

Myers, M. D. (2020). *Qualitative Research in Business and Management*. SAGE.

Nasri, N., Mohamad Nasri, N., & Abd Talib, M. A. (2023). Developing an inclusive curriculum: Understanding co-creation through cultural lens. *International Journal of Inclusive Education*, 27(9), 1072–1083. doi:10.1080/13603116.2021.1880652

Pordelan, N., Sadeghi, A., Abedi, M. R., & Kaedi, M. (2020). Promoting Student Career Decision-Making Self-Efficacy: An Online Intervention. *Education and Information Technologies*, 25(2), 985–996. doi:10.1007/s10639-019-10003-7

Purohit, D., & Jayswal, R. (2022). Developing and Validating Protean and Boundaryless Career Scale for College Passing Out Students. *European Journal of Training and Development*. . doi:10.1108/EJTD-07-2021-0115

Quinlan, K. M., & Renninger, K. A. (2022). Rethinking Employability: How Students Build on Interest in a Subject to Plan a Career. *Higher Education*, 84(4), 863–883. doi:10.1007/s10734-021-00804-6

Scully-Russ, E., & Torraco, R. (2020). The Changing Nature and Organization of Work: An Integrative Review of Literature. *Human Resource Development Review*, 19(1), 66–93. doi:10.1177/1534484319886394

Steup, M., & Neta, R. (2020). Epistemology. *Stanford Encyclopedia of Philosophy*. https://plato.stanford.edu/entries/epistemology/

Sultana, R., & Malike, O. F. (2019). Is Protean Career Attitude Beneficial for Both Employees and Organizations? Investigating the Mediating Effects of Knowing Career Competencies. *Frontiers in Psychology*, 10, 1284. doi:10.3389/fpsyg.2019.01284 PMID:31214088

Tan, L. M., Laswad, F., & Chua, F. (2022). Bridging the Employability Skills Gap: Going Beyond Classroom Walls. *Pacific Accounting Review*, 34(2), 225–248. doi:10.1108/PAR-04-2021-0050

UCL. (n.d.). What we Mean by Co-Creation. *UCL ChangeMakers*. https://www.ucl.ac.uk/changemakers/what-we-mean-co-creation

Valiente-Riedl, E., Anderson, L., & Banki, S. (2021). Practicing What We Teach: Experiential Learning in Higher Education That Cuts Both Ways. *Review of Education, Pedagogy & Cultural Studies*, *44*(3), 231–25. doi:10.1080/10714413.2021.1985372

Van Buren, H. J. III. (2003). Boundaryless Careers and Employability Obligations. *Business Ethics Quarterly*, *13*(2), 131–149. doi:10.5840/beq20031329

Vulperhorst, J. P., van de Rijst, R. M., & Akkerman, S. F. (2020). Dynamics in Higher Education Choice: Weighing One's Interests in Light of Available Programmes. *Higher Education*, *79*(6), 1001–1021. doi:10.1007/s10734-019-00452-x

Wiernik, B. M., & Kostal, J. W. (2019). Protean and Boundaryless Career Orientations: A Critical Review and Meta-Analysis. *Journal of Counseling Psychology*, *66*(3), 280–307. doi:10.1037/cou0000324 PMID:30777774

Williams, M. K. (2017). John Dewey in the 21st Century. *Journal of Inquiry and Action in Education*, *9*(1), 91–101.

Wood, L., & Louw, I. (2018). Reconsidering Postgraduate "Supervision" from a Participatory Action Learning and Action Research Approach. *South African Journal of Higher Education*, *32*(4), 284–297. doi:10.20853/32-4-2562

## ADDITIONAL READING

Forehand, M. (2005). Bloom's taxonomy: Original and revised. *Emerging perspectives on learning, teaching, and technology, 8*, 41-44.

Hall, D. T. (2002). Careers in and out of organizations. *Sage (Atlanta, Ga.)*.

Hoidn, S., & Klemenčič, M. (Eds.). (2020). *The Routledge international handbook of student-centered learning and teaching in higher education*. Routledge. doi:10.4324/9780429259371

Kochan, T., & Dyer, L. (2020). *Shaping the future of work: A handbook for action and a new social contract*. Routledge. doi:10.4324/9781003050001

Lowe, T., & El Hakim, Y. (Eds.). (2020). *A handbook for student engagement in higher education: theory into practice*. Routledge. doi:10.4324/9780429023033

Maher, C. (2015). Students as Active Participants in Curriculum Design: Exploratory Implications for Career Path Choices. ReflectEd, St Mary's. *Journal of Education*, *5*, 1–12.

Nguyen, D. J., & Yao, C. W. (Eds.). (2023). *A handbook for supporting today's graduate students*. Taylor & Francis.

# APPENDIX 1: STUDENTS' RESPONSES

*Table 1. Student responses*

| Appendix 1: Modes of Students Participation in Curriculum Co-creation ||
|---|---|
| **PARTICIPANT** | **Examples of how students participated in curriculum co-creation** |
| 1 | Fieldwork research |
| 2 | feedback questionnaire for a module |
| 3 | Suggesting types of assessments |
| 4 | End of term module evaluation |
| 5 | Completing a module evaluation form |
| 6 | Participation in program re-validation |
| 7 | Finding a company for a placement |
| 8 | Suggested fieldwork as part of a Module. |
| 9 | Putting ideas forward for research projects |
| 10 | Participation in new module development |
| 11 | Suggesting development of practical skills for a module |
| 12 | Participating in re-assessment panel review |
| 13 | Field work research |
| 14 | Review of assessment briefs |
| 15 | Suggesting organizations for placements |
| 16 | Participation in program re-validation |
| 17 | Review of assessment briefs |
| 18 | Suggesting organizations for placements |
| 19 | Participation in program re-validation |
| 20 | Suggesting journal articles |
| 21 | Review of assessment briefs |
| 22 | Contributed to scheme of work for a module |
| 23 | Was not asked to participate in co-creation of the curriculum |
| 24 | End of term course evaluation |
| 25 | Reviewing assessments |
| 26 | Suggesting organizations for placements |
| 27 | Completing end of term evaluation |
| 28 | End of term course evaluation |
| 29 | Reviewing journal articles for a module reading lists |
| 30 | I was not asked to participate in co-creation of the curriculum |
| 31 | I was not asked to participate in co-creation of the curriculum |
| 32 | Suggesting organizations for placements |
| 33 | Reviewing case studies for term two |

*continued on following page*

*Table 1. Continued*

| Appendix 1: Modes of Students Participation in Curriculum Co-creation ||
|---|---|
| **PARTICIPANT** | **Examples of how students participated in curriculum co-creation** |
| 34 | Review of assessment briefs |
| 35 | Review of assessment briefs |
| 36 | Reviewing assessments briefs |
| 37 | Reviewing case studies for term two |
| 38 | Participation in program re-validation |
| 39 | Reviewing case studies for term two |
| 40 | Suggesting organizations for placements |
| 41 | Was not asked to participate in co-creation of the curriculum. |
| 42 | Did not have a say |
| 43 | Review of assessment briefs |
| 44 | I was not asked to participate in co-creation of the curriculum. |
| 45 | Participation in program re-validation |
| 46 | I was not asked to participate in co-creation of the curriculum. |
| 47 | Review of assessment briefs |
| 48 | Suggesting organizations for placements |
| 49 | Reviewing case studies for the next term |
| 50 | Participation in program re-validation |
| 51 | Was not asked to participate in co-creation of the curriculum. |
| 52 | Participated in end of term course review |
| 53 | Review of assessment briefs |
| 54 | Reviewing journal articles for a module reading list |

## APPENDIX 2: INTERVIEW QUESTIONS

To explore the stated aim, objectives and questions, the researchers conducted fifty-four semi-structured interviews using the following questions:

1. Could you briefly tell me about your main jobs since finishing your bachelor's degree?
2. Does any of these jobs fit in with your career path needs?
3. What are your career path preferences?
4. Are there specific initiatives in this University that has supported your preferred career path?
5. Do you have experience of collaborating with a tutor or Programme leader to co-design curriculum content?
6. Can you provide an example of types of co-creation of the curriculum you have been involved with?
7. Has participation in co-designing the curriculum made you more aware of the link between your university studies and your chosen career path?

## PERSONAL PROFILE

8. Do you have other Professional Qualification?
   8b. Please state the name of the qualification.
   8c. What was your reason(s) for obtaining this qualification?
9. Do you belong to or attend any networking events or associations?
   9b. If so, what are your reasons for attending?
10. Could you tell me your age?
11.. How would you describe your gender?
12. Are there any other issues you wish to raise which you feel were not covered in this interview and which in your opinion, could benefit small our research.

Thank you for taking part in this interview. Your input is valued.

## APPENDIX 3: KEY TERMS AND DEFINITIONS

**Career Path**: A series of job roles and work experiences that enables an individual to achieve their career objectives and future goals.

**Co-Curriculum Design**: Students and tutors working in partnership in designing the curriculum.

**Student Engagement**: Is the degree of attention, interest, and passion students show when they are being taught, which elevates the level of motivation they need to learn and progress in their course.

**Inclusive Learning:** Providing learning environments that contribute to an overall inclusive learning environment in which all students perceive themselves to be valued and able to succeed.

**Student Voice:** Allowing students to express their opinions and perspectives on University policies and strategies based on their interests, passions, and ambitions.

**Student Co-Creation:** When students and tutors collaborate with one another to create parts and components of the curricula and/or pedagogical approaches.

**Higher Education Institutions:** Includes a wide range of institutions providing courses beyond the level of secondary education, such as colleges, universities, community colleges, and polytechnics.

# Chapter 4
# Interdisciplinary Curriculum for Engineering Graduates:
## A Constructive Alignment With Career Competency

**Swati Gupta**
*Universal AI University, India*

## ABSTRACT

*Interdisciplinary teaching combines multiple subjects. Business, communication, and sustainability may be part of an interdisciplinary engineering curriculum. An interdisciplinary curriculum can help engineering students learn more. Students can prepare for more careers by combining engineering with other subjects. Employers value interdisciplinary skills and competencies. Interdisciplinary coursework helps students develop critical thinking, problem-solving, communication, and collaboration skills. Effective interdisciplinary engineering curricula align. This means the curriculum should match employers' career competencies so students can succeed. Interdisciplinary education helps engineering graduates develop career-ready skills. An interdisciplinary curriculum aligns with employer needs to prepare students for engineering careers.*

## INTRODUCTION

In the evolving landscape of higher education, there is an amplified need to equip students with skills that resonate with real-world job demands. This has spurred numerous initiatives to revamp curricula, ensuring that they not only impart academic knowledge but also enhance career readiness (Stoner and Milner, 2010). The two fields at the crossroads of this transformation are Engineering and Accounting.

For engineers, the mandate is clear: they must possess competencies that allow them to devise solutions addressing both local and global challenges. Their role is pivotal, as society relies on their expertise to innovate, design, and implement solutions that cater to diverse societal needs (Lavadia et al., 2018). However, a gap exists. Research indicates that students might not fully nurture these competencies un-

DOI: 10.4018/978-1-7998-7999-2.ch004

less they are explicitly educated about their significance and the methodologies used to develop them (Rhee et al., 2020; Lavadia et al., 2018; Choi et al., 2018).

However, the Accounting and Finance sectors witnessed a surge in the value of critical reflection. This competency empowers students to dissect the foundational principles of their field, fostering a deeper and more critical understanding of their societal implications (Rhee et al., 2020).

This chapter delves into the pivotal role of interdisciplinary curricula in bridging this gap. This underscores the challenges and rewards of integrating critical reflection into the Accounting and Finance syllabus. Furthermore, it emphasizes the alignment of academic outcomes with industry demands and advocates for educators to champion the development of holistic competencies, ensuring that students are not just job-ready but future-ready. In conclusion, this chapter serves as a roadmap for educators, guiding them towards curricular excellence that aligns with the dynamic demands of today's professional landscape.

## IMPORTANCE OF INTERDISCIPLINARY EDUCATION

The engineering field demands technical expertise and analytical skills, yet traditional engineering curricula often overlook the importance of interdisciplinary knowledge (Hall and Seth, 2022). Consequently, engineering graduates may struggle to meet the expectations of their prospective employers. This chapter critically examines the profound impact of an interdisciplinary curriculum designed through intentional alignment with career competencies desired by employers on students' skills, knowledge acquisition, and readiness for diverse career paths in the engineering industry.

An interdisciplinary curriculum broadens engineering students' skill sets beyond their core discipline, empowering them with multifaceted problem-solving abilities, critical thinking, creativity, and adaptability (Zhang, 2021). By integrating various disciplines such as business, communication, analytics, humanities, and social sciences, students acquire well-rounded expertise that enables them to tackle complex challenges from diverse perspectives. Employers actively seek engineers with diverse proficiencies, recognizing their versatility and ability to holistically address intricate problems.

Interdisciplinary education facilitates the exploration of diverse fields, fostering a comprehensive understanding of the interconnected nature of engineering and other domains. By appreciating the social, ethical, economic, and environmental dimensions of their work, graduates have emerged as well-rounded professionals capable of effectively addressing real-world complexities. This broader perspective equips them with acumen to navigate the multifaceted challenges and develop sustainable solutions that positively impact society.

The CA ensures that the interdisciplinary curriculum precisely aligns with the competencies desired by employers, ensuring that students are well prepared for the workforce. By incorporating industry-relevant projects, internships, and cooperative educational experiences, the curriculum provides students with practical exposure to authentic engineering challenges. This experiential learning enhances their readiness for the industry, making them highly sought-after candidates with both theoretical knowledge and practical skills. Tailoring their education to career goals through specialized programs further augments their expertise and employability.

An interdisciplinary curriculum nurtures agility and adaptability among engineering graduates, enabling them to thrive in the rapidly evolving engineering landscape. By acquiring knowledge from various disciplines, graduates possess the flexibility to seamlessly integrate insights and techniques across various domains. This interdisciplinary approach is equipped with the capability to contribute effectively to multidisciplinary teams, enabling smooth transitions between different roles and industries throughout their careers.

Interdisciplinary curricula foster innovation by encouraging the fusion of ideas and methodologies from various fields. Graduates exposed to interdisciplinary approaches demonstrate enhanced creative thinking skills, enabling them to identify unconventional solutions and explore entrepreneurial opportunities. This mindset aligns with the demands of the engineering landscape, in which innovation and entrepreneurial thinking are vital drivers of progress. Such graduates possess the ability to push boundaries, drive technological advancements, and contribute to industry growth.

An interdisciplinary curriculum meticulously designed through CA with employer competencies offers substantial benefits to engineering students' readiness for diverse career paths. By developing a versatile skill set, cultivating holistic understanding, providing career-focused preparation, promoting agility and adaptability, and fostering innovation and entrepreneurship, graduates have emerged as well-rounded professionals capable of addressing complex engineering challenges. These curricula bridge the gaps present in traditional engineering education, empowering graduates to excel in multidimensional roles and make significant contributions to the engineering field. By embracing interdisciplinary approaches, educational institutions can enhance students' employability and ensure that they are equipped to meet the evolving demands of the industry.

## MAPPING COMPETENCIES WITH AN INTERDISCIPLINARY CURRICULUM

Employers are increasingly seeking engineering graduates who possess a diverse range of competencies that extend beyond technical knowledge (Chenicheri et al., 2009). To meet these industry demands and enhance the employability of engineering students, universities are mapping their desired competencies with an interdisciplinary curriculum. This approach equips students with a comprehensive skill set that prepares them for the challenges of the modern engineering workforce (Robert and Siva, 2022).

Effective communication is one of the competencies highly valued by employers (Azmi et al., 2018; Ebrahiminejad, 2017). Engineering students must develop strong written and verbal communication skills to convey technical information to various stakeholders effectively. By incorporating interdisciplinary coursework that emphasizes communication across different fields, students can learn how to communicate effectively with professionals from diverse backgrounds. This fosters collaboration and enhances their ability to bridge the gap between technical jargon and layman terms, which is a crucial skill in real-world engineering settings (Ebrahiminejad, 2017; Raj et al., 2015).

Critical thinking and problem solving are also sought-after competencies (Ebrahiminejad, 2017). Interdisciplinary coursework encourages students to approach problems from multiple perspectives, thereby allowing them to develop a broader understanding of complex issues. By integrating knowledge from various disciplines, students can holistically analyze problems and devise innovative solutions (Robert & Siva, 2022). Incorporating interdisciplinary projects and case studies into the curriculum provides students with the opportunity to address real-world challenges that require a multidisciplinary approach. This nurtures their ability to think creatively, adapt to different contexts, and solve complex problems effectively (Hanapi et al., 2015).

Collaboration and teamwork are competencies highly valued by employers of engineering graduates (Azmi et al., 2018; Ebrahiminejad, 2017). Interdisciplinary coursework provides students with opportunities to work in diverse teams, thus reflecting the collaborative nature of the engineering profession. By engaging in interdisciplinary projects, students learn to appreciate diverse viewpoints, leverage the strengths of team members from different disciplines, and foster effective collaborations (Azmi et al., 2018; Hanapi et al., 2015). This competency is vital in today's globalized engineering industry, where projects often require collaboration across geographical and disciplinary boundaries.

Employers also seek graduates who possess adaptability and willingness to learn. The dynamic nature of the engineering field demands continuous learning and the ability to adapt to emerging technologies and industrial trends. Interdisciplinary coursework equips students with the ability to integrate knowledge from different disciplines and prepare them to embrace new challenges and technologies. By exposing students to interdisciplinary concepts and methodologies, universities ensure that graduates are equipped with a mindset of lifelong learning and adaptability, which enables them to stay relevant and thrive in their careers (Azmi et al., 2018; Hanapi et al., 2015; Robert & Siva, 2022).

Ethical and professional responsibility is another competency that employers prioritize. Interdisciplinary education provides a broader understanding of the social, environmental and ethical implications of engineering projects. By integrating ethical considerations from different disciplines, students develop a strong sense of responsibility and are better equipped to address ethical challenges that arise in their professional practice. This competency is crucial for building trust and maintaining integrity in the engineering profession (Azmi et al., 2018; Ebrahiminejad, 2017).

Employers today seek engineering graduates who possess a range of competencies beyond their technical knowledge. By mapping these competencies with an interdisciplinary curriculum, universities can equip students with a well-rounded skill set that aligns with industrial demands. One framework that can be utilized to map these competencies is the Definition and Selection of Competencies (DeSeCo) framework (Midhat et al., 2021). The DeSeCo framework, developed by the Organization for Economic Co-operation and Development (OECD), provides a comprehensive set of key competencies that individuals need to thrive in a rapidly changing world. These competencies are divided into three broad domains: using tools interactively, interacting with heterogeneous groups, and acting autonomously.

The first domain, using tools interactively, encompasses competencies such as problem solving, critical thinking, and communication. By integrating interdisciplinary coursework that emphasizes these competencies, engineering students can develop the ability to identify and solve complex problems by drawing on knowledge from various fields (Midhat et al., 2021; Male et al., 2011). Students learn to think critically, analyze information, and effectively communicate their ideas to diverse audiences. This interdisciplinary approach helps students develop a strong foundation in technical skills, while honing their ability to think creatively and apply their knowledge in real-world contexts.

The second domain, interacting in heterogeneous groups, focused on competencies related to collaboration, teamwork, and cultural sensitivity. Engineering projects often require collaboration with professionals from various disciplines and cultural backgrounds. By incorporating interdisciplinary projects and group assignments into the curriculum, universities can provide students with opportunities to develop these competencies (Suleiman & Abahre, 2020; Male et al., 2011). By working in diverse teams, students learn to appreciate different perspectives, effectively communicate and cooperate with others, and leverage the strengths of team members from various disciplines. Such experiences foster cultural sensitivity, enhance interpersonal skills, and prepare students to thrive in multicultural work environments.

The third domain, acting autonomously, highlights competencies such as adaptability, lifelong learning, and ethical responsibility (Midhat et al., 2021). The engineering field is constantly evolving with

*Interdisciplinary Curriculum for Engineering Graduates*

emerging technologies and changing industry trends (Male et al., 2011). To succeed in this dynamic environment, engineering graduates must have the ability to adapt to new situations, learn independently, and embrace lifelong learning. Interdisciplinary coursework can foster these competencies by exposing students to different disciplines and encouraging them to integrate their knowledge from diverse sources. Additionally, incorporating ethical considerations into the curriculum ensures that students develop a strong sense of responsibility towards society and the environment, preparing them to make ethical decisions, and contributing to sustainable and socially responsible engineering practices (Midhat et al., 2021).

By mapping these competencies from the DeSeCo framework to an interdisciplinary curriculum, universities can provide engineering students with a well-rounded education that meets the expectations of their employers. This approach equips graduates with the necessary skills to excel in their careers and to adapt to the evolving demands of the engineering profession. Employers value graduates who not only possess technical expertise, but also demonstrate effective communication, critical thinking, collaboration, adaptability, and ethical responsibility. Through an interdisciplinary curriculum that aligns with the DeSeCo framework, universities can ensure that engineering graduates are equipped with the competencies needed to succeed in a competitive job market and make meaningful contributions to the society.

## CONSTRUCTIVE ALIGNMENT

Reflective changes in the business environment, such as globalization, swelling business complexity, shifting demographic patterns, and emerging technologies, supply businesses with a rock-solid signal to change. Hence, in a VUCA[1] world (Bennis & Nanus, 1985), technological advancement ignites changes in the business environment, together with the marketization of higher education (Hemsley & Oplatka, 2006). These changes require business faculties to adjust their educational practices to meet the needs of the business world. This adjustment includes the provision of relevant data, skills, and analyses that are beneficial to the stakeholders being served (McHann, 2012; McCune & Entwistle, 2000). A significant advancement in this direction is that outcome-based education (OBE) has gained widespread acceptance over the last few decades (Gurukkal, 2018; Spady, 1994). OBE reflects an exemplar shift in academic philosophy. It is necessary to explicitly differentiate the training outcomes that indicate students' development or growth in completing a study program (Spady, 1994). These intended learning outcomes ought to guide the program, learning, and assessment of the study program (Walker & Leary, 2009; Spady, 1994). At present, these changes have created widespread interest in the outcomes of academic experiences in business education schemes in instruction and a transparent tendency for instruction institutes in business to follow international and native academic standards.

Masie (2007) insists on the importance of giving students the right tools to keep up with current and valid technology and training them with habits to continue as lifelong learners. He emphasizes the decreased sense of certainty about what tomorrow will bring, especially concerning the technological changes that we have witnessed in the last few years, especially during COVID time.

The accreditation standards pay more attention to the OBE to eliminate the traditional teacher-centered model, in which teachers play a central role in imparting knowledge to learners and require the curriculum, teaching and learning (TLA), and assessment techniques of a program (Spady, 1994; Tam, 2014; Treleaven & Voola, 2008). Although the OBE is of great significance to business education, there is still a lack of research on its practical application in various disciplines, such as the impact of accounting and education standards on the OBE.

*Figure 1. OBE vs. traditional education system*

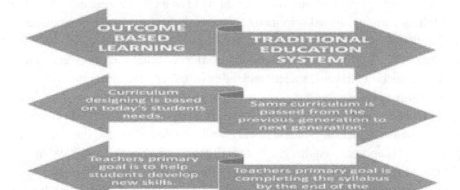

CA has two aspects. The 'constructive' aspect refers to what the learner does, which is to construct meaning through relevant learning activities. The 'alignment' aspect refers to what the teacher does, which is to set up a learning environment that supports the learning activities appropriate to achieving the desired learning outcomes. The key is that the components in the teaching system, especially the teaching methods used and the assessment tasks, are aligned to the learning activities assumed in the intended outcomes. The learner is in a sense 'trapped' and finds it difficult to escape without learning what is intended should be learned. (Biggs, 2003)

Because of the disconnect between accounting education in universities and the demands of the profession, which has been highlighted since the mid-1980s (Bedford et al., 1986; Kullberg et al., 1989),

*Figure 2. Constructive alignment in accounting*

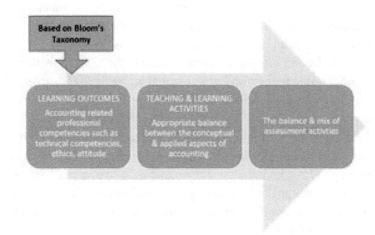

there is widespread demand that degree programs concentrate on key learning outcomes. The results are addressed in terms of the competencies that university accounting graduates need to build to achieve the accounting profession's goals (Lawson et al., 2014). These competencies encompass the knowledge and skills anticipated by companies for accounting professionals to possess and utilize as graduates engage in various tasks throughout the organization (Lawson et al., 2014). The Managerial Accounting curriculum under review explores CA in accounting education, focusing on an OBE model.

Hence, CA is a key principle in designing an interdisciplinary curriculum that aligns with career competencies. This ensures that ILOs, teaching strategies, and assessment methods are all aligned to support students' acquisition of the desired competencies (Entwistle, 2000). Educational institutions can bridge the gap between academic knowledge and real-world applications by carefully mapping the curriculum to industry needs.

A well-structured curriculum framework provides a foundation for CA. It involves selecting and sequencing courses that integrate various disciplines and incorporate industry-relevant projects, internships, and cooperative educational experiences. The framework also allows for flexibility, enabling students to tailor their education to their career goals and specialize in specific areas of engineering (Lucas & Mladenovic, 2007).

Through CA and a robust curriculum framework, students gain a comprehensive skill set; a holistic understanding of engineering's interconnections; career-focused preparation, agility, and adaptability; and a mindset that fosters innovation and entrepreneurship. These elements significantly enhance their readiness for diverse career paths, making them highly sought-after candidates in a competitive engineering industry.

## BLOOM'S TAXONOMY

Bloom's revised taxonomy (Anderson et al., 2001) has been universally employed in course design to evaluate and shape learning opportunities that enhance deep learning[2]. This approach supports educators in intentionally embedding integrative learning into the curriculum. It serves as a vital tool for achieving alignment within an interdisciplinary curriculum by linking educational objectives to career competencies (Bloom et al., 1984).

The revised taxonomy has two dimensions: cognitive processing and knowledge. The cognitive processing dimension reflects the type of knowledge involved in a particular learning activity, with six categories spanning lower-order thinking through higher-order thinking: remember, understand, apply, analyze, evaluate, and create. The latter categories of analyzing, evaluating, and creating are closest to describing integrative learning activities. The knowledge dimension describes the degree to which students know or are aware of their cognition with four types of knowledge: factual, conceptual, procedural, and metacognitive.

The latter is aligned with the knowledge acquired through integrative learning. By aligning learning objectives and assessments with the revised taxonomy, educators can ensure that students' progress through increasingly complex cognitive tasks (MacDonald et al. 2022). This alignment ensures that students acquire the necessary skills, from foundational knowledge to higher-order thinking abilities, that are sought after by employers in the engineering field. The revised taxonomy provides a roadmap for designing an interdisciplinary curriculum that fosters the development of critical thinking, problem solving, and creativity. By systematically addressing each level of taxonomy, students are equipped with

*Figure 3. Bloom's revised taxonomy*

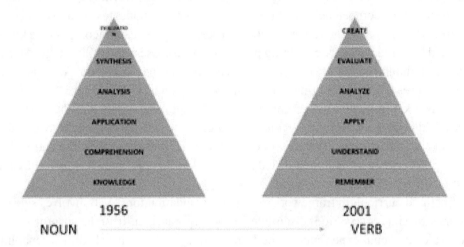

*Figure 4. Levels of knowledge dimension of the revised Bloom's taxonomy*

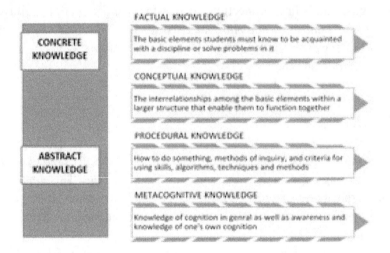

the cognitive abilities necessary to excel in diverse engineering roles and adapt to the evolving demands of the industry.

Hence, the revised Bloom's taxonomy offers a valuable analytical framework for aligning an interdisciplinary curriculum with career competencies. By incorporating taxonomy into curriculum design, educators can guide the cognitive progression of students and ensure that students acquire the essential skills and knowledge necessary for success in the engineering field (MacDonald et al., 2022; Sung et al., 2022). This alignment enables students to develop a comprehensive skill set and readiness for diverse career paths, enhance their employability, and prepare them for challenges in the engineering industry.

## RELATIONSHIP BETWEEN CONSTRUCTIVE ALIGNMENT & INTENDED LEARNING OUTCOME

Constructive Alignment and Intended Learning Outcomes are intricately connected to the design and implementation of a curriculum. Constructive Alignment ensures that teaching methods, learning activities, and assessments are aligned with the desired Intended Learning Outcomes, which define the specific knowledge, skills, and competencies that students should acquire (Leber et al., 2018). By aligning the curriculum with Intended Learning Outcomes, Constructive Alignment provides a clear focus and direction for educators and learners. It allows educators to design instructional strategies and assessment tasks that directly contribute to achieving desired learning outcomes (Weimer, 2013; Habel, 2012). This alignment enhances the coherence and consistency of students' learning experiences.

In turn, they play a crucial role in shaping Constructive Alignment. Well-defined Intended Learning Outcomes that are specific, measurable, attainable, relevant, and time-bound (SMART) provide a foundation for curriculum development (Biwer et al., 2020; Larkin & Richardson, 2013; Habel, 2012). Taxonomy assists educators in defining the knowledge and skills that students should achieve by completing the curriculum. These outcomes act as benchmarks against which teaching methods and assessments can be evaluated to ensure their effectiveness (Baeten et al., 2010).

The relationship between Constructive Alignment and Intended Learning Outcomes is dynamic and iterative. During the implementation of the curriculum and the assessment of students' progress (Kandlbinder, 2014), educators may identify areas that require adjustments. Continuous evaluation and refinement of Intended Learning Outcomes based on assessment feedback and the evolving needs of the engineering field ensure that the curriculum remains aligned with the expectations of employers and industry demands (Kandlbinder, 2014; Stamov et al., 2021).

Research has demonstrated the positive impact of Constructive Alignment on students' learning experience. Studies have shown that it increases students' confidence in their ability to succeed and improves their academic self-efficacy. The implementation of such principles has resulted in higher student satisfaction, greater clarity in assessment, and improved grades. Redesigning assessment tasks to better reflect Intended Learning Outcomes and graduate attributes has been appreciated by students, thereby enhancing their overall learning experience (Entwistle, 2000). Furthermore, studies comparing aligned and misaligned learning conditions have consistently shown that aligned Constructive Alignment leads to higher levels of learning motivation and better learning outcomes (Pretorius et al., 2013). Students in aligned conditions demonstrated a higher level of competence and understanding than those in the misaligned conditions.

Thus, both are interdependent components of the curriculum design. Constructive Alignment ensures that teaching, learning activities, and assessments are aligned with the desired Intended Learning Outcomes, providing a clear direction for educators and learners. Simultaneously, well-defined Intended Learning Outcomes guide the development of Constructive Alignment, shape the curriculum, and serve as benchmarks for evaluation. The symbiotic relationship between them enhances the effectiveness of teaching and learning, ultimately equipping students with the knowledge, skills, and competencies required for success in the engineering field.

## CURRICULUM DEVELOPMENT PROCESS: THE PRESENT STUDY

The university follows a rigorous curriculum development process. The curriculum flow from 3 committees, starting from DCC[3], then BOS[4] and Academic Council Final Approval. These committees embody the faculty fraternity of universities, other prestigious universities, industrial experts, alumni, and student representatives.

## LEARNING OUTCOME

Universities have adopted newly found, time-tested, and well-researched teaching-learning methodologies, practiced internationally across eminent institutes. For effective teaching and learning, the courses have been structured on the 'Blooms Taxonomy' (Revised). The course outcomes[5] are arrived at and mapped with Program Outcomes (POs)[6] and Program Specific Outcomes (PSOs)[7]. The same is further mapped with assessment tools and teaching tools (part of the teaching-learning methodologies).

POs are attained through program-specific Core Courses that have their own previously set outcomes. Course-specific outcomes are called Course Outcomes. Each Course is designed to meet (about 4–6) Course Outcomes. These competencies are developed through consultation with Heads of Departments

*Figure 5. Curriculum development process at university*

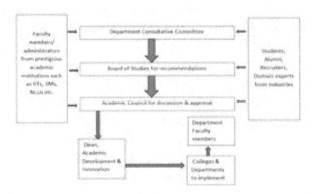

*Figure 6. Outcome mapping process at university*

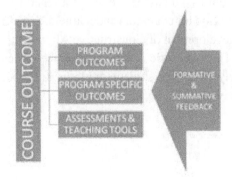

(HODs), domain faculties, and engineering graduates, ensuring that the competencies are defined in a way that allows for effective measurement.

At the University, student-centric methods such as experiential learning (Butler, 2022), participative learning, and problem-solving methodologies are used (Li et al., 2022). Simultaneously, preparing the course plan, the faculty handbook teaching tool for each topic is most suited to teach that topic and generate the best student learning experience. PPT Presentation, Chalk & Talk, Examples, Discussion, Reflections, Random questions, Case study, Simulation, Experiment are commonly using teaching tools to ensure a better student-learning experience.

1) Experiential Learning- 'Doing is the new learning.' University is of the view that hands-on practical learning is a far superior way to develop knowledge, skills, and values beyond the confines of classroom learning. Of the host of experiential learning tools, a few of the widely practiced ones at the University are internships, industry trips, exchange programs, working on projects, career development activities, field research, incubation and entrepreneurial engagement, participation in cultural programs, creativity, and leadership activities (Fredricks et al., 2016).

In the School of Business, case study pedagogy is adopted for teaching management subjects that enhance engineering graduates' problem-solving skills and application orientation (Pan et al., 2023). Simulations such as Ceteris Paribus and Flexsim exercises provide students with an opportunity for "learning by doing" as if in a real-life situation. The use of role-play, business games, and field projects employed while teaching management courses encourages engineering graduate participation and fosters experiential learning (Butler, 2022). Capstone dissertation projects and internships provide engineering graduates with integrative learning experiences.

2) Participative learning: The activities adopted by faculty members develop an applied approach for engineering graduates.
    a) Integration of Flipped Sessions, continuous assessment, and computational tools in laboratory engineering education–the Flipped Session Approach conventionally employed for theory sessions–can be advantageous when used in laboratories. In these flipped videos, the faculty covers the relevance, practical illustrations, theory, methodology, and a deliberate emphasis on the analysis of data using computational tools. Engineering graduates have also been given access to the required computational skills developed by the faculty, enabling them to learn analytical skills. Hybrid-Blended Learning 100% of the engineering graduates and faculty use Blackboard as a Learning Management System tool for teaching & learning.
    b) Projects and Field Practical

Around 90% of engineering graduates enrolled under various programs in university go for a field visit and on industry projects supported by the Faculty and Career Services to obtain hands-on practical experience.

## CURRICULUM FRAMEWORK

Building engineering graduates' capacities for integrative learning is a crucial feature of effective curriculum (Higgs et al., 2010). An integrative learning curriculum enables engineering graduates to be 'fully engaged in practical and breakthrough learning that sticks and engages the body, mind, heart, and spirit of the learners' (Ryan et al., 2010). It is intended that through experiencing these curricula and upon graduation, meaning making is replicated to synthesize different perspectives and ways of knowing, laying the groundwork for personal growth and responsible citizenship (Huber and Hutchings, 2004)

Curriculum design is based on Biggs's (2003) framework. The framework provides a model for designing effective teaching and learning experiences aligned with Intended Learning Outcomes (Alfauzan & Tarchouna, 2017). The framework comprises three key components: Intended Learning Outcomes (ILOs), teaching and learning activities (TLAs), and assessment tasks (ATs). ILOs specify the knowledge, skills, and attitudes that engineering graduates should acquire, while TLAs support their development. ATs assess engineering graduates learning and measure progress towards the desired outcomes. By aligning these components, educators can create a cohesive learning experience that helps engineering graduates achieve ILOs. This framework ensures that teaching and assessment are directly connected to desired learning goals, promoting a focused and effective educational experience.

1. Presage: POs, PSOs and content development of the Course

The course curriculum has the following salient features:

- English as the medium of instruction.
- Excel was used as a core component.
- Business communication skills development

POs have been developed, demarcating them as knowledge-, skill-, and attitude-based outcomes.

*Figure 7. Model of teaching and learning by Biggs, Kember, and Leung*

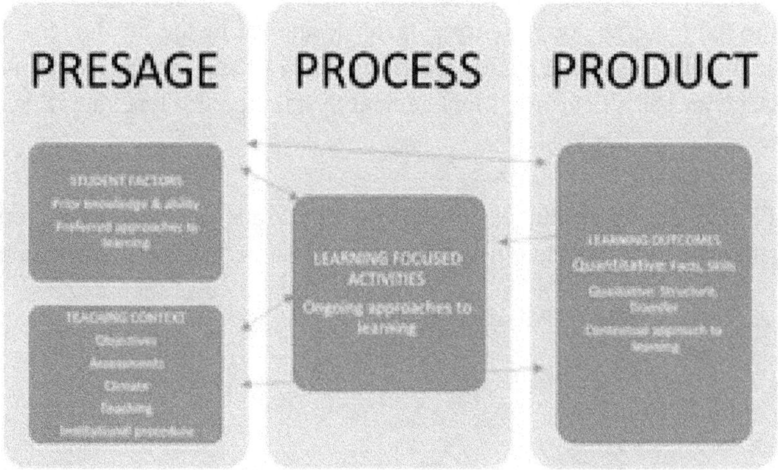

2. Process: Teaching Learning Activities (TLA) of the Course

Under the Course, lectures are the primary pedagogical methods. Additionally, engineering graduates are provided with more opportunities for constructive learning with the use of excel practical sessions, lectures, and group work as instructional methods. A group project is also an important component, as it enables engineering graduates to actively participate in learning. In group projects, engineering graduates must study annual reports and write company analyses highlighting the company's financial position through Excel modelling.

3. Product: Mix of assessments of the Course

A couple of years ago, the assessment was conducted through a midterm exam, internals, and final examination. The emphasis shifted to the final review through continuous evaluation because of the current market demand and the introduction of quality assurance. Continuous appraisal is an essential part of the evaluation process. There is a growing preference for practice-based evaluations (i.e., engineering graduates have been assessed based on problem-based[8] Practical/Field Studies). Consequently, engineering graduates' ability to incorporate theoretical principles in realistic situations increased, as did their ability to learn generic and implementation skills. Furthermore, the rubric of question papers has improved over time, with more case/scenario-based organized questions. In-class evaluations such as presentations related to engineering graduate group assignments are also widely used.

The course plan determines the nature of the content presented, the instructional methods[9] employed and the types of assessments. Engineering graduates ' prior knowledge and preferred approaches to learning affect their ability to achieve learning goals (Weimer, 2013). The process consists of engineering graduates' learning activities, including reading, home assignments, in-class exercises, cases, and projects. The faculty defines the learning outcomes (product) of the course regarding knowledge, facts, procedures, and thinking skills transferrable to other contexts. Hence, each component of the model affects the other.

## COURSE CURRICULUM: REFLECTIVE ANALYSIS

The course highlighted in this chapter is "Accounting for Managers," offered during the first semester of the MBA program for the 2020–2021 academic sessions. This course was selected for its universal appeal across all MBA specializations, making it a focal point for assessing engineering graduates' skill development. As a foundational course in first-year curriculum, it encompasses a broad spectrum of learning objectives and outcomes.

Designed with an instructional approach, the course integrates learning exercises and assessments tailored to foster research and application of managerial skills in real-world settings. Traditional accounting pedagogies, which often rely on textbook narratives and end-of-chapter materials, starkly contrast with the innovative teaching methodologies and evaluations employed in this course (Walker & Leary,2009; Davidson & Baldwin, 2005; Spiceland et al., 2015).

Throughout the semester, I employed action research methodologies to address the following research questions.

1. How does a hands-on systematic problem-solving project enhance engineering graduates' critical thinking abilities?
2. What challenges do instructors face when integrating a comprehensive problem-based project throughout the semester?
3. How do engineering graduates' perceptions of managerial challenges evolve after undertaking a detailed problem-based project complemented by reflection essays?
4. How can teaching enhancements related to reflection papers foster engineering graduates' understanding of managerial decision making?
5. What impact does transitioning from traditional assessments to a comprehensive problem-based project with reflection essays have on engineering graduates' proficiency in accounting procedures?

The diverse content of the course allows engineering graduates to hone skills from various angles, underscoring their universal applicability (Lucas & Mladenovic, 2007). Jack and McCartney (2007) emphasized the significance of qualitative learning outcomes, particularly critical analysis and thinking skills. They championed these competencies as foundational for "argumentative accountants."

In this course, the acquisition of critical analysis and decision-making skills is partly driven by the aspiration to nurture engineering graduates' ethical and intellectual growth (Perry, 1970; Kenefelkamp, 1999). Over time, the course encouraged engineering graduates to transition from a dualistic learning approach, where answers are often binary, to a more nuanced, relativistic perspective, where they evaluate multiple viewpoints in real-world scenarios.

In Managerial Accounting, where answers are not always clear-cut, critical evaluation becomes paramount, especially when choosing between alternative methodologies in various contexts. Furthermore, a problem-solving approach that uses models is central to the course. This approach is pivotal for understanding and critically assessing the various techniques. Skills essential for employability were progressively introduced and intertwined with the core subject skills and objectives. Diverse offline and online skill development exercises were embedded in each lesson. Engineering graduates were urged to assimilate these skills and adapt their learning strategies to bolster their employability and academic maturity.

Each tutorial clearly outlined the skill components of both preparatory and in-class activities. Real-world data or mini-cases often serve as the backdrop for analysis and evaluation. Engineering graduates were consistently tasked with modelling financial data or solution processes with spreadsheets aiding their modelling endeavors.

## LEARNERS' LANDSCAPE

The "Accounting for Managers" course, offered by the Department of General Management, is tailored to cater to a diverse student body, including engineering graduates. Since its inception, the course has seen a steady influx of students, with the latest enrollment statistics indicating 90 students, of which 40% are engineering graduates. This significant percentage underscores the course's interdisciplinary appeal.

Engineering graduates, with their analytical and problem-solving abilities, play a pivotal role in MBA courses. Their technical backgrounds often provide a unique perspective, especially when juxtaposed with the financial and managerial concepts taught in the course. For instance, in modules that delve into cost analysis or financial optimization, engineering graduates often lead discussions and draw paral-

*Figure 8. Skill development components*

lels between engineering principles and financial management. Their participation not only enriched classroom discussions, but also fostered cross-disciplinary collaborations on projects and case studies.

Upon enrollment, irrespective of their background, all students received an introduction to foundational concepts in finance and accounting. The primary objective is to equip them with essential knowledge while honing skills such as critical and analytical thinking, problem-solving, etc. Given the diverse backgrounds of students, standardizing their understanding of accounting is a challenge. However, the course's structure, which comprises five escalating modules, ensures a comprehensive blend of theoretical, design, technical, and communication contexts, catering to the varied expertise of enrolled students.

I have had the privilege of instructing this course over the past three years, marking my fourth consecutive batch. Each year offers a fresh perspective and renewed opportunity for growth. As highlighted by Toohey (2002), every teaching cycle provides a chance for reflection, planning, and application. Each engineering graduates's unique learning journey, especially the significant contribution from engineering graduates, enriches their experience and debunks the myth of monotony in repetitive teaching.

## ENGINEERING COMPETENCIES MAPPING: REFLECTIVE ANALYSIS

Course curriculum competency mapping is a process of aligning the course curriculum with the competencies required for graduates to succeed in their careers. This process involves identifying the necessary competencies, analyzing the course curriculum, and mapping the competencies to the curriculum to ensure that engineering graduates acquire the required skills and knowledge. Reflecting on this process, it becomes apparent that course curriculum competency mapping is a vital component of modern education, as it helps to produce competent and skilled graduates.

The first step in curriculum competency mapping is to identify the required competencies. For engineering graduates, employers expect a wide range of competencies beyond technical skills. Communication skills, problem-solving abilities, critical thinking, teamwork, leadership, and ethical conduct are essential competencies that engineers must possess. By incorporating these competencies into the course curriculum, engineering graduates can develop a well-rounded skill set essential for their career success.

The second step involves an analysis of the course curriculum to identify gaps and areas in need of improvement. This entails a thorough examination of the course content, instructional strategies, and methods to assess their alignment with the identified competencies. Reflective analysis of the course curriculum reveals that many accounting courses often place more emphasis on technical skills while overlooking other critical competencies. For instance, most accounting courses focus heavily on financial reporting, auditing, and taxation while giving minimal attention to competencies such as communication and leadership.

The third step involved mapping the identified competencies to the course curriculum. This step holds great significance, as it guarantees that engineering graduates acquire the necessary competencies throughout their progression in the curriculum. Reflecting on this process, it is apparent that mapping competencies to the course curriculum is not always straightforward. This requires a deep understanding of the course content, instructional strategies, and assessment methods. Mapping should be performed systematically, and care should be taken to avoid overlaps or omissions.

Table 1 explores the competencies that employers look for among engineering graduates and how the accounting course curriculum should incorporate these competencies, teaching strategies, and course outcomes to prepare graduates for a successful career.

## LEARNING OUTCOME: REFLECTIVE ANALYSIS

The Co-relationship matrix (Table 2) clearly defines the significance level of the relationship between Cos, POs, and PSOs, highlighting the key outcomes of the course.

*Table 1. Competency mapping (author compilation)*

| COMPETENCY | EMPLOYER EXPECTATION | CURRICULUM MAPPING |
|---|---|---|
| Technical Skill | Employers expect engineering graduates to have a strong foundation in technical skills, including mathematics, physics, and computer programming. These skills enable graduates to design and develop engineering solutions and communicate them effectively to stakeholders. | Focus on providing graduates with a strong foundation in mathematics, financial analysis, and computer skills. Engineering graduates should be encouraged to take courses in computer programming and data analysis to enhance their technical skills. |
| Critical Thinking | Critical thinking is the ability to analyze information, evaluate its quality, and make decisions based on evidence. Employers seek graduates who can think critically to solve complex problems, develop new ideas, and innovate. | Incorporate problem-solving exercises, case studies, and discussions to enhance students' critical thinking skills. Engineering graduates should be encouraged to analyze financial statements and develop innovative solutions to financial problems. |
| Communication | Effective communication is vital for engineers to share their ideas, present solutions, and collaborate with peers and stakeholders. Employers look for graduates who can communicate effectively, both orally and in writing. | Emphasize the importance of effective communication, both oral and written. Engineering graduates should be encouraged to present their ideas and solutions to peers and instructors and receive feedback to improve their communication skills. |
| Teamwork | Engineers often work in teams to complete projects. Employers seek graduates who can work well in a team, collaborate, and manage conflicts. | Provide opportunities for Engineering graduates to work in teams to complete assignments and projects. Teamwork exercises should be designed to enhance collaboration, communication, and conflict management skills. |
| Leadership | Leadership skills are essential for engineers to take charge of projects, manage teams, and drive innovation. Employers look for graduates who can lead and inspire others. | Include leadership development activities, such as group projects, mentorship programs, and guest speaker sessions. These activities can help Engineering graduates develop leadership skills, build professional networks, and gain real-world experience. |

*Interdisciplinary Curriculum for Engineering Graduates*

*Table 2. Co-relationship matrix*

| Program Outcomes<br>Course Outcomes | PO1 | PO2 | PO3 | PO4 | PO5 | PO6 | PO7 | PSO1 | PSO2 | PSO3 |
|---|---|---|---|---|---|---|---|---|---|---|
| CO 1 | 3 | - | - | 3 | 2 | 3 | 1 | 1 | 3 | 2 |
| CO 2 | 1 | - | - | 2 | 1 | 1 | 2 | 1 | 1 | 2 |
| CO 3 | 1 | 1 | 3 | 2 | 1 | 1 | 1 | 2 | 1 | 3 |
| CO 4 | 1 | 1 | 2 | 2 | 3 | 1 | 3 | 1 | 1 | 3 |
| Average | 1.5 | 1 | 2.5 | 2.2 | 1.7 | 1.5 | 1.7 | 1.2 | 1.5 | 2.5 |

Hence, my observations on CO are as follows, and have been redefined based on Bloom's taxonomy. While reading Bloom's Taxonomy, it was enriching to understand that the quality of the outcome is more important than the quantity, as depicted in Tables 3 and 4. As indicated by Biggs and Tang (2011), certain insights emerged, specifically regarding the limitations of verbs such as "understand," "comprehend," and "be aware of" in the classroom environment. These verbs do not effectively convey the desired level of performance necessary to fulfil the ILOs (ILOs).

## ASSESSMENT: REFLECTIVE ANALYSIS

To meet my learning goals, I needed to divert students' attention away from memorizing all the facts, processes, and equations, and instead evaluate their ability to apply the intellectual skills required for professional work. Student assessments encompassed objective examinations, short problems, short writing assignments, and presentations (Treleaven and Voola, 2008). Engineering graduates were expected to complete a semester-long authentic comprehensive project that required them to practice analytical, consistent, and reflective thinking by the end of the semester (Facione, 1990; Mezirow, 1991). Hence, Table 5 demonstrates that incorporating a diverse range of skills and knowledge areas into the accounting curriculum has a direct impact on graduates' employability. By assessing and developing skills such as critical thinking, problem solving, communication, collaboration, digital literacy, ethics, and leadership, the curriculum prepares graduates to meet the demands of the accounting profession. This

*Table 3. Cognitive process dimension*

| | | REMEMBER10 | UNDERSTAND11 | APPLY12 | ANALYZE13 | EVALUATE14 | CREATE |
|---|---|---|---|---|---|---|---|
| KNOWLEDGE DIMENSION | FACTUAL | | | | | | |
| | CONCEPTUAL | | CO 1<br>CO 4 | | CO 4 | | |
| | PROCEDURAL | | | CO 2 | CO 3 | CO 3<br>CO 4 | |
| | META COGNITIVE | CO1 | | | CO 3 | CO 3<br>CO 4 | |
| | | | KNOWLEDGE | SKILL | ABILITY | | |

*Table 4. COs observations*

| CO | Observation | Recommendation |
|---|---|---|
| Demonstrate the applicability of the concept of accounting to understand the Managerial decisions and financial statements. | "Demonstrate" is about understanding the concept. Its more than understanding, where Engineering graduates must present and defend his opinion by making judgments about financial information | Appraise the applicability of the concept of accounting to understand Managerial decisions and financial statements. |
| Apply the Financial Statement Analysis associate with Financial Data in the Organization. | Verb 'apply' is one of the standard verbs, but it is too wide-ranging on its own and is focused down to apply something or someone (Biggs & Tang 2011) | Analyze financial data and interpret financial statements |
| Analyse the complexities associated with management of cost of product and services in the Organization. | The outcome is particular and limited, whereas Engineering graduates is expected to do more than defined. Word like 'formulate' would have fed onto the learning outcome more appropriately | 1. Critically evaluate and analyze the complexities associated with the management of cost in the Organization. 2. Formulate persuasive solutions for the complexities associated with cost. |
| Integrate how the concepts of accounting and costing could integrate while identification and resolution of problems pertaining to Management Sector | Integrate is the wrong verb used to formulate outcome, rather | Demonstrate the need for a balance between financial and non-financial information in decision making, control and performance evaluation applications of management accounting |

comprehensive approach enhances graduates' ability to succeed in the workplace, and increases their prospects for employment.

Instructors assessed the engineering graduates based on their performance on case-related assignments (40%) and objective examinations (60%). Instructors noted using the textbook for reference, objective testing of accounting procedures, and continuous improvement of the case materials necessary to meet learning objectives.

*Table 5. Assessment analysis*

| LEARNING OUTCOME | BLOOM'S TAXONOMY | TEACHING LEARNING ACTIVITIES | ASSESSMENT METHODS |
|---|---|---|---|
| Knowledge and understanding | Cognitive -LOTS | Lecture/Tutorial | Written Tests/ Quiz |
| Cognitive Skills | Cognitive-HOTS | Case Study/ Project/ Tutorial/ Group Work | Written Tests/Presentation/ Essay |
| Practical Skills | Psychomotor | Practical/ Demonstration | Practical Tests |
| Interpersonal Skills | Affective | Case Study/ Project/ Tutorial/ Group Work | Assessing how individual members of the group, works to achieve: Presentation/ Project |
| Communication Skills | Affective | Case Study/ Project/ Tutorial | Presentation (individual) |
| Digital Skills | Affective | Case Study/ Project/ Group Work | Project/ Portfolio (individual) |
| Numeracy Skills | Cognitive-HOTS | Case Study/ Project/ Tutorial/ Group Work | Written Tests/Presentation/ Essay |
| Leadership, Autonomy and Responsibility | Affective | Case Study/ Project/ Group Work/ Industrial Attachment/ Discussion | Assessing how individual members of the group, lead the group to achieve: Project/Group work |
| Personal Skills | Affective | Case Study/ Project/ Group Work | Project/ Portfolio (individual) |
| Entrepreneurial Skills | Affective | Case Study/ Project/ Group Work/ Industrial Attachment/ Discussion | Project/Presentation/ Essay (individual) |
| Ethics and Professionalism | Affective | Case Study/ Project/ Industrial Attachment/ Tutorial/ Discussion | Essay/Presentation/ Project (individual) |

The findings led to the perseverance of application issues associated with using a project. Engineering graduates incapability instigates most implementation issues in learning from working-structured problems to unstructured accounting work. Short reflection papers (RPs) have replaced periodic objective tests to encourage deep and meaningful learning. The engineering graduates' responses to question prompts provided evidence of Mezirow's (1991) four stages of professional reflection.

Engineering graduates were expected to read annual report footnotes that outlined a company's accounting practices and answer questions about public company financials. Engineering graduates considered how the accountants' choice of accounting methods affected the items listed on the financial statements after reading the footnotes. The task seemed insurmountable. For the course topic, I needed to create a work environment that allowed engineering graduates to do the work of a skilled accountant.

In contrast to engineering graduates ' previous experience in the introductory accounting course, it becomes essential to persuade engineering graduates that the standardized homework completed outside the class represents only the foundational information necessary for proficiently carrying out the tasks of an accountant, rather than constituting the primary goal of their learning. It will be challenging to know when to let engineering graduates fail, and when to provide further assistance to advance their work. To ensure that engineering graduates practice critical thinking and reflection, reasonable and supported responses will have to substitute the correct answer. I would have to work under the constraints of limited class time, engineering graduates' expectations of accounting from the introductory class, grade issues, and departmental peer pressure to adhere to the conventional accounting teaching system.

## STUDENT FEEDBACK ON CURRICULUM

Problem-solving and modelling were given significant emphasis in the newly developed interventions, namely Excel and asynchronous sessions. The modelling process itself serves as a means to support problem-solving, which is recognized as a crucial employability skill (Stoner & Milner, 2010). Moreover, these abilities are explicitly and systematically integrated as essential requirements within the subjects covered by courses.

After discussion (ANNEXURE I) with a couple of engineering graduates, it was ostensible that the engineering graduates found it challenging to participate in the modelling process and identified that financial data modelling supports problem-solving. In addition, due to the pandemic, online classes for such courses made them less participative and interactive. Engineering graduates also found it challenging to move away from their search for 'the correct' answer, which is counter-intuitive to model building, emphasizing processes and alternatives (Cleveland, 2005).

Furthermore, the engineering graduates expressed that the vastness of the curriculum content made it difficult for them to understand and incorporate each topic effectively. A specific concern pertained to time management, as they encountered difficulties in completing their assessment tasks within the allocated time frame.

Moreover, post-interaction observations revealed that they faced challenges in actively engaging with and developing all subsets of employability skills emphasized in the curriculum. Specifically, difficulties were encountered in managing time, especially when attending online classes, participating in modelling exercises, and problem-solving activities. Additionally, there was reluctance to take personal responsibility for their learning and to adopt a positive attitude towards the process of acquiring learning-to-learn skills.

## MY LEARNING

Moon (2002) states that Intended Learning Outcomes are written in terms of 'what the learners are expected to do' since the teacher has no real control over engineering graduates' learning. No one can make an engineering graduate learn but can only hope that learning will occur. Intended Learning Outcome focuses on the learning experience of learners. Learning aims should possess three characteristics: observable, measurable, and student-centered (Goodyear & Dudley, 2015; McNeill et al., 2012).

While going through POs and PSOs with COs in the course plan, I, as a faculty, always assumed that 'content to be taught' defines outcomes. However, after reviewing the literature, I learned that appropriately written outcomes derive content from being taught. While implying good teaching, the following phenomena should be considered.

What? What are the learning outcomes?

How? - The learning outcome can be achieved through medium (content).

But how? - How can we give the 'ownership to students' so that ILO could be achieved

Selecting the actual topics to be taught is a matter of specific content, expertise, and judgment. A curriculum is a rectangular area (breadth × depth) (Biggs and Tang, 2011). Most educators focus on breadth and depth. Learning Outcomes must be validly assessed and need to be S.M.A.R.T, an acronym meaning Specific, Measurable, Attainable, Relevant, Time-Bound which are 'ILOs' (Biwer & et al., 2020). However, it now needs to be 'SMARTER' - specific, measurable, attainable, relevant, time-bound, evaluate, and re-evaluate.

The evaluation of the Course that I have taught for three consecutive years has helped me to critically analyze and reflect on the course and identify the gaps that I was unable to dig out. CA also allowed me to bridge the gap between the planned course, the delivered Course, and Course. Thereby, I look at myself as a reflective practitioner and continue to re-examine the gaps and misalignment in the modules to bridge the gap and ensure students' learning.

## RECOMMENDATION

The contemporary landscape of education and employment underscores the imperative of a holistic approach to curriculum design, particularly in disciplines like accounting that have traditionally been viewed through a narrow, technical lens. As the boundaries between disciplines blur in the professional world, it becomes paramount for educational institutions to ensure that their curricula are both comprehensive and adaptive. For engineering graduates transitioning into or intersecting with the realm of accounting, this is even more crucial. The following recommendations aim to bridge this interdisciplinary gap, drawing on the synthesis of technical prowess inherent in engineering and the analytical depth required in accounting.

1. Holistic Curriculum Design:
    - Technical and Soft Skills Integration: While accounting courses have traditionally emphasized financial knowledge, it's essential to integrate soft skills such as communication, leadership, and ethical conduct. These competencies, often highlighted in engineering curricula, ensure that graduates are equipped to navigate the multifaceted challenges of the modern workplace.

- Case Study Approach with Engineering Context: Incorporate case studies that require engineering graduates to analyze real-world scenarios, such as evaluating a company's financial health or determining the viability of a new product launch. These case studies should be tailored to resonate with an engineering mindset, perhaps focusing on industries or sectors where engineering and finance intersect.
2. Experiential Learning and Real-world Application:
    - Internships and Cooperative Education: Facilitate partnerships with industries to offer internships or cooperative education opportunities. Such hands-on experiences allow engineering graduates to apply theoretical knowledge, bridging the academic-industry gap. For engineering graduates, placements in sectors like tech finance or industrial accounting can provide invaluable insights.
    - Service Learning: Encourage engineering graduates to undertake community projects where they can apply their accounting skills in real-world contexts. This not only enhances their practical knowledge but also instills a sense of ethical responsibility, a competency highly sought after in both engineering and accounting professions.
3. Innovative Teaching Strategies Tailored for Engineers:
    - Utilizing Technology and Software Tools: Integrate tools or software commonly used in engineering into the accounting curriculum. For instance, using data visualization tools to interpret financial data can make the content more relatable and engaging for engineering graduates.
    - Emphasizing the Modelling Process: Given that problem-solving and modelling are foundational in engineering, emphasize these aspects in the accounting curriculum. Use platforms like Excel for financial modelling, allowing them to draw parallels between engineering simulations and financial projections.
4. Continuous Feedback and Iteration:
    - Feedback Mechanisms: Establish robust feedback mechanisms where engineering graduates and industry professionals can provide insights into the curriculum's relevance and effectiveness. This iterative approach ensures that the curriculum remains attuned to industry demands and evolving pedagogical best practices.
    - Faculty Development: Regularly update faculty on the latest trends at the intersection of engineering and accounting. Workshops or seminars focusing on interdisciplinary teaching methods can be invaluable.
5. Course Objectives and Outcomes Alignment:
    - Explicit Competency Mapping: Clearly map the identified engineering competencies to course objectives and outcomes. This systematic approach ensures that there are no overlaps or omissions and that engineering graduates are progressively acquiring the desired competencies.
    - Assessment Reforms: Re-evaluate assessment methods to ensure they align with the integrated competencies. For instance, instead of traditional exams, consider project-based assessments where they might design a financial model for an engineering project.

# CONCLUSION

The integration of engineering competencies into the accounting curriculum is not merely an academic exercise but a forward-looking strategy to prepare graduates for the multifaceted challenges of the 21st-century workplace. As disciplines converge in the professional realm, it is incumbent upon educational institutions to anticipate these shifts and adapt accordingly. The recommendations provided herein offer a comprehensive roadmap for such an integration, emphasizing a holistic, experiential, and iterative approach. By weaving together, the analytical rigor of engineering with the nuanced depth of accounting, we can foster a new generation of professionals, adept at navigating the intricate interplay of numbers, ethics, and innovation. This interdisciplinary synergy, if executed with intentionality and foresight, holds the promise of not just producing competent professionals but pioneering thinkers at the nexus of engineering and finance.

# REFERENCES

Alfauzan, A. A., & Tarchouna, N. (2017). The role of an aligned curriculum design in the achievement of learning outcomes. *Journal of Education and e-learning Research, 4*(3), 81–91. doi:10.20448/journal.509.2017.43.81.91

Azmi, A. N., Kamin, Y., & Noordin, M. K. (2018). Competencies of engineering graduates: what are the employer's expectations. *International Journal of Engineering & Technology, 7*(2.29), 519-523.

Baeten, M., Kyndt, E., Struyven, K., & Dochy, F. (2010, January). Using student-centred learning environments to stimulate deep approaches to learning: Factors encouraging or discouraging their effectiveness. *Educational Research Review, 5*(3), 243–260. doi:10.1016/j.edurev.2010.06.001

Biggs, J. (2003). Aligning teaching and assessing to course objectives. *Teaching and learning in higher education: New trends and innovations, 2*(4), 13-17.

Biggs, J., & Tang, C. (2011). Teaching for Quality Learning at University. McGraw-Hill Education (UK).

Biwer, F., Egbrink, M. G. A., Aalten, P., & de Bruin, A. B. H. (2020). Fostering effective learning strategies in higher education–a mixed-methods study. *Journal of Applied Research in Memory and Cognition, 9*(2), 186–203. doi:10.1016/j.jarmac.2020.03.004

Bloom, B. S., Krathwohl, D. R., & Masia, B. B. (1984). Bloom taxonomy of educational objectives. In *Allyn and Bacon*. Pearson Education.

Butler, M. (2022). Interdisciplinary experiential learning during COVID-19: Lessons learned and reflections for the future. *Journal of Environmental Studies and Sciences, 12*(2), 369–377. doi:10.1007/s13412-021-00734-w PMID:35013697

Choi, Han, Lee, & Rhee. (2018). Effects of Interdisciplinary Courses on Engineering Students' Competencies. *TENCON 2018 - 2018 IEEE Region 10 Conference*, 793-797.. doi:10.1109/TENCON.2018.8650133

Ebrahiminejad, H. (2017, June), *A Systematized Literature Review: Defining and Developing Engineering Competencies* Paper presented at 2017 ASEE Annual Conference & Exposition, Columbus, OH. 10.18260/1-2--27526

Entwistle, N. (2000). Approaches to studying and levels of understanding: The influences of teaching and assessment. *Higher Education-New York-Agathon Press Incorporated, 15*, 156–218.

Fredricks, J. A., Filsecker, M., & Lawson, M. A. (2016). Student engagement, context, and adjustment: Addressing definitional, measurement, and methodological issues. *Learning and Instruction, 43*, 1–4. doi:10.1016/j.learninstruc.2016.02.002

Goodyear, V., & Dudley, D. (2015). "I'm a facilitator of learning!" Understanding what teachers and students do within student-centered physical education models. *Quest, 67*(3), 274–289. doi:10.1080/00336297.2015.1051236

Gurukkal, R. (2018). Towards outcome-based education. *Higher Education for the Future, 5*(1), 1–3. doi:10.1177/2347631117740456

Habel, C. (2012). 'I can do it, and how!' Student experience in access and equity pathways to higher education. *Higher Education Research & Development, 31*(6), 811–825. doi:10.1080/07294360.2012.659177

Hall, O., & Seth, D. (2022). Role of Interdisciplinarity and Collaboration in Engineering Design Curriculum. *2022 IEEE Integrated STEM Education Conference (ISEC)*, 285-292. 10.1109/ISEC54952.2022.10025305

Hanapi, Z., Nordin, M. S., & Khamis, A. (2015). Challenges Faced by Engineering Lecturers in Integrating Technical and Employability Skills in the Curriculum: A Case Study in Community College, Malaysia. *International Journal of Social Science and Humanity, 5*(5), 483–486. doi:10.7763/IJSSH.2015.V5.504

Hemsley-Brown, J., & Oplatka, I. (2006). Universities in a competitive global marketplace: A systematic review of the literature on higher education marketing. *International Journal of Public Sector Management, 19*(4), 316–338. doi:10.1108/09513550610669176

Huber, M. T., & Hutchings, P. (2004). *Integrative Learning: Mapping the Terrain. The Academy in Transition.* Association of American Colleges and Universities.

Kandlbinder, P. (2014). CA in university teaching. *HERDSA News, 36*(3), 5–6.

Larkin, H., & Richardson, B. (2013). Creating high challenge/high support academic environments through CA: Student outcomes. *Teaching in Higher Education, 18*(2), 192–204. doi:10.1080/13562517.2012.696541

Lawson, R. A., Blocher, E. J., Brewer, P. C., Cokins, G., Sorensen, J. E., Stout, D. E., Sundem, G. L., Wolcott, S. K., & Wouters, M. J. (2014). Focusing accounting curricula on students' long-run careers: Recommendations for an integrated competency-based framework for accounting education. *Issues in Accounting Education, 29*(2), 295–317. doi:10.2308/iace-50673

Leber, J., Renkl, A., Nückles, M., & Wäschle, K. (2018). When the type of assessment counteracts teaching for understanding. *Learning: Research and Practice, 4*(2), 161–179. doi:10.1080/23735082.2017.1285422

Li, Y., Liu, Y., Nguyen, K., Shi, H., Vuorenmaa, E., Jarvela, S., & Zhao, G. (2022). Exploring Interactions and Regulations in Collaborative Learning: An Interdisciplinary Multimodal Dataset. *arXiv preprint arXiv:2210.05419*.

Lucas, U., & Mladenovic, R. (2007). The potential of threshold concepts: An emerging framework for educational research and practice. *London Review of Education*, *5*(3). Advance online publication. doi:10.1080/14748460701661294

MacDonald, L., Thomas, E., Javernick-Will, A., Austin-Breneman, J., Aranda, I., Salvinelli, C., Klees, R., Walters, J., Parmentier, M. J., Schaad, D., Shahi, A., Bedell, E., Platais, G., Brown, J., Gershenson, J., Watkins, D., Obonyo, E., Oyanedel-Craver, V., Olson, M., ... Linden, K. (2022). Aligning learning objectives and approaches in global engineering graduate programs: Review and recommendations by an interdisciplinary working group. *Development Engineering*, *7*, 100095. doi:10.1016/j.deveng.2022.100095

Male, S. A., Bush, M. B., & Chapman, E. S. (2011). Understanding generic engineering competencies. *Australasian Journal of Engineering Education*, *17*(3), 147–156. doi:10.1080/22054952.2011.11464064

Mariasse, A. L. (1985). Vision and leadership: Paying attention to intention. *Peabody Journal of Education*, *63*(1), 150–173. doi:10.1080/01619568509538505

McCune, V., & Entwistle, N. (2000, August). The deep approach to learning: analytic abstraction and idiosyncratic development. In *Innovations in Higher Education Conference* (Vol. 30). University of Helsinki.

McHann, J. C. (2012). Changed learning needs: some radical reflections on B-School education. *Business Administration Education: Changes in Management and Leadership Strategies*, 105-128.

McHenry, R., & Krishnan, S. (2022). A conceptual professional practice framework for embedding employability skills development in engineering education programmes. *European Journal of Engineering Education*, *47*(6), 1296–1314. doi:10.1080/03043797.2022.2164255

McNeill, M., Gosper, M., & Xu, J. (2012). Assessment choices to target higher order learning outcomes: The power of academic empowerment. *Research in Learning Technology*, *20*, 20. doi:10.3402/rlt.v20i0.17595

Midhat Ali, M., Qureshi, S. M., Memon, M. S., Mari, S. I., & Ramzan, M. B. (2021). Competency framework development for effective human resource management. *SAGE Open*, *11*(2), 21582440211006124. doi:10.1177/21582440211006124

Nair, C. S., Patil, A., & Mertova, P. (2009). Re-engineering graduate skills – a case study. *European Journal of Engineering Education*, *34*(2), 131–139. doi:10.1080/03043790902829281

Pan, Q., Zhou, J., Yang, D., Shi, D., Wang, D., Chen, X., & Liu, J. (2023). Mapping Knowledge Domain Analysis in Deep Learning Research of Global Education. *Sustainability (Basel)*, *15*(4), 3097. doi:10.3390/su15043097

Pretorius, L., Bailey, C., & Miles, M. (2013). CA and the Research Skills Development Framework: Using Theory to Practically Align Graduate Attributes, Learning Experiences, and Assessment Tasks in Undergraduate Midwifery. *International Journal on Teaching and Learning in Higher Education*, *25*(3), 378–387.

Raj, V., Hardik, P., Puranik, P. S., & Acharya, G. D. (2015). *Engineering Graduates Competence and Employability*. Academic Press.

Ramsden, P. (2003). *Learning to teach in higher education*. Routledge. doi:10.4324/9780203507711

Ramsden, P., Beswick, D. G., & Bowden, J. A. (1986). Effects Of Learning-Skills Interventions On 1st Year University-Students Learning. *Human Learning*, *5*(3), 151–164.

Rhee, H., Han, J., Lee, M., & Choi, Y. W. (2020). Effects of interdisciplinary courses on future engineers' competency. Higher Education. *Skills and Work-Based Learning*, *10*(3), 467–479. doi:10.1108/HESWBL-05-2019-0071

Spady, W. G. (1994). *Outcome-Based Education: Critical Issues and Answers*. American Association of School Administrators.

Spady, W. G. (1995, June 1). *Outcome-Based Education: Critical Issues and Answers*. https://doi.org/doi:10.1604/9780614251012

Stamov Roßnagel, C., Fitzallen, N., & Lo Baido, K. (2021). CA and the learning experience: Relationships with student motivation and perceived learning demands. *Higher Education Research & Development*, *40*(4), 838–851. doi:10.1080/07294360.2020.1787956

Stamov Roßnagel, C., Lo Baido, K., & Fitzallen, N. (2021). Revisiting the relationship between CA and learning approaches: A perceived alignment perspective. *PLoS One*, *16*(8), e0253949. doi:10.1371/journal.pone.0253949 PMID:34428210

Stoner, G., & Milner, M. (2010). Embedding generic employability skills in an accounting degree: Development and impediments. *Accounting Education*, *19*(1-2), 123–138. doi:10.1080/09639280902888229

Suleiman, A., & Abahre, J. (2020). Essential competencies for engineers from the perspective of fresh graduates. *Engineering Management in Production and Services*, *12*(1), 70–79. doi:10.2478/emj-2020-0006

Sung, S., Alon, L., Cho, J. Y., & Kizilcec, R. (2022). How to Assess Student Learning in Information Science: Exploratory Evidence from Large College Courses. *Proceedings of the Association for Information Science and Technology*, *59*(1), 500–504. doi:10.1002/pra2.659

Treleaven, L., & Voola, R. (2008). Integrating the development of graduate attributes through CA. *Journal of Marketing Education*, *30*(2), 160–173. doi:10.1177/0273475308319352

Van Rossum, E. J., & Schenk, S. M. (1984). The relationship between learning conception, study strategy and learning outcome. *The British Journal of Educational Psychology*, *54*(1), 73–83. doi:10.1111/j.2044-8279.1984.tb00846.x

Walker, A., & Leary, H. (2009). A problem based learning meta analysis: Differences across problem types, implementation types, disciplines, and assessment levels. *The Interdisciplinary Journal of Problem-Based Learning, 3*(1), 6. doi:10.7771/1541-5015.1061

Weimer, M. (2013). *Learner-centered teaching: Five key changes to practice.* John Wiley & Sons.

Zhang, J. (2021, September). Research on the interdisciplinary competence and its influencing factors of engineering college students under the emerging engineering education. In *Proceedings of the 5th International Conference on Digital Technology in Education* (pp. 163-169). 10.1145/3488466.3488486

## ENDNOTES

1. World that is Volatile, Uncertain, Complex and Ambiguous, the acronym is popularly used to describe the contemporary workplaces and current state of education.
2. Students who use a deep approach to learning search for meaning integrate old knowledge with new knowledge, synthesize information, and look for ways to apply knowledge (Biggs 1987; Entwistle and Ramsden 1983; Entwistle et al. 2000; Trigwell and Prosser 1991).
3. Department Consultative Committee
4. Board of Studies
5. The principles of CA are reflected in the undergraduate and postgraduate curriculum frameworks which require faculty to map out very clearly the alignment between assessment and learning outcomes in the course specification forms.
6. Statements about the knowledge, skills, and attitudes (attributes) the graduate of the program should have.
7. Statements that describe the career and professional accomplishments that the program is preparing graduates to achieve.
8. Problem-based learning is a student-centered instructional method that requires students to work together to investigate unstructured problems (Baeten, Kyndt, Struyven, & Dochy, 2010; Barrows, 1986; Prince, 2004).
9. An instructional method is a specifically designed interaction between an instructor, students, and a task to enhance learning (Weimer, 2013).
10. Remembering involves recall of factual knowledge.
11. Understanding is the ability to interpret, summarize, infer, compare, and explain
12. Applying occurs through implementation of a concept.
13. Analyzing involves determining relationships and differentiating ideas.
14. Evaluating requires a judgment and creating results in an original idea or product.

## APPENDIX I

Student Interaction Records

a) I'd say about 7 hours a week at the most. I'll work on the tutorials and workshop for about 4 hours a week, only in managerial accounting, then maybe an hour in statistics, just…. work, and maybe half an hour in finance, if anything. I usually devote about an hour to economics, and if I miss a lecture during the week, I can do some reading, but I usually combine that with some tutorial workings... about 6/7 hours.

b) You must be able to prepare and control your time, as well as take notes in class. It's not like going to a traditional school where you can get a lot of support.

c) It may be an exercise in perception, figuring out what the lecturers want, but we're looking for something a little more precise. To tell, "Ok, if you want us to do that, can we go ahead and do it instead of you picking the three easiest?"


## APPENDIX II

### Course Plan

Year: 1st
    Semester: I
    Name of the Faculty: Course Code:
    Course: Accounting for Managers L:3
    Program: MBA Power Management T:0
    Target: Level 2 P:0
    C:3
    1. Pedagogy

Due to Covid19 pandemic and subsequent government guidelines, teaching learning will be conducted through synchronous and asynchronous online sessions on Blackboard that will include the following components.

- Lecture/Class Participation
- Group discussion
- Online videos
- Case study
- Group Project and Presentation
- Test

*Table 6. Level and population percentage*

| Target | 50% (marks) |
|---|---|
| Level-1 | 40% (population) |
| Level-2 | 50% (population) |
| Level-3 | 60% (population) |

*Table 7. Method of evaluation*

| PG |
|---|
| Quizzes/Tests, Assignments, seminar (50%) |
| End semester (50%) |

*Table 8. Passing criteria*

| Scale | PG |
|---|---|
| **Out of 10-point scale** | SGPA – "6.00" in each semester<br>CGPA – "6.00"<br>Min. Individual Course Grade – "C"<br>Course Grade Point – "4.0" |

*For PG, passing marks are 40/100 in a paper

*Table 9. References*

| Textbooks | Web Resources | Journals | Reference Books |
|---|---|---|---|
| 1. Sehgal, Deepak (2019), *"Financial Accounting"*, Vikas Publishing H House, 5th Edition, New Delhi.'<br>2. Goyal, Bhushan Kumar; Tiwari, HN (2019), *"Financial Accounting"*, 5th Edition Taxmann Publications<br>3. Goldwin, Alderman ; Sanyal (2019), *"Financial Accounting"*, 2nd Edition, Cengage Learning. | www.orsoc.org.uk<br>www.elsevier.com | Journal of Finance Vikalpa Journals published by ICAI, ICWAI | 1. Lal, J ; Srivastava, S (2019), " Financial Accounting; Principles and Practices", 4th Edition, S Chand, New Delhi<br>2. Robert N Anthony, David Hawkins, Kenneth A. Merchant(2019), *"Accounting: Text and Cases"*, 13th Ed, McGraw-Hill Education<br>3. Charles T. Horngren and Donna Philbrick (2019), *"Introduction to Financial Accounting"*, 11th Edition, Pearson Education.<br>4. Monga, J, R, *"Financial Accounting: Concepts and Applications"* (2019) Mayur Paper Backs, 2th Edition, New Delhi.<br>5. Tulsian, P.C; Tulsia, Bharat (2019)., *"Financial Accounting"*, 10th Edition, Pearson Education |

## GUIDELINES TO STUDY THE SUBJECT

Instructions to Students

1. Go through the 'Syllabus' in the Black Board section of the website in order to find out the Reading List.
2. Get your schedule and try to pace your studies as close to the timeline as possible.

3. Get your online lecture notes (Content, videos) at <u>Lecture Notes</u> section. These are our lecture notes. Make sure you use them during this course.
4. Check your blackboard regularly.
5. Go through study material.
6. Check mails and announcements on blackboard.
7. Keep updated with the posts, assignments and examinations which shall be conducted on the blackboard
8. Be regular, so that you do not suffer in any way
9. **E-Mail and online learning tool:** Each student in the class should have an e-mail id and a pass word to access the LMS system regularly. Regularly, important information – Date of conducting class tests, guest lectures, via online learning tool. The best way to arrange meetings with us or ask specific questions is by email and prior appointment. All the assignments preferably should be uploaded on online learning tool. Various research papers/reference material will be mailed/uploaded on online learning platform time to time.
10. **Attendance:** Students must have minimum attendance of 75% in each subject. Students with less than said percentage shall NOT be allowed to appear in the end semester examination.

This much should be enough to get you organized and on your way to having a great semester! If you need us for anything, send your feedback through e-mail <u>to your concerned faculty.</u> Please use an appropriate subject line to indicate your message details.

## RELATED OUTCOMES

**1. Co-Relationship Matrix** Indicate the relationships by 1- Slight (low) 2- Moderate (Medium) 3-Substantial (high)

*Table 10. The expected outcomes of the program are*

| PO1 | Apply knowledge of management theories and practices to solve business problems |
|---|---|
| PO2 | Foster Analytical and critical thinking abilities for databased decision-making |
| PO3 | Develop Value based Leadership ability |
| PO4 | Ability to understand, analyze and communicate global, economic, legal, and ethical aspects of business. |
| PO5 | Ability to lead themselves and others in the achievement of organizational goals, contributing effectively to a team environment. |
| PO6 | Understand the impact of the professional management solutions in societal and environmental contexts and need for inclusive and sustainable development |
| PO7 | Recognize the need for, and have the preparation and ability to engage in independent and life-long learning in the broadest context of technological and managerial change. |

*Table 11. The expected outcomes of the specific program are*

| PSO1 | Apply decision-support tools to decision making in Power Sector |
|---|---|
| PSO2 | Apply conceptual knowledge of Power Sector in an integrated manner |
| PSO3 | Demonstrate Employability Skills for appropriate roles in Power Sector |

*Table 12. The expected outcomes of the course are (minimum 3 and maximum 6)*

| CO 1 | Demonstrate the applicability of the concept of Accounting to understand the Managerial decisions and financial statements . |
|---|---|
| CO 2 | Apply the Financial Statement Analysis associate with Financial Data in the organization. |
| CO 3 | Analyze the complexities associated with management of cost of product and services in the Organization. |
| CO 4 | Integrate how the concepts of accounting and costing could integrate while identification and resolution of problems pertaining to Management Sector |

*Table 13. Co-relationship matrix*

| Program Outcomes / Course Outcomes | PO1 | PO2 | PO3 | PO4 | PO5 | PO6 | PO7 | PSO1 | PSO2 | PSO3 |
|---|---|---|---|---|---|---|---|---|---|---|
| CO 1 | 3 | - | - | 3 | 2 | 3 | 1 | 1 | 3 | 2 |
| CO 2 | 1 | - | - | 2 | 1 | 1 | 2 | 1 | 1 | 2 |
| CO 3 | 1 | 1 | 3 | 2 | 1 | 1 | 1 | 2 | 1 | 3 |
| CO 4 | 1 | 1 | 2 | 2 | 3 | 1 | 3 | 1 | 1 | 3 |
| Average | 1.5 | 1 | 2.5 | 2.2 | 1.7 | 1.5 | 1.7 | 1.2 | 1.5 | 2.5 |

*Table 14. Course outcomes assessment plan:*

| components | Assignment | Test/Quiz | End Semester | Case Study Analysis | Practical Application of Concepts | Live Project |
|---|---|---|---|---|---|---|
| CO 1 | √ | X | √ | X | X | X |
| CO 2 | √ | X | √ | X | √ | X |
| CO 3 | X | √ | √ | √ | X | √ |
| CO 4 | X | √ | √ | √ | √ | √ |

## BROAD PLAN OF COURSE COVERAGE

Sessions: Total No. of Instructional periods available for the course

*Table 15. Course activities*

| S. No. | Description | Planned | | | Remarks |
|---|---|---|---|---|---|
| | | From | To | No. of Sessions | |
| | Group Project (10% weightage) | | | 2 | Online discussion over Blackboard (Bb) |
| | Assignment (10% weightage) | | | 1 | Online over Blackboard |
| | Innovative Tool-Practical Application of Accounting Concepts -Reflection (5% weightage) and Application (5% weightage) | | | 3 | Online over Blackboard |
| | Quiz/Test (10% weightage) | | | 3 | Online over Blackboard |
| | Case Study Presentation (10%) | | | 5 | Online over Blackboard |
| | Total no. of sessions | 60 | | | |

*Interdisciplinary Curriculum for Engineering Graduates*

## SESSION PLAN

*Table 16. UNIT-I*

| Lecture No. | Topics to be Covered | Mode | CO Mapped |
|---|---|---|---|
| 1. | Sharing Syllabus and Course plan. Introducing Black board and the pedagogy with Students Introduction to Course | Synchronous | 1 |
| 2. | Meaning, Need, Role and Significance of Accounting | Synchronous | 1 |
| 3. | https://www.accountingcoach.com/accounting-principles/explanation https://www.toppr.com/guides/principles-and-practice-of-accounting/meaning-and-scope-of-accounting/meaning-of-accounting/ | Asynchronous | 1,2,3,4. |
| 4. | Discussion Session | Synchronous | 3 |
| 5. | Basic Accounting Concepts (AS-1 & 9) and Conventions | Synchronous | 1 |
| 6. | Basic Accounting Concepts (AS-1 & 9) and Conventions | Synchronous | 1 |
| 7. | https://www.accountingcoach.com/accounting-principles/explanation https://www.toppr.com/guides/principles-and-practice-of-accounting/meaning-and-scope-of-accounting/meaning-of-accounting/ | Asynchronous | 1,2,3,4. |
| 8. | Discussion Session | Synchronous | 3 |
| 9. | (Overview of Indian GAAP, US GAAP, IAS, IFRS), Asset-Liability Equity Relationship (ALE) | Synchronous | 1 |
| 10. | (Overview of Indian GAAP, US GAAP, IAS, IFRS), Asset-Liability Equity Relationship (ALE) | Synchronous | 1 |
| 11. | https://www.accountingcoach.com/accounting-principles/explanation https://www.toppr.com/guides/principles-and-practice-of-accounting/meaning-and-scope-of-accounting/meaning-of-accounting/ | Asynchronous | 1,2,3,4. |
| 12. | Discussion Session | Synchronous | 3 |

## SESSION PLAN

*Table 17. UNIT-II*

| Lecture No. | Topics to be Covered | Mode | CO Mapped |
|---|---|---|---|
| 13. | Introduction to Accounting Cycle-Preparation of Journal, Ledger, Trial Balance | Synchronous | 1 |
| 14. | Introduction to Accounting Cycle-Preparation of Journal, Ledger, Trial Balance | Synchronous | 1 |
| 15. | https://courses.lumenlearning.com/sac-finaccounting/chapter/ledgers-journals-and-accounts/ | Asynchronous | 1,2,3,4. |
| 16. | Discussion Session | Synchronous | 3 |
| 17. | Introduction to Accounting Cycle-Preparation of Journal, Ledger, Trial Balance | Synchronous | 1 |
| 18. | Depreciation, Depletion and Amortization (AS-6), Preparation of financial statements with adjustments. | Synchronous | 1 |
| 19. | https://www.double-entry-bookkeeping.com/depreciation/depreciation-depletion-and-amortization/ | Asynchronous | 1,2,3,4. |
| 20. | Discussion Session | Synchronous | 3 |
| 21. | Depreciation, Depletion and Amortization (AS-6), Preparation of financial statements with adjustments. | Synchronous | 1 |
| 22. | Depreciation, Depletion and Amortization (AS-6), Preparation of financial statements with adjustments. | Synchronous | 1 |
| 23. | https://www.economicshelp.org/blog/4890/economics/types-of-costs/ | Asynchronous | 1,2,3,4. |
| 24. | Discussion Session | Synchronous | 3 |

## SESSION PLAN

*Table 18. UNIT-III*

| Lecture No. | Topics to be Covered | Mode | CO Mapped |
|---|---|---|---|
| 25. | Understanding & Analysis of Company Accounts | Synchronous | 1 |
| 26. | Understanding & Analysis of Company Accounts | Synchronous | 1 |
| 27. | Non-manufacturing unit: https://resource.cdn.icai.org/55008bosfndnov19-p1-cp7u1.pdf  Manufacturing unit: https://resource.cdn.icai.org/55009bosfndnov19-p1-cp7u2.pdf | Asynchronous | 1,2,3,4. |
| 28. | Discussion Session | Synchronous | 3 |
| 29. | Understanding & Analysis of Company Accounts | Synchronous | 1 |
| 30. | Understanding & Analysis of Company Accounts | Synchronous | 1 |
| 31. | https://byjus.com/commerce/trading-and-profit-and-loss-account/ | Asynchronous | 1,2,3,4. |
| 32. | Discussion Session | Synchronous | 3 |
| 33. | Analysis of Financial statements of Holding & Subsidiary Companies. | Synchronous | 1 |
| 34. | Analysis of Financial statements of Holding & Subsidiary Companies. | Synchronous | 1 |
| 35. | https://sites.google.com/a/tges.org/accountancy/trading-and-profit-and-loss-account  https://www.playaccounting.com/explanation/fa-exp/profit-and-loss-account/ | Asynchronous | 1,2,3,4. |
| 36. | Discussion Session | Synchronous | 3 |

## SESSION PLAN

*Table 19. UNIT-IV*

| Lecture No. | Topics to be Covered | Mode | CO Mapped |
|---|---|---|---|
| 37. | Analysis and Interpretation of Financial Statements-Ratio Analysis, | Synchronous | 1 |
| 38. | Analysis and Interpretation of Financial Statements-Ratio Analysis, | Synchronous | 1 |
| 39. | https://corporatefinanceinstitute.com/resources/knowledge/finance/ratio-analysis/ https://resource.cdn.icai.org/56013bosinter45376-p8-seca-cp3.pdf | Asynchronous | 1,2,3,4. |
| 40. | Discussion Session | Synchronous | 3 |
| 41. | Common-Size Statement, Du-Pont Analysis, Cash-Flow Statement (AS-3) | Synchronous | 1 |
| 42. | Common-Size Statement, Du-Pont Analysis, Cash-Flow Statement (AS-3) | Synchronous | 1 |
| 43. | Case Study- Maruti Udyog | Asynchronous | 1,2,3,4. |
| 44. | Discussion Session | Synchronous | 3 |
| 45. | Common-Size Statement, Du-Pont Analysis, Cash-Flow Statement (AS-3) | Synchronous | 1 |
| 46. | Common-Size Statement, Du-Pont Analysis, Cash-Flow Statement (AS-3) | Synchronous | 1 |
| 47. | https://taxguru.in/income-tax/applicability-cash-flow-statement-caro-2016-2020-internal-financial-control.html | Asynchronous | 1,2,3,4. |
| 48. | Discussion Session | Synchronous | 3 |

## SESSION PLAN

*Table 20. UNIT-V*

| Lecture No. | Topics to be Covered | Mode | CO Mapped |
|---|---|---|---|
| 49. | Cost Concepts, Cost Sheet, Material Costing | Synchronous | 1 |
| 50. | Cost Concepts, Cost Sheet, Material Costing | Synchronous | 1 |
| 51. | https://www.economicshelp.org/blog/4890/economics/types-of-costs/ | Asynchronous | 1,2,3,4. |
| 52. | Discussion Session | Synchronous | 3 |
| 53. | Labour and Overhead Costing, Absorption Costing, Activity Based Costing | Synchronous | 1 |
| 54. | Inventory Valuation (AS-2) | Synchronous | 1 |
| 55. | https://www.economicshelp.org/blog/4890/economics/types-of-costs/ | Asynchronous | 1,2,3,4. |
| 56. | Discussion Session | Synchronous | 3 |
| 57. | Marginal Costing- PV Ratio, BEP Analysis, Relevant Costing, Standard Costing, Budgetary Control, EVA, MVA | Synchronous | 1 |
| 58. | Marginal Costing- PV Ratio, BEP Analysis, Relevant Costing, Standard Costing, Budgetary Control, EVA, MVA | Synchronous | 1 |
| 59. | https://www.economicshelp.org/blog/4890/economics/types-of-costs/ | Asynchronous | 1,2,3,4. |
| 60. | Discussion Session | Synchronous | 3 |

# Chapter 5
# The Interplay Between Career Adaptability and Foreign Language Skills in an Unstable Labor Market

**Maria-Anca Maican**
https://orcid.org/0000-0002-8120-3955
*Transilvania University of Braşov, Romania*

**Elena Cocoradă**
*Transilvania University of Braşov, Romania*

**Felicia Constantin**
https://orcid.org/0000-0002-3964-7974
*University of Oradea, Romania*

## ABSTRACT

*Career adaptability is a soft skill that allows people to cope with professional tasks in an unpredictable labor market. Today's global labor market also requires language skills to facilitate employees' collaboration across linguistic boundaries. The chapter is built around a quantitative study with participants from a large public university in the south-eastern part of Central Europe, and it aims to analyze the connection between career adaptability, foreign languages, and personal traits. The results show significant gender differences regarding adaptability and the perceived role of foreign languages for employability and in one's career development, all in favor of girls. Concerning students' status as employed/unemployed, the tendencies regard only unemployed students' stronger confidence in and lower concern with the future. Career adaptability is predicted by foreign language anxiety, conscientiousness, openness to experience, and self-perceived FL proficiency. Some implications for teachers are presented at the end of the chapter.*

DOI: 10.4018/978-1-7998-7999-2.ch005

*The Interplay Between Career Adaptability and Foreign Language Skills in an Unstable Labor Market*

## INTRODUCTION

European statistics and institutional reports have shown an increase in the employment rate for recent graduates of tertiary education compared to pre-pandemic times, especially for male graduates, but they have also pointed to a shortage of skills in the labor market (European Commission [EC], 2023a; EC, 2023b). Hard skills continue to be important in employment, but soft skills are constantly gaining prominence for employability, work performance, and advancement (LaPrade et al., 2019).

Soft skills, such as adaptability, critical and analytical thinking, teamwork, time management, the ability to cooperate and communicate, computer skills, as well as foreign languages (FLs), have the advantage of being transferrable from one field to another, facilitating performance in social contexts, and benefiting one's professional life at large (Poláková et al., 2023). The importance of these skills has emerged more forcefully recently, as work, traditionally seen as a stable environment for individuals' maturation, has become a dynamic and unpredictable environment that forces people to adapt to new working environments (Fusco et al., 2019). Consequently, young people are far from the comfort and security that they should enjoy once they finish higher education (HE) and get a job (Savickas, 2013). The COVID-19 pandemic and the recent international conflicts have added even more challenges and distress to the existing uncertainty in the job market (International Labour Organization, 2022).

Career adaptability, a part of the individuals' psychological capital, has been indicated as a key resource for coping with present and anticipated professional tasks and job-related transitions and difficulties, underlying professional success at both corporate and individual levels (Savickas, 2005; Savickas & Porfeli, 2012). Given that the mission of HE is to prepare young people for the labor market and global challenges (Guichard, 2018), career adaptability should be one of the soft skills to be considered for development during university studies.

Another soft skill that is particularly valued in the labor market nowadays is the ability to effectively communicate in foreign languages (LaPrade et al., 2019). In this respect, meaningful communicative competence in FLs in addition to one's mother tongue has become a desideratum at the European Union (EU) level and a requirement in the labor market (Commission of the European Communities, 2003). Across the EU member states and the United Kingdom, over 10% of the vacancies that were posted online in 2021 explicitly demanded language skills (Marconi et al., 2023). FL skills are necessary for various positions in the labor market, but especially for those involving complex cognitive tasks (Marconi et al., 2023). They are considered a driving force for graduate employability, career growth, labor force mobility, and immigration, but also for interpersonal communication and student education and mobility (Badescu et al., 2019; British Academy, 2020; Council of Europe, 2003; EC, 2017; Shepperd, 2021).

At the EU level, FLs are part of the students' curriculum from primary education or even kindergarten to higher education, where they are taught at different proficiency levels, either as mandatory or elective courses (Kortmann, 2019; Maican, 2019). At present, statistics show that 73.3% of young European adults (aged 25–34) have a command of at least one FL, with about 30% of them knowing their best-known FL at a proficient level and another 30% at a good level. Individuals with a tertiary level of education, employed, and with a higher labor market status have a higher language proficiency level (EC, 2019).

Given the above, the authors consider that bringing the two soft skills, i.e., career adaptability and FL skills, into the same research area may reveal new insights into the mutual influences between HE, students' socio-economic environment, and their individual characteristics. It may also contribute to a better understanding of the role these skills have in the undergraduates' future professional lives.

Taking into consideration that career construction is a dynamic process between individuals and the environment, which begins before they enter the labor market, the authors chose to analyze the relationships between career adaptability and a set of psychosocial factors, as antecedents of career adaptability, especially students' FL skills and some important dimensions involved in students' learning at university. Designing teaching and learning and other dedicated pedagogical interventions in HE based on the findings in the present research can optimize students' academic performance and enhance their career adaptability and chances for employability, in the context of socio-economic uncertainty.

## BACKGROUND

### Career Adaptability

Research has revealed the importance of adaptability in today's complex and rapidly changing labor market, which requires the harmonization of individual needs and social expectations (Savickas & Porfeli, 2012). Career adaptability has been found to offer an important competitive advantage, predicting job efficacy, employability, employment status, and career development (Guan et al., 2013; Sidiropoulou-Dimakakou et al., 2018). In addition, adaptability has been acknowledged as a key resource in the recent COVID-19 pandemic for coping with numerous changes and challenges, being associated with more positive reactions, higher levels of self-esteem and mattering, and lower dependency, self-criticism, and distress (Besser et al., 2020).

Career adaptability is a self-regulatory ability, depending on personal and contextual resources, which allows individuals to cope with the predictable and unpredictable tasks and problems encountered at different stages in their career, including job trauma (Savickas & Porfeli, 2012; Tolentino et al., 2014). In Savickas and Porfeli's approach (Savickas & Porfeli, 2012), this ability is part of the human capital developed throughout one's life, depending on the socioeconomic and cultural context, different countries providing different opportunities for individual development. Career adaptability comprises four distinct resources, i.e., concern, control, curiosity, and confidence ("the 4Cs"). These represent strengths or capacities that allow individuals to successfully integrate into one of their life roles, the work role. Concern refers to the individuals' interest in their career development and the awareness of the need to make adjustments in it, control refers to the people's belief that they can influence and shape their career path, curiosity refers to the openness to explore new career options and willingness to learn from different experiences, while confidence refers to the individuals' belief in their capacity to overcome job-related challenges and uncertainties (Chen et al., 2020b; Savickas & Porfeli, 2012).

The career construction theory (Savickas, 2005) states that career adaptabilities influence the individuals' capacity to tackle professional tasks and trigger different adaptive responses regarding planning, decision-making difficulties, exploration, and occupational self-efficacy beliefs, having core self-evaluations and proactivity as antecedents (Hirschi & Valero, 2015). Job satisfaction and work success are examples of adaptive results in one's career, as they indicate a good fit between the person and the environment (DiMaggio et al., 2020). It can be supposed that, in the academic field, adaptive results could include academic achievement as indicated by grades, positive emotions, and the favorable perception of one's competences.

Certain research studies have not identified significant gender differences in career adaptability among college students (Rottinghaus et al., 2005; Rudolph et al., 2017), but others point to a close relationship between general career adaptability on the one hand, and gender and emotional intelligence on the other, showing that these two can predict how students will cope with the challenges of the business world (Cizel, 2018). Other studies have revealed that the female gender positively impacts only certain dimensions of career adaptability, such as concern (Fernandes & Carvalho, 2020). In contrast, another study has highlighted that male students have higher career adaptability than their female peers (Hou et al., 2012).

Career adaptability is associated with higher levels of academic engagement (Merino-Tejedor et al., 2018), motivation (Pouyaud et al., 2012), and academic achievement (Rottinghaus et al., 2005). It is also linked to engagement in adaptive behaviors, lowering the levels of anxiety connected to one's future objectives (Jia et al., 2020; Pouyaud et al., 2012). Moreover, career adaptability produces effects not only at the individual level but also shapes sustainable education (Chen et al., 2020b) and social interactions (Chen et al., 2020a).

## FL Achievement and Self-Perceived FL Proficiency

FL academic achievement represents students' performance in mastering language elements that have been taught, measured against objectives set by the teacher, generally using achievement, attainment, or progress tests (Harmer, 2015; Takahashi, 2009). FL language proficiency is a similar concept, which is defined as the students' general ability to use language skills effectively in different communicative situations. The latter is assessed using comprehensive standardized tests and is generally required by employers and universities (Council of Europe, 2003; Harmer, 2015).

Students' FL achievement is impacted by students' emotions, engagement in learning, and exposure to the target language, but also by external factors, such as the educational setting (Oruç & Demirci, 2020). Research has highlighted gender differences concerning students' achievement, showing that female students generally outperform their male peers academically, this being even more obvious in the case of FLs (Davies, 2004).

Self-perceived FL proficiency refers to one's self-assessed proficiency level (Council of Europe, 2003) or (self-) perceived language ability (Takahashi, 2008). It has a dynamic structure, being built against both internal and external criteria, and is influenced by the students' critical thinking, practice in self-assessment, attitude towards FL learning (Argondizzo et al., 2020; Boekaerts, 1991), academic results (Zhang et al., 2020), personality, age (Cook, 2000), and self-esteem (Rubio-Alcalá, 2017). It is also shaped by evaluations and feedback from teachers and peers throughout the entire teaching-learning-evaluation process, as well as from parents (Takahashi, 2008).

In turn, self-perceived FL proficiency strongly impacts the overall FL learning outcomes and the FL learning process. The students who have a favorable opinion of their foreign language skills are more motivated to learn and show higher confidence and more positive attitudes towards learning (Botes et al., 2020; Takahashi, 2008; Takahashi, 2009). It is interesting to note that the students' willingness to communicate is influenced to a greater extent by their perceived proficiency than by their actual proficiency (Baker & Macintyre, 2002).

To the authors' knowledge, the connection between students' self-perceived FL proficiency and career adaptability has not been studied yet, previous research having revealed only the direct correlation between FL proficiency and positive career prospects (Uber Grosse, 2004).

## Motivation in FL Learning

Research on language learning has revealed that motivation is a major contributor to the acquisition of good language skills, as it provides the impetus to initiate language learning, the background for the actions students take throughout the learning process, the persistence and the effort they put in it (Dörnyei et al., 2006). Motivation theories in FL learning have identified numerous pragmatic benefits that the command of FLs brings to students (Dörnyei, 2005). The Expectancy-Value Theory posits that motivation to engage in specific tasks or activities can be explained by two primary components: task value and expectancy. Task value represents the perceived importance or significance of a task or activity, comprising several subcomponents: intrinsic value, utility value, attainment value, and cost. Expectancy refers to an individual's perception of their capabilities or competence in performing a specific task or achieving a particular goal (Wigfield & Eccles, 2020). FL learners who attribute more intrinsic value to FLs or exhibit intrinsic motivation are inherently interested in the learning process, which brings them satisfaction and joy (Shan, 2020). In contrast, a high level of utility value is indicative of the students' preoccupation with the relevance or usefulness of learning for their short and long-term goals, as they consider FL learning contributes to their success in life (Q. Wang & Xue, 2022).

Students' FL language learning motivation is directly associated with their self-perceived and actual FL proficiency (Takahashi, 2008; Zhang et al., 2020), positive emotions (H. Wang et al., 2023), and negatively associated with FL anxiety (C. Li & Xu, 2019). Academic motivation has been proven to impact educational attainment, school attendance, classroom behavior (Vecchione et al., 2014), career decidedness, and choices (Eccles & Wigfield, 2002; Koyuncuoğlu, 2021).

## Learning Behaviors

Positive learning behavior or behavioral engagement refers to the students' classroom conduct, participation in school-related activities and compliance with the tasks assigned to them (Kang &Wu, 2022). Positive behaviors with respect to language learning refer to in-class actions that facilitate the improvement or development of grammar, vocabulary, and language skills. They include practicing the language during the classes, doing the homework, checking work against instructions, or using a strategy before starting the work (Borg, 2014; Boyle et al., 2001).

Misbehaviors, considered a challenge in the teaching profession, involve students' passive and disruptive behaviors during classes. The former are regarded as inappropriate in the classroom setting (for example, lack of and concentration, inattentiveness, task avoidance, late assignments), but they are seen by students as non-problematic (Debreli & Ishanova, 2019; Sun & Shek, 2012). Low motivation is sometimes considered the main source of students' passive engagement. Disruptive behaviors, on the other hand, impinge on the overall teaching and learning process. Examples include mobile phone use, inappropriate turn-taking, resisting authority, practicing plagiarism in homework and research (Debreli & Ishanova, 2019; Üstünlüoğlu, 2013). Girls tend to report more positive behaviors than boys (Wagner & Ruch, 2015), while misbehaviors have generally been connected to boys (Erdem & Koçyiğit, 2019; Zhang et al., 2020). However, there are studies in which gender difference in this respect tends to level off (Borg, 2014; Maican & Cocoradă, 2023).

Positive behaviors have been shown to influence students' academic achievement, positive emotions in the FL class, and the development of professional skills (Borg, 2014; Kang & Wu, 2022), while misbehaviors are conducive to academic underachievement, poor development of professional skills, and indiscipline (Bhatnagar, 2021).

## Emotional Factors

After emotions have been ignored or avoided for many years (Boekaerts, 1991; Dewaele & Li, 2020), they are now considered inseparable from the learning process, as they can enhance learning or impinge on it, influencing both students' individual learning process and the dynamic of the learning environment (Osika et al., 2022).

The positive emotions acknowledged to have a fundamental role in language learning include curiosity, enjoyment, excitement, and optimism. They enhance students' resources and focus, trigger a positive behavioral intention, make the learning experience desirable and the coping with failure effective (Boekaerts, 1991; Dewaele & Li, 2020; Osika et al., 2022). On the other hand, negative emotions, such as shame, anxiety, fear, and nervousness diminish students' attention and the efficacy of coping mechanisms, being related to underachievement (Dewaele & Li, 2020; Pekrun & Stephens, 2012).

FL enjoyment (FLE), the most researched positive emotion in the field of language learning, involves an interplay of pleasure, increased attention, goals met, and a constructive attitude towards the language learning process, peers, and the teacher (Botes et al., 2020; Dewaele & Li, 2020; Dewaele & MacIntyre, 2014), amplified learning motivation, proficiency, and achievement concerning FLs (Jin & Zhang, 2018). It is strongly connected to the learning context and is enhanced by multilingualism and a favorable perception of one's FL proficiency (Botes et al., 2020). But FLE also triggers higher self-perceived FL proficiency (Dewaele & MacIntyre, 2019), their influence on each other being mutual.

Conversely, FL anxiety (FLA) has a debilitating effect in the FL class. It is more prominent for speaking and listening, and in cultures scoring higher for uncertainty avoidance and restraint (Botes et al., 2020; Hofstede et al., 2010; X. Wang & Zhang, 2021). FLA may originate in the students' beliefs related to language learning, inappropriate teaching methods, and fear of negative evaluation, but it is also influenced by students' gender (Botes et al., 2020; X. Wang & Zhang, 2021). Female students seem to score significantly higher in FLA than male students (Maican & Cocoradă, 2021), but the findings in this respect are not always consistent (Dewaele & MacIntyre, 2019). FLA is also strongly predicted by neuroticism, by students' actual and self-perceived FL proficiency, the difference between upper levels of self-rated proficiency and lower levels being particularly significant (Botes et. al., 2020; Dewaele, 2021; Dewaele & MacIntyre, 2019; Takahashi, 2008). In turn, FLA has a negative predictive value for academic achievement (Cocoradă & Maican, 2013), self-perceived FL proficiency, and motivation (Horwitz et al., 1986; Oruç & Demirci, 2020). Nevertheless, some studies have mentioned a possible facilitating role of FLA in the FL learning process (Dewaele & MacIntyre, 2014; Takahashi, 2009; Turner & Waugh, 2007); being an ambivalent emotion, FLA can be used by certain students to improve their academic results (Pekrun et al., 2007).

## Personality Traits

Personality traits are relatively stable characteristics of individuals, the coherence of behaviors being given by the interaction of the attributes with the situations people are in. One of the most widely used models for analyzing personality traits is the Five-Factor Model (Big Five), which considers personality from five major dimensions: Openness, Conscientiousness, Extraversion/ Introversion, Agreeableness, and Emotional stability/ Neuroticism, which allow the prediction of behaviors (McCrae & Sutin, 2018).

The vast body of literature on the relationship between personality traits and school performance has revealed that conscientiousness is the most important predictor of academic achievement, followed by openness to experience (Hakimi et al., 2011; O'Connor & Paunonen, 2007; Poropat, 2014). Research has also shown weaker positive associations with agreeableness, and most often negative associations with neuroticism and extraversion, but there is not full consensus in this respect, as findings seem to be influenced by the level of education and self-rated measures (Hakimi et al., 2011; John et al., 2020; Poropat, 2014).

Other factors which undergo a significant influence from personality traits are learning behavior and motivation. Thus, agreeable students are more willing to comply with the tasks set and score higher for extrinsic motivation, conscientious students exhibit behaviors that support the learning process and persist when difficulties arise, extroverts contribute spontaneously and actively to class activities, less emotionally-stable students have lower motivation and are more easily distracted from learning tasks, just like the less conscientious ones (Fuertes et al., 2020; Dewaele, 2021; Poropat, 2016).

Some personality traits also have a predicting value for students' emotions during the teaching-learning-evaluation process, including FL classes. As already stated, FLA is strongly predicted by lower emotional stability (neuroticism) and, to a smaller extent, by introversion (Dewaele, 2021; Dewaele & MacIntyre, 2019), while personality factors influence FLE to a smaller extent.

As far as individuals' professional life is concerned, personality traits can predict occupational attainment, career satisfaction, self-rated performance, as well as other important life outcomes directly, or through complex mechanisms (McCrae & Sutin, 2018; Roberts et al., 2007; Zacher, 2014). Certain personality traits directly correlate with career adaptability; thus, there is a positive association with openness, extraversion, agreeableness, and conscientiousness, and a negative one with neuroticism. Openness to experience, agreeableness, conscientiousness, and emotional stability have also been found to be significant predictors of overall career adaptability (Y. Li et al., 2015; Martin et al., 2013; Zacher, 2014), while the dimensions of career adaptability (4Cs) are influenced by all personality traits (Dursun & Argan, 2017). Other research has revealed that the direct effect is visible only in the case of extraversion, the effects of the other personality traits over career adaptability being explained through mediators, such as proactive personality, core self-evaluation, or learning goal orientation (Guan et al., 2017).

To sum up, the literature review highlights the importance of career adaptability for today's labor market, analyzing the relationships between adaptability and students' academic engagement, motivation, outcomes, personality traits, and their variance by gender. The authors could not identify any previous research on the relationships between career adaptability and FL skills, which are required for effective communication in the world of work, or various aspects directly related to FL learning, such as FL proficiency, self-perceived FL proficiency, learning behaviors, and emotions (FL enjoyment and FL anxiety). Similarly, the data about students' job experience and career adaptability are scarce. That is why the data extracted from the literature in the field to introduce these constructs are only convergent with the objective of the present chapter.

The authors aim to bridge the existing gap in the literature by guiding the research using the following questions:

**Q1**. What are the differences concerning career adaptability, personality traits, and some important dimensions related to the development of FL skills at university between male and female students, and between employed and unemployed students, respectively?

**Q2.** What are the relevant factors that can predict students' career adaptability in the aforementioned context?

## METHODS AND MATERIALS

### Research Context

The study was conducted in a Romanian public comprehensive university with almost 20,000 students, which offers study programs in over 40 domains. Romania is a former communist country located in the south-eastern part of Central Europe, which underwent a strong ideological influence from the Soviet Union for more than forty years. Starting with the 1990s, Romania has undergone tremendous economic and political changes aimed at achieving sustainable economic growth and meeting the criteria for accession to the EU (The Adecco Group, 2022). In 2022, the GDP per capita in Romania was €10,080, while the average gross monthly salary in September 2023 was a little over €1,400 (EC, 2023c; National Institute of Statistics, 2023). The overall employability rate in Romania in 2022 was almost 70%, close to the European average (74.6%), but the employment rate of recent graduates (69.9%) is much below the European average (82.4%) (Trading Economics, 2023). Migration has been extensive over the last twenty years, being considered a survival strategy due to the low wages, low income, and lack of employment opportunities (EC, 2023d; Iacob, 2018; Pripoaie et al., 2022). It is considered that 75% of the decline in population in Romania from 22.4 million in 2000 to 19.5 million in 2018 is due to outward migration, the high flow towards other countries concerning especially young people. About 25% of Romanian migrants are highly educated, while 30% of them have a low level of education (OECD, 2019).

After 1990, things radically changed from the perspective of FL learning, as a wide range of FLs became available in the school curriculum at all educational levels, with English, French, German, and Spanish prevailing. Knowledge of these international languages had been considered a form of resistance through culture under communism and the languages themselves had long been associated by the oppressed people with Western economies and a high standard of living. Consequently, they immediately started to gain ground, as people became more and more aware of the benefits that can be reaped through their command, such as opportunities for better employment on the domestic market, employment opportunities abroad, promotion prospects, or business opportunities overseas.

The interest in FL learning has become even more overt since 2007, when Romania joined the EU and started to implement its policies, including FL ones. Thus, at present, Romania comes third in Europe with respect to the number of students studying two or more languages in upper secondary education (EC, 2023e). At the HE level in Romania, FLs continue to be taught in compliance with European policies, being a compulsory part of the curriculum. The main aim of the FL courses for non-language study programs is two-fold: to endow students with the FL competences necessary for their academic life and to prepare students for the world of work (Ambrósio et al., 2014; Lauridsen, 2013; Tudor, 2009). Mastering an FL can be considered a survival strategy, ensuring adaptation when leaving the country or working for an international company.

The decision on the languages taught, their place in the university curriculum and the level are made based on the university's mission, vision and human resources, the students' FL repertoire, and economic realities (Lauridsen, 2013). It should be added that, in Romania, students are allowed to work full-time or part-time, but universities have a mandatory attendance policy for all classes involving practical activities (laboratory works, projects, internships) (Transilvania University of Brasov, 2023).

Considering the above context, the teaching of FLs in the university under consideration aims to develop students' linguistic, discourse, and intercultural competences, which entails a focus on a combination of grammar structures, receptive and productive skills, general vocabulary (language for general purposes), and specialized vocabulary in the occupational fields the students prepare for (e.g., English for Science and Technology, French for Medical Purposes etc.) (Dudley-Evans & St. John, 1998; Frendo, 2005; Maican, 2019).

## Hypotheses

Considering the research questions (shown in brackets), the following hypotheses were formulated:

**Hypothesis One**: Career adaptability and its dimensions (concern, control, curiosity, and confidence) are (a) positively associated with FL Enjoyment, FL learning motivation, the perceived role of FLs for employability (employment prospects, access to famous companies, and a big salary), the perceived importance of specific FL skills for professional tasks, positive behaviors during FL classes, the FL grade, and self-perceived FL proficiency, and (b) negatively associated with FL Anxiety and misbehaviors during FL classes (Q2).

**Hypothesis Two**: There are statistically significant differences regarding the variables explored between the means of the groups created by (a) students' gender and (b) students' status as employed/ unemployed (Q1).

**Hypothesis Three**: Career adaptability is predicted (a) directly by gender and the students' status as employed/ unemployed, positive behaviors during FL classes, personality traits, FL learning motivation, the FL grade, and the self-perceived FL proficiency, and (b) negatively by FL Anxiety and misbehaviors during FL classes (Q2).

**Hypothesis Four**: Academic achievement, expressed by (a) FL grades and (b) self-perceived FL proficiency, is predicted by career adaptability (Q2).

## Participants

The participants are 328 Bachelor's degree students, out of whom 65.5% are female. The participant's mean age is 21.4 (SD = 4.7), the students in the 19-30 age range prevailing (94%). In the entire sample, 22% of the students are simultaneously enrolled in full-time educational programs and employed, either full-time or part-time. The ratio of employed male students is significantly higher (29.2%) than that of female students (18.1%) ($\chi2 = 5.29$, $p = 0.02$). The mean of the self-reported FL grade is 8.97 (SD = 1.27, 5 being the minimum passing grade and 10 the highest grade), while the self-perceived FL proficiency for writing, listening, reading, spoken production, and spoken interaction has a means of 17.8 points (SD = 6.8, min = 5, max = 30). The multilingual competence is reported by most of the respondents (91.7%). The ratio of multilingual girls (68.9%) is significantly higher than that of multilingual boys (31.1%) ($\chi2 = 16.93$, $p < 0.001$).

## Procedure

The data were collected at the end of the second semester of the academic year 2019–2020, as well as during the first semester of the subsequent academic year (2021). Participation in the study was entirely voluntary, with no compensation. The research received approval from the Research Ethics Committee of the University. The present chapter uses data from a larger research study and some of the findings of this research have already been presented in scientific works (Maican & Cocoradă, 2021; Maican & Cocoradă, 2023).

In the recruitment process, the institutional e-mail addresses of the participants were used. The authors sent an email to all undergraduate students, in which they provided the link to an internal secured website of the university, which hosted the survey tools. The first procedural step for the participants was to thoroughly read the informed consent. After giving their consent, the students provided the required socio-demographic information and then proceeded to complete research questionnaires anonymously.

The data set underwent analysis using the IBM SPSS version 26. The statistical analysis encompassed the calculation of means and standard deviations, comparisons of means, Pearson correlation coefficients, and the application of hierarchical regression equations.

## Research Tools

The following instruments were used, translated into Romanian:

- *The Career Adapt-Abilities and Cooperation Scale – Short Form (CAAS-SF)* (12 items), designed by Maggiori, Rossier and Savickas (2015). It measures psychosocial resources that individuals need to cope with professional transitions, tasks, and problems (Savickas & Porfeli, 2012). It has four sub-scales, each one with three items: F1-Concern (Cronbach's Alpha = 0.88), F2-Control (Cronbach's Alpha = 0.85), F3-Curiosity (Cronbach's Alpha = 0.80), and F4-Confidence (Cronbach' Alpha = 0.87). It was used with the authors' consent, in translated form. The internal consistency for the General Adaptability (12 items) is 0.93, so a very good one. The tool has a 5-point Likert scale, from 1- not strong to 5- strongest. Examples of items: *"Thinking about what my future will be like"*, *"Making decisions by myself"*, *"Becoming curious about new opportunities"*, *"Looking for opportunities to grow as a person"*.
- *The Foreign Language Enjoyment Questionnaire* (29 items), designed by Dewaele and MacIntyre (2014). It was used with the authors' consent, in translated form. The tool has a 5-point Likert scale, from 1- absolutely disagree to 5- strongly agree. Both subscales of the tool were used: (a) Foreign Language Classroom Anxiety, which measures foreign language anxiety (Cronbach's Alpha = 0.66), based on eight items extracted from the Scale - FLCAS (Horwitz et al., 1986), and (b) Foreign Language Enjoyment-Total (21 items, Cronbach' Alpha = 0.84). The latter measures the enjoyment towards FL learning, the favorable atmosphere in the FL class, the positive presence of the teacher and peers, their encouragement, and personal reactions to FL learning. Examples of items: (a) *"Even if I am well prepared for FL class, I feel anxious about it"*, *"It embarrasses me to volunteer answers in my FL class"*; (b) *"I can laugh off embarrassing mistakes in the FL"*, *"It's a positive environment"*.
- *The IPIP-50 Inventory* (55 items), designed by (Goldberg et al., 2006), and adapted to Romanian participants (Rusu et al., 2012). The tool has a 5-point Likert scale, from 1- very inaccurate to

5- very accurate. The instrument measures the five dimensions of personality: Emotional stability (lower scores of emotional stability show Neuroticism, as opposed to Stability), Extraversion (lower scores show Introversion, as opposed to Extraversion), Openness, Agreeableness, and Conscientiousness. Examples of items: *"Am the life of the party"*, *"Get stressed out easily"*, *"Worry about things"*, *"Am quick to understand things"*.

- *Students' Self-Perceived FL Proficiency Scale* is an adapted form of the *Self-assessment grid* in the Common European Framework of Reference for Languages (2003), designed to aid language learners in evaluating their own language proficiency. Similarly, the tool elaborated for the current study comprises six different descriptors for each of the five major categories of language use (Listening, Reading, Spoken interaction, Spoken production, and Writing). Six language proficiency levels result: Basic user (A1 and A2 levels), Independent user (B1 and B2 levels), and Proficient user (C1 and C2 levels). Its Cronbach's Alpha coefficient is very good (0.95). Examples of items: *"I can understand familiar words and very simple sentences about myself and concrete surroundings when people speak slowly and clearly"*, *"I can understand familiar words and very simple sentences (for example on notices and or in catalogues)"*, *"I can write a short and simple postcard"*, *"I can fill in forms with personal details"*.

The other instruments were elaborated by two of the authors for the present study:

- *The Foreign Language Learning Motivation Scale/ Self-Perceived Task Value* (19 items), inspired by Eccles (2005) and considered as an aggregated scale. It refers to the intrinsic task value and the utility value. The tool uses a 5-point Likert scale, from 1- unimportant to 5- very important, and its Cronbach's Alpha is 0.81. Examples of items: *"I can improve the range of specialized vocabulary"*, *"I can improve grammar structures"*, *"I can get a job in an international company"*, *"I can get a higher salary"*.
- *FL Skills for Professional Tasks* (FLS-PT) (8 items) measures students' perception of the importance of FL skills in accomplishing tasks at the workplace. The tool uses a 5-point Likert scale, from 1- unimportant to 5- very important. Its Cronbach's Alpha coefficient is 0.93. Examples of items: *"Rank the importance of the reading skills for your future professional tasks"*, *"Rank the importance of spoken interaction skills for your future professional tasks"*, *"Rank the importance of specialized vocabulary in the field for your future professional tasks"*.
- *FLs for Employability* (FLECS) (3 items) measures the importance students attach to the command of FLs for employment prospects, access to famous companies, and a big salary. The tool uses a 5-point Likert scale, from 1- unimportant to 5- very important. Its Cronbach's Alpha coefficient is 0.93. Examples of items: *"Rank the importance of FL skills for finding a job easily"*, *"Rank the importance of FL skills for finding a job in a famous company"*, *"Rank the importance of FL skills for earning a big salary"*.
- *Positive Behaviors in FL Learning* (4 items) concerns students' activities in the FL class which help them learn the FL. Its Cronbach's Alpha is 0.80. Examples of items: *"Mark the answers that are true for you: I have initiatives/ I carry out additional activities to develop my skills"*.
- *Misbehaviors in FL Learning* (4 items) refers to the students' passive engagement or disengagement in class activities, which hinders the learning of the FL. Its Cronbach's Alpha is 0.47. Examples of items: *"Mark the answers that are true for you: I prefer to do things unrelated to the foreign language class/ I skip classes"*.

- A questionnaire comprising demographic questions on gender, year of study, grade obtained for the FL for the previous semester of the corresponding academic year, and students' status as employed/ unemployed.

## RESULTS AND DISCUSSION

The authors analyzed the relationships between career adaptability (4Cs and overall adaptability) and a set of psychosocial factors, such as in-class behaviors, motivation, emotions, self-perceived and actual FL proficiency, and personality traits. The data were compared by students' gender and by their position as employed or not; the former criterion has been frequently used in previous research, while the latter has been introduced by the authors of this chapter.

The results will be presented and discussed in order of the hypotheses. It is worth noting that in the first two hypotheses, career adaptability, as the main concept, was treated both as a composite score (sum of the four dimensions), and separately, on the four dimensions (concern, control, curiosity, and confidence). In the last two hypotheses, career adaptability was considered only as a composite score, to avoid multicollinearity.

### Descriptive Statistics

The participants score higher for the dimensions career curiosity, career confidence, and positive behaviors during classes. They are very demanding when it comes to their FL skills, as they score 17.8 out of max. 30 for their self-rated FL proficiency, while the average grade received is 8.9 out of max. 10 (Table 1).

The first hypothesis is partially confirmed, the direction of the associations being the one supposed in H1a. However, the second part of the hypothesis was not validated, since career adaptability positively correlates with the variable FL Anxiety. The negative correlation with misbehaviors is present, but it is very small and not significant (Table 1).

The direct association between adaptability and FL anxiety is unexpected. More specifically, in the sample researched, students with higher anxiety towards FL learning are more sensitive and more strained regarding the development of their careers. The present finding is in contrast with a meta-analysis (Rudolf et al., 2017) and with other previous studies which have found an indirect association of negative affect, including anxiety, with adaptability (Jia et al., 2020; Shin & Lee, 2019). In line with other studies (Dewaele & MacIntyre, 2014; Takahashi, 2009; Turner & Waugh, 2007), the present findings prove that FLA is an ambivalent emotion with complex effects, which certain students may use to enhance adaptability and learning, provided its motivational energy is implied.

It can also be supposed that today's unstable and unpredictable labor market (Fusco et al., 2020) and the need for language competences can lead to an increase in students' general anxiety and anxiety towards the FL, which is often involved in the staff selection requirements for employment (Marconi et al., 2023). The labor market seems to be even more unpredictable and demanding with respect to FLs in the case of Romania, due to the high migration rate and particularly to the brain drain phenomenon (Iacob, 2018; Pripoaie et al., 2022). The authors suppose that the adaptation process required in this situation is even more challenging and may generate anxiety, as Romania is a country with high uncertainty avoidance, favoring structure and predictability, and showing low tolerance for uncertainty and ambiguity (Hofstede et al., 2010).

Table 1. Means, standard deviations, and Pearson's correlations between the variables explored

| | 1 | 2 | 3 | 4 | 5 | 6 | 7 | 8 | 9 | 10 | 11 | 12 | 13 | 14 | 15 |
|---|---|---|---|---|---|---|---|---|---|---|---|---|---|---|---|
| 1. Career concern | 1 | | | | | | | | | | | | | | |
| 2. Career control | .56** | 1 | | | | | | | | | | | | | |
| 3. Career curiosity | .54** | .74** | 1 | | | | | | | | | | | | |
| 4. Career confidence | .55** | .64** | .85** | 1 | | | | | | | | | | | |
| 5. Overall career adaptability | .80** | .86** | .90** | .87** | 1 | | | | | | | | | | |
| 6. FL Enjoyment | .18** | -.02 | .04 | .04 | .08 | 1 | | | | | | | | | |
| 7. FL Anxiety | .17** | .18** | .30** | .28** | .27** | -.02 | 1 | | | | | | | | |
| 8. FL skills for employability | .10 | .06 | .10 | .16** | .12* | .37** | -.02 | 1 | | | | | | | |
| 9. FL skills for professional tasks | .11* | .12* | .12* | .12* | .17* | .22** | -.01 | .58** | 1 | | | | | | |
| 10. FL learning motivation | .15** | .07 | .12* | .13* | .14* | .407** | .03 | .64** | .89** | 1 | | | | | |
| 11. Positive behaviors | .21** | .04 | .13* | .13* | .15** | .68** | .02 | .34** | .23** | .40** | 1 | | | | |
| 12. Misbehaviors | -.10 | -.05 | -.08 | -.07 | -.09 | -.40** | .28** | -.25** | -.17** | -.24** | -.29** | 1 | | | |
| 13. FL grades | .05 | -.06 | -.02 | .01 | -.01 | .46** | -.25** | .24** | .13* | .19** | .39** | -.37** | 1 | | |
| 14. Self-perceived FL proficiency | .11* | .08 | .06 | .06 | .09 | .23** | -.37** | .40** | .26** | .23** | .21** | -.32** | .37** | 1 | |
| 15. Age | .09 | .02 | -.04 | -.07 | .01 | .14* | .05 | .01 | .08 | .03 | .12* | .03 | .04 | .05 | 1 |
| Mean | 11.6 | 12.8 | 13.2 | 13.3 | 50.9 | 33.2 | 25.9 | 34.5 | 12.8 | 56.8 | 9.8 | 8.3 | 8.9 | 17.8 | 21.4 |
| SD | 3.5 | 3.1 | 2.7 | 2.7 | 10.2 | 10.2 | 4.3 | 6.9 | 3.0 | 11.6 | 3.1 | 2.4 | 1.3 | 6.9 | 4.7 |

Note: *p < 0.05, ** p < 0.01

The positive relationship between FL anxiety and low grades, and FL anxiety and the unfavorable perception of FL proficiency is confirmed. However, the current results did not support the finding that students with higher academic achievements have better self-reported foreign language proficiency (Zhang et al., 2020). When the language competences are perceived as lower than those anticipated as necessary, students can experience negative emotions, as emphasized in other studies (Pekrun et al., 2007; Wigfield & Eccles, 2020).

It is also likely that the economic and socio-political context of the recent past has favored FL learning in Romania and has made the benefits of language proficiency even more overt. Thus, students acknowledge the importance of language skills for employment prospects, a better salary, or openings for working in a famous company, considering the linguistic and communication competence relevant to their future careers. As these variables directly correlate with career adaptability, it follows that raising awareness about the opportunities offered by multilingual competence and enhancing students' motivation entail better chances for them to develop the resources they need to cope with present or future job-related difficulties (Savickas & Porfeli, 2012).

## Gender Differences

In the sample investigated, female students report higher concern with the preparation for future job-related tasks, more confidence in their ability to solve problems connected to their future job, exploring career opportunities more forcefully, being more curious, and perceiving a greater control over their careers compared to male peers (Table 2). The present findings are different from those suggested in previous studies, some of which support the absence of gender differences regarding career adaptability (Rottinghaus et al., 2005), or higher adaptability in the case of male students compared to female students, on all dimensions of CAAS, except for Concern (Hou et al., 2012).

In the current study, gender differences are not significant concerning students' school performance in the FL, so the results do not support the findings that female students have high academic achievement in FLs (Davies, 2004). Although the findings in the present research show that female students are significantly more motivated in the FL class and attach greater importance to FLs for employability and careers than boys, the grade-related difference is not statistically significant. An explanation of the findings could reside in the male students' higher self-esteem (Rubio-Alcalá, 2017) or the great variations existing with respect to girls' and boys' academic achievement depending on the country, subject, or skill assessed (Eriksson et al., 2020). Another variable for which the findings contradict the general opinion (Erdem & Koçyiğit, 2019; Zhang et al., 2020) is misbehaviors, as male students in the sample investigated do not display more misbehaviors when compared to female students. For male students, the importance of FLs in finding a job and in having a higher labor market status is likely to trigger better command of the FL and fewer unfavorable behaviors.

## Differences by Students' Status as Employed or Unemployed

The differences in the means by students' status as employed or unemployed, although few and a little significant, do show that the students who were employed at the moment when the research was conducted (so students possessing both learning experience and work experience) tend to be less confident in the future, but more concerned with their career, being probably more responsible compared to their peers who only have academic experience (Table 3). The current result regarding unemployed students' higher confidence in the future is consistent with the difference between college students and their non-college peers obtained in a previous study on emerging adults (Reifman et al., 2007), as the former exceeded the latter in the sense of life possibilities.

The only variables which have significantly different means are personality traits, except for agreeableness. Employed students report being more conscientious, more emotionally stable, more extrovert, and more open to new experience and knowledge compared with the other group, the effect size reaching the highest values concerning the variables compared (between 0.39 and 0.56). Based on the authors' information, studies with such participants have not been performed so far, so no point of reference is available.

## Predicting Career Adaptability

To check the third hypothesis, a hierarchical regression was calculated, with three blocks:

1. Socio-demographic characteristics;

*Table 2. Differences in means by students' gender (H2a)*

| Variables | Gender | Mean | SD | t | p | d Cohen |
|---|---|---|---|---|---|---|
| Career concern | F | 11.86 | 3.49 | 1.743 | .08 | 0.21 |
| | M | 11.15 | 3.47 | | | |
| Career control | F | 13.16 | 2.76 | 2.753 | .006 | 0.30 |
| | M | 12.18 | 3.62 | | | |
| Career curiosity | F | 13.55 | 2.31 | 3.662 | .001 | 0.40 |
| | M | 12.42 | 3.26 | | | |
| Career confidence | F | 13.67 | 2.29 | 3.334 | .001 | 0.41 |
| | M | 12.55 | 3.17 | | | |
| Overall career adaptability | F | 52.24 | 8.85 | 3.067 | .002 | 0.37 |
| | M | 48.29 | 12.09 | | | |
| FL skills for employability | F | 13.13 | 2.86 | 2.742 | .006 | 0.27 |
| | M | 12.17 | 3.26 | | | |
| FL skills for professional tasks | F | 35.26 | 6.56 | 2.878 | .004 | 0.33 |
| | M | 32.96 | 7.48 | | | |
| Positive behaviors | F | 10.07 | 3.15 | 1.82 | .07 | 0.22 |
| | M | 9.43 | 2.82 | | | |
| Misbehaviors | F | 8.39 | 2.46 | 0.498 | .619 | 0.05 |
| | M | 8.26 | 2.27 | | | |
| Emotional stability | F | 26.90 | 8.00 | 4.796 | .001 | 0.57 |
| | M | 30.85 | 6.93 | | | |
| Extraversion | F | 30.71 | 8.36 | 1.985 | .049 | 0.23 |
| | M | 28.81 | 7.91 | | | |
| Openness | F | 35.62 | 5.38 | 1.586 | .114 | 0.19 |
| | M | 34.67 | 4.70 | | | |
| Agreeableness | F | 39.37 | 5.24 | 7.236 | .001 | 0.84 |
| | M | 34.92 | 5.38 | | | |
| Conscientiousness | F | 36.74 | 6.14 | 1.697 | .09 | 0.20 |
| | M | 35.56 | 5.78 | | | |
| FL Enjoyment | F | 33.33 | 10.63 | .396 | .692 | 0.05 |
| | M | 32.88 | 9.27 | | | |
| FL Anxiety | F | 26.85 | 4.36 | 5.77 | .001 | 0.65 |
| | M | 24.27 | 3.54 | | | |
| FL learning motivation | F | 58.64 | 10.97 | 4.018 | .001 | 0.46 |
| | M | 53.34 | 12.07 | | | |
| FL grades | F | 8.94 | 1.3 | -.681 | .50 | 1.18 |
| | M | 9.04 | 1.2 | | | |
| Self-perceived FL proficiency | F | 17.20 | 6.92 | -2.221 | .027 | 0.26 |
| | M | 18.96 | 6.56 | | | |

Note: F -215. M-113; Some of the data in this table can be found in Maican & Cocoradă (2023), but in other patterns of variables.

*Table 3. Differences in means by students' status as employed/unemployed (H2b)*

|  | Are You Employed? | Mean | SD | t | p | d Cohen |
|---|---|---|---|---|---|---|
| Career concern | No | 11.42 | 3.48 | 1.912 | .057 | 0.26 |
|  | Yes | 12.31 | 3.49 |  |  |  |
| Career control | No | 12.81 | 2.91 | -.138 | .89 | 0.02 |
|  | Yes | 12.88 | 3.78 |  |  |  |
| Career curiosity | No | 13.32 | 2.34 | 1.592 | .12 | 0.24 |
|  | Yes | 12.58 | 3.75 |  |  |  |
| Career confidence | No | 13.46 | 2.29 | 1.775 | .08 | 0.26 |
|  | Yes | 12.65 | 3.67 |  |  |  |
| Overall career adaptability | No | 51.01 | 9.01 | .345 | .73 | 0.05 |
|  | Yes | 50.42 | 13.82 |  |  |  |
| Positive behaviors | No | 9.81 | 3.00 | -.435 | .66 | 0.06 |
|  | Yes | 9.99 | 3.25 |  |  |  |
| Misbehaviors | No | 8.38 | 2.46 | .391 | .69 | 0.06 |
|  | Yes | 8.25 | 2.16 |  |  |  |
| FL skills for employability | No | 12.82 | 3.03 | .276 | .78 | 0.04 |
|  | Yes | 12.71 | 3.06 |  |  |  |
| FL skills for professional tasks | No | 34.54 | 6.81 | .336 | .74 | 0.04 |
|  | Yes | 34.22 | 7.56 |  |  |  |
| Emotional stability | No | 27.34 | 7.83 | -3.148 | .002 | 0.42 |
|  | Yes | 30.61 | 7.68 |  |  |  |
| Extraversion | No | 29.38 | 8.27 | -2.847 | .005 | 0.39 |
|  | Yes | 32.47 | 7.73 |  |  |  |
| Openness | No | 34.84 | 5.14 | -3.075 | .002 | 0.41 |
|  | Yes | 36.93 | 4.99 |  |  |  |
| Agreeableness | No | 37.66 | 5.71 | -1.028 | .31 | 0.14 |
|  | Yes | 38.44 | 5.61 |  |  |  |
| Conscientiousness | No | 35.62 | 5.91 | -4.165 | .001 | 0.56 |
|  | Yes | 38.89 | 5.82 |  |  |  |
| FL Enjoyment | No | 32.73 | 10.19 | -1.495 | .14 | 0.20 |
|  | Yes | 34.75 | 9.99 |  |  |  |
| FL Anxiety | No | 26.16 | 4.30 | 1.545 | .12 | 0.21 |
|  | Yes | 25.28 | 4.12 |  |  |  |
| FL learning motivation | No | 56.80 | 11.77 | -.039 | .97 | 0.005 |
|  | Yes | 56.86 | 11.19 |  |  |  |
| FL grades | No | 8.95 | 1.26 | -.688 | .49 | 0.09 |
|  | Yes | 9.07 | 1.35 |  |  |  |
| Self-perceived FL proficiency | No | 17.58 | 6.72 | -1.132 | .26 | 0.15 |
|  | Yes | 18.61 | 7.27 |  |  |  |

Note: Employed = 72. Unemployed = 256

2. FL grade, and self-perceived FL proficiency;
3. Behaviors during FL classes, personality traits, FL Enjoyment, and FL Anxiety.

The hypothesis is partially confirmed. The significant predictors for overall Career adaptability are FL Anxiety, Conscientiousness, Openness, and Self-perceived FL proficiency (Table 4). All three models are statistically significant, the highest R Square being obtained for the third model (R = 0.48, R2 = 0.23, F = 19.058, p < 0.001). The students' status as employed/ unemployed, the FL motivation, the FL grade, and the behaviors during FL classes do not significantly predict career adaptability. Tolerance and VIF values are in the reference range, being lower than 1, and lower than 5, respectively.

The students who are FL anxious, show openness and conscientiousness and perceive their FL skills favorably have higher career adaptability. The involvement of conscientiousness and openness in predicting adaptability has also been mentioned in some previous research (Storme et al., 2020; Zacher, 2014). It can be supposed that, in the context of an unpredictable labor market and the ensuing necessary adjustments, the interactions between individuals and their environment can produce high worry and uncertainty. The increasing role of FLs in staff selection, determined by the growing global mobility in international companies may lead to an increase in the importance attached to FLs for employability and professional success and, implicitly, to an increase in the responsibility feeling and FL anxiety in the case of students concerned with career adaptability and the successful interaction with the work environment. The relationship can also be due to the research procedure, as a convenience sample.

The present findings are convergent with those in other studies which show that FL skills also have a significant influence on broader outcomes, such as sociocultural and academic adaptation or social satisfaction, especially in international settings (Wilczewski & Alon, 2022). It can be supposed that female students, as they are likely to have a high emotional intelligence level, show higher adaptability to career challenges, whereas male students have low career adaptability because they have lower emotional intelligence (Cizel, 2018).

## Predicting Academic Achievement

To check the fourth hypothesis, a symmetrical hierarchical regression was calculated, with three blocks:

1. Socio-demographic characteristics;

*Table 4. Overall career adaptability as a dependent variable (H3)*

| Model | | Coefficients | | t | p | Correlations | | |
|---|---|---|---|---|---|---|---|---|
| | | B | Beta | | | Zero-Order | Partial | Part |
| 3 | (Constant) | 5.51 | | .924 | .356 | | | |
| | Gender* (1-F, 2-M) | -1.73 | -.080 | -1.561 | .120 | -.18 | -.09 | -.08 |
| | Self-perceived FL proficiency | .22 | .145 | 2.653 | .008 | .09 | .15 | .13 |
| | FL Anxiety | .71 | .296 | 5.428 | .000 | .27 | .29 | .27 |
| | Conscientiousness | .41 | .244 | 4.601 | .000 | .33 | .25 | .23 |
| | Openness | .29 | .148 | 2.720 | .007 | .28 | .15 | .13 |

Note: *t is significant in Models 1 and 2.

2. Adaptability;
3. Behaviors during FL classes, personality traits, FL Enjoyment, FL Anxiety, and FL learning motivation.

The hypothesis is partially confirmed. The significant direct predictors of Self-perceived FL proficiency are FL learning motivation, Openness, Adaptability, and FL Enjoyment and gender to a lesser extent. FL Anxiety has a negative influence. All three models are statistically significant, the highest R Square being obtained for the third model ($R = 0.51$, $R2 = 0.26$, $F = 19.73$, $p < 0.001$). More specifically, students self-rate their FL competences higher when they show stronger career adaptability, are more motivated, less anxious concerning FL learning, score higher for openness, and tend to have higher enjoyment during their formal training in FLs (Table 5). The FL grade is not significantly predicted by overall career adaptability, which is in accordance with other studies (Alahdadi & Ghanizadeh, 2017). At the same time, there is little evidence for the positive influence of FL Enjoyment and gender (marginal significance) on self-perceived FL proficiency, but FL Anxiety has the strongest influence in the set of predictors for the dependent variable.

It is worth noting that, in the case of FLA, more data values are located near the mean and fewer data values are located on the tails, so probably the students may use the motivational energy implied by FLA, a negative and activating emotion (Pekrun et al., 2007). In the case of the two predictions, gender tends to act as an inverse predictor: female students tend to show higher career adaptability than male students, while male students tend to have a more favorable perception of their FL competences.

## LIMITATIONS AND FUTURE RESEARCH

Several limitations in the present study need to be addressed. First of all, the research involved just one higher education institution, so the sample may be under-represented at the national or international level. The research can be performed again on a larger sample, possibly in a cross-cultural study. Because the data were collected only from the authors' university, in a culture characterized by Collectivism, high Power Distance, low Indulgence, high Uncertainty Avoidance, and high anxiety in the formal learning

*Table 5. Self-perceived FL proficiency as a dependent variable (H4)*

| | Model | Coefficients | | | | Correlations | | |
|---|---|---|---|---|---|---|---|---|
| | | B | Beta | t | p | Zero-Order | Partial | Part |
| 3 | (Constant) | 11.837 | | 3.039 | .003 | | | |
| | Gender* (1-F, 2-M) | 1.334 | .093 | 1.796 | .073 | .122 | .100 | .086 |
| | Overall career adaptability | .090 | .134 | 2.564 | .011 | .091 | .142 | .123 |
| | FL Enjoyment | .069 | .103 | 1.912 | .057 | .230 | .106 | .092 |
| | FL Anxiety | -.600 | -.375 | -7.232 | .000 | -.365 | -.374 | -.347 |
| | Openness | .198 | .150 | 2.856 | .005 | .252 | .157 | .137 |
| | FL Motivation | .104 | .176 | 3.271 | .001 | .234 | .180 | .157 |

environment (Maican & Cocoradă, 2021; Maican & Cocoradă, 2023), the results can be generalized for other cultural contexts only cautiously.

Secondly, the research has explored only some of the individual resources, but it is possible that other variables also play a role regarding career adaptability, such as self-esteem, the family's socioeconomic status, or the students' aspirations regarding their careers.

Then, the results have been obtained on a sample of students, so they cannot be generalized to the working population. And, although the research comprises a sub-sample of employed students, a small-size one compared to the sample of unemployed students, this can threaten the validity of the independent samples t-test used. It should also be specified that the instruments designed for the needs of the present research could be further validated to check the reliability of the results.

Future research will consider the inclusion of Romanian graduates in the research. The analysis of the graduates' retrospective view on FL learning at university, of the factors that influenced the learning process, and of the importance of FLs in their getting employed and career advancement will provide the input for the comparison with the undergraduates' sample, with presumably interesting results for students, FL teachers, and academic institutions.

## CONCLUSIONS AND IMPLICATIONS

The research investigated a sample of undergraduate students and analyzed a variety of personal factors possibly involved in developing career adaptability. Based on the authors' information, this is the first study which has analyzed the relationships between FL learning and career adaptability, in a dynamic labor market in which communication in an FL is already an important criterion in staff selection for employment and an important contributor to professional success. The present study can also be distinguished through the analysis of a wide range of psychological and psychosocial factors that can lead to a better understanding of the relationships between career adaptability and other personal resources.

The main results show that there is a significant gender difference in favor of girls concerning the respondents' overall career adaptability and three of its dimensions (control, curiosity and confidence). The same holds for the perceived role of FLs for employability and professional tasks. From the perspective of the students' status as employed/ unemployed, there is only a tendency for unemployed students to be more confident in the future and for employed students to be more concerned with the future. On the entire sample, the students who report higher career adaptability are more conscientious, more anxious, more open to experience, and perceive their FL skills more favorably. The study confirms the existence of a mutual influence between career adaptability and self-perceived FL proficiency, each of these variables being a significant predictor for the other one, in constellations of slightly different independent variables.

The findings also suggest that career adaptability directly correlates with FLA, positive behaviors during the class, FL learning motivation, and the importance attached to FL for professional tasks. Male students outperform female students with respect to the role of FLs for employment prospects, their self-rated FL proficiency, and emotional stability. Female students are more adaptable, attach greater importance to FL learning in their future careers, enjoy the FL classes more, and show more positive behaviors during the class, but score higher than their male peers for FLA. Employed students are more concerned with their future careers and are extrovert, more conscientious, more open, and more emotionally stable than their unemployed peers, but show lower confidence in their career future.

Considering the present research and findings, the following implications can be formulated, which would benefit FL teachers, future graduates, and academic institutions:

- Universities should provide supportive environments to raise students' awareness about their own resources and career-related opportunities, so as for them to be able to better cope with career-related challenges. The Career Counselling and Guidance Centers in universities and high schools could offer valuable assistance for students' career orientation and for enhancing their understanding of the factors that could impact their future professional life, including FLs and career adaptability.
- Career adaptability is not taught in school as a distinct subject, but it can be indirectly touched upon during the teaching-learning-evaluation process of the different subjects in the curriculum. Consequently, the objective of the FL classes should go beyond the development of language skills, towards offering learning opportunities for other relevant skills in the labor market, including career adaptability.
- In the elaboration of FL syllabuses, emphasis should be put on contents and skills specific to the students' field of study and their future work environment. Receptive and productive skills (listening, reading, speaking, and writing) should be developed in an integrated manner, to enhance students' communicative competence and facilitate effective communication with clients and colleagues from different cultures.
- The inclusion in the FL classes of debates, input texts, audio/ video materials, and case studies on the impact of transversal competences, including language ones, could further raise students' awareness. This requires FL teachers to make themselves aware of the role FLs play in future graduates' professional lives.
- An accurate self-assessment of one's FL proficiency is useful both for the students' adaptation during studies and for the subsequent fostering of their career prospects. Special attention should be given to the self-assessment and assessment of FL skills in the case of female students, who are concerned with developing their career adaptability, but who are disadvantaged in the labor market.
- FL teachers should support students in coping with FL anxiety, by avoiding too high requirements, maintaining optimum motivation, enhancing positive behaviors, and encouraging progress. The increase of FLA in the case of female students and of their maladjustment should be particularly considered.
- Students should be engaged in the construction of their professional identity, by harmonizing career concern, control, curiosity, and confidence with the preoccupation for FL learning.
- FL teachers should regard FL classes as a means to contribute to the attainment of the United Nations' Quality Education Goal, i.e., to increase the number of youth and adults who have relevant knowledge, skills, and attitudes for employment, and, eventually, decent jobs and better lives (EC, 2020).

The authors consider that the findings contribute to a better understanding of career adaptability and of possible ways to enhance it. In addition, it advances knowledge concerning the interplay between two of the skills that are now in particularly high demand in the labor market, i.e., career adaptability and FL competences, and it draws attention to the need to gear the curriculum in higher education with the demands in the labor market.

## REFERENCES

Alahdadi, S., & Ghanizadeh, A. (2017). The dynamic interplay among EFL learners' ambiguity tolerance, adaptability, cultural intelligence, learning approach, and language achievement. *Iranian Journal of Language Teaching Research*, *5*(1), 37–50. https://api.semanticscholar.org/CorpusID:52061020

Ambrósio, S., Araújo e Sá, M., Pinto, S., & Simões, A. (2014). Perspectives on educational language policy: Institutional and students' voices in higher education. *European Journal of Language Policy*, *6*(2), 175–194. doi:10.3828/ejlp.2014.4

Argondizzo, C., De Bartolo, A. M., Fazio, A., Jimenez, J. M., & Ruffolo, I. (2020). Academic, cultural and social growth through the language of websites: A challenge for European University Language Centres. *Language Learning in Higher Education*, *10*(2), 341–355. doi:10.1515/cercles-2020-2023

Badescu, G., Sandu, D., Angi, D., & Greab, C. (2019). *Youth Study Romania 2018/2019*. Friedrich-Ebert-Stiftung. https://library.fes.de/pdf-files/bueros/bukarest/15294.pdf

Baker, S. C., & MacIntyre, P. D. (2000). The Role of Gender and Immersion in Communication and Second Language Orientations. *Language Learning*, *50*(2), 311–341. doi:10.1111/0023-8333.00119

Besser, A., Flett, G. L., Nepon, T., & Zeigler-Hill, V. (2022). Personality, Cognition, and Adaptability to the COVID-19 Pandemic: Associations with Loneliness, Distress, and Positive and Negative Mood States. *International Journal of Mental Health and Addiction*, *20*(2), 971–995. doi:10.1007/s11469-020-00421-x PMID:33230393

Bhatnagar, H. (2021). Study of student behaviour in Indian higher education - A broad perspective of teacher. *International Journal of Multidisciplinary Research and Development*, *8*(7), 49–52. https://www.allsubjectjournal.com/assets/archives/2021/ vol8issue7/8-6-66-291.pdf

Boekaerts, M. (1991). Subjective competence, appraisals and self-assessment. *Learning and Instruction*, *1*(1), 1–17. doi:10.1016/0959-4752(91)90016-2

Borg, E. (2014). Classroom behaviour and academic achievement, how classroom behaviour categories relate to gender and academic performance. *British Journal of Sociology of Education*, *36*(8), 1127–1148. doi:10.1080/01425692.2014.916601

Botes, E., Dewaele, J. M., & Greiff, S. (2020). The Power to improve, effects of multilingualism and perceived proficiency on enjoyment and anxiety in foreign language learning. *European Journal of Applied Linguistics*, *8*(2), 279–306. doi:10.1515/eujal-2020-0003

Boyle, S., Fahey, E., Loughran, J., & Mitchell, I. (2001). Classroom research into good learning behaviours. *Educational Action Research*, *9*(2), 199–224. doi:10.1080/09650790100200149

British Academy, American Academy of Arts, Sciences, Academy of the Social Sciences in Australia, Australian Academy of the Humanities and The Royal Society of Canada. (2020). *The Importance of Languages in Global Context: An International Call to Action*. https://www.thebritishacademy.ac.uk/publications/the-importance-of-languages-in-global-context-an-international-call-to-action/

Chen, H., Fang, T., Liu, F., Pang, L., Wen, Y., Chen, S., & Gu, X. (2020a). Career Adaptability Research: A Literature Review with Scientific Knowledge Mapping in Web of Science. *International Journal of Environmental Research and Public Health, 17*(16), 5986. Advance online publication. doi:10.3390/ijerph17165986 PMID:32824717

Chen, H., Ling, L., Ma, Y., Wen, Y., Gao, X., & Gu, X. (2020b). Suggestions for Chinese University Freshmen Based on Adaptability Analysis and Sustainable Development Education. *Sustainability (Basel), 12*(4), 1371. Advance online publication. doi:10.3390/su12041371

Cizel, R. B. (2018). Gender and Emotional Intelligence as Predictors of Tourism Faculty Students' Career Adaptability, Advances in Hospitality and Tourism Research (AHTR) *An International Journal of Akdeniz University Tourism Faculty, 6*(2), 188-204. http://www.ahtrjournal.org

Cocoradă, E., & Maican, M. A. (2013). A study of foreign language anxiety with Romanian students. *Bulletin of the Transilvania University of Braşov, Series VII: Social Sciences & Law, 6*(55), 9-18. http://rs.unitbv.ro/BU2013/Series%20VII/BULETIN%20VII/01_Cocorada%20&%20Maican%202-2013.pdf

Commission of the European Communities. (2003). *Communication from the Commission to the Council, the European Parliament, the Economic and Social Committee and the Committee of the Regions - Promoting Language Learning and Linguistic Diversity: an Action Plan 2004 – 2006.* https://eur-lex.europa.eu/legal-content/EN/TXT/PDF/?uri=CELEX:52003DC0449

Cook, V. (2000). *Linguistics and second language acquisition.* Bloomsbury Publishing.

Council of Europe. (2003). *The Common European Framework of Reference for Languages, Teaching, Learning, Assessment.* https://rm.coe.int/1680459f97

Davies, B. (2004). The gender gap in modern languages, a comparison of attitude & performance in year 7&year 10. *Language Learning Journal, 29*(1), 53–58. doi:10.1080/09571730485200111

Debreli, E., & Ishanova, I. (2019). Foreign language classroom management: Types of student misbehaviour and strategies adapted by the teachers in handling disruptive behaviour. *Cogent Education, 6*(1), 1–21. doi:10.1080/2331186X.2019.1648629

Dewaele, J. M. (2021). Personality. In T. Gregersen & S. Mercer (Eds.), *The Routledge Handbook of the Psychology of Language Learning &Teaching* (pp. 112–123). Routledge. doi:10.4324/9780429321498-12

Dewaele, J. M., & Li, C. (2020). Emotions in second language acquisition: A critical review and research agenda. *Foreign Language World, 196*(1), 34–49. https://eprints.bbk.ac.uk/id/eprint/32797

Dewaele, J. M., & MacIntyre, P. (2019). The predictive power of multicultural personality traits, learner and teacher variables on foreign language enjoyment and anxiety. In M. Sato & S. Loewen (Eds.), *Evidence-based second language pedagogy: A collection of Instructed Second Language Acquisition studies* (pp. 263–286). Routledge. doi:10.4324/9781351190558-12

Dewaele, J. M., & MacIntyre, P. D. (2014). The two faces of Janus? Anxiety & enjoyment in the foreign language classroom. *Studies in Second Language Learning and Teaching, 4*(2), 237–274. doi:10.14746/ssllt.2014.4.2.5

DiMaggio, I., Ginevra, M. C., Santilli, S., Nota, L., & Soresi, S. (2020). The Role of Career Adaptability, the Tendency to Consider Systemic Challenges to Attain a Sustainable Development, and Hope to Improve Investments in Higher Education. *Frontiers in Psychology*, *7*(11), 1926. Advance online publication. doi:10.3389/fpsyg.2020.01926 PMID:32849132

Dörnyei, Z. (2005). *The Psychology of the Language Learner. Individual Differences in Second Language Acquisition*. Lawrence Erlbaum Associates. doi:10.4324/9781410613349

Dörnyei, Z., Csizer, K., & Nemeth, N. (2006). *Motivational dynamics, language attitudes and language globalization: a Hungarian perspective*. Multilingual Matters. doi:10.21832/9781853598876

Dudley-Evans, T., & St. John, M. J. (1998). Developments in English for Specific Purposes: A multi-disciplinary approach. Cambridge University Press.

Dursun, M. T., & Argan, M. T. (2017). Does Personality Affect Career Adaptability? *International Journal of Humanities Social Sciences and Education*, *4*(10), 107–115. doi:10.20431/2349-0381.0410014

Eccles, J. S. (2005). Subjective Task Value and the Eccles et al. Model of Achievement-Related Choices. In A. J. Elliot & C. S. Dweck (Eds.), *Handbook of competence and motivation* (pp. 105–121). Guilford Publications.

Eccles, J. S., & Wigfield, A. (2002). Motivational beliefs, values and goals. *Annual Review of Psychology*, *53*(1), 109–132. doi:10.1146/annurev.psych.53.100901.135153 PMID:11752481

Erdem, C., & Koçyiğit, M. (2019). Student Misbehaviors Confronted by Academics and Their Coping Experiences. *Educational Policy Analysis and Strategic Research*, *14*(1), 98–115. doi:10.29329/epasr.2019.186.6

Eriksson, K., Björnstjerna, M., & Vartanova, I. (2020). The relation between gender egalitarian values and gender differences in academic achievement. *Frontiers in Psychology*, *11*, 236. Advance online publication. doi:10.3389/fpsyg.2020.00236 PMID:32153461

European Commission. (2017). *Key Data on Teaching Languages at School in Europe – 2017*. Education, Audiovisual and Culture Executive Agency. https://data.europa.eu/doi/10.2797/62028https://doi.org/10.3389/fpsyg.2020.00236

European Commission. (2019). *Foreign language skills statistics*. Eurostat. https://ec.europa.eu/eurostat/statistics-explained/index.php?title=Foreign_language_skills_ statistics

European Commission. (2020). *The 2030 Agenda for Sustainable Development & the SDGs*. https://ec.europa.eu/environment/sustainable-development/SDGs/index_en.htm

European Commission. (2023a). *Employment rates of recent graduates*. Eurostat. https://ec.europa.eu/eurostat/statistics-explained/index.php?title=Employment_rates _of_recent_graduates#Employment_rates_of_recent_graduates

European Commission. (2023b). *European Year of Skills 2023,* https://commission.europa.eu/strategy-and-policy/priorities-2019-2024/europe-fit-digital-age/european-year-skills-2023_en

European Commission. (2023c). *Real GDP per capita*. Eurostat. https://ec.europa.eu/eurostat/databrowser/view/sdg_08_10/default/table

European Commission. (2023d). *Labour market information: Romania*. EURES. https://eures.ec.europa.eu/living-and-working/labour-market-information/labour-market-information-romania_ro

European Commission. (2023e). *Foreign language learning increases among EU students*. Eurostat. https://ec.europa.eu/eurostat/web/products-eurostat-news/w/edn-20230926-1

Fernandes, E. M., & Carvalho, R. G. (2020). The relation between sociodemographic and school path variables, and career adaptability of high school students. *Psychologica, 63*(1), 83–100. doi:10.14195/1647-8606_63-1_5

Frendo, E. (2005). *How to Teach Business English*. Pearson Education.

Fuertes, A. M. de C., Blanco Fernández, J., García Mata, M. Á., Rebaque Gómez, A., & Pascual, R. G. (2020). Relationship between Personality and Academic Motivation in Education Degrees Students. *Education Sciences, 10*(11), 327. Advance online publication. doi:10.3390/educsci10110327

Fusco, L., Parola, A., & Sica, L. S. (2019). From creativity to future: the role of career adaptability. *CEUR Workshop Proceeding*. https://ceur-ws.org/Vol-2524/paper24.pdf

Goldberg, L. R., Johnson, J. A., Eber, H. W., Hogan, R., Ashton, M. C., Cloninger, C. R., & Gough, H. G. (2006). The international personality item pool and the future of public-domain personality measures. *Journal of Research in Personality, 40*(1), 84–96. doi:10.1016/j.jrp.2005.08.007

Guan, Y., Dai, X., Gong, Q., Deng, Y., Hou, Y., Dong, Z., Wang, L., Huang, Z., & Lai, X. (2017). Understanding the trait basis of career adaptability: A two-wave mediation analysis among Chinese university students. *Journal of Vocational Behavior, 101*, 32–42. doi:10.1016/j.jvb.2017.04.004

Guichard, J. (2018). Final Purposes for Life-and-Career Design Interventions in the Anthropocene Era. In V. Cohen-Scali, L. Nota, & J. Rossier (Eds.), *New Perspectives on Career Guidance and Counseling in Europe. Building Careers in Changing and Diverse Societies* (pp. 189–204). Springer International Publishing. doi:10.1007/978-3-319-61476-2_12

Hakimi, S., Hejazi, E., & Lavasani, M. G. (2011). The Relationships Between Personality Traits and Students' Academic Achievement. *Procedia: Social and Behavioral Sciences, 29*, 836–845. doi:10.1016/j.sbspro.2011.11.312

Harmer, J. (2015). *The practice of English language teaching (with DVD)* (4th ed.). Pearson.

Hirschi, A., & Valero, D. (2015). Career adaptability profiles and their relationship to adaptivity and adapting. *Journal of Vocational Behavior, 88*, 220–229. doi:10.1016/j.jvb.2015.03.010

Hofstede, G., Hofstede, G. J., & Minkov, M. (2010). *Software of the Mind, Intercultural Cooperation &Its Importance for Survival*. McGraw-Hill Comp.

Horwitz, E. K., Horwitz, M. B., & Cope, J. (1986). Foreign Language Classroom Anxiety. *Modern Language Journal, 70*(2), 125–132. doi:10.1111/j.1540-4781.1986.tb05256.x

Hou, Z. J., Leung, S. A., Li, X., Li, X., & Xu, H. (2012). Career Adapt-Abilities Scale—China Form: Construction and initial validation. *Journal of Vocational Behavior, 80*(3), 686–691. doi:10.1016/j.jvb.2012.01.006

Iacob, R. (2018). Brain Drain Phenomenon in Romania: What Comes in Line after Corruption? *Romanian Journal of Communication and Public Relations, 20*(2), 53–78. doi:10.21018/rjcpr.2018.2.259

International Labour Organization. (2022). *Monitor on the world of work. Tenth edition. Multiple crises threaten the global labour market recovery*, https://www.ilo.org/wcmsp5/groups/public/---dgreports/---dcomm/---publ/documents/briefingnote/wcms_859255.pdf

Jia, Y., Hou, Z.-J., Zhang, H., & Xiao, Y. (2020). Future time perspective, career adaptability, anxiety, and career decision-making difficulty: Exploring mediations and moderations. *Journal of Career Development, 49*(2), 282–296. doi:10.1177/0894845320941922

Jin, Y., & Zhang, L. J. (2018). The dimensions of foreign language classroom enjoyment and their effect on foreign language achievement. *International Journal of Bilingual Education and Bilingualism, 24*(7), 948–962. doi:10.1080/13670050.2018.1526253

John, R., John, R., & Rao, Z.-R. (2020). The Big Five personality traits and academic performance. *Journal of Law & Social Studies, 2*(1), 10–19. doi:10.52279/jlss.02.01.1019

Kang, X., & Wu, Y. (2022). Academic enjoyment, behavioral engagement, self-concept, organizational strategy and achievement in EFL setting: A multiple mediation analysis. *PLoS One, 17*(4), e0267405. doi:10.1371/journal.pone.0267405 PMID:35486654

Kortmann, B. (2019). *Language Policies at the LERU Member Institutions*, LERU Briefing Paper (4). https://www.leru.org/files/Publications/Language-Policies-at-LERU-member-institutions-Full-Paper.pdf

Koyuncuoğlu, Ö. (2021). An Investigation of Academic Motivation and Career Decidedness among University Students. *International Journal of Research in Education and Science, 7*(1), 125. doi:10.46328/ijres.1694

LaPrade, A., Mertens, J., Moore, T., & Wright, A. (2019). *The enterprise guide to closing the skills gap. Strategies for building and maintaining a skilled workforce*, IBM Institute for Business Value. https://www.ibm.com/thought-leadership/institute-business-value/en-us/report/closing-skills-gap

Lauridsen, K. M. (2013). Higher education language policy- Report of European Language Council working group. *European Journal of Language Policy, 5*(1), 128. https://www.liverpooluniversitypress.co.uk/journals/id/73/

Li, C., & Xu, J. (2019). Trait emotional intelligence and classroom emotions: A positive psychology investigation and intervention among Chinese EFL learners. *Frontiers in Psychology, 10*, 2453. Advance online publication. doi:10.3389/fpsyg.2019.02453 PMID:31736840

Li, Y., Guan, Y., Wang, F., Zhou, X., Guo, K., Jiang, P., Mo, Z., Li, Y., & Fang, Z. (2015). Big-five personality and BIS/BAS traits as predictors of career exploration: The mediation role of career adaptability. *Journal of Vocational Behavior, 89*, 39–45. doi:10.1016/j.jvb.2015.04.006

Maggiori, C., Rossier, J., & Savickas, M. L. (2015). Career Adapt-Abilities Scale–Short Form (CAAS-SF). *Journal of Career Assessment*, *25*(2), 312–325. doi:10.1177/1069072714565856

Maican, M. A. (2019). European Language Policies and the Development of Language Competences in Higher Education. *Bulletin of the Transilvania University of Brasov. Series V : Economic Sciences*, *12*(2), 127–132. doi:10.31926/but.es.2019.12.61.2.16

Maican, M. A., & Cocoradă, E. (2021). Online Foreign Language Learning in Higher Education and Its Correlates during the COVID-19 Pandemic. *Sustainability (Basel)*, *13*(2), 781. doi:10.3390/su13020781

Maican, M. A., & Cocoradă, E. (2023). University students' foreign language learning behaviours in the online environment. In T. D. Neimann, L. L. Hindman, E. Shliakhovchuk, M. Moore, & J. J. Felix (Eds.), *Multifaceted Analysis of Sustainable Strategies and Tactics in Education* (pp. 32–67). IGI Global. doi:10.4018/978-1-6684-6035-1.ch002

Marconi, G., Vergolini, L., & Borgonovi, F. (2023). *The demand for language skills in the European labour market: Evidence from online job vacancies.* OECD Social, Employment and Migration Working Papers, No. 294. doi:10.1787/1815199X

Martin, A. J., Nejad, H. G., Colmar, S., & Liem, G. A. D. (2013). Adaptability: How students' responses to uncertainty and novelty predict their academic and non-academic outcomes. *Journal of Educational Psychology*, *105*(3), 728–746. doi:10.1037/a0032794

McCrae, R. R., & Sutin, A. R. (2018). A Five-Factor Theory Perspective on Causal Analysis. *European Journal of Personality*, *32*(3), 151–166. doi:10.1002/per.2134 PMID:30140117

Merino-Tejedor, E., Hontangas, P. M., & Petrides, K. V. (2018). Career adaptability mediates the effect of trait emotional intelligence on academic engagement. Revista de Psicodidáctica, 23(2), 77–85. doi:10.1016/j.psicoe.2017.10.002

National Institute of Statistics. (2023). *Monthly average earning*. https://insse.ro/cms/ro/tags/comunicat-castig-salarial

O'Connor, M. C., & Paunonen, S. V. (2007). Big Five personality predictors of post-secondary academic performance. *Personality and Individual Differences*, *43*(5), 971–990. doi:10.1016/j.paid.2007.03.017

Organisation for Economic Co-operation and Development (OECD). (2019). *Talent Abroad: A Review of Romanian Emigrants*. OECD Publishing. doi:10.1787/bac53150-

Oruç, E., & Demirci, C. (2020). Foreign Language Anxiety and English Language Achievement in Higher Education: The Mediating Role of Student Engagement. *European Journal of Education Studies*, *7*(3), 199–212. https://zenodo.org/records/3756910

Osika, A., MacMahon, S., Lodge, J. M., & Carro, A. (2022). Emotions and learning: what role do emotions play in how and why students learn? *Times Higher Education*. https://www.timeshighereducation.com/campus/emotions-and-learning-what-role-do-emotions-play-how-and-why-students-learn

Pekrun, R., Frenzel, A. C., Goetz, T., & Perry, R. P. (2007). The control-value theory of achievement emotions: An integrative approach to emotions in education. In P. A. Schutz & R. Pekrun (Eds.), *Emotion in education* (pp. 13–36). Elsevier Academic Press., doi:10.1016/B978-012372545-5/50003-4

Pekrun, R., & Stephens, E. J. (2012). Academic emotions. In K. R. Harris, S. Graham, T. Urdan, S. Graham, J. M. Royer, & M. Zeidner (Eds.), APA educational psychology handbook: Vol. 2. *Individual differences and cultural and contextual factors* (pp. 3–31). American Psychological Association. doi:10.1037/13274-001

Poláková, M., Suleimanová, J. H., Madzík, P., Copuš, L., Molnárová, I., & Polednová, J. (2023). Soft skills and their importance in the labour market under the conditions of Industry 5.0. *Heliyon*, *9*(8), e18670. doi:10.1016/j.heliyon.2023.e18670 PMID:37593611

Poropat, A. E. (2014). Other-rated personality and academic performance: Evidence and implications. *Learning and Individual Differences*, *34*, 24–32. doi:10.1016/j.lindif.2014.05.013

Poropat, A. E. (2016). Beyond the shadow: The role of personality and temperament in learning. In L. Corno & E. M. Anderman (Eds.), Handbook of educational psychology (pp. 172–185). Routledge/Taylor & Francis Group.

Pouyaud, J., Vignoli, E., Dosnon, O., & Lallemand, N. (2012). Career adapt-abilities scale-France form: Psychometric properties and relationships to anxiety and motivation. *Journal of Vocational Behavior*, *80*(3), 692–697. doi:10.1016/j.jvb.2012.01.021

Pripoaie, R., Crețu, C., Turtureanu, A. G., Sîrbu, C., Marinescu, E. Ș., Talaghir, L., Chițu, F., & Robu, D. M. (2022). A Statistical analysis of the migration process: A Case study—Romania. *Sustainability (Basel)*, *14*(5), 2784. doi:10.3390/su14052784

Reifman, A., Arnett, J. J., & Colwell, M. J. (2007). Emerging adulthood: Theory, assessment, and application. *Journal of Youth Development, 2*(1), Article 0701FA003. https://www.nae4ha.org/ directory/jyd/index.html

Roberts, B. W., Kuncel, N. R., Shiner, R. L., Caspi, A., & Goldberg, L. R. (2007). The Power of Personality: The comparative validity of personality traits, socioeconomic status, and cognitive ability for predicting important life outcomes. *Perspectives on Psychological Science*, *2*(4), 313–345. doi:10.1111/j.1745-6916.2007.00047.x PMID:26151971

Rottinghaus, P. J., Day, S. X., & Borgen, F. H. (2005). The Career Futures Inventory: A Measure of Career-Related Adaptability and Optimism. *Journal of Career Assessment*, *13*(1), 3–24. doi:10.1177/1069072704270271

Rubio-Alcalá, F. D. (2017). The Links between Self-Esteem and Language Anxiety and Implications for the Classroom. In C. Gkonou, M. Daubney, & J.-M. Dewaele (Eds.), *New Insights into Language Anxiety: Theory, Research, and Educational Implications* (pp. 198–206). Multilingual Matters. doi:10.21832/9781783097722-012

Rudolph, C. W., Lavigne, K. N., & Zacher, N. (2017). Career adaptability: A meta-analysis of relationships with measures of adaptivity, adapting responses, and adaptation results. *Journal of Vocational Behavior*, *98*, 17–34. doi:10.1016/j.jvb.2016.09.002

Rusu, S., Maricuțoiu, L. P., Macsinga, I., Vîrgă, D., & Sava, F. A. (2019). Evaluarea personalității din perspectiva modelului Big Five. Date privind adaptarea chestionarului IPIP-50 pe un eșantion de studenți români. *Psihologia Resurselor Umane*, *10*(1), 39–56. https://www.hrp-journal.com/index.php/pru/article/view/148/152

Savickas, M. L. (2005). The theory and practice of career construction. In R.W. Lent & S.D. Brown (Eds.), Career development and counseling: Putting theory and research to work. (pp. 42–70). John Wiley & Sons, Inc.

Savickas, M. L. (2013). Career construction theory and practice. In S. D. Brown & R. W. Lent (Eds.), *Career development and counseling: Putting theory and research to work*. John Wiley & Sons, Inc.

Savickas, M. L., & Porfeli, E. J. (2012). Career Adapt-Abilities Scale: Construction, reliability, and measurement equivalence across 13 countries. *Journal of Vocational Behavior*, *80*(3), 661–673. doi:10.1016/j.jvb.2012.01.011

Shan, Y. (2020). Whether successful language learners require intrinsic motivation. *Open Journal of Modern Linguistics*, *10*(05), 549–559. doi:10.4236/ojml.2020.105031

Shepperd, L. (2021). *Foreign languages: skills in the workforce*. UK Parliament. House of Lords Library. https://lordslibrary.parliament.uk/foreign-languages-skills-in-the-workforce/

Shin, Y.-J., & Lee, J.-Y. (2019). Self-Focused Attention and Career Anxiety: The Mediating Role of Career Adaptability. *The Career Development Quarterly*, *67*(2), 110–125. doi:10.1002/cdq.12175

Sidiropoulou-Dimakakou, D., Mikedaki, K., Argyropoulou, K., & Kaliris, A. (2018). A Psychometric Analysis of the Greek Career Adapt-Abilities Scale in University Students. *International Journal of Psychological Studies*, *10*(3), 95–108. doi:10.5539/ijps.v10n3p95

Storme, M., Çelik, P., & Myszkowski, N. (2020). A forgotten antecedent of career adaptability: A study on the predictive role of within-person variability in personality. *Personality and Individual Differences*, *160*(1), 109936. doi:10.1016/j.paid.2020.109936

Sun, R., & Shek, D. T. L. (2012). Student Classroom Misbehavior: An exploratory study based on teachers' perceptions. *TheScientificWorldJournal*, *2012*, 1–8. doi:10.1100/2012/208907 PMID:22919297

Takahashi, A. (2008). Learners' Self-perception of English Ability: Its relationships with English language anxiety and strength of motivation for learning the language. *Departemental Bulletin Paper,* (1), 57-69. https://niigata-u.repo.nii.ac.jp/records/27414

Takahashi, A. (2009). Self-perception of English Ability: Is it related to proficiency and/or class performance? *Psychology*. https://www.semanticscholar.org/paper/Self-perception-of-English-Ability%3A-Is-it-related-Takahashi-%E9%AB%98%E6%A9%8B/98ed59be9cf961fa46ca4846b2569044e2f1f396

The Adecco Group. (2022). *Guidebook for investors in Romania.* http://investromania.gov.ro/web/wp-content/uploads/2022/11/Guidebook-for-investors-nov.2022.compressed.pdf

Tolentino, L. R., Garcia, P. R. J. M., Lu, V. N., Restubog, S. L. D., Bordia, P., & Plewa, C. (2014). Career adaptation: The relation of adaptability to goal orientation, proactive personality, and career optimism. *Journal of Vocational Behavior*, *84*(1), 39–48. doi:10.1016/j.jvb.2013.11.004

Trading Economics. (2023). *European Union - Employment rates of recent graduates - 2023 Data 2024 Forecast 2006-2022 Historical.* https://tradingeconomics.com/european-union/employment-rates-of-recent-graduates-eurostat-data.html

Transilvania University of Brasov. (2023). *Regulation on students' professional activity.* https://www.unitbv.ro/documente/despre-unitbv/regulamente-hotarari/ regulamentele-universitatii/studenti/Regulament_activitate_profesionala_a_studentilor_ 2023-2024_22.05.2023.pdf

Tudor, I. (2009). Promoting language learning in European higher education: An overview of strategies. *European Journal of Language Policy, 1*(2), 188–205. link.gale.com/apps/doc/A243358479/AONE?u =anon~30fa6f62&sid=googleScholar&xid=7ca6bfb8

Turner, J. E., & Waugh, R. M. (2007). A dynamical systems perspective regarding students' learning processes: Shame reactions and emergent self-organizations. In P. A. Schutz & R. Pekrun (Eds.), *Emotion in education* (pp. 125–145). Elsevier Academic Press. doi:10.1016/B978-012372545-5/50009-5

Uber Grosse, Ch. (2004). The Competitive Advantage of Foreign Languages and Cultural Knowledge. *Modern Language Journal, 88*(3), 351–373. doi:10.1111/j.0026-7902.2004.00234.x

Üstünlüoğlu, E. (2013). Understanding misbehavior at university level: Lecturer perceptions from the US and Turkey. *Education in Science, 38*(169), 224–235.

Vecchione, M., Alessandri, G., & Marsicano, G. (2014). Academic motivation predicts educational attainment: Does gender make a difference? *Learning and Individual Differences, 32*, 124–131. doi:10.1016/j.lindif.2014.01.003

Wagner, L., & Ruch, W. (2015). Good character at school: Positive classroom behavior mediates the link between character strengths and school achievement. *Frontiers in Psychology, 6*. Advance online publication. doi:10.3389/fpsyg.2015.00610 PMID:26029144

Wang, H., Xu, L., & Li, J. (2023). Connecting foreign language enjoyment and English proficiency levels: The mediating role of L2 motivation. *Frontiers in Psychology, 14*, 1054657. Advance online publication. doi:10.3389/fpsyg.2023.1054657 PMID:36844295

Wang, Q., & Xue, M. C. (2022). The implications of expectancy-value theory of motivation in language education. *Frontiers in Psychology, 13*, 992372. Advance online publication. doi:10.3389/fpsyg.2022.992372 PMID:36425822

Wang, X., & Zhang, W. (2021). Psychological anxiety of college students' foreign language learning in online course. *Frontiers in Psychology, 12*, 598992. Advance online publication. doi:10.3389/fpsyg.2021.598992 PMID:34122211

Wigfield, A., & Eccles, J. S. (2020). 35 years of research on students' subjective task values and motivation: A look back and a look forward. *Advances in Motivation Science.* doi:10.1016/bs.adms.2019.05.002

Wilczewski, M., & Alon, I. (2022). Language and communication in international students' adaptation: A bibliometric and content analysis review. *Higher Education, 85*(6), 1235–1256. doi:10.1007/s10734-022-00888-8 PMID:35855684

Zacher, H. (2014). Career adaptability predicts subjective career success above and beyond personality traits and core self-evaluations. *Journal of Vocational Behavior*, *84*(1), 21–30. doi:10.1016/j.jvb.2013.10.002

Zhang, H., Dai, Y., & Wang, Y. (2020). Motivation and second foreign language proficiency: The mediating role of foreign language enjoyment. *Sustainability (Basel)*, *12*(4), 1302. doi:10.3390/su12041302

## ADDITIONAL READING

Akkermans, J., Paradniké, K., Van der Heijden, B. I., & De Vos, A. (2018). The best of both worlds: The role of career adaptability and career competencies in students' well-being and performance. *Frontiers in Psychology*, *9*, 1678. Advance online publication. doi:10.3389/fpsyg.2018.01678 PMID:30258381

Barabadi, E., & Khajavy, G. H. (2020). Perfectionism and foreign language achievement: The mediating role of emotions and achievement goals. *Studies in Educational Evaluation*, *65*, 100874. doi:10.1016/j.stueduc.2020.100874

Fortanet-Gómez, I., & Räisänen, Ch. A. (Eds.). (2008). *ESP in European higher education. (2008)*. AILA Applied Linguistics Series. doi:10.1075/aals.4

Hahm, S., & Gazzola, M. (2022). The value of foreign language skills in the German labor market. *Labour Economics*, *76*, 102150. doi:10.1016/j.labeco.2022.102150

Hirschi, A. (2009). Career adaptability development in adolescence: Multiple predictors and effect on sense of power and life satisfaction. *Journal of Vocational Behavior*, *74*(2), 145–155. doi:10.1016/j.jvb.2009.01.002

Lee, A., & Jung, E. (2022). University students' career adaptability as a mediator between cognitive emotion regulation and career decision-making self-efficacy. *Frontiers in Psychology*, *13*, 896492. Advance online publication. doi:10.3389/fpsyg.2022.896492 PMID:36275236

Peng, P., Song, Y., & Yu, G. (2021). Cultivating proactive career behavior: The role of career adaptability and job embeddedness. *Frontiers in Psychology*, *12*, 603890. Advance online publication. doi:10.3389/fpsyg.2021.603890 PMID:34690849

Pourfeiz, J. (2015). Exploring the relationship between global personality traits and attitudes toward foreign language learning. *Procedia: Social and Behavioral Sciences*, *186*, 467–473. doi:10.1016/j.sbspro.2015.04.119

Sandu, D., Stoica, C. A., & Umbres, R. (2014). *Romanian Youth: concerns, aspirations, attitudes and lifestyle*. București Friedrich Ebert Stiftung.

Scott, F. J., & Willison, D. (2021). Students' reflections on an employability skills provision. *Journal of Further and Higher Education*, *45*(8), 1118–1133. doi:10.1080/0309877X.2021.1928025

## KEY TERMS AND DEFINITIONS

**Behaviors in Foreign Language Learning:** Actions students undertake during the FL classes, which can facilitate the development of language competences (positive behaviors) or hinder it through passive engagement or disengagement (misbehaviors).

**Career Adaptability:** A part of the individuals' psychological capital, which helps them cope with present and anticipated professional tasks and job-related transitions and difficulties required in an unstable labor market.

**FL Anxiety:** Unpleasant feeling of fear, worry and uneasiness, with debilitating effects especially for speaking and listening in an FL, and with a possible facilitating role for improving results, provided its motivational energy is implied.

**FL Language Proficiency:** Students' general ability to use language skills effectively in different communicative situations, externally assessed using comprehensive standardized tests.

**Foreign Language Outcomes:** language skills, knowledge and attitudes developed by FL learners that help them communicate effectively in various personal, academic, public and professional contexts, and develop an interest in other cultures.

**Importance of FL Skills for Employability:** Individuals' perception of the role FL skills (listening, reading, speaking, and writing) play for good employment prospects, access to famous companies, and a big salary.

**Importance of FL Skills for Professional Tasks:** Individuals' perception of the role FL skills (listening, reading, speaking and writing) play in accomplishing tasks at the workplace.

**Labor Market:** A component of any economy, which involves the supply of and demand for work. Today's labor market is an unstable and unpredictable environment, requiring employees' continuous adaptability to insecure jobs, sometimes with negative consequences for their health and life satisfaction, or with favorable consequences at social and personal levels.

**Self-Perceived FL Proficiency:** The results of one's self-assessed FL skills, influenced by the individuals' critical thinking, practice in self-assessment, attitude towards FL learning, academic results, personality, and shaped by evaluations from significant adults or peers.

# Chapter 6
# Reflecting on Empowering Students in Museum Work Through Federal Work-Study Positions:
## A USA Case Study

**Kathryn Medill**
*Rocky Mountain College of Art and Design, USA*

## ABSTRACT

*This chapter serves as a reflective case study, in which ex-colleagues, who held different institutional roles—federal work study student worker and manager—discuss their experiences as part of the visitor engagement team at a university art museum in relation to their transition from academia to their professional fields. These conversations serve as anecdotes other professionals can reference when building student work study positions for universities. The conversation is a unique opportunity to unpack the impact a student work study program had from the perspective of its participants. Specific themes explored are 1) the expectations of participants' regarding their role at the museum, 2) reflections from participants about their lived experiences as museum employees, 3) the transferable skills participants feel they developed as a result of their role, 4) if/how they utilize those transferable skills in their current professional practice, and 5) suggestions for institutions who have or would like to build similar roles.*

## INTRODUCTION

In 2016 I started my first full-time job in my career sector, museums. The primary purpose of my role, which was new to the museum, was to manage a team of front-of-house staff at a university art museum employed through Federal Work Study (FWS). Seven of the eight student workers from the seminal cohort were first-generation, four of the students identified as white, and four identified as Hispanic or

DOI: 10.4018/978-1-7998-7999-2.ch006

Latino. I was a 25-year-old Ph.D. candidate who knew she would graduate without accruing debt and had only ever worked part-time or unpaid internships in the museum sector.

My journey from academia to a professional career was such a pivotal experience that it inspired my dissertation research in 2018 (Medill, 2018). The transition from academia to the professional sector, in which students apply what they learned in their degree, is not a clear path nor a sequential experience. Instead, many students begin to weave themselves into their respective professional sectors via required internships for degree programs, volunteering, and part-time and/or full-time positions before they earn their diplomas.

The shift from higher education to ones' respective career sector is a layered process shaped by access to institutional support, socio-economic conditions, individuals' lived experiences, and personal interests (Croteau & Velez, 2006). Understanding these conditions is vital to institutions and businesses that interface with and employ students pursuing degrees in higher education. While some students might easily transition into their desired careers, others face obstacles like unemployment, underemployment, or uncertainty about their career direction (Gore, 2019). It is crucial that those preparing students to transition from academia to the workplace recognize these disparities and work to address them when structuring courses, curricula, internships, and other modes supporting future student career readiness.

Selecting a career path is fundamental to transitioning from higher education to a professional career. Students preparing to enter the workforce navigate many choices, such as selecting a degree program, the industry in which they wish to work, and how to balance school, work, and life. Students might also consider long-term career goals, work values, personal interests, and alignment with their educational experiences (Brown & Lent, 2016). Career interventions, counseling services, and experiential learning opportunities provided by educational institutions play a crucial role in assisting students with these decisions (Krumboltz et al., 1976).

Students' acquisition of and ability to apply skills and competencies unique to their sector and transferable skills, such as communication, teamwork, problem-solving, and adaptability (Fugate et al., 2004), are central to a successful transition. These skills enhance graduates' prospects in the job market. Additionally, discipline-specific knowledge and technical expertise acquired in academia contribute significantly to students' ability to meet industry-specific requirements (Rothwell et al., 2008). Preparing students with a holistic skill set is paramount in ensuring a smooth entrance into the workforce.

Educational institutions, career services, faculty mentors, and peer networks are essential support systems for students in transition. Career services departments offer guidance on resume building, job searching, interview preparation, and networking (Hartung et al., 2002). Faculty members can provide mentorship, professional advice, and opportunities for research or internships. Peer networks allow students to exchange experiences, insights, and job leads, facilitating a sense of belonging and mutual assistance (Rivera, 2011). Furthermore, familial and societal expectations can influence students' career choices and transitions (Tracey & Sedlacek, 1984). Understanding and addressing these support systems' roles in the transition process is critical for facilitating students' success.

This chapter unpacks a conversation between myself and three of the members of the first cohort of student Federal Work Study workers called Student Ambassadors at the museum–Elise, Al, and Ted. In this work, I utilize the relational lens of discussions with my colleagues to have an open conversation about our experiences—a conversation that, given our respective roles within the institution during our time of employment, would have been difficult to navigate. Readers should approach the data through our subjective lenses; they should not view this document as an objective study that judges the individuals who participated or the institution where the study was conducted.

The call for chapters for this book served as a guide to reflect on our experiences being employed at a university art museum. I explored my time as a new museum sector professional tasked with creating and managing a program that served the museum's array of needs and cultivated a beneficial experience for the student workers. Elise, Al, and Ted discuss questions I crafted using seven general themes/categories: 1) General/contextual, 2) Federal Work Study, 3) Museums, 4) The student worker role, 5) Transferable skills, 6) Reflections, and 7) Any other thoughts/comments (see Appendix 1 for specific questions). Elise, Al, and Ted also answered follow-up questions after the first group interview was coded (see Appendix 2 for specific questions). Using the voices of participants of a Federal Work-Study position (the manager [the author] and student worker [Elise, Al, and Ted]) at a university art museum. This chapter contributes to the exploration of how institutions that employ students through Federal Work Study positions can assist students in transitioning from academia to their chosen field of practice—from a managerial lens. The specific objectives of the chapter are to utilize the relational dynamic between FWS students and their manager as a mechanism to assess the efficacy of FWS programs, and share examples of resources similar programs might use when building and/or reimagining their own programming.

## BACKGROUND

This chapter uses narrative inquiry and autoethnography to explore the concept of preparing minority and first-generation students to transition from the academic world into their chosen career path from the perspective of student managers and students. As the focus of this chapter is multifaceted, existing literature about both the book's general theme–preparing students to transition from university to careers– and literature specific to the focus of chapter participants–federal work-study students' positions within museums– are presented next. General topics include Social Cognitive Career Theory (SCCT) and the importance of internships and experiential learning. Specific areas of interest explored are Federal Work Study positions and the lack of diversity in museum staff. While each of these topics intersects with the focus of this chapter, it is essential to note that retroactive explorations of these processes from the participants' perspectives, especially within the museum sector, are limited. This chapter aims to model how discursive assessment of FWS program from the perspectives of managers and student workers —as seen in the *Results, Discussion, and Suggestions* section—can aid in creating evaluative practices for institutions that manage FWS positions and have the goal of supporting students' transitions from higher education to full time professional practice.

### Social Cognitive Career Theory (SCCT)

Social Cognitive Career Theory (SCCT) is a framework that suggests ones' sense of self-efficacy in the workforce is influenced by environmental factors like personal experiences, and personal and communal behavior. These factors, paired with an individuals' outcome expectations, shape individuals' career development (Bandura, 1986, Lent et al., 2002; Wang et al., 2022). In this framework, self-efficacy, goal setting, and outcome expectations change dynamically as learning experiences change.

SCCT provides a comprehensive framework for understanding career decision-making processes among undergraduate students. Research suggests that students who apply SCCT principles in decision-making exhibit greater clarity and confidence in their career paths (Betz & Voyten, 1997; Wang et al., 2022).

Four central tenets of SCCT apply to this chapter:

- The concept of self-efficacy–an individuals' belief in their capacity to execute actions required to achieve desired career goals and how high career self-efficacy tends to set more ambitious career goals and are more resilient in the face of setbacks (Lent et al., 1994).
- Defining and setting personal goals by expanding interests and promoting choices (Barnard et al., 2008 as cited in Wang, et al., 2022).
- How the tone of personal and professional relationships (e.g., mentorship) impact students' future success.
- The importance of observational learning (Lent et al., 2000).

Critiques of SCCT include an overemphasis on cognitive processes and neglect of the role of affective factors in shaping behavior (Bandura, 2004), inadequate attention or lack of a framework for understanding emotional regulation (Caprara et al., 2000), limited consideration of how cultural and social contexts impact the development of social cognitive processes (Gutchess & Rajaram, 2022), an underemphasis of how unconscious processes impact decision making (Chartrand & Bargh, 1999), limited attention to structural inequalities and power dynamics that shape social cognition (Foucault & Gordon, 2015), and a lack of qualitative research methods— specifically how individuals understand their career development in relation to self-efficacy, setting expectations, and overall experience The limited amount of qualitative research impacts how these aspects are or are not assessed. Simultaneously, it can be difficult to create longitudinal studies that follow the career development of specific groups as seen in Yuen et al.'s study from 2022 (Yuen et al., 2022). As such, it can be a challenge to map and expand the generalized findings in studies of specific groups.

While SCCT offers a theoretical foundation for understanding and forecasting academic and career outcomes, quantitative and qualitative studies investigating the correlation between self-efficacy, setting expectations, and overall experience have yet to produce consistent findings (Garriott et al. 2014, Sheu et al. 2010). Moreover, a need exists for research to explore the intersection of SCCT with emerging career challenges, such as the gig economy, remote work, as well as the role of technology, and online resources in shaping career self-efficacy and decision-making. SCCT is an appropriate theory for this chapter because it offers a general framework and vocabulary to examine the experiences of the chapter participants in relation to their professional development.

## The Importance of Internships and Experiential Learning

### General

While the traditional focus on academic achievement can sometimes overshadow career preparation efforts (Dolan et al., 2011), numerous studies highlight the importance of internships and experiential learning opportunities as a way to begin to bridge the gap between academia and the workforce (e.g., Weeden et al., 2019; Kim et al., 2020). Experiential learning is a broader educational approach encompassing various hands-on experiences, including internships. It involves any learning that arises from direct engagement in real-world activities or experiences (Kolb, 2015). Internships are a specific form of experiential learning typically involving structured, supervised work experiences in a professional setting. Internships are often undertaken for academic credit or as part of a formal educational program (Yates, 2017).

## Benefits for Students

Internships encourage students to apply and question the content of their academic courses and theoretical knowledge within new professional contexts (Gault et al., 2010). Research has shown that integrating experiential learning, such as internships, with traditional coursework can deepen students' understanding of theoretical concepts and increase academic engagement (Lester & Costley, 2010). This practice reinforces the relevance and applicability of students' education to real-world contexts.

Experiential learning and internships also create opportunities for students to gain practical skills (Hartung & Taber, 2008), network with other professionals (Knouse et al., 2016), participate in formal and informal mentorship (Jacobi, 1991; Ragins & Cotton, 1999), clarify their professional goals (Erdogan et al., 2012) and better understand the complex interpersonal and professional aspects of their chosen fields.

Internships provide a unique opportunity for students to connect with experienced mentors and peers who can offer guidance, support, and valuable career advice (Villarreal et al., 2016). These relationships can extend beyond the internship period, serving as ongoing sources of support and guidance. Positive relationships with supervisors and colleagues can lead to valuable job referrals and mentorship opportunities (Allen et al., 2004). These networks can enhance immediate job prospects and improve long-term career success (Rivera, 2011; VanMaaren & Hooley, 2018).

In fact, students who complete internships are more likely to make informed career choices and pursue careers aligned with their interests (Colarelli et al., 2015). Moreover, internships foster students' personal growth and confidence (Blickenstaff & Sweeney, 2019). They gain a sense of self-efficacy as they navigate professional challenges and responsibilities (Bingham & Moore, 2014). This increased confidence positively impacts students' ability to secure and excel in their careers.

Experiential learning significantly boosts employability by providing students a competitive edge in the job market (Ployhart et al., 2003). Applied practice through experiential learning, like internships, can facilitate experience with industry-specific tools and techniques, making graduates more job-ready (Villano et al., 2016). These skill sets can lead to higher starting salaries and shorter job search periods (Vigoda-Gadot et al., 2017). Research indicates that students who engage in internships demonstrate improved problem-solving abilities, communication skills, and adaptability (Collier & Morgan, 2008).

Despite the benefits, several challenges and barriers exist to successful internships and experiential learning. These include issues related to access, diversity, compensation, and quality supervision (Knouse et al., 2016; Velez & Gray, 2019). To maximize the benefits of these experiences, institutions must address access, diversity, and quality supervision challenges.

## Benefits for First-Generation College Students

First-generation college students, whose parents have not completed a bachelor's degree, often face unique challenges and barriers as they navigate higher education and transition into the workforce. Creating access to educational opportunities assists in rupturing the cycle of generational poverty (Pascarella et al., 2004). Internships are a powerful tool in bridging the gap between academia and career success. Internships for first-generation students can enhance academic outcomes, foster professional development, and contribute to long-term career success.

First-generation students often lack access to social networks and resources that can provide insight into career options and pathways (Pascarella et al., 2004). Internships can provide a structured opportunity for students to explore potential career fields, build professional networks, and gain exposure to workplace environments (Gibbs et al., 2016). These experiences can help first-generation students make informed decisions about their future careers, providing clarity and direction they might not have otherwise. Additionally, as seen with research on internships in general, first-generation students who complete internships are more likely to secure job offers before or shortly after graduation (Zafar, 2013).

Finally, first-generation students often bring diverse perspectives, backgrounds, and experiences to the workplace. By offering internships to first-generation students, organizations contribute to creating a more inclusive and diverse workforce.

## Benefits for Museum Studies Majors

Historically, internships have been an integral part of degree programs for students majoring in an applied social science field like Museum Studies (Beckmann, 2013). While I agree with the potential positive outcomes of thoughtful internship programs as well as the gaps addressed, it is essential to note that the cultural expectation of unpaid or low-paid internships in museums has led to homosocial reproduction in museums (Luke, 2018; Dean and Fiore, 2016; Saldaña, 2014). That is, museums lack diversity within their internal staff structures and collections.

Preparing students for careers in an increasingly globalized job market has gained importance. Research emphasizes the need for global competencies, intercultural awareness, and adaptability (Wilkins et al., 2015). Museums and the material culture they house offer a unique opportunity for students to hone their cultural competencies.

## Federal Work Study

Federal Work Study (FWS) is a federal financial aid initiative in the United States. It provides part-time jobs for undergraduate and graduate students with financial needs [determined by income], allowing them to earn money to help pay education expenses. The program encourages community service work and work related to the course of study (Federal Student Aid, n.d.). FWS is primarily intended to assist students with their educational expenses and mitigate the long-term burden of student loan debt (Cunningham & Kienzl, 2011).

Numerous studies suggest that FWS positions offer students opportunities to develop transferable skills (Johnson & McCabe, 2008; Toth, 2010). These skills include communication, time management, problem-solving, teamwork, and adaptability. FWS positions often expose students to diverse work environments, enhancing their ability to navigate various professional settings–all components that effective internships and experiential learning aim to do.

Research about FWS positions reiterates the advantages discussed in "the importance of experiential learning: general." That is, FWS students can gain practical skills that enhance their resumes (Burrus et al., 2012; Leonard et al., 2021; Shriver, 2018), network with other professionals (Kuh, 2008; Shepard, 2015), participate in formal and informal mentorship (Shapiro et al., 2015) and clarify their professional goals (Meyers, 2005; Field, 2009). Additional research on FWS positions asserts that these programs help students foster financial responsibility (Kuh, 2008) and develop a strong work ethic (Pascarella et al., 2004; Brown & Watson, 2010).

Federal Work-Study programs frequently connect students with their campus community. Whether working in academic departments, student organizations, or administrative offices, students build relationships with faculty, staff, and fellow students. This engagement can lead to mentorship opportunities, networking connections, and a more enriching college experience (Yu et al., 2020).

FWS programs also contribute to the broader goal of increasing access to higher education. These programs help address socio-economic disparities in college attendance and completion by providing financial support to low-income and underrepresented students. FWS can be pivotal in making higher education more accessible and equitable (Long & Kurlaender, 2009).

However, it is essential to recognize that not all students have equal access to FWS positions or internships, potentially perpetuating disparities in career preparation (Shapiro et al., 2015). Addressing issues related to access and opportunities for marginalized students remains a challenge.

## The Lack of Diversity in Museum Staff

The participants in this chapter were/are all members of the art sector and museums. As such, we must briefly consider museums' diversity, or lack thereof. Museums play a crucial role in preserving and presenting cultural heritage and art. However, there has been growing concern and discussion about the lack of diversity in museum staff, which does not adequately reflect the multicultural societies they serve.

Several studies have documented the stark underrepresentation of racial and ethnic minorities in museum staff across the United States. Research shows that Black, Indigenous, and People of Color (BIPOC) are disproportionately absent from curatorial, leadership, and managerial positions (Benoit-Bryan, et al., 2023; Middleton, 2020). This lack of diversity and internal support of diversity within museums (MMF Report, 2023) is particularly concerning given museums' cultural/social role as visitor-centric (Weil, 1999; Falk, 2016; Simon, 2016).

The lack of diversity among museum staff directly impacts the representation of diverse voices, perspectives, and stories in museum collections, exhibitions, and programs. Museums often struggle to present a comprehensive and inclusive portrayal of history and culture, as staff demographics influence decision-making processes (Anderson, 2017). Museum staff diversity is linked to the narratives that museums choose to highlight. A homogeneous staff may unintentionally or intentionally perpetuate biases and gaps in the representation of marginalized communities, limiting the ability of museums to engage a broad and diverse audience (Bennett, 2018).

Research suggests that various barriers prevent BIPOC individuals from pursuing careers in museums. These barriers include limited access to educational opportunities, unpaid or low-paid internships, and implicit bias in hiring practices (Middleton, 2020). As a result, many potential museum professionals from underrepresented backgrounds are deterred from entering the field.

A lack of diversity among museum staff can affect the visitor experience, making some individuals, particularly those from underrepresented groups, feel unwelcome or disconnected from museum spaces. Research indicates that diverse staff can lead to more inclusive programming and outreach efforts, ultimately broadening the museum's audience (Roberts, 2016).

Efforts to address the lack of diversity in museum staff include mentorship programs, internship stipends, diversity and inclusion training, and targeted recruitment efforts. Additionally, some institutions are reevaluating their collections and exhibition strategies to better reflect diverse narratives (Anderson, 2017; Middleton, 2020).

The lack of diversity in museum staff is a pressing issue that has far-reaching implications for the cultural sector. To fulfill their missions effectively, museums must prioritize diversifying their staff to better reflect the communities they serve. Addressing this issue requires systemic change, including reforms in hiring practices, greater financial support for emerging museum professionals, and a commitment to telling more inclusive and representative stories. Ultimately, increased diversity in museum staff is an ethical imperative and essential for museums' continued relevance and sustainability. Appendix 3 provides more information about formal museum studies program structures in the United States and Europe.

The aforementioned literature demonstrates to the reader: the importance of internships and experiential learning—like Federal Work Study positions, the tenets of SCCT and the lack of diversity in museums. The Student Ambassador program discussed in this chapter represents a space where these three themes, which are usually examined discretely, intersect—a space with limited research. As such, this chapter aims to examine how these intersections are perceived from managerial and student perspectives. Moreover, this chapter aims to model how the process of intentional, reflective discourse between Federal Work Study students and managers can be used to deepen students' sense of self efficacy during their experiential learning experience and utilize Federal Work Study positions as a way to hire more minority and/ or first-generation students within museums.

## SETTING AND PARTICIPANT PROFILES

My primary task at the museum was to train and manage the front-of-house staff (Student Ambassadors) in a way that promotes visitor engagement while maintaining the safety of the artwork. I approached my role through my lens as a museum educator and worked to cultivate programs that are responsive to the museum's needs while also providing professional learning experiences for the students. In order to be eligible for the Student Ambassador role, applicants needed to be eligible for FWS, have an interest in museums, and could be from any major (arts based and non-arts based).

In my position, I managed between seven and ten FWS-eligible students from various degree program backgrounds. Seventy five percent of the student workers were minorities and 90% were first generation students. Students were cross-trained in security and visitor services. I tried to create a program that provided them with real-world experience within the museum sector, was sensitive to their personal interests, and addressed the museum's needs for front-of-house staff. Table 1 provides brief participant profiles from 2016, and Table 2 shares updated profiles for participants in 2023. Reference Appendix 4 for a discussion on the lack of diversity demonstrated by study participants.

It is important to note that the participants in this story were all colleagues who interacted on different professional and social levels. While these dynamics were not explicitly explored in the research, they emerge as significant factors in the creation of relational space of the Federal Work-Study position. All names, excluding mine, have been changed to protect participants' privacy.

## THEORETICAL AND METHODOLOGICAL FRAMEWORK

I utilized SCCT to frame my methodology. Qualitative research is a tool researchers utilize to investigate how people interpret their lived experiences and that "the experience a person has includes the way in which the experience is interpreted" (Merriam & Tisdell, 2016, p. 9). I posit that using an auto-ethnographic lens and narrative prose to present a case study written in narrative prose embodies SCCT's dynamic framework. Using a case study strengthened my understanding of the Federal Work-Study student position's perceived impact on three of my former colleagues through a retroactive reflective

*Table 1. Participant profile from 2016*

| Name | Pronouns | Age | First Generation/ Minority | Age When Hired | Academic Year/Major | Year Hired |
|---|---|---|---|---|---|---|
| Elise | She/her | Federal Work Study Student Ambassador | Yes/No | 28 | Junior/Fine Arts Major, Film and Digital Media Minor | 2016 |
| Al | He/him | Federal Work Study Student Ambassador | Yes/No | 30 | Junior/Fine Arts Major | 2016 |
| Ted | He/him | Federal Work Study Student Ambassador | Yes/Yes | 21 | Junior/ Art major with an emphasis in drawing | 2016 |
| Kat | She/her | Manager of Federal Work Study Student Ambassadors | No/No | 25 | ABD in a Ph.D. program/Art and Visual Culture Education and Art History | 2016 |

*Table 2. Participant profile from 2023*

| Name | Pronouns | Age | Current Career Description and Title |
|---|---|---|---|
| Elise | She/her | 35 | Elise has a BFA in Photography, a Film and Media production minor, and an MFA. She works as a multimedia artist focusing on video, photography, and installation. Elise's research unpacks ideas about gender, desire, consumerism, memory, and technology. She is also a photo technician and instructor for a university in the Western United States. |
| Al | He/him | 38 | Al has a BFA in Printmaking, a minor in Art History, and an MFA. He works as a multimedia artist focusing on printmaking, collage, collaborative sound, and video installation. His research focuses on contemporary consumerism, American culture, ideology, nostalgia, and the spaces between high and low culture. Al is also a photo technician and instructor for a university in the Western United States. |
| Ted | He/him | 28 | Ted has a BFA in Drawing and a MEd in Secondary Education with K-8 Art Endorsement. He has worked as a full-time elementary school art teacher for over five years. |
| Kat | She/her | 33 | Kat is a fully remote assistant professor of Art History at a private college in Lakewood, Colorado. She continues contributing to the museum sector through contract and volunteer work. |

conversation. In future research, with a different theoretical lens, I could craft a more generalizable study. Auto-ethnography enabled me to respect the duality of narrative inquiry as both a method and a phenomenon by encouraging me to reflect on the research experience (see Appendix 4 for the discussion on the limitations and delimitations of this study).

## Data Collection Methods

A group interview functioned as my primary source of data collection. I conducted two sets of interviews–one as a group and one as a setup follow-up questions in a shared Google document with member checks after each interview. Codes were created based on SCCT. The themes uncovered in the first round of interviews were member checked before continuing to the second round. The four key codes/ themes were mentorship, observational learning, self-efficacy, and suggestions. (See Appendix 5 for an in-depth discussion of data collection methods).

## RESULTS, DISCUSSION, AND SUGGESTIONS

The data is presented and organized in this section using four codes that became the subheadings: mentorship, observational learning, self-efficacy, and suggestions from Student Ambassadors. Sections are supported with quotes from participants, summaries of key ideas, and a discussion of how the findings intersect with SCCT. To bolster the discursive and autoethnographic framing of this chapter, I also insert additional context, feedback, and suggestions from my perspective as a museum professional and the manager of the program into this section of the chapter.

## Mentorship

The provided quotes effectively exemplify the theme of "mentorship" in career development, which aligns with SCCT. SCCT emphasizes the role of mentorship and guidance from experienced professionals in shaping individuals' career paths. "I wish at times that there would have been more education about the exhibits and artists that came from them directly and more intimately, so the ambassadors could ask questions and get all of the information necessary so they felt confident in informing the public" (Elise, follow up interview, 2023). Elise mentions a desire for more education and direct communication about the exhibits and artists from the museum staff. She believes that a more intimate and direct exchange of information with curators and other museum professionals would have helped students feel confident in their roles as ambassadors. Mentorship can significantly impact self-efficacy, as individuals gain confidence in their abilities when they receive guidance and support from mentors. Elise's desire for a more intimate exchange of information indicates her belief that such mentorship would enhance her confidence and competence as an ambassador. An increase in confidence and connection with staff through mentorship could bolster Elise's feelings of self-efficacy and create positive interest.

As mentioned earlier, research utilizing SCCT to the connections between self-efficacy, interest, learning experiences, and outcomes is inconsistent. However, in this case study, Elise's comments suggest that students' connections with staff through mentorship have a potential to serve as a mechanism to foster self-efficacy for student workers. This positions mentorship as a positive aspect of FWS positions which institutions that facilitate FWS could consider defining internally, assessing and tracking as a metric of success for preparing students to transition into professional spaces.

While I fully agree that more mentorship would benefit student ambassadors, actualizing this practice would require a shift within the internal expectations of staff at the institution. Many staff members performed roles positioned as hybrid—meaning they worked between different departments. The heavy workload and low pay (See Appendix 6 for information on the average pay of employees at this museum in 2016) created tension among the staff and led to burnout. An expectation of mentorship would add to the overburdening (Benoit-Bryan et al., n. d.) that exists within the institutional culture. Crafting more opportunities for students to observe the museum staff at work is an alternative option that could benefit students, but not add to staff expectations. For example, requiring students to observe staff members and take notes/ document questions for a set amount of time every semester. Then, meeting with each department where students could share their observations and ask questions could be built into the Student Ambassador position.

Another approach to bolster the mentorship aspect of the ambassador program could be to have program alums come and discuss their experiences with the position and what they are doing professionally with current ambassadors.

## Observational Learning

The quotes aptly exemplify the theme of "observational learning," which is central to SCCT's emphasis on the role of observation and modeling in career development. According to SCCT, individuals often acquire knowledge, skills, and self-efficacy through observing the experiences and behaviors of others. The theme of "observational learning" is evident in the provided quotes as they collectively offer insights into how individuals acquire knowledge and perspectives through observing the art world, museum culture, and the roles within it. This section demonstrates the importance of environmental factors (SCCT) and how the observation and experience within professional contexts contributes to an individual's learning and experiences.

### Initial Perceptions of Museums

My family has an attitude toward museums that is this standard attitude applied to many things that are like considered cultured that they think the institution thinks it's better than them, so they don't even want to participate... But anyway, I learned from my family's attitude toward museums. I just never really understood contemporary art for a really long time until I started college. I liked low brow forms of art a lot, right, or other lowbrow like pop cultural expressions, right. But it took me a really, really long time to come around to the fine or realm of visual expression (Al, group interview, 2023).

Much like Al, like I didn't go to a lot of museums when I was a kid. I don't think I went to my first art museum until going to community college. My interactions with art were, you know, really like going to the movies every week you know because I really enjoyed film or taking photos and pinning them on my wall and like creating my own museum, right? I mean I think everybody has kind of been talking about this kind of the inaccessibility of the space. Not always financially because some museum spaces like, you know, were free to the public, but inaccessible maybe in the sense that there is that aura, right? There's that energy and I think it's the fact that museums are silent and the walls are white and it's a very large kind of daunting space and you're only one person, right? (Elise, group interview, 2023).

The interviewees discuss their initial perceptions of museums as intimidating or elitist. This observation demonstrates how people initially form opinions about cultural institutions like museums based on the outward appearance and stereotypes they encounter. Observational learning comes into play as these perceptions may be informed by what they have seen, heard, or understood from others, as was the case with Al and his family or Elise's perception of museums as spaces with an uninviting aura.

Al and Elise's experience serve as evidence of how the social perception of institutional spaces might impact an individual's subconscious interest in that space. Moreover, these comments create an opportunity for museums as institution to consider how informal experiences with their constructed spaces might impact the development of an individual's interest in becoming a part of that space as a professional. Put another way, reviewed through the lens of SCCT and interest, Elise and Al's comments support the critique of SCCT regarding the need for more research on how cultural and social contexts impact the development of social cognitive processes, as well as how unconscious processes impact decision making (Chartrand & Bargh, 1999).

## Complexity of Museums

I just thought like well you just find some pretty pictures and you put them on a wall and there you go that's a museum but I didn't realize so much work went into how to put up a collection and like what the how to arrange the you know all the different exhibitions and things. Like that I didn't realize is that so much psychology of the patrons and like what they were looking for, and also just like the business side of it in sense of like how do we find ways to get people to come in here and enjoy the content of the museum in interesting ways and think about all the different audiences. Like, okay, do we focus on families? Do we focus on 20- to 30-year-olds? Do we focus on like richer older people. How do you get all these audiences while sometimes maybe realizing that you can only really focus on one and especially like well this person who works with the museum is more focused on this and then this person works in the museum is more focused on this audience... It made me appreciate it a lot more once I started working (Ted, group interview, 2023).

The interviewees gain a deeper appreciation for the complexities of museums, acknowledging that there is more to them than just displaying art. This learning process involves observing and recognizing the various aspects of museum operations, including administration, patronage, and visitors' psychology. Their understanding evolves through observation and exposure.

The reflection demonstrated in the students' responses highlights another potential category museums that have FWS programs could track and assess while students are employed with them in the form of a recurring semesterly survey which records students' understandings of sector specific roles and challenges. Other sectors could develop similar surveys with the goal of assessing FWS student's understanding of the complexities they identify which are specific to their sector. Tracing these understandings serves as qualitative data that could be used to identify potential strengths and weaknesses of these programs regarding how prepared students are or are becoming to effectively execute sector specific tasks in a specific institutional space or professional practice.

## Catering to Various Visitors

Observational learning is evident in the discussion of museums' challenges in catering to diverse audiences. The interviewees observed the tension between focusing on different demographics and the difficulty of making museums accessible to everyone. They learn from their observations of how museums adapt and evolve to serve a broader public.

Interviewees also thought critically about their experiences working with a business contracted to "teach" them strategies to better engage with visitors. All interviewees expressed their negative experiences working with an external consulting firm. Their disappointment is rooted in their observations of the business' behavior and approach to the training and how they acted during the event they helped the museum create. When speaking about his experience Al shared, "Yeah, they were hacks. They made us feel uncomfortable in our own space [the museum]" (group interview, 2023). Ted shared his critique of the experience when he stated, "If we had acted how they did during the opening, we would have been fired!" (group interview, 2023). This experience shapes their perception and understanding of what is and is not respectful or professional behavior within museums.

While I, too, was disappointed in our experience with the consultants, I was proud to see our team critique the experience and choose not to emulate the behaviors modeled for them. From a SCCT lens, these comments highlight the sense of ownership, agency and self-efficacy the students felt regarding their roles at the museum. Moreover, students felt comfortable questioning the power dynamics between themselves and the consultants. The comments also showcase, to me as the manager, that the students had cultivated a sense of what professional practice within the context of the museum was and was not.

## Curatorial Work

*It's [curating] is like a mixtape right. It's somebody's opinion of a theme and they found somebody else's work to illustrate their point, right? So, there's some artistic bitterness coming through about curators I suppose, I guess, I don't know. Right, but also from an artist's point of view, once you build something and put it out there, my opinion is not yours anymore. It's like it's subjected to the open interpretations and thoughts of every person on the planet, right? It's not yours. (Al, group interview, 2023)*

The interviewees discuss the role of curators and express a desire for more inclusive approaches to curatorial work. Through observation, they realize that some curators tend to center their voices in exhibitions, leading to a call for more public-centered curation. Al's comment also demonstrates how he utilized what he observed during his time in the museum environment to inform his own practice as an artist and approach to curating.

## Art Literacy, Anxiety, and Art's Value in Society

*After watching people at the museum, I think that walking into a museum space, the environment, the literacy, right, or even just how to look at something, right, it just becomes kind of this anxiety-filled experience that I think is kind of a turn-off for people. (Elise, group interview, 2023)*

*Museums would be scary, like haunted houses if we didn't give them cultural value. (Al, group interview, 2023)*

The interviewees highlight the fear and intimidation some people feel when entering museum spaces due to a lack of art literacy. The comments are a clear example of observational learning, as the students recognize the anxiety caused by a lack of understanding the social value assigned to art in society. The students observe how art is perceived by others and its impact on individuals' museum experiences.

*I think ultimately what it comes down to really is that the arts aren't valued, right? Like it's not something that, you know, is as important as engineering or for healthcare, like these other things, right? It's kind of seen as this kind of extra fun luxury kind of thing, right? So that informs how people come into these spaces, right? (Elise, group interview, 2023)*

The broader issue of how art is valued in society is also explored. The interviewees observe how art is often seen as a luxury compared to other fields. As a museum professional, these observations exemplify a larger gap with the art education—the lack of funding and support for art education and opportunities to develop art literacy. The student workers observed the results of this gap during their time at the museum and their interactions with visitors. Moreover, the students' comments show how they used their observations to reach larger conclusions regarding: the value of the arts in society. That is students observed that visitors can be anxious in museums because they do not have the appropriate vocabulary and context to utilize museum spaces. They then concluded that these experiences indicate a larger gap in how society does or does not value the arts.

## Learning From Ambassador Position

*Showing in a professional space and just observing sometimes, I really enjoyed, because like for me, it was training, right? Like I wanna be an artist, how do artists work? Like there aren't a lot of opportunities to kind of shadow or you know intern with a working kind of mid-career artist so yeah, I mean I really enjoyed those moments when there were artists in the spaces like installing or whatever the case was. Those kinds of opportunities, like we're not, that was not an opportunity that anybody else in the school was getting, right? (Elise, group interview, 2023).*

Elise reflects on her learning experience in the position, where she interacted with mid-career artists and observed installations. Her growth in the art world directly results from observational learning, as she gained knowledge by observing and engaging with experienced artists and their processes.

Despite their negative experience with a consulting company specializing in visitor engagement, Al and Elise admire a resident artist duo–Las Hermanas Iglesias. This admiration results from their observations of the artist duo's philosophy and approach to art, emphasizing the impact of learning through observation and peer inspiration. Moreover, they discuss the importance of play and humility in art. They have observed these qualities in Las Hermanas Iglesias and have come to appreciate them as valuable attributes in art.

## Art as a Vehicle for Ideologies

*I mean, I have learned so many things from the curators. Not just about art, but about, like, history, different places, their governments and political struggles. I didn't know much about decolonization when I started, but now I can talk about it. I think we show really cool, unique stuff that a "traditional" museum person might not know about. (Ted, group interview, 2023)*

The interviewees discuss the role of museums in presenting different ideologies through art. Their observations in the art world have contributed to their appreciation of art's role in expressing and examining ideologies.

I must note that the internal interests of curators and the staff demographics at the museum in this case study are unique in that there was more diversity in upper-level positions than in other institutions (Benoit-Bryan et al., n. d.). Considering interviewee's comments, this diversity deepened their knowledge acquisition and exposure to new ideas.

## Hierarchical Treatment of Museum Employees

*I definitely felt uncomfortable during events, because I left like the donors saw us as "the help". On tours, I was able to do my own thing and share my knowledge. But events could be uncomfortable because it felt like I was not respected. (Ted, group interview, 2023)*

*Sometimes your opinions are valuable in a private setting or conversation, but when it comes to the presentation and performance of rank in front of donors, [Student Ambassador] employees were told to be quiet and blend into the wall. I was told multiple times that my clothing was not professional enough as well. That distinction between behaving in a proper manner was something I had never really experienced before. I felt picked on, but then again, it probably would have been a similar situation at any art museum, there is a traditional manner of expectations of speech and behavior in institutions like this. I felt like Tonya Harding, like I was too low class to be taken seriously even though I was extremely interested in the subject of art history and I consider myself fairly knowledgeable in the field. I was the ice skater who smoked cigarettes and cursed, but I felt like this wasn't in-line with the image that the museum wanted to portray of its employees. (Al, follow up interview, 2023)*

*I think the times that I did not feel supported were from employees that were not directly associated with the Student Ambassador position- like the director and curators. I think this is to be expected since they have large projects that they are managing, but as the Student Ambassadors we were the "face" of the museum, and I wish at times that there would have been more education about the exhibits and artists that came from them directly and in a more intimate way, so the ambassadors could ask questions and get all of the information necessary so they felt confident in informing the public. (Elise, follow up interview, 2023)*

Interviewees' observations of the hierarchical treatment of lower-level employees by museum donors and staff reveal how observational learning can also encompass learning about power dynamics and the workplace environment. The students' feeling of not being adequately supported by certain staff members in the museum is a reflection of how they observed the dynamics within the institution.

As someone who has dedicated their professional career to studying museums and the use of public space, these observations demonstrate that while the role of students might be positioned as "entry-level" within an institutional structure, through observation, students learn about the primary issues which museums face, such as understanding the visitor base and connecting with them, hierarchical staff structures, professional attitudes and a lack of diversity in curatorial practices. From a managerial perspective, these comments highlight an opportunity to find ways to educate internal staff about how student workers contribute to the work of the institution. They also support an earlier assertion that a need to explore power dynamics is needed in the discussion and use of SCCT.

## Self-Efficacy

The code self-efficacy comprises the three intersecting themes: transferable skills, sector-specific skills, and agency.

### Transferable Skills: Public Speaking, and Time Management

*Although the tours made me very nervous, like it was good practice, right, like I needed to do it, right, because it was going to be what I was going to be doing after graduation. (Elise, group interview, 2023)*

*The practice in public speaking, right? So, it's like, no, the word teachers, it's like, that's basically our entire job. It's public speaking, right? So, to be able to see people entering that already feel very little anxiety about those kinds of situations was also really helpful. (Al, group interview, 2023)*

*I mean, I talk all day now, that is my job. Tours really helped me grow that comfort, or skill, that I now use daily in my work. (Ted, group interview, 2023)*

Interviewee's initial discomfort with public speaking and their concerns about effectively communicating complex ideas to museum visitors reflect a common fear and challenge. Their experiences as Student Ambassadors involved significant development of public speaking skills, a transferable skill that can be applied to various professions. This aligns with SCCT, highlighting skills acquisition through observation and practice as a critical career development component.

Elise and Ted's progression from discomfort with public speaking to addressing complex ideas demonstrates the development of self-efficacy. Ted's comment demonstrate that as students gain experience and expertise, their confidence in public speaking will likely increase. SCCT underscores that self-efficacy beliefs are crucial for individuals to pursue and succeed in their chosen careers.

*One more thing that I think it really prepared me for graduate school because I had to work as a teacher assistant during graduate school, so I was already used to being at school all the time, basically, right? (Al, group interview, 2023)*

Al discussed how his experience as a Student Ambassador prepared him for graduate school by honing his time management, teaching, and public speaking skills. This underscores the transferability of skills. Time management is crucial for many careers, while teaching and public speaking skills can be applied in various educational and professional settings.

Al's statement about how his ambassador experience prepared him for graduate school exemplifies the role of self-efficacy in career development. By acquiring transferable skills and adapting to new challenges, he likely developed a stronger belief that he could excel in a higher education setting.

*Managing school and work at the museum and museum events was stressful. But I also now know I can manage my time and prioritize what needs to get done. (Ted, group interview, 2023)*

Several participants mentioning the balance they struck between work and study at the museum highlights a critical transferable skill. Balancing multiple responsibilities is valuable in any career and crucial to adaptability and effective time management.

Participants' ability to balance work and study suggests the development of self-efficacy in managing multiple responsibilities. Successfully navigating this balance can boost individuals' confidence in their ability to handle challenges and succeed in their careers.

## Transferable Skills: Professionalism

*It definitely, it taught me to kind of work in a professional environment which like I had never really done before, like working retail, working in food service. I mean, there's a certain level of professionalism that you need to bring to the job, but you're working in the service industry. Like, you're not expected to be like, "My lady", you know, like, how are you today? But working in the museum, you know, it was a professional environment. So, it taught me how to behave, right, in certain circumstances. Like when to flip that switch, right? So, you can kind of kiss [butt] a little bit because that's so much what working in the arts is about. It's who you know, it's being a good person and a hard-working person so people recognize that and remember it later, right? Like so it did teach me working in that kind of environment. So, I thought that that was really important. It made me feel a little bit more professional, which I, which I've carried with me, right? And to my, like, teaching career and all of that. (Elise, group interview, 2023)*

The interviewees' discussion of developing the ability to interact with the public and professionalism in a work environment aligns with SCCT's focus on skill development. These skills, such as effective communication and professionalism, are foundational for career success and are transferable to various professional roles. The interviewees emphasized how the experience prepared them for professional development and taught them the importance of professionalism in a work setting. They learned to navigate professional environments, participate in meetings, and observe how different departments operate, including how professionals handle both good and challenging days.

The interviewees' emphasis on how their experience prepared them for professional development highlights the role of self-efficacy. By observing professionals and engaging in various work-related tasks, they likely gained confidence in navigating professional environments and contributing effectively. SCCT recognizes that self-efficacy beliefs are influenced by observational learning and personal experiences.

## Transferable Skills: Simplifying Complex Topics

*I think that touring and even just engaging with the public as it is, because you're getting a bunch of random people who are like, I don't know what this is. And it's like, well, let me find ways to relate this to you. Let me break it down so it's very engaging. And I found that so helpful. It really helped me figure out what I wanted to do for my Masters [teaching]. (Ted, group interview, 2023)*

The capacity to break down complex topics, like art and art history, into more understandable and engaging forms for different audiences is a valuable skill. This skill resonates with SCCT's emphasis on individuals acquiring problem-solving and communication skills to succeed in their careers. The interviewees' ability to engage with a diverse audience and make art more accessible reflects their self-efficacy in interpersonal communication. They gained the confidence to navigate challenging or sensitive topics, illustrating how self-efficacy plays a pivotal role in their roles as ambassadors. SCCT acknowledges the importance of self-efficacy in career success, especially in roles involving interaction with diverse stakeholders.

Ted's comments allude to how his experiences at the museum gave him insights into teaching and the art field, inspiring them to pursue further education and consider careers in these areas.

## Sector Specific Skills: Directly Related Work-Study Experience

*I got to work with education, the print room and the preparators. It was like behind-the-scenes access to artists and museums. (Al, group interview, 2023)*

*Just the exposure to so many, like, amazing pieces of artwork. I didn't know it at the time. Like because the caliber of artists that were coming through the museum, top-notch, dude, like I to this day speak about my experience there as just like there's only so much you can learn in the classroom, right? (Elise, group interview, 2023)*

Al and Elise's comments emphasize the advantage of gaining valuable experience through work-study programs, especially in environments related to students' fields of study. He appreciates that the job was directly related to his academic pursuits. These quotes highlight the significance of sector-specific skills acquired through work-study programs directly related to one's academic field. SCCT underscores the importance of acquiring field-specific expertise to enhance one's career prospects.

### Sector-Specific Skills: Unique Perspective on Art Interaction

Al talks about how his work-study experience at the Art Museum gave him a unique perspective on how people interact with art, which has been valuable in his professional artistic practice and teaching. Al's work-study experience provided him with sector-specific insights into art interaction. These unique perspectives are essential for professionals in the art field and are indicative of how work experiences can contribute to specialized knowledge. SCCT acknowledges that sector-specific skills play a critical role in career development.

### Sector Specific Skills: Exposure to Different Aspects of the Art World

*So, I think the programming that was at the museum while I was there was really important and prepared me for kind of knowing the difference between, like, good and bad art, right? Like what is to be expected in these kinds of institutions because that's what the public deserves to see. I think that that was something that I recognize. So yeah, just kind of learning professionalism kind of in a, in that kind of setting was something that I've taken with me. (Al, group interview, 2023)*

Al mentions that he took on the ambassador position to explore whether it was something he might want to pursue. He highlights how the role allowed him to gain exposure to different aspects of the art world, including curation and art handling. Working as ambassadors exposed them to a wide range of art and artists, helping them understand what is expected in cultural institutions and distinguishing between good and bad art. The experiences also provided insights into various roles within a museum, such as curators, directors, and conservators, enhancing their understanding of the art world. Their exposure to different facets of the art world through the STUDENT AMBASSADOR position demonstrates the acquisition of sector-specific skills. This exposure enriched his understanding of various roles within the art world, contributing to his sector-specific knowledge. SCCT recognizes that exposure to diverse aspects of a sector can lead to career clarity and success.

### Agency: Reframing the Value of Skills and Contributions

Elise reflects on the financial challenges in the arts and mentions the prevalent notion of the 'starving artist.' She discusses her experiences with low income and the financial bonus of participating in work-study programs. Elise also shares that her work-study experience changed her mind set about the value of her skills and contributions. She mentions that this experience helped her realize that she should not give away her labor for free.

Elise's reflection on her work-study experience demonstrates her agency in reevaluating the value of her skills and contributions. This transformative shift in perspective aligns with the theme of agency, as she actively took steps to recognize the worth of her work. SCCT emphasizes that agency plays a vital role in career development, allowing individuals to assert control over their career choices.

Elise mentions that she has grown more comfortable with public speaking and would approach the role differently if given the chance again, demonstrating personal growth and development. Her growth in comfort with public speaking demonstrates the development of self-efficacy. Her evolving self-belief in her public speaking abilities aligns with SCCT's emphasis on self-efficacy as a driving force in career development.

## Agency: Empowerment in Museum Roles

Al and Elise both mention feeling empowered when taking on specific roles within the museum, such as security, because it allowed them to assert ownership over the space and feel more confident in their positions. The feeling of empowerment and ownership over specific roles within the museum underscores the agency theme. Al and Elise actively embraced these roles and derived confidence from them, reflecting their ability to take control of their professional development. The interviewees reflect on their journeys in breaking down the barriers they initially felt in museums. They mention that their experiences working in museums have demystified these spaces and made them feel more comfortable, but there are still lingering feelings of intimidation in certain situations. The interviewees' reflection on breaking down barriers and gaining comfort within museums signifies the development of self-efficacy. Overcoming initial discomfort and intimidation reflects their growing confidence in the art world. SCCT recognizes the importance of self-efficacy in influencing career choices and success. SCCT highlights the importance of empowering individuals to make choices that align with their career goals.

## Agency: Personalized Student Ambassador Role for Career Goals

Elise believes that a successful Student Ambassador role should challenge participants to meet the expectations of the position while allowing them to take initiative and work on tasks that align with their interests in the arts. Providing a sense of agency and ownership over specific projects during the experience is essential. Elise's emphasis on the need for a personalized role that aligns with the individual's career goals resonates with the concept of agency. She advocates empowering individuals to design their roles to reflect their interests and aspirations. SCCT recognizes the importance of personal agency in tailoring career experiences to one's goals.

In summary, the provided quotes exemplify the themes of "agency" and "self-efficacy" as outlined in Social Cognitive Career Theory (SCCT). They illustrate how individuals actively assert control over their career paths, reframe their perspectives, and gain confidence through their experiences, aligning with the principles of agency and self-efficacy central to SCCT. These elements underscore the significance of self-directed actions and self-belief in career development.

## Suggestions From Student Ambassadors

This section both presents suggestions from the Student Ambassador of how to strengthen the FWS position, and serves as an example of how to incorporate students' voices into the process of evaluating a program using SCCT.

### Listen to Students' Needs and Aspirations

Elise emphasizes the importance of actively listening to the needs and aspirations of students participating in the program. Institutions should:

- Understand the unique approaches and experiences that students seek beyond traditional roles.
- Recognize the importance of understanding the unique needs and aspirations of participating students.
- Go beyond traditional roles and tailor the program to challenge students intellectually. Align their contributions with the institution's goals to provide a more meaningful experience that boosts self-efficacy.
- Acknowledge that a successful role may vary among individual students.
- Personalize the position to help students gain specific skills and experiences that align with their post-graduation aspirations.

By doing so, institutions can help students build self-efficacy based on their individual goals. Institutions could provide additional projects or tasks for students to work on during their downtime to enhance self-efficacy. This approach prevents students from feeling bored and allows them to contribute more to the institution, further boosting their sense of competence and self-efficacy.

A specific approach that institutions could use to support students' needs and advance the goals of the institution is to schedule semesterly check-ins between the manager and students which resemble the quarterly and/or annual reviews staff complete. In the suggested model students would fill out a self-assessment (See Figures 1-5 in Appendix 7 for an example of a potential self-assessment for student workers) and the manager would fill out an assessment form for each Student Ambassador (See Figures 6-9 Appendix 8 for an example of a potential self-assessment for student workers). Then they would meet to discuss the content. In these reviews students gain applied practice with the formal review process which supports their transition from academia to applied practice. The institution gains valuable feedback from students regarding: the effectiveness of the FWS position. These interviews could be used by administration to support requests to increase the budget for FWS positions.

### Raise Awareness of Federal Work-Study Programs

*So, I didn't know anything about work study at all. I mean I knew this area type of like students had jobs that's college but I didn't know that it was actually through sort of like FAFSA and stuff like that. I just kind of assumed it was just normal in a normal job. So, I remember it was a big battle like a lot. I remember I was going to financially a lot and like basically they're trying to see like, well, do you qualify? Do you not qualify? And it was like really it I remember there was kind of sometimes a lot of hiccups with it, trying to just get eligible just to work, because I remember you're being like, man, I wish*

*I could just work here and not have to worry about if I'm eligible or not in terms of FAFSA and all that stuff. (Ted, group interview, 2023)*

Institutions should actively promote awareness of federal work-study programs among students. Ted's initial lack of awareness underscores the importance of making such programs well-known. This includes providing clear and accessible information about eligibility requirements and program details. Moreover, the fact that during my 6 years at the museum 75% of the student workers were minorities and 90% were first generation students, indicates the potential for FWS students to highlight diverse and underrepresented voices with the museum institution. However, the reader must note that filling entry level jobs with underrepresented demographics is not a solution for the lack of diversity within museums—rather FWS positions have the potential to introduce these groups to institutions and give them the room to experiment with their own self efficacy within an institutional space. Incorporating semesterly reviews also serves as a strategy to ensure student voices are considered by administration and the institution.

Ted's experience navigating eligibility criteria highlights the need for transparency. It is necessary to communicate the financial aspects of the federal work-study program, including compensation. Students should have a realistic understanding of the financial benefits and limitations.

Two suggestions for other institutions with similar programming are to create a one-page resource potential FWS students can download and reference when applying to the position. The document would provide: steps for applying for the position with a timeline, important contact information at the institution and the financial aid office. Additionally, once hired, students should have access to a handbook, and a section outlining FWS should be included.

## Define Successful Student Worker Roles

Define what constitutes a successful student worker role within the institution, emphasizing adaptability, leadership, and an interest in the field. This definition serves as a guideline for students. Communicate the role of student workers, such as Student Ambassadors, clearly to staff members and visitors. It is crucial to convey that they are not just security guards or general student workers but are there to answer questions about the artwork. The use of visual cues can help visitors recognize their role and purpose.

Consider evolving student worker roles, such as the role explored in this chapter, focus on:

- Engagement with visitors rather than solely emphasizing security.
- Provide clear role definitions and use visual cues to help other stakeholders understand the role of the students.
- Recognize that the definition of a successful role may vary among individual students. The role should be personalized to help students gain specific skills and experiences aligned with their post-graduation aspirations.
- Aim to place students who genuinely have an interest in the field in relevant roles. Genuine interest greatly enhances the effectiveness of the program and the students' experience. The role should be personalized to help students gain specific skills and experiences aligned with their post-graduation aspirations.
- Provide more projects or tasks for students to work on during their downtime. This approach can prevent students from feeling bored and make better use of their time, allowing them to contribute more to the institution.

These suggestions aim to create a more effective and engaging experience for student workers, emphasizing personalization, alignment of goals and expectations, empowerment, and clarity in roles and responsibilities.

## Fair Wages and Recognition

While livable wages are a gap in contemporary museum practice (Benoit-Bryan et al., n.d.). Institutions could create an environment where student workers feel supported and recognized for their contributions. Celebrate students' knowledge and passion for their roles and ensure that their work is valued as an integral part of the museum's operations internally and with the public. Internally, the museum could recognize ambassadors and demonstrate respect by addressing the issue of fair wages for student workers. For example, student worker wages could become a line item in each exhibition budget. Or the museum's development department could add an annual goal of obtaining at least one grant a year to assist with funding the program. Additionally, students could be acknowledged by their names internally on platforms like email or slack as well as publicly by adding their names to content they create for the institution. The museum can further support the professional development of students by noting students' contributions on public content and encouraging them add the experience to their resumes. Internally and externally acknowledging students' contributions is one tactic institutions might use to begin to address power discrepancies between senior staff and student workers.

## Redefine Role Perceptions

*Well, I think that I definitely have a complex relationship with museums where I think seeing now that it's just a bunch of people who are all just trying to find a way to keep this museum going basically and they are trying to find new ways to do it. I think that it has helped to kind of break that seal. But then I do the some of the memories about the museum that were kind of hard and a little more like made me put off a little bit by experience was like whenever we had to do like the opening receptions and it was like the people, the donors and like that and I just felt so like I don't belong here, I don't this isn't where I'm supposed to be and I have to try to like talk to these people who like they probably don't see me as anything. (Ted, group interview, 2023)*

Institutions should work on redefining the perception of student workers, such as ambassadors, within the organization. Encourage a shift from seeing them as non-sector specific staff to recognizing them as essential contributors to the museum's mission of connecting guests with artwork. This could be achieved by providing training and clear role definitions that emphasize their role in visitor engagement. Institutions should actively address class-based perceptions that may affect how student workers are seen within the organization. Ensure that students are not viewed as "low-class" and work on aligning their roles with the desired employee image of the museum. This could involve professional development and training to enhance students' confidence and professionalism. Additionally, staff could be required to engage with the student workers at least once a term (see Appendix 9 for an example of a form museums could use to promote and define engagement with Student Ambassadors for staff), and staff could also be asked to reflect on their professional relationship with the student workers in their quarterly and annual reviews (see Appendix 10 for an example of potential questions that could be added to staff reviews). Integrating requirements for staff to interact with student workers increases students' potential to learn through observation and modeling. Requiring staff to reflect on their interactions with student workers demonstrates the importance of the student worker role within the larger ecosystem of the institution to staff.

Finally, creating more opportunities to weave Student Ambassadors into the internal fabric of the everyday practices of the museum would offer students the ability to observe more aspects of professional practice. For example, including Student Ambassadors in staff meetings would provide a unique opportunity for students observe professional practice and engage in professional conversations. This deepens students' ability to cultivate their professionalism and also demonstrates to other museum staff that the Student Ambassadors should be treated as colleagues.

In summary, the suggestions aim to promote a shift in the perception and treatment of student workers, fostering an environment of respect within the institution. This respect, in turn, can enhance the effectiveness and satisfaction of student workers in their roles.

## CONCLUSION

The interviewees reflect on their time as Student Ambassadors with fondness despite facing challenges and working with various personalities. They recognize the unique opportunities and experiences that working in a museum provided and express gratitude for those experiences. The findings support the study's chosen theoretical framework—SCCT. Specifically, the idea that effective ways to support students' transitions from academia to professional practice include: growing students' options, building support, and promoting work satisfaction (Lent, 2013, as cited in Wang et al., 2022).

From a managerial lens, it was a privilege to use this chapter as the impetus to reflect on a program I managed and hear about my former colleagues' current professional practice. This process also helped me recognize that formal assessment and goal setting could have been built into the Student Ambassador program as a strategy to support students' needs. At the same time, the institutional history of museums being poorly funded and lacking diversity leads me to question how institutions can balance their pragmatic needs, the shifting focus on their respective sector, and the needs of students who contribute to the institutional fabric as they transition from academia to professional practice.

To me, this study highlights untapped resources those who build and manage FWS positions can utilize to strengthen their programs—student perspectives and the relationship between managers and student workers. Additionally, while the study in this chapter is a small case study, it demonstrates that collecting the perspectives of student participants through various stages of their experience with FWS programs and how the experience impacted their careers holds great potential in regards to assessing if/how FWS positions assist student with transitioning to academia to their respective professional sectors through a qualitative process.

## REFERENCES

Allen, T. D., Eby, L. T., Poteet, M. L., Lentz, E., & Lima, L. (2004). Career benefits associated with mentoring for proteges: A meta-analysis. *The Journal of Applied Psychology, 89*(1), 127–136. doi:10.1037/0021-9010.89.1.127 PMID:14769125

Anderson, G. (2017). *Reinventing the museum: Historical and contemporary perspectives on the paradigm shift*. Rowman & Littlefield.

Anderson, S. (2020). Unsettling national narratives and multiplying voices: The art museum as renewed space for social advocacy and decolonization–a Canadian case study. *Museum Management and Curatorship*, *35*(5), 488–531. doi:10.1080/09647775.2020.1803111

Bandura, A. (1986). *Social Foundations of Thought and Action: A Social Cognitive Theory*. Prentice Hall.

Bandura, A. (1997). *Self-Efficacy: The Exercise of Control*. Freeman.

Bandura, A. (2004). Health Promotion by social cognitive means. *Health Education &amp. Behaviour*, *31*(2), 143–164. doi:10.1177/1090198104263660 PMID:15090118

Barnard, G. W., Lent, R. W., & Akamatsu, T. J. (2008). Predicting academic and job performance: The contribution of math and science interests, goals, and self-efficacy. *Journal of Vocational Behavior*, *73*(1), 47–55.

Beckmann, E. (2013). Internships in museum studies: Learning at the interface. In A. Boddington, J. Boys, & C. Speight (Eds.), *Museums and higher education working together: Challenges and opportunities* (pp. 39–53). Routledge.

Bennett, T. (2018). *Museums, equality and social justice*. Routledge.

Benoit-Bryan, J., Jean-Mary, D., & Locks, M. (2023). *Museums Moving Forward Workplace Equity and Organizational Culture in US Art Museums 2023 Report*. Museums Moving Forward.

Betz, N. E., & Voyten, K. K. (1997). Efficacy and outcome expectations influence career exploration and decidedness. *The Career Development Quarterly*, *45*(2), 176–186. doi:10.1002/j.2161-0045.1997.tb01004.x

Bingham, M., & Moore, M. R. (2014). The present state of career preparation for communication students: Preparing for a future in flux. *Journal of Applied Communication Research*, *42*(1), 3–22.

Blickenstaff, J. C., & Sweeney, K. M. (2019). The impact of structured university internships on diversity and career trajectory. *Innovative Higher Education*, *44*(5), 407–420.

Bourke, B. (2014). Positionality: Reflecting on the research process. *The Qualitative Report*, *19*(33), 1–9.

Brown, S. D., & Lent, R. W. (2016). *Career development and counseling: Putting theory and research to work* (2nd ed.). John Wiley & Sons.

Brown, S. D., & Watson, M. B. (2010). Bidirectional relations between work and personality development: Delineating personality-related work behaviors. *Journal of Vocational Behavior*, *76*(3), 458–472.

Burrus, J., Hardin, E. E., & Butz, A. (2012). Impact of student employment on career development: Differences between work-study and non-work-study participants. *NASPA Journal*, *49*(1), 106–125.

Caprara, G. V., Barbaranelli, C., Pastorelli, C., Bandura, A., & Zimbardo, P. G. (2000). Prosocial foundations of Children's Academic Achievement. *Psychological Science*, *11*(4), 302–306. doi:10.1111/1467-9280.00260 PMID:11273389

Chartrand, J. M., & Rose, M. L. (1996). Career interventions for at-risk populations: Incorporating social cognitive influences. *The Career Development Quarterly, 44*(4), 341–353. doi:10.1002/j.2161-0045.1996.tb00450.x

Chartrand, T. L., & Bargh, J. A. (1999). The chameleon effect: The perception–behavior link and social interaction. *Journal of Personality and Social Psychology, 76*(6), 893–910. doi:10.1037/0022-3514.76.6.893 PMID:10402679

Colarelli, S. M., Dean, R. L., & Konstans, C. (2015). Retaining the next generation of employees: The relationship between work/family balance and turnover intentions. *Group & Organization Management, 40*(3), 282–319.

Collier, P. J., & Morgan, D. L. (2008). "Is that paper really due today?": Differences in first-generation and traditional college students' understandings of faculty expectations. *Higher Education, 55*(4), 425–446. doi:10.1007/s10734-007-9065-5

Coombes, A. E., & Phillips, R. B. (Eds.). (2020). *Museum transformations: Decolonization and democratization*. John Wiley & Sons.

Creswell, J. W. (2012). *Educational research: Planning, conducting, and evaluating quantitative and qualitative research* (4th ed.). Pearson.

Croteau, J. M., & Velez, B. L. (2006). A social cognitive framework for career interventions. *The Career Development Quarterly, 54*(3), 198–211.

Cunningham, A. F., & Kienzl, G. S. (2011). The use of federal work-study funds for service-learning. *Michigan Journal of Community Service Learning, 18*(1), 61–75.

Dean, A., & Fiore, R. (2016). The problem of diversity in museum internship programs: A case study of NYU's Institute of Fine Arts. *Collections, 12*(4), 375–384.

Dolan, J. M., Matthews, G., & Healy, C. C. (2011). Career development learning and employability. *Education + Training, 53*(7), 635–649.

Erdogan, B., Bauer, T. N., Truxillo, D. M., & Mansfield, L. R. (2012). Whistle while you work: A review of the life satisfaction literature. *Journal of Management, 38*(4), 1038–1083. doi:10.1177/0149206311429379

Falk, J. H. (2016). *Identity and the museum visitor experience*. Routledge. doi:10.4324/9781315427058

Federal Student Aid. (n.d.). *Federal Work-Study jobs help students earn money to pay for college or career school*. https://studentaid.gov/understand-aid/types/work-study

Foucault, M., & Gordon, C. (2015). *Power/Knowledge: Selected interviews and other writings 1972-1977*. Vintage Books.

Garriott, P. O., Flores, L. Y., Prabhakar, B., Mazzotta, E. C., Liskov, A. C., & Shapiro, J. E. (2014). Parental support and underrepresented students' math/science interests: The mediating role of learning experiences. *Journal of Career Assessment, 22*(4), 627–641. doi:10.1177/1069072713514933

Gault, J., Leach, E., & Duey, M. (2010). Effects of business internships on job marketability: The employers' perspective. *Education + Training, 52*(1), 76–88. doi:10.1108/00400911011017690

Gibbs, P., & Appleton, J. (2016). Foundation degree and internship programmes for widening participation students: A UK case study. *Widening Participation and Lifelong Learning : the Journal of the Institute for Access Studies and the European Access Network, 18*(3), 8–25.

Gore, P. A. (2019). Disparities in career readiness and employment outcomes for college graduates. *The Career Development Quarterly, 67*(3), 235–249.

Gutchess, A., & Rajaram, S. (2022). Consideration of culture in cognition: How we can enrich methodology and theory. *Psychonomic Bulletin & RE:view, 30*(3), 914–931. doi:10.3758/s13423-022-02227-5 PMID:36510095

Hartung, P. J., Subich, L. M., Bagley, S. B., & Liu, Y. (2002). Exploring congruence between work values and personality: Do congruent people achieve more satisfaction, commitment, and success? *Journal of Career Assessment, 10*(2), 156–177.

Hartung, P. J., & Taber, B. J. (2008). Career construction and subjective well-being. *Journal of Career Assessment, 16*(1), 75–85. doi:10.1177/1069072707305772

Hooper-Greenhill, E. (2015). *Museums and the shaping of knowledge*. Routledge.

Jacobi, M. (1991). Mentoring and undergraduate academic success: A literature review. *Review of Educational Research, 61*(4), 505–532. doi:10.3102/00346543061004505

Johnson, M. (2007). *The meaning of the body: Aesthetics of human understanding*. University of Chicago Press. doi:10.7208/chicago/9780226026992.001.0001

Johnson, M. R., & McCabe, R. H. (2008). Federal work-study participants' and employers' perceptions of skill development. *Journal of College Student Development, 49*(4), 363–382.

Jung, Y., & Love, A. R. (2017). *Systems thinking in museums: theory and practice*. Rowman & Littlefield.

Kim, J., Hagedorn, L. S., Williamson, J. H., & Aquino, J. (2020). The effects of cooperative education participation on student employment and starting salary: A propensity score matching analysis. *Journal of College Student Retention, 22*(1), 61–77.

Knouse, S. B., Tanner, J. R., & Harris, E. W. (2016). Behavioral outcomes of the interview: An examination of college internship programs and student selections. *The Psychologist Manager Journal, 19*(4), 196–220.

Kolb, D. A. (2015). *Experiential learning: Experience as the source of learning and development*. FT Press.

Krumboltz, J. D., Mitchell, A. M., & Jones, G. B. (1976). A social learning theory of career selection. *The Counseling Psychologist, 6*(1), 71–81. doi:10.1177/001100007600600117

Kuh, G. D. (2008). *High-impact educational practices: What they are, who has access to them, and why they matter*. Association of American Colleges and Universities. https://www.aacu.org/publication/high-impact-educational-practices-what-they-are-who-has-access-to-them-and-why-they-matter

Lent, R. W., Brown, S. D., & Hackett, G. (2000). Contextual supports and barriers to career choice: A social cognitive analysis. *Journal of Counseling Psychology, 47*(1), 36–49. doi:10.1037/0022-0167.47.1.36

Lent, R. W., Brown, S. D., & Hackett, G. (2002). Social cognitive career theory. In D. Brown (Ed.), *Career choice and development* (4th ed., pp. 255–311). Jossey-Bass.

Leonard, A. J., Akos, P., & Hutson, B. (2021). The impact of work-study participation on the career readiness of undergraduates. *Journal of Student Financial Aid, 52*(1). Advance online publication. doi:10.55504/0884-9153.1758

Lester, J., & Costley, C. (2010). Work-based learning at higher education level: Value, practice and critique. *Teaching in Higher Education, 15*(3), 291–302.

Long, B. T., & Kurlaender, M. (2009). Do community colleges provide a viable pathway to a baccalaureate degree? *Educational Evaluation and Policy Analysis, 31*(1), 30–53. doi:10.3102/0162373708327756

Lorente, J. P. (2012). The development of museum studies in universities: From technical training to critical museology. *Museum Management and Curatorship, 27*(3), 237–252. doi:10.1080/09647775.2012.701995

Luke, C. (2018). *Museum studies: An anthology of contexts*. John Wiley & Sons.

Merriam, S. B., & Tisdell, E. J. (2016). *Qualitative research: A guide to design and implementation*. Jossey-Bass.

Meyers, S. A. (2005). Part-time work and university students' success: A daily diary analysis. *Journal of Employment Counseling, 42*(2), 74–83.

Middleton, D. (2020). The art museum as educator: A constructive study on African American youth. *Museum Management and Curatorship, 35*(3), 220–234.

Pascarella, E. T., Pierson, C. T., Wolniak, G. C., & Terenzini, P. T. (2004). First-generation college students: Additional evidence on college experiences and outcomes. *The Journal of Higher Education, 75*(3), 249–284. doi:10.1080/00221546.2004.11772256

Ployhart, R. E., Ziegert, J. C., & McFarland, L. A. (2003). Understanding racial differences on cognitive ability tests in selection contexts: An integration of stereotype threat and applicant reactions research. *Human Performance, 16*(3), 231–259. doi:10.1207/S15327043HUP1603_4

Ragins, B. R., & Cotton, J. L. (1999). Mentor functions and outcomes: A comparison of men and women in formal and informal mentoring relationships. *The Journal of Applied Psychology, 84*(4), 529–550. doi:10.1037/0021-9010.84.4.529 PMID:10504893

Rivera, L. A. (2011). Ivies, extracurriculars, and exclusion: Elite employers' use of educational credentials. *Research in Social Stratification and Mobility, 29*(1), 71–90. doi:10.1016/j.rssm.2010.12.001

Roberts, L. (2016). Addressing the lack of diversity in museums: The role of museum studies programs. *American Studies (Lawrence, Kan.), 54*(4), 123–143.

Rose, G. (1997). Situating knowledges: Positionality, reflexivities and other tactics. *Progress in Human Geography, 21*(3), 305–320. doi:10.1191/030913297673302122

Rothwell, W. J., Benscoter, B., King, R., & King, S. (2008). *Beyond training: The rise of learning and performance support*. Human Resource Development Press.

Saldaña, J. (2014). *Ethnodrama: An anthology of reality theatre*. Rowman & Littlefield.

Samis, P. S., & Michaelson, M. (2017). *Creating the visitor-centered museum*. Routledge.

Shapiro, D., Dundar, A., Wakhungu, P. K., Yuan, X., Nathan, A., & Hwang, Y. (2015). Deficit or advantage? The role of federal work-study participation in student outcomes. *ASHE Conference*, 40.

Shepard, L. (2015). Measuring the impact of work-study participation on post-college earnings. *The Annals of the American Academy of Political and Social Science*, 657(1), 160–179.

Sheu, H., & Bin, L. (2010). Testing the choice model of social cognitive career theory across Holland themes: A meta-analytic path analysis. *Journal of Vocational Behavior*, 76(2), 252–264. doi:10.1016/j.jvb.2009.10.015

Shriver, L. H. (2018). Work-study students and the labor market: Do they experience improved employment outcomes? *Journal of College Student Development*, 59(4), 471–476.

Simon, M., & Atkins, J.R. (2011). *The participatory museum*. Museum 2.0.

Simon, N. (2016). *The art of relevance*. Museum 2.0.

Simpson, A. (2019). Why academic museums matter: Four frameworks for considering their value. *University Museums and Collections Journal*, 11(2), 196–202.

Toth, E. L. (2010). Federal Work-Study employment and college students' success. *Review of Higher Education*, 33(3), 399–425.

Tracey, T. J., & Sedlacek, W. E. (1984). Factor structure of the Career Factors Inventory. *Journal of Counseling Psychology*, 31(2), 209–212.

VanMaaren, R. L., & Hooley, T. (2018). 'He is always in my corner': Mentorship support for career development. *Journal of Vocational Behavior*, 105, 1–11.

Velez, W., & Gray, D. E. (2019). Collaborative social class transitioning: Navigating higher education with intersectionality. *Journal of College Student Development*, 60(3), 375–394.

Vigoda-Gadot, E., Grimland, S., & Shoham, A. (2017). The effect of internships on students' career aspirations. *Journal of Education for Business*, 92(5), 221–230.

Villano, R. A., & Patrick, S. W. (2016). The impact of structured university internships on diversity and career trajectory. *Innovative Higher Education*, 44(5), 407–420.

Villarreal, A., Broido, E. M., & Moore, K. B. (2016). Student outcomes of co-curricular involvement: The role of gender, class level, and pre-college experiences. *Journal of College Student Development*, 57(4), 411–427.

Villeneuve, P. (2008). *From periphery to center: Art museum education in the 21st century*. National Art Education Association.

Villeneuve, P., & Love, A. R. (2017). *Visitor-centered exhibitions and edu-curation in art museums*. Rowman and Littlefield.

Wang, Y., Niu, W., & Lent, R. W. (2022). Social cognitive career theory. In P. Robertson, T. Hooley, & P. McCash (Eds.), *The Oxford Handbook of Career Development* (pp. 51–66). Oxford University Press.

Weeden, K., Reed, D., & Espinoza, A. (2019). Internship participation, high-impact educational practices, and student learning. *The Journal of Higher Education*, *90*(3), 348–374.

Weil, S. E. (1999). From being about something to being for somebody: The ongoing transformation of the American museum. *Daedalus*, *128*(3), 229–258.

Yates, M. S. (2017). *Internships: Theory and practice*. Routledge.

Yu, H., Mckinney, L., & Carales, V. D. (2020). Do community college students benefit from Federal Work-study participation? *Teachers College Record*, *122*(1), 1–36. doi:10.1177/016146812012200111

Yuen, M., Zhang, J., Man, P. K. W., Mak, J., Chung, Y. B., Lee, Q. A. Y., Chan, A. K. C., So, A., & Chan, R. T. H. (2022). A strengths-based longitudinal career intervention for junior secondary school students with special educational needs: A mixed-method evaluation. *Applied Research in Quality of Life*, *17*(4), 2229–2250. doi:10.1007/s11482-021-10028-6 PMID:35035601

Zafar, B. (2013). College major choice and the gender earnings gap. *The Journal of Human Resources*, *48*(3), 545–595. doi:10.3368/jhr.48.3.545

## KEY TERMS AND DEFINITIONS

**Auto-Ethnography:** A qualitative research method that utilizes the researcher's personal/ lived experiences as a reflective lens to better understand different social and cultural phenomena.

**Experiential Learning:** An educational approach that emphasizes the acquisition of knowledge and skills through direct engagement with real-world experiences.

**Federal Work Study (FWS):** A U.S. government-funded program that provides part-time employment opportunities for undergraduate and graduate students with demonstrated financial need. Eligible students can secure on-campus or off-campus jobs, typically related to their field of study or community service.

**Internship:** A temporary, supervised work experience that provides students or recent graduates with practical exposure to a specific industry or profession. Internships can be paid or unpaid and fall under the broader umbrella of experiential learning.

**Mentorship:** A developmental relationship in which a more experienced individual (the mentor) provides guidance, support, and advice to a less experienced or individual (the mentee). These relationships can be formal, time bound and/or informal with no set timeframe.

**Narrative Inquiry:** A qualitative research method which focuses on the human experience through the exploration and analysis of stories and narratives. This method allows the researcher to consider the intersection(s) between personal narratives and mezzo and macro social, cultural, political, and economic contexts.

**Self-Efficacy:** An individual's belief in their capacity to successfully execute specific actions or tasks to achieve desired outcomes.

**Social Cognitive Career Theory (SCCT):** A psychological theory that emphasizes the role of social and cognitive factors in shaping an individual's career development and decision-making process. SCCT posits that people's career choices are influenced by their self-efficacy beliefs, outcome expectations, personal goals, and the social context in which they operate, including role models, mentors, and societal expectations. It underscores the significance of observational learning, self-efficacy, and goal setting in career development, highlighting the interplay between individual agency and environmental influences.

**Transferable Skill:** Are versatile proficiencies that can be applied across various roles, industries, and contexts, enabling individuals to adapt to different work environments and tasks. E.g., critical thinking, teamwork, and problem-solving.

## APPENDIX 1

General

- When did you start at the museum?
- What was your major, minor, age, and academic year?
- How long were you at the museum? Did your role change?

On FWS

- From your perspective and experience, what are the advantages of federal work study programs?
- From your perspective and experience, what are the gaps of/in federal work study programs?

On Museums

- What was your understanding of/ or relationship to museums before you became employed?

On Student Ambassador Role

- Why did you initially want to be employed at the museum?
- What was your understanding of the position? How did it change during your employment?
- What did you hope to experience in your role when you were first hired?
- What did you experience in your role? What was your favorite part of your experience? What was your least favorite part of your experience?

Transferable Skills+ Reflections

- What transferable skill did you hope to cultivate when you were first hired at the museum?
- How did your time being employed at the museum inform your future career choices?
- If you were to describe the role of museums and what it is like to work for a museum to a stranger what would you say?

## What Else?

## APPENDIX 2

- Y'all mentioned that, at times, you did not feel supported by some staff at the museum. Could you elaborate on this and provide examples?

- Reflecting on your experience, how would you define a successful Student Ambassador role? What would it look like? How would participants feel during and after their experience?
- What is some advice you would give, or suggestions you would offer to admin to make the STUDENT AMBASSADOR role more effective?
- What is some advice you would give other institutions who were interested in building a similar program?
- Any other thoughts/ comments?

## APPENDIX 3

## Museum Studies Courses in the USA and Europe

While we have considered informal education in regards to preparing students for a career in the museum sector. Here we briefly review literature on formal degree programs in museology and/or museum studies in the USA and Europe.

In both the USA and Europe, Museum Studies programs typically offer a multidisciplinary curriculum that covers various aspects of museum management, curation, conservation, community programming, and education. In Europe, Museum Studies programs frequently offer one-year master's degrees. In contrast, American programs tend to offer both master's and graduate certificate options, with varying program lengths, catering to a wider range of career goals and backgrounds (Middleton, 2020).

European Museum Studies programs often strongly emphasize cultural heritage preservation and management, reflecting museums' traditional and colonial history. These programs may offer specialized courses on heritage conservation, archaeology, art museums/ galleries, and cultural policy (Simpson, 2019). In the USA, Museum Studies programs focus more broadly on museum management, policy, and public engagement.

Museum Studies programs in both regions increasingly recognize the importance of global perspectives. European programs may emphasize international collaborations and the impact of globalization on museums (Lorente, 2012). American programs often incorporate discussions of global trends in museology and cultural heritage.

Both American and European Museum Studies programs are increasingly addressing issues of diversity, equity, accessibility and inclusion in the museum field. Courses on cultural sensitivity, repatriation, and decolonization are becoming more prevalent in response to growing awareness of these issues (Anderson, 2020; Coombes et al, 2020).

Museum Studies courses in the USA and Europe aim to prepare professionals for careers in the museum and cultural heritage sector. However, they exhibit differences in curriculum, pedagogical approaches, program duration, and cultural heritage emphasis. Regional educational traditions, museum landscapes, and broader cultural contexts influence these distinctions.

These programs vary from the program discussed in the chapter, in that, they are considered formal education. FWS programs offer students who are not seeking a specific Museum Studies degree, experience within the museum sector. This approach to informal education allows students to cultivate experience in an area—museums—that intersects with their formal degree program or personal interest. This exposure can potentially help them set future personal and professional goals.

## APPENDIX 4

### Limitations/Delimitations of the Study

#### Limitations

This research is grounded in qualitative research, reflecting case studies and auto-ethnographic methods. The findings are not intended to be generalizable to all university museum federal work-study programs. Instead, I share a case study of contemporary professional practice for other institutions to reference as they build or modify their programs.

I also recognize my positionality–how I view and engage with the world from a specific and perpetual fluctuating space (Bourke, 2014, Rose, 1997)—impacts how the data was interpreted. Additionally, while the chapter highlights a lack of diversity within professional museum practice and states that participants of the Student Ambassador are a diverse demographic, the socio economic, cultural and ethnic diversity of the participants who agreed to be interviewed for this chapter is limited.

Finally, the reader must acknowledge that my choice to focus on a case study informs the breadth and scope of the responses and conclusions discussed in the chapter. If I were to expand upon this study, I would interview student workers from similar programs in different countries.

#### Delimitations

I crafted the guiding questions for my first interview set based on the call to chapters guidelines. As mentioned in the chapter, the informal dynamics of internal staff are explored in my presentation of my relationships with my colleagues as reflected in the character profiles I wrote, and in the notes taken during data collection regarding the transformation of interviews into dialogues with colleagues. It must be understood that the four characters have their own professional and personal relationships that they have formed with their colleagues and may have influenced comments about work peers.

If I were to pursue a study of this nature again, I would consider interviewing at least one student worker from each year of the program as well as the new program manager. I would also consider interviewing faculty from Museum Studies programs to explore if/how FWS or similar programs might be embedded into degree programs.

## APPENDIX 5

My research was conducted using text-based coding and data analysis adhering to the following steps:

- transcription of interview one

- first read-through of group interview
- second read-through with coding notes of selected SCCT themes
- expansion of coding themes
- follow up questions in shared Google documents
- read-through of the second interview with coding notes from interview one to check for consistency and inconsistency in themes (Creswell, 2012).

To include my perspective and experience and create an audit trail, I journaled about my assumptions, thoughts, hunches, questions, methodological concerns, and realizations made throughout the coding process.

Coding is "an interpretive act" that can "summarize, distill, or condense data, not simply reduce them" (Saldaña, 2016, p. 5). Or put another way, coding is a process that looks for patterns in using words, ideas, or themes. As such, other codes emerged due to the repetition of ideas of themes that emerged during the group interview. The codes were used to analyze the interviews and my research journal. The first round of coding categories are listed below:

- P-positive
- N-negative
- NT-Neutral
- Mentorship
- observational learning
- self-efficacy
- goal setting
- MQ-Memorable quotes

After my initial round of coding, *goal setting* was removed from the code, and two sub-codes emerged related to self-efficacy:

- transferable skills
- sector-specific skills

This approach uncovered new topics or concerns that framed my follow-up questions in the Google document. The questions asked in the follow-up were:

- Y'all mentioned that, at times, you did not feel supported by some staff at the museum. Could you elaborate on this and provide examples?
- Reflecting on your experience, how would you define a successful student ambassador role? What would it look like? How would participants feel during and after their experience?
- What is some advice you would give, or suggestions you would offer to admin to make the student ambassador role more effective?
- What is some advice you would give other institutions who were interested in building a similar program?
- Any other thoughts/ comments?

To maintain consistency, responses were coded using the same categories as the updated initial group interview, and the category of *suggestions* was added as a code to ensure that the students' voices and suggestions were presented. As such, the codes became:

- Mentorship
- Observational learning
- Self-efficacy
  - transferable skills
  - sector-specific skills
- Suggestions

## APPENDIX 6

In 2016, the average median income in the United States was 59,039 USD or 28.38 USD hourly for 40 hours a week. The average annual salary of staff eligible for benefits at the museum in the case study–defined by the institution as working 20+ hours a week–was 39,776.44 USD annually or 19.12 USD hourly. The highest hourly salary of this sample was 34 USD hourly (71,671 USD annually) for the Associate Director and lead curator. The lowest hourly salary was for the head of Marketing and Communications, at 18.26 hourly (38,000 USD annually).

# APPENDIX 7

*Figure 1. Section one of an example of an annual student ambassador performance self-assessment—formatted as a Google form*

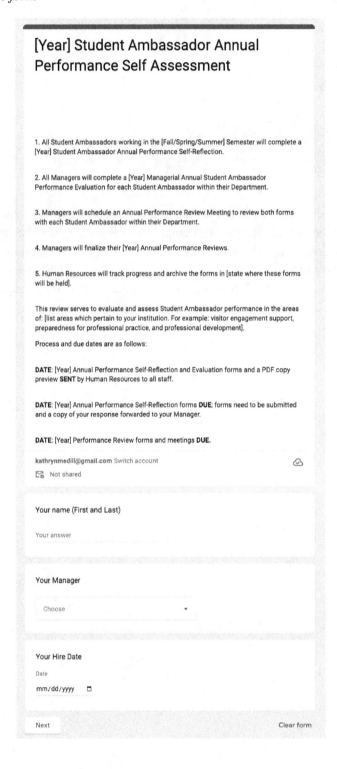

*Figure 2. Section two of an example of an annual student ambassador performance self-assessment—formatted as a Google form*

**Visitor Engagement Support**

Visitor engagement support is a key element of your role at the museum. The museum defines best practices in Visitor Engagement as, per the Student Ambassador handbook as:

- Interpretive Programming: Assist with the creation, implementation and or assessment of diverse programs such as guided tours, interactive workshops, and artist talks to provide visitors with a deeper understanding of the artworks and the context in which they were created.
- Interactive Exhibits: Assist with the creation, implementation and or assessment of interactive elements like touch screens, multimedia installations, and hands-on activities to encourage active participation and a more immersive experience for visitors.
- Digital Integration: Assist with the creation, implementation and or assessment of technology to enhance visitor engagement through mobile apps, virtual reality experiences, and augmented reality features that provide additional information and insights about the artworks on display.
- Diverse Perspectives: Assist with the creation, implementation and or assessment of presenting a variety of perspectives and narratives in the exhibits to cater to a diverse audience, fostering inclusivity and promoting a more comprehensive understanding of art and culture.
- Visitor-Friendly Signage: Assist with the creation, implementation and or assessment of clear and concise signage with engaging content that provides relevant information without overwhelming visitors, helping them navigate the museum and understand the significance of the displayed artworks.
- Community Involvement: Assist with the creation, implementation and or assessment of fostering community engagement by organizing community-based programs, collaborations with local artists, and outreach initiatives that encourage participation and collaboration from the local community.
- Hands-On Learning: Assist with the creation, implementation and or assessment of offering interactive educational activities, workshops, and art-making sessions that enable visitors, especially children and families, to actively participate in the creative process and gain a deeper appreciation for the arts.
- Personalized Experiences: Assist with the creation, implementation and or assessment of providing customizable experiences through personalized tours, audio guides, and tailored content that cater to the specific interests and preferences of individual visitors, enhancing their overall museum experience.
- Visitor Feedback: Assist with the creation, implementation and or assessment of visitor feedback through surveys, comment boxes, and online platforms to understand their needs and preferences, allowing the museum to continuously improve its offerings and enhance visitor engagement.
- Accessibility and Inclusivity: Assist with the creation, implementation and or assessment of ensuring that the museum is accessible to all visitors, including those with disabilities, by offering wheelchair accessibility, braille materials, audio descriptions, and other accommodations to make the museum experience inclusive and welcoming for everyone.

Visitor Engagement Support

1. Below Average / Sometimes Misses Expectations
2. Average / Usually Meets Expectations
3. Above Average / Often Exceeds Expectations
4. Exceptional / Always Exceeds Expectations
5. Sets a New Standard of Performance

|   | 1 | 2 | 3 | 4 | 5 |   |
|---|---|---|---|---|---|---|
| Below Average | ○ | ○ | ○ | ○ | ○ | Sets a New Standard of Performace |

Assess your Visitor Engagement Support and your ability to incorporate best practices in Visitor Engagement Support in [current year]. Assess your ability to adhere to the Museum's policies that reinforce these practices. Address what areas of Visitor Engagement Support you excel in and what specific improvements you would like to make moving into [the next year/term].

*Figure 3. Section two of an example of an annual student ambassador performance self-assessment—formatted as a Google form*

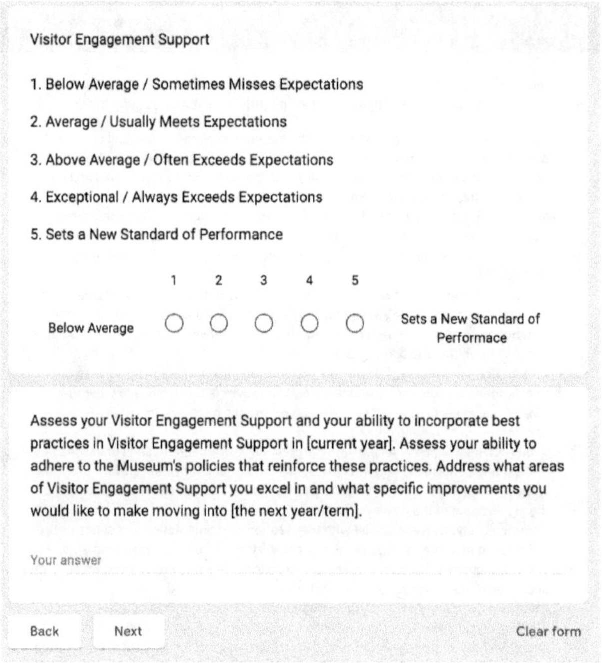

*Figure 4. Section three of an example of an annual student ambassador performance self-assessment—formatted as a Google form*

**Preparedness for Professional Practice**

Preparedness for Professional Practice is a key element of the Student Ambassador role. That is, the Museum works to create a position which supports your transition from academia to professional practice. The Museum defines best practice for Preparedness for Professional Practice as, per the Student Ambassador handbook as:

- Time Management: Plan and prioritize your tasks by setting clear goals and deadlines, and use time management techniques such as creating to-do lists and using digital calendars to stay on track.
- Effective Communication: Practice clear and concise communication with colleagues, supervisors, and visitors, both verbally and in written correspondence, to ensure that everyone is on the same page and expectations are well understood.
- Continuous Learning: Stay updated with the latest industry trends and developments by engaging in continuous learning through professional development courses, workshops, webinars, and industry-related literature.
- Adaptability: Be open to change and willing to adapt to new technologies, work processes, and challenges in the workplace to demonstrate your flexibility and problem-solving skills.
- Professional Etiquette: Maintain a professional demeanor by adhering to workplace etiquette, dressing appropriately, being punctual, and respecting the boundaries of colleagues and visitors.
- Collaboration: Foster a collaborative work environment by actively participating in team discussions, sharing ideas, and supporting your colleagues to achieve common goals and foster a positive work culture.
- Organization: Keep your workspace organized and clutter-free, and develop a systematic approach for managing files, documents, and digital data to facilitate easy access and retrieval when needed.
- Attention to Detail: Pay close attention to detail in your work to ensure accuracy and precision, and double-check your work before submitting it to avoid errors and unnecessary rework.
- Problem-Solving Skills: Cultivate strong problem-solving skills by analyzing complex situations, identifying potential challenges, and implementing effective solutions that align with the organization's goals and objectives.
- Networking: Build and maintain professional relationships by networking with peers, mentors, and industry professionals to expand your professional network, gain valuable insights, and create potential career opportunities.

Preparedness for Professional Practice

1. Below Average / Sometimes Misses Expectations

2. Average / Usually Meets Expectations

3. Above Average / Often Exceeds Expectations

4. Exceptional / Always Exceeds Expectations

5. Sets a New Standard of Performance

|  | 1 | 2 | 3 | 4 | 5 |  |
|---|---|---|---|---|---|---|
| Below Average | ○ | ○ | ○ | ○ | ○ | Sets a New Standard of Performace |

Assess your Preparedness for Professional Practice and your ability to incorporate best practices in Visitor Engagement Support in [current year]. Assess your ability to adhere to the Museum's policies that reinforce these practices. Address what areas ofPreparedness for Professional Practice you excel in and what specific improvements you would like to make moving into [the next year/term].

Your answer

Back    Next                                                    Clear form

*Figure 5. Section four of an example of an annual student ambassador performance self-assessment—formatted as a Google form*

## APPENDIX 8

*Figure 6. Section one of an example of an annual student ambassador performance managerial-assessment—formatted as a Google form*

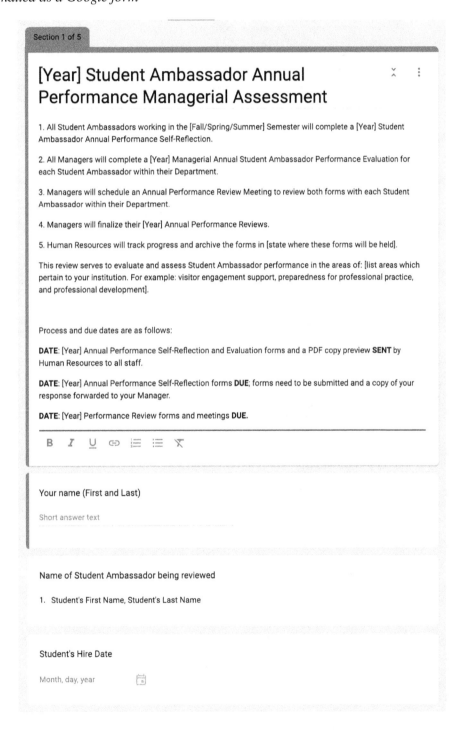

*Figure 7. Section two of an example of an annual student ambassador performance managerial-assessment—formatted as a Google form*

*Figure 8. Section three of an example of an annual student ambassador performance managerial-assessment—formatted as a Google form*

*Figure 9. Sections four and five of an example of an annual student ambassador performance managerial-assessment—formatted as a Google form*

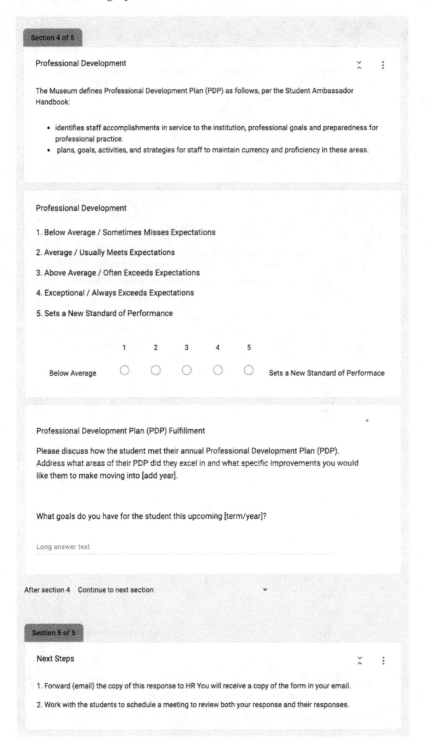

## APPENDIX 9

Below is an example of a form museums could use to promote and define engagement with Student Ambassadors for staff.

### Context

As a way to ensure that our institutional support of Student Ambassadors' transitions from academia to professional practice each semester departments are required to determine how they will create opportunities for engagement and mentorship with our Student Ambassadors. Each department must offer at total [state the number of hours the institution requires] amount of engagement hours per semester for the Student Ambassadors. Engagement is broken down into three categories: observation, mentorship and applied practice.

- Observation: Staff provide students with a list of dates/times/location in which they can observe career specific moment. I.e., the curatorial department could list dates and times when artists are installing, the development office could invite students to sit in and observe a meeting with donors or a grant review.
- Mentorship: Staff initiate and schedule discussions with Student Ambassadors pertaining to your specialties, upcoming work and lived experiences within the museum sector.
- Applied Practice: Opportunities for Student Ambassadors to contribute to your work. I.e., the curatorial department could ask Student Ambassadors to write one wall label per exhibition. The preparators could ask students to install one piece of art per semester. The registrar could ask students to write one condition report for a piece in the permanent collect each semester.

    Questions

1. List the tentative titles and dates for your upcoming exhibitions, or major projects.
2. Share which type(s) of engagement you could cultivate for each exhibition or project.
3. State roughly how many hours of engagement you can offer per exhibition/project.
4. What support do you need in order to offer engagement to the Student Ambassadors?

## APPENDIX 10

Examples of potential questions that could be added to staff reviews to support staffs' reflection on their professional relationship with the student workers.

Questions

1. Describe the ways in which you engaged with the Student Ambassadors this semester. Provide at least one specific example.
2. Describe how working with the Student Ambassadors impacted your professional practice this semester. What went well/expanded your practice? What needs to be reconsidered for next semester?

# Chapter 7
# Student Challenges During COVID-19:
## Can Experiential Learning Be Effective Online?

**Erika Galindo-Bello**
https://orcid.org/0000-0002-5465-0434
*Universidad de las Américas, Puebla, Mexico*

## ABSTRACT

*During the COVID-19 pandemic, internships were translated into home office modality; organizations, universities, and students faced significant challenges to which they had to adapt in a short period of time. This chapter describes the effects of COVID-19 in the experiential learning activities, specifically the case of internship programs for marketing students at an emerging market university, in order to learn about their experiences during the pandemic and incorporate the lessons in post pandemic experiences. Students and organizations were surveyed to know about their internship experiences and perceptions. Results indicate that under certain conditions, online internship experiences can be successful.*

## INTRODUCTION

The Labor market is highly competitive, and there is a need to provide students with practical experience and adequate skills (Edmondson, D., & Matthews, L., 2021; Cerych, L., & Frost-Smith, B., 1985; Asmara, A., & Ming-Chang, W., 2020). Latin America is home to diverse natural hazards including recurrent climate shocks earthquakes, droughts, floods, landslides, tropical storms, and hurricanes. For example, the smaller-scale antecedents such SARS-CoV of 2003 the H1N1 pandemic of 2009, or the Spanish Influenza (1918-1919). It seems relevant that students must be prepared to understand and overcome the effects disasters can have on academics and career paths. Building a resilient education system is compulsory for all countries.

DOI: 10.4018/978-1-7998-7999-2.ch007

In the early months of the pandemic, UNESCO estimated that at least 1.3 billion children and youth were out of school and that school closures occurred in at least 138 countries (UNESCO Institute for Statistics 2020). Due to COVID-19 school closures ran longer in Latin America and the Caribbean than anywhere in the world, leaving 86 million children out of classrooms (OCHA, 2021).

The pandemic covid-19 represented a challenge for education (The World Bank, UNESCO, and UNICEF, 2021) the crisis exacerbated inequality in education. The mental health crisis among young people has reached unprecedented levels. Advances in gender equality are threatened, with school closures placing an estimated 10 million more girls at risk of early marriage in the next decade and at increased risk of dropping out of school. According to Unesco, (The World Bank, UNESCO, and UNICEF, 2021) the COVID-19 crisis forced the global education community to learn some critical lessons but also highlighted that transformation and innovation are possible. Countries have an opportunity to accelerate learning and make schools more efficient, equitable, and resilient by building on investments made and lessons learned during the crisis. The faculty had to adapt their teaching practices to new technologies and distance learning. Otherwise, Companies faced important challenges taking actions such as reducing costs, looking for new opportunities, and adapting to the new context for survival.

Unesco defines the term "learning loss" as any loss of knowledge or skills and/or deceleration of or interruption to academic progress, most commonly due to extended gaps or discontinuities in a student's education (The World Bank, UNESCO, and UNICEF, 2021).

The pandemic reveals that digital technologies make the world more deeply interconnected and interdependent than ever before, but also more divided. Remote and Hybrid education is here to stay (The World Bank, UNESCO, and UNICEF (2021). School closures are not unique to COVID-19 and are likely to occur in the future as a result of climate-related natural disasters, conflicts, and public health emergencies (The World Bank, UNESCO, and UNICEF, 2021) it seems necessary to be prepared to avoid the learning loss.

The drastic changes in the learning environment and learning methods have led to student resilience (Meshram, K., Paladino, A., & Cotronei-Baird, V. S.; 2022). Remote learning requires considerable effort by a student about how much time to invest in learning (Núñez Pérez, J. C., et al., 2011), students had to improve some skills like time management, technology skills, self-learning, and self-evaluation. Also, previous research indicates that students' growing anxiety related to remote learning (Peltier, J. W., Chennamaneni, P. R., & Barber, K. N., 2022). Students also had to deal with social distancing, social desirability, and social information in a significant way (Meshram, K., 2022) the situation of confinement during the most restrictive period of the pandemic led to situations of social isolation that caused emotional problems for the students and influenced their performance (Sáiz-Manzanares M-C, et al., 2022). Internship experiences help students integrate into the world of work in a guided way, from the Academic World to Career Paths. At the beginning of the pandemic, students were reluctant to do an internship online. Some students considered the option of delaying their plan to participate in an internship, bearing in mind that the contingency was temporary. However, over time they had to do an internship online in order not to affect their graduation process.

According to the report of the World Economic Forum (2020), the pandemic has left a displacement of the labor market and employers are making post-covid adaptations to their strategies, among which are, firstly, the acceleration of the automation of the work process (e.g. use of digital tools, video conferencing) and secondly, 80% of companies plan to provide more opportunities to work remotely. The demand from employers for remote-based work is increasing rapidly across economies, also has nearly doubled the demand from job seekers. There is an emerging marketplace for remote work. The pandemic shows a new hybrid way of working is possible at a greater scale than imaged in previous years.

According to the world economic forum report (2020), during the pandemic, new skills in self-management such as active learning, resilience, stress tolerance, and flexibility. Manpower group (2020), indicates that 3 in 4 employers report difficulty finding the talent they need, with the right blend of technical skills and human strengths. In the same report, indicates that human strengths stand out in the digital age and the main skills identified in order of importance are: 1. reliability & self-discipline, 2. resilience & adaptability, 3. reasoning & problem-solving, creativity & originality, and critical thinking & analysis.

According to the Organization for Economic Co-operation and Development (OECD), many young people put their life on hold during the pandemic, the people who are now ending their university education or finishing during the pandemic are particularly exposed to unemployment in the short term. Young people will need particular attention. The consequences of COVID-19 have fallen disproportionately on the young's livelihoods and labor market prospects. OECD (2021), specifies the importance, of developing a program of measures to protect these young workers and provide them with an initial foothold in the labor market, preparing them for future opportunities.

The COVID-19 pandemic raised major challenges for the delivery of career guidance services particularly relevant to ensure that workers' skills remain up to date and to help them match with the most suitable jobs by facilitating better matches between workers and jobs. According to Quintini, et al., (2022) the most relevant career guidance activities young people needs for the near future are Individual information and advice, Job-search assistance, Career education and training, Skills assessment/career assessments, and tests, Networking with professionals and employers. It seems necessary that universities help students with a transition model from academic to the labor market, students must adapt to the emerging needs of the global labor market. According to World Economic Forum (2022), most jobs performed in 2018 did not exist in 1940 and close to 60% of jobs done in 2018 had not yet been "invented" in 1940. The skills and competencies required for the future are changing.

The first objective of the chapter is to understand the effects of Covid-19 pandemic on academic and career paths, specifically the case of internship as a transition model from the academic world to the labor market, for marketing students of an emerging market university. The second objective is to impart knowledge about considerations that educators, students, and companies must incorporate into their internship programs and experiences to improve career paths. The research questions that will be addressed in this chapter are: Can experiential learning be effective online? what are the lessons for marketing educators, students, and companies after the pandemic Covid-19?. The results will be used to learn about the experience during the pandemic and incorporate the lessons into post-pandemic experiences, to help students to incorporate successful internship experiences into career paths.

## BACKGROUND

The university at which this research was carried out is a Mexican private university located in San Andrés Cholula, near Puebla. It is considered to be one of the most prestigious universities in Latin America, as well as being one of the only seven universities in Latin America accredited by the Southern Association of Colleges and Schools. The campus is made up of 38 buildings on 180 acres (728,000 m2). The School of Business and Economics (SBE) is the largest of the five Schools at Universidad de las Américas Puebla (UDLAP). SACSCOC accredits the university since 1959, currently as a level VI institution. The SBE was founded in 1970 and now offers eight undergraduate and seven master's programs. The school of Business and Economics (SBE) is AACSB accredited since March 2021. All programs offered by the SBE are accredited by National agencies.

The marketing department offers the Marketing undergraduate degree, which has been ranked first place in Mexico for 8 years and has had a sustained growth in enrolment. It has two innovative laboratories in Mexico, the Laboratory of Qualitative Research and Innovation and the market intelligence laboratory, The marketing students have to do an internship in an external organization, in a mandatory way as part of the marketing curricula.

Through time and experience, the process that students must follow to do an internship has been improved, the students have to plan their internship period and start the process one semester before initiation. *Figure 1*, shows the main components and steps of the process marketing students follow to ensure their successful internship experiences. During the application process, the student receives online training on topics such as how to prepare a CV or letter position, and how to prepare for an interview. On the other hand, the administrative staff of the university carries out a process of promotion and search for opportunities in the organization. Each organization presents documentation accrediting its existence, and its official registration with the government authorities and presents the internship project or mission, administrative staff, and faculty review each organization and each internship vacancy to ensure that the mission or project is aligned with the profile and learning needs of the students.

Students must enroll in an internship course, which is compulsory for all students. In this course, the teacher asks for reports and advises the student if necessary, during the internship in the selected organization. In the reports, the student identifies a problem in the organization and proposes solutions under the problem-solving methodology. At the end of the internship period, the student makes a self-reflection about his/her performance, learning, shortcomings, and opportunities.

An important component of an internship program is the evaluation, companies evaluate the performance of the students and students evaluate their placement. The final grade students receive in the internship course is a weighting between the assessment received from the organization and the grades assigned by the faculty to the reports submitted.

The internship course is a capstone course in the curricula, in this course learning outcomes are measured by faculty, to identify opportunities for improvement and for plan closing the loop actions, for process improvement or curriculum improvement. The expectation is that students can link theory with practice by first understanding and then solving a real problem inherent to marketing, proposing a solution, and being aware of the impact and changes this solution may bring about.

## ISSUES, CONTROVERSIES, PROBLEMS

Pandemic COVID-19 has changed learning and working conditions. The managers of the analyzed university decided to continue with the academic activities in an online mode to meet the planned learning objectives. To understand the problems, issues, and controversies faced during the pandemic by managers, students, and university managers some semi-structured interviews were conducted. The director of the marketing department and some students from the marketing department who completed internships during the pandemic period were interviewed and company managers were interviewed. According to the results of interviews, the opportunities for internship companies offered were scarce and limited to

*Figure 1. The internship program, steps students follow up https://www.udlap.mx/practicasprofesion/*

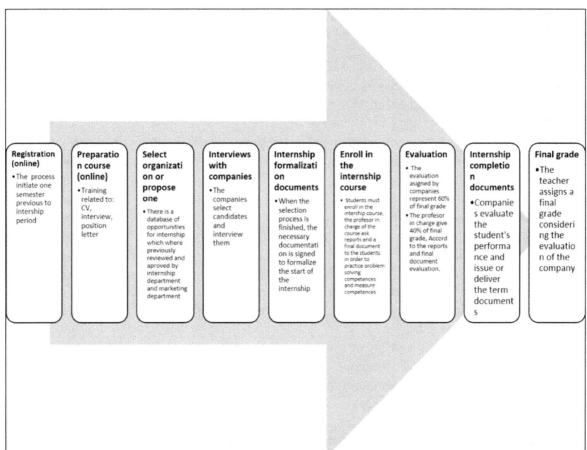

digital activities. Some students decided to wait for the contingency to pass and for commercial activities to be reactivated on a face-to-face basis or change their academic plans delaying their graduation date. Others students decided to continue with their plans and look for an online internship. The first work experience regularly excites students and many of them expect it can be a great opportunity to have a presence in the labor market, apply their knowledge, and meet professionals in the field. The closure of opportunities for face-to-face internships represented a great disappointment for many students.

*"I was looking forward to doing an internship, so during the pandemic, I decided not to do an internship and while the contingency passed, I enrolled in more advanced semester courses"- Paulina, last year student*

*"The opportunities offered by the companies for internships were few and the activities to be carried out did not seem interesting to me"- Jose Luis, Last year´s student*

In times of crisis, there are opportunities and important changes, students and faculty had to make decisions between adapting to new opportunities and continuing with curricular training through experiential learning or suspending and continuing with traditional learning models.

*"During the first months of the pandemic, most students decided to stop their plans for internships, but as the months passed and the contingency continued, students had to adapt and do internships online"- Director of the marketing department*

The companies were focused on migrating their operations to a digital form at a lower cost. Time passed and organizations faced a strong digital and marketing need, which translated into online internship opportunities for students.

*"We had to reinforce in a few months the sale of products through the web and we faced logistical problems because we were not prepared for the growth in online sales and home delivery"- Ghary Director of Departmental Retail store*

On the other hand, organizations were not prepared for the home office mode, in many cases, they did not have the technological tools, training, and management skills to manage their human resources in a home office environment.

*"During the first months of the pandemic, we had to suspend the internship and trainee opportunities, but over time we found ways to organize our processes, and the opportunities for remote work increased"- Pedro, Director of a Consulting company*

The faculty was skeptical of the scope and success that could be obtained by carrying out an online internship in such a critical environment. For the students, it was already a challenge to continue their studies in the online modality and they were facing difficulties, in addition to this, their first online work experience represented a great challenge for all.

In an interview, the Director of the Marketing Department mentioned that during the pandemic, all the processes and steps students have to do to apply for an internship were online, the training, the documents, the interviews, etc. the problem for some disciplines were the lack of opportunities and vacancies for online internships, it was necessary to reinforce the search for opportunities. At the most critical moment of the pandemic, it was considered the possibility of generating internal applied projects to meet the demand of students, to complete their internships and finish their studies. In the case of marketing students, it was not necessary to generate internal projects because there were always unmet needs on the part of the companies for marketing students to help them in their online survival.

Currently, the pandemic is controlled, and commercial and educational activities have returned to the face-to-face modality, however, there is a new normal environment, organizations and individuals have changed, and is necessary to stop for learn from the experience and adapt experiential learning to the new normal (Krishnamurthy, S., 2020).

## CAN EXPERIENTIAL LEARNING BE EFFECTIVE ONLINE?

The research efforts about online learning during Covid-19 indicate that a fully online blended learning course can be designed and delivered effectively, the problems with technology or software are significant factors for dissatisfaction (Carouglu, 2022). The success of online activities is highly dependent on faculty time and effort. Online experiential learning tools are crucial for effective learning experiences in skill-based disciplines, however, most courses are not designed for experiential learning, and this narrowed the present experiences with online experiential learning (Daalhuizen, 2018)

In the literature the benefits of online learning tools in the support of experiential learning have recently emerged, there is some disagreement about how much technology can and should be used, o due to the idea that teacher education cannot be effectively accomplished in an online setting (Snow, 2029). The transition of courses to an online setting has enabled the sharing of experiences and a sense of community among the students and provided significant flexibility (Snow, 2019). Otherwise, the asynchronous environments, punctuated with critical deadlines, create space for students to develop time management and self-directed learning skills. Literature indicates that the online mode can play an important role in skills development and fostering an authentic learning experience (Snow, 2019).

Without experiential learning, the online classroom environment can easily become a closed-off place (Kaminstein et al., 2022). Real-time learning is not available through lecture discussions, which is the format most often used in virtual settings. The need for research on conducting experiential education online is urgent. Too little research exists that examines experiential learning in an online environment, most of the studies use asynchronous solutions (Carver et al., 2007). More research to compare and contrast asynchronous and synchronous online learning is needed to examine what is working and what is not (Kaminstein et, al., 2022)

After the spread of COVID-19, Remote work has become increasingly popular and important. The research indicates that employees are more productive when they work from home and that, they can improve their work-life balance by working this way Technology favors remote work, makes the time of the employees more flexible (Xu, S. et al. 2018; Reshma et al, 2015; Mostafa, 2021). Other authors declare vice versa (Mostafa, 2021). The research identifies some disadvantages of working from home, even if it is related to job satisfaction working longer hours than employees are paid, which can generate family problems, and also can lead to more stress, work-life conflicts, and negative well-being (Jehanzeb et al, 2012). Remote work brings time flexibility but managing time is a concern for employees due to personal and professional duties (Mostafa, 2021). Psychological well-being might be affected due to loneliness feelings and missing human interaction (Mostafa, 2021; Grzegorz Kowalski, 2022). The work-life balance can be achieved by distinguishing: personal space and time, care time and space, and work time and space (Turnea, 2021).

Understanding remote work effectiveness is crucial, especially since remote working offers indisputable convenience, which will contribute to its expansiveness in the organizational setting compared to the pre-COVID-19 level (Grzegorz Kowalski, 2022). The COVID-19 pandemic compels organizations to develop work-from-home policies, working online is experiencing a crucial boost, there is a possibility that this crisis will permanently change the way we work. There may be no going back as the pandemic has shown that working from home is possible and employees can achieve their goals (Mirabela-Constanta et al. 2020). The labor market is highly competitive, and there is a need to provide students with practical experience, the pandemic covid-19 represented a challenge for education. The future of jobs after the pandemic includes a significant expansion of remote work, with the potential to move 44% of their workforce to operate remotely (World Economic Forum, 2020). Some questions are relevant for creating a new normality for experiential learning through internships, first is necessary to know if experiential learning is effective online. What are the lessons for marketing educators and companies after the pandemic Covid-19?

## THEORETICAL FRAMEWORK

### Experiential Learning

Literature learning theories can be divided into two categories, the first is cognitivist which refers to learning as internal meaning-making structures of an adult. The second is constructivism, which refers to learning as a reflective process of personal interpretation of experience. Experiential learning is part of Constructivism (Kumar, S., et al. 2020).

Marketing education literature moves from traditional passive knowledge transfer to an experimental and interactive method for learning (Frontczak, 1998). A trend in the 1990s in marketing education literature was experiential Learning, the variety and scope of new experiential learning activities have grown in variety over time. There is no single definition for Experiential Learning, most of them include a direct and real experience with reflection and analysis (Frontczak, 1998; Kumar, S., & Bhandarker, A., 2020).

Kolb (1984) defined Experiential learning as "the process whereby knowledge is created through the transformation of experience. Kolb´s model (2005) is one of the most relevant in the literature, presenting learning as a cyclical process with four stages: experiencing, reflecting, thinking, and acting. Kolb's Model and its Learning theory have been applied by various researchers (Young, M. R., 2002; Frontczak, N. T., 1998; Satyam, & Aithal, R. K., 2022; Hayden, S. C., & Osborn, D. S., 2020; Colombari, R., D'Amico, E., & Paolucci, E., 2021). Greene (2011) mentioned that "Experiential Learning is learning by doing". Previous researchers applied Kolb's model for designing teaching experiences, to test the efficacy of experiences in different disciplines (Kumar, S., et al., 2020)

### Internships as a Transition Model to the World of Work

Doing an internship is a great opportunity for students to have a high-impact learning experience is a link between knowledge and real life (O'Neill, N., 2010; Lastner, M. M., & Rast, R. (2016; Binder, J. F., Baguley, T., Crook, C., & Miller, F., 2015). The internship literature explores the knowledge and skills practiced (Johansson, I., et al., 2020; Varghese, M. E., et al., 2012; Hergert, M., et al., 2009; Lopes, B., et al., 2019), link industry-university (Virolainen, M. H., et al., 2011; Cojocariu, V. M., et al., 2019), the contribution of internship experience to career development and employability (O'Neill, N., 2010; Gault, J., et al., 2000; O'Connor, H., et al., 2017; Helyer, R., et al., 2014; Bittmann, F., et al., 2020; Hergert, M., 2009; Virolainen, M. H. et al 2011; Silva, P., et al., 2018).

There are different research efforts to determine the nature and conditions of a successful internship program, some of them explore if internships must be mandatory or voluntary (Bittmann, F., 2020), whether they must be structured for short periods at different points in the curriculum or as a single period towards the end of the curriculum (Bittmann, F. et al., 2020; Varghese, M. E., et al., 2012), there are also opposing views on the perception of students (O'Connor, H., 2017; Hergert, M., 2009; Gault, J., et al., 2000) some students see it as an opportunity and others as exploitation, and there are also different views from employers (Virolainen, M. H., 2011; Cojocariu, V. M, 2019; Sanahuja Vélez, G., et al., 2015; Helyer, R., et al., 2014).

Research confirms that there are great benefits for students to undertake an internship, for those who have not had experience or awareness of opportunities in the labor market, it can help them understand "the world of work and build professional experience and sometimes discover what they do not want to do (O'Neill, N., 2010). Researchers have also been concerned about achieving high-impact internships (Helyer, R., et al. D., 2014; O'Neill, N., 2010; Bittmann, F., et al., 2020; Johansson, I., et al., 2020).

Students' transition into a labor world has been identified as problematic by both graduates and employers, main problems are insufficient preparation for the culture of the workplace, unrealistically high expectations of work, and more. The internships may help reduce the discrepancy between the expectations of graduates and the requirements of managers (Auburn, T., et al. 1993). Work experience contributes to the development of career management competencies and reinforces student and graduate employability (Jackson, D., & Wilton, N. (2016).

## Capstone Course and Career Competences

The literature on school-to-work transitions has primarily focused on the preparation of students, for entering the workforce. Emphasis has been on how youth develop skills through education and training to support their future employment (Popadiuk N. E., 2014).

The literature evidences the importance of planning capstone courses in the undergraduate curricula, as a terminal experience for integrating knowledge and preparing students for their transition to the professional environment (McNamara, J., et al. 2011). The definition of a capstone course is *"a crowning (unit) or experience coming at the end of a sequence of (units) with the specific objective of integrating a body of relatively fragmented knowledge into a unified whole. As a rite of passage, this (unit) provides an experience through which undergraduate students both look back over their undergraduate curriculum to make sense of that experience, and look forward to life by building on that experience"*. (Durel, 1993, p. 223).

Previous research indicates that the final year is critical for students. The end of the student stage and the beginning of their incursion into the world of work demand that universities provide them with specific support to assist them to deal with the changes (McNamara, J., et al. 2011). Assessment and critical self-reflection can promote reflection on what has been learned throughout the degree and on the transition to post-university life (McNamara, J., et al. 2011)

Career management consists of career planning where students have to identify career goals and pathways for achieving them. Career development for the acquisition of skills and competencies. Previous studies show a range of conceptual frameworks summarizing the competencies considered important for self-managing one's career (Jackson, D., et al. 2016; Blustein, D. L., et al. 1997).

A common definition of career competencies is "knowledge, skills, and abilities central to career development, which can be influenced and developed by the individual" (Presti, A. L., et al. 2022, p. 110). Career competencies allowed young workers to craft their jobs, which then positively related to career success. Previous studies have shown that graduates must develop their career competencies early on and engage in career self-management during the school-to-work transition (Presti, A. L., et al. 2022; Jackson, D., et al. 2016). Previous researchers have shown that students have a proximal awareness of a desire for assistance with job searching, and university career guidance is often not available to them. Career management skill development needs to begin in university programs (Bridgstock, R.; 2009).

## ASSESSMENT METHODOLOGY

The Marketing Department of a private emerging market university has implemented some changes to improve the quality of student learning. The faculty of the marketing department defined seven learning objectives for a bachelor of marketing. A curricular map was created to illustrate in which courses' learning objectives are introduced, practiced, and mastered or courses where there is an assessment opportunity (capstone course). Each course in the curricula contributes to developing learning outcomes in a unique way (Ayers, D. J., & Underwood, R. L., 2007).

There are capstone courses, in which students are expected to integrate the knowledge acquired throughout the curriculum to carry out marketing strategies. In this course, the measurement of learning outcomes is carried out. Additionally, there is an external evaluation where managers in the companies evaluate the performance and competencies of the students at the end of the internship. An internal evaluation, where students evaluate the organization and a self-reflection on the concepts, applied theories, their learning, and deficiencies experimented on during the internship. The results are analyzed by the faculty of a marketing program, to plan short-term actions and/or define curriculum improvements to improve the program's performance. During the pandemic the process of collecting data and evaluating was not suspended, the technology was used to take place in the same way but online. The objective of this chapter is to understand the effects of covid-19 pandemic on experiential learning activities, specifically the case of internship as a transition model from the academic world to the labor market, for marketing students of an emerging market university. The research questions that will be addressed in this chapter are: Can experiential learning be effective online? what are the lessons for marketing educators and companies after the pandemic Covid-19?. To respond to the research question and objectives of this chapter, the data collected and analyzed were about the internship experiences of all students participating in the following periods: Autumn 2020, spring 2021, summer 202, autumn 2021, and spring 2022, which is the pandemic COVID-19 period. The 100% of marketing students were surveyed and all the students wrote a self-reflection. The 100% of the managers responsible for the supervision of students during their internship in the organization were surveyed, and 162 questionnaires were collected, and after the cleaning process where incomplete questionnaires were eliminated, a total of 156 questionnaires were analyzed. On the other hand, all students who did internships during the same period were surveyed to find out their perception of the experience, a total of 178 questionnaires and self-reflection were responded to by students.

## DATA ANALYSIS AND RESULTS

A descriptive analysis was developed to confirm if the performance of students during the pandemic COVID-19, where students have to do a home-office internship meets their expectations or not. Minitab Statistical Software was used for analyzing quantitative data. A content analysis was developed for qualitative responses. The results show the perceptions of students and managers.

## Managers' Perceptions of Online Internships

All the managers in charge of student internships answer a survey. *Table 1*, contains descriptive statistics of the evaluation results, the mean of 156 responses is 3 (good) the mode is 4(excellent) which is a good result.

The goal established by faculty is that 70% of students in an internship have to be evaluated with a score of 3 (good) and 4 (excellent) by the companies. The results in table 1, indicate that all the criteria evaluated by companies during the pandemic period meet expectations.

As part of the survey applied to company executives, they were asked if they were interested in receiving more students of the same university for an internship, the majority responded "yes" they are interested and 129 executives gave some reasons for their interest, a summary of their comments are presented in appendix 1, *table 5*. The comments made by executives indicate a high degree of satisfaction with the skills, knowledge, attitudes, and performance of the participating students during the pandemic. Some statements that show this:

*"Students have shown excellent skills, competencies and initiative, which are important for the performance of activities in our company"- FULFILLMENT coordinator*

*"The profiles of the students are quite complete and help make the day-to-day easier for coordination, they can learn and complement their fairly good theoretical knowledge"-Commercial Director*

*Table 1. Managers evaluation: Frequency distributions. It shows the 11 outcomes evaluated by the managers. The first 6 are related to the performance of each practitioner, and the remaining 7 are learning outcomes. A 4 points scale was used.*

| Outcomes | Poor (1) | Fair (2) | Good (3) | Very Good (4) | Number of Evaluations |
|---|---|---|---|---|---|
| 1. Punctuality | 0.64% | 3.85% | 30.77% | 64.74% | 156 |
| 2. Attendance | 0.64% | 2.56% | 19.23% | 77.56% | 156 |
| 3. Fulfilment of objectives | 1.28% | 5.13% | 23.72% | 69.87% | 156 |
| 4. Efficient use of resources | 0.00% | 1.92% | 18.59% | 79.49% | 156 |
| 5. Adherence to standards | 1.28% | 1.28% | 11.54% | 85.90% | 156 |
| 6. Initiative with judgement | 1.28% | 3.85% | 24.36% | 70.51% | 156 |
| 7. LO1 | 0.64% | 3.21% | 35.90% | 60.26% | 156 |
| 8. LO2 | 0.64% | 3.21% | 32.05% | 64.10% | 156 |
| 9. LO3 | 1.92% | 7.05% | 33.97% | 57.05% | 156 |
| 10. LO4 | 0.64% | 3.21% | 26.28% | 69.87% | 156 |
| 11. LO5 | 0.64% | 3.21% | 25.64% | 70.51% | 156 |
| 12. LO6 | 0.64% | 1.28% | 12.18% | 85.90% | 156 |
| 13. LO7 | 3.85% | 0.64% | 24.36% | 71.15% | 156 |

*During the pandemic, institutional guidelines did not allow face-to-face internships. The pandemic was a period of adaptation and change for everyone and some company leaders were exceptionally critical of the success of online internships. This commentary is related:*

*"They have a lot of initiative; however, I consider that the modality home office is not a sign of commitment"- Public Relations Director*

Although the results of evaluation by companies, show areas for improvement, the expectations established by faculty for 70% of the students were met therefore, it can be affirmed that the online internships during the covid-19 period were successful and met the experiential learning expectations set by the faculty and companies.

## Students' Perceptions of Online Internships

All marketing students who did an internship during covid-19 were surveyed. A total of 178 responses were obtained, the descriptive statistics are *in table 2*. On a four-point scale, results show a mean of around 3 (good).

The expectations established previously by faculty was 70% of companies receiving students for an internship have to be evaluated with a score of 3 (good) and 4 (excellent) by the students. The results displayed in *table 3* indicate that the faculty and students' expectations are met for questions 1 to 8, where at least 70% of respondents select 3 or 4. Contrary, to the answers to the following question, *"Does the organization provide you with the benefits (canteen, transport, financial remuneration, etc.) that were agreed at the beginning of your internship?"* the expectations of the faculty and students were not met. It is worth mentioning that in Mexico there is no obligation for organizations to pay or give financial incentives during the internship, very few organizations pay or give any other benefits to students. Also, is important to consider that during the pandemic some benefits like travel expenses, food, and others which some companies usually offer to students, were suspended due to working from home.

The students were asked about their perception related to the question "Do you think your internship experience complements your professional training? The students responded that their participation in the internship, almost always (35.96% of students) and always (52.81% of students) opened up different learning opportunities for them. Another question was "During your internship, did you apply knowl-

*Table 2. Student perceptions. The table concentrates data about marketing student perception of the organizations in which they did internships. A four-point scale was used.*

| Variable | N | Mean | StDev | Minimum | Maximum | Mode | N for Mode |
|---|---|---|---|---|---|---|---|
| 1. Rules and guidelines | 178 | 3.5225 | 0.7226 | 1.0000 | 4.0000 | 4 | 116 |
| 2. Training | 178 | 3.3090 | 0.9144 | 1.0000 | 4.0000 | 4 | 99 |
| 3. Resources needed | 178 | 3.5281 | 0.7455 | 1.0000 | 4.0000 | 4 | 118 |
| 4. Activities | 178 | 3.5899 | 0.6767 | 1.0000 | 4.0000 | 4 | 122 |
| 5. Working time | 178 | 3.5337 | 0.6901 | 1.0000 | 4.0000 | 4 | 113 |
| 6. Organizational environment | 178 | 3.5112 | 0.7534 | 1.0000 | 4.0000 | 4 | 115 |
| 7. Adequate supervision | 178 | 3.6461 | 0.6409 | 1.0000 | 4.0000 | 4 | 128 |

edge related to your degree?" 28.65% of students responded that the activities almost always required them to apply skills related to their degree, and 61.24% of students mentioned that always required the application of skills related to their degree. At the end of the internship period, 25% of the students had received a contract offer from the organization despite the labor situation that the pandemic caused, 72% of students who received a job offer accepted.

Some general comments made by the students at the end of their internships indicate that they enjoyed and learned of the experience during the pandemic, here are the most representative comments:

*"Even though all my internships were online, communication with my coordinator was always adequate, I felt satisfied with the activities I did and I was able to develop different skills in the development of my internships"- Andrea- marketing student.*

*"The experience is good; the advantage is that there are several areas in which you can learn and apply what you have learned in different ways. Online work limits certain opportunities, but there is still learning"-Ana Paola- marketing student.*

*"The truth is I liked to do my internship at the agency, I would have liked more in-person, but I learned a lot and I liked what I did over these months. I liked it a lot" -Valeria Rodríguez*

## LEARNING AND RECOMMENDATIONS

The objective of the chapter was to understand the effects of Covid- 19 pandemic on experiential learning activities, specifically internship programs for marketing students. In this context, opportunities for internships in organizations decreased and migrated to an online modality. In addition, students and

*Table 3. Students' perceptions about internship organization. The table summarizes frequencies of each criterion evaluated by students participating in an internship during the pandemic.*

| Criteria | Poor (1) | Fair (2) | Good (3) | Very Good (4) | Number of Evaluations |
|---|---|---|---|---|---|
| 1. Did the organization make you aware of the rules, guidelines, and directives relating to your duties? | 0.56% | 11.8% | 22.47% | 65.17% | 178 |
| 2. Did the organization train you to carry out your activities? | 6.18% | 12.36% | 25.84% | 55.62% | 178 |
| 3. Did the organization provide you with the necessary resources to carry out your activities? | 1.69% | 10.11% | 21.91% | 66.29% | 178 |
| 4. Did the organization respect the activities described in the offered project? | 1.12% | 7.30% | 23.03% | 68.54% | 178 |
| 5. Did the organization respect work schedules, appointments, and meetings? | 1.12% | 7.87% | 27.53% | 63.48% | 178 |
| 6. Did the organizational environment make it easier for you to live and work in the organization? | 2.25% | 8.99% | 24.16% | 64.61% | 178 |
| 7. Was your line manager's supervision adequate in time and form? | 1.69% | 3.93% | 22.47% | 71.91% | 178 |
| 8. Does the organization provide you with the benefits (canteen, transport, financial remuneration, etc.) that were agreed upon at the beginning of your internship? | 28.25% | 71.75% | 00.00% | 0.00% | 177 |

organizations were not habituated to home office modality and were unenthusiastic to do so. It was necessary to reinforce the search for internship vacancies and to motivate students and companies to participate in an online internship.

## Students' Perceptions of Online Internships

The perception of the students about their online internship indicates that they are satisfied with what they have learned, applied, and achieved, although they would have liked to have some moments of physical interaction in the organization.

Another objective for this chapter was to learn about the experience during the pandemic and incorporate the lessons into post-pandemic experiences. According to the data collected the online internship experiences during the pandemic COVID 19 were mostly satisfactory for students and companies, some learnings and recommendations can be incorporated for new normality:

- To make the bridge from their student lives to their post-university lives is an important challenge for universities, governments, and employers
- To be clear about career competencies, skills, or application of knowledge would like to practice during the internship experience. Competences and learning objectives should be aligned with the graduate profile and learning objectives of each course included in the curriculum.
- To evaluate the internship experience. Assign an academic to monitor and support students' performance during the internship. The academic must evaluate and assign a grade to the internship course, this is essential to ensure student commitment, resolve special cases, and identify areas for improvement. Students have the opportunity for self-assessment and reflection on what they learned.
- To care about the mission of the internship. The companies should be clear about the internship mission, projects or objectives to be covered by the participating students. This will allow them to make better use of the students' time, to have clarity about the knowledge and skills required and to be practiced by the students, and to measure more objectively the performance of the participants.
- Results indicate an opportunity to improve student's experience, the students perceive that companies do not give enough benefits to motivate students' performance. This can be a consequence of the home office modality, where there is no necessity to offer food, transportation, or other benefits. It is important, for the new normal to consider that if companies and universities want to continue offering online internships, must create benefits or compensations for remote working.
- According to the results of the research, there is a perceived acceptance and preference by organizations and students towards the opportunity to carry out online internships, due to the advantages that this can represent, therefore it seems to be relevant to adapt to this new environment and promote the participation of students in online internships, mixed internships (some periods or days face-to-face and others online), on-site internships to have a real learning experience, ad-hoc to the trends in the labor market.

Educators and students need to consider the following considerations when moving from academics to career path(s). Students who graduate with a Bachelor of Marketing degree moving in a career path will need to consider the following:

- Building networks and doing an internship, participating in applied projects before and after graduation
- Taking assessments to assist in choosing the career of choice (e.g. Self-Directed Search, etc.)
- Attend certain conferences and presentations that can inspire and give greater clarity on career development opportunities in the discipline
- Actively participate in research with a faculty member.
- Visit careers fairs to obtain knowledge about career development opportunities, job opportunities, and professional requirements in the labor market.
- Research internships that can propel them into a long-standing career.

For educators working with students who are transitioning from academics to careers, here are some considerations:

- Advise on the existing fields of development in the discipline and the search for job opportunities, the search for postgraduate studies, the search for scholarships, and research opportunities.
- Offer training on the tools and topics related to recruitment and selection carried out by organizations (e.g. how to write a CV, relevant aspects to prepare for an interview, etc.).
- Form alliances with companies, job boards, government chambers, research institutions, and Organizations that provide support for graduate education, to concentrate opportunities so that candidates can make more informed decisions
- Strengthen internships and trainee programs to offer experiential learning and networking opportunities to participants.
- Measure the performance and competency assessment of final-year students and develop curricular improvement actions to ensure that graduates have the required competencies, knowledge, and skills demanded in the market

## FUTURE RESEARCH DIRECTION

Due to time and resource constraints, the study focused on marketing students, but it would be interesting to include other disciplines, as there may be important differences like the activities within the discipline. A post-pandemic study would help to understand in more detail the challenges and conditions of the new normal for adapting internship programs. A comparative study before, during, and post-pandemic would be enriching to understand the changes. Extending the scope of the study to an international setting would be enriching, given the cultural, institutional, and occupational differences that exist in different countries. For future research, a comparative study across different disciplines would be helpful.

## CONCLUSION

According to the result, experiential learning can be effective in an online mode under certain conditions: To be clear about competencies, skills, and knowledge would like to practice during the internship, to provide helpful information to students related to the mission of the experiences, evaluate students and organizations, allow students of reflection about their experience and lack of knowledge or skills to improve, motivate students and look for benefits for home office modality. Students and employers have experienced the benefits and advantages of a home office, and the trend in the labor market indicates that companies and talents are ready to take advantage of the benefits of remote work opportunities around the world.

If there is no funding information they should simply state:

This research received no specific grant from any funding agency in the public, commercial, or not-for-profit sectors. The research was supported by Universidad de las Américas, Puebla.

## REFERENCES

Akkermans, J., Paradniké, K., Van der Heijden, B. I., & De Vos, A. (2018). The best of both worlds: The role of career adaptability and career competencies in students' well-being and performance. *Frontiers in Psychology*, *9*, 1678. doi:10.3389/fpsyg.2018.01678 PMID:30258381

Asmara, A., & Ming-Chang, W. (2020). An analytical study on the effective approaches to facilitate higher education cooperate with industry: Based on faculty members perspective. *TEM Journal*, *9*(4), 1721–1731. doi:10.18421/TEM94-53

Auburn, T., Ley, A., & Arnold, J. (1993). Psychology Undergraduates' Experience of Placements: a role-transition perspective. *Studies in Higher Education*, *18*(3), 265–285. https://doi-org.udlap.idm.oclc.org/10.1080/03075079312331382211

Ayers, D. J., & Underwood, R. L. (2007). Integrating concepts across marketing courses via experiential learning. *Journal for Advancement of Marketing Education*, *11*(1), 63–68.

Binder, J. F., Baguley, T., Crook, C., & Miller, F. (2015). The academic value of internships: Benefits across disciplines and student backgrounds. *Contemporary Educational Psychology*, *41*, 73–82. doi:10.1016/j.cedpsych.2014.12.001

Bittmann, F., & Zorn, V. S. (2020). When choice excels obligation: About the effects of mandatory and voluntary internships on labour market outcomes for university graduates. *Higher Education*, *80*(1), 75–93. doi:10.1007/s10734-019-00466-5

Blustein, D. L., Phillips, S. D., Jobin-Davis, K., Finkelberg, S. L., & Roarke, A. E. (1997). A theory-building investigation of the school-to-work transition. *The Counseling Psychologist*, *25*(3), 364–402. doi:10.1177/0011000097253002

Bridgstock, R. (2009). The graduate attributes we've overlooked: Enhancing graduate employability through career management skills. *Higher Education Research & Development*, *28*(1), 31–44. doi:10.1080/07294360802444347

Carver, R., King, R., Hannum, W., & Fowler, B. (2007). Toward a model of experiential e-learning. *Journal of Online Learning and Teaching*, *3*(3), 247–256.

Cerych, L., & Frost-Smith, B. (1985). Collaboration between higher education and industry: An overview. *European Journal of Education*, *20*(1), 7–18. doi:10.2307/1502999

Cojocariu, V. M., Cîrțiță-Buzoianu, C., & Mareș, G. (2019). Opportunities and Difficulties in Conducting Internships in Higher Education from the Employers' Perspective. *Postmodern Openings/Deschideri Postmoderne, 10*(2).

Colombari, R., D'Amico, E., & Paolucci, E. (2021). Can challenge-based learning be effective online? A case study using experiential learning theory. *CERN ideaSquare Journal of Experimental Innovation, 5*(1), 40–48.

Daalhuizen, J., & Schoormans, J. (2018). Pioneering Online Design Teaching in a MOOC Format: Tools for Facilitating Experiential Learning. *International Journal of Design, 12*(2), 1–14.

Durel, R. J. (1993). The capstone course: A rite of passage. *Teaching Sociology, 21*(3), 223–225. doi:10.2307/1319014

Edmondson, D., & Matthews, L. (2021). Developing marketing curriculum to make students workforce ready. *International Journal of Educational Management, 35*(5), 969–983. doi:10.1108/IJEM-10-2019-0370

Frontczak, N. T. (1998). A paradigm for the selection, use and development of experiential learning activities in marketing education. *Marketing Education Review, 8*(3), 25–33. doi:10.1080/10528008.1998.11488641

Gault, J., Redington, J., & Schlager, T. (2000). Undergraduate business internships and career success: Are they related? *Journal of Marketing Education, 22*(1), 45–53. doi:10.1177/0273475300221006

Hayden, S. C., & Osborn, D. S. (2020). Using experiential learning theory to train career practitioners. *Journal of Employment Counseling, 57*(1), 2–13. doi:10.1002/joec.12134

Helyer, R., & Lee, D. (2014). The role of work experience in the future employability of higher education graduates. *Higher Education Quarterly, 68*(3), 348–372. doi:10.1111/hequ.12055

Hergert, M. (2009). Student Perceptions Of The Value Of Internships In Business Education. *American Journal of Business Education, 2*(8), 9–14. doi:10.19030/ajbe.v2i8.4594

Jackson, D., & Wilton, N. (2016). Developing Career Management Competencies among Undergraduates and the Role of Work-Integrated Learning. *Teaching in Higher Education, 21*(3), 266–286. doi:10.1080/13562517.2015.1136281

Jehanzeb, K., Rasheed, M. F., & Rasheed, A. (2012). Impact of rewards and motivation on job satisfaction in banking sector of Saudi Arabia. *International Journal of Business and Social Science, 3*(21).

Johansson, I., & Winman, T. (2020). Orchestrating of Learning in Higher Education Through Internships. *Educational Review, 4*(5), 101–112. doi:10.26855/er.2020.05.001

Kaminstein, D. S., Stevens, A., & Forst, M. (2022). Experiential Work in a Virtual World: Impactful and Socially Relevant Experiential Learning. *The Journal of Educators Online, 19*(2), n2. doi:10.9743/JEO.2022.19.2.6

Kolb, A. Y., & Kolb, D. A. (2005). Learning styles and learning spaces: Enhancing experiential learning in higher education. *Academy of Management Learning & Education, 4*(2), 193–212. doi:10.5465/amle.2005.17268566

Kolb, D. A. (1984). *Experiential learning: Experience as the source of learning and development.* Prentice Hall.

Kowalski, G., & Ślebarska, K. (2022). Remote Working and Work Effectiveness: A Leader Perspective. *International Journal of Environmental Research and Public Health, 19*(15326), 15326. doi:10.3390/ijerph192215326 PMID:36430045

Krishnamurthy, S. (2020). The future of business education: A commentary in the shadow of the Covid-19 pandemic. *Journal of Business Research, 117*, 1–5. doi:10.1016/j.jbusres.2020.05.034 PMID:32501309

Kumar, S., & Bhandarker, A. (2020). Experiential learning and its efficacy in management education. PURUSHARTHA-A journal of Management. *Ethics and Spirituality, 13*(1), 35–55. doi:10.21844/16201913103

Lastner, M. M., & Rast, R. (2016). Creating win-win collaborations for students: An immersive learning project for advanced sales courses. *Journal for Advancement of Marketing Education, 24*, 43–48.

Lopes, B., Silva, P., Melo, A. I., Brito, E., Paiva Dias, G., & Costa, M. (2019). The 'lunar side' of the story: Exploring the sustainability of curricular internships in higher education. *Sustainability (Basel), 11*(21), 5879. doi:10.3390/su11215879

Manpower, I. (2020). *The 2022 global talent shortage survey result.* Retrieved November, 9, 2022 from https://go.manpowergroup.com/talent-shortage

McNamara, J., Brown, C., Field, R., Kift, S., Butler, D., & Treloar, C. (2011). Capstones: Transitions and professional identity. In *Proceedings of the World Association for Cooperative Education (WACE) 17th World Conference on Cooperative & Work Integrated Education* (pp. 1-12). World Association for Cooperative Education, Inc.

Meshram, K., Paladino, A., & Cotronei-Baird, V. S. (2022). Don't Waste a Crisis: COVID-19 and Marketing Students' Self-Regulated Learning in the Online Environment. *Journal of Marketing Education, 44*(2), 285–307. doi:10.1177/02734753211070561

Mirabela-Constanta, M., Maria-Madela, A., & Leonard-Calin, A. (2020). The Future of Work in the Post-Pandemic Era. Annals of the University of Oradea. *Economic Science Series, 29*, 49–50.

Mostafa, B. A. (2021). *The effect of remote working on employees wellbeing and work-life integration during pandemic in Egypt.* Academic Press.

Núñez Pérez, J. C., Cerezo Menéndez, R., Bernardo Gutiérrez, A. B., Rosário, P. J. S. L. D. F., Valle Arias, A., Fernández Alba, M. E., & Suárez Fernández, N. (2011). Implementation of training programs in self-regulated learning strategies in Moodle format: Results of a experience in higher education. *Psicothema, 23*, 274–281. PMID:21504681

O'Connor, H., & Bodicoat, M. (2017). Exploitation or opportunity? Student perceptions of internships in enhancing employability skills. *British Journal of Sociology of Education, 38*(4), 435–449. doi:10.1080/01425692.2015.1113855

O'Neill, N. (2010). Internships as a high-impact practice: Some reflections on quality. *Peer Review : Emerging Trends and Key Debates in Undergraduate Education, 12*(4), 4–9.

OCHA. (2021). *Year in Review 2021: Regional Office for Latin America and the Caribbean*. Regional Office for Latin America & the Caribbean.

Peltier, J. W., Chennamaneni, P. R., & Barber, K. N. (2022). Student anxiety, preparation, and learning framework for responding to external crises: The moderating role of self-efficacy as a coping mechanism. *Journal of Marketing Education, 44*(2), 149–165. doi:10.1177/02734753211036500

Popadiuk, N. E., & Arthur, N. M. (2014). Key relationships for international student university-to-work transitions. *Journal of Career Development, 41*(2), 122–140. doi:10.1177/0894845313481851

Reshma, P. S., Aithal, P. S., & Acharya, S. (2015). An empirical study on Working from Home: A popular e-business model. *International Journal of Advance & Innovative Research, 2*(2).

Sáiz-Manzanares, M.-C., Casanova, J.-R., Lencastre, J.-A., Almeida, L., & Martín-Antón, L.-J. (2022). Satisfacción de los estudiantes con la docencia online en tiempos de COVID-19. *Comunicar., 30*(70), 35–45. doi:10.3916/C70-2022-03

Sanahuja Vélez, G., & Ribes Giner, G. (2015). Effects of business internships on students, employers, and higher education institutions: A systematic review. *Journal of Employment Counseling, 52*(3), 121–130. doi:10.1002/joec.12010

Satyam & Aithal, R. K. (2022). Reimagining an Experiential Learning Exercise in Times of Crisis: Lessons Learned and a Proposed Framework. *Journal of Marketing Education*.

Silva, P., Lopes, B., Costa, M., Melo, A. I., Dias, G. P., Brito, E., & Seabra, D. (2018). The million-dollar question: Can internships boost employment? *Studies in Higher Education, 43*(1), 2–21. doi:10.1080/03075079.2016.1144181

Snow, K., Wardley, L., Carter, L., & Maher, P. (2019). Lived experiences of online and experiential learning in four undergraduate professional programs. *Collected Essays on Learning and Teaching, 12*, 79–93. doi:10.22329/celt.v12i0.5388

Turnea, E.-S. (2021). Organizational Rewards in the Online Work Environment. Is There Any Chance of Full Accomplishment? Ovidius University Annals. *Series Economic Sciences, 21*(1), 434–438.

Varghese, M. E., Parker, L. C., Adedokun, O., Shively, M., Burgess, W., Childress, A., & Bessenbacher, A. (2012). Experiential internships: Understanding the process of student learning in small business internships. *Industry and Higher Education, 26*(5), 357–367. doi:10.5367/ihe.2012.0114

Virolainen, M. H., Stenström, M. L., & Kantola, M. (2011). The views of employers on internships as a means of learning from work experience in higher education. *Journal of Vocational Education and Training, 63*(3), 465–484. doi:10.1080/13636820.2011.580360

World Economic Forum. (2020). *The future of jobs report 2020*. Author.

World Economic Forum. (2022). *Centre for the New Economy and Society Accenture (Firm). Jobs of tomorrow: the triple returns of social jobs in the economic recovery*. World Economic Forum.

Xu, S., Van Hoof, H., & Nyheim, P. (2018). The effect of online scheduling on employees' quality of life. *Journal of Foodservice Business Research*, *21*(2), 172–186. doi:10.1080/15378020.2017.1364592

Young, M. R. (2002). Experiential learning= hands-on+ minds-on. *Marketing Education Review*, *12*(1), 43–51. doi:10.1080/10528008.2002.11488770

## ADDITIONAL READING

Presti, A. L., Capone, V., Aversano, A., & Akkermans, J. (2022). Career competencies and career success: On the roles of employability activities and academic satisfaction during the school-to-work transition. *Journal of Career Development*, *49*(1), 107–125. doi:10.1177/0894845321992536

Shetty, S., Shilpa, C., Dey, D., & Kavya, S. (2022). Academic Crisis During COVID 19: Online Classes, a Panacea for Imminent Doctors. *Indian Journal of Otolaryngology and Head and Neck Surgery*, *74*(1), 45–49. doi:10.1007/s12070-020-02224-x PMID:33102186

Tan, L. M., Laswad, F., & Chua, F. (2022). Bridging the employability skills gap: Going beyond classroom walls. *Pacific Accounting Review*, *34*(2), 225–248. doi:10.1108/PAR-04-2021-0050

Virtue, D. C. (2022). Exploring experiential learning processes in the context of an international school–university partnership. *New Directions for Teaching and Learning*, *2022*(169), 99–108. doi:10.1002/tl.20485

Wurdinger, S., & Allison, P. (2017). Faculty perceptions and use of experiential learning in higher education. *Journal of e-learning and Knowledge Society, 13*(1).

## KEY TERMS AND DEFINITIONS

**Competences:** Abilities that a professional needs to perform a job.
**Experiential Learning:** A experience of learning by doing and reflecting about the learning.
**Home Office:** Remote work for an organization or self-employed.
**Internship Program:** A service to support students to do a period of work experience in an organization for a limited period.
**New Normal:** The pandemic COVID-19 changed the way many activities are currently carried out. The new way is the new normal.
**Online Learning:** Take courses online.
**Pandemic COVID-19:** Global pandemic of coronavirus, caused by severe acute respiratory syndrome coronavirus 2 (SARS-CoV-2).

## APPENDIX 1: TABLES

*Table 4. Managers' responses. The table concentrates on the descriptive statistics of the responses obtained from the managers of the organizations that received students for an internship during the pandemic COVID-19 period.*

| Variable | N | Mean | SE Mean | StDev | Mode | N for Mode |
|---|---|---|---|---|---|---|
| 1. Punctuality | 156 | 3.5962 | 0.0479 | 0.5987 | 4 | 101 |
| 2. Attendance | 156 | 3.7372 | 0.0428 | 0.5342 | 4 | 121 |
| 3. Fulfilment of objectives | 156 | 3.6218 | 0.0517 | 0.6460 | 4 | 109 |
| 4. Efficient use of resources | 156 | 3.7756 | 0.0370 | 0.4624 | 4 | 124 |
| 5. Adherence to standards | 156 | 3.8205 | 0.0401 | 0.5014 | 4 | 134 |
| 6. Initiative with judgment | 156 | 3.6410 | 0.0498 | 0.6216 | 4 | 110 |
| 7. LO1: Mastery of theoretical, methodological, and/or technological aspects. | 156 | 3.5577 | 0.0475 | 0.5929 | 4 | 94 |
| 8. LO2: Critical, creative, and interdisciplinary capacity to identify, analyze and solve the problems and challenges that arise during the execution of his/her activities. | 156 | 3.5962 | 0.0471 | 0.5878 | 4 | 100 |
| 9. LO3: Shared leadership capacity. | 156 | 3.4615 | 0.0571 | 0.7129 | 4 | 89 |
| 10. LO4: Ability to complement their autonomous learning. | 156 | 3.6538 | 0.0461 | 0.5753 | 4 | 109 |
| 11. LO5: Ability to communicate orally and in writing. | 156 | 3.6603 | 0.0459 | 0.5736 | 4 | 110 |
| 12. LO6: Ethical and/or socially responsible behavior. | 156 | 3.8333 | 0.0362 | 0.4520 | 4 | 134 |
| 13. LO7: Proficiency in English or another language. | 156 | 3.5833 | 0.0692 | 0.8648 | 4 | 111 |

*Table 5. Summary of qualitative responses. The table summarizes the comments of managers.*

| We are interested in receiving more UDLAP students as collaborators in our company because: | Company |
|---|---|
| "give good results" | Account Manager |
| "We believe that the talent that UDLAP students have is very high since they show a very good degree of interest in learning and growing" | Associate director |
| "With Dania's example, we hope that all students are of that level" | Operations Coordinator |
| "highly prepared students" | Digital coordinator |
| "They have great qualities and skills that are reflected when requesting support for daily activities" | Digital coordinator |
| "They are very responsible people" | Communications Executive |
| "They have great skills and abilities" | Director |
| "It was the first time that we participated in the UDLAP marketing area, it was an excellent experience" | General Director |
| "Most students have a high sense of responsibility. | Country manager LATAM |
| "High responsability level." | Country manager LATAM |
| "It is a proactive, purposeful, and dedicated staff." | Marketing Director |
| "The profiles of the students are quite complete and help make the day-to-day easier for coordination, they can learn and complement their fairly good theoretical knowledge" | Commercial Director |
| "Because they have proven to be very responsible, professional, and committed to their learning" | Marketing Director |
| "Students who are of great help to our company" | Marketing department |

*continued on following page*

*Table 5. Continued*

| We are interested in receiving more UDLAP students as collaborators in our company because: | Company |
|---|---|
| "They know how to find the solution to the problem and know how to be a project leader" | New projects Director |
| "Because of their dedication, knowledge, and contributions during the internship" | Operations Director |
| "Because we loved to receive a student as committed as Grecia Jaime" | Logistic and planning director |
| "They have a lot of initiative; however, I consider that the modality from home is not a sign of commitment". | Public Relations Director |
| "We like the quality of knowledge and training of its students" | Marketing Coordinator |
| "If the other students are as enthusiastic as Regina, they will be very supportive" | Project leader |
| "In general, they have a good attitude, they like to learn, they are very willing and their knowledge is excellent" | Implementation coordinator |
| "I have had in my last experiences boys with the intention of learning and doing things" | Client services Chief |
| "They have a good academic level, are responsible and fulfilled." | Community Manager |
| "Excellent students, with great capacity and solid values." | Co-Founder |
| "Udlap students have shown excellent skills, competencies and initiative, which are important for the performance of activities in our company. | FULFILLMENT coordinator |
| "We have collaborated with your students in past years, we like their performance and some have even stayed collaborating with us" | Marketing Manager |
| "They are very supportive of our company." | Digital marketing Director |
| "They are of great help, Innovation and learning in the company" | Managing Director |
| "Students are responsible, they are attentive to the needs and above all it gives us security and confidence that the students are constantly monitored by the university for the correct fulfilment of their work in the company" | Creative Director |
| "We really like the fact that the students are constantly monitored by the university, as well as the fact that they work with a lot of willingness" | Creative Manager |
| "The quality of their students is excellent, very responsible people and people we would like to integrate into our team" | Digital Campaigns Manager |
| "Students are always proactive and have a lot of quality" | KEY ACCOUNT MANAGER |
| "We think it's a mutually beneficial the internship program and we think that by collaborating with us, students can learn about aspects of everyday work that cannot be learned at the University through the experience of the working world alone" | Regional Manager |
| "Students show a high level of knowledge in their studies and thus add value to the organization" | General Manager |
| "They are student leaders, eager to learn and share knowledge and capable of bringing learning to the Blanck team" | Marketing Manager |
| "The interns we have received have performed efficiently" | Marketing Manager |
| "They are outstanding students with quality education" | Marketing Chief |
| "They are students, with good knowledge and willingness to learn, which is good to share in the agency" | Brand Manager |
| "GOOD ACADEMIC STRUCTURE AND INITIATIVE TO CREATE OR PROVIDE SOLUTIONS" | Director |
| "The students can learn and implement great strategies, leading projects in an effective way" | Director |
| "After having some negative experiences with other students years ago, the students have responded favorably" | Qualitative research Manager |
| "They seem to me to be highly prepared students with the intention of learning to enter the labor market" | Content Manager |
| "We are convinced that any good internship is the door to a job and business reality for all students" | Creative director |

*continued on following page*

*Table 5. Continued*

| We are interested in receiving more UDLAP students as collaborators in our company because: | Company |
|---|---|
| "Excellent interns" | Social media manager |
| "It is good that the students are monitored by the university. Most of them have a good attitude to participating" | Marketing Manager |
| "The performance of your students has been satisfactory and we are interested in continuing to collaborate for the development of the students" | Human Resources |
| "Noelia has left us with a great experience of having UDLAP students collaborating in the agency" | Awards Manager |
| "Karla demonstrated the commitment and high level of knowledge that UDLAP teaches its students" | Public Relations and Communication Manager |
| "Your students have the necessary competencies to carry out the assigned activities efficiently in the work area" | Marketing Manager |

# Chapter 8
# From University to the Labour Market:
## Assisting Students Through Personal Career Maps

**Elena Ramona Richiteanu-Nastase**
https://orcid.org/0000-0003-0105-1697
*Bucharest University of Economic Studies, Romania*

**Monica Elisabeta Paduraru**
*Bucharest University of Economics Studies, Romania*

## ABSTRACT

*Adjusting to university life is a challenge for many students, who find it difficult to cope with academic demands and complete their studies. Preparing for a career can generate anxiety, stress, maladjustment, vulnerability. At university level, students` counselling can be a solution to help students adapt to the demands of this environment and their future career. This chapter clarifies concepts such as academic adjustment, career counselling strategy, and institutional support. Furthermore, the authors will present the Personal Career Map as a specific theory and instrument that can be used in counselling students. The structure of the career map, the career profiling questionnaire, the benefits, and limitations of this approach will be highlighted. Personal Career Map offers suggestions for student`s counselling plan, detailing concrete steps that can be taken at personal and university level to enhance students' academic and professional insertion. Discussions and recommendations on the use of this approach at university level will be addressed.*

## INTRODUCTION

Adjusting to university life is a challenge for many students, who find it difficult to cope with academic demands, complete their studies, and prepare for a job. Preparing for a future professional career can generate anxiety, stress, maladjustment, and vulnerability (Zhang, 2022; Jungbluth et al., 2011). A

DOI: 10.4018/978-1-7998-7999-2.ch008

survey conducted by the National Union of Students Scotland on 1872 students from 19 colleges and 15 university campuses shows that examinations were found to be the biggest concern for students. An overwhelming 90% of students reported this caused them more stress than expected" (Paduraru, 2019, p. 65). Studies show that adjustment disorder has a calculable incidence of 5–21% in psychiatry consultation services for adults (Glenn, 2011).

Students can overcome these negative states if they manage to adjust psychologically, develop appropriate coping mechanisms, or if they are helped by universities, through different counseling services to identify these difficulties and challenges, and are assisted in a smooth transition to their chosen career. At the university level, career counseling for students can help them identify their gaps and suggest different routes that will facilitate a better insertion into their chosen careers.

The purpose of this chapter is the following:

1) To analyze the current context of the difficulties faced by students emphasizing the need for various counseling activities;
2) To offer a capable integrative theory and tool taking into consideration different career factors;
3) Formulate a coherent counseling strategy that can be used by universities and student career counseling centers to facilitate better integration of students in the university and the workplace.

To meet these objectives, the authors propose this chapter, which can be a real guide for career counseling specialists at the university level or other career counseling specialists interested in a better insertion of graduates.

This chapter is structured into three parts.

*In the first part, the background* clarifies concepts such as academic adjustment and career counseling activities as a way for universities to support students in adapting to academic demands and facilitate professional insertion. Theories and approaches used in counseling are mentioned, to highlight the need for a complex, integrative theory.

*In the second part*, *Assisting Students Through Personal Career Maps* the authors present the Personal Career Map as a specific theory and instrument that can be used in counseling students. The structure of the career map (career facets), the career profile questionnaire, and the benefits and limitations of this approach are highlighted. The authors present the Personal Career Map counseling strategy detailing concrete steps that were taken at the university level to enhance students' adjustment and insertion.

*The last part* of the paper will address *discussions* and *recommendations* on the use of career counseling for students to assist them in their transition to the labor market. Issues of the usefulness of this approach at the university level are addressed by the authors, as well as ways for future development.

## BACKGROUND

The academic demands, especially for the first year of college, and later adapting to a career, are serious challenges for many students to overcome. Students experience several problems when transitioning from high school to university, such as the failure to undergo a suitable orientation regarding academic expectations and social integration.

A key factor in determining whether students remain and succeed in postsecondary education is their ability to adapt to an often-complex environment ("postsecondary adjustment") (Lipka et al., 2020).

Academic adjustment is a complex concept that has been approached in a variety of ways over time.

Whereas in the past, academic adjustment was seen as a single variable, today it is considered a concept involving four distinct functions in four distinct domains: "academic achievement", "social adjustment", "personal emotional adjustment" and "institutional adjustment" (Mooney et al., 1991). Each of the four areas in which academic adjustment manifests itself can be detailed, giving teachers and counselors a clearer perspective on concrete areas of intervention to support students. Thus, within the first domain, academic achievement, motivation for learning, appropriateness of skills to academic requirements, and the ability to achieve satisfactory grades are included. The second domain, social adjustment, includes aspects such as involvement in the learning environment and the ability to establish social networks. The third domain, personal emotional adjustment, refers to the ability to cope with challenges related to learning activities, which may generate stress and anxiety. The fourth domain, institutional adjustment, refers to students' perceptions of their relationship with teachers and academics (Lipka et al., 2020, p. 3).

According to Gerdes and Mallinckrodt (1994, p. 282), academic adjustment includes academic abilities, motivational factors, and institutional commitment. Other studies (Gerdes & Mallinckrodt, 1994) identify motivation to learn, acting to meet academic demands, a clear sense of purpose, and general satisfaction with the academic environment as important components of **academic adjustment.**

The system of academic requirements presents students with new challenges, with some students finding it difficult to adapt during their academic journey.

In terms of solutions regarding adaptation into the first year, we have identified in the literature review the following:

- Having positive interactions with lecturers and fellow students and being able to handle the increased complexity and quantity of the learning content (determines whether or not a student is satisfied with the first-year experience and whether he or she obtains good grades, passes his or her courses and persists to the second year (Astin, 1999; Pascarella & Terenzini, 2005; Sevinç & Gizir, 2014; Rooij et al., 2018).
- Stimulating metacognitive and learning skills (Costabile et al., 2013).
- Counseling services for first-year students (Renuka et al., 2013; Kivlighan et al., 2021).

Overcoming academic difficulties is necessary but not sufficient for students' long-term success. Facing the challenges of university life can be more easily addressed if students receive expert support and intervention in this area. That means counseling services and activities.

Counseling activities can be carried out in different ways: individual or group counseling, coaching, mentoring, training, courses, and workshops, by different specialists with different levels of training and quality standards, but that in principle all aim to achieve the same goals: promotion of well-being and health (optimal functioning from a somatic, physiological, mental, emotional, social, and spiritual point of view), personal development (self-knowledge, harmonious interpersonal relationships, stress management, techniques of creative attitudes, realistic career choices), and prevention (of negative affective mood, lack of self-confidence, risk-taking behavior, interpersonal conflicts, learning difficulties, social maladjustment, crises).

Many theories attempt to provide a more complete perspective on choosing, pursuing, and developing a career. Each identifies various career factors and attempts to formulate a more complete explanation. An interesting classification in approaching and interpreting career theories is that offered by Patton and

*From University to the Labour Market*

McMahon (2006). The two authors consider that there are content-centered career theories, process-focused theories, both content- and process-focused theories, and integrative career theories.

The literature reflects the multifaceted complexity of the concept of career development, but until recently, efforts to synthesize theories have been minimal. Brown (Patton & McMahon, 2006, p.148) points out in this regard that 'integrationists' and 'constructionists' are the current key leaders in the construction of career development theory. The systems theory of career counseling has been proposed by McMahon and Patton and emphasizes the importance of society and environment as well as individual differences (gender, age, values, sexual orientation, abilities, disabilities, interests, physical attributes, skills, ethnicity, self-concept, personality, beliefs, and health) in career choice, and the analysis of elements such as geographical location, political decisions, historical trends, globalization, socio-economic status, labor market, indicate that these external, contextual factors can influence the choice, pursuit, and development of a career. This theory has the advantage of a global perspective and of considering a very large number of factors that influence the choice and pursuit of a career.

Alongside systemic theory, Career Anchor Theory is another major contribution to understanding an individual's career paths and was proposed by Edgard Schein. Schein identifies eight distinct patterns of talents, goals, needs, and values in self-perception that emerge from early career experiences. (Schein et al., 2010) The term "anchor" is used to designate consistent individual-specific cores that are part of the individual's occupational identity and over time manifest as anchors. As they are formed, these anchors determine powerful influences on career choice and direction. (Coetzee & Roythorne-Jacobs, 2007, p.59).

Postmodern approaches focus on the subjective experience of career development, with individuals being the agents who build their careers. They are treated as individuals who attach meanings to the reality in which they live, and not as identifiable objects on a normal distribution curve. Two approaches are best known from this point of view: logotherapy (Frankl, 1963) and the narrative approach.

The career theories reviewed propose a complex, but often facetted, one-sided approach to careers. In an attempt to have a comprehensive and integrative view of career factors, it is important to see the pluses and limitations. Each of these theories expounds and recommends complex modalities and counseling services alike, requiring a certain behavior from career counselors, which makes it even more difficult to choose the optimal ways to act.

Starting from these theories, the authors of this chapter propose another one, which seeks to provide an integrative view of career factors and a useful, easy-to-use tool that describes in terms of profiles and suggestions for effective ways of career counseling activities that will facilitate academic adjustment and the professional insertion of students.

The Personal Career Map theory and instrument (the Personal Career Map Questionnaire- Appendix 1. Personal Career Map Questionnaire) were proposed and intensively studied as a result of a doctoral thesis of one of the authors (Richiteanu-Nastase, 2011, 2019) and later developed by the authors of this chapter to propose a career counseling program and a counseling strategy that will help students adapt to university life and further to professional life (measured as professional insertion).

In this chapter, we address the usefulness and importance of counseling students, by using an integrative theory on career counseling and an instrument (Personal Career Map) to help them adapt to academic requirements and meet future labor market demands for a better career insertion.

# ASSISTING STUDENTS THROUGH PERSONAL CAREER MAPS

## Personal Career Map (the Theory and the Instrument)

The "Personal Career Map" is a mental model consisting of an individual's way of positioning himself concerning the set of career factors that delimit a stable, undecided, or unstable profile.

The facets that make up the personal career map are internal representations of the individual concerning the essential factors of the choice and pursuit of a career (Richiteanu-Nastase, 2019).

These representations form an individual's career map that serves to organize information, attitudes, or values concerning a career. The authors believe that this map is formed over time and is defined with the professional insertion of the individual.

The authors identified four functions of the personal career map: informational (it provides knowledge for students for each facet concerning the stable profile), diagnostic (offers a diagnosis/profile on the individual to certain factors/facets), remedial (suggests career counseling activities for each facet), forecasting (the student's career insertion) (Richiteanu-Nastase, 2019, p.244).

From the authors` perspective, a personal career map includes the following dimensions/facets/career factors: motivations, values, career plan, decision-making aspects, expectations, and training needs.

The proposed theory is based on career theories, considering the mentioned factors, but these factors are not static but are shaped like cognitive maps, mental representations of the individual, which help him or, on the contrary, hinder him in choosing and pursuing a career.

The starting point of this theory and tool was the attempt to find out what differentiates students and graduates from having a better insertion in the labor market. Career theories try to explain choice and path maintenance, but not success. How can we characterize this profile, capable of knowing very well what it wants and what motivates it, that analyzes obstacles, and makes rational decisions? And above all, can such a profile be formed?

The research carried out by the authors of this chapter, in a 4-year longitudinal study, on 100 students, and 50 counseling specialists, using qualitative methods (interview-based survey, focus group) and quantitative methods (questionnaire-based survey, the study of documents), later statistical methods, reveals the fact that this stable profile exists and that it has a very good professional insertion. Research data (Richiteanu-Nastase, 2011, 2012) allowed us to outline the most effective career counseling activities for each career facet/factor analyzed.

Below, the authors analyze the factors that make up the personal career map.

We can define motivation as the set of states of need that require to be satisfied and which drive, stimulate, and determine the individual to satisfy them (Zlate, 2000, p. 152). The reasons why individuals choose a career lie in the importance of personal preferences (e.g., interests) or external influences (labor market trends and family expectations) (UNESCO, 2002).

The literature distinguishes several types or forms of motivation (positive/negative motivation, cognitive/affective motivation). The most common form of classification of motivation is to divide it into intrinsic and extrinsic motivation.

Frederic Guay proposes and validates a tool for measuring motivation towards decision-making activities: the autonomy scale in career decision-making (2005, p. 78). This instrument aims to measure the following dimensions: intrinsic motivation, identified regulators, embodied regulators, and external regulators.

An interesting theoretical position on motivation (and one that Frederic Guay also uses) is the self-determination theory (Guay, 2005, p. 78). This theory focuses not only on the intensity of the motivational process, but also on the quality of this process, emphasizing the importance of three psychological needs that have to be met to experience being motivated: autonomy (the sense of freedom in initiating, maintaining, and controlling own behavior), competence (the perceived effectiveness to the environment), relational needs (the positive relationships with others).

Deci and Ryan (1985) proposed that there are several types of motivation along the self-determination continuum. Therefore, intrinsic motivation reflects the highest level of self-determination or autonomy. It considers engagement in activity for the sake of the experience and satisfaction that comes from it. Extrinsic motivation refers to external reasons. The author believes that extrinsic motivation can also have varying degrees of autonomy and that on a scale of autonomy from low to high there are different types of extrinsic motivation: external regulation (regulating behavior through external means such as rewards and constraints), embodied regulation (those behaviors that are partially internalized by the individual) and identified regulation (behaviors performed at the choice of the individual because they are considered important by the individual). According to self-determination theory, those who behave driven by the intrinsic or extrinsic motivation of an identified regulation type satisfy their need for autonomy. The stable profile is characterized by intrinsic motivation or extrinsic motivation of the identified regulation type.

The second dimension of the personal career map, values, is defined as a set of beliefs that influence human behavior and decision-making. As these develop, values are crystallized and prioritized forming a value system. A value system contains those values that are desired to be satisfied by the individual. Individual values can be satisfied through a range of activities: at work, leisure activities, interpersonal activities, etc.

There are many classifications of human values in the literature.

Meglino (1998) identified the values of individuals at work. He distinguishes the following values: getting something done, helping and caring for others, honesty (telling the truth and doing what the individual considers to be right), impartiality, and professionalism. For example, work-related values learned in the family have a strong influence on vocational choice.

To observe students' values orientation, the Personal Career Map uses values from the Life Values Inventory (Duane & Crace, 1996), an inventory that assesses the values involved in decision-making.

Analyzing this inventory and following the typologies used, the authors propose the following classification of values: professional, work-related, and career values: being successful at work, speaking my mind at work, being independent in decision-making, working in a team, being ambitious in my career, taking responsibility, being persistent in pursuing my desired career, being serious about my chosen profession;

The Personal Career Map differentiates professional values from other values.

Another career factor of the personal career map is the career plan. The authors think that the career plan is a progressive construction of the career, developed throughout school and life, a construction that allows countless possible scenarios to unfold.

In the Personal Career Map, a well-established, flexible career plan corresponds to a stable profile.

Decision-making is a form of problem-solving in which we try to make the best choice from several alternatives. The authors think that there is a distinction between decision-making and problem-solving, in that decision-making involves exploring a variety of possibilities to formulate a satisfactory solution, whereas problem-solving does not focus on 'positive' or 'negative' solutions. Two factors are usually involved in the decision-making: utility and probability. Decisions are usually made in the direction of increased utility and probability. Interestingly, indecision is now seen as a normal stage in an individual's life and not as an individual's inability to make important decisions.

An interesting tool to measure career decisions was developed by Lawrence K. Jones in 1989. The Career Decision Profile (CDP) is a 16-item inventory designed to measure the status of career decision-making in terms of three dimensions: decisiveness, comfort, and reasons for indecision (Jones, 1989). Another useful instrument for investigating career decision-making difficulties is the one proposed by Gati, Krausz, and Osipow (1996) called the Career decision-making difficulties questionnaire (CDDQ). Consisting of 44 items, it investigates the following dimensions: lack of preparation, lack of information, and heterogeneous information.

The Personal Career Map focuses on the degree of decision-making, the degree of comfort with the decision made (items adapted from Career decision profile, Jones, 1988), to what extent the decisions made are responsible ones, and whether or not the short-and long-term consequences of the action are considered.

Another dimension/career factor of the personal career map is that of expectations and the balance between aspirations and expectations.

Metz et al. (2009, p.155) see career aspirations as "vocational possibilities or work preferences in the context of ideal conditions". Johnson (Metz et al., 2009, p. 155) described career aspirations as "point-in-time expressions of career goals". While aspirations refer to a set of ideal conditions for the manifestation of the desired career, expectations refer to a much more concrete, real, and attainable plan from the individual's point of view. Career expectations have a much more direct link to career choice.

Rojewski (Metz et al., 2009, p. 157) stressed the importance of examining the congruence or discrepancy between individual aspirations and individual expectations because we can identify the factors that may lead individuals to compromise their aspirations or to act in the full realization of their aspirations. According to Rojewski, these factors include beliefs about self-efficacy, support from family and friends, and perceptions of social opportunities and barriers. (2005, Metz et al., 2009, p. 157).

In addition to these factors, the Personal Career Map includes the balance between aspirations and expectations, the realism of expectations to see to what extent the choice made is a real or fantasy one, thus considering that real expectations correspond to the stable profile, while fantasy expectations highlight an unstable profile. Also, the authors focused on two aspects of expectations: expectations of the workplace and expectations of career development. The instrument takes into consideration only medium-level expectations that express a realistic and perfectly valid position for a stable profile, while over- or under-expectations lead to extreme, unrealistic aspects.

A first factor that can be analyzed following the discrepancy between aspirations and expectations is the individual's beliefs about career decision self-efficacy (CDSE) (Metz et al., 2009). This construct was introduced by Bandura (1977; 1982) and refers to "the degree of confidence in accomplishing a task relevant to career decision-making" (Metz et al., 2009, p. 158). Research indicates that CDSE is a good predictor of career exploration behavior as well as career decision-making.

A second factor that emerges from the discrepancy between aspirations and expectations is the support of family and friends. The family is the most important social system that influences an individual's vocational development. Emotionally, the role of family and friends is very important in choosing and pursuing a career. Parental neglect, rejection, overprotection, conflicts between parents, and sibling rivalry can create a person who is insecure and difficult to integrate. Cultural stimulation in the family or religion also plays an important role. We often hear expressions such as "an appetite for books", and "a desire for self-improvement" which are developed in the family. However, not only the support of family and friends is important, but also the reference group or the individual role model (not always from the family: teacher, trainer, and so on) that can be significant in choosing and pursuing a career.

Perceptions of social opportunities and barriers are the third factor that can be highlighted in the balance between aspirations and expectations. It considers how the individual relates to the socio-economic level of the family, which affects the possibilities of financially supporting the individual's education and a certain lifestyle, but also how the individual assesses the employment opportunities in the labor market, the social or economic barriers that may exist at a given time.

A.K Nayak finds that individuals tend to identify with professions from their socio-economic background (2016, p. 61). When choosing and pursuing a career, an individual may be influenced by social prestige, but also by the salary offered for that job. The health of family members can also indirectly affect vocational development (sick parents, death of a parent).

Physical factors such as geographical location influence an individual's vocational development in terms of restrictions and opportunities (e.g. rural/urban).

To investigate perceived barriers, Luzzo & McWhirter (Metz et al., 2009, p. 160) propose an instrument comprising 64 items. To investigate beliefs about self-efficacy Personal Career Map includes three relevant items in the questionnaire: adaptation to the workplace, perceived self-efficacy, family and friends support, perceptions of social opportunities and barriers (family socioeconomic level, the health status of family members, geographical location, minority group membership, gender differences, and labor market barriers.

To study job expectations and career development expectations, the Personal Career Map includes several response options (9) from which the respondents choose as many options as they wish. 1-3 variants correspond to low expectations, 4-6 variants consider average expectations (stable profile), and the choice of 7-9 variants corresponds to above-average expectations.

A final career factor highlighted in the Personal Career Map is analyzing self-training needs. This aspect has been marginalized in career studies and career counseling. Therefore, the perspective the authors promote is that a person oriented towards continuous improvement, and able to identify their training needs will correspond to a stable profile of the career map career and will have a better chance of finding a job than the other profiles identified.

Identified profiles and specific facets are described in Table 1 (Appendix 2. Table 1. Personal Career Map profiles).

After applying the questionnaire, the interpretation will be made according to the 3 profiles and following the previous point. It is recommended to discuss each item individually precisely to see nuanced aspects of the decision and factors influencing the career, other problems to be solved, and suggestions for advice using the table below.

Research data (Richiteanu-Nastase, 2011) reveal that people with a stable profile have a better insertion in the labor market (maximum 6 months after graduation).

The Personal Career map studies professional insertion as the time interval between graduation and employment, insertion during studies, the efficiency of studies programs (working in the studied specialization, the knowledge gained in college about job requirements, the knowledge gained in college concerning career development) and the level of insertion in postgraduate and master programs.

This should be seen as a challenge to build stable profiles, but also to intervene through tailored counseling for the other profiles. The research data (Richiteanu-Nastase, 2011) provides counseling support suggestions according to the diagnosed problem. Table 2 (Appendix 3. Table 2. Designing a personalized career counseling pathway) provides suggestions for counseling in this regard.

The authors think that using the Personal Career Map can be very helpful because it provides information about the individual's positioning concerning each facet and concerning stable profile, it offers clear and varied career counseling suggestions activities and can be an indicator of a student`s professional insertion if the profile is stable or through counseling so it becomes stable.

The limits of the tool concern its wide-scale applicability. It was tested in a longitudinal study including one hundred students (in the first year of college, in the third year of college, and 6 to 8 months after graduation to measure the degree of professional insertion). The authors believe that the tool can be improved, but even in the absence of a strong correlation, all the facets offer discussion points for counseling from the perspective of various career factors.

## Using Personal Career Maps to Enhance Adjustment and Insertion

Based on the difficulties faced by students and the potential solutions identified in the previous sections, the authors propose a counseling strategy that can be used at the university level to support students to better adapt to their academic and career preparation pathways. To this end, the authors of this chapter propose five steps to assist students in their adaptation to student life and later to their jobs:

- Identifying the dimensions of the personal map at the beginning of the academic year by applying the Personal Career Map Questionnaire during the first week of the academic year in the introductory course.
- Applying the Personal Career Map Questionnaire after Big Brother week.
- Applying the Personal Career Map Questionnaire in individual career counseling, to establish the individual counseling plan.
- Participating in counseling sessions where counseling strategies will be applied, according to the individual counseling plan that has been established.
- Measuring students` professional insertion into the labor market.

In the first stage, we recommend that at the beginning of the academic year, in addition to the general information that students receive regarding the university campus, there should also be an application of the Personal Career Map Questionnaire.

The application of the Personal Career Map Questionnaire during the first week of the academic year in the introductory course offers the possibility of identifying unstable profiles, which require immediate counseling or which are in situations of possible university dropout. For example, item 5 of the instrument provides important information regarding the support of the family, the group of friends, and other socio-economic factors, which can represent obstacles in pursuing university studies and subsequently a career in the field. The authors consider that the tool can be applied in any year for a bigger effect.

The second stage of the proposed strategy considers a relatively common event in universities that facilitates the integration and adaptation of first-year students. In Bucharest University of Economic Studies, this is called" Big Brother week".

In principle, this week involves meetings between the 1st and 3rd year students, in which the 3rd year students inform the 1st year students about different tips and tricks for academic survival/academic adjustment and professional insertion. Beyond information, the 3rd year students are a model for the

1st year students and can provide educational advice to the 1st year students regarding the factors that contribute to academic and professional success.

The authors recommend that the presentations and exercises proposed in the workshops connect to the facets of the Personal Career Map. For example, debates regarding myths/obstacles/expectations related to the university and the labor market, analysis of personal values, and activities asking to share the motivation of the choice of specialization and career can be used.

At the end of this week, the instrument can be applied again to notice an improvement in the profile, at least on one or more aspects.

The third stage can be applied at any time during the studies and aims to achieve at least one individual counseling session in which the establishment of an individual career plan is sought. The instrument can be applied as it is or can be the base for individual discussions. After establishing a career plan, the student can participate in various counseling activities, so that his/her profile becomes stable in all aspects. The counseling activities for students may include activities such as (the fourth stage):

- Active listening: allowing students to express themselves and giving them undivided attention to better understand their concerns.
- Solution-focused therapy: helping students identify and build on their strengths to find solutions to their problems.
- Cognitive-behavioral therapy: teaching students to identify and challenge negative thought patterns and behaviors.
- Mindfulness and relaxation techniques: promoting mental and emotional well-being through meditation, deep breathing, and other practices.
- Play and art therapy: using creative expression to help students communicate their thoughts and feelings.
- Group counseling: providing a supportive and safe environment for students to share their experiences and learn from each other.
- Referral to outside resources: connecting students with community services or other resources when necessary.
- Behavior modification: encouraging positive behavior through rewards and consequences.

In the fifth stage, to prove the effectiveness of the proposed strategy, the authors recommend measuring the degree of professional insertion of the students who participated in counseling.

This approach is relatively easy to achieve because the universities already measure the degree of professional insertion, and the Counselling and Orientation Center at the university level can have access to the respective database. However, the correct measurement of professional insertion is important.

The authors consider that the following should be considered when measuring professional insertion:

- the time interval between graduation and employment.
- employability during studies.
- the effectiveness of study programs in terms of employability in the specialization studied (level of knowledge acquired in college concerning job requirements, level of knowledge acquired in college concerning development) and
- the percentage of participation in postgraduate and master's programs (concern for professional development).

## SOLUTIONS AND RECOMMENDATIONS

The authors think that the proposed tool offers a viable counseling strategy, with broad career counseling suggestions and activities (from individual or group counseling to coaching, mentoring, training, courses, and workshops) capable of developing a more stable profile.

Taking as a starting point the issues outlined above, the authors believe it is useful to make some suggestions on measures that can be taken at the university level to make it easier for students to adapt to academic life and, subsequently, to professional life:

- Orientation programs for new students.
- Providing a clear course syllabus & academic calendar.
- Encouraging student-faculty interaction.
- Developing courses and workshops for first-year students (about: adapting to student life, and knowledge of educational opportunities offered on campus) and others for those approaching graduation (about: writing a resume, and making a career plan).
- Offering various counseling services: individual or group activities on career topics suggested by students, occasional group activities offered by teachers or invited experts, conferences, and so on.
- Offering peer support and mentorship programs.
- Offering flexible scheduling and accommodations for students with disabilities or special needs.
- Encouraging students to get involved in campus activities and clubs.
- Periodical testing of students' career needs.
- Organizing practice programs based on a partnership between the university and other organizations.
- Counselling and guidance of students throughout the practice.
- Delivering responsibility to teachers to act as a coach/mentor.
- Studying professional insertion of graduates to indicate the effectiveness of the educational programs.

We highlight the importance of universities in recognizing the positive effects of career counseling services and strengthening the efforts of multiplication by building partnerships with the labor market (formal internship programs, coaching, mentoring). We consider that it is desirable to transform the university into an initiator and promoter of career counseling and a partner in a relationship with the labor market.

## FUTURE RESEARCH DIRECTIONS

Research should undertake a comprehensive examination of the instrument's efficacy in predicting successful professional integration aligned with a stable profile. Certain aspects, such as peer group support and perceptions of the labor market, exhibit more robust correlations, warranting further investigation to validate these associations. To optimize outcomes, the authors suggest implementing the instrument following the aforementioned counseling strategy or as an integral component of a multifaceted support strategy provided by the university.

## CONCLUSION

The authors consider that the theory and the proposed tool are a real help for the student's academic adjustment and professional insertion. The counseling effort should start as early as the first year, to avoid the dropout phenomenon, with a focus on preventing and overcoming academic difficulties, and should continue throughout the university career, to support students' well-being, career orientation, and increased adaptability for their future careers.

The current chapter is written in the same direction as the book focusing on guiding students in their transition from the academic environment to the professional world. It offers strategies, advice, and tools to help students navigate their career paths successfully.

## REFERENCES

Brown, D. (1996). *Life Values Inventory*. Retrieved 6 December 2022. https://bhmt.org/wp-content/uploads/2016/04/BHMT_CC_Life-Values_Inventory.pdf

Brown, D., & ... (2002). *Career choice and development* (4th ed.). Jossey-Bass.

Cleland, J., Arnold, R., & Chesser, A. (2005). Failing finals is often a surprise for the student but not the teacher: Identifying difficulties and supporting students with academic difficulties. *Medical Teacher*, 27(6), 504–508. doi:10.1080/01421590500156269 PMID:16199356

Coetzee, M., & Roythorne-Jacobs, H. (2007). *Career counseling and guidance in the workplace: a manual for career practitioners*. Juta&Co. Ltd.

Deci, E. L., & Ryan, R. M. (1985). *Intrinsic Motivation and Self-Determination in Human Behavior*. Springer Science & Business Media. doi:10.1007/978-1-4899-2271-7

Gati, I., Krausz, M., & Osipow, S. (1996). A Taxonomy of Difficulties in Career Decision Making. *Journal of Counseling Psychology*, 43(4), 510–526. doi:10.1037/0022-0167.43.4.510

Gerdes, H., & Mallinckrodt, B. (1994). Emotional, social, and academic adjustment of college students: A longitudinal study of retention. *Journal of Counseling and Development*, 72(3), 281–288. doi:10.1002/j.1556-6676.1994.tb00935.x

Glenn, M. C. (2011). Academic achievement and academic adjustment difficulties among college freshmen. *Journal of Arts, Science, and Commerce*, 2, 72–76.

Guay, F. (2005). Motivations Underlying Career Decision-Making Activities: The Career Decision-Making Autonomy Scale (CDMAS). *Journal of Career Assessment*, 13(1), 77–97. doi:10.1177/1069072704270297

Guo, P. (2021). Research on the Strategy of Improving College Students' Career Adaptability in Application-oriented Colleges and Universities. *Journal of Education. Teaching and Social Studies*, 3(3), 54–63. doi:10.22158/jetss.v3n3p54

Jigău, M. (2003). *Consilierea carierei adulților*. Editura Afir.

Jones, L. K. (1989). Measuring a three-dimensional construct of career indecision among college students: A revision of the Vocational Decision Scale: The Career Decision Profile. *Journal of Counseling Psychology, 36*(4), 477–486. doi:10.1037/0022-0167.36.4.477

Jungbluth, C., MacFarlane, I. M., Veach, P. M., & LeRoy, B. S. (2011). Why is Everyone So Anxious?: An Exploration of Stress and Anxiety in Genetic Counseling Graduate Students. *Journal of Genetic Counseling, 20*(3), 270–286. doi:10.1007/s10897-010-9348-3 PMID:21264500

Kirtchuk, D., Wells, G., Levett, T., Castledine, C., & de Visser, R. (2022). Understanding the impact of academic difficulties among medical students: A scoping review. *Medical Education, 56*(3), 262–269. doi:10.1111/medu.14624 PMID:34449921

Kris Metz, A. J. (2009). Career aspirations and expectations of college students: Demographic and labor. *Journal of Career Assessment, 17*(2), 155–171. doi:10.1177/1069072708328862

Lipka, O., Sarid, M., Aharoni Zorach, I., Bufman, A., Hagag, A. A., & Peretz, H. (2020). Adjustment to higher education: A comparison of students with and without disabilities. *Frontiers in Psychology, 11*(923), 1–11. doi:10.3389/fpsyg.2020.00923 PMID:32670127

Meglino, B. M., & Ravlin, E. C. (1998). Individual values in organizations: Concepts, controversies, and research. *Journal of Management, 24*(3), 351–389. doi:10.1177/014920639802400304

Mooney, S. P., Sherman, M. F., & Lopresto, C. T. (1991). Academic locus of control, self-esteem, and perceived distance from home as predictors of college adjustment. *Journal of Counseling and Development, 69*(5), 445–448. doi:10.1002/j.1556-6676.1991.tb01542.x

Nayak, A. K., & Neill, J. T. (2016). The University Student Satisfaction and Time Management Questionnaire v.9. In *Time Management*. InTech. idl.isead.edu.es:8080/jspui/bitstream/10954/1767/1/9789535103356.pdf

Noveanu, E., & Potolea, D. (2016). *Education sciences. Encyclopedic Dictionary*. Sigma.

Patton, W., & McMahon, M. (2006). *Career development and system theory. Connecting theory and practice*. Sense Publishers. doi:10.1163/9789087903343

Richiteanu-Nastase, E. R. (2011). *Modalități de realizare a consilierii pentru carieră a studenților* [Doctoral dissertation]. Universitatea din Bucuresti. https://www.scribd.com/doc/138482571/Rezumat-Ramona-Stoiculescu-c-richiteanu-Nastase

Richiteanu-Nastase, E.R. (2019) *Consiliere și orientare pentru carieră și viață Fundamente teoretice și metodologice*. Editura ASE.

Richiteanu-Nastase, E. R., Cace, C., & Staiculescu, C. (2012). E-learning about self-career. An analysis of Romanian e-counselling services. *The International Scientific Conference eLearning and Software for Education, Carol I" National Defence University, 1*, 282-288. https://www.ceeol.com/search/article-detail?id=41722

Richiteanu-Nastase, E. R., & Staiculescu, C. (2015). The impact of career factors on students' professional insertion. What measures are to be taken by the university? *Procedia: Social and Behavioral Sciences, 180*, 1102–1108. doi:10.1016/j.sbspro.2015.02.216

Savickas, M. L. (1997). Career adaptability: An integrative construct for life-span, life-space theory. *The Career Development Quarterly, 45*(3), 247–259. doi:10.1002/j.2161-0045.1997.tb00469.x

Schein, E. H. (2010). Career Anchors for Leaders. In F. Bournois, J. Duval-Hamel, S. Roussillon, & J. L. Scaringella (Eds.), *Handbook of Top Management Teams* (pp. 126–133). Palgrave Macmillan. doi:10.1057/9780230305335_14

Swanson, J. L., & Fouad, N. A. (1999). *Career theory and practice: learning through case studies.* Sense Publishers.

UNESCO. (2002). *Handbook on career counseling. A practical manual for developing, implementing, and assessing career counseling services in higher education settings.* UNESCO. https://unesdoc.unesco.org/images/0012/001257/125740e.pdf

van Rooij, E. C. M., Jansen, E. P. W. A., & van de Grift, W. J. C. M. (2018). First-year university students' academic success: The importance of academic adjustment [Correction]. *European Journal of Psychology of Education, 33*(4), 769. doi:10.1007/s10212-017-0364-7

Zhang, Z. M., Yu, X., & Liu, X. H. (2022). Do I decide my career? Linking career stress, career exploration, and future work self to career planning or indecision. *Frontiers in Psychology, 13*, 997984. doi:10.3389/fpsyg.2022.997984 PMID:36081730

Zlate, M. (2000). *Fundamentele psihologiei.* Editura Pro Humanitate.

## ADDITIONAL READING

Guo, P. (2021). Research on the Strategy of Improving College Students' Career Adaptability in Application-oriented Colleges and Universities. *Journal of Education. Teaching and Social Studies, 3*(3), 54–63. doi:10.22158/jetss.v3n3p54

Paduraru, M. E. (2019). Coping strategies for exam stress. *Mental Health: Global Challenges Journal, 1*(1), 64–66. doi:10.32437/mhgcj.v1i1.26

Patton, W. (2006). *Overview of career development theory. Connecting theory and practice.* Sense Publishers.

Richiteanu-Nastase, E.-R. (2019). *Consiliere și orientare pentru carieră și viață. Fundamente teoretice și metodologice.* Editura ASE.

Richiteanu-Nastase, E. R., Mihaila, A. R., Staiculescu, C., & Paduraru, M. E. (2013). Gamification in career e-counselling. *eLearning & Software for Education*, (1), https://www.proquest.com/openview/33292c482c8d7d6c470fd3995ceb8214/1?pq-origsite=gscholar&cbl=1876338

UNESCO. (2002), *Handbook on career counseling. A practical manual for developing, implementing, and assessing career counseling services in higher education settings.* UNESCO. https://unesdoc.unesco.org/images/0012/001257/125740e.pdf

van Rooij, E. C. M., Jansen, E. P. W. A., & van de Grift, W. J. C. M. (2018). First-year university students' academic success: The importance of academic adjustment [Correction]. *European Journal of Psychology of Education, 33*(4), 769. doi:10.1007/s10212-017-0364-7

Wendlandt, N. M., & Rochlen, A. B. (2008). Addressing the College-to-Work Transition. Implications for University Career Counselors. *Journal of Career Development, 35*(2), 151–165. doi:10.1177/0894845308325646

## KEY TERMS AND DEFINITIONS

**Academic Adjustment:** The student's ability to develop coping mechanisms and learning strategies that will help him/her achieve satisfactory results concerning academic demands.

**Career Counselling:** The process of assisting the individual in choosing, following, and developing their career.

**Career Counselling Theories:** Explanatory models for conceptualizing career counseling that has one or more career factors at its center.

**Career Factors:** Various internal and external individual factors that influence the choice and pursuit of a career.

**Counseling strategy:** The approach or the plan a counselor uses to assist students in resolving their problems, achieving their goals, or improving their mental health and well-being. This can involve a combination of techniques, theories, and interventions tailored to the individual's needs and preferences.

**Personal Career Map:** A tool and a theory developed to explain a series of factors that lead to the choice of a career and to support the career counseling process toward a stable profile.

**Professional Insertion:** The employment of the individual at the workplace in the profile, the pursued specialization, in a short time after graduation. It is considered that is a good insertion if the time is shorter and respects the profile/specialization of the individual.

## APPENDIX 1. PERSONAL CAREER MAP QUESTIONNAIRE

The personal Career Map Questionnaire aims to explore, through your opinions, the different factors that determine your choice and pursuit of a career.
Also, your honest answers will help identify your career counseling needs and propose concrete ways of career counseling.
* Mandatory question

Section 1

1. Have you chosen a career? Think for a moment and then identify the reasons why you have chosen this career * (tick a maximum of 4 options):
    - Different reward packages: bonuses, work phone, car, etc.
    - I was constrained by certain material issues.
    - Parents suggested it as a good career.
    - Friends suggested it as a good career.
    - Other people suggested to me that it would be a good choice.
    - Salary commensurate with skills/responsibilities.
    - Decent, open working environment.
    - I have a career model.
    - Fits my skills and competencies.
    - Best expresses my skills and talents.
2. The values that guide me in life are * (tick maximum 6 values):

To be modest; Live a healthy life; be liked by others; be rich; To protect the environment; To be honest; To perform well at work; Have a sense of belonging; Belief in God; Speak my mind at work; Being sociable; Be financially independent; Have independence in decision-making; To help others; To be healthy; Work as part of a team; Be ambitious in my career; Take responsibility; Be open to new things; Be fair; Have time for myself; To be loyal; To be persistent in the pursuit of my desired career; To be creative; To respect family traditions; To be serious about my chosen profession.

3.1. Do you have a career plan * (tick one):
    - I have a well-established career plan.
    - I have an outline plan; I know where I would like to end up.
    - I don't have a well-defined plan; I have several options.
    - I don't have a well-defined plan; I'm trying to see what my options are.
    - I haven't thought about that.
    - I'm not interested in that at the moment, I'm concentrating on my studies.
3.2. I can adapt to changes in career plans/flexibility of plans: If you ticked the first or second option to the above question, please answer this question as well. If no, go to the next question:
    - Yes
    - No

4.1. Have you decided on a career? How decided are you? Think for a moment and then tick all the options that suit your situation. * You can tick as many options as suit your situation.
- I've decided what field I'm going to work in.
- I've decided on the type of company I want to work for.
- I've decided what specialization I'd like to pursue.
- I have decided to work full-time and continue my studies.
- I've decided what I want to do with my life and that decision will be the same next year.

4.2. I feel * (tick one) about the decision to choose and pursue a career:
- comfortable with my decision.
- Uncomfortable because I have not yet made a decision.
- Comfortable, even though I have not yet made a decision.

4.3. About the consequences of the career decision * (tick one):
- I always analyze the consequences (risks/benefits/long-term effects).
- I analyze the consequences and consult with other important people; the final decision is mine.
- I make decisions based on my intuition, following my interests/needs.

5.1. How quickly do you think you will adapt to the university life/workplace * (tick one):
- Very quickly.
- Quickly.
- Relatively quickly.
- Slowly, I need more time to settle in.
- Very slowly, I find it hard to integrate into new groups.
- Very slowly, I learn more slowly.

5.2. Do you consider yourself to be competent in your field * (tick one):
- I am a competent person and able to overcome any obstacles.
- I am a competent and responsible person.
- I am not very satisfied with my professional competence.
- I consider myself incompetent in my field.

5.3. To what extent do you agree with the following statement: Success in my career will be determined by my efforts * (tick one):
- To a very large extent.
- To a large extent.
- To a fair extent.
- To a small extent.
- To a very small extent.

5.4. How would you rate your family's support in choosing and pursuing your chosen career * (tick one):
- My family has always supported me in my chosen career.
- Family has not always supported me in my chosen career.
- Family has been indifferent to my career choice.
- Family was against this choice.

5.5. How would you rate the support of your friends in choosing and pursuing your chosen career * (tick one):
- Friends have always supported me in my chosen career.
- Friends have not always supported me in my chosen career.
- Friends have been indifferent to my career choice.

- Friends have been against this choice.
5.6. Socio-economic level of family is/impeded pursuing the desired career * (tick one):
    - Is/impeded pursuing a desired career.
    - Is/was it an obstacle that the family, through their efforts, managed to overcome.
    - It has not negatively influenced the pursuit of the desired career.
5.7. The health status of family members is/was an impediment to pursuing the desired career * (tick one):
    - Is/was an impediment to pursuing the desired career.
    - Is/was it an obstacle that the family, through their efforts, managed to overcome.
    - It has not negatively influenced the pursuit of the desired career.
5.8. Geographical location (rural residence, small town, undeveloped) is/impeded pursuing the desired career * (tick one):
    - Is/was an impediment to pursuing the desired career.
    - Is/was an obstacle that, through my efforts, I managed to overcome.
    - It has not negatively influenced the pursuit of the desired career.
5.9. Belonging to a minority group (ethnic group, religious group) is/impedes pursuing the desired career * ((tick one):
    - Is/was an obstacle to pursuing the desired career.
    - It has been an obstacle that, through my efforts, I managed to overcome.
    - It has not negatively influenced the pursuit of the desired career.
5.10. Gender differences are/impeded pursuing the desired career * (tick one):
    - Are/have been a hindrance to pursuing the desired career.
    - They are/were an obstacle that, through my efforts, I managed to overcome.
    - Have not negatively influenced the pursuit of the desired career.
5.11. Over-saturation of the labor market (too many economists) is/impeded the pursuit of the desired career * (tick one):
    - Is/was an impediment to pursuing the desired career.
    - It is/was an obstacle that, through my efforts, I managed to overcome.
    - It has not negatively influenced the pursuit of the desired career.
5.12. How do you perceive the current labor market * (tick one):
    - There are few jobs, but you can get them if you "know the right people".
    - There are few jobs for very good/competent people.
    - There are quite a lot of jobs, but they all require experience.
    - There are plenty of jobs if you know how to look.
    - There are no jobs available, and the job market is blocked.
5.13. My most important expectations of the job where I will/am employed are * (tick the options that characterize you):
    - Very good communication with superiors.
    - Decent working conditions.
    - Very good relations with colleagues.
    - Being respected.
    - Salary commensurate with responsibilities/effort.
    - Professional people.
    - Transparency in decision-making.

- Opportunities for advancement.
- Decent salary.

5.14. My most important career development expectations are * (tick the options that characterize you):
- To be in line with my training.
- To move up the social ladder.
- Financial independence.
- Career advancement based on work done.
- Continued specialization in a particular field.
- Job stability.
- More jobs where I can gain experience.
- A job I enjoy.
- Being very well off.

6. 1. Do you think you need further training? *
- Yes
- No

6.2. If you answered Yes to the above question, list your training needs: If you answered No to the above question go to the next question.

## APPENDIX 2

*Table 1. Personal career map profiles*

| Type of Profile | Motivation in Choosing Career | Values | Plan of Career | Decision-Making | Expectations (Balance Aspirations-Expectations) | Needs Training (Lifelong Learning) |
|---|---|---|---|---|---|---|
| Stable | Predominantly intrinsic or extrinsic type identified regulation | In favor of labor | Its presence, flexible plan | ● Decided and comfortable with the decision taken. ● Analyzing the consequences of the action | ● Beliefs about self-efficacy: above average ● Support from family and friends: above average ● Perceptions of social opportunities and barriers (obstacles) average/low ● Towards the workplace (medium, low) Career development (medium) | Listing training needs (self-analysis capacity) |
| Undecided | Predominantly extrinsic: built-in adjustment or external adjustment | Other values | Its absence | ● Undecided and uncomfortable with the decision taken. ● Analyzing consequences of action/ Unable to forecast consequences | ● Beliefs about self-efficacy: above average/medium/ low ● Support from family and friends: above average/ average/low ● Perceptions of social opportunities and barriers: above average/average/low ● Towards the workplace (high - idealistic, medium, low - pessimistic) ● Career development (high - idealistic, medium, low - pessimistic) | Listing training needs (self-analysis capacity) |
| Unstable | Predominantly extrinsic: built-in adjustment or external adjustment | Other values | Its absence | ● Indecisive and comfortable with the decision taken ● Unable to forecast consequences | ● Beliefs about self-efficacy: above average/ /low ● Support from family and friends: low ● Perceptions of social opportunities and barriers: low ● Towards the workplace (high - idealistic, low - pessimistic) ● Career development (high - idealistic, low - pessimistic) | Inability to self-assess training needs |

# APPENDIX 3.

*Table 2. Designing a personalized career counseling pathway*

| Profile Type/ Facets of a Personal Career Map | Motivation in Career Choice Item 1 | Values Item 2 | Career Plan Item 3 | Decision-Making Item 4 | Expectations (Aspirations-Expectations Balance) Item 5 | Training Needs (Lifelong Learning) Item 6 |
|---|---|---|---|---|---|---|
| **Stable profile** | No counseling required | No counseling required | No counseling required | No counseling required | No counseling required | No counseling required |
| **Undecided profile Unstable profile - Suggestion 1** | Internships | Internships | Individual counseling | Individual counseling | Internships | Internships |
| **Suggestion 2** | Courses, workshops on career/personal development topics | Courses, workshops on career/personal development topics | Courses, workshops on career/personal development topics | Internships | Visits to different organizations/potential employers | Courses, workshops on career/personal development topics |
| **Suggestion 3** | Internship programs | Individual counseling | Internships | Courses, workshops on career/ personal development topics | programs | Individual counseling |
| **Suggestion 4** | Individual counseling | Internship programs | Visits to different organizations/ potential employers | Internship programs | Individual counseling | Internship programs |

# Chapter 9
# The Undergraduate Career Compass:
## A Seven-Step Plan for Navigating the Transition From Academia to the World of Work

**Randika Perera**
 https://orcid.org/0000-0002-4398-624X
*Gampaha Wickramarachchi University of Indigenous Medicince, Sri Lanka*

## ABSTRACT

*Higher education's ultimate achievement is to position the undergraduate towards professionalism successfully. Recently, higher education institutes have recognized this need and offered various services to realistically place students in the world of work. Throughout the academic journey, undergraduates acquire the hard and soft skills to meet the demands of the work world. Nevertheless, properly positioning undergraduates in the world of work is a self-responsibility and exploration journey. Therefore, this chapter introduces a self-directed mechanism under the title of career compass and elaborates on seven steps that undergraduates need to follow for success in their career or professional development. These seven steps positively contribute to lifelong personal and professional development.*

## INTRODUCTION

The principal objective of each undergraduate is to position themselves in the world of work. Undergraduate success in their future endeavors lies in proper career planning and readiness on their academic journey. To address this need contemporary higher education institutes have developed the curriculums of academic programs according to the demands of the work world. Higher education institutions are providing career guidance services, mentoring, and internship opportunities for undergraduates to make this adaptation more effective (Stebleton & Kaler, 2020). Moreover, contemporary technological transformations are making an impact on the changes in the work world. Such as technological integra-

DOI: 10.4018/978-1-7998-7999-2.ch009

tion will develop a multi-talent workforce and open to distance work with technology. The result of this technological transformation is work world will be more globalized. The future work world will provide more access to innovations and cutting-edge technologies will rapidly change the demand of the work world (Lewis, 2020). Apart from this perspective positing in the work world is a challenging task in the 21st century. Undergraduates will receive guidance supervision from their institutions. However, adapting to this climate in the work world will be a self-directed process (Ogunlana, 2023). Through this chapter, undergraduates gain an informative understanding of career development according to the several theories and practical dimensions present work world and facilitation provided by the higher education institutes. Ultimately, this chapter will give undergraduates a pragmatic way towards professionalism under the approach of career compass and empower the individual to meet the demands and cope with the changes and challenges that occur in the work world.

The career development mechanism's success lies in sound knowledge of career developmental theories. Scholars who belong to the disciplines of psychology, sociology, and human resource management have explored individual interaction in the work world and introduced various career developmental theories. These career development theories have revealed that career development is associated with each human development stage. In each human development, stage individuals develop career-related ideation and act purposefully (Lent & Brown, 2012). To recognize own ideation about the career throughout individual human development these theories provide a practical direction. Further recognizing the weaknesses and strengths of individual ideation of the career will benefit in developing effective ideation about career or professionalism. The ideation of career is a developed through the influence of various psychological and social factors. However, according to human development theories, the transformation from adolescence to adulthood majorly lies in career development (Havighurst, 1972). Pragmatically, this is fulfilled with the individual interaction in higher education institutes. Therefore, preparing for the work world and creating economic independence knowledge about career development theories is essential.

Contemporary, individuals are unable to effectively adapt to professionalism due to the adequate knowledge about the world of work. The most significant feature is the work world is dynamic. Due to this dynamic nature of career-specific things also change rapidly. This has been more critical with the technological influence of digitalization, decreased manpower need, and economic changes in the global context (Parker & Grote, 2022). However, higher education institutes working towards the development of requirement competencies in undergraduates through the curriculum and learning exposure. Further, before the completion of the academic programs individual will receive industrial exposure through their internship placements. This process grooms the undergraduates accordingly and ensures preparing the undergraduates for the demands of the world of work (Ordine & Rose, 2015). knowledge about such opportunities will help undergraduates to adapt the learned and use the developed skills to fit the work world and survive the changes that occur in the work world.

The undergraduate inadequate knowledge about these two dimensions increases the rate of graduate unemployment. The below diagram indicates the severity of this condition:

Several factors influence undergraduate unemployment such as mismatch between qualifications and jobs, adequate competency, loss of skills, lack of soft skills, lack of emotional intelligence abilities, and lack of technological skills. The most critical factor is the preparation for the demands of the work world. When the individual is empowered to adapt work world with the acquired competencies in the tertiary of higher education individual can be free from unemployment (Alolaqi & Yusof, 2022). To acquire the maximum benefits from the undergraduate programs enrolled the student needs to have proper ideology about the nature of the higher education. The knowledge about the nature and services offered in higher

*Figure 1. World youth unemployment rate 1991 - 2024*
Source: Macro Trends (2024)

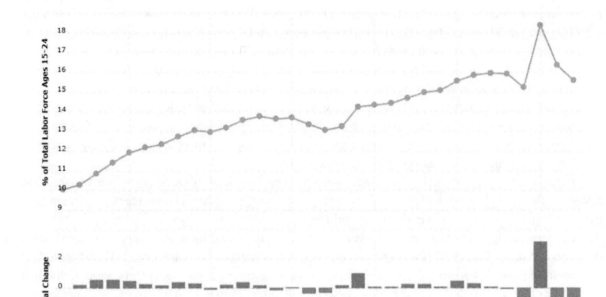

education institutes makes better association with such activities and enables them to achieve the fullest outcome from their undergraduate program (John & Villiers, 2022). The content in the third heading will illustrate how to utilize the features of academia to make a positive transformation to the world of work. This makes a motivation on undergraduates to extract the maximum essence from their learning experience in higher education.

Looking at the success stories of the work world, such as Steve Jobs, Mark Zuckerberg, and Bill Gates took several challenges to position at the highest in the work world. The have utilized serval concepts which are illustrated in the above. For example, Mark Zuckerberg had the opportunity to take advice from his mentor Steve Jobs. Bill Gates also maximized the opportunities he had at the university. This chapter empowers each an ever individual student to prepare for the work world with the proper ideation of career development, the dynamic nature of the work world, and several techniques to maximize the experience in higher education institutes. To pragmatically put these into practice the approach of career compass has been introduced in this chapter. Therefore career compass will help students to pragmatically way to understand their strengths and weaknesses related to professionalism. Then, direct to the proper way to collect information on the world of work. The third step will direct the individual to temporary career decision making. Before decision making on a specific career compass direct individuals to the networking with the professionals. This knowledge acquisition will direct individuals to the proper career decision making. Further, the career compass's sixth step directs individuals to develop a plan for career success. The ultimate goal of career development is the develop a proper balance between personal and professional life. The final step of the career compass directs the individual to create a balance state

*The Undergraduate Career Compass*

between the professional and personal life on the period of the undergraduate. Therefore, making the undergraduate transformation and positioning in the world of work according to their expected career or occupation aspiration is a reproving need in the present academia. Achieving this goal efficiently and productively lies in the self-management of individual professionalism. The teachings and strategies discussed in the chapters and career compass will direct undergraduates to achieve professional and personal success in their future endeavors.

## THEORIES ON CAREER DEVELOPMENT

The influential career development process lies in a realistic understanding of career development theories. These theories provide intellectual guidance to the career seeker and mentor to make more reliable career decisions and develop productive career plans. Scholars who have explored the career development process of an individual introduced several theories on career development (Osipow & Fitzgerald, 1996: Robertson et al., 2021). The concept and theories of career development were introduced by Frank Parson in the 20th century. The approach of professional help in career development was first propagated as vocational guidance. Expansion of the economy and industrialization have been majorly influenced by this evolution. The major goal of the first-era career development theories is to help individuals provide proper guidance on the choice of the proper career or vocational decision-making. Later, scholars who have explored career development theories have direct attention towards the link between career and personal characteristics. Further, these theories have explored the influence of the environmental factor on career development. Contemporary, scholars explored the association between career and human development under the psychological perceptive of self and personality traits (Patton & McMahon, 2021). The developed theories have been more oriented towards making a positive career development on individuals adhering to the psychological principles of human attitudes, motivation, personality, self-concepts, human development, and social interaction and work environment. The career development theories have illustrated career ideation, career readiness, professionalism, and self-concept-related career development processes that occur throughout the life span with special reference to late adolescence and transition to adulthood. The career theories which align with the described nature are as follows:

### Theory of Occupational Choice

Eli Ginzenberg (1951) introduced the theory of occupational career choice. This theory emphasizes occupational or career choice development throughout human development, which will conclude with the choice of realistic career possibility. Accordingly, this theory elaborates that career choice development occurs from birth to the early 20's (Brown, 2002). The first period of fantasy choice belongs to the birth to the age of 10. During this age, the child does not have a reflection about their personality, choices, values, and prospects. They attract dynamic career choices based on their day-to-day life experience. At the end of this period, individuals may have multiple career choices and experiences in an unrealistic manner. However, this influences the development of the remaining stages.

The second stage is known as the period of tentative choice. During this stage, the child begins to explore their future career preference depending on their interests and chosen careers. Then, they compare their career choices with their intellectual abilities and competencies. This mismatch will lead them to seek other available career choices. Children develop their value system by transitioning to adolescence and socialization. Adolescents work towards conceptually identifying realistic career choices by synthesizing their values and self throughout this transformation process.

This third stage is known as the period of the realistic choice, between the ages of 17 and early 20. In this stage, individuals develop their ideal career choices. Then, explore the pragmatic aspects of achieving career opportunities and prospects. The period of realistic choice is alternatively known as the specification stage, and individuals commit towards one specific career choice. They hinge on preferred career choices as individuals from other activities. According to Pattaon and McMahon (2006, p.52), Ginzenberg highlights three perspectives on career growth, the first fact is that occupational choice is a process that remains open as long as one makes and expects to make decisions about his work and career. In many instance it is coterminous with his work life. The second fact is while the successive decisions that a young person makes during the preparatory period will have a shaping influence on his later career, so will the continuing changes that he undergoes in work and life. The third fact is people make decisions about jobs and career with an aim of optimizing their satisfactions by finding the best possible fit between their priority needs and desires and opportunities and constraints that they confront in the world of work.

Thus, the theory of career choice significantly highlights the individual interaction with their social group, cultural factors, and personal exploration, and can be influenced towards the development of career choices. However, this theory indicates that throughout the later experience of career development, several changes may occur, and this will be sharper with future influences coming from social, cultural, and economic factors.

## John Holland's Theory of Vocational Choice

John Holland (1973) has recognized that individual career decision-making critically influences the association between individual personality and environment. The career potential towards fulfilling personal interests will influence career expectation development. Under several assumptions, personality is the primary factor in career choice. The remaining psychological attributes of personal inventories, stereotypical views of the profession, career goals, and personal characteristics also influence career interests or preferences (Gregoire & Jungers, 2013). According to these assumptions, John Holland has developed a personality-based career choice theory that includes six personality types within the career and environment. The preferred six types of personalities are as follows:

John Holland (as cited in Lent & Brown, 2012, pp. 62 -64) has further illustrated the most suitable career option for individuals according to their personality traits:

**Realistic:** Individuals with a high intellectual level and competency toward experimental work belong to this personality category, and their preferred career options are pilot, agriculture, and technology-related job prospects.

**Integrative:** Individuals with the innovation potential to explore new ideas and solve problems belong to this category, and career options are scientist, medical and health professional, and technology-related job prospects.

**Artistic:** Individuals with more potential towards aesthetic activities belong to this category, and the suitable career prospects are photographer, singer player, dancer, and fashion designer.

**Social:** Individuals who are extroverted and socialize belong to this category, and professions of teacher, nurse, counselor, psychologist, social worker, and socially engaging careers are preferred.

*Figure 2. Holland hexagon*
Source: Holland (1973)

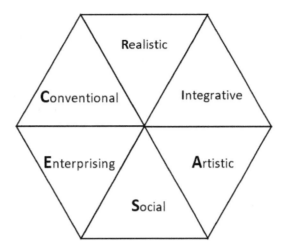

**Enterprising**: An individual who can innovate and deal with people to achieve any goal belongs to this category, and managers, lawyers, politicians, and businessmen are the preferred career prospects.

**Conventional**: Individuals who have the potential to organize, be accurate, and work according to the procedures belong to this category, and preferred career prospects are secretary, receptionist, librarian, and office clerk.

Holland's theory indicates that the nature of individual personality will be directly associated with career prospects. This study has extended, and contemporary researchers have developed a psychometric assessment of *The Occupational Finder* and *My Vocational Situation Tool* to evaluate the link between personality and a suitable career. Further, web applications have also developed, and any individual can easily recognize their nature and the most relevant career. Some of those web tools are:

Holland Code Career Quiz - https://www.truity.com/test/holland-code-career-test

The Holland Code Career Test - https://www.careerfitter.com/career-tests/desires-career-test/holland-code-test

Holland Code (RIASEC) Test - https://openpsychometrics.org/tests/RIASEC/

## Gottredson's Theory of Circumscription and Compromise

The development of the psychological attribute of self-concept is a significant psychological development of any individual. This development and nature of the self-concept influence several aspects of life. As Gottredson (1981) highlights, the individual's psychological and social self majorly influences career choices and professional development (Swanson & Fouad, 2009). This psychological development is majorly associated with the cognitive development and appraisal of the individual. Through human development, children learn about several segments of human life and collect information related to the occupations to determine the quality of the matches. When the child has recognized their occupational choices, such individuals develop a cognitive complexity regarding their expected career or occupation. The development of the mental map regarding the work and career-related self-concept majorly influenced this exploration. Modern theories of personality highlight that genetic and environmental factors influence the development of the individual character.

However, the humanistic psychologist has shown that the development of the self or the character is a self-creation that affects pragmatic career inspiration. This theory highlights that every individual has a development need of niche seeking or finding their place in the world. The seeker's association with self-concept and career choice may shape this exploration behavior. Social factors make this need sharper (Brott, 1993). For example, the prestige received from the occupation or gender suitability may affect the career choice. Later, the period of adolescent development shapes this need more realistically. Mental complex about career choice, interests, values, and abilities will contribute to developing occupational aspirations and alternative career options. In addition, self-exploration about the career may be positively beneficial toward making effective career choices and future career development steps.

## Super's Developmental Theory

Donald E. Super (1980) built upon the developmental psychological principles and stressed that career development aligns with life span development. According to Super's theory, every individual holds a role in their life stages, and the effectiveness of their life role may direct individuals towards satisfaction or dissatisfaction. The introduced five developmental stages depend on career aspirations and environmental factors (Patton & McMahon, 2021). The first stage is the growth stage from the age of 4 to 13. During this period, the child develops their self-concept and fulfills their psychological and physical needs and mental formation through socialization. The second stage is the exploration, between the ages of 12 and 24. Throughout this period, individuals experience life and develop the needed skills according to their tentative choices. The third stage is the establishment period, the age of 25 to 44. During this period individuals have moved forward with life choices and worked toward achieving life goals. The age of 45 to 65 is known as the maintenance period. During this period, individuals focus on maintaining their life standards and moving toward achieving life goals. The final stage is the disengagement period, the individual prepares for retirement and withdraws from his professional and career-related activities. This theory is known as the rainbow of life (Gothard et al., 2001). Individual representation of each developmental stage influences the development of career choice and career-related behavior. Therefore, in the initial stage, the child will develop the idealization of the virtue and career. Then, individuals move toward selecting their respective career choices and working toward achieving career expectations. The journey of career propagated with the interaction of higher education. Depending on the later experience changes may occur in professionalism.

Contemporary, scholars on vocation and career psychology have further explored the human career development process. Recent research studies have been majorly focused on linking career theories and adapting these teachings to the actual conditions of career development (Patton & McMahon, 2021). Early theories on career development have revealed more teaching related to the find out most suitable career options, but at present scholars are focused have driven towards grooming the future generation as entrepreneurs. Apart from the teachings of career theories and career development, the association within the scope of entrepreneurship related to career has been an upcoming trend (Burnette et al., 2020). The present work word is looking for organizational development through career enhancement. Scholars have explored enhancement of the level of performance with career development, through the approaches of training, positive work environment, sustaining career development, employee engagement and career learning has been the major perspectives of career development at present (Robertson, 2021). Further, presently career researchers have directed their attention toward making a positive career transition in career change (Steindórsdóttir et al., 2023)

The contemporary theories on career development also highlight the pragmatic dimension of career development. Career choice and attainment theory have highlighted that the ideology of career development is associated with the occupation self-concept. Social factors such as sex role, size and power, social value, and unique self will determine career choices. The attainment of the career aspiration will depend upon the social attitude, bias, cultural expectation, and stereotyped experience of the gender race ethnicity will determine the level of career achievement (Lent & Brown, 2012). Another recent theory on career development is the career self-determination theory, this theory emphasizes utilizing individual potential and strengths to achieve the expectations of life endeavors. This theory empowered individuals to achieve career expectations with positive psychological abilities. According to this theory achieving career success is fully responsible by the job seeker (Chen, 2017). When looking at an individual who is successful in the work world their personality shows this quality of determination for the achievement the career goals. For Example, author J.K Rowling has faced many challenges in finding a publisher for her book. But with self-determination, she has success in her profession with a billion-worth book series. Another critical theory of career development is The Chaos Theory of Careers. We all experience uncertainties in our day-to-day lives. This condition is common even in career development. Previous theories have highlighted the theme was career development systematically and explained certain conditions. However, our existence is full of uncertainties, and synthesizing these uncertain conditions with our possibilities helps to secure us from career growth vulnerability. This theory is emphasize utilize the obstacles, challenges, and threats as an opportunity to growth (Pryor & Bright, 2011). Another successful individual who aligns with this theory is founder of the Amazon. Jeff Bezos has taken challenges as opportunities and develop his venture. In addition, social and cultural factors such as ethnicity, nationality, religion, social class, values, childhood experience gender social and economic condition, and life roles will play a significant role in transformations of professional development.

Thus, career development theories have highlighted that the individual career development process is a significant developmental task. Each development stage may develop the career-related self-concept. Throughout human development, every individual enrolls in numerous career development tasks. During the progressive development stages, adolescents may develop more realistic and alternative career choices. Then, the individual is directed towards achieving future career aspirations. These theories have shown that the nature of the individual achievement of their career goals shapes the life prospects and total life span. The insight into career development theories makes a solid foundation for career progression. Contemporary, there is a growing demand to adapt these teachings to positively adapt to the work world and enrich the career development of the individual. However, the knowledge of the above theories provides an informative way to orient toward career success according to the universally accepted theories. While looking more inwardly several occasions, undergraduates experience deficits in career development due to not having proper knowledge about the work world. The below heading will elaborate on the nature of the world of work, which helps with adaptation and resilience in career progression according to the dynamic nature of the work world.

## NATURE OF THE WORD OF WORK

We are interacting with the fourth industrial revolution or technology-based industrial era in the contemporary world. Human needs and services are wholly filled through a technological orientation. The development process of professionals for the present world of work is challenging due to this rapid change of industries with technological transformation. Making more resilient towards the world of work challenges, knowledge about the respective industries is essential for higher education policymakers, teachers, and career decision-making students.

According to the interpretations of the World Economic Forum (2022), the world of work has been mainly affected by the COVID-19 pandemic, and remote working and digitalized industries will dominate the world of work. Adapting more positively towards rapid changes in industries, acquiring new career-related knowledge, and developing skills are essential. Since, a career is a cultural phenomenon, which helps towards fulfills the needs of the day to day life. But contemporary career has transformed into a globalized phenomenon, career opportunities have been propagated worldwide and help to connect with the world through the technological infrastructure.

Further, employees are highly interested in the transition to new industries, and starting a new career has been a trend in the future world of work. As a result of the changes occurring in the world of work, some professions will disappear or become less demanding. New occupations or careers will be propagated depending on human needs and services. Due to the advancement of technology, most traditional occupations and job tasks will be automated and computerized. Considering this nature, undergraduates must understand that the demand for careers or professions will disappear with time and the industrial revolutions (Godfrey, 2021).

The technological influence of the fourth industrial revolution has made this condition more critical. The nature of the fourth industrial revolution will be connected with the digital domain and technological infrastructural development. This means the industries will be converted from the machines to the robots. Artificial intelligence platforms are playing a major role in the present work world. Higher education academic programs must be adapted according to the opportunities and prospects of the fourth industrial revolution (Xu et al., 2018). The future opportunities in the fourth industrial revolution will be knowledge-driven and skill-demanded. The prospects of the fourth industrial revolution are making fewer barriers with the inventors and markets. The more active role of artificial intelligence and quality lifestyle with robotics and the internet will be witnessed.

Moreover, technology will change the working environment of the future work world. Traditionally individuals will went a location to perform their job-orient works. But presently, this has transformed into distance work or work from home. This has converted the work career into a globalized phenomenon. The person can work in any organization anywhere in the world. Through the automation of the industry, most traditional jobs will disappear with the replacement of the reboots. Even this can affect the service-oriented career with the integration of artificial intelligence. Career outlook will further evolve with the economic transformation and most of the time future work world will exist with short-term job placements (Younus, 2021).

However, the challenges of the fourth industrial revolution are the complexity and the technological initiation. As described above, more significant job displacement will occur, and technological-related matters will be raised further. Nevertheless, changes occur in the world of work, and adapting to the respective changes in higher education is necessary. This adaptation must be filled with the expected knowledge and skill. According to Pandya et al. (2020, p.55) have predicted the demanding skills for the fourth industrial era and 2030 as Cognitive and Metacognitive skills (critical thinking, Learning to learn, and self-regulation), Creativity and Innovation, Social and emotional skills (empathy, self-efficacy, and collaboration), technology-related skills and the remaining skills are hard to automate. The nature of the future world of work is ever-changing, and the demands of the future workforce will be competing and complex forces. According to the geographical difference, this may be further dynamic. Due to this demand, the future workforce needs to be more empowered through education and skills to contribute to the economic growth of the region (Kubicek & Korunka, 2017).

In conclusion, the future work will be more dynamic and challenging with the technological evolving and economic growth. Through the traditional viewpoint of career individuals will inadequate to survive in the work world, multiple skills and technological interaction is an essential needs in the work world. This modification happens in the work world and the future workforce is majorly served by higher education institutions. The development of academic programs, teachings, and learning experiences, which need to fulfill the needs of the future demands of the world of work. Students' orientation toward the future world of work for achieving career aspirations, expected skill development, and direction toward exploring new career opportunities are needed. Otherwise, students will face many challenges in the future due to a mismatch of the academic qualifications and skills demanded by the world of work.

## MOVING ACADEMIA TO PROFESSIONALISM

The career development theories have highlighted that individuals develop career ideations, during adolescence and establish realistic concepts about careers, then work towards achieving their career goals. The most significant feature is individuals must enroll actively in higher education to achieve career goals successfully. Undergraduates understanding of the procedures of higher education institutes assist in preparing for the world of work demand. This understanding may direct the undergraduate towards making a balance between academic activities and resilience in a dynamic work world. According to Chu et al. (2016, p.20) highlight contemporary educational policy and academic programs need to be developed depending on the following framework of 21st-century education:

This diagram highlights the educationist's role in the development of academic programs according to the needs of the 21st-century educational policy. Significant recognition is given to curriculum development and assessments. According to this diagram, professional development and the working environment are the most critical factors. This diagram shows that higher education has to give more recognition to professional development in curriculum with a hands-on learning experience. The expected skill development process can be recognized from personal and professional development perspectives. From a personal perspective, life and career skills, and a professional perspective, critical thinking, communication, collaboration, creativity, information, and technology skills have been highlighted. Literature highlights that throughout the higher education process, educationists need to focus on developing skills in teamwork, problem-solving, social skills, and innovation (Dunne et al., 2000).

Learning experience of higher education individuals need to be aware of these dimensions and acquire the needed potential as much as they can. However, the needed skill may be changed according to the expectations of the economy of the respective society (Bagci & Kocyigit, 2019). Higher education curricula need to be developed to achieve the expectations of the world of work. This needs is in three dimensions: pedagogical, content, and technological knowledge. Through the learning experience of higher education, educationists have to focus on developing these three dimensions (Gollnick et al.,

*Figure 3. P21 framework for 21st century learning*
Source: Chu et.al (2016)

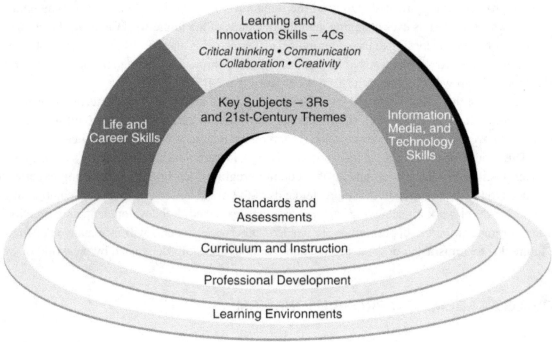

2018). The undergraduate responsibility is harnessing and inculcating professional competencies in the curriculum. The major problem in present academics is most undergraduates are not aware of these aspects and the consequence is individuals will lack the demanding competencies.

To adapt the graduates to the work world properly higher education institutes are offered mentoring services. The scholars have provided several answers to the question of what is mentoring. Considering all the definitions mentoring can be recognized as providing information, developing skills, and directing individuals toward impactful transformation (Laverick, 2016). Generally, this mentoring ship support can be provided by an academic member or professional individual. Throughout the mentoring service, the student can plan their career according to the guidelines and directions given by the mentor. Continues relationship collaboration with the mentor individual able to achieve their career and academic goals according to the instructions given by the mentor. Moreover, the mentor will help to shape the individual personality through his expertise and knowledge. Therefore, mentoring services help students to make the proper transition from word of work with the proper directions with all the necessary potential (Miller, 2004). However, present higher education most student are not taking directions from these services for their career enhancement.

In addition, the higher education process needed to focus on fulfilling the needs of the world of work. This will positively contribute to the economic growth of the respective nation and address the shortages of human capital development (Teichler, 2009). Contemporary researchers have recognized that there is a gap between graduates' skills, quality, and quantity-wise gaps, and research and innovation ability-related weaknesses may be represented (Ordine & Rose, 2015). The linkage between industries, research institutes, and training-providing institutions may depend on effectively delivering the teachings and grooming of undergraduates to the world of work (Di Gropello & Tandon, 2011). Undergraduates can have this exposure through their internship placements. This professional placement focuses on growing student knowledge and adaptation to the work world with hands-on experience and making a proper transition from the university to the work environment (International Labor Organization, 2021). Generally, these internship opportunities are provided by the university, or according to student preference they can find these opportunities via serval web sites. This will be a temporary job placement, student will gain the opportunity to enhance their ability and apply what they have acquired in higher education. On some occasions, this can perform as work while learning. Further, while internship students have the opportunity to shift between the various departments in the organization. According to student preference, Students can continue this internship as their career according to their preference (Cooper et al., 2013).

Thus, the student's behavior toward achieving their career goals in higher educational institutes plays a significant role. Individuals start the journey of professionalism, acquiring qualifications and skills developed through the experience and exposure received through higher education institutes and academic programs. Therefore, the practical function of higher education institutes in the above-mentioned dimensions positively and effectively contributes to grooming the future workforce. Contemporary, major challenges experienced by graduates is not gaining the fullest from the available sources and services in higher education institutes. The negative consequence of these actions is graduate output will conclude with minimum competencies. However, the awareness of the above-described paradigms of higher education helps individuals to move toward academia to professionalism productively. The knowledge about above the dimensions gives a proper insight into the psychological development of the career self, the dynamic nature of the work world, and available options in higher education for grooming the future workforce. Founding this knowledge individuals gain proper insight into professionalism and by maximizing this knowledge and achieving the goals in professionalism the below seven strategies described under the career compass will give empirical directions.

## PREPARING FOR THE WORLD OF WORK

The individual career development process is a lifelong process. Career readiness is majorly presented in the period of late adolescence or the period of engagement in higher education. Through the higher education journey, every undergraduate prepares to achieve future career expectations. According to the nature of the individual career readiness, their success in future careers may depend. Considering this, higher education institutes are responsible for grooming undergraduates for the world of work with the expected intellect and skills. Contemporary world higher education institutes have introduced several programs for career development and career counseling services for students. Through the support of these services, undergraduates can achieve their career goals effectively. However, the result of achieving career success, self-preparation, and self-management are vital tasks (Conley, 2010).

The undergraduates' transition to the work world is presented through the psychological process of career readiness. While looking through the undergraduate's behavior related to career readiness and preparation shows several deficits. According to the studies related to the challenges of undergraduates' career readiness shows, most undergraduates experience career choice-related anxiety, lack of self-knowledge in career preparation, career indecision, and a mismatch between expected career goals and academic programs (Salleh et al., 2017). Another study that has shown undergraduates' lack of career readiness has majorly affected the career decision-making process. The unemployed undergraduates have shown a low rate of career readiness and most of them have experienced dysfunctional career thinking. As a result of these conditions career-related self-efficacy also shows a lack of functions. The major causes for these deficits are a lack of self-knowledge, career information, and improper career selection and planning (Mahmud et al., 2019).

Further, scholars have shown these career readiness-related issues can be solved through internships and short-term working opportunities. Through these approaches, undergraduates can experience the real nature of the work world. This has made a greater impact on undergraduates to make their career decisions with appropriate knowledge and exposure (Leonard et al., 2023). Providing opportunities for the students to enhance their career readiness and preparation by providing career-related information, development of transferable skills, developing insight about the dynamic employment landscape, and industrial exposure developed the undergraduate's potential for career readiness. The positive consequences are effective career choices, evidence-based career decision making, and planning (Stebleton et al., 2020). Likewise, higher education institutes have introduced several programmes and services to enhance the undergraduate potential of career readiness. However, studies have shown that interventions related to enhancement of the career readiness may show a significant development of career perception and active preparation, but these interventions are doing surface learning. There is a serious need from the undergraduate corner to compare their ideation with the real-world nature and become more prepared to achieve their career goals within deep learning and realistically adapting towards the dynamic nature of the landscape of the work world (Siby et al., 2023).

This evidence shows at present most undergraduates experience career-related matters due to a lack of career readiness. The root cause for career readiness is a lack of self-knowledge and career knowledge. This may negatively affect career decision making, career choices, proper adaptation to the work world, lack of competencies, and lack of soft skills. The interventions utilized to overcome these gaps have made a greater contribution towards the development of career perceptions and readiness. However, from the undergraduate's corner, a significant self-contribution needs to be made toward their professionalism (Jackson & Wilton, 2017).

Therefore, the career readiness of undergraduates is an essential cognitive attribute on undergraduates towards preparing for the work world. The information gathering related to self and career is the essential task in career readiness, then synthesizing the information within the real work world decision making and developing the career plans direct individual to success in professionalism. This complete process consists of self-preparation, self-management, and a self-responsible process, and the illustrated seven realistic steps may help to address all these needs and be able to pragmatically transform individuals from academia to the work world. These steps are as follows:

The overview and function of each step are as follows:

## Step 1: Self-Evaluation and Self-Understanding

To successfully make career choices and adapt to the world of work, first proper self-evaluation and self-understanding are essential. Inadequate understanding of personality, individuals are unable to move toward professional development. The self-evaluation task can be completed with the analysis of strengths, weaknesses, opportunities, and threats (SWOT). Through the SWOT analysis, an individual can understand the spectrum of personality. However, here individuals are mainly directed toward identifying and evaluating the career-related SWOT analysis. Schermerhorn and Bachrah (2017, p.18) have introduced the following model for this analysis:

*The Undergraduate Career Compass*

*Figure 4. Seven steps of the career compass*
Source: Author Created (2023)

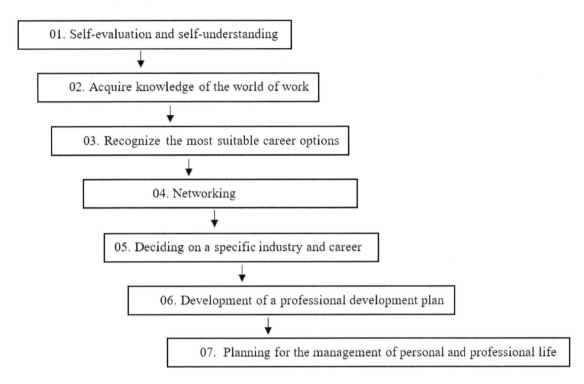

*Table 1. SWOT analysis for the career planning*

| Career and Personality | |
|---|---|
| **Strengths** <br> • Identification of the strengths and further strengthening them | **Weaknesses** <br> • Identification of the weaknesses and overcome the weaknesses |
| **Opportunities** <br> • Recognizing the opportunities available and strengths them | **Threats** <br> • Recognizing the threats that occur and helping to overcome them |
| Career and environment | |

Source: Schermerhorn & Bachrach (2017)

By assessing the dimensions of the diagram individuals can recognize the prospects for career planning. The first two domains evaluate the individual personality and career-related strengths and weaknesses according to the skills, intellectuality, and personal choice, preference related to the career or occupation. Through the evaluation of these two dimensions, individuals can comparatively recognize the variance between career choices and interests. For example some occasions individuals may interested in one specific career, but the demand for skill may not be with them. This analysis will give a complete idea about individual personality and career aspirations. Further, this will not limited to the individual career-related assessment. The seeker can explore their strengths and utilize them to overcome their career and personality-related weaknesses. At present, several online tools are available for self-exploration and undergraduates can utilize those resources to recognize their potential. A few prominent tools are:

Myers Briggs Type Indicator – https://www.16personalities.com/

Recognizing strengths - https://high5test.com/
Recognize strengths related to career - https://www.redbull.com/int-en/wingfinder
Career interest and personality test - https://www.truity.com/view/tests/personality-career

This analysis process's second dimension is recognizing the job environment-related opportunities and threats. Since a career is not bound to the individual domain, it is interrelated with several external factors. The awareness of the external factors under the dimensions of the opportunities and threats is essential to gain proper steps toward career development. This evaluation can be done through knowledge and information they have gathered on the work world and their relationship with external factors. By exploring these two factors, individuals can recognize the career environment-related influence on achieving career goals. Individuals must overcome career-related threats through the available opportunities. Thus, by completing the first step, individuals can develop a good understanding of their needs and career-orientated strengths and weaknesses. While individuals wish to achieve their career goals, they must balance internal and external factors to move towards their goals without any disturbance or barriers. This process can be further strengthened with the use of personality and career choice assessments (Barrett, 2009). The successful outcome may be beneficial for the remaining steps of the career compass (Cambers, 2005).

## Step 2: Acquire Knowledge of the World of Work

The second step is acquiring knowledge about the world of work. When individuals have good insight and understanding of the world of work, they can make a successful step toward professionalism. Through this step, the individual becomes a knowledge-driven person, and further actions may be performed with the proper understanding and insight. According to Peacock et al (2020), individuals need to focus on the collected information from two perspectives, those are industry and career-related information.

Under the information gathering on industry-related information, individual findings need to highlight the nature of the respective industry globally and nationally. The information gathering may be evident about the reputed organizations, changes that occur in the respective industry, and available opportunities in the industry. Especially the number of jobs available and the increment of the job opportunities. Then, the expected skills in the industry and discerning professionals or careers in the respective industry need to be identified. To collect this information individuals can access the websites of the organization, professional bodies, and blogs that discuss the economic and industry transformation. Acquiring the proper knowledge about the industry allows individuals to have a more insightful perception of the preferred industry for effective decision-making.

The second category of career-related information is collected through a similar process of job analysis in human resource management (Nankervis et al, 2019). The expected outcome will be collecting the information related to the several tasks that need to be performed in the respective career, available responsibilities, the level of the workload the individual needs to handle, physical and mental courage needed for the career, skills, competencies needed for the career, hierarchy of the career, risk available in the job, salary scales and qualifications needed for the job (Kumar, 2010). For this individuals can reefer several job posting websites and referee the job advertisement posts on the websites, such websites are:

Indeed Job Search – https://www.indeed.com/
Glassdoor Job Search – https://www.glassdoor.com/index.htm
Google jobs - https://jobs.google.com
Simply hired - https://www.simplyhired.com

Career builder - https://www.careerbuilder.com

Further, an individual can collect information related to the industry and career by utilizing the methods of interviewing the individual in the industry to identify the information related to the industry and career. This information collection process needs to be a continuous and renewing process. Ensuring the reliability and validity of collected information may be beneficial for making temporary career decisions in the third step and proper career decision making in the fifth step.

## Step 3: Recognize the Most Suitable Career Options

The third step is focused on recognizing the most suitable career options available for the undergraduate. These career options are selected with the proper knowledge of the self and world of work. In this step, the individual is not making an exact career decision. Individuals must go through the fourth step to make a proper or exact career decision. According to Hassna et al (2022), social and psychological factors of social cognition, sex difference, self-efficacy, future academic achievement, and experience received through academic activities make multiple career decisions (Morgan et al., 2001). As described by Dick and Rallis (1991) due to the re-definable ideation having multiple career decisions and choices may be beneficial. The utility of selecting multiple careers may be beneficial towards matching the individual potentials with various career options available.

According to the career principles if an individual is inadequate to achieve the expected career outcome having an optional career may beneficial to survive in the professional world. The temporary career decisions and multiple career options may sustain individual career progression without any doubt or challenge. From a social perspective, individual occupational motivation, job satisfaction, job continuity, and fulfilling life goals through the respective occupation may depend. Individual interests, job-specific traits, self-concepts and self-perception, advancement in life and career, seeking different options, and improvement of abilities and experience may create a dynamic nature in career decisions.

In addition, presently most students experience obstacles related to their career choices due to their psychology foundation. The psychological foundation of career choice consists of personality traits and social factors. Individual differences are the major factors that influence career choices. Individual childhood experiences, personal preferences, traumatic experiences, and IQ will influence individual career choices. Apart from this several social factors may also influence career choices such as gender, ethnicity, and social and economic background (Rakhmanova & Meylieva, 2021). The psychological states of positive and negative emotions, fear, and anxiety also lead toward a dynamic nature of career. These factors can be recognized as the obstacles we experience in career choices and a proper understanding of these facts will lead to the most suitable career choices.

Therefore, in the initial stage, making multiple career options depending on the insight about self and knowledge of the world of work will be more effective than selecting one specific career and developing plans according to the respective career. Further, knowledge about the psychological and sociological foundation of career choices may lead towards the make an appropriate career decision free from prejudice. The third step of the career compass is making an experimental career decision with an opening toward change in future possibilities. To make the proper career decision actual knowledge about the work world and aligning individual interests with the demands of the work world are essential. This knowledge only can be acquired through networking with individuals in the work world. The fourth steps provide proper directions related to the network with professionals and acquiring essential information.

## Step 4: Networking

An individual needs to develop a professional network before deciding about a specific career option and working toward achieving career goals. Networking does not belong to an activity related to the undergraduate learning experience of higher education. On most occasions, networking is utilized in graduate and professional education. However, this step suggests that individuals build up their network at their undergraduate level, which will benefit them in many aspects. This process is similar to mentoring, which is focused on obtaining support from industry professionals to develop career decisions and plans. The present professional world has plenty of networking opportunities. Professionals welcome those who are willing to network. Through the networking process, individuals gain sound knowledge about the success of professionalism. To develop effective networking with professionals, individuals need to have proper awareness about the nature of people, strategies for maintaining social relationships, and communication ability, (Fishers, 2011).

Initial stage, individuals need to recognize the available opportunities for the development of the network and the types of actions utilized to maintain the relationship with the respective professionals. The effectiveness of the networking process, undergraduates can participate in events in the industry, perform freelance work, engage in social media networking, and have internship opportunities provided by higher educational institutes. Present work word has established several platforms for professional networking, such as;

LinkedIn- https://www.linkedin.com/
Meetup - https://www.meetup.com/
Job case - https://www.jobcase.com/

Further, to sustain the relationship with their network, students can participate in the events conducted by the respective organization, doing collaborative work with the professionals and asking for information related to the industry and career. The most important thing is expanding the individual network. Through this networking process, individuals need to collect reliable information flow for making proper decisions in the fifth step. Therefore, networking is a principal obligation of the undergraduate career development process (Faulkner et al., 2010).

## Step 5: Deciding on a Specific Industry and Career

The principal step of the undergraduates' career compasses is decision-making on a career in a specific industry. Traditionally, individuals make career decisions without a proper understanding of self and knowledge of the world of work. Undergraduates do not give much more attention to the dynamic changes in their career decisions. The fifth step is working on actual or permanent career decisions making. The distinguishing feature of this step from the third step is, that individuals are free from the multiple career options. Undergraduates are not making exact decisions on their career, throughout the third step, undergraduates go through several career options and synthesize them with their preferences.

Then, under the fifth step, the individual makes the evidential decision. This decision becomes evidential due to the collected information in self-understanding and knowledge of the world of work. Further, an individual is empowered with the assistance of networking. Then, the first task of the fifth step is individual decision-making in the respective industry. Recognizing industry is essential because all occupations are based on the specific industry, and changes in the industry majorly influence the occupation. Sometimes, a few careers may belong to several industries. The second step is career decision-making. This is a complex intellectual process, which may influence several factors. The decision-making process must be done based on the information collected from the above steps. Reliable information is needed to make a more realistic and satisfied decision (Harren, 1979).

In proper career decision making individuals have to consider the social and cultural factors that influence career decision making. On, some occasions individual has an insightful ideology about their career decision, but they become victims of their social and cultural identities. For example, Thomas Edison came from a low social statues but he used to manage his social and economic status in the growth of his career. Culture also limits human potential and in career decision making some cases, individuals may have to beyond the stigmas of culture. For example, females enrolling in some professions and becoming entrepreneurs in society are seen as challenges for cultural values (Lent & Brown, 2020).

The potential to select a specific industry and career with proper insight and planning indicates individual career maturity. Moreover, scholars highlight that this decision-making process will be weak due to factors such as lack of readiness, inconsistent information, and gender stereotypes (Albion & Fogarty, 2002). There are several career decision-making styles known as rational, intuitive, and dependent, the decision must be rational (Gati et al., 2010).

Contemporary career seekers experience difficulties making decisions due to an improper understanding of the dynamic nature of career preferences and a lack of information. In the effective formation of the fifth step, undergraduates will overcome the illusion of career dynamics and make an exact and effective career decision rather than working towards the career aspiration in the initial stages of professional development.

## Step 6: Development of a Professional Development Plan

Individuals who have completed the above steps must work towards developing a result-based plan for their professional development in this step. Here, individuals must focus on academic qualifications, job-oriented skills, experience, soft skills, and professional qualifications expected for the relevant career and the progression of career development according to the career ladder. Depending on the collected information on the above themes, undergraduates have to develop a career development plan according to the below steps:

To successfully implement this process, individuals must evaluate and map their developmental path. Preparing the timeline progression with key performance indicators, modularizing, and checking the

*Figure 5. The progressive steps of the professional development plan*
Source: Author Created (2023)

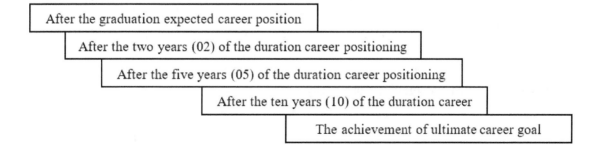

hazards is essential. Throughout the planning process, individuals need to explore the gaps available and take action to address those gaps. This will be beneficial for the overcome future needs and threats (Sangster, 2017). Moreover, transforming this planning into an action plan is the most needed part, and predicting the utilization of the resources will assist in successfully achieving the goals of professionalism.

The success of a career is deepening upon the qualification and job-oriented skills acquired by the individual. But to achieve real success in their careers, the individual has to develop their soft skills or enhance their capacity for emotional intelligence. Individual empowered with the emotional intelligence capacity or EQ, plays a significant role in building a career (Tripathy, 2020). Potentials such as self-awareness, self-regulation, self-motivation, empathy, positive social interaction, and communication are essential for career success. Individuals who are working towards professional success need their emotional intelligence (EQ) during the period of professional development planning (Goleman, 2012).

Proper preparation for professionalism according to the above highlighted will ensure the professional success of the individual. However, throughout the preparation for professionalism, individuals have to shape both personal and professional outlooks. This has been a unique need because most individuals success in their profession but face may difficulties in their personal lives. Therefore, from the undergraduate period proper mechanisms for stress management and resilience towards keeping the balance between personal and professional life is an essential need. The following step directs the individual toward for achievement of that prospect.

## Step 7: Plan for the Management of Personal and Professional Life

The undergraduate's ultimate goal is to position themselves in their expected career aspiration after graduation. But undergraduate's genuine enthusiasm is to succeed in both professional and personal life. Considering this need, an effective plan for balancing personal and professional life is essential. The development process of the individual career development plan must consist of the parameters for managing the personal and professional life. Professional development and personal development are two distinctive approaches. Professional development is known as achieving the expected pursuits in a career or occupation. Personal development can be recognized as enriching and satisfying personal life wishes. Proper management of emotions and motivations is essential for the success of professionalism and personal life (Tipton, 2015).

Contemporary world most professionals are suffering from stress due to their job roles. Developing an effective mechanism of stress management on the student's time makes a great effort towards the betterment of future life. Giving recognition for the management of work-life stress from the early stages of career development planning leads to future satisfaction. Moreover, personal and professional life consists of complex life challenges and an effective life philosophy helps to develop resilience. Individuals can develop their own set of habits and read the self helps books to develop this knowledge and skill. This can be more effective with having proper insight and effective behaviors on positive attitude, time management, self-motivation, and self-care. Adaptation of these qualities, individuals can develop a positive spectrum of work-life balance in the future. Also benefited the success of the student life. Therefore, working towards a balance in personal and professional life in the initial stage of career development may enrich undergraduate prosperity.

## FUTURE RESEARCH DIRECTIONS

Contemporary, undergraduates may experience numerous challenges regarding their professional development. The teachings of this chapter emphasize pragmatic ways to overcome those challenges. Undergraduate can utilize the mentioned seven steps for their career development process pragmatically. This chapter has illustrated the most practical aspects related to career development. Any undergraduate who has already worked towards their career goals can adapt these teachings to make their career plans effective. Moreover, the individual who has already developed career development plans can evaluate the reliability of their plans by synthesizing the steps of the career compass. Presently, career counselors and mentors are making a greater contribution toward individual professional development. The illustrated seven steps of the career compass can be utilized for career counseling and mentoring to direct clients toward professional development. The significant feature of the career compass is this approach is free from the directive approach. Through a non-directive approach, a career compass directs individuals toward professional growth. In addition, higher education institutes can adopt this framework for the professional development of undergraduates within their teachings and learning exposure. After the utilization of the career compass future, empirical studies can evaluate the efficacy of these seven steps in an evidence-based manner and develop a reliable framework for navigating undergraduates for career succession.

## CONCLUSION

The ultimate goal of the undergraduate diary is to successfully position in the work world. To effectively position in the world of work, properly developed plans and relevant actions are needed. Presently, undergraduates who are enrolled in higher education are unable to effectively enter the work world due to not having proper guidance for professionalism. This may occur as the consequence of unemployment, dissatisfaction, work stress, turnover, and issues in personal life. The concepts illustrated in the chapters have given an effective way to overcome these challenges pragmatically. On most occasions, undergraduates are directed toward professional planning without the insight of career development theories. The knowledge acquisition of the career development theories makes proper ideation about the comparative process of career and human development. Secondly, for the success of professionalism, the knowledge of the work world is essential. Since all professional-related behaviors are associated with the work world. The significant feature of the work world is dynamic. To effectively adapt towards professionalism knowledge about the work world is essential. Otherwise, individuals may be unable to survive in the world of work. Moreover, present academic undergraduates were inadequate to gain the maximum opportunities available in higher education institutes and academic programs. To gain maximum from the academic diary and move towards a professional outlook of higher education needs to be communicated. These three dimensions empowered the undergraduates with the essential knowledge and a clear view of professionalism.

After the acquisition of knowledge about the above dimension, an individual can properly move toward career planning. In any context, career planning needs to start with self-evaluation and an overall understanding of internal and external factors associated with career development. Individual career decision making is a significant action related to career progression. However, according to the career compass individuals make career decisions with the understating of the work world and professional networking. Also, undergraduates can address the obstacle of multiple career choices with the help of a career compass. Then, individuals move towards the development of career development plans in a result-based manner with the management of their personal and professional lives. The described approach of the career compass gives giving greater contribution towards overcoming the challenges related to undergraduate career succession.

Through the described steps of the career compass undergraduate will be able to make their career decision and plans with a proper understanding of their inner and outer world related to professionalism. The limitation of this approach can be recognized as while the implementation of the strategies of the career compass individuals need to have proper ideation about the career concepts. Individuals may implement these steps with their potential without any guidance and supervision, in realistic conditions several challenges may occur by the undergraduates. The nature of the work world and frameworks of higher education institutes in respective societies may weaken the efficacy of the career compass. This chapter has addressed the common issues experienced by undergraduates in career readiness. Through the described concepts individuals can generate insightful knowledge about career development, the dynamic nature of the work world, and harnessing the fullest from the higher education interaction. Ultimately described seven will be beneficial for undergraduates to develop the psychological ability of career readiness with proper self and career-related knowledge. Further, an individual can make proper career decisions according to their career choices and develop plans for achieving their career goals in professional and personal endeavors.

The present higher education sector is majorly focused on transferring undergraduates toward the work world. Throughout the process of grooming undergraduates toward the work world, several potentials need to develop within the undergraduates. Apart from several attributes career readiness is the most essential pillar. The success of an undergraduate's career path lies in the proper career readiness. Therefore, this chapter pragmatically contributes to the theme of the book chapter, providing an evidence-based mechanism for preparing the first generation students to work world self-directed approach, and the teachings of the career compass may enrich career efficacy and contribute towards effective adaptation to the work world.

## REFERENCES

Albion, M. J., & Fogarty, G. J. (2002). Factors influencing career decision making in adolescents and adults. *Journal of Career Assessment*, *10*(1), 91–126. doi:10.1177/1069072702010001006

Alolaqi, S. A., & Yusof, R. B. (2022). Youth Unemployment and Role of Entrepreneurship: Factors Influencing Students' Entrepreneurial Intention. *Global Business and Management Research*, 14.

Bagci, H., & Kocyigit, M. (2019). *21st Century Skills and Education*. Cambridge Scholars Publisher.

Barrett, J. (2009). *Career Aptitude and Selection Tests: Match Your IQ Personality and Abilities to Your Ideal Career*. Kogan Page Publishers.

Brott, P. E. (1993). *Gottfredson's Theory of Circumscription and Compromise: Implications for Career Counseling*. Educational Resources Information Center.

Brown, D. (2002). *Career Choice and Development*. Wiley Publications.

Burnette, J. L., Pollack, J. M., Forsyth, R. B., Hoyt, C. L., Babij, A. D., Thomas, F. N., & Coy, A. E. (2020). A growth mindset intervention: Enhancing students' entrepreneurial self-efficacy and career development. *Entrepreneurship Theory and Practice*, *44*(5), 878–908. doi:10.1177/1042258719864293

Cambers, R. (2005). *Career Planning for Everyone in the NHS: The Toolkit*. Radcliffe Publications.

Chen, C. P. (2017). Career self-determination theory. *Psychology of career adaptability, employability and resilience*, 329-347.

Chu, S. K. W., Reynolds, R. B., Tavares, N. J., Notari, M., & Lee, C. W. Y. (2016). *21st Century Skills Development Through Inquiry-Based Learning: From Theory to Practice*. Springer Nature.

Conley, D. T. (2010). *College and Career Ready: Helping All Students Succeed Beyond High School*. Wiley Publications. doi:10.1002/9781118269411

Cooper, D. L., Saunders, S. A., Winston, R. B. Jr, Hirt, J. B., Creamer, D. G., & Janosik, S. M. (2013). *Learning Through Supervised Practice in Student Affairs*. Taylor & Francis. doi:10.4324/9780203890332

Di Gropello, E., & Tandon, P. (2011). *Putting Higher Education to Work: Skills and Research for Growth in East Asia*. World Bank Publications.

Dick, T. P., & Rallis, S. F. (1991). Factors and influences on high school students' career choices. *Journal for Research in Mathematics Education*, *22*(4), 281–292. doi:10.2307/749273

Dunne, E., Bennett, N., & Carre, C. (2000). *Skill development in higher education and employment*. Society for Research into Higher education and Open University Press.

Faulkner, M. L., Faulkner, D. M. L., & Nierenberg, A. (2010). *Networking for College Students (and Recent Graduates): Nonstop Business Networking That Will Change Your Life*. Pearson Learning Solutions.

Fisher, D. (2011). *Professional Networking For Dummies*. Wiley Publications.

Gati, I., Landman, S., Davidovitch, S., Asulin-Peretz, L., & Gadassi, R. (2010). From career decision-making styles to career decision-making profiles: A multidimensional approach. *Journal of Vocational Behavior*, *76*(2), 277–291. doi:10.1016/j.jvb.2009.11.001

Ginzberg, E. (1951). *Occupational Choice: An Approach to a General Theory*. Columbia University Press.

Godfrey, N. (2021, September 13). *Dying careers you may want to Steer Clear of*. Kiplinger. https://www.kiplinger.com/personal-finance/careers/603424/dying-careers-you-may-want-to-steer-clear-of

Goleman, D. (2012). *Emotional Intelligence: Why It Can Matter More Than IQ*. Random House Publishing Group.

Gollnick, D. M., Hall, G. E., & Quinn, L. F. (2018). *The Wiley Handbook of Teaching and Learning*. Wiley Publications.

Gothard, W. P., Mignot, P., Offer, M., & Ruff, M. (2001). *Careers Guidance in Context*. SAGE Publications. doi:10.4135/9781446220399

Gottfredson, L. S. (1981). Circumscription and compromise: A developmental theory of occupational aspirations. *Journal of Counseling Psychology*, *28*(6), 545–579. doi:10.1037/0022-0167.28.6.545

Gregoire, J., & Jungers, C. (2013). *The Counsellor's Companion: What Every Beginning Counselor Needs to Know*. Taylor & Francis.

Harren, V. A. (1979). A model of career decision making for college students. *Journal of Vocational Behavior, 14*(2), 119–133. doi:10.1016/0001-8791(79)90065-4

Hassan, H., Hussain, M., Niazi, A., Hoshino, Y., Azam, A., & Kazmi, A. S. (2022). Career Path Decisions and Sustainable Options. *Sustainability (Basel), 14*(17), 10501. doi:10.3390/su141710501

Havighurst, R. J. (1972). *Developmental Tasks and Education*. D. McKay Company.

Holland, J. L. (1973). *Making Vocational Choices: A Theory of Careers*. Prentice-Hall.

International Labour Organization. (2021). *Internships, Employability and the Search for Decent Work Experience*. Edward Elgar Publishing Limited.

Jackson, D., & Wilton, N. (2017). Perceived employability among undergraduates and the importance of career self-management, work experience and individual characteristics. *Higher Education Research & Development, 36*(4), 747–762. doi:10.1080/07294360.2016.1229270

John, S. P., & De Villiers, R. (2022). Factors affecting the success of marketing in higher education: A relationship marketing perspective. *Journal of Marketing for Higher Education*, 1–20. doi:10.1080/08841241.2022.2116741

Kubicek, B., & Korunka, C. (2017). *Job Demands in a Changing World of Work: Impact on Workers' Health and Performance and Implications for Research and Practice*. Springer International Publishing.

Kumar, R. (2010). *Human Resource Management: Strategic Analysis Text and Cases*. I.K. International Publishing House Pvt. Limited.

Laverick, D. M. (2016). *Mentoring Processes in Higher Education*. Springer International Publishing. doi:10.1007/978-3-319-39217-2

Lent, R. W., & Brown, S. D. (2020). Career decision making, fast and slow: Toward an integrative model of intervention for sustainable career choice. *Journal of Vocational Behavior, 120*, 103448. doi:10.1016/j.jvb.2020.103448

Lent & Steven. (2012). Career Development and Counselling: Putting Theory and Research to Work. Wiley Publications.

Leonard, A. J., Akos, P., & Hutson, B. (2023). The Impact of Work-Study Participation on the Career Readiness of Undergraduates. *Journal of Student Financial Aid, 52*(1). Advance online publication. doi:10.55504/0884-9153.1758

Lewis, K. (2020). Technology in the workplace: Redefining skills for the 21st century. *The Midwest Quarterly, 61*(3), 348–356.

Mahmud, M. I., Noah, S. M., Jaafar, W. M. W., Bakar, A. Y. A., & Amat, S. (2019). The career readiness construct between dysfunctional career thinking and career self-efficacy among undergraduate students. *Strategies (La Jolla, Calif.), 7*(1), 74–81.

Miller, A. (2004). *Mentoring Students and Young People: A Handbook of Effective Practice*. Taylor & Francis. doi:10.4324/9780203417188

Morgan, C., Isaac, J. D., & Sansone, C. (2001). The role of interest in understanding the career choices of female and male college students. *Sex Roles, 44*(5/6), 295–320. doi:10.1023/A:1010929600004

Nankervis, A., Baird, M., Coffey, J., & Shields, J. (2019). *Human resource management*. Cengage.

Ogunlana, B. E. (2023). *The Career Success Formula: Proven Career Developmental Advice and Finding Rewarding Employment of Young Adults and College Graduates*. TCEC Publisher.

Ordine, P., & Rose, G. (2015). Educational mismatch and unemployment scarring. *International Journal of Manpower, 36*(5), 733–753. doi:10.1108/IJM-03-2013-0048

Osipow, S. H., & Fitzgerald, L. F. (1996). *Theories of Career Development*. Allyn and Bacon.

Pandya, Patterson, & Ruhi. (2022). The readiness of workforce for the world of work in 2030: perceptions of university students. *International Journal of Business Performance Management, 23*(1-2), 54-75.

Parker, S. K., & Grote, G. (2022). Automation, algorithms, and beyond: Why work design matters more than ever in a digital world. *Applied Psychology, 71*(4), 1171–1204. doi:10.1111/apps.12241

Patton, W., & McMahon, M. (2006). *Career Development and Systems Theory: Connecting Theory and Practice*. Sense Publishers. doi:10.1163/9789087903343

Patton, W., & McMahon, M. (2021). *Career Development and Systems Theory: Connecting Theory and Practice* (4th ed.). Brill. doi:10.1163/9789004466210

Peacock, M., Stewart, E. B., & Belcourt, M. (2020). *Understanding Human Resources Management: A Canadian Perspective*. Nelson Education Limited.

Pryor, R., & Bright, J. (2011). *The Chaos Theory of Careers: A New Perspective on Working in the Twenty-First Century*. Taylor & Francis. doi:10.4324/9780203871461

Rakhmanova, M., & Meylieva, M. (2021). Socio-Psychological Features of the Formation of a System of Attitudes to Career Choice in Adolescents. *Indiana Journal of Humanities and Social Sciences, 2*(12), 4–7.

Robertson, P. J., Hooley, T., & McCash, P. (2021). *The Oxford Handbook of Career Development*. Oxford University Press.

Salleh, N. M., Prikshat, V., Nankervis, A., & Burgess, J. (2017). Undergraduate Career-Readiness Challenges in Malaysia. *World Applied Sciences Journal, 35*(12), 2659–2664.

Sangster, C. (2017). *Planning and Organizing Personal and Professional Development*. Taylor & Francis. doi:10.4324/9781315246734

Schermerhorn, J. R., & Bachrach, D. G. (2017). *Exploring Management*. Wiley Publications.

Stebleton, M. J., & Kaler, L. S. (2020). Preparing college students for the end of work: The role of meaning. *Journal of College and Character, 21*(2), 132-139. doi:10.1080/2194587X.2020.1741396

Stebleton, M. J., Kaler, L. S., Diamond, K. K., & Lee, C. (2020). Examining career readiness in a liberal arts undergraduate career planning course. *Journal of Employment Counseling, 57*(1), 14–26. doi:10.1002/joec.12135

Steindórsdóttir, B. D., Sanders, K., Arnulf, J. K., & Dysvik, A. (2023). Career transitions and career success from a lifespan developmental perspective: A 15-year longitudinal study. *Journal of Vocational Behavior, 140*, 103809. doi:10.1016/j.jvb.2022.103809

Super, D. E. (1980). A life-span, life-space approach to career development. *Journal of Vocational Behavior, 16*(3), 282–298. doi:10.1016/0001-8791(80)90056-1

Swanson, J. L., & Fouad, N. A. (2009). *Career Theory and Practice: Learning Through Case Studies.* SAGE Publications.

Teichler, U. (2009). *Higher Education and the World of Work: Conceptual Frameworks, Comparative Perspectives, Empirical Findings.* Sense Publishers. doi:10.1163/9789087907563

Tipton, D. J. (2015). *Personal and Professional Growth for Health Care Professionals.* Jones & Bartlett Learning, LLC.

Trends, M. (2024). *World Youth Unemployment Rate 1991 – 2024.* Macro Trends. https://www.macrotrends.net/global-metrics/countries/WLD/world/youth-unemployment-rate

Tripathy, M. (2020). Relevance of soft skills in career success. *MIER Journal of Educational Studies Trends and Practices*, 91-102.

World Economic Forum. (2022, Jan 18). *5 forces driving the new world of work.* https://www.weforum.org/agenda/2022/01/the-5-forces-driving-the-new-world-of-work/

Xu, M., David, J. M., & Kim, S. H. (2018). The fourth industrial revolution: Opportunities and challenges. *International Journal of Financial Research, 9*(2), 90-95.

Younus, A. M. (2021). Technological Advancement and Economic Growth for The Business Sector. *Academic Journal of Digital Economics and Stability, 10*, 56–62.

## ADDITIONAL READING

Beltran, E. (2023). *Career Development - Tips for Finding Purpose, Advancing in a Career, and Achieving Success.* Draft2digital.

Burtnett, F. (2020). *Bound-for-Career Guidebook: A Student Guide to Career Exploration, Decision Making, and the Job Search.* Rowman & Littlefield Publishers.

Campbell, E. L. (2022). *101 Career Myths Debunked: The Ultimate Career Planning Workbook.* Taylor & Francis Group. doi:10.4324/9780429261770

Cook, S. (2022). *Effective Career Development: Advice for Establishing an Enjoyable Career.* Walter de Gruyter GmbH. doi:10.2307/j.ctv2rtgp25

Felten, P., & Lambert, L. M. (2020). *Relationship-Rich Education: How Human Connections Drive Success in College*. Johns Hopkins University Press. doi:10.1353/book.78561

Harris, M., & Westermann, G. (2014). *A Student's Guide to Developmental Psychology*. Taylor & Francis. doi:10.4324/9781315867212

Hennessee, K. (2020). *Career Development Mastery: The Last Recession-Proof Career Book You'll Ever Need*. KDP Publishers.

Light, C. (2021). *Professional Networking*. Rosen Publishing Group.

McNeff, D. J. (2021). *The Work-Life Balance Myth: Rethinking Your Optimal Balance for Success*. McGraw Hill LLC.

## KEY TERMS AND DEFINITIONS

**Career:** Performing a group of tasks for the achievement of goals through the developed knowledge and skill in a progressive manner.

**Career Maturity:** Individual level of empowerment for the future occupation career or job.

**Career Planning:** Forecasting the need required to fulfill the future occupation and conceptually developing the relevant actions.

**Career Readiness:** Level of preparation and acquisition of the needed knowledge and skills required for the future occupation.

**Personal Development:** Fulfillment of the desires of secular living and spending a satisfied lifestyle.

**Professional Development:** Acquiring the knowledge and skills required for a certain occupation and continuously developing the competencies directed towards enhancing the level of occupation.

**Professionalism:** Individual occupation-related personality and nature of the collective works performed by an individual in respective occupation.

**World of Work:** A combination of several industries and occupations.

# Chapter 10
# From Classroom to Career:
## A Holistic Approach to Student Preparedness

**Ruby Jindal**
*Department of Physics, School of Basic and Applied Sciences*
*K.R. Mangalam University, Gurugram, India*

## ABSTRACT

*Within this chapter, the exploration focuses on the varied journey students undertake when transitioning from their academic endeavors to the professional sphere. The emphasis lies in acknowledging the importance of embracing a holistic perspective that incorporates their academic foundation, skill development, practical experiences, mentorship, and fostering a growth-oriented mindset. Practical real-world examples and strategies are provided to aid students in effectively navigating this transitional phase. This chapter serves as an invaluable resource for educators, career advisors, and students navigating the dynamic and ever-evolving job market.*

## 1. INTRODUCTION

In today's dynamic and rapidly evolving world, the path from the classroom to a successful career has never been more challenging or essential. The traditional journey of acquiring academic knowledge and expecting it to seamlessly translate into professional success is no longer sufficient. Employers increasingly seek graduates who possess not only academic excellence but also a diverse set of skills, adaptability, and a proactive mindset. This chapter, titled "From Classroom to Career: A Holistic Approach to Student Preparedness," embarks on a journey to explore the profound shift in how students must prepare themselves for the professional world.

The traditional academic approach has its merits, providing a solid foundation of knowledge. However, the changing landscape of the job market demands a broader perspective. The paces of technological advancement, shifting industry landscapes, and global connectivity have transformed the very nature of work and career paths. This transformation necessitates a reevaluation of how students are prepared for life beyond the classroom. In this chapter, the concept of holistic student preparedness, which transcends

DOI: 10.4018/978-1-7998-7999-2.ch010

the confines of textbooks and lectures has been underscored. The need for students has been emphasized to equip themselves with not only academic knowledge but also a diverse skill set that includes critical soft skills such as communication, adaptability, and teamwork. Additionally, the importance of practical experiences, internships, mentorship, networking, and the cultivation of a growth-oriented mindset in building a successful career has been explored (Fajaryati et al., 2020).

## 2. ACADEMIC FOUNDATIONS

Academic excellence forms the bedrock of a student's journey from the classroom to a successful career. While the concept of holistic student preparedness extends beyond academics, a strong foundation in academic knowledge remains an indispensable cornerstone (Black & Wiliam, 1998). A solid academic foundation provides students with the fundamental knowledge, critical thinking skills, and problem-solving abilities required in the workplace. It equips them with the subject matter expertise essential for their chosen fields, making them valuable contributors from day one. However, the goal is not merely to encourage rote memorization of facts and figures. Instead, it's about fostering a deep understanding of concepts and the ability to apply them in practical situations. Students are encouraged to engage actively with their coursework, ask questions, and explore topics in depth. Recognizing that academic success entails more than just achieving grades, the chapter advocates for a holistic approach to student preparedness, promoting the cultivation of well-rounded individuals proficient in critical thinking, effective communication, and collaborative work. This comprehensive approach further underscores the importance of a balanced amalgamation of academic prowess and practical skill development through participation in extracurricular activities, internships, and real-world projects (OECD, 2015). It highlights the pivotal role of Educators and educational institutions in facilitating this balance. They should provide a supportive environment that encourages students to excel academically while also fostering personal and professional growth.

Hence, academic foundations are the starting point of a student's journey towards a successful career. However, they are just one piece of the puzzle. The holistic approach to student preparedness, as explored in this chapter, encompasses a broader set of skills and experiences that go beyond the confines of the classroom. It is through the integration of academic excellence with practical skills, soft skills, and a growth-oriented mindset that students can truly thrive in the ever-changing landscape of the modern workforce (Keiler, 2018; Lee, 2019; Siddiqui & Ahamed, 2020).

## 3. SKILL DEVELOPMENT BEYOND THE CLASSROOM

While academic knowledge is essential, it is often the soft skills that set individuals apart in the professional world. In the pursuit of holistic student preparedness, the development of skills that extend beyond the boundaries of the classroom is paramount. This section of the chapter delves into the significance of skill development beyond academic knowledge and emphasizes the critical role of soft skills and practical competencies in preparing students for successful careers (OECD, 2015).

### a) The Significance of Soft Skills

Effective communication, adaptability, teamwork, problem-solving, and leadership are among the soft skills that employers highly value. These skills enhance a student's ability to collaborate with colleagues, navigate workplace challenges, and contribute positively to their organizations (Wats & Wats, 2009). Beyond acknowledging the importance of soft skills, students are encouraged to actively cultivate these skills during their academic journey. This involves participating in group projects, extracurricular activities, and workshops that promote skill development. Additionally, seeking out leadership roles and opportunities for public speaking can significantly enhance these capabilities.

### b) Interdisciplinary Competence

Interdisciplinary Competence" refers to the ability to work across different disciplines or fields of study. It involves integrating knowledge, methods, and insights from multiple disciplines to solve complex problems or address multifaceted issues that cannot be adequately addressed by a single discipline alone. Interdisciplinary competence typically involves understanding the fundamental principles of various fields, recognizing the connections between them, and effectively applying this integrated knowledge to real-world situations. This ability is becoming increasingly crucial in the modern world, where many challenges require a comprehensive, multifaceted approach that draws upon expertise from different domains. Developing interdisciplinary competence often involves fostering skills such as critical thinking, creativity, adaptability, communication, and collaboration, as well as a willingness to engage with diverse perspectives and information across disciplines. Students are encouraged to explore a broad range of subjects and engage in cross-disciplinary activities. This allows them to adapt to various professional environments and contribute innovative solutions that draw from different fields of knowledge.

### c) Problem-Solving and Critical Thinking

Problem-solving and critical thinking serve as vital components in the development of skills that extend beyond the classroom. These skills enable students to navigate complex challenges and find innovative solutions in diverse professional environments. By honing their problem-solving abilities, students learn to approach issues methodically, analyze them from various angles, and propose effective strategies. Similarly, fostering critical thinking empowers students to evaluate information critically, discern underlying assumptions, and make informed decisions. The application of these skills outside academic settings facilitates the adaptation of theoretical knowledge to practical scenarios, thus preparing students for the multifaceted demands of the contemporary workforce. These skills also foster resilience and the capacity to thrive in dynamic and unpredictable professional landscapes, contributing significantly to a student's holistic development. The ability to think critically and solve complex problems is a skill highly sought after by employers. Students should encouraged to engage in analytical thinking and engage in projects or research that requires creative problem-solving (Bariyyah, 2021; M. Aldiono et al., 2023).

### d) Adaptability and Resilience

The modern job market is characterized by change and uncertainty. Therefore, cultivating adaptability and resilience is crucial. Students are encouraged to embrace challenges, learn from failures, and view setbacks as opportunities for growth.

Skill development is an ongoing process. In the dynamic job market, individuals must commit to lifelong learning. Students are encouraged to stay curious, seek out new experiences, and continuously refine their skill set to remain competitive throughout their careers. So, skill development beyond the classroom is integral to holistic student preparedness. While academic foundations provide essential knowledge, it is the acquisition and refinement of practical skills, particularly soft skills that empower students to excel in their chosen careers. This chapter underscores the importance of an active, well-rounded approach to skill development, equipping students with the tools they need to thrive in the ever-evolving landscape of the professional world.

## 4. PRACTICAL EXPERIENCES AND INTERNSHIPS

The transition from the classroom to a successful career is significantly enriched through practical experiences and internships. This section of the chapter delves into the profound value of hands-on learning opportunities and the pivotal role they play in preparing students for the complexities of the professional world (Anjum, 2020).

### a) Bridging Theory and Practice

Practical experiences and internships serve as a bridge between academic knowledge and its real-world application. These opportunities provide students with hands-on exposure to real-world scenarios, enabling them to apply theoretical knowledge in practical settings. By engaging in internships, students gain valuable insights into the intricacies of their chosen fields, refine their skill sets, and develop a nuanced understanding of industry practices. Practical experiences offer a platform for students to test their theoretical understanding, problem-solving capabilities, and critical thinking skills in authentic professional environments. This integration of theoretical concepts with practical applications fosters a deeper comprehension of the subject matter and equips students with the competencies required for seamless integration into the workforce. Moreover, these experiences cultivate adaptability, resilience, and a proactive approach to learning, preparing students to navigate the complexities and challenges of their future careers with confidence and proficiency.

### b) Exposure to Professional Environments

Exposure to professional environments plays a pivotal role in preparing students for the transition from academia to the workplace. This exposure offers students firsthand insights into the dynamics, expectations, and practices of various professions. By immersing themselves in professional settings, students gain a comprehensive understanding of the industry's operational aspects, workplace culture, and professional etiquette. Such exposure fosters the development of essential interpersonal skills, including effective communication, teamwork, and adaptability to diverse work environments. Additionally, it provides students with the opportunity to observe and learn from seasoned professionals, facilitating the acquisition of industry-specific knowledge and practical insights that complement their academic learning. Exposure to professional environments not only enhances students' employability but also nurtures a sense of professional identity and confidence, enabling them to make informed career choices and thrive in their chosen fields.

## c) Skill Enhancement

Practical experiences and internships serve as invaluable platforms for skill enhancement, providing students with the opportunity to apply theoretical knowledge in real-world settings and cultivate a diverse range of professional competencies. Through these experiences, students can refine their technical skills, such as data analysis, research methodologies, or industry-specific tools, under the guidance of seasoned professionals. Additionally, practical experiences and internships foster the development of essential soft skills, including effective communication, teamwork, adaptability, and problem-solving, which are integral to successful collaboration and navigating complex work environments. The exposure to practical challenges and day-to-day operations not only enhances students' understanding of industry practices but also encourages a proactive approach to learning and a deeper integration of classroom theories with practical applications. By actively participating in practical experiences and internships, students can significantly enrich their skill sets, strengthen their professional acumen, and better prepare themselves for the demands and expectations of the contemporary workforce.

## d) Resume Building

By listing relevant internships and practical experiences on their resumes, students can showcase their hands-on skills, industry-specific competencies, and demonstrated ability to thrive in professional settings. Additionally, the inclusion of practical experiences and internships highlights a student's proactive approach to learning, adaptability to diverse work environments, and capacity for effective problem-solving. This not only enriches the content of the resume but also signals to potential employers the candidate's readiness and potential to make immediate contributions in the workplace. Furthermore, highlighting the key responsibilities and accomplishments during these practical experiences in a well-structured resume underscores the practical relevance of the student's academic background and positions them as a competitive and promising candidate in the job market.

## e) Clarifying Career Goals

Clarifying career goals is a significant outcome of practical experiences and internships, as these opportunities offer students firsthand insights into the realities of various professions. Through active engagement in practical settings, students can gain a clearer understanding of their professional interests, strengths, and areas of development. By experiencing the day-to-day responsibilities and challenges of a specific role or industry, students can assess their compatibility with different career paths and make informed decisions about their future endeavors. Practical experiences and internships provide a platform for students to explore different facets of their chosen fields, identify their passions, and align their career aspirations with their personal values and skills. Additionally, these experiences encourage students to reflect on their experiences, assess their professional development, and refine their long-term career objectives. By gaining a deeper understanding of their career goals through practical experiences and internships, students can chart a more focused and purposeful trajectory, maximizing their potential for success and satisfaction in their chosen professions.

### f) Securing Future Employment

Many students secure full-time employment with the organizations where they interned. Employers often prefer candidates who are already familiar with their company's culture and operations.

### g) Diversity of Experience

Encouraging students to seek diverse internship experiences broadens their horizons. It exposes them to various facets of their field and can lead to unexpected and rewarding career opportunities.

In a nutshell, practical experiences and internships are instrumental in the holistic preparation of students for their future careers. They provide a unique opportunity for students to apply their academic knowledge, develop critical skills, and gain a deeper understanding of their chosen fields. By actively seeking out and maximizing these opportunities, students not only enhance their career prospects but also embark on a journey of self-discovery and professional growth.

## 5. MENTORSHIP AND NETWORKING

### a) The Role and Benefits of Mentorship

Seeking guidance and mentorship is an integral and proactive step in a student's journey toward a successful career. These relationships are akin to beacons of light in the often complex and dynamic world of professional development. Mentors, who have traversed similar paths and gathered a wealth of experiences, willingly share their knowledge, insights, and advice with students. Their wisdom provides invaluable guidance on career choices, offers perspectives on industry trends, and illuminates the pathways to success.

Students are encouraged to take an active role in seeking out mentors who align with their career aspirations and values. It's not merely about finding a mentor but about actively engaging and demonstrating a sincere commitment to learning and growth. By setting clear objectives for mentorship relationships, students can tailor their learning experiences and ensure that they gain the knowledge and insights they need.

Mentorship is not just about theory; it's about learning from the real-world experiences and practical wisdom of those who have walked the path before. Mentors impart not only the successes but also the invaluable lessons learned from failures and challenges. This knowledge helps students make informed career decisions and navigate their chosen industries with confidence (Fallon, 2023). Moreover, mentorship is a gateway to expanding one's professional network. Mentors often introduce students to their own networks, providing access to valuable industry connections and potential job opportunities. These relationships open doors and offer insights into the unwritten rules and nuances of their respective fields. Building self-confidence is another significant aspect of mentorship. Encouragement and constructive feedback from experienced professionals boost a student's belief in their abilities and their potential for success. As students grow and learn under the guidance of their mentors, they not only gain practical skills but also develop the self-assuredness needed to make bold career choices. In the spirit of reciprocity, students should recognize that mentorship is a two-way exchange. While they receive guidance and support, they should also be open to providing value to their mentors when opportunities arise. Expressing gratitude for mentorship is not only polite but also reinforces the importance of these relationships.

## b) Building Professional Networks

Networking and cultivating professional relationships are essential components of a student's journey toward a successful career. These connections open doors to opportunities, offer valuable insights, and contribute to personal and professional growth. Effective networking involves more than collecting business cards or adding connections on social media. Students are guided on how to build meaningful and mutually beneficial relationships within their chosen industries. Expanding one's professional network begins with a proactive mindset. Students learn to attend industry events, conferences, seminars, and workshops relevant to their fields of interest. These gatherings provide fertile ground for connecting with like-minded professionals and potential mentors.

Students are encouraged to join professional organizations and associations related to their career goals. These groups not only facilitate networking but also offer access to valuable resources, industry trends, and opportunities for skill development. Building professional relationships is a two-way street. Students are advised to approach networking with a genuine interest in others and a willingness to offer support and assistance when possible. Nurturing these connections through regular communication and follow-ups is crucial for maintaining strong relationships. Alumni networks are a valuable resource for students. Graduates who have successfully transitioned to careers can provide guidance, mentorship, and insider knowledge of the job market. Students are encouraged to leverage these networks for valuable insights and connections. Peer networking is equally important. Students can learn from their classmates, share experiences, and collaborate on projects. Building strong relationships with peers can lead to future collaborations, referrals, and a support system throughout one's career. Effective networking etiquette is emphasized, including professionalism, respect, and integrity. Students learn to communicate clearly and concisely about their career goals and aspirations, as well as the value they bring to potential employers or collaborators. Mentorship relationships are a key aspect of networking. Students are encouraged to seek mentors who can provide guidance, share experiences, and offer advice on career development. These mentorship connections often have a profound impact on a student's career trajectory.

So, mentorship and networking are essential components of holistic student preparedness. They provide students with access to valuable guidance, industry insights, and career opportunities. By actively seeking out mentors and building professional networks, students not only enhance their readiness for the workforce but also establish a foundation for ongoing career success and growth (Bolton-King, 2022; Cutillas et al., 2023).

## 6. MINDSET AND CAREER READINESS

In the pursuit of a successful transition from the classroom to the professional realm, one's mindset and approach to career readiness are foundational. This section of the chapter delves into the pivotal role of mindset in shaping a student's preparedness for a career and explores the proactive steps necessary for success (Yavuz, 2019).

## a) The Power of Mindset

Understanding the significance of mindset is the first step towards holistic student preparedness. A positive and growth-oriented mindset sets the stage for success by fostering resilience, adaptability, and a profound belief in one's capacity to overcome challenges. In the face of setbacks and obstacles, which are bound to arise in the professional world, a growth-oriented mindset encourages students to view these hurdles as opportunities for personal and professional growth. This mindset enables them to embrace change and uncertainty with a sense of curiosity and an eagerness to learn. It instills the belief that abilities and intelligence can be cultivated through dedication and effort, motivating students to take proactive steps towards achieving their career goals. By recognizing the power of mindset, students not only enhance their career readiness but also embark on a lifelong journey of self-discovery and continuous improvement, ensuring their resilience and adaptability in the ever-evolving landscape of the professional world.

## b) Resilience in the Face of Challenges

Resilience is a fundamental attribute that students must cultivate as they prepare to transition from the classroom to their future careers. In the professional world, challenges and setbacks are inevitable; they are an integral part of the journey. Resilience equips students with the mental fortitude to face adversity with determination and grace. It encourages them to view challenges not as insurmountable obstacles, but as opportunities for personal and professional growth. By developing resilience, students learn to bounce back from setbacks, persevere in the face of adversity, and maintain a positive attitude even in challenging circumstances. This attribute is not only crucial for individual well-being but also for career success, as it enables students to navigate uncertainty and change with confidence. It empowers them to embrace challenges as stepping stones to greater achievements and reinforces their belief in their ability to overcome any obstacle that comes their way on their journey to a successful career.

## c) Proactive Career Readiness

Proactive career readiness is the cornerstone of a student's preparedness for the professional world. It goes beyond simply acquiring knowledge and skills; it involves taking deliberate, forward-looking steps to shape one's career path and ensure success. This proactive approach empowers students to seize opportunities and effectively navigate the complexities of the job market. Proactivity begins with setting clear career goals. Students are encouraged to define their objectives, both short-term and long-term, and create actionable plans to achieve them. This involves setting milestones, establishing timelines, and tracking progress (Casillas et al., 2019).

Lifelong learning and adaptation are central components of proactive career readiness. Students understand that the modern workplace is dynamic and ever-changing. To remain competitive, they embrace ongoing learning, seek professional development opportunities, and stay attuned to industry trends. Effective goal setting and planning are complemented by the development of a personal brand. Students recognize the importance of creating an online presence, such as a LinkedIn profile, that showcases their skills and achievements. This personal brand not only enhances visibility but also communicates their unique value to potential employers and professional networks. Proactive students also understand the significance of networking and building professional relationships. They actively expand their networks by attending industry events, joining relevant organizations, and connecting with peers, professors, and professionals in their field. They recognize that these relationships can lead to valuable career opportunities and insights. Seeking guidance and mentorship is another proactive step in career readiness. Students actively seek out mentors and advisors who can provide them with valuable insights and advice based on their own experiences. They understand that mentorship relationships can accelerate their professional growth and development. Confidence and self-efficacy play a critical role in proactive career readiness. Students develop a strong belief in their capabilities and their potential for success. This confidence empowers them to pursue their career goals with enthusiasm and resilience.

## d) Goal Setting and Planning

Goal setting and planning are pivotal components of a student's journey toward a successful career. These processes provide students with the structure and direction needed to transform their aspirations into tangible achievements. At the core of effective career readiness is the establishment of clear and meaningful career goals. Students are encouraged to define their objectives, both short-term and long-term, with precision and clarity. These goals act as beacons, guiding their actions and decisions throughout their academic and professional pursuits. Setting career goals involves identifying what one aims to achieve in terms of job positions, skills, or personal accomplishments. Whether it's securing a specific job role, attaining a particular level of expertise, or making a meaningful contribution to a chosen field, well-defined goals provide motivation and purpose. Once goals are established, the next critical step is creating actionable plans to achieve them. Planning involves breaking down long-term goals into smaller, manageable steps and setting achievable milestones. It includes setting deadlines, identifying necessary resources, and outlining the specific actions required to move closer to the desired outcomes. By creating a roadmap for their career journey, students gain a sense of direction and control over their professional development. They can systematically track their progress, evaluate their strategies, and make adjustments as needed to stay on course.

Moreover, effective goal setting and planning foster a sense of accountability. Students understand that they are responsible for their own success and that consistent effort and dedication are required to reach their objectives. This sense of ownership instills discipline and a commitment to their chosen career path. Goal setting and planning also enhance decision-making. When students have a clear vision of their career goals, they can make informed choices about coursework, extracurricular activities, internships, and networking opportunities that align with their aspirations.

## e) Building a Personal Brand

Building a personal brand is a strategic and essential aspect of a student's journey toward a successful career in the modern professional landscape. It involves crafting a unique and compelling identity that not only showcases one's skills and achievements but also leaves a lasting impression on potential employers, colleagues, and professional networks. One of the foundational steps in building a personal brand is self-reflection. Students are encouraged to identify their strengths, passions, values, and career aspirations. Understanding one's unique qualities and what sets them apart from others is the first step toward crafting a distinct personal brand. An online presence is a vital component of personal branding in today's digital age. Students are guided on how to create and maintain professional profiles on platforms like LinkedIn. These profiles serve as a digital resume and an opportunity to showcase their expertise, experiences, and accomplishments. Consistency is key to effective personal branding. Students learn to maintain a consistent and professional online presence across all platforms, ensuring that their personal brand remains cohesive and recognizable.

Content creation is another avenue for building a personal brand. Students are encouraged to share their knowledge and insights through blog posts, articles, or videos on relevant topics in their field. Creating valuable content establishes them as thought leaders and experts in their chosen area. Networking plays a crucial role in personal branding. Students are taught how to engage with peers, professors, professionals, and industry influencers in meaningful ways. Building strong relationships within their professional networks not only expands their reach but also enhances their personal brand through positive associations. In addition to creating an online presence, students are advised to proactively seek opportunities for showcasing their expertise. This might involve presenting at conferences, participating in panel discussions, or contributing to industry publications.

Feedback and self-assessment are integral to personal branding. Students are encouraged to seek constructive feedback from mentors, peers, and colleagues to refine and strengthen their personal brand continuously. Ultimately, building a personal brand is about creating a reputation and image that aligns with one's career goals and values. It empowers students to communicate their unique value proposition effectively and stand out in a competitive job market.

### f) Confidence and Self-Efficacy

Confidence and self-efficacy serve as the bedrock of a student's journey towards a successful career. Confidence, the unwavering belief in one's abilities and self-worth, is a driving force that propels individuals to take on challenges, seize opportunities, and persevere through setbacks. Similarly, self-efficacy, a subset of confidence, is the conviction that one possesses the skills and capabilities necessary to accomplish specific tasks and achieve defined goals. These attributes, when nurtured and cultivated, empower students to step boldly into the professional world. Fostering confidence and self-efficacy is a multifaceted process. Constructive feedback, whether from mentors, peers, or personal reflection, plays a vital role in helping individuals recognize their strengths and identify areas for improvement. It's through acknowledging these areas of growth that individuals can focus their efforts on personal development and skill enhancement.

Celebrating small victories and personal achievements is another strategy to reinforce self-belief. These successes act as building blocks, gradually constructing a foundation of confidence and self-efficacy. Each accomplishment, no matter how minor, serves as evidence that one's efforts can yield positive outcomes. Despite these strategies, moments of self-doubt may still arise. However, students are equipped with the tools to manage and overcome these doubts. They learn to challenge negative self-talk and replace it with affirmations of their capabilities. Through a combination of reflection, practice, and the support of mentors and peers, students continuously strengthen their confidence and self-efficacy.

### g) Embracing Change

Embracing change is a vital mindset and skill set that every student must cultivate as they prepare for a successful career in the dynamic and ever-evolving professional landscape. Change is a constant in today's world, and the ability to adapt and even thrive amidst uncertainty is a hallmark of a resilient and forward-thinking professional. First and foremost, students are encouraged to recognize change as an inevitable part of the modern job market. Industries, technologies, and market trends continuously shift, and the most successful professionals are those who not only accept but also welcome these changes as opportunities for growth and innovation. Adaptation is a key component of embracing change. Students learn to be flexible in their approaches and open to new ideas and methods. They understand that what worked yesterday may not work tomorrow, and they actively seek out ways to adjust and pivot when necessary. Moreover, students are taught to stay proactive and stay ahead of the curve. This involves staying informed about emerging trends in their field, seeking out professional development opportunities, and actively positioning themselves to leverage new developments to their advantage. Resilience is another critical aspect of embracing change. Students understand that challenges and setbacks may accompany change, but they view these as valuable learning experiences. They develop the mental fortitude to bounce back from setbacks, persevere through adversity, and maintain a positive attitude even in the face of uncertainty. Furthermore, embracing change is not limited to external factors; it also encompasses personal growth and development. Students are encouraged to continuously seek out opportunities for self-improvement, whether through further education, skill enhancement, or expanding their comfort zones

## 7. ROLE OF CASE STUDIES AND SUCCESS STORIES

case studies and success stories play a crucial role in preparing students for their future careers, serving as valuable tools for practical learning and inspiration. These resources provide students with real-world examples of challenges, strategies, and solutions encountered in various industries and professions. By examining case studies, students can develop critical thinking skills and analytical abilities, learning to apply theoretical knowledge to practical scenarios. They can gain insights into the complexities of decision-making, problem-solving, and effective management within different organizational contexts. Success stories, on the other hand, offer students role models and exemplars to emulate. They demonstrate the journey of individuals or organizations that have achieved notable success, highlighting the strategies, skills, and attributes that contributed to their accomplishments. By studying success stories, students can glean valuable lessons, identify key factors for success, and cultivate a proactive and goal-oriented mindset. Both case studies and success stories contribute to a comprehensive understanding of the challenges and opportunities that await students in their chosen careers. They inspire students to think creatively, strategically, and adaptively, fostering a deeper appreciation for the practical application of knowledge and the importance of perseverance and innovation in achieving professional success

## 8. CHALLENGES AND FUTURE TRENDS

Challenges and future trends in the realm of student preparedness for successful careers represent crucial considerations that are shaping education and career development strategies. To understand the landscape that students must navigate, it is essential to examine the key challenges and emerging trends that will influence the way they prepare for their future careers. The first challenge is the rapid pace of technological advancements, which demands that students continually update their skills to remain relevant in an ever-evolving job market. Globalization has intensified the competition for jobs, necessitating a global perspective and intercultural competence. Moreover, economic uncertainty resulting from fluctuations and the changing nature of work has made career planning and job security more unpredictable for students. The burden of student debt is another significant challenge, impacting students' ability to make career choices based on their interests and passions, rather than purely financial considerations. Additionally, the balancing act between academic pressures and career expectations can take a toll on students' mental health, emphasizing the need for institutions to prioritize student well-being and provide comprehensive support services.

Looking ahead, several key future trends are expected to shape the landscape of student preparedness. The COVID-19 pandemic accelerated the adoption of remote work and digital tools, making proficiency in remote collaboration and digital skills a necessity for students. Lifelong learning is emerging as the norm, as professionals must continually upskill and reskill to adapt to evolving job requirements. Data-driven decision-making is becoming increasingly vital, with organizations relying on data analytics skills for informed strategic choices. Furthermore, students are prioritizing careers that align with their values, particularly in areas such as sustainability, environmental responsibility, and social impact. Hybrid learning models, combining in-person and online education, are continually evolving, providing students with enhanced flexibility and accessibility. With the rise of Artificial Intelligence (AI) and automation, students must adapt to work alongside these technologies, presenting both opportunities and challenges. More students are also exploring entrepreneurial ventures and participating in the gig economy, necessitating a different set of skills and mindsets. Soft skills such as communication, empathy, and adaptability are increasingly valued, as automation handles routine tasks, emphasizing the importance of emotional intelligence in the workforce.

## 9. CONCLUSION

In conclusion, the journey from the academic world to a successful career is a multifaceted and dynamic process, requiring a holistic approach to student preparedness. Throughout this chapter, various components and strategies that contribute to this holistic preparation has been explored the. From establishing a strong academic foundation to developing essential skills beyond the classroom, engaging in practical experiences and internships, seeking guidance and mentorship, and cultivating a growth-oriented mindset, each aspect plays a vital role in equipping students for the challenges and opportunities they will encounter in their professional lives. Furthermore, building a personal brand, expanding one's network, embracing change, and fostering confidence and self-efficacy are essential attributes that empower students to not only enter the workforce but to thrive in it. The inclusion of case studies and success stories serves as a bridge between theoretical knowledge and practical application, offering students real-world insights, inspiration, and actionable strategies to navigate the complexities of their future careers. In the ever-evolving landscape of professions and industries, adaptability, continuous learning, and a proactive mindset are key drivers of success. By embracing the holistic approach to student preparedness outlined in this chapter, individuals can embark on their career journeys with confidence, resilience, and a clear sense of purpose. Ultimately, the transition from the academic world to a successful career is not a destination but a continuous journey of growth, development, and discovery. It is a journey that promises challenges, opportunities, and the potential for meaningful impact. With the right foundations, skills, mindset, and support systems, students are well-equipped to embark on this journey and forge their paths toward rewarding and fulfilling careers.

## REFERENCES

Aldiono, M., Purnomo, T., & Prastowo, T. (2023). Profile of Problem-Solving Ability in Junior High School Students on Global Warming Lesson Material. *IJORER : International Journal of Recent Educational Research*, *4*(3), 355–364. doi:10.46245/ijorer.v4i3.301

Anjum, S. (2020). Impact of internship programs on professional and personal development of business students: A case study from Pakistan. *Future Business Journal*, *6*(1), 2. doi:10.1186/s43093-019-0007-3

Bariyyah, K. (2021). Problem solving skills: Esssential skills challenges for the 21st century graduates. *Jurnal EDUCATIO: Jurnal Pendidikan Indonesia*, *7*(1), 71. doi:10.29210/120212843

Black, P., & Wiliam, D. (1998). Assessment and Classroom Learning. *Assessment in Education: Principles, Policy & Practice*, *5*(1), 7–74. doi:10.1080/0969595980050102

Bolton-King, R. S. (2022). Student mentoring to enhance graduates' employability potential. *Science & Justice*, *62*(6), 785–794. doi:10.1016/j.scijus.2022.04.010 PMID:36400500

Casillas, A., Kyllonen, P. C., & Way, J. D. (2019). Preparing Students for the Future of Work. In F. Oswald, T. S. Behrend, & L. Foster (Eds.), *Workforce Readiness and the Future of Work* (1st ed., pp. 35–52). Routledge. doi:10.4324/9781351210485-3

Cutillas, A., Benolirao, E., Camasura, J., Golbin, R. Jr, Yamagishi, K., & Ocampo, L. (2023). Does Mentoring Directly Improve Students' Research Skills? Examining the Role of Information Literacy and Competency Development. *Education Sciences*, *13*(7), 694. doi:10.3390/educsci13070694

Fajaryati, N., Budiyono, Akhyar, M., & Wiranto. (2020). The Employability Skills Needed To Face the Demands of Work in the Future: Systematic Literature Reviews. *Open Engineering*, *10*(1), 595–603. doi:10.1515/eng-2020-0072

Fallon, M. E. (2023). A Graduate Student's Mentorship Pedagogy for Undergraduate Mentees. *Biomedical Engineering Education*. doi:10.1007/s43683-023-00121-7

Keiler, L. S. (2018). Teachers' roles and identities in student-centered classrooms. *International Journal of STEM Education*, *5*(1), 34. doi:10.1186/s40594-018-0131-6 PMID:30631724

Lee, J. C.-K. (2019). Teachers' work, change and learning: Roles, contexts and engagement. *Teachers and Teaching*, *25*(4), 399–403. doi:10.1080/13540602.2019.1625616

OECD. (2015). *Skills for Social Progress: The Power of Social and Emotional Skills*. OECD. doi:10.1787/9789264226159-

Siddiqui, S., & Ahamed, M. (2020). Teachers' Roles Beyond and Within the Context: An Ever-Changing Concept. *Arab World English Journal*, *11*(1), 282–296. doi:10.24093/awej/vol11no1.21

Wats, R. K., & Wats, M. (2009). Developing Soft Skills in Students. *International Journal of Learning*, *15*(12), 1–10. doi:10.18848/1447-9494/CGP/v15i12/46032

Yavuz, O. (2019). A Quantitative Exploration of Students' Mindsets and Behaviors: A Whole Child Academic, Emotional, and Career Development. *International Journal of Educational Reform*, *28*(4), 319–347. doi:10.1177/1056787919856735

## ADDITIONAL READING

Kuep, J. R., & Young, D. G. (2018). Investigating the first-year seminar as a high-impact practice. In *The first year of college: Research, theory, and practice on improving the student experience and increasing retention* (pp. 93–125). Cambridge University Press.

Liu, J. C., & Adams, A. (2017). Design of online student orientation with conceptual and procedural scaffolding. In F. Lai & J. Lehman (Eds.), *Learning and knowledge analytics in open education* (pp. 41–68). Springer. doi:10.1007/978-3-319-38956-1_5

McFarland, J., Hussar, B., de Brey, C., Snyder, T., Wang, X., Wilkinson-Flicker, S., Gebrekristos, S., Zhang, J., Rathbun, A., Barmer, A., Bullock Mann, F., & Hinz, S. (2017). *The condition of education 2017 (NCES 2017-144). U.S. Department of Education*. National Center for Education Statistics.

Stephen, J. S., & Rockinson-Szapkiw, A. J. (2021). A high-impact practice for online students: The use of a first-semester seminar course to promote self-regulation, self-direction, online learning self-efficacy. *Smart Learning Environments, 8*(1), 1–18.

Stephen, J. S., Rockinson-Szapkiw, A. J., & Dubay, C. (2020). Persistence model of nontraditional online learners: Self-efficacy, self-regulation, and self-direction. *American Journal of Distance Education*, *34*(4), 306–321. doi:10.1080/08923647.2020.1745619

## KEY TERMS AND DEFINITIONS

**Critical Thinking:** Critical thinking involves analyzing information, evaluating arguments, and making reasoned judgments to solve problems and make informed decisions.

**Holistic Approach:** A holistic approach considers all aspects of a situation, emphasizing the interconnectedness of various factors.

**Problem-Solving:** Problem-solving is the process of finding effective solutions to challenges or obstacles by analyzing the situation, identifying options, and implementing strategies to achieve a resolution.

**Skill Development:** Skill development is the intentional process of acquiring, enhancing, or refining abilities and competencies, often to improve performance in various tasks or professions.

**Student Preparedness:** Student preparedness is the readiness of students to navigate the transition from classroom learning to the demands of the working world.

**Transition to Career:** The transition to a career is the shift from education to applying acquired skills in a professional work setting.

# Chapter 11
# The Intersection of Academics and Career Readiness

**Ranjit Singha**
 https://orcid.org/0000-0002-3541-8752
*Christ University, India*

**Surjit Singha**
 https://orcid.org/0000-0002-5730-8677
*Kristu Jayanti College (Autonomous), India*

**Elizabeth Jasmine**
*Indian Institute of Psychology and Research, India*

## ABSTRACT

*This chapter emphasizes the significant correlation between vocation readiness and academic achievement, highlighting the thoughtful consequences for students' triumphs. This highlights the significance of effectively integrating theoretical knowledge with hands-on vocational training, cultivating aptitudes for analysis, resolution of challenges, and flexibility. Case studies that have achieved success serve as illustrations of successful integration, highlighting the cooperative nature of academic departments and career services. Exploration of early career options, practical experience, and transferable skills are crucial components. Collaborative platforms, curricular redesign, and technology integration are all reasonable solutions. Notwithstanding the obstacles encountered, educators are motivated to maintain their commitment to this incorporation as a top priority, guaranteeing that students are adequately equipped to confront the workforce's ever-changing demands and facilitate a smooth transition into the professional realm.*

## INTRODUCTION

Central to this chapter is a thorough examination of the complex correlation between scholarly endeavours and the preparedness to confront professional obstacles. The chapter acknowledges that the academic trajectory encompasses more than a mere accumulation of courses; it is a critical factor that shapes a

DOI: 10.4018/978-1-7998-7999-2.ch011

## The Intersection of Academics and Career Readiness

student's ability to flourish in a highly competitive professional environment. Through deciphering this correlation, our objective is to provide mentors and academic support staff with a sophisticated comprehension of how scholastic experiences can advantageously correspond with the competencies and expertise required for a wide range of professional trajectories. The narrative underscores the reciprocal relationship between academic achievement and professional success. It promotes an all-encompassing educational methodology that cultivates abilities such as critical thinking, problem-solving, communication, and adaptability, in addition to imparting subject-specific knowledge. Significant emphasis is placed on the dynamic unity of academic curricula with the ever-changing requirements of the professional realm. Educators are encouraged to remain updated on industry trends to enhance their relevance. The chapter explores the pragmatic dimensions of practising academic knowledge via apprenticeships, projects, and hands-on experiences. Critically, it emphasizes the importance of soft skills in augmenting preparedness for the workforce and deliberates on approaches to smoothly incorporate their cultivation into scholarly curricula. The chapter highlights the critical role that educators and support staff play and the significance of proficient career guidance and counselling services in connecting academic ambitions with the complex realities of various career trajectories. By examining these pivotal aspects, the chapter furnishes an all-encompassing manual, imparting pragmatic wisdom that instructors and assistance personnel may utilize to galvanize pupils for triumph in their educational and prospective vocational undertakings.

Understanding the complex interplay between academics and vocation readiness is crucial for support staff and educators, as it confers numerous advantages. Such an understanding enables educators to provide students with a comprehensive repertoire of abilities that transcends scholarly comprehension and is crucial for traversing the complex realm of work (Naylor et al., 2021). By acknowledging this correlation, educators guarantee that educational material continues to be congruent with the ever-changing labour market requirements, augmenting its pragmatic applicability. The intersection of these factors highlights the significance of comprehensive development, compelling educators to foster cognitive advancement and acquire crucial interpersonal abilities, thereby more effectively equipping students for the multifaceted obstacles they will encounter throughout their professional lives. By incorporating industry-relevant projects, practical experiences, and real-world case studies, educators strategically develop curricula that facilitate a smooth transition from the classroom to the workplace. Equipped with the knowledge of this convergence, student support personnel can provide individualized career counselling, aiding pupils in identifying their strengths, passions, and areas requiring development, thereby harmonizing guidance with specific vocational aspirations. This sophisticated comprehension empowers proficient career counselling, which assists pupils in making well-informed choices regarding academic trajectories, extracurricular engagements, and internships following their professional ambitions. With the ever-changing nature of work, educators and support staff impart to students a mindset of adaptability, continuous learning, and a willingness to confront novel challenges guided by this knowledge. The support provided by these individuals not only improves students' academic performance but also facilitates the acquisition of essential skills highly sought after by employers in an ever-evolving labour market (Akosah-Twumasi et al., 2018).

Furthermore, understanding the intersection facilitates cooperation between academic establishments and businesses, bridging the divide between academia and the business sector. When it comes to influencing pupils' educational trajectories and prospective professional trajectories, educators and student support personnel who are well-informed regarding intersectionality assume critical functions. They direct pupils towards comprehensive growth, enabling them to thrive in the demanding and varied professional environment. This chapter establishes a conceptual framework by drawing upon various educational and career development theories. An example of a foundational approach in this regard is the Human Capital Theory, which asserts that education facilitates the acquisition of knowledge and skills, consequently augmenting the employability and productivity of an individual. This theoretical perspective places significant emphasis on the economic worth of education as a determinant of professional paths. An additional pivotal viewpoint is the Social Cognitive Career Theory, which posits that people acquire knowledge and develop their career expectations and beliefs by observing and imitating successful individuals and participating in experiences that influence these perceptions. This highlights the importance of self-efficacy and the constructive impact of mentors and educators in steering students towards prosperous professional trajectories. Constructivism grounds the guide, acknowledging learning as an active and experiential process. It emphasizes establishing environments that facilitate students in constructing their understanding of academic material and applying it to practical situations.

Life Design Theory is a significant framework that actively influences the development of individuals' lives and career trajectories. It highlights the crucial role of educators and support personnel in assisting students in their journey of self-discovery, focusing on exploring their passions, values, and personal aspirations. This chapter is a pragmatic handbook intended to equip stakeholders with the requisite knowledge and resources, facilitate practical advice for students, and match their educational paths with crucial competencies for successful jobs. Acknowledging the intricate dimensions of success extends beyond scholastic accomplishments, emphasizing the development of pragmatic information, life skills, and the cultivation of enduring inquisitiveness. Research has shown that tailored career advising services significantly contribute to students' overall performance by effectively targeting their specific ambitions and areas of development.

This chapter covers an extensive range of subjects fundamental to comprehending the convergence of academia and preparedness for the workforce. This study explores approaches to effectively incorporating career-relevant skills and experiences into academic curricula, guaranteeing that graduates possess practical and pertinent knowledge. The investigation further examines the promotion of critical soft skills, including adaptability, communication, and collaboration, acknowledging their importance in the workplace. Furthermore, the manual recommends cultivating partnerships between academic establishments and business sectors, facilitating the vital link between academia and the ever-evolving professional environment. It provides perspectives on providing adequate career counselling services customized to each student's specific requirements and aspirations, considering their varied professional objectives.

The manual probes into strategies for integrating practical skills development by integrating real-world initiatives and hands-on experiences into scholarly work. It facilitates dialogues concerning cultivating an adaptable mentality among students and the criticality of ongoing education to thrive in ever-changing professional environments. The guide endeavours to be an indispensable and practical resource for educators and student support staff by covering these exhaustive aspects. Its purpose is to facilitate students' successful transition from academic environments to a wide range of rewarding career paths, thereby contributing to their holistic development.

## DEFINING CAREER READINESS

Career readiness is an all-encompassing concept that entails attaining essential competencies, understanding, and qualities vital for success in the business world. Furthermore, it involves acquiring practical and intangible proficiencies, understanding the standards set by the business sector, and cultivating a mindset dedicated to ongoing education and flexibility (Akosah-Twumasi et al., 2018). This comprehensive readiness enables individuals to seamlessly transition from academic to professional environments, equipping them with the skills and knowledge to navigate real-life situations effectively. In addition to augmenting employability through developing valuable technical competencies, career readiness fosters the cultivation of critical soft skills such as effective communication and collaborative collaboration. It promotes a mentality of adaptability, which is crucial in a society where swift technological progress alters employment demands. Beyond facilitating success in academia and the workplace, career readiness promotes comprehensive development in both personal and professional spheres. It enables students to harmonize their professional trajectories with their interests and principles, resulting in a more gratifying professional existence. Career-ready individuals demonstrate elevated levels of self-assurance, proficiency in navigating obstacles encountered in the workplace, and effective communication capabilities. By fostering a dedication to ongoing education, career readiness empowers pupils to devise their professional trajectories strategically, capitalize on networking prospects, and comprehend the routes leading to their desired professional outcomes. It emphasizes cultural competency in an interconnected world and prepares students for diverse work environments by strongly emphasizing global and cultural dimensions.

Career readiness is fundamental to ensuring enduring and prosperous professional trajectories and equipping students with the essential skills required for success in their chosen vocations. Within educational and vocational development theories, the conceptualization of career preparedness necessitates a comprehensive comprehension of the fundamental abilities, information, and traits vital for success in professional endeavours. Super's career development theory posits that job preparedness encompasses more than professional skills. It includes elements such as self-concept, adaptability, and the ability to engage in lifelong learning. The educational and career development theories proposed by Holland emphasize the congruence between an individual's preferences and work surroundings. By incorporating various theoretical perspectives, career preparedness is a multifaceted construct that highlights acquiring technical expertise and cultivating interpersonal competencies, emotional intelligence, and adaptability in response to changing work environments. Essentially, it signifies a comprehensive approach that connects fundamental academic principles with the diverse requirements of the modern professional environment.

Career readiness is an all-encompassing notion comprising a varied collection of competencies, understanding, and a mentality vital for success in the business world. A foundational element is possessing field-specific skills, encompassing technical abilities such as programming or laboratory techniques and project management. Interpersonal competencies are equally important, including problem-solving, communication, collaboration, adaptability, and emotional intelligence. A comprehensive comprehension of scholarly subjects, acquired via coursework and practical engagements, enhances this preparedness in an academic sense. Demonstrating knowledge of industry trends, market dynamics, and emerging technologies signifies a proactive mindset. The capacity to accept and integrate change, demonstrate flexibility, and adopt a proactive problem-solving attitude facilitates adaptability in dynamic environments (Ferreira, 2022). Akosah-Twumasi et al. (2018) present a comprehensive definition of career preparedness that incorporates ethical behaviour, continuous education, and a deep sense of accountability. The framework encompasses activities such as goal setting, strategic planning, and the development of professional networks, in addition to job proficiency. Career preparedness includes a broader scope beyond conventional boundaries within the context of life design theory. The process entails actively developing one's life and professional trajectory by aligning personal passions, values, and ambitions. The central focus of Life Design Theory is the recognition that job preparedness extends beyond the acquisition of specific skills, encompassing a continuous journey of self-exploration and purposeful decision-making. This approach promotes exploring individual interests and potentials, cultivating adaptability and a dedication to lifelong learning. Within the framework of this paradigm, the notion of career preparedness is a fluid and multifaceted term that encompasses both individual goals and the ever-changing requirements of the professional sphere. The approach emphasizes equipping individuals with the skills and knowledge to pursue fulfilling and meaningful jobs through a comprehensive strategy.

The framework emphasizes proficiently utilizing digital tools and effective oral and written communication. To underscore the global economy's interdependence, the focus is on nurturing respect for diversity, cultivating adaptability in various contexts, and promoting a nuanced understanding of international perspectives. In addition to leadership abilities, the decision-making process, collaboration, critical analysis, and resiliency in the face of adversity are all components of the holistic approach to career readiness. In addition, a comprehensive understanding of financial principles and an innovative approach to problem-solving enhance one's readiness. This guarantees that individuals achieve exceptional performance in their respective domains and possess the moral underpinnings, flexibility, and dedication to continuous education indispensable for long-term career success.

## ACADEMIC FOUNDATIONS FOR CAREER READINESS

Solid academic groundwork is crucial for individuals, as it furnishes them with an all-encompassing collection of knowledge indispensable for achieving success in their chosen realm. In addition to fostering comprehension of fundamental principles, theories, and practices, this foundation provides a solid groundwork for developing career-specific expertise. In addition to imparting subject-specific knowledge, academic endeavours foster the growth of analytical, research, critical thinking, and problem-solving abilities. Transferable skills are of the utmost importance in ensuring adaptability and effective decision-making within the professional domain. An extensive academic record indicates to employers that a person has achieved a specific level of proficiency, thereby establishing them as valuable resources for organizations. It fosters confidence, credibility, and dedication to academic rigour and diligence. Thorough academic instruction enhances problem-solving capabilities, equipping individuals with the skills to tackle intricate professional challenges using a systematic and discerning approach. This characteristic is greatly valued in a professional setting. The scholarly pursuit cultivates an attitude of flexibility and perpetual education, encouraging consistent encounters with novel insights, developing methodologies, and emergent technologies. Adopting this perspective enables individuals to navigate the ever-changing professional environment effectively.

As espoused by Bandura's social cognitive theory and Vygotsky's sociocultural theory, Profound academic foundations are critical for achieving career success in educational and professional development theories. They develop abilities in collaboration, critical thinking, and communication, in addition to subject-matter expertise. By incorporating many theoretical frameworks, academic institutions can design curricula that provide specialized knowledge and cultivate comprehensive skills applicable to various career paths. Within the domain of Life Design Theory, educational foundations surpass traditional criteria, functioning as conduits through which individuals construct significant life narratives. According to this theory, academic endeavours aim to enable individuals to discover and pursue their interests and values, thereby directing them towards rewarding professional paths. This viewpoint emphasizes the significance of educational foundations as essential elements in the broader framework of an individual's life trajectory. Establishing a solid academic foundation facilitates personal achievement and grants access to a wide array of prospects within the professional sphere. People who get access to research positions, apprenticeships, and networking opportunities and improve their analytical and problem-solving skills through rigorous academic pursuits become invaluable assets to organizations. This shows that a solid educational background and professional success go hand in hand.

Moreover, a robust academic foundation grants access to many prospects, including research positions, apprenticeships, and networking engagements that augment one's preparedness for the professional world. A strong educational background guarantees international competitiveness in an era of globalization, enabling individuals to make valuable contributions in multicultural and diverse professional environments. Fundamentally, solid academic groundwork serves as the bedrock of career preparedness, imparting indispensable knowledge and competencies and moulding the mindset and qualities critical for achieving triumph in the professional realm. Critical thinking is an essential component of strategic planning, as it significantly influences an individual's capacity to make valuable contributions to formulating and implementing strategic initiatives internally in an organization. Those who can analyze data, evaluate risks, and predict potential outcomes contribute a significant viewpoint to making strategic decisions. Critical thinkers are valuable contributors to collaborative problem-solving within team environments, cultivating a culture that appreciates and incorporates diverse perspectives into decision-making.

Ethical decision-making and critical thinking are inextricably linked, as the former empowers individuals to evaluate the ethical ramifications of their selections and guarantees that decisions are consistent with ethical principles; thus, it contributes to the organization's integrity. Critical components of career readiness include the development of subject-specific knowledge and the refinement of thinking abilities. These components not only endow individuals with the knowledge and skills required to thrive in their selected domains but also foster the critical thinking and resolution aptitudes indispensable for professional achievement. Constructing a prosperous and influential professional trajectory necessitates integrating subject-matter expertise and analytical reasoning (Bonn, 2001; Sinnaiah et al., 2023; Dinsmore & Fryer, 2023).

The attainment of subject-specific knowledge is fundamental to developing expertise in a specific domain, enabling individuals to enhance their comprehension and establish themselves as highly regarded specialists in the labour market. This knowledge and skill set are crucial for fulfilling employer demands and contributing to the organization's objectives by approaching practical obstacles with a resolution-oriented approach. In addition, expertise in a particular field can catalyze innovation, resulting in novel resolutions and progress within the industry. Individuals with specialized knowledge in competitive job markets possess a distinct advantage, making them attractive candidates to employers. Concurrently, the ability to think critically is essential for the examination of data, the formulation of well-informed judgments, and the navigation of intricate professional situations. Proficient critical thinking cultivates adaptability, empowering individuals to manoeuvre through ever-changing professional environments adeptly.

Furthermore, it facilitates improved communication, transforming individuals into valuable participants in collaborative environments and emphasizing articulate and reflective discourse. Critical thinkers foster an innovative organizational culture by adopting a creative, continuous-improvement, and hypothesis-challenging mindset. A penchant for ongoing education guarantees that they remain well-informed regarding industry developments and optimal methodologies, which are essential for their professional progress and flexibility. Critical thinking significantly aids strategic planning, contributing to the conception and implementation of strategic initiatives. Critical thinkers promote collaborative problem-solving in team settings by appreciating and incorporating diverse perspectives into decision-making. Finally, ethical decision-making requires critical thinking to ensure that options adhere to ethical standards and contribute to the organization's integrity. Combining subject-specific knowledge with thinking skills creates a solid foundation for workforce preparation. It gives people the skills they need to do well in their chosen fields and the analytical and problem-solving skills they need to have successful and influential careers (Cheng et al., 2021).

Transferrable skills, frequently denoted as soft or generic skills, are fundamental abilities and qualities that surpass particular circumstances and demonstrate universal worth in diverse spheres of life. These abilities bestow upon individuals a sense of flexibility, adaptability, and overall efficacy in scholarly and occupational settings. For example, proficient communication skills, refined via educational presentations and group endeavours, are essential for success in the professional environment when engaging with peers, customers, and superiors. Cultivating critical thinking skills through academic coursework is fundamental for effective problem-solving and strategic planning in professional capacities (Bonn, 2001; Olesen et al., 2020; Sinche et al., 2017). Proficiency in time management, adaptability, collaboration, and leadership, developed within academic environments, effortlessly transitions into productive professional contexts. Educational values, which prioritize ethical decision-making and accountability, are consistent with the professional standards expected in the workplace. Transferrable skills are crucial in bridging the gap between academic and professional achievement, enhancing an individual's flexibility and readiness to navigate the complexities inherent in both domains. In addition to imparting technical knowledge, attaining these abilities promotes comprehensive growth, which is critical for ongoing education in academia and the workplace. Transferrable skills are precious assets that bridge the divide between scholastic distinction and thorough readiness for the complexities and prospects that define the professional sphere (Nagele & Stalder, 2016).

Participating in academic coursework promotes the growth of critical transferable skills indispensable for achieving academic excellence and preparing for professional endeavours. This encompasses the capacity to effectively communicate discoveries and concepts to colleagues and professors while also expressing reasoning and ideas succinctly and unambiguously. Analyzing and evaluating information refines problem-solving skills and applying critical thinking to address complex issues. Effectively managing coursework deadlines and scheduling time for exam preparation are essential practices that cultivate significant time management abilities. Systematically investigating particular subjects and proficiently collecting, synthesizing, and citing data facilitate the development of research and information literacy. One develops adaptability by navigating diverse academic issues and teaching methodologies and adjusting to various intellectual challenges. Participating in collective learning experiences and joint project work with peers strengthens teamwork and collaboration abilities. One can develop and refine leadership abilities by participating in or leading clubs and organizations and assuming leadership roles in group initiatives. Integrating theoretical knowledge into practical scenarios and resolving real-world issues enhances problem-solving skills. One can instil integrity by considering ethical implications in academic work and demonstrating professionalism in collaboration. One exhibits flexibility and dedication to ongoing education when one can adjust educational plans in response to changes and integrate constructive criticism. Digital proficiency is enhanced by using technology for presentations and navigating digital platforms for coursework. Engagement with diverse perspectives and consideration of global contexts in coursework foster the development of global awareness. Developing relationships with colleagues and establishing connections with experts in the field are essential elements that significantly contribute to comprehensive personal and professional growth.

The proficient management and resolution of conflicts arising during collaborative endeavours are essential to fostering strong collaboration and interpersonal abilities. Effectively managing disagreements, divergent viewpoints, and misunderstandings constructively is critical for sustaining a productive and positive workplace. Effectively addressing conflicts proactively not only improves the overall outcome of the current project but also fosters greater collaboration among professionals in a variety of contexts. Proficiency in this area is crucial for cultivating an environment that promotes transparent dialogue, collaborative efforts, and effective dispute resolution—attributes fundamental for achievement in scholarly undertakings and prospective vocational pursuits. These transferable skills are advantageous resources for attaining scholastic distinction and lay the groundwork for individuals to thrive in diverse professional capacities. Educational institutions guarantee that students are not only proficient in their academic pursuits but also adequately equipped to confront the ever-changing demands of the professional environment by incorporating these competencies into coursework and assignments (Meißner et al., 2022; Shonk, 2023; Stepanova et al., 2019).

Developing a curriculum that effectively combines professional and academic rigour necessitates educators adopt a strategic stance. Fundamental methodologies encompass structured group initiatives, essential for encouraging teamwork, communication, and problem-solving via clearly defined responsibilities. Implementing peer review assignments promotes the development of communication skills and fosters a culture of ongoing improvement by motivating students to offer constructive feedback. Case studies and practical implementations of theoretical concepts ignite students' critical thinking and problem-solving abilities. Including leadership development programs in extracurricular leadership positions enhances the comprehensive skill set essential for success in one's professional endeavours. Workshops on conflict resolution afford students a regulated setting in which they can resolve conflicts, thereby enhancing their interpersonal proficiencies. Time management exercises are essential for success in academic and professional spheres, as they cultivate practical allocation skills. Integrating ethical considerations into research endeavours fosters professionalism and ethical decision-making. Using digital communication platforms to facilitate collaborative assignments improves students' digital literacy, communication, and collaboration proficiencies. Organizing seminars on professional development and facilitating international collaborations exposes students to a variety of viewpoints, thereby preparing them for the global professional landscape. Simulations and role-playing exercises enhance practical skills, whereas reflective assignments foster self-awareness and ongoing progress (Meng et al., 2022; Xing, 2022; Morrison-Smith & Ruiz, 2020). Mentorship initiatives and specialized courses in professional ethics guarantee that pupils acquire practical knowledge and ethical direction. Fostering interdisciplinary cooperation facilitates the adoption of a comprehensive methodology for addressing challenges (Brodin & Avery, 2020; Nurius & Kemp, 2019; Vogel et al., 2021).

By employing these methodologies strategically, educators promote the comprehensive growth of students, endowing them not solely with academic understanding but also with critical transferable competencies vital for achievement in various professional environments. Ethical decision-making is a process through which individuals evaluate multiple options and choose actions that align with moral principles and values. It involves considering the potential consequences of actions on oneself, others, and society as a whole and making choices that promote the greater good. Ethical decision-making empowers individuals to make moral decisions by providing a framework for evaluating alternatives and actions. This framework typically considers stakeholder impact, adherence to ethical standards and principles, and alignment with personal and organizational values. Individuals develop the skills and mindset necessary to navigate complex moral dilemmas and act following their principles by engaging in ethical decision-making. The chapter emphasizes that social cognitive and social learning theories and ethical behaviour may be influenced by observing and imitating the behaviour of others. However, societal approval does not determine whether the behaviour is considered moral. While societal norms and values shape perceptions of what is ethical, ethical decision-making goes beyond mere conformity to social norms. It involves critical reflection, moral reasoning, and a commitment to upholding ethical principles despite societal pressures or expectations. An organization's integrity refers to its commitment to ethical behaviour and adherence to moral principles and values. It encompasses honesty, transparency, fairness, and accountability in the organization's operations. Maintaining integrity requires consistent efforts to uphold ethical standards, cultivate a culture of integrity among employees, and hold individuals accountable for unethical behaviour. Organizations with solid integrity are more likely to earn the trust and respect of stakeholders, build sustainable relationships, and achieve long-term success.

## BRIDGING THE GAP: CONNECTING ACADEMIC LEARNING TO CAREER GOALS

There are numerous compelling reasons students must recognize the practical implications of their academic studies for their prospective careers. To begin with, this correlation cultivates a more profound comprehension and admiration for the significance of their academic training. Students' understanding and application of theoretical and conceptual knowledge in the real world elevate the importance and purpose of their academic endeavours. This comprehension, consequently, stimulates enthusiasm and involvement as learners become aware of the pragmatic ramifications of their educational expedition. Furthermore, establishing a concrete connection between scholarly pursuits and prospective professional endeavours fosters a profound sense of direction. Motivating and enlightening students regarding the practical applications of their education, such as effecting positive change in their respective industries, enables them to envision how their studies contribute to these ends. This transparency serves as a catalyst for their dedication to acquiring knowledge and attaining exceptional results.

Integrating academic learning and career goals is crucial to educational and career development ideas. Super's career development theory emphasizes integrating academic experiences with job aspirations, advocating for a seamless connection between educational endeavours and professional objectives. By integrating courses with practical applications in real-world contexts, individuals can augment their preparedness for their professional endeavours. Krumboltz's social learning theory emphasizes the importance of a wide range of learning experiences in influencing job choices and the necessity of exposure to many domains. Hence, the crucial aspect resides in cultivating a dynamic educational milieu that effectively harmonises academic learning with ever-evolving vocational aspirations.

Moreover, exposure to the pragmatic implementation of theoretical concepts equips learners with the ever-evolving demands of the professional environment. It gives them a practical understanding of the obstacles and prospects that may be present in their professional endeavours. This consciousness empowers individuals to acquire expertise in a particular field and the universal competencies—proficient communication, problem-solving, and critical thinking—indispensable for success in a professional environment. Students must comprehend the theoretical and be equipped with a sense of purpose, motivation, and practical preparedness (Amerstorfer & Von Münster-Kistner, 2021; Han et al., 2021). This correlation converts education into a significant means of equipping individuals for the trials and obligations that accompany them throughout their vocational trajectories.

*The Intersection of Academics and Career Readiness*

Educators possess a critical capacity to direct pupils towards a smooth progression from academic study to their prospective professional endeavours. The effective integration of diverse approaches is essential for cultivating a solid correlation between abstract concepts and real-world implementation. By integrating industry-specific scenarios, real-world examples, and case studies into the curriculum, instructors demonstrate the practical manifestations of academic concepts, thus establishing a foundation for learning grounded in tangible applications. Including guest speakers and industry experts introduces a dynamic element, providing students firsthand accounts of how academic knowledge has contributed to professionals' success. Practical applications and apprenticeships offer invaluable hands-on experience, strengthening theoretical knowledge's pragmatic applicability. Capstone projects further narrow the divide by requiring students to apply their acquired knowledge and demonstrate their aptitude for resolving practical issues. Mentorship programs and workshops focused on professional development and emphasizing transferable skills all enhance students' comprehension of the broader relevance of their academic endeavours. This comprehensive approach concludes with networking opportunities and encouragement of self-reflection, which fosters a greater understanding of the practical implications of education and equips students with the functional readiness required for professional success (Kim & Kim, 2022). When implemented together, these approaches enable instructors to establish a stimulating atmosphere that actively aids pupils in traversing the convergence of scholarly pursuits and prospective professional paths. Real-world examples effectively demonstrate the seamless transition of academic knowledge to professional success, substantiating the practical applications of education.

For example, the accomplishments of computer science graduates from Christ University in Bangalore testify to the significant influence of a solid academic background in the ever-evolving technology industry. This case study examines the interdependent connection between academic achievement and professional success, specifically emphasizing individuals possessing a comprehensive knowledge of programming languages and algorithms. Individuals who have completed their studies at Christ University, equipped with a well-rounded education have established themselves as prominent personalities in the technological sector. Individuals in this context effectively navigate and achieve success within the dynamic and ever-changing technical environment, demonstrating the substantial impact of academic principles. Drawing upon their extensive expertise, alums from Christ University have taken on crucial positions in developing innovative software solutions. This not only demonstrates their exceptional individual abilities but also contributes to the transformation of the digital realm and exerts a significant influence on the direction of technology companies. In addition to adhering to conventional career trajectories, confident graduates have chosen to pursue entrepreneurial endeavours by establishing their startups. This strategic manoeuvre highlights their belief in utilizing scholarly expertise to investigate technological boundaries, thereby making significant contributions to the advancement and expansion of the sector. The evident consequences of the mutually beneficial association between educational background and professional achievement are undeniable. The computer science graduates of Christ University have demonstrated exceptional performance in their respective positions and have emerged as influential catalysts for innovation, expansion, and entrepreneurial initiatives within the technology industry. The achievements of computer science graduates from Christ University provide a convincing illustration of how a strong academic background may significantly propel professional paths towards positive transformation. This expedition highlights the persistent significance of intellectual brilliance from Christ University in promoting innovation, contributing to the expansion of organizations, and influencing the future of an industry that flourishes through continuous change.

Life Design Theory emphasizes the intricate correlation between vocational aspirations and academic learning, conceptualizing education as a mechanism through which one can purposefully construct one's life. In this context, bridging the gap entails harmonizing scholarly coursework with individual aspirations and integrating education with the progression of life narratives. According to the theory, education should seamlessly integrate academic experiences and an individual's genuine identity rather than segregating them. This perspective perceives the correlation between academic achievement and professional ambitions not solely as a practical matter but as an in-depth investigation of an individual's authentic identity. According to this purpose-driven education, every academic pursuit substantially contributes to continuous self-exploration and the deliberate formation of a satisfying professional trajectory, as conceptualized in the framework of Life Design Theory.

Theoretical knowledge acquired through rigorous study has formed the foundation for revolutionary discoveries and progress in biomedical research. Prominent figures in biology, genetics, and related academic studies have been instrumental in developing life-saving medications, resolving disease complexities, and advancing global healthcare. Likewise, those with a foundation in environmental science and sustainability studies have effectively applied their scholarly understanding to productive professional endeavours. Professionals in this domain have influenced corporate sustainability endeavours, moulded ecological policies, and spearheaded causes for a more environmentally friendly and sustainable future through their comprehension of environmental systems, climate change dynamics, and sustainable practices. Entrepreneurial success tales also illustrate the correlation between scholarly understanding and professional accomplishments. Numerous entrepreneurs attribute their achievements to developing strategic thinking, problem-solving abilities, and financial knowledge acquired through their educational endeavours. These individuals, holding business degrees or other relevant credentials, have effectively utilized their academic backgrounds to traverse intricate markets, pioneer advancements in their respective industries, and establish prosperous enterprises. These instances clearly illustrate the correlation between scholarly expertise and professional achievement. Academic pursuits function as an initial platform, equipping individuals with the cognitive resources, aptitudes for critical analysis, and specialized knowledge essential for producing significant advancements in their chosen disciplines. The concrete examples solidify the lasting significance of scholarly expertise in the quest for professional distinction and emphasize the profound impact that education can have on the career paths of individuals.

## ACADEMIC ADVISING FOR CAREER READINESS

Academic advisors play a critical role throughout the complex fabric of a student's academic trajectory, serving as essential architects, mentors, and advocates for career preparedness. In addition to course selection, their responsibility encompasses the crucial aspect of harmonizing academic endeavours with prospective professional ambitions. Advisors guide students through the uncharted waters of career exploration by facilitating conversations regarding their interests, aspirations, and long-term objectives. Operating in the capacity of architects, they carefully construct strategic plans that link academic decisions with particular professional paths, thereby illuminating how extracurricular engagements and courses contribute to one's employability. Admitting that intellectual prowess is not enough, advisors proactively promote the growth of adaptable proficiencies, including communication and critical thinking, to guarantee a comprehensive repertoire of abilities that augments overall preparedness for the workforce. Mentors fulfil the role of intermediaries, connecting students with networking prospects

## The Intersection of Academics and Career Readiness

and suggesting events that enhance their professional visibility; thus, they cultivate a feeling of inclusion and connection within their respective industries. In preparation for the competitive job market, advisors fulfil a critical function by offering individualized resume construction and interview readiness guidance, augmenting students' marketability. With a forward-thinking perspective, they provide astute advice regarding graduate school for individuals contemplating pursuing advanced degrees. Advisors fulfil the role of vigilant overseers by monitoring students' academic progress, proactively adapting career goals, and providing expeditious support to ensure students' trajectories remain aligned with their evolving aspirations. Advisors facilitate mentorship opportunities by capitalizing on alumni networks; these connections connect students with accomplished alumni who offer practical advice and insights, cultivating a supportive community. Academic advisors serve as crucial figures who enable students to achieve academic excellence and enter the professional world with the requisite abilities, understanding, and self-assurance required for a prosperous and gratifying vocation. Within the framework of educational and career development theories, academic advising assumes a crucial role in promoting the preparedness of individuals for their professional paths.

Academic advising, informed by Holland's vocational personality theory and founded on Super's career development theory, is critical in assisting students in navigating their academic pursuits in pursuit of changing career goals. This procedure customizes guidance according to individual preferences and capabilities, exemplifying individualized support. As Bandura's social cognitive theory emphasizes, skill development, mentoring, and guidance are essential components. Customized academic guidance enables people to effectively navigate the complexities of higher education, hone critical abilities, and arrive at well-informed vocational choices, guaranteeing a smooth progression from academia to the working world. Academic advising assumes a transformative role within the framework of life design theory by facilitating the alignment of individual values with educational decisions. As co-designers, Advisors foster deliberate decision-making, cultivating readiness for a profession that aligns with individuals' fundamental values and ambitions. Academic advisors are critical in directing students towards prosperous professional paths by incorporating career discussions into their interactions. Initiating these dialogues early in a student's academic trajectory is crucial, as it fosters introspection regarding long-term objectives and hobbies to harmonize educational decisions with prospective professional ambitions. Assessment instruments offer invaluable insights by facilitating the identification of strengths and potential career paths. Advisors augment comprehension by integrating concrete illustrations from the real world, demonstrating the pragmatic implications of scholastic decisions via success narratives. Advisors establish connections between academic pursuits and industry developments by highlighting students' contributions to progressive sectors by applying transferable competencies like critical thinking and communication. Advisors achieve a comprehensive approach by promoting internships and experiential learning, facilitating networking opportunities, and providing guidance about graduate education. Facilitating skill-enhancement workshops and conducting periodic evaluations enables sustained progress and assistance. By sharing the success stories of alums, we can highlight the tangible outcomes of a well-coordinated academic and professional journey. Fostering a supportive environment facilitates candid dialogues regarding professional matters, cultivating confidence and optimizing the efficacy of these interactions with a focus on one's career. By employing these tactics, academic advisors encourage students to conceptualize and achieve prosperous professional trajectories.

Advisors and educators serve a crucial function in assisting students in effectively aligning their academic and professional ambitions. Through early exploration, goal-setting, and self-evaluation, pupils can make well-informed educational choices that align with their long-term objectives. The divide between theoretical knowledge and practical requirements can be narrowed by linking academic advisors and career services in collaboration, utilizing career development resources, and participating in practical experiences such as internships. A dedication to ongoing education, consistent monitoring, and exposure to various viewpoints strengthens the correlation between theoretical understanding and practical professional achievement. By implementing these tactics, educators and guidance counsellors enable pupils to merge their scholastic and vocational aspirations successfully.

## COLLABORATIONS WITH CAREER SERVICES

Amidst the ever-evolving realm of education and professional development, it becomes increasingly vital for students' achievements that academic departments and career services offices cultivate strong partnerships. This chapter explores the inherent worth of these collaborations, shedding light on their critical function in effectively bridging scholarly education with practical preparedness for the workforce. The crucial aspect is recognizing the reciprocal connection between theoretical understanding and the pragmatic requirements of the professional domain. Through emphasizing this collaboration, institutions establish a cohesive educational strategy that acknowledges the mutual reliance between scholastic distinction and comprehensive professional growth. Institutions can enhance the educational experiences of their students by selecting a framework that promotes collaboration through practical strategies such as transparent communication channels, shared initiatives, and mutual understanding. By combining career-oriented events and incorporated curricular experiences, this partnership facilitates a smooth progression from academic success to preparedness for the labour market.

Career services and educational and career development theories must collaborate to ensure that academic pursuits align with long-term objectives. Consistent with Super's career development theory, these collaborations afford concrete prospects for individuals to establish connections between their academic endeavours and future aspirations. Using observational learning and mentoring, career services, informed by Bandura's social cognitive theory, significantly impact workforce readiness. Career services are considered essential collaborators in Life Design Theory, which promotes collaborative platforms beyond traditional planning by incorporating self-discovery and personal values. Under the guidance of principles of life design, these collaborative endeavours pool collective knowledge to assist individuals in translating their aspirations into tangible career trajectories. Academic advising, informed by life design theory, serves as an individualized catalyst by emphasizing purposeful decision-making and equipping students for careers that align with their most profound aspirations. To bridge the divide between theory and practice and address the challenges of educational and vocational development theories, incorporating experiential learning guided by Krumboltz's social learning theory. By integrating multiple theories, Super's career development theory addresses career indecision through comprehensive counselling. By adopting a holistic perspective, students can confront challenges proactively, ensure they are in line with the ever-changing professional environment, and improve their adaptability and prospects for success.

Through disseminating these narratives, institutions strive to foster a culture of collaboration, thereby strengthening the tangible advantages they offer and motivating others to undertake comparable transformative alliances. The practical cooperation between academic departments and career services offices constitutes a formidable entity that moulds an educational milieu in which pupils prosper scholastically and acquire the pragmatic competencies and mentorship critical for a triumphant ascent into their selected professional vocations. Promoting cooperation between academic departments and career

## The Intersection of Academics and Career Readiness

services agencies is crucial to augmenting students' preparedness for the workforce. To accomplish this, it is imperative to establish unambiguous channels of communication that foster open discourse and the exchange of knowledge via routine formal and informal gatherings. Joint endeavours, including workshops and events concentrating on careers, can effectively merge scholarly education with hands-on career readiness, thereby addressing particular deficiencies in skills or knowledge. To foster collaboration, curricula must incorporate career development elements that provide practical applications and valuable insights via pertinent assignments or guest lectures. Opportunities for professional development, such as conferences and training sessions, foster a collective comprehension of the requirements of academic and career services personnel. The establishment of cross-functional teams allows for collaborative endeavours such as industry research and internship programs, while the application of technology streamlines communication in institutions with varying characteristics. By involving faculty members in the collaborative process, it is possible to ensure that academic insights remain current with the ever-changing expectations of careers. Consistent feedback loops and ongoing development initiatives, driven by agreed-upon objectives and metrics, enhance the collaborative methodology. Honouring success tales highlight the concrete results of these combined efforts, demonstrating how students effortlessly transition from academic achievements to significant professional paths. By implementing these tactics, educational establishments can foster a cooperative atmosphere that maximizes learners' readiness for prosperous and gratifying careers.

Numerous academic institutions have demonstrated effective collaborations between career services and educational personnel, fostering a synergistic environment that augments students' preparedness for the workforce. An exceptional collaborative effort entails the incorporation of career development modules into scholarly curricula. The academic and career services staff at Christ University have effectively bridged the divide between theoretical learning and practical career preparation through the collaborative design of coursework that integrates real-world applications and industry insights. Furthermore, the academic institution orchestrates an annual career symposium through a collaborative effort between career services, academic departments, and employer panels. This event features seminars and networking opportunities. This endeavour facilitates direct student-professional interaction, imparting invaluable insights regarding prospective career trajectories. A distinctive collaboration occurs at Kristu Jayanti College in Bangalore, where cross-functional teams of academic and career services representatives are involved. These teams collaborate on various endeavours, including establishing specialized internship programs, collaborative research on industry trends, and developing resources that aid in the seamless transition of individuals from academia to the professional world. This collaborative model has effectively promoted a comprehensive approach to career readiness.

Bangalore's Christ University demonstrates an effective faculty engagement initiative. Faculty members engage in collaborative endeavours by remaining well-informed regarding contemporary industry trends, providing career services with pertinent insights, and actively participating in initiatives that bolster students' career readiness. The amalgamation of scholarly knowledge and initiatives to foster professional growth has notably enhanced students' educational experiences. With the establishment of a comprehensive and supportive atmosphere that maximizes students' readiness for prosperous and gratifying professional journeys, academic and career services personnel have proven in each of these fruitful collaborations that this is possible. These instances function as paradigms for alternative establishments aiming to forge productive alliances between academic and career services personnel.

## CASE STUDIES AND SUCCESS STORIES

Christ University demonstrated a comprehensive methodology for incorporating career readiness and academics, utilizing a strategic partnership between career services and academic departments. The educational establishment formed interdisciplinary groups of faculty members and career advisors who collaborated to strategize and execute a sequence of specialized seminars and events emphasizing professional growth. Students experienced an easier transition from their academic studies to the professional realm due to this initiative. Significantly, internship participation increased substantially, as did the rate of successful employment placements following graduation. At Christ University, EK, a computer science major, exemplifies the efficacy of this integrated approach. She gained theoretical understanding and practical experience following industry standards through her academic pursuits. Because of this all-encompassing groundwork, EK obtained a highly desirable internship during her junior year, culminating in a permanent employment offer from the same organization when she graduated. The success of EK unmistakably demonstrates the favourable consequences that can arise from Christ University's effectively integrated academic and career readiness approach.

Kristu Jayanti College has effectively implemented a novel strategy to incorporate vocation readiness into its syllabi by strategically revising its curriculum. By strategically modifying particular courses to include industry-specific projects, case studies, and practical applications, the institution ensured that students achieved academic excellence and acquired valuable experience immediately relevant to their prospective careers. This progressive approach has contributed to the college's exceptional history of alumni achievement in diverse sectors. JL, an entrepreneur enrolled at Kristu Jayanti College, effectively illustrates the efficacy of this methodology. JL effectively initiated operations for his startup by capitalizing on the robust academic groundwork provided by the program. The program's focus on practical business situations allowed JL to implement his acquired knowledge in his entrepreneurial pursuits immediately. Through mentorship from the college's career services, JL successfully overcame the obstacles of launching a business and converting his academic background into a prosperous enterprise. The case studies and success tales presented herein vividly illustrate the concrete advantages of integrating academics and career readiness. Institutions and programs that prioritize this integration foster academic excellence and equip students with the means to transition seamlessly into successful and satisfying careers.

## CHALLENGES AND SOLUTIONS

Several obstacles complicate the effective integration of academics and career readiness initiatives, each necessitating well-considered resolutions. A notable obstacle pertains to compartmentalization between career services and academic departments, wherein a lack of communication hinders the smooth integration of theoretical knowledge with hands-on career readiness. Furthermore, an inherent shortcoming of conventional curriculum design is its preoccupation with theoretical understanding to the detriment of practical implementation, which impedes students' ability to fulfil the ever-evolving demands of the professional realm. The challenges posed by opposition to change among faculty and institutional stakeholders hinder the implementation of novel strategies designed to emphasize career preparedness. Limited exposure to real-world scenarios inhibits the transition from academic studies to the professional environment; this obstacle necessitates implementing strategic solutions to facilitate a more seamless progression. An additional challenge arises when attempting to accommodate students' varied aims and aspirations, as a standardized approach might need to attend to their unique requirements adequately. The importance of faculty training increases significantly, as the inability of instructors to integrate career-oriented discussions and activities into their teaching approaches presents a significant obstacle. The insufficient integration of technology and the absence of practical industry experience in specific academic programs exacerbate these challenges. Comprehensive strategies are required to reconcile these gaps effectively.

Theories of vocational and educational development confront the challenge of equipping individuals for academic endeavours in contrast to the rigours of the real world. Integrating Krumboltz's social learning theory into experiential learning enrichment is crucial for bridging the divide between theory and practice. Super's theory of career development tackles ambivalence using comprehensive counselling, which facilitates productive introspection and decision-making. Academic establishments proactively modify curricula to correspond with ever-changing professional environments by incorporating various theoretical perspectives. As posited by Life Design Theory, collaborative career services involve individuals constructing their trajectories, emphasizing self-reflection and harmonizing personal beliefs with vocational choices to create a dynamic trajectory. Under the guidance of Life Design Theory, academic advising encourages conscientious decision-making consistent with an individual's values. The effective incorporation of Krumboltz's theory addresses challenges, guarantees congruence with the ever-changing professional landscape, and equips students with fundamental capabilities for achievement.

To tackle the obstacles associated with the misalignment of educational pursuits and career readiness, academic establishments may implement collaborative platforms that facilitate integrating career services and academic departments. Curriculum restructuring that incorporates industry-specific initiatives imparts practical experience and promotes innovative pedagogical approaches. Coordination is improved by employing customized career readiness initiatives, faculty development programs, and technology-driven experiential learning opportunities, facilitating successful student transitions and bridging the divide between theoretical academic knowledge and its practical application.

## DISCUSSION

This chapter explores the intricate convergence of academics and career preparation, emphasizing its profound influence on students' achievement. The thorough emphasis on effectively integrating theoretical knowledge with hands-on career readiness highlights the comprehensive approach required to foster well-rounded individuals. Case studies effectively illustrate the successful collaborations between academic departments and career services, providing tangible examples of the benefits of these types of partnerships. By strategically emphasizing early career exploration, real-world examples, and transferable skills, this program ensures that students have a strong foundation for success in the ever-changing professional landscape. The discourse surrounding collaborations with career services underscores the critical significance of these alliances in connecting theoretical understanding with the pragmatic requirements of the professional realm. The chapter advocates for a unified educational approach by emphasizing the symbiotic relationship between academic excellence and holistic career development. Effective methods for cultivating collaboration, such as establishing transparent channels of communication and coordinating collaborative endeavours, furnish institutions with a structure to elevate the educational experiences of their pupils. The chapter emphasizes the concrete results of joint efforts utilizing compelling success tales and partnerships, motivating institutions to initiate comparable transformative collaborations.

Numerous academic institutions and career services departments serve as paradigms for productive collaborations, showcasing the efficacy of a synergistic strategy in augmenting students' career preparedness. These collaborative efforts, which encompass cross-functional teams and integrated curricula, demonstrate the vast array of approaches academic institutions can employ to foster inclusive and encouraging atmospheres. The chapter acknowledges the significance of faculty engagement, citing institutions such as Christ University that exemplify it through the active participation of faculty members in endeavours that improve students' preparedness for the workforce.

Ethical decision-making involves evaluating options based on moral principles, considering consequences for oneself, others, and society, and choosing actions that promote the greater good. It provides a framework for assessing choices, evaluating stakeholder impact, and aligning with personal and organizational values. Social cognitive theories suggest that observing others can influence behaviour, but ethics is not solely defined by societal approval; it requires critical reflection and adherence to principles. An organization's integrity involves a commitment to ethical behaviour, including honesty, transparency, fairness, and accountability. Upholding integrity fosters trust, builds relationships, and contributes to long-term success.

The incorporated case studies and success tales demonstrate the importance of integrating academics and career readiness. Instances from Christ University and Kristu Jayanti College illustrate how strategic collaboration and curriculum redesign can yield concrete student advantages, such as heightened engagement in internships and prosperous employment placements. These instances provide persuasive proof regarding the beneficial effects of effectively incorporating academic and career readiness approaches. The discourse surrounding challenges and potential remedies offers a pragmatic evaluation of the barriers that educational institutions might encounter when attempting to harmonize curriculum with initiatives promoting career preparedness. Practical resolutions address the identified challenges, including resistance to change and institutional isolation. The chapter espouses the implementation of collaborative platforms, curricular redesign, faculty development programs, and technology utilization as practical strategies to surmount these challenges. The chapter emphasizes once more the critical significance of the academic-career readiness intersection. They include the idea that academic instruction and hands-on job readiness should work together, that students should learn skills that can be used in different situations, and that academic departments and career assistance should work together to help students do well. In the face of obstacles, the chapter offers pragmatic resolutions and motivates educators to maintain their commitment to prioritizing this integration. The commitment to shaping students' future success in a constantly shifting global environment reaffirms the constraints educational institutions and their stakeholders face in integrating academics and career preparedness.

## CONCLUSION

Placing significant emphasis on the critical correlation between academic achievement and career preparation highlights its profound influence on students' success. This underscores the necessity of establishing a unified link between theoretical knowledge and hands-on vocational competencies. A solid academic foundation fosters critical thinking, problem-solving, and adaptability—qualitative attributes for achieving success in the workplace—in addition to subject-specific expertise. By bridging the divide between theory and practice, the collaboration between academic departments and career services propels students toward influential careers. Academics emphasize early career exploration, practical examples, and transferable skills for workforce readiness. Academic advisors fulfil a crucial function by ensuring that the decisions made by students align with their long-term aspirations and by attending to the industry's requirements. By tailoring readiness programs, encouraging creativity, and leveraging technology, institutions guarantee that students are prepared to confront the ever-changing demands of the workforce. Students are better equipped to successfully transition into a competitive global environment when academics and career readiness are integrated.

## REFERENCES

Akosah-Twumasi, P., Emeto, T. I., Lindsay, D., Tsey, K., & Malau-Aduli, B. S. (2018). A systematic review of factors that influence youths career choices—the role of culture. Frontiers in Education, 3. doi:10.3389/feduc.2018.00058

Amerstorfer, C. M., & Von Münster-Kistner, C. F. (2021). Student Perceptions of Academic Engagement and Student-Teacher Relationships in Problem-Based Learning. Frontiers in Psychology, 12, 713057. Advance online publication. doi:10.3389/fpsyg.2021.713057 PMID:34777094

Bonn, I. (2001). Developing strategic thinking as a core competency. Management Decision, 39(1), 63–71. doi:10.1108/EUM0000000005408

Brodin, E., & Avery, H. (2020). Cross-disciplinary collaboration and scholarly independence in multidisciplinary learning environments at the doctoral level and beyond. Minerva, 58(3), 409–433. doi:10.1007/s11024-020-09397-3

Cheng, M., Adekola, O., Albia, J. E., & Cai, S. (2021). Employability in higher education: A review of key stakeholders' perspectives. Higher Education Evaluation and Development, 16(1), 16–31. doi:10.1108/HEED-03-2021-0025

Dinsmore, D. L., & Fryer, L. K. (2023). Critical thinking and its relation to strategic processing. Educational Psychology Review, 35(1), 36. Advance online publication. doi:10.1007/s10648-023-09755-z

Ferreira, N. (2022). Career adaptability as a predictor of employees' career agility and career embeddedness. In Springer eBooks (pp. 229–248). doi:10.1007/978-3-031-09803-1_13

Han, J. H., Kelley, T. R., & Knowles, J. G. (2021). Factors influencing student STEM learning: Self-Efficacy and outcome expectancy, 21st century skills, and career awareness. Journal for STEM Education Research, 4(2), 117–137. doi:10.1007/s41979-021-00053-3

Kim, N., & Kim, M. K. (2022). Teachers' perceptions of using an artificial intelligence-based educational tool for scientific writing. Frontiers in Education, 7, 755914. Advance online publication. doi:10.3389/feduc.2022.755914

Meißner, F., Weinmann, C., & Vowe, G. (2022). Understanding and Addressing Problems in Research Collaboration: A Qualitative interview study from a Self-Governance perspective. Frontiers in Research Metrics and Analytics, 6, 778176. Advance online publication. doi:10.3389/frma.2021.778176 PMID:35224422

Meng, J., Kim, S., & Reber, B. H. (2022). Ethical challenges in an evolving digital communication era: Coping resources and ethics training in corporate communications. *Corporate Communications*, *27*(3), 581–594. doi:10.1108/CCIJ-11-2021-0128

Morrison-Smith, S., & Ruiz, J. (2020). Challenges and barriers in virtual teams: A literature review. *SN Applied Sciences*, *2*(6), 1096. Advance online publication. doi:10.1007/s42452-020-2801-5

Nägele, C., & Stalder, B. E. (2016b). Competence and the need for transferable skills. In Technical and vocational education and training (pp. 739–753). doi:10.1007/978-3-319-41713-4_34

Naylor, R., Bird, F. L., & Butler, N. E. (2021). Academic expectations among university students and staff: Addressing the role of psychological contracts and social norms. *Higher Education*, *82*(5), 847–863. doi:10.1007/s10734-020-00668-2

Nurius, P. S., & Kemp, S. P. (2019). Individual-Level Competencies for Team Collaboration with Cross-Disciplinary Researchers and Stakeholders. In Springer eBooks (pp. 171–187). doi:10.1007/978-3-030-20992-6_13

Olesen, K. B., Christensen, M. K., & O'Neill, L. D. (2020). What do we mean by "transferable skills"? A literature review of how the concept is conceptualized in undergraduate health sciences education. *Higher Education, Skills and Work-based Learning*, *11*(3), 616–634. doi:10.1108/HESWBL-01-2020-0012

Shonk, K. (2023, March 24). *How to Handle Conflict in Teams: Lessons from Scientific Collaborations*. PON - Program on Negotiation at Harvard Law School. https://www.pon.harvard.edu/daily/conflict-resolution/how-to-handle-conflict-in-teams-lessons-from-scientific-collaborations/

Sinche, M., Layton, R. L., Brandt, P. D., O'Connell, A. B., Hall, J. D., Freeman, A. M., Harrell, J. R., Cook, J. G., & Brennwald, P. (2017). An evidence-based evaluation of transferrable skills and job satisfaction for science PhDs. *PLoS One*, *12*(9), e0185023. doi:10.1371/journal.pone.0185023 PMID:28931079

Sinnaiah, T., Adam, S., & Mahadi, B. (2023). A strategic management process: The role of decision-making style and organizational performance. *Journal of Work-Applied Management*, *15*(1), 37–50. doi:10.1108/JWAM-10-2022-0074

Stepanova, O., Polk, M., & Saldert, H. (2019). Understanding mechanisms of conflict resolution beyond collaboration: An interdisciplinary typology of knowledge types and their integration in practice. *Sustainability Science*, *15*(1), 263–279. doi:10.1007/s11625-019-00690-z

Vogel, A. L., Knebel, A. R., Faupel-Badger, J. M., Portilla, L., & Simeonov, A. (2021). A systems approach to enable effective team science from the internal research program of the National Center for Advancing Translational Sciences. *Journal of Clinical and Translational Science*, *5*(1), e163. Advance online publication. doi:10.1017/cts.2021.811 PMID:34527302

Xing, S. (2022). Ethical Conflict and Knowledge Hiding in Teams: The moderating role of workplace friendship in the Education sector. Frontiers in Psychology, 13. doi:10.3389/fpsyg.2022.824485

## ADDITIONAL READING

Campbell, M., Cooper, B., Rueckert, C., & Smith, J. E. (2019). Reimagining student employability: A case study of policy and practice transformation. *Journal of Higher Education Policy and Management*, *41*(5), 500–517. doi:10.1080/1360080X.2019.1646379

Courtois, A. (2018). From 'academic concern' to work readiness: Student mobility, employability and the devaluation of academic capital on the year abroad. *British Journal of Sociology of Education*, *40*(2), 190–206. doi:10.1080/01425692.2018.1522241

Dodd, V., Hanson, J., & Hooley, T. (2021). Increasing students' career readiness through career guidance: Measuring the impact with a validated measure. *British Journal of Guidance & Counselling*, *50*(2), 260–272. doi:10.1080/03069885.2021.1937515

Fox, K. F. (2018). Leveraging a leadership development framework for career readiness. *New Directions for Student Leadership*, *2018*(157), 13–26. doi:10.1002/yd.20276 PMID:29451730

Mayes, R. D., Hines, E. M., Bibbs, D. L., & Rodman, J. (2019). Counsellors and psychologists are mentoring gifted Black males with disabilities to foster college and career readiness. *Gifted Child Today*, *42*(3), 157–164. doi:10.1177/1076217519843150

Pak, K., & Desimone, L. M. (2018). How do states implement College- and Career-Readiness Standards? A Distributed Leadership Analysis of Standards-Based Reform. *Educational Administration Quarterly*, *55*(3), 447–476. doi:10.1177/0013161X18799463

Quarles, A. M., Conway, C. S., Harris, S. M., Osler, J. E. II, & Rech, L. (2022). Integrating Digital/Mobile Learning Strategies With Students in the Classroom at the Historical Black College/University (HBCU). In J. Keengwe (Ed.), *Handbook of Research on Digital Content, Mobile Learning, and Technology Integration Models in Teacher Education* (Vol. 1, pp. 390–408). IGI Global. https://www.igi-global.com/chapter/integrating-digitalmobile-learning-strategies-with-students-in-the-classroom-at-the-historical-black-collegeuniversity-hbcu/186260

Waite, A. M., & McDonald, K. S. (2018). Exploring challenges and solutions facing STEM careers in the 21st century: A Human Resource Development perspective. *Advances in Developing Human Resources*, *21*(1), 3–15. doi:10.1177/1523422318814482

Winterton, J., & Turner, J. J. (2019). Preparing graduates for work readiness: An overview and agenda. *Education + Training*, *61*(5), 536–551. doi:10.1108/ET-03-2019-0044

## KEY TERMS AND DEFINITIONS

**Academic and Career Integration:** The seamless alignment of academic learning with practical career preparation to enhance students' overall readiness for professional success.

**Adaptability:** The capacity to adjust and thrive in changing circumstances, demonstrating flexibility, resilience, and openness to new ideas and approaches.

**Career Exploration:** The active investigation and assessment of various professions and industries to make informed decisions about future career paths and aspirations.

**Collaborative Learning:** A cooperative approach to education where students engage collectively in the learning process, promoting teamwork, shared understanding, and knowledge exchange.

**Critical Thinking:** The ability to analyze, evaluate, and synthesize information, fostering informed decision-making and problem-solving skills in diverse situations.

**Problem-Solving:** Addressing challenges or obstacles through analytical thinking and creative strategies to achieve effective and practical solutions.

**Student Success:** The achievement of positive academic, personal, and career outcomes, indicating effective learning, growth, and accomplishment for students.

# Chapter 12
# Impact of Frequency and Consistency in Preparing Students for Career Paths

**Saptarshi Kumar Sarkar**
*Brainware University, India*

**Piyal Roy**
*Brainware University, India*

**Shivnath Ghosh**
*Brainware University, India*

**Amitava Podder**
*Brainware University, India*

**Subrata Paul**
*Brainware University, India*

## ABSTRACT

*The modern labor market is constantly evolving, making it challenging to prepare students for rewarding career paths. This chapter emphasizes the importance of consistency and regularity in career preparation, highlighting the impact on educators, career counselors, and students. It explores how frequency and consistency shape students' preparedness for the changing world of work, drawing on research and real-world experiences. Consistency in learning and skill development leads to greater proficiency and adaptability and is crucial in setting objectives, habit formation, and time management. This understanding can help educators, career advisors, and students navigate the intricacies of the modern labor market with greater resilience and confidence. The chapter also lays the groundwork for future research and real-world implementations, providing a strong foundation for improving job readiness in a time of innovation and transition.*

DOI: 10.4018/978-1-7998-7999-2.ch012

## 1. INTRODUCTION

More complex and difficult than ever in a fast-changed environment and labour market is the process of preparing students for future success along chosen career pathways. The present study seeks to explore the importance of consistency and frequency principles toward the challenging career preparation cycle. It sheds light on the vast importance of these two issues and how they affect teachers and career counsellors as well as students. This paper provides an exposition and evaluation of the role played by the aspects of frequency and consistency in preparing students for the challenges that exist within the current workforce environment. This is why it relies on a lot of research and practical experience as well. Modern labour market is inherently volatile, characterized by constant evolution of technology, economic ups and downs, and fluctuating needs of different sectors. Hence, it becomes very difficult to equip the students well enough for prosperous employment.

In a holistic study on the influence of frequency and regularity, this paper considers such matters as continued skills development, memory retention, flexibility, and self-confidence. Examining if repeated exposure to a topic helps to improve the corresponding skills. Moreover, the psychological theory of spaced repetition stresses on the importance of being exposed to information throughout your lifetime to make sure that you remember it and put it into practice productively during your career. Consistency with regard to goal setting and habit formation forms the basis for successful career preparation as opposed to mere acquisition of skills and knowledge. Students are motivated because they can work towards small pieces of their long term career objectives, increasing the sense of competence. Pursuing specific goals will help in converting students' not so focused careers objectives into tangible goals while at the same time forming good practices.

Yet, another important aspect of consistency is time management which helps students find balance between their extracurricular, job-related, and academic demands. Regularly, those students who have certain chores concerning their careers have less attitude towards defer their obligations and therefore they are better equipped with this respect.

Professional networks play an important role in any society, with consistency in networking efforts being identified as crucial in such a setting. In order for a student to have a successful career, he or she should ensure that they attend job-related activities regularly, maintain an active online presence, and develop professional networks. Creating and maintaining such links on a regular basis can benefit pupils who would get a valuable understanding from experienced individuals. Figure 1 shows the basic diagram to prepare students for future success in placement.

This article also provides tips for the educators, career counsellors, and students that can help them implement the concepts highlighted above regarding the value of periodicity and continuity during job readiness pre-planning processes. It stresses on the need for institutions of learning to introduce job oriented exercises that will provide students with enough chances to put into practice whatever they learn. It should also be emphasized to mentors and consultants about the need to maintain the same attitude, goal setting and continuous skills enhancement.

Students have various avenues and means at their disposal during the digital age, allowing them to make career preparations systematically. Apps and other tools that assist students in setting goals, managing time, and developing skills help students track their progress towards a career-ready state.

*Figure 1. The basic diagram to preparing students for future success*

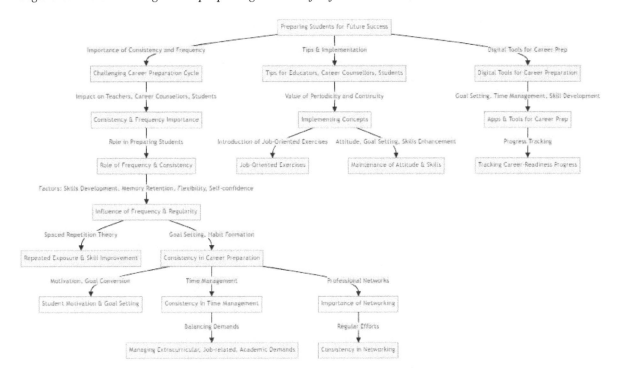

## 2. SIGNIFICANCE OF FREQUENCY

In this article, we focus on the important idea of periodicity in relation to job training. This highlights the fact that it is crucial for students to keep interacting with subject matter, content, and skills so as to be thoroughly ready for their future career paths. It is also important in aiding learners join the competitive job market as well as ensure they do not fail after the job. In this way through continuous practice and living in their own subjects students develop their skills, extend knowledge on the branch and keep abreast of trends in the branch of study. The principle of frequency is also important because frequent exposure ensures that what one learns can be retained and applied in the professional area. Similarly, frequent participation enables students to be more adaptive such that they are able to respond quickly to changes and developments within their areas of studies. Finally, continuous practice and involvement in occupation oriented tasks assist students to boost their confidences, who in reality is one of most significant factors required in work environment that let them confronts challenges and grasp opportunities with certainty.

As such, an important aspect of successful career preparation involves how often learning and skill acquisition is done in order to ensure that each student's first job will be suitable for them and is also an initial step towards a prosperous working life path in a quickly evolving labour environment market.

### 2.1 Continuous Improvement of Skill

This explains why frequency is a sine qua non to preparing the students for their future jobs. This philosophy centers on the fact that continuous skill development is crucial for learners' ability to compete within a highly demanding job market. Skill acquisition and mastery require continuous involvement with areas of expertise for sustained skills. Consistent practice allows students understand more about their professions. Take a case of a programmer who needs routine coding to remain abreast with changing programming languages and technologies, as this also improves skills. Consistent improvement in students is also important for students to be ready to withstand the requirements and challenges in their future profession.

### 2.1.1 Constant Skill Improvement

The process of improving student skill sets as they continue towards their career paths remains one of the crucial ways of preparing them for their future job pathways. Besides gaining basic information, students need to build up their technical skills and capabilities that keep changing in today's dynamic labour markets. The concept highlights that it important to periodically or constantly explore with subjects, knowledge, and skills. Interaction with these learning components is an inherent feature toward skill growth and proficiency. The strategy is useful across industry lines in situations where an individual's width or range of abilities may dictate upward versus horizontal motion.

### 2.1.2 Mastery Through Consistent Practice

Consistent exposure of any subject area is what develops new skill in any field. In essence, this means constant involvement with the content, which should be done through regular practice in the real settings. An example is the need for uniform coding practices in the software arena. As students solve their problems, they become more proficient in one programming language. Students who continuously and systematically code, develop insight into the language besides mastering skills to face more complicated activities.

### 2.1.3 Keeping Up to Date in Changing Fields

It is necessary to be in the know as far as industries such as business, medical and technology that are experiencing accelerated changes. However, students who receive ongoing skill development are more likely to be able to adapt to changing trends within their area of learning. They remain relevant by continually acquiring new skills and improving on those that they already possess. A seasoned web designer that keeps learning and applying a new frame work will easily design more relevant contemporary sites and apps hence remain competitive in the evolving field of web development.

### 2.1.4 Proficiency and Problem-Solving

These two concepts cannot be separated since they deal with developing skills and being a specialist at the same time. When skill development is consistent, proficiency comes after mastery. The capability to overcome problems makes them feel confident that this skill will be useful for their career life as well. As an example, a health care provider will diagnose and treat a patient more precisely if they constantly improve their knowledge and skills. This will enhance trust between the patient and the provider.

## 2.1.5 Competitive Edge

The dedicated students in this quest are more competitive in this cutthroat labour market than any other learner in this quest. Rather, employers search for applicants that evidence willingness to learn as well as a flexibility in addition to qualifying the minimal requirements for a position. Pro-activeness leads by example as students who are constantly sharpening their skills or keeping abreast of industry trends are more likely to attract potential employers.

## 2.1.6 Transferability and Career advancement

It is still necessary for career growth and expansion past just being ready for a first job. Demographics of the workforce and the current work practices in that specific field. The students broadening their skills every time can take on more responsibilities and even assume new roles in their organizations. Such a flexible career gives an opportunity for many different career pathways and allows to find new possibilities for life.

In conclusion, an important aspect of job planning is ongoing skills development. It reflects a notion that learning, as well as the development of skills, are continuous endeavours which should extend beyond schoolwork and continue through one's entire working life. One must engage into his field continuously if he is to gain skills, stay abreast, counter complex problems, have an edge over competitors and support his career success. The commitment to continuous skill development shows a person's passion for professional excellence and one's determination to face different challenges of the ever-changing labour market.

## 2.2 Memory and Retention

This other way importance of frequency relates to memory retention which also affects job preparation. Spaced repetition as a method is highlighted in cognitive psychology research; this approach involves reviewing the knowledge by taking longer and longer breaks over time. Spaced repetition concept ensures pupils remember what they have learnt thus leading to an enhanced understanding of the subject matter. Consequently, they can retain and take advantage of this knowledge when they start work, as well as adjust to new information in their jobs. In short, exposure to information on a day to day basis enables one to memorize it and utilise it better at his/her daily work.

## 2.2.1 Basis of Knowledge

Retention and memorization have a significant bearing on effective learning that results in job preparation. These capabilities encompass the capacity to recall knowledge, acquired skills, and learned information developed in course of education as well as life experiences. This set of cognitive skills will be useful for them when they set out on their career paths. Knowledge must be effectively recalled and retrieved when needed in order to utilize it efficiently at the workplace.

## 2.2.2 Function of Spaced Repetition

As evidenced by the psychological principle of spaced repetition, constant exposure to knowledge in time proves essential. Repetition of information in order for it to be embedded into long-term memory.

This helps students retain knowledge which they may use throughout their professional lives, and by visiting content frequently. For instance, scientists and medical practitioners believe that fundamental information builds up on more sophisticated learning.

### 2.2.3 Practical Application in Professional Settings

The importance of memory retention in the workplace can also be understood when one thinks about jobs which require quicker decision making (Harren et al., 1979) and ready access to essential information. Healthcare provider should have been in a position to quickly assess and give treatment basing on past knowledge and level of medical training. On the other hand, lawyers depend on their recollection of previous court cases while practicing whereas engineers utilize their understanding of complex technical issues. The ability to remember and summon this information is what makes the experts succeed in their respective fields.

### 2.2.4 Adaptation to Evolving Fields

Memory recall is just as vital as memory storage when dealing with modern day business organizations that operate on fluidity. Although specific principles of certain professions are subject to change with circumstances, many universal issues and knowledge keep constant. For instance, learning the basics of programming facilitates software developers to quickly adapt to new programming or frameworks as the technological world is always dynamic.

### 2.2.5 Retention and Lifelong Learning

Career preparation is a dynamic process that occurs during a person's entire professional career, and not just on academic settings. As such, professionals who are able hold their memory and retain information in their minds have a higher likelihood of pursuing a lifelong process of education or professional development. This will help them blend the new skills they have learnt with those they already possess and be well-positioned for the ever evolving job environment.

### 2.2.6 Problem-Solving and Confidence

Good memory enhances your confidence. Those who have a good memory find it easy to accept challenges in an assured manner. It is, therefore, extremely important that people take on their trust when it comes to making a decision under stress by people like emergency responders, financial analysts, or health care professionals who deal with matters that do not tolerate time wastage.

### 2.2.7 Enhanced Creativity

Retaining information may also enhance creativity. With lots of information and experience accumulated in their memory banks, individuals can create innovative thoughts and approaches towards promoting their career moves.

These two elements make up important aspects of career preparation as they assist the ability to use knowledge and skills at work. Memorization-enhancement approaches, such as spaced repetition, ensure the information remains for a longer period of time and the understanding becomes firm. In numerous professions, memory retention becomes critical, however when making crucial decisions based on instant recollection is imperative. Strong memory recall abilities makes it possible for individuals to keep learning new things right through their lifespan. One is also able to easily adapt to various fields, undertake challenges confidently and even come up with creative ideas that lead to success within a highly competitive work place.

## 2.3 Adaptability

The employment market is constantly evolving, hence professionals need to possess this ability of being flexible. Exposure to several aspects of one's profession and keeping abreast of advances in the field is crucial to career preparation. This clearly illustrates the importance of periodicity for learning. The students who keep practicing what they love acquire appropriate methods of adaptation that allow them to respond quickly to any alterations and progress encountered on the market. Developed through continuous participation, this flexibility will make someone relevant in a very dynamic work place. It also ensures students' have permanent jobs and easy movement whenever necessary, making certain their careers are long-lasting.

### 2.3.1 Key to Career Survival

People must possess an innate characteristic, which should enable them to be ready for new careers and adapt to changing jobs environments. This is the capacity to work in a changing environment arising from an industry transformation, technological innovations or shifts in demand for labour. Flexibility is also an imperative trait for success on top of being one of the skills that are often demanded by the modern workforce because change is inherent in contemporary workforce (Arthur et al., 2005).

### 2.3.2 Constant Learning and Skill Updating

Adaptability develops through an ongoing education process and on-going skills training. However, employees keep on being open and ready for more ideas, innovations, and anything new and development in their field of specialization. A good example of an adaptive software engineer or a data analyst is somebody who keeps studying new skills and technologies to remain relevant in an ever changing industry. They include various professionals who are involved in technology-oriented industries.

### 2.3.3 Problem-Solving and Innovation

The last two skills are associated with adaptive capacity (Taber et al., 2015). Flexible professionals often approach problems from different perspectives, have little hesitation of trying new approaches. In this way, they help to come up with new ideas that could shape their careers and industries.

## 2.3.4 Career Transition and Expansion

Adaptability is crucial when considering a job change or taking on additional responsibilities. Successful adapters do better in changing careers or leadership (Salisbury et al., 2012) roles as it calls for creativity in dealing with problems and management.

## 2.3.5 Resilience and Stress Management

However, resilience can be regarded as one of the aspects contributing to adaptability. Resilience is essential in maintaining one's sense of wellness and mental stability amidst the twists and turns of a career. People work in such stressful environments as healthcare and rescue services need to be adaptable, since this quality helps them cope with tough circumstances.

## 2.3.6 Interpersonal Skills

Adaptability encompasses interpersonal skills as well. It is evident that employees who can fit into various organizational environments and work in multi-cultural teams have a clear edge. Such ability to adapt when working with different colleagues in different environments also may foster better team dynamics as well as stronger professional relationships.

## 2.3.7 Entrepreneurship and Risk-Taking

Being adaptable is important for both new business owners and entrepreneurs in general. If one company has a strong enough resolve, it will always know when to change direction and adjust its plans in accordance with sudden occurrences or changing markets. Adaptors who do this well have greater resistance toward changes in the economy, and more opportunities arise for them.

In any case, one important feature when it comes to preparation is also when it comes to promotion is flexibility. This practice allows people to excel in the changing professional environment via resilience, creativity, problem solving, and continuous learning. As new trends emerge in different sectors and careers go off course, resilience will help stay relevant, take advantage of opportunity and ultimately succeed. Adaptability is one of the vital factors that determine excellence in any industry such as technology, health care or simply business.

## 2.4 Building Confidence

Involving pupils in different activities related to their careers and making them practice regularly also helps build their confidence. Workplace confidence is critical as it empowers a person to meet new challenges and overcome obstacles and also creates room for innovation within one's career. Relevant jobs, projects, and situations help build self-confidence. Regular homework assignments and academic issues offer pupils a strong sense of how they are likely to cope with everyday problems outside the classroom environment. Psychologically and practically, people with this level of confidence are successful in their work environments. In essence, one of the essential elements of professional training is appreciating how frequency influences confidence formation. Confidence becomes a key aspect for their career development when students are constantly exposed to their obstacles and opportunities within the industry of interest.

### 2.4.1 Foundation of Success

Confidence is what lays down a path toward a good career. Self-efficacy signifies a belief in one's own judgement/problem solving skills and capabilities. Such a person will be able to step in front of challenges and stick to their pursuit for professional target by dint of being confident. If one has to achieve a successful and gratifying job, confidence is essential.

### 2.4.2 Regular Practice and Mastery

In many cases, building up of confidence rests on regular practice and skill mastery. On taking such tasks or difficulties associated with people's interest; this makes individuals to have confidence on themselves for them to work towards improving such skills that give individuals sense of achievement, therefore improving learning levels. Proficiency breeds confidence, and perfection is achieved through practice. As for example, when an experienced graphic designer works frequently with different design assignments, they acquire self-confidence as regards their ability to solve creative problems as well as mastering design skills.

### 2.4.3 Positive Feedback Loop

Confidence creates a positive feedback loop. Such positive feedback could be in the form of job offers, promotion, or a recognition of the person showcasing proficiency in his/her field of specialization and acquiring more experience. This additional feedback further builds their confidence in addition to creating a cycle of growth and confidence, subsection. Moreover, their self-confidence is boosted with time making them more adventurous thus; ready to explore new avenues of career success.

### 2.4.4 Innovation and Risk-Taking

It often means being prepared to go out on a limb, knowing fully well that one cannot be confident. A confident professional has the zeal to explore new areas of unchartered territory as he tries new ideas and exceeds his daily limitations. For example, self-confidence pushes entrepreneurs to develop new products, and enter into new areas hitherto unexploited.

### 2.4.5 Overcoming Obstacles

Developing confidence has to include overcoming obstacles, and frustrations as well. A confident individual rarely finds failures and failures as things that can be discouraging. Instead, they perceive each interaction as an opportunity to grow up and be enlightened. It becomes more significant in sectors such as scientific research and art where difficulties are common.

### 2.4.6 Effective Leadership and Communication

Confidence ranks highly among the top factors for both. It is also worth noting that confident professionals are more likely to conduct themselves boldly and inspire confidence in their respective teams. Sometimes confidence is what determines whether an organization gets success in areas such as management that involve team commanding and decision making (Gu et al., 2020).

### 2.4.7 Mental Health and Stress Reduction

Mental health can be improved by building and maintaining self-confidence and reducing stress levels through this. Such kind of work usually entails a lot of pressure and stress, thus a confident individual is in the best position to deal with it. Mental toughness enables them to concentrate on producing top quality work despite a high stress environment.

### 2.4.8 Professional Image

The way people come across you at work really matters in building your professional image, and a good part of it is determined by how confident or not you are. Confident people are often perceived to be competent, intelligent, and trustworthy. A good reputation for professionals can give those opportunities for career progression because colleagues and employers trust them more.

Job advancement and preparation also depends on gaining confidence. It builds up courage for conquering barriers, exploring new ideas, overcoming barriers, and achieving success in one's fields.3. Success and healthiness are always associated with confidence at work if you are an artist, leader, or an entrepreneur. Confidence is not limited to being just a personality trait, but it also functions as a determinant of career success (Heslin et al., 2005) and satisfaction.

## 3. POWER OF CONSISTENCY

A strong power of turning ones dreams come true by preparing systematically towards a profession. This involves a tendency for setting clear, attainable targets and transforming ambitious career achievements into manageable steps. It enhances the belief of possibility in achievement, which helps build self-efficacy and motivation for this pursuit. Secondly, habitual behaviours that contribute towards efficient use for work are created by consistency. Consequently, it becomes the backbone of successful time management resulting in balance between academic, work, and private activities. Moreover, sustaining consistency in networking and relationship building as significant professional ties are forged with time. Regular good judgment forms the basis for resilience, enabling people to persist in achieving long-term goals. Consistency provides a foundation for continued learning and development so that people remain adaptable and viable in an ever-changing job market.

### 3.1 Goal Setting and Achievement

The process of setting up goals in a systematic manner becomes essential to a successful career preparation programme. One has to set attainable and measurable specific objectives every day in order to be consistent. This type of activity gives students an opportunity to break down their long-term career objectives into smaller manageable tasks. The pursuit of those aims regularly enhances self-efficacy and motivation. Achieving some of smaller goals make them think they will be able handle bigger and greater professional goals. In fact, all that one requires in order for wide dreams to transform to achievable career objectives is consistency.

### 3.1.1 Clarity and Direction

Creating goals is a crucial part of preparing for a successful career. It gives people direction and clarity so they may set out to achieve their desired career results. Clear objectives act as a road map, assisting students as they navigate the challenging process of developing their careers. Fundamental inquiries like "Where do I want to be in my career?" and "What steps do I need to take to get there?" are addressed by them.

### 3.1.2 Motivation and Focus

They provide goal-directed behaviour. This helps people to know where they want to go and what to do to reach their goals. Pursuance of an objective helps get over roadblocks and detours as it instils a sense of urgency and commitment. Through goal setting, students have been able to use this beacon as they persistently pursue success in their respective professions.

### 3.1.3 Measurable Progress

Measurability of goals helps in monitoring and tracking the progress made. Determining how much one has achieved towards a targeted achievement serves as a motivation towards achieving success. Furthermore, observable outcomes and achievements increase student's confidence and drive even more. Further, reviewing the progress also enables one to adjust and remain in track with the chosen path which is practical and cost effective.

### 3.1.4 Confidence and Self-Efficacy

Self-efficacy (Borgen et al., 2008) is achieved during goal setting and goal attainment processes. The confidence in their ability provides individuals this needed courage, to venture into new ventures which will eventually help them towards a career. The modern business world relies on two fundamental characteristics-resilience and adaptability. In turn, these attributes can be strengthened by another trait self-confidence.

### 3.1.5 Balance Between the Short- and Long-Term

Good goals are set through evaluating short and long-term goals. The short term goals make small portions out of the journey while long terms give a sight for the career. Such an equilibrium ensures that a student has something to contemplate about in relation to his or her current state of learning instead of focusing solely on the far flung future.

### 3.1.6 Flexibility and Customization

Goal setting has proven to be highly flexible procedure. It empowers students to tailor their job training according to their own desires, goals, and weaknesses. This personalization will make sure that their goals are driven by what they have a passion for and believe in. Setting goals also makes individuals able to turn aside in case of priority changes or circumstance changes.

### 3.1.7 Responsibility and Accountability

The objectives bring about individual responsibility and personal accountability. Setting specific goals enables students to initiate control on the own growth as professionals. They know that what they do has direct impact upon arriving at their goals fast. It makes people engage more in improving themselves professionally; they become result oriented but proactive.

### 3.1.8 Success as a Stepping Stone

To hit one target usually serves as leverage toward another goal. Achieving a goal becomes the beginning point in terms of further development and aspiration, not the end of the travel. Each achievement encourages individuals to strive for greater heights as it opens up doors to fresh doors that bring together new prospects and challenges.

Goal setting and achievement are the building blocks upon which a proper career preparations rests. Confidence, self-efficacy, motivation, clarity, and quantifiable progress are among factors that they provide. These give people control over their career development, enable individualisation of their journey, and help to reconcile near term and distant visions. Furthermore, when they set and achieve objectives it is the first step on the ladder towards lifelong education for achievement and future progress.

## 3.2 Habit Formation

Consistency plays an important part in building a habit. Repeating certain routine/behaviour forms it as beneficial habit. These habits grow roots into a person's daily life and dictate much of his or her decisions and actions. For instance, one can automate the process of scheduling by undertaking career related endeavours on a routine basis such as scheduling an informational interview with another person every month or so. This method ensures that despite contradicting objectives, students always strive towards their careers.

### 3.2.1 Automated Action

Becoming ready for a profession includes establishing habits. To start with, it refers to automatic programming of automatic behaviours and habits that individuals systematically follow as a matter of course. Particularly in this case of preparation for work or any other act where one has a number of decisions to make at once, habits prove very efficient as they diminish the necessity not only of a continuous decision making but also of using physical and mental resources that can be otherwise saved for something else.

### 3.2.2 Regular Practice

Habits are normally developed with the help of regular practice. The repetition of an activity ensures that they become part of the day-to-day habits of a person aimed at enhancing their time management skills, acquiring skills, and personal self-organization. For example, setting apart a defined portion of time daily dedicated towards learning or tasks related to one's job forms the habit eventually.

### 3.2.3 Effective Time Management

Time management involves developing good habits. Habits ensure proper utilization of time as a scarce and valuable resource. those who get in the habit of making daily to-do lists first write down as much time as they can, then set aside time each day to prepare for a task.

### 3.2.4 Mastery and Skill Development

Professional preparation includes developing skills. Learning skills is achieved through repetition, which leads to habit formation that becomes a routine for one. Practice and honing skills by people, they become experts. To excel at anything you do whether it's learning a new programming language, improving communication skills or enhancing analytical skills, you need to practice consistently.

### 3.2.5 Diminished Procrastination

Having good habits can be an effective form of treatment against procrastination. The habit of career preparation has reduced procrastinate tendencies among many people in their critical tasks. The behaviours act like a mental switch in triggering these actions. Among the strategies to get motivated in having a great morning is setting up goal-oriented activities towards careers that can become a daily routine.

### 3.2.6 Decrease in Procrastination

This is particularly useful when fighting procrastination. Once job preparation becomes a habit, it will be hard for people to postpone their important acts. Such behaviours are the psychological trigger points that make someone to act. This would be for example creating work specific goals as one starts his/her work to push oneself towards finishing off the duties before the due time has elapsed.

### 3.2.7 Improved Efficiency

Habits lead to increased efficiency. Doing simple repeating tasks helps finish work faster and takes away mental fatigue of decision making. There is this advantage of effectiveness that makes it very easy with other tasks such as work, schooling and preparation for career.

### 3.2.8 Personal Development

This is one of powerful drivers of self-development. Moreover, engaging in career-related activities also encourages self-discipline, self-motivation and time management in addition to developing professional skills. Characteristics like these are so vital and they influence greatly on personal as well as professional life of man.

### 3.2.9 Adaptability

Routines are flexible. They can fit into changing circumstances and goals. People are able to change their habits as well as update them according to various shifts in the business goals they might have or take up as well as to better match these with evolving work environment demands.

Professional preparation includes developing of habits. It involves the creation of automated behaviours and routines that help in managing time effectively, acquiring new skills as well as achieving set goals through frequent practice. Habits also make it possible to sidestep procrastination, increase performance, improve development, and accommodate ongoing changes in what business wants from its employees. Individuals establish a platform on which they build success in their personal and professional lives through developing good habit into daily schedule.

## 3.3 Time Management

Effective time management is closely related with consistency in career preparation. Children that have a habit of leaving career tasks aside when it comes to other engagements have been rarely found. The consistent persons on time have more success in dealing with extraneous, employment, and academic tasks. Time management is indeed important if one wants to keep being productive and prepared for career advancement.

### 3.3.1 Maximization of Resources

Time is a crucial if not limited resource when preparing oneself for professional performance. The only way to have good time management then, is by using the resource that we have made for this, optimally. This refers to planning out work and tasks with a view towards productivity and progression towards personal career targets. Optimizing available time leads people to do much more within shortest possible time that also enhances their capability.

### 3.3.2 Prioritization

Time management entails having prioritization. However, not all tasks and activities are equally important. It allows people put their time and energy where they matter most in their career. For example, something as crucial as getting prepared for a job interview might be of prime importance than something casual like making use of social media.

### 3.3.3 Objective-Oriented Focus

The element of time management complements objective-oriented vision. Proficient temporal practitioners also allocate time for activities that propel individual's career development. It helps in staying focused on long term goals and ensures that the daily activities are consistent with the big picture goals.

### 3.3.4 Decreased Procrastination

The reduction in procrastination is a major benefit associated with time management. When people are organized and have a plan, it becomes more difficult to put off or post-date professional tasks. Good management of time promotes responsibility and cuts down on procrastination.

### 3.3.5 Productivity and Efficiency

A well-crafted time management strategy enhances one's productivity and efficiency. This enhances systematic approach to work, ensuring time is put into use. A clearly ordered program ensures that people do activities fast without unnecessary disturbances hence gaining more time for career improvement.

### 3.3.6 Task Completion

Time management is critical when completing tasks. Such people are likely to achieve their target if they allocated certain time-slots for jobs and activities they wanted to do. This ensures that time is taken to carry out vital occupational obligations, thereby assuring their promptness.

### 3.3.7 Work-Life Balance

However, time management is also about balancing one's professional and personal life. Those who have mastered time management will always have sufficient time for family life, hobbies, and health maintenance. Mental and physical welfare is very important because it facilitates their balance leading to professional readiness (Melvin et al., 2012).

### 3.3.8 Adaptation

Adaptation happens when time management techniques that work well are implemented. There is also an upside to being organized. In case of any sudden incidents, or new career objectives; it makes easy modification of one's plans and schedules. Such people are sure to remain agile and responsive to fluctuating job demands.

### 3.3.9 Stress Reduction

Ineffective time management often makes people anxious and tense. However, efficient time management helps to reduce stress because it ensures that everything is planned appropriately in terms of allocating sufficient time to handle duties. The lower level of stress is needed as it maintains mental focus and clear thinking are critical for readiness (Almalki et al., 2022) to work.

### 3.3.10 Long-Term Success

Effective time management is what leads to long-term success. People who spend a considerable amount of time participating in activities related to careers will be moving toward achieving their goals. Even small advances contribute over time to big achievements and readiness for employment in the long term.

One of the important job preparation abilities is time management. Time management encompasses the ability to take advantage of every minute available, prioritize responsibilities through a focus on achieving outcomes rather than a mere list of duties, limit procrastination and improve output and efficiency leading to accomplishing a task, encouraging flexibility at the workplace which eventually goes hand in Effective time management also allows an individual to take advantage of every opportunity or overcome each difficulty that comes with his/her job.

## 3.4 Building Relationships and Networking

Regular network helps you have a successful career. The students who always involve themselves in career related activities, have an online presence which remain active all the time and build relations with professionals gain an upper hand in the competitive job market. Their constant hard work enables them to use such chances and benefit significantly from older individuals' knowledge in order to do so. Figure 2 shows the simple diagram of building relationships and networking.

### 3.4.1 Connections in Professional World

Career planning includes making contacts and building networks. These include establishing relationship with colleagues, supervisors, domain experts, and potential employers. These contacts come in handy throughout one's career.

### 3.4.2 Information Exchange

The process of networking simplifies dissemination of useful information and thoughts among people sharing the same market or discipline. The engagement with such expert, who has specialised knowledge or experience is crucial as they play a substantial role in enabling people to develop important insights, trends and best practise. This enables individuals to remain informed while they make healthy choices about their careers.

### 3.4.3 Opportunity Identification

Networking can often lead to career prospects. It is possible for one to find some relevant positions, internships and projects in their career field from their professional networks. This aspect of networking can be particularly useful to students as well as job-seeking graduates looking to fast-track their careers.

*Figure 2. Building relationships and networking*

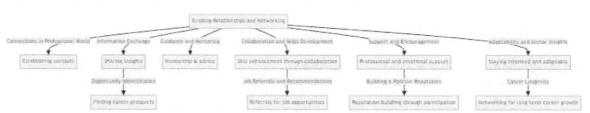

### 3.4.4 Guidance and Mentoring

This may lead to networking with experienced business people that could end up in mentorship & guidance. Mentors provide wise and supportive advice, lots of experience that can be invaluable to those about to get into the workplace. It is through such advice that individuals overcome challenges at the workplace, make good decisions, and increase their job performance.

### 3.4.5 Collaboration and Development of Skills

Chances of collaboration that enhance skills development through networking. Working on projects or initiatives with other experts help such individuals develop new talents and polish old ones. They help in personal and professional growth.

### 3.4.6 Job Referrals and Recommendations

Job referrals and recommendation also result from strong business connection. People with experience about one's abilities and attitude towards work will be much willing to refer you to colleagues and connections who suggest people for vacant positions and profession opportunities. This could be an asset of a fierce competitive job market.

### 3.4.7 Support and Encouragement

A network provides for both professional and emotional support. Friends and guides come in handy during difficulties, talk over work issues and offer their experiences in such moments. Resilience and motivation are maintained in this social support system.

### 3.4.8 Building a Positive Reputation

Networking is an important factor towards building a sound professional reputation. Participating in industry events such as conferences, debates, and giving views in this direction helps people gain prestige and acclaim within the sphere of their occupation. Getting a good reputation may bring more job opportunities as well as promotion in one's career.

### 3.4.9 Adaptability and Sector Insights

That is why network keep its users informed and adapted. This way it is possible for a person to keep track of industry trends, new tech, as well as the latest information about a given market. Their adaptability allows them to respond to changing career needs.

### 3.4.10 Career Longevity

Relationships building as well as networking is important not only for career preparation, but for successful careers as well. In addition, such networks remain valuable even throughout one's professional life, providing new perspectives, opportunities, and support as a professional growth advances.

Building linkages and friendships in preparation for a job. They enable networking of professionals and exchange of ideas, they help to identify opportunities, avail mentorship services, cooperation on professional skill growth, job referrals, seek support, establish credibility, be adaptable and have a long-term career. Networking is effective for both career mobility as well as providing individuals with necessary resources and connections to overcome jobs market uncertainties.

## 4. IMPLEMENTING FREQUENCY AND CONSISTENCY

However, applying frequency and consistent professional preparation becomes a successful and intentional way toward the goal. This involves setting out a unique long term goal before decomposing them to smaller, achievable short- term objectives. to write essay The objectives form the basis of a properly structured daily routine enabling the application of concerted and resolute moves towards the career advancement. Practice, participation in career-related activities, and a periodic review of one's goals promote skill growth, competency, and flexibility.

The way this plan works is by making each day count towards your professional path, helping you keep track yourself and reduce procrastination. Using frequency and constancy they establish the infrastructure which leads them to their work goals; turning dreams into actual achievements. Figure 3 shows the flow from implementing frequency and consistency towards various strategies regarding placement and success in there career.

### 4.1 Integration of Career-Oriented Activities Into Curriculum

Career oriented activities ought to be integrated in education curriculum to ensure students have periodical chance of applying whatever which is learnt on the day to day basis. Capstone projects, internship programs, and practical learn can help this endeavour.

*Figure 3. The flow from implementing frequency and consistency towards various strategies*

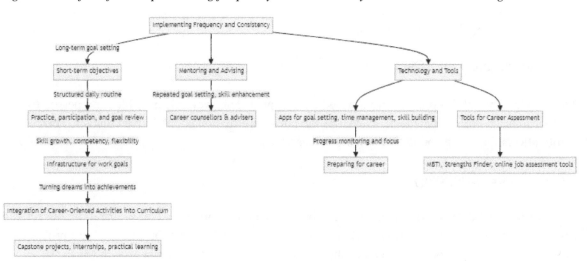

### 4.1.1 Early Career Exposure

Career-related aspects of studies should be added to curricula so as to give children pre-career experience by taking them into the adult world of work. This exposes them to practical world situations where they can explore on how what they learned in books relates to practical life. For example, students studying computing sciences can engage in simulated coding exercises that recreate the workplace environment in order to enhance the understanding of future careers in software.

### 4.1.2 Relevance and Practicality

Career-related activities give relevancy to and usability of the curriculum. Ensures that students are taught lessons relevant to their future endeavours. This relationship allows students to perceive importance of the topic and makes studying it more appealing. For instance, in a business program, students may consider case studies or engage in internships where they have to solve actual business issues that would add more value to their learning process.

### 4.1.3 Skill Development

The curriculum activities aimed at careers equip students with necessary skills. On the other hand, students develop important skills for any work place like problem solving, teamwork, and communication. Moreover, these skills will make them better prepared for work thus enable them to succeed in all jobs and industries.

### 4.1.4 Networking Possibilities

This can also provide a lot of career networking possibilities, for example when it is important to take into account any relevant activities. Group projects, guest lectures and industry events allow students to access professionals and prospective workplace partners. Such contacts may lead to an opportunity for internship and employment as well as a valuable mentor who is extremely helpful when it comes to furthering one's career path.

### 4.1.5 Critical Thinking and Application

Career minded activities promote critical thinking as well as information processing. This, in turn, encourages students to explore complex questions and devise feasible solutions to those questions. For example, health care program students could engage in clinical simulation wherein the students would make the diagnosis based on their observations and give treatment.

### 4.1.6 Job Growth

The mixing of jobs' activities may serve as a basis for career growth. Resume writing, assistance with employment search, practice session before interviews, and career advising are the services included in this category. Such support facilitates smooth transition of students from school to work environment resulting in greater success.

### 4.1.7 Innovation and Creativity

Career-focused activities promote innovation and creativity. They need to provide realistic solutions that answer problem questions which students often face in real life. For instance, students pursuing engineering studies could develop prototypes that could be applied to solve specific industrial problems, thereby cultivating their creativity and problem solving skills.

### 4.1.8 Adaptability

Career preparation includes teaching students to be flexible and make the necessary adjusts in response to changing labour market dynamics. Such students get information about modern technologies, changing occupations' requirements and dynamics of the labour market. The gradual exposure ensures flexibility for graduates and equips them with the necessary skills to deal with future career variations.

### 4.1.9 Building Confidence

Activities related to careers boost students' confidence. It helps them realize the value of their information as far as they can use it for work and its importance. When confronting real-life issues and completing these endeavours, the students gain confidence, enabling them to become confident, forward thinkers in their future endeavours.

### 4.1.10 Student-Centric Learning

Away from a "one size fits all" approach, activities geared towards career change emphasize the student centric leaning paradigm. It addresses individual goals, aptitudes and skills of every child. Such activities can be integrated into students' education programs in a way that makes it possible for them to personalize and match their own job goals.

Career-oriented activities like critical thinking enhance the educational opportunities, providing early career exposure, relevance, skill development, networking chances, critical thinking, career development (Arulmani et al. 2014) support, innovation, adaptability, and confidence, and student centred learning. The all-embracing approach ensures that students get the knowledge, skills as well as mind-sets required for a smooth transition from their learning life to real employment opportunities.

## 4.2 Mentoring and Advising

Career counsellors and advisers help to promote students in schools. Thus, they should place an emphasis on such matters as repeated goal setting, continued skill enhancement, and behavioural continuity.

### 4.2.1 Advice and Direction

The importance of mentoring and advising cannot be overemphasized; it is imperative in career preparation as well as giving useful ideas and guidance to the students. Academic counsellors and mentors enable people to choose the right courses, majors and careers depending on their strengths and interests.

This helps to guide the students on various available academic as well as career choices and ensure that these are informed decisions.

### 4.2.2 Individualized Assistance

The fact that mentorship and advice is individualized is one of its most significant advantages. Student's specific objectives and stumbling blocks are carefully understood in conjunction with mentors and advisors. They make sure that they tailor their advice depending on their specific needs which include academic, professional and personal development. Personalised approach provides the most relevant direction, assistance, and support to children.

### 4.2.3 Clarification of Career Routes

Career counsellors and mentors facilitate choice of the careers that each student intends to venture in to. People help individuals explore possible careers among other things like evaluating interests, strengths and weaknesses. Talks and tests will help students have an idea on the professions that they can do best depending on their objectives and talents.

### 4.2.4 Developing Skills

This requires mentorship and advice. A mentor is likely to be endowed with so many careers' experiences which provide valuable information on the capabilities and qualification needed by different professions. Students gain these skills with help of these professors as they prepare them to face the job market.

### 4.2.5 Networking and Industry Knowledge

Usually, advisors and mentors have broad networks and deep knowledge of the industry. Through the internet, they could link students to specialist in particular fields which would also allow them to engage in networking as well as learn from experienced persons. Networking can help one secure an internship, employment, and mentorship from established experts.

### 4.2.6 Resume Building and Interview Preparation

Career counsellors assist students in making strong, powerful resumes as well as preparing them for job interviews. These assist in emphasizing any related academic and extracurricular achievements, personalization of resumes for varying jobs scenarios, as well as preparation of appropriate interview approaches the help is important as it enables the students to find internships and jobs.

### 4.2.7 Internship and Job Placement

Advice and mentoring might open doors of opportunity including internships and jobs. The career counsellors usually are in touch with employers searching for qualified people. This helps them identify suitable placements for students in terms of internships and job placement that increases the possibility of having meaningful employment.

### 4.2.8 Personal and Professional Development

Often mentors are considered models which provide guidance to students as they mature not only personally but also professionally as well. In this regard they guide on how to lead effectively, time management, communication, as well as soft skills needed for successful careers. Moreover, they often give tips on how to deal with work-life balance.

### 4.2.9 Support and Encouragement

Their advisers and mentors keep on encouraging and pushing them forward all through. This allows them to be sympathetic listeners during unfamiliar or difficult times in students' careers(Walker et al. 2022), keeping up the motivation and resilience of the learners. Sustaining attention and good mental health should be supported throughout the whole job preparation.

### 4.2.10 Long-Term Partnership

Mentoring and advice are not confined to the class only. A lot of students stay connected with their mentors until they even become professionals. This lasting relationship ensures continued support, guidance on career path, and reliable contact for any post-career decision and problem.

Both mentoring and advice constitute professional preparation. They offer counselling, customized guidance on careers, help in clarifying their career paths, skills training, networking chances, development of their resumes, internship and jobs placement, aftercare and long-term partnerships. Advisers and mentors give students what they need to have success in their studies, choosing the field, which would be right for them, and laying down a good basis for their professional career.

## 4.3. Technology and Tools

There are various tools and platforms available in our digital world that could assist students to plan ahead towards careers and remain organised through all their efforts to prepare for jobs. Apps that set goals, manage time and build skills are very helpful resources. They help students monitor their progress, and stay focused on preparing for their career.

### 4.3.1 Tools for Career Assessment

Technology has helped in developing of complex equipment that can help students and job seekers discover themselves by understanding what they are good at or not. Such programs usually provide job tailoring recommendations via algorithms and psychometric procedures based on one's profile. Some examples include MBTI and Strengths Finder, or several online job assessment tools.

### 4.3.2 Builders and Templates for Resumes

Online resume builders and templates, however, have proved invaluable in coming up with professionally looking and catching to the eye resumes. They include ready-made resume templates as well as

*Impact of Frequency and Consistency in Preparing Students for Career Paths*

guidelines on developing specific profession and situation appropriate resumes. They also give tips on how to style and write the text appropriately.

### 4.3.3 Job Search Platforms

With increased internet job search sites, job seeking process has transformed. Websites and smartphone apps like Monster, Indeed, Glassdoor, LinkedIn, and Indeed allow companies to list jobs across diverse industries in great detail. They also boast of more refined search engine and categorisation tools that enable job seekers to focus on what interests them the most.

### 4.3.4 Platforms for Professional Networking

Many sites like LinkedIn have become vital sources of connections as far as doing business goes. On these networks, users will be able to create digital profile to get connected to their peers and other business leaders where they will discuss achievements and also check for jobs. They are an avenue of communication through forums, and a form of learning while exchanging knowledge among industries.

### 4.3.5 Learning Management Systems

Educational institutions use learning management systems commonly known as LMS in order to support one online learning. These portals make it possible for students to upload and retrieve course material, assignment and examination questions anytime at their convenience. Asynchronous learning allows people to learn at their own pace, therefore they also promote it. Zero upgrading of skills and ongoing education heavily rely on this technology.

### 4.3.6 Online Course Delivery Systems

Some of these programs such as Coursera, edx, Udemy offers multiple categories of courses ranging from technical and vocational skills up to some other kinds and different modes. This is in line with the way these platforms have made it easy for people to learn new skills or acquire new knowledge on their way and in most cases within their timeframe.

### 4.3.7 Video Conferencing Solutions

Video conferencing solutions, such as Zoom, Microsoft Teams, and Skype, have risen in popularity, especially after remote work and virtual interviews. Such programs allow people to network with professionals worldwide and hold virtual meetings, interviews, and so on.

### 4.3.8 Electronic Portfolios (or ePortfolios)

E-portfolio gives people an opportunity to showcase their work, talent and achievements in digital form. These give the users chance to compile their best works, credentials, and experience in one attractive presentation of credential.

### 4.3.9 Personal Branding Tools

These social media platforms and tools are essential in building and sustaining peoples' personal branding through their own brands. In other words, these blogs give an opportunity for users to tell fellow human beings what they have achieved, how they see things, or what they know. The use of personal branding in creating posts or contents can be achieved using tools such as Canva among other devices.

### 4.3.10 Software for Career Management

Career management software is inclusive of tracking one's professional goals, job applications, and networking purposes. Some of these programs often include sections that help users set their goals, manage their resumes, and track their job objectives so as to keep them focused on their mission.

### 4.3.11 Software Tailored to a Particular Industry

One can benefit his/her career if he/she adopts special software used in many fields. Such as while data analysts use Python, R, and SQL, graphic designers apply on the Adobe Creative Cloud system. Awareness of specific software in an industry will add weight to one's credentials with respect to a particular profession.

The way people prepare themselves for careers has been impacted by new technologies and instruments. These include career assessment tools, resume builders, job search and professional networking platforms, learning management systems, online course platforms, video conferencing tools, portfolios, tools for personal branding, etc., career management software as well as industry targeted software to mention but a few. The use of these tools in negotiating through the competitive labour market and keeping on top is important to be adequately prepared for a chosen profession.

## 5. CONCLUSION

However, preparations of prospective careers need not forget about frequent and regular occurrence. That's not just mere acquisition of the knowledge but also developing it and utilising it. Teachers and careers counsellors can help to equip students with the necessary tools for overcoming the problems faced in the labour market through the emphasis on skills improvement, goal plotting, habit development and time management. At last, the students acquire the necessary knowledge that enables them to launch high-flown careers and prosper in a challenging marketplace.

## REFERENCES

Almalki, O. S., Alqarni, T. A., Alharthi, R. M., Algarni, M. A., Mohamed Ibrahim, M. I., Asiri, Y. A., & Fathelrahman, A. I. (2022). Career Readiness Among Saudi Pharmacy Students: Exploring the Need for and the Impact of Career Counseling Services. *Advances in Medical Education and Practice, 13*, 1267–1277. doi:10.2147/AMEP.S375929 PMID:36254266

Arthur, M. B., Khapova, S. N., & Wilderom, C. P. (2005). Career success in a boundaryless career world. Journal of Organizational Behavior: The International Journal of Industrial. *Journal of Organizational Behavior*, *26*(2), 177–202. doi:10.1002/job.290

Arulmani, G. (2014). The cultural preparation process model and career development. In *Handbook of career development: International perspectives* (pp. 81–103). Springer New York. doi:10.1007/978-1-4614-9460-7_6

Borgen, F. H., & Betz, N. E. (2008). Career self-efficacy and personality: Linking career confidence and the healthy personality. *Journal of Career Assessment*, *16*(1), 22–43. doi:10.1177/1069072707305770

Gu, X., Tang, M., Chen, S., & Montgomery, M. L. (2020). Effects of a Career Course on Chinese High School Students' Career Decision-Making Readiness. *The Career Development Quarterly*, *68*(3), 222–237. doi:10.1002/cdq.12233

Harren, V. A. (1979). A model of career decision making for college students. *Journal of Vocational Behavior*, *14*(2), 119–133. doi:10.1016/0001-8791(79)90065-4

Heslin, P. A. (2005). Conceptualizing and evaluating career success. Journal of Organizational Behavior: The International Journal of Industrial. *Journal of Organizational Behavior*, *26*(2), 113–136. doi:10.1002/job.270

Melvin, B., Galles, J. A., & Lenz, J. G. (2012). Assessing career readiness in culturally and ethnically diverse populations. *Career Planning and Adult Development Journal*, *28*(1).

Salisbury, M. H., Pascarella, E. T., Padgett, R. D., & Blaich, C. (2012). The effects of work on leadership development among first-year college students. *Journal of College Student Development*, *53*(2), 300–324. doi:10.1353/csd.2012.0021

Taber, B. J., & Blankemeyer, M. (2015). Future work self and career adaptability in the prediction of proactive career behaviors. *Journal of Vocational Behavior*, *86*, 20–27. doi:10.1016/j.jvb.2014.10.005

Walker, B., Bair, A. R., & Macdonald, R. H. (2022). Supporting students' career development: A call to action. *New Directions for Community Colleges*, *2022*(199), 93–106. doi:10.1002/cc.20526

## KEY TERMS AND DEFINITIONS

**Adaptation:** The ability to adjust plans and strategies in response to changing circumstances, fostering agility in dealing with unexpected events.

**Career Readiness:** The state of being well-prepared and equipped with the necessary skills and mindset for entering and succeeding in the workforce.

**Guidance and Mentoring:** Receiving advice and support from experienced individuals, often leading to personal and professional development.

**Information Exchange:** The sharing of valuable insights, trends, and best practices among individuals within a particular market or industry.

**Long-Term Success:** Achievement and accomplishment sustained over an extended period, often resulting from consistent efforts toward career goals.

**Networking:** Building and maintaining relationships with professionals in one's field, often for mutual benefit in terms of career opportunities and knowledge exchange.

**Objective-Oriented Focus:** Concentrating efforts on activities and tasks that align with specific goals and contribute to long-term objectives.

**Prioritization:** The act of assigning degrees of importance to tasks or activities, ensuring that efforts are focused on the most critical elements.

**Procrastination:** The act of delaying or postponing tasks, often resulting from poor time management or a lack of motivation.

**Productivity and Efficiency:** The measure of how effectively tasks are completed within a given time frame, often influenced by strategic time management.

**Stress Reduction:** The process of minimizing or eliminating anxiety and tension through effective time management and planning.

**Task Completion:** Successfully finishing assigned or planned activities within specified timeframes.

**Technology and Tools:** The various applications, platforms, and software that assist individuals in planning, organizing, and enhancing their career preparation efforts.

**Time Management:** The process of planning and organizing one's activities and tasks in a way that maximizes productivity and efficiency.

**Work-Life Balance:** The equilibrium between professional responsibilities and personal life, ensuring well-being and preventing burnout.

# Compilation of References

Akkermans, J., Paradniké, K., Van der Heijden, B. I., & De Vos, A. (2018). The best of both worlds: The role of career adaptability and career competencies in students' well-being and performance. *Frontiers in Psychology*, 9, 1678. doi:10.3389/fpsyg.2018.01678 PMID:30258381

Akosah-Twumasi, P., Emeto, T. I., Lindsay, D., Tsey, K., & Malau-Aduli, B. S. (2018). A systematic review of factors that influence youths career choices—the role of culture. Frontiers in Education, 3. doi:10.3389/feduc.2018.00058

Alahdadi, S., & Ghanizadeh, A. (2017). The dynamic interplay among EFL learners' ambiguity tolerance, adaptability, cultural intelligence, learning approach, and language achievement. *Iranian Journal of Language Teaching Research*, 5(1), 37–50. https://api.semanticscholar.org/CorpusID:52061020

Albion, M. J., & Fogarty, G. J. (2002). Factors influencing career decision making in adolescents and adults. *Journal of Career Assessment*, 10(1), 91–126. doi:10.1177/1069072702010001006

Aldiono, M., Purnomo, T., & Prastowo, T. (2023). Profile of Problem-Solving Ability in Junior High School Students on Global Warming Lesson Material. *IJORER : International Journal of Recent Educational Research*, 4(3), 355–364. doi:10.46245/ijorer.v4i3.301

Alfauzan, A. A., & Tarchouna, N. (2017). The role of an aligned curriculum design in the achievement of learning outcomes. *Journal of Education and e-learning Research*, 4(3), 81–91. doi:10.20448/journal.509.2017.43.81.91

Allen, T. D., Eby, L. T., Poteet, M. L., Lentz, E., & Lima, L. (2004). Career benefits associated with mentoring for proteges: A meta-analysis. *The Journal of Applied Psychology*, 89(1), 127–136. doi:10.1037/0021-9010.89.1.127 PMID:14769125

Almalki, O. S., Alqarni, T. A., Alharthi, R. M., Algarni, M. A., Mohamed Ibrahim, M. I., Asiri, Y. A., & Fathelrahman, A. I. (2022). Career Readiness Among Saudi Pharmacy Students: Exploring the Need for and the Impact of Career Counseling Services. *Advances in Medical Education and Practice*, 13, 1267–1277. doi:10.2147/AMEP.S375929 PMID:36254266

Alolaqi, S. A., & Yusof, R. B. (2022). Youth Unemployment and Role of Entrepreneurship: Factors Influencing Students' Entrepreneurial Intention. *Global Business and Management Research*, 14.

Ambrósio, S., Araújo e Sá, M., Pinto, S., & Simões, A. (2014). Perspectives on educational language policy: Institutional and students' voices in higher education. *European Journal of Language Policy*, 6(2), 175–194. doi:10.3828/ejlp.2014.4

Amerstorfer, C. M., & Von Münster-Kistner, C. F. (2021). Student Perceptions of Academic Engagement and Student-Teacher Relationships in Problem-Based Learning. *Frontiers in Psychology*, 12, 713057. Advance online publication. doi:10.3389/fpsyg.2021.713057 PMID:34777094

Anderson, G. (2017). *Reinventing the museum: Historical and contemporary perspectives on the paradigm shift*. Rowman & Littlefield.

Anderson, L. (2006). Analytic autoethnography. *Journal of Contemporary Ethnography*, *35*(4), 373–395. doi:10.1177/0891241605280449

Anderson, S. (2020). Unsettling national narratives and multiplying voices: The art museum as renewed space for social advocacy and decolonization–a Canadian case study. *Museum Management and Curatorship*, *35*(5), 488–531. doi:10.1080/09647775.2020.1803111

Anjum, S. (2020). Impact of internship programs on professional and personal development of business students: A case study from Pakistan. *Future Business Journal*, *6*(1), 2. doi:10.1186/s43093-019-0007-3

Argondizzo, C., De Bartolo, A. M., Fazio, A., Jimenez, J. M., & Ruffolo, I. (2020). Academic, cultural and social growth through the language of websites: A challenge for European University Language Centres. *Language Learning in Higher Education*, *10*(2), 341–355. doi:10.1515/cercles-2020-2023

Arthur, M. B. (2014). The Boundaryless Career At 20: Where Do We Stand, and Where Can We Go? *Career Development International*, *19*(6), 627–640. doi:10.1108/CDI-05-2014-0068

Arthur, M. B., Khapova, S. N., & Wilderom, C. P. (2005). Career success in a boundaryless career world. Journal of Organizational Behavior: The International Journal of Industrial. *Journal of Organizational Behavior*, *26*(2), 177–202. doi:10.1002/job.290

Arthur, M. B., & Rousseau, D. M. (1996). *The Boundaryless Career: A New Employment Principle for a New Organizational Era*. OUP. doi:10.1093/oso/9780195100143.001.0001

Arulmani, G. (2014). The cultural preparation process model and career development. In *Handbook of career development: International perspectives* (pp. 81–103). Springer New York. doi:10.1007/978-1-4614-9460-7_6

Asmara, A., & Ming-Chang, W. (2020). An analytical study on the effective approaches to facilitate higher education cooperate with industry: Based on faculty members perspective. *TEM Journal*, *9*(4), 1721–1731. doi:10.18421/TEM94-53

Auburn, T., Ley, A., & Arnold, J. (1993). Psychology Undergraduates' Experience of Placements: a role-transition perspective. *Studies in Higher Education*, *18*(3), 265–285. https://doi-org.udlap.idm.oclc.org/10.1080/03075079312331382211

Austin, J., & Hickey, A. (2007). Autoethnography and teacher development. *The International Journal of Interdisciplinary Social Sciences: Annual Review*, *2*(2), 369–378. doi:10.18848/1833-1882/CGP/v02i02/52189

Ayers, D. J., & Underwood, R. L. (2007). Integrating concepts across marketing courses via experiential learning. *Journal for Advancement of Marketing Education*, *11*(1), 63–68.

Azmi, A. N., Kamin, Y., & Noordin, M. K. (2018). Competencies of engineering graduates: what are the employer's expectations. *International Journal of Engineering & Technology*, *7*(2.29), 519-523.

Bacon, M., & Sloam, J. (2010). John Dewey and the Democratic Rose of Higher Education in England. *Journal of Political Science Education*, *6*(4), 336–352. doi:10.1080/15512169.2010.518087

Badescu, G., Sandu, D., Angi, D., & Greab, C. (2019). *Youth Study Romania 2018/2019*. Friedrich-Ebert-Stiftung. https://library.fes.de/pdf-files/bueros/bukarest/15294.pdf

Baeten, M., Kyndt, E., Struyven, K., & Dochy, F. (2010, January). Using student-centred learning environments to stimulate deep approaches to learning: Factors encouraging or discouraging their effectiveness. *Educational Research Review*, *5*(3), 243–260. doi:10.1016/j.edurev.2010.06.001

Bagci, H., & Kocyigit, M. (2019). *21st Century Skills and Education*. Cambridge Scholars Publisher.

Baker, S. C., & MacIntyre, P. D. (2000). The Role of Gender and Immersion in Communication and Second Language Orientations. *Language Learning*, *50*(2), 311–341. doi:10.1111/0023-8333.00119

Bandura, A. (1986). *Social Foundations of Thought and Action: A Social Cognitive Theory*. Prentice Hall.

Bandura, A. (1997). *Self-Efficacy: The Exercise of Control*. Freeman.

Bandura, A. (2004). Health Promotion by social cognitive means. *Health Education &amp. Behaviour*, *31*(2), 143–164. doi:10.1177/1090198104263660 PMID:15090118

Bariyyah, K. (2021). Problem solving skills: Esssential skills challenges for the 21st century graduates. *Jurnal EDUCATIO: Jurnal Pendidikan Indonesia*, *7*(1), 71. doi:10.29210/120212843

Barnard, G. W., Lent, R. W., & Akamatsu, T. J. (2008). Predicting academic and job performance: The contribution of math and science interests, goals, and self-efficacy. *Journal of Vocational Behavior*, *73*(1), 47–55.

Barrett, J. (2009). *Career Aptitude and Selection Tests: Match Your IQ Personality and Abilities to Your Ideal Career*. Kogan Page Publishers.

Beckmann, E. (2013). Internships in museum studies: Learning at the interface. In A. Boddington, J. Boys, & C. Speight (Eds.), *Museums and higher education working together: Challenges and opportunities* (pp. 39–53). Routledge.

Bedwei-Majdoub, C. (2023). *An Aquinian Virtue Ethics Approach to Action Learning Sets on Postgraduate Business Programmes Attracting International Students* [Paper Presentation]. International Action Learning Conference. Action Learning Research and Practice.

Bell, E., Bryman, A., & Harley, B. (2022). *Business Research Methods*. OUP. doi:10.1093/hebz/9780198869443.001.0001

Bennett, T. (2018). *Museums, equality and social justice*. Routledge.

Benoit-Bryan, J., Jean-Mary, D., & Locks, M. (2023). *Museums Moving Forward Workplace Equity and Organizational Culture in US Art Museums 2023 Report*. Museums Moving Forward.

Bernard, D. L., Hoggard, L. S., Neblett, E. W. Jr, & Neblett, E. W. (2018). Racial discrimination, racial identity, and impostor phenomenon: A profile approach. *Cultural Diversity & Ethnic Minority Psychology*, *24*(1), 51–61. doi:10.1037/cdp0000161 PMID:28414495

Bernard, D. L., Lige, Q. M., Willis, H. A., Sosoo, E. E., & Neblett, E. W. (2017). Impostor Phenomenon and Mental Health: The Influence of Racial Discrimination and Gender. *Journal of Counseling Psychology*, *64*(2), 155–156. doi:10.1037/cou0000197 PMID:28182493

Bernard, D., & Lowe, T. (2019). Impostor Syndrome, Black College Students and How Administrators Can Help. *Diverse Issues in Higher Education*, *36*(14), 40.

Bernard, N. S., Dollinger, S. J., & Ramaniah, N. V. (2002). Applying the Big Five Personality Factors to the Impostor Phenomenon. *Journal of Personality Assessment*, *78*(2), 321–333. doi:10.1207/S15327752JPA7802_07 PMID:12067196

Besser, A., Flett, G. L., Nepon, T., & Zeigler-Hill, V. (2022). Personality, Cognition, and Adaptability to the COVID-19 Pandemic: Associations with Loneliness, Distress, and Positive and Negative Mood States. *International Journal of Mental Health and Addiction*, *20*(2), 971–995. doi:10.1007/s11469-020-00421-x PMID:33230393

Betz, N. E., & Voyten, K. K. (1997). Efficacy and outcome expectations influence career exploration and decidedness. *The Career Development Quarterly*, *45*(2), 176–186. doi:10.1002/j.2161-0045.1997.tb01004.x

Bhatnagar, H. (2021). Study of student behaviour in Indian higher education - A broad perspective of teacher. *International Journal of Multidisciplinary Research and Development*, *8*(7), 49–52. https://www.allsubjectjournal.com/assets/archives/2021/ vol8issue7/8-6-66-291.pdf

Biggs, J. (2003). Aligning teaching and assessing to course objectives. *Teaching and learning in higher education: New trends and innovations*, *2*(4), 13-17.

Biggs, J., & Tang, C. (2011). Teaching for Quality Learning at University. McGraw-Hill Education (UK).

Binder, J. F., Baguley, T., Crook, C., & Miller, F. (2015). The academic value of internships: Benefits across disciplines and student backgrounds. *Contemporary Educational Psychology*, *41*, 73–82. doi:10.1016/j.cedpsych.2014.12.001

Bingham, M., & Moore, M. R. (2014). The present state of career preparation for communication students: Preparing for a future in flux. *Journal of Applied Communication Research*, *42*(1), 3–22.

Bittmann, F., & Zorn, V. S. (2020). When choice excels obligation: About the effects of mandatory and voluntary internships on labour market outcomes for university graduates. *Higher Education*, *80*(1), 75–93. doi:10.1007/s10734-019-00466-5

Biwer, F., Egbrink, M. G. A., Aalten, P., & de Bruin, A. B. H. (2020). Fostering effective learning strategies in higher education–a mixed-methods study. *Journal of Applied Research in Memory and Cognition*, *9*(2), 186–203. doi:10.1016/j.jarmac.2020.03.004

Black, P., & Wiliam, D. (1998). Assessment and Classroom Learning. *Assessment in Education: Principles, Policy & Practice*, *5*(1), 7–74. doi:10.1080/0969595980050102

Blickenstaff, J. C., & Sweeney, K. M. (2019). The impact of structured university internships on diversity and career trajectory. *Innovative Higher Education*, *44*(5), 407–420.

Bloom, B. S., Krathwohl, D. R., & Masia, B. B. (1984). Bloom taxonomy of educational objectives. In *Allyn and Bacon*. Pearson Education.

Blustein, D. L., Phillips, S. D., Jobin-Davis, K., Finkelberg, S. L., & Roarke, A. E. (1997). A theory-building investigation of the school-to-work transition. *The Counseling Psychologist*, *25*(3), 364–402. doi:10.1177/0011000097253002

Bochner, A. P. (2007). Notes toward an ethics of memory in autoethnographic inquiry. In N. K. Denzin & M. D. Giardina (Eds.), *Ethical futures in qualitative research: Decolonizing the politics of knowledge* (pp. 197–208). Routledge.

Boekaerts, M. (1991). Subjective competence, appraisals and self-assessment. *Learning and Instruction*, *1*(1), 1–17. doi:10.1016/0959-4752(91)90016-2

Bolton-King, R. S. (2022). Student mentoring to enhance graduates' employability potential. *Science & Justice*, *62*(6), 785–794. doi:10.1016/j.scijus.2022.04.010 PMID:36400500

Bonn, I. (2001). Developing strategic thinking as a core competency. *Management Decision*, *39*(1), 63–71. doi:10.1108/EUM0000000005408

Borg, E. (2014). Classroom behaviour and academic achievement, how classroom behaviour categories relate to gender and academic performance. *British Journal of Sociology of Education*, *36*(8), 1127–1148. doi:10.1080/01425692.2014.916601

Borge, M., Toprani, D., Yan, S., & Xia, Y. (2020). Embedded Design: Engaging Students as Active Participants in the Learning of Human-Centered Design Practices. *Computer Science Education*, *30*(1), 47–71. doi:10.1080/08993408.2019.1688592

Borgen, F. H., & Betz, N. E. (2008). Career self-efficacy and personality: Linking career confidence and the healthy personality. *Journal of Career Assessment, 16*(1), 22–43. doi:10.1177/1069072707305770

Botes, E., Dewaele, J. M., & Greiff, S. (2020). The Power to improve, effects of multilingualism and perceived proficiency on enjoyment and anxiety in foreign language learning. *European Journal of Applied Linguistics, 8*(2), 279–306. doi:10.1515/eujal-2020-0003

Bourke, B. (2014). Positionality: Reflecting on the research process. *The Qualitative Report, 19*(33), 1–9.

Bovill, C. (2020). Co-Creation in Learning and Teaching: The Case for Whole Class Approach in Higher Education. *Higher Education, 79*(6), 1023–1037. doi:10.1007/s10734-019-00453-w

Bovill, C., Cook-Sather, A., & Felten, P. (2011). Students as Co-Creators of Teaching Approaches, Course Design, and Curricula: Implications for Academic Developers. *The International Journal for Academic Development, 16*(2), 133–145. doi:10.1080/1360144X.2011.568690

Bovill, C., Cook-Sather, A., Felten, P., Millard, L., & Moore-Cherry, N. (2016). Addressing Potential Challenges in Co-creating Learning and Teaching: Overcoming Resistance, Navigating Institutional Norms, and Ensuring Inclusivity in Student–Staff Partnerships. *Higher Education, 71*(2), 195–208. doi:10.1007/s10734-015-9896-4

Boyle, S., Fahey, E., Loughran, J., & Mitchell, I. (2001). Classroom research into good learning behaviours. *Educational Action Research, 9*(2), 199–224. doi:10.1080/09650790100200149

Bredin, K., & Söderlund, J. (2013). Project Managers and Career Models: An Exploratory Comparative Study. *International Journal of Project Management, 31*(6), 889–902. doi:10.1016/j.ijproman.2012.11.010

Bridgstock, R. (2009). The graduate attributes we've overlooked: Enhancing graduate employability through career management skills. *Higher Education Research & Development, 28*(1), 31–44. doi:10.1080/07294360802444347

British Academy, American Academy of Arts, Sciences, Academy of the Social Sciences in Australia, Australian Academy of the Humanities and The Royal Society of Canada. (2020). *The Importance of Languages in Global Context: An International Call to Action.* https://www.thebritishacademy.ac.uk/publications/the-importance-of-languages-in-global-context-an-international-call-to-action/

British Academy. (2021). Business and Management Provision in UK Higher Education. *The British Academy.* https://www.thebritishacademy.ac.uk/publications/business-and-management-provision-in-uk-higher-education/

Brodin, E., & Avery, H. (2020). Cross-disciplinary collaboration and scholarly independence in multidisciplinary learning environments at the doctoral level and beyond. *Minerva, 58*(3), 409–433. doi:10.1007/s11024-020-09397-3

Bron, J., & Veugelers, W. (2014). Why We Need to Involve Our Students in Curriculum Design: Five Arguments for Student Voice. *Curriculum and Teaching Dialogue, 16*(1/2), 125.

Brott, P. E. (1993). *Gottfredson's Theory of Circumscription and Compromise: Implications for Career Counseling.* Educational Resources Information Center.

Brown, D. (1996). *Life Values Inventory.* Retrieved 6 December 2022. https://bhmt.org/wp-content/uploads/2016/04/BHMT_CC_Life-Values_Inventory.pdf

Brown, D., & ... (2002). *Career choice and development* (4th ed.). Jossey-Bass.

Brown, D. (2002). *Career Choice and Development.* Wiley Publications.

Brown, S. D., & Lent, R. W. (2016). *Career development and counseling: Putting theory and research to work* (2nd ed.). John Wiley & Sons.

Brown, S. D., & Watson, M. B. (2010). Bidirectional relations between work and personality development: Delineating personality-related work behaviors. *Journal of Vocational Behavior, 76*(3), 458–472.

Burnette, J. L., Pollack, J. M., Forsyth, R. B., Hoyt, C. L., Babij, A. D., Thomas, F. N., & Coy, A. E. (2020). A growth mindset intervention: Enhancing students' entrepreneurial self-efficacy and career development. *Entrepreneurship Theory and Practice, 44*(5), 878–908. doi:10.1177/1042258719864293

Burrus, J., Hardin, E. E., & Butz, A. (2012). Impact of student employment on career development: Differences between work-study and non-work-study participants. *NASPA Journal, 49*(1), 106–125.

Butler, M. (2022). Interdisciplinary experiential learning during COVID-19: Lessons learned and reflections for the future. *Journal of Environmental Studies and Sciences, 12*(2), 369–377. doi:10.1007/s13412-021-00734-w PMID:35013697

Byrnes, H. (2020). Engaging with professional organizations. In L. Plonsky (Ed.), *Professional development in applied linguistics* (pp. 139–152). John Benjamins. doi:10.1075/z.229.10byr

Cambers, R. (2005). *Career Planning for Everyone in the NHS: The Toolkit*. Radcliffe Publications.

Canagarajah, A. S. (2012). Teacher development in a global profession: An autoethnography. *TESOL Quarterly, 46*(2), 258–279. doi:10.1002/tesq.18

Caprara, G. V., Barbaranelli, C., Pastorelli, C., Bandura, A., & Zimbardo, P. G. (2000). Prosocial foundations of Children's Academic Achievement. *Psychological Science, 11*(4), 302–306. doi:10.1111/1467-9280.00260 PMID:11273389

Carver, R., King, R., Hannum, W., & Fowler, B. (2007). Toward a model of experiential e-learning. *Journal of Online Learning and Teaching, 3*(3), 247–256.

Casillas, A., Kyllonen, P. C., & Way, J. D. (2019). Preparing Students for the Future of Work. In F. Oswald, T. S. Behrend, & L. Foster (Eds.), *Workforce Readiness and the Future of Work* (1st ed., pp. 35–52). Routledge. doi:10.4324/9781351210485-3

Cerych, L., & Frost-Smith, B. (1985). Collaboration between higher education and industry: An overview. *European Journal of Education, 20*(1), 7–18. doi:10.2307/1502999

Chartrand, J. M., & Rose, M. L. (1996). Career interventions for at-risk populations: Incorporating social cognitive influences. *The Career Development Quarterly, 44*(4), 341–353. doi:10.1002/j.2161-0045.1996.tb00450.x

Chartrand, T. L., & Bargh, J. A. (1999). The chameleon effect: The perception–behavior link and social interaction. *Journal of Personality and Social Psychology, 76*(6), 893–910. doi:10.1037/0022-3514.76.6.893 PMID:10402679

Chen, C. P. (2017). Career self-determination theory. *Psychology of career adaptability, employability and resilience*, 329-347.

Cheng, M., Adekola, O., Albia, J. E., & Cai, S. (2021). Employability in higher education: A review of key stakeholders' perspectives. *Higher Education Evaluation and Development, 16*(1), 16–31. doi:10.1108/HEED-03-2021-0025

Chen, H., Fang, T., Liu, F., Pang, L., Wen, Y., Chen, S., & Gu, X. (2020a). Career Adaptability Research: A Literature Review with Scientific Knowledge Mapping in Web of Science. *International Journal of Environmental Research and Public Health, 17*(16), 5986. Advance online publication. doi:10.3390/ijerph17165986 PMID:32824717

Chen, H., Ling, L., Ma, Y., Wen, Y., Gao, X., & Gu, X. (2020b). Suggestions for Chinese University Freshmen Based on Adaptability Analysis and Sustainable Development Education. *Sustainability (Basel), 12*(4), 1371. Advance online publication. doi:10.3390/su12041371

Choi, Han, Lee, & Rhee. (2018). Effects of Interdisciplinary Courses on Engineering Students' Competencies. *TENCON 2018 - 2018 IEEE Region 10 Conference*, 793-797. . doi:10.1109/TENCON.2018.8650133

Chuang, N. K., Lee, P. C., & Kwok, L. (2020). Assisting students with career decision-making difficulties: Can career decision-making self-efficacy and career decision-making profile help? *Journal of Hospitality, Leisure, Sport and Tourism Education*, *26*(4), 1–15. doi:10.1016/j.jhlste.2019.100235

Chu, S. K. W., Reynolds, R. B., Tavares, N. J., Notari, M., & Lee, C. W. Y. (2016). *21st Century Skills Development Through Inquiry-Based Learning: From Theory to Practice*. Springer Nature.

Cizel, R. B. (2018). Gender and Emotional Intelligence as Predictors of Tourism Faculty Students' Career Adaptability, Advances in Hospitality and Tourism Research (AHTR) *An International Journal of Akdeniz University Tourism Faculty*, *6*(2), 188-204. http://www.ahtrjournal.org

Clance, P. R. (1985). *The Impostor Phenomenon*. Peachtree.

Clance, P. R., & Imes, S. A. (1978). The imposter phenomenon in high achieving women: Dynamics and therapeutic intervention. *Psychotherapy (Chicago, Ill.)*, *15*(3), 241–247. doi:10.1037/h0086006

Cleland, J., Arnold, R., & Chesser, A. (2005). Failing finals is often a surprise for the student but not the teacher: Identifying difficulties and supporting students with academic difficulties. *Medical Teacher*, *27*(6), 504–508. doi:10.1080/01421590500156269 PMID:16199356

Cocoradă, E., & Maican, M. A. (2013). A study of foreign language anxiety with Romanian students. *Bulletin of the Transilvania University of Braşov, Series VII: Social Sciences & Law*, *6*(55), 9-18. http://rs.unitbv.ro/BU2013/Series%20VII/BULETIN%20VII/01_Cocorada%20&%20Maican%202-2013.pdf

Coetzee, M., & Roythorne-Jacobs, H. (2007). *Career counseling and guidance in the workplace: a manual for career practitioners*. Juta&Co. Ltd.

Cojocariu, V. M., Cîrtiţă-Buzoianu, C., & Mareş, G. (2019). Opportunities and Difficulties in Conducting Internships in Higher Education from the Employers' Perspective. *Postmodern Openings/Deschideri Postmoderne*, *10*(2).

Colarelli, S. M., Dean, R. L., & Konstans, C. (2015). Retaining the next generation of employees: The relationship between work/family balance and turnover intentions. *Group & Organization Management*, *40*(3), 282–319.

Collier, P. J., & Morgan, D. L. (2008). "Is that paper really due today?": Differences in first-generation and traditional college students' understandings of faculty expectations. *Higher Education*, *55*(4), 425–446. doi:10.1007/s10734-007-9065-5

Collins, H., & Callaghan, D. (2018). The Role of Action Learning in Supporting Cross-Cultural Adaptation of International Students. *Action Learning*, *15*(3), 267–275. doi:10.1080/14767333.2018.1510633

Colombari, R., D'Amico, E., & Paolucci, E. (2021). Can challenge-based learning be effective online? A case study using experiential learning theory. *CERN ideaSquare Journal of Experimental Innovation*, *5*(1), 40–48.

Commission of the European Communities. (2003). *Communication from the Commission to the Council, the European Parliament, the Economic and Social Committee and the Committee of the Regions - Promoting Language Learning and Linguistic Diversity: an Action Plan 2004 – 2006*. https://eur-lex.europa.eu/legal-content/EN/TXT/PDF/?uri=CELEX:52003DC0449

Conley, D. T. (2010). *College and Career Ready: Helping All Students Succeed Beyond High School*. Wiley Publications. doi:10.1002/9781118269411

Cook-Sather, A. (2018). Listening to Equity-Seeking Perspectives: How Students' Experiences of pedagogical Partnership Can Inform Wider Discussions of Student Success. *Higher Education Research & Development*, *37*(5), 923–936. doi:10.1080/07294360.2018.1457629

Cook-Sather, A., Bovill, C., & Felten, P. (2014). *Engaging Students as Partners in Learning and Teaching: A Guide for Faculty.* Jossey-Bass.

Cook, V. (2000). *Linguistics and second language acquisition.* Bloomsbury Publishing.

Coombes, A. E., & Phillips, R. B. (Eds.). (2020). *Museum transformations: Decolonization and democratization.* John Wiley & Sons.

Cooper, D. L., Saunders, S. A., Winston, R. B. Jr, Hirt, J. B., Creamer, D. G., & Janosik, S. M. (2013). *Learning Through Supervised Practice in Student Affairs.* Taylor & Francis. doi:10.4324/9780203890332

Cooper, J. N., & Hawkins, B. (2016). An anti-deficit perspective on black male student athletes' educational experiences at a historically black college/university. *Race, Ethnicity and Education, 19*(5), 950–979. doi:10.1080/13613324.2014.946491

Council of Europe. (2003). *The Common European Framework of Reference for Languages, Teaching, Learning, Assessment.* https://rm.coe.int/1680459f97

Creswell, J. W. (2012). *Educational research: Planning, conducting, and evaluating quantitative and qualitative research* (4th ed.). Pearson.

Croteau, J. M., & Velez, B. L. (2006). A social cognitive framework for career interventions. *The Career Development Quarterly, 54*(3), 198–211.

Cunningham, A. F., & Kienzl, G. S. (2011). The use of federal work-study funds for service-learning. *Michigan Journal of Community Service Learning, 18*(1), 61–75.

Cutillas, A., Benolirao, E., Camasura, J., Golbin, R. Jr, Yamagishi, K., & Ocampo, L. (2023). Does Mentoring Directly Improve Students' Research Skills? Examining the Role of Information Literacy and Competency Development. *Education Sciences, 13*(7), 694. doi:10.3390/educsci13070694

Daalhuizen, J., & Schoormans, J. (2018). Pioneering Online Design Teaching in a MOOC Format: Tools for Facilitating Experiential Learning. *International Journal of Design, 12*(2), 1–14.

Davies, B. (2004). The gender gap in modern languages, a comparison of attitude & performance in year 7&year 10. *Language Learning Journal, 29*(1), 53–58. doi:10.1080/09571730485200111

De Costa, P. I. (2020). Making the most of your applied linguistic conference experience: Things to do before, during, and after the event. In L. Plonsky (Ed.), *Professional development in applied linguistics* (pp. 41–48). John Benjamins. doi:10.1075/z.229.04dec

De Costa, P. I. (2022). Opening the gates for the next generation of scholars. In P. Habibie & A. K. Hultgren (Eds.), *The Inner World of Gatekeeping in Scholarly Publication* (pp. 83–98). Springer Nature. doi:10.1007/978-3-031-06519-4_6

Dean, A., & Fiore, R. (2016). The problem of diversity in museum internship programs: A case study of NYU's Institute of Fine Arts. *Collections, 12*(4), 375–384.

Debreli, E., & Ishanova, I. (2019). Foreign language classroom management: Types of student misbehaviour and strategies adapted by the teachers in handling disruptive behaviour. *Cogent Education, 6*(1), 1–21. doi:10.1080/2331186X.2019.1648629

Deci, E. L., & Ryan, R. M. (1985). *Intrinsic Motivation and Self-Determination in Human Behavior.* Springer Science & Business Media. doi:10.1007/978-1-4899-2271-7

DeFillippi, R. J., & Arthur, M. B. (1994). The Boundaryless Career: A Competency-Based Perspective. *Journal of Organizational Behavior, 15*(4), 307–324. doi:10.1002/job.4030150403

Dewaele, J. M., & Li, C. (2020). Emotions in second language acquisition: A critical review and research agenda. *Foreign Language World, 196*(1), 34–49. https://eprints.bbk.ac.uk/id/eprint/32797

Dewaele, J. M. (2021). Personality. In T. Gregersen & S. Mercer (Eds.), *The Routledge Handbook of the Psychology of Language Learning &Teaching* (pp. 112–123). Routledge. doi:10.4324/9780429321498-12

Dewaele, J. M., & MacIntyre, P. (2019). The predictive power of multicultural personality traits, learner and teacher variables on foreign language enjoyment and anxiety. In M. Sato & S. Loewen (Eds.), *Evidence-based second language pedagogy: A collection of Instructed Second Language Acquisition studies* (pp. 263–286). Routledge. doi:10.4324/9781351190558-12

Dewaele, J. M., & MacIntyre, P. D. (2014). The two faces of Janus? Anxiety & enjoyment in the foreign language classroom. *Studies in Second Language Learning and Teaching, 4*(2), 237–274. doi:10.14746/ssllt.2014.4.2.5

Di Gropello, E., & Tandon, P. (2011). *Putting Higher Education to Work: Skills and Research for Growth in East Asia*. World Bank Publications.

Dick, T. P., & Rallis, S. F. (1991). Factors and influences on high school students' career choices. *Journal for Research in Mathematics Education, 22*(4), 281–292. doi:10.2307/749273

DiMaggio, I., Ginevra, M. C., Santilli, S., Nota, L., & Soresi, S. (2020). The Role of Career Adaptability, the Tendency to Consider Systemic Challenges to Attain a Sustainable Development, and Hope to Improve Investments in Higher Education. *Frontiers in Psychology, 7*(11), 1926. Advance online publication. doi:10.3389/fpsyg.2020.01926 PMID:32849132

Dinsmore, D. L., & Fryer, L. K. (2023). Critical thinking and its relation to strategic processing. *Educational Psychology Review, 35*(1), 36. Advance online publication. doi:10.1007/s10648-023-09755-z

Dolan, J. M., Matthews, G., & Healy, C. C. (2011). Career development learning and employability. *Education + Training, 53*(7), 635–649.

Dörnyei, Z. (2005). *The Psychology of the Language Learner. Individual Differences in Second Language Acquisition*. Lawrence Erlbaum Associates. doi:10.4324/9781410613349

Dörnyei, Z., Csizer, K., & Nemeth, N. (2006). *Motivational dynamics, language attitudes and language globalization: a Hungarian perspective*. Multilingual Matters. doi:10.21832/9781853598876

Doyle, E., Buckley, P., & McCarthy, B. (2021). The Impact of Content Co-creation on Academic Achievement. *Assessment & Evaluation in Higher Education, 46*(3), 494–507. doi:10.1080/02602938.2020.1782832

Dudley-Evans, T., & St. John, M. J. (1998). *Developments in English for Specific Purposes: A multidisciplinary approach*. Cambridge University Press.

Duke, N. N., Campbell, S. D., Sauls, D. L., Stout, R., Story, M. T., Austin, T., Bosworth, H. B., Skinner, A. C., & Vilme, H. (2021). Prevalence of food insecurity among students attending four Historically Black Colleges and Universities. *Journal of American College Health*, 1–7.

Dunne, E., Bennett, N., & Carre, C. (2000). *Skill development in higher education and employment*. Society for Research into Higher education and Open University Press.

Durel, R. J. (1993). The capstone course: A rite of passage. *Teaching Sociology, 21*(3), 223–225. doi:10.2307/1319014

Dursun, M. T., & Argan, M. T. (2017). Does Personality Affect Career Adaptability? *International Journal of Humanities Social Sciences and Education, 4*(10), 107–115. doi:10.20431/2349-0381.0410014

Ebrahiminejad, H. (2017, June), *A Systematized Literature Review: Defining and Developing Engineering Competencies* Paper presented at 2017 ASEE Annual Conference & Exposition, Columbus, OH. 10.18260/1-2--27526

Eccles, J. S. (2005). Subjective Task Value and the Eccles et al. Model of Achievement-Related Choices. In A. J. Elliot & C. S. Dweck (Eds.), *Handbook of competence and motivation* (pp. 105–121). Guilford Publications.

Eccles, J. S., & Wigfield, A. (2002). Motivational beliefs, values and goals. *Annual Review of Psychology*, *53*(1), 109–132. doi:10.1146/annurev.psych.53.100901.135153 PMID:11752481

Edmondson, D., & Matthews, L. (2021). Developing marketing curriculum to make students workforce ready. *International Journal of Educational Management*, *35*(5), 969–983. doi:10.1108/IJEM-10-2019-0370

Ellis, C. (2004). *The ethnographic I: A methodological novel about autoethnography.* Altamira Press.

Entwistle, N. (2000). Approaches to studying and levels of understanding: The influences of teaching and assessment. *Higher Education-New York-Agathon Press Incorporated*, *15*, 156–218.

Erdem, C., & Koçyiğit, M. (2019). Student Misbehaviors Confronted by Academics and Their Coping Experiences. *Educational Policy Analysis and Strategic Research*, *14*(1), 98–115. doi:10.29329/epasr.2019.186.6

Erdogan, B., Bauer, T. N., Truxillo, D. M., & Mansfield, L. R. (2012). Whistle while you work: A review of the life satisfaction literature. *Journal of Management*, *38*(4), 1038–1083. doi:10.1177/0149206311429379

Eriksson, K., Björnstjerna, M., & Vartanova, I. (2020). The relation between gender egalitarian values and gender differences in academic achievement. *Frontiers in Psychology*, *11*, 236. Advance online publication. doi:10.3389/fpsyg.2020.00236 PMID:32153461

European Commission. (2017). *Key Data on Teaching Languages at School in Europe – 2017.* Education, Audiovisual and Culture Executive Agency. https://data.europa.eu/doi/10.2797/62028https://doi.org/10.3389/fpsyg.2020.00236

European Commission. (2019). *Foreign language skills statistics.* Eurostat. https://ec.europa.eu/eurostat/statistics-explained/index.php?title=Foreign_language_skills_ statistics

European Commission. (2020). *The 2030 Agenda for Sustainable Development & the SDGs.* https://ec.europa.eu/environment/sustainable-development/SDGs/index_en.htm

European Commission. (2023a). *Employment rates of recent graduates.* Eurostat. https://ec.europa.eu/eurostat/statistics-explained/index.php?title=Employment_rates _of_recent_graduates#Employment_rates_of_recent_graduates

European Commission. (2023b). *European Year of Skills 2023,* https://commission.europa.eu/strategy-and-policy/priorities-2019-2024/europe-fit-digital-age/european-year-skills-2023_en

European Commission. (2023c). *Real GDP per capita.* Eurostat. https://ec.europa.eu/eurostat/databrowser/view/sdg_08_10/default/table

European Commission. (2023d). *Labour market information: Romania.* EURES. https://eures.ec.europa.eu/living-and-working/labour-market-information/labour-market-information-romania_ro

European Commission. (2023e). *Foreign language learning increases among EU students.* Eurostat. https://ec.europa.eu/eurostat/web/products-eurostat-news/w/edn-20230926-1

Fajaryati, N., Budiyono, Akhyar, M., & Wiranto. (2020). The Employability Skills Needed To Face the Demands of Work in the Future: Systematic Literature Reviews. *Open Engineering*, *10*(1), 595–603. doi:10.1515/eng-2020-0072

Falk, J. H. (2016). *Identity and the museum visitor experience.* Routledge. doi:10.4324/9781315427058

Fallon, M. E. (2023). A Graduate Student's Mentorship Pedagogy for Undergraduate Mentees. *Biomedical Engineering Education*. doi:10.1007/s43683-023-00121-7

Faulkner, M. L., Faulkner, D. M. L., & Nierenberg, A. (2010). *Networking for College Students (and Recent Graduates): Nonstop Business Networking That Will Change Your Life*. Pearson Learning Solutions.

Federal Student Aid. (n.d.). *Federal Work-Study jobs help students earn money to pay for college or career school*. https://studentaid.gov/understand-aid/types/work-study

Fernandes, E. M., & Carvalho, R. G. (2020). The relation between sociodemographic and school path variables, and career adaptability of high school students. *Psychologica*, *63*(1), 83–100. doi:10.14195/1647-8606_63-1_5

Ferreira, N. (2022). Career adaptability as a predictor of employees' career agility and career embeddedness. In Springer eBooks (pp. 229–248). doi:10.1007/978-3-031-09803-1_13

Fisher, D. (2011). *Professional Networking For Dummies*. Wiley Publications.

Flowerdew, J. (2013). English for research publication purposes. In B. Paltridge & S. Starfield (Eds.), *The handbook of English for specific purposes* (pp. 301–321). Wiley.

Flowerdew, J., & Habibie, P. (2022). *Introducing English for research publication purposes*. Routledge.

Foucault, M., & Gordon, C. (2015). *Power/Knowledge: Selected interviews and other writings 1972-1977*. Vintage Books.

Franklin, R., Younge, S., & Jensen, K. (2023). The role of historically Black colleges and universities (HBCUs) in cultivating the next generation of social justice and public service-oriented moral leaders during the racial reckoning and COVID-19 pandemics. *American Journal of Community Psychology*, *71*(1-2), 1. doi:10.1002/ajcp.12648 PMID:36661445

Fredricks, J. A., Filsecker, M., & Lawson, M. A. (2016). Student engagement, context, and adjustment: Addressing definitional, measurement, and methodological issues. *Learning and Instruction*, *43*, 1–4. doi:10.1016/j.learninstruc.2016.02.002

Frendo, E. (2005). *How to Teach Business English*. Pearson Education.

Frontczak, N. T. (1998). A paradigm for the selection, use and development of experiential learning activities in marketing education. *Marketing Education Review*, *8*(3), 25–33. doi:10.1080/10528008.1998.11488641

Fuertes, A. M. de C., Blanco Fernández, J., García Mata, M. Á., Rebaque Gómez, A., & Pascual, R. G. (2020). Relationship between Personality and Academic Motivation in Education Degrees Students. *Education Sciences*, *10*(11), 327. Advance online publication. doi:10.3390/educsci10110327

Fusco, L., Parola, A., & Sica, L. S. (2019). From creativity to future: the role of career adaptability. *CEUR Workshop Proceeding*. https://ceur-ws.org/Vol-2524/paper24.pdf

Galer-Unti, R. A., & Tappe, M. K. (2009). Demystifying the abstract submission and conference presentation process. *Health Educator : Journal of Eta Sigma Gamma*, *41*(2), 64–67.

Garriott, P. O., Flores, L. Y., Prabhakar, B., Mazzotta, E. C., Liskov, A. C., & Shapiro, J. E. (2014). Parental support and underrepresented students' math/science interests: The mediating role of learning experiences. *Journal of Career Assessment*, *22*(4), 627–641. doi:10.1177/1069072713514933

Gati, I., Krausz, M., & Osipow, S. (1996). A Taxonomy of Difficulties in Career Decision Making. *Journal of Counseling Psychology*, *43*(4), 510–526. doi:10.1037/0022-0167.43.4.510

Gati, I., Landman, S., Davidovitch, S., Asulin-Peretz, L., & Gadassi, R. (2010). From career decision-making styles to career decision-making profiles: A multidimensional approach. *Journal of Vocational Behavior*, *76*(2), 277–291. doi:10.1016/j.jvb.2009.11.001

Gault, J., Leach, E., & Duey, M. (2010). Effects of business internships on job marketability: The employers' perspective. *Education + Training*, 52(1), 76–88. doi:10.1108/00400911011017690

Gault, J., Redington, J., & Schlager, T. (2000). Undergraduate business internships and career success: Are they related? *Journal of Marketing Education*, 22(1), 45–53. doi:10.1177/0273475300221006

Gerdes, H., & Mallinckrodt, B. (1994). Emotional, social, and academic adjustment of college students: A longitudinal study of retention. *Journal of Counseling and Development*, 72(3), 281–288. doi:10.1002/j.1556-6676.1994.tb00935.x

Gerli, F., Bonesso, S., & Pizzi, C. (2015). Boundaryless Career and Career Success: The Impact of Emotional and Social Competencies. *Frontiers in Psychology*, 6. Advance online publication. doi:10.3389/fpsyg.2015.01304 PMID:26388809

Gibbs, P., & Appleton, J. (2016). Foundation degree and internship programmes for widening participation students: A UK case study. *Widening Participation and Lifelong Learning : the Journal of the Institute for Access Studies and the European Access Network*, 18(3), 8–25.

Ginzberg, E. (1951). *Occupational Choice: An Approach to a General Theory*. Columbia University Press.

Gironella, F. (2023). Gamification Pedagogy: A Motivational Approach to Student-Centric Course Design in Higher Education. *Journal of University Teaching & Learning Practice*, 20(3), 4.

Glenn, M. C. (2011). Academic achievement and academic adjustment difficulties among college freshmen. *Journal of Arts, Science, and Commerce*, 2, 72–76.

Godfrey, N. (2021, September 13). *Dying careers you may want to Steer Clear of*. Kiplinger. https://www.kiplinger.com/personal-finance/careers/603424/dying-careers-you-may-want-to-steer-clear-of

Goldberg, L. R., Johnson, J. A., Eber, H. W., Hogan, R., Ashton, M. C., Cloninger, C. R., & Gough, H. G. (2006). The international personality item pool and the future of public-domain personality measures. *Journal of Research in Personality*, 40(1), 84–96. doi:10.1016/j.jrp.2005.08.007

Goleman, D. (2012). *Emotional Intelligence: Why It Can Matter More Than IQ*. Random House Publishing Group.

Gollnick, D. M., Hall, G. E., & Quinn, L. F. (2018). *The Wiley Handbook of Teaching and Learning*. Wiley Publications.

Goodyear, V., & Dudley, D. (2015). "I'ma facilitator of learning!" Understanding what teachers and students do within student-centered physical education models. *Quest*, 67(3), 274–289. doi:10.1080/00336297.2015.1051236

Gore, P. A. (2019). Disparities in career readiness and employment outcomes for college graduates. *The Career Development Quarterly*, 67(3), 235–249.

Gothard, W. P., Mignot, P., Offer, M., & Ruff, M. (2001). *Careers Guidance in Context*. SAGE Publications. doi:10.4135/9781446220399

Gottfredson, L. S. (1981). Circumscription and compromise: A developmental theory of occupational aspirations. *Journal of Counseling Psychology*, 28(6), 545–579. doi:10.1037/0022-0167.28.6.545

Gregoire, J., & Jungers, C. (2013). *The Counsellor's Companion: What Every Beginning Counselor Needs to Know*. Taylor & Francis.

Guan, Y., Arthur, M. B., Karpova, S. N., Hall, R. J., & Lord, R. G. (2019). Career boundarylessness and career success: A review, integration, and guide to future research. *Journal of Vocational Behavior*, 110, 390–402. doi:10.1016/j.jvb.2018.05.013

**Compilation of References**

Guan, Y., Dai, X., Gong, Q., Deng, Y., Hou, Y., Dong, Z., Wang, L., Huang, Z., & Lai, X. (2017). Understanding the trait basis of career adaptability: A two-wave mediation analysis among Chinese university students. *Journal of Vocational Behavior*, *101*, 32–42. doi:10.1016/j.jvb.2017.04.004

Guay, F. (2005). Motivations Underlying Career Decision-Making Activities: The Career Decision-Making Autonomy Scale (CDMAS). *Journal of Career Assessment*, *13*(1), 77–97. doi:10.1177/1069072704270297

Guichard, J. (2018). Final Purposes for Life-and-Career Design Interventions in the Anthropocene Era. In V. Cohen-Scali, L. Nota, & J. Rossier (Eds.), *New Perspectives on Career Guidance and Counseling in Europe. Building Careers in Changing and Diverse Societies* (pp. 189–204). Springer International Publishing. doi:10.1007/978-3-319-61476-2_12

Guo, P. (2021). Research on the Strategy of Improving College Students' Career Adaptability in Application-oriented Colleges and Universities. *Journal of Education. Teaching and Social Studies*, *3*(3), 54–63. doi:10.22158/jetss.v3n3p54

Gurukkal, R. (2018). Towards outcome-based education. *Higher Education for the Future*, *5*(1), 1–3. doi:10.1177/2347631117740456

Gutchess, A., & Rajaram, S. (2022). Consideration of culture in cognition: How we can enrich methodology and theory. *Psychonomic Bulletin & RE:view*, *30*(3), 914–931. doi:10.3758/s13423-022-02227-5 PMID:36510095

Gu, X., Tang, M., Chen, S., & Montgomery, M. L. (2020). Effects of a Career Course on Chinese High School Students' Career Decision-Making Readiness. *The Career Development Quarterly*, *68*(3), 222–237. doi:10.1002/cdq.12233

Habel, C. (2012). 'I can do it, and how!' Student experience in access and equity pathways to higher education. *Higher Education Research & Development*, *31*(6), 811–825. doi:10.1080/07294360.2012.659177

Habibie, P., Sawyer, R. D., & Norris, J. (2021). Thinking beyond ourselves: Career reflections on the Trojan Horse of Hegemonic Discourses. In P. Hibibie & S. Burgess (Eds.), *Scholarly publication trajectories of early-career scholars: insider perspectives* (pp. 299–320). Springer. doi:10.1007/978-3-030-85784-4_17

Habibie, P., & Starfield, S. (2022). English for research publication purposes: Two significant exigencies. *Journal of English for Research Publication Purposes*, *3*(2), 165–168. doi:10.1075/jerpp.00012.edi

Hakimi, S., Hejazi, E., & Lavasani, M. G. (2011). The Relationships Between Personality Traits and Students' Academic Achievement. *Procedia: Social and Behavioral Sciences*, *29*, 836–845. doi:10.1016/j.sbspro.2011.11.312

Hall, O., & Seth, D. (2022). Role of Interdisciplinarity and Collaboration in Engineering Design Curriculum. *2022 IEEE Integrated STEM Education Conference (ISEC)*, 285-292. 10.1109/ISEC54952.2022.10025305

Hanapi, Z., Nordin, M. S., & Khamis, A. (2015). Challenges Faced by Engineering Lecturers in Integrating Technical and Employability Skills in the Curriculum: A Case Study in Community College, Malaysia. *International Journal of Social Science and Humanity*, *5*(5), 483–486. doi:10.7763/IJSSH.2015.V5.504

Han, J. H., Kelley, T. R., & Knowles, J. G. (2021). Factors influencing student STEM learning: Self-Efficacy and outcome expectancy, 21st century skills, and career awareness. *Journal for STEM Education Research*, *4*(2), 117–137. doi:10.1007/s41979-021-00053-3

Harmer, J. (2015). *The practice of English language teaching (with DVD)* (4th ed.). Pearson.

Harren, V. A. (1979). A model of career decision making for college students. *Journal of Vocational Behavior*, *14*(2), 119–133. doi:10.1016/0001-8791(79)90065-4

Hartung, P. J., Subich, L. M., Bagley, S. B., & Liu, Y. (2002). Exploring congruence between work values and personality: Do congruent people achieve more satisfaction, commitment, and success? *Journal of Career Assessment*, *10*(2), 156–177.

Hartung, P. J., & Taber, B. J. (2008). Career construction and subjective well-being. *Journal of Career Assessment, 16*(1), 75–85. doi:10.1177/1069072707305772

Haskins, N. H., Hughes, K. L., Crumb, L., Smith, A. R., Brown, S. S., & Pignato, L. (2019). Postmodern Womanism: Dismantling the Imposter Phenomenon for Black American College Students. *Negro Educational Review, 70*(1–4), 5–25.

Hassan, H., Hussain, M., Niazi, A., Hoshino, Y., Azam, A., & Kazmi, A. S. (2022). Career Path Decisions and Sustainable Options. *Sustainability (Basel), 14*(17), 10501. doi:10.3390/su141710501

Havighurst, R. J. (1972). *Developmental Tasks and Education*. D. McKay Company.

Hayden, S. C., & Osborn, D. S. (2020). Using experiential learning theory to train career practitioners. *Journal of Employment Counseling, 57*(1), 2–13. doi:10.1002/joec.12134

Helyer, R., & Lee, D. (2014). The role of work experience in the future employability of higher education graduates. *Higher Education Quarterly, 68*(3), 348–372. doi:10.1111/hequ.12055

Hemsley-Brown, J., & Oplatka, I. (2006). Universities in a competitive global marketplace: A systematic review of the literature on higher education marketing. *International Journal of Public Sector Management, 19*(4), 316–338. doi:10.1108/09513550610669176

Hennink, M., Hutter, I., & Bailey, A. (2020). *Qualitative Research Methods*. Sage.

Hergert, M. (2009). Student Perceptions Of The Value Of Internships In Business Education. *American Journal of Business Education, 2*(8), 9–14. doi:10.19030/ajbe.v2i8.4594

Heslin, P. A. (2005). Conceptualizing and evaluating career success. Journal of Organizational Behavior: The International Journal of Industrial. *Journal of Organizational Behavior, 26*(2), 113–136. doi:10.1002/job.270

Hirschi, A., & Valero, D. (2015). Career adaptability profiles and their relationship to adaptivity and adapting. *Journal of Vocational Behavior, 88*, 220–229. doi:10.1016/j.jvb.2015.03.010

Hofstede, G., Hofstede, G. J., & Minkov, M. (2010). *Software of the Mind, Intercultural Cooperation &Its Importance for Survival*. McGraw-Hill Comp.

Holland, J. L. (1973). *Making Vocational Choices: A Theory of Careers*. Prentice-Hall.

Hood, S., & Forey, G. (2005). Introducing a conference paper: Getting interpersonal with your audience. *Journal of English for Academic Purposes, 4*(4), 291–306. doi:10.1016/j.jeap.2005.07.003

Hooper-Greenhill, E. (2015). *Museums and the shaping of knowledge*. Routledge.

Horwitz, E. K., Horwitz, M. B., & Cope, J. (1986). Foreign Language Classroom Anxiety. *Modern Language Journal, 70*(2), 125–132. doi:10.1111/j.1540-4781.1986.tb05256.x

Hou, Z. J., Leung, S. A., Li, X., Li, X., & Xu, H. (2012). Career Adapt-Abilities Scale—China Form: Construction and initial validation. *Journal of Vocational Behavior, 80*(3), 686–691. doi:10.1016/j.jvb.2012.01.006

Hsu, J., Lin, L. C., & Stern, M. (2023). Curriculum Co-Creation: Knowledge Co-Creation in an Educational Context. *International Journal of Knowledge-Based Organizations, 13*(1), 1–24. doi:10.4018/IJKBO.317116

Huber, M. T., & Hutchings, P. (2004). *Integrative Learning: Mapping the Terrain. The Academy in Transition*. Association of American Colleges and Universities.

Hyland, K. (2004). *Disciplinary discourses: Social interactions in academic writing*. University of Michigan Press.

Hyland, K. (2012). *Disciplinary identities: Individuality and community in academic discourse.* Cambridge University Press. doi:10.1017/9781009406512

Hyland, K. (2015). *Academic publishing: Issues and challenges in the construction of knowledge.* Oxford University Press.

Iacob, R. (2018). Brain Drain Phenomenon in Romania: What Comes in Line after Corruption? *Romanian Journal of Communication and Public Relations, 20*(2), 53–78. doi:10.21018/rjcpr.2018.2.259

Ichikawa, J. J., & Steup, M. (2017). The Analysis of Knowledge. *Stanford Encyclopedia of Philosophy.* https://plato.stanford.edu/entries/knowledge-analysis/#LighKnow

International Labour Organization. (2021). *Internships, Employability and the Search for Decent Work Experience.* Edward Elgar Publishing Limited.

International Labour Organization. (2022). *Monitor on the world of work. Tenth edition. Multiple crises threaten the global labour market recovery,* https://www.ilo.org/wcmsp5/groups/public/---dgreports/---dcomm/---publ/documents/briefingnote/wcms_859255.pdf

Jackson, D., & Tomlinson, M. (2019). Career Values and Proactive Career Behavior Among Contemporary Higher Education Students. *Journal of Education and Work, 32*(5), 449–464. doi:10.1080/13639080.2019.1679730

Jackson, D., & Wilton, N. (2016). Developing Career Management Competencies among Undergraduates and the Role of Work-Integrated Learning. *Teaching in Higher Education, 21*(3), 266–286. doi:10.1080/13562517.2015.1136281

Jackson, D., & Wilton, N. (2017). Perceived employability among undergraduates and the importance of career self-management, work experience and individual characteristics. *Higher Education Research & Development, 36*(4), 747–762. doi:10.1080/07294360.2016.1229270

Jacobi, M. (1991). Mentoring and undergraduate academic success: A literature review. *Review of Educational Research, 61*(4), 505–532. doi:10.3102/00346543061004505

Jehanzeb, K., Rasheed, M. F., & Rasheed, A. (2012). Impact of rewards and motivation on job satisfaction in banking sector of Saudi Arabia. *International Journal of Business and Social Science, 3*(21).

Jia, Y., Hou, Z.-J., Zhang, H., & Xiao, Y. (2020). Future time perspective, career adaptability, anxiety, and career decision-making difficulty: Exploring mediations and moderations. *Journal of Career Development, 49*(2), 282–296. doi:10.1177/0894845320941922

Jigău, M. (2003). *Consilierea carierei adulților.* Editura Afir.

Jin, Y., & Zhang, L. J. (2018). The dimensions of foreign language classroom enjoyment and their effect on foreign language achievement. *International Journal of Bilingual Education and Bilingualism, 24*(7), 948–962. doi:10.1080/13670050.2018.1526253

Jo, H., Park, M., & Song, J.H. (2023). Career Competencies: An Integrated Review of Literature. *European Journal of Training and Development.* . doi:10.1108/EJTD-04-2023-0052

Johansson, I., & Winman, T. (2020). Orchestrating of Learning in Higher Education Through Internships. *Educational Review, 4*(5), 101–112. doi:10.26855/er.2020.05.001

John, R., John, R., & Rao, Z.-R. (2020). The Big Five personality traits and academic performance. *Journal of Law & Social Studies, 2*(1), 10–19. doi:10.52279/jlss.02.01.1019

John, S. P., & De Villiers, R. (2022). Factors affecting the success of marketing in higher education: A relationship marketing perspective. *Journal of Marketing for Higher Education,* 1–20. doi:10.1080/08841241.2022.2116741

Johnson, M. (2007). *The meaning of the body: Aesthetics of human understanding*. University of Chicago Press. doi:10.7208/chicago/9780226026992.001.0001

Johnson, M. R., & McCabe, R. H. (2008). Federal work-study participants' and employers' perceptions of skill development. *Journal of College Student Development*, *49*(4), 363–382.

Jones, L. K. (1989). Measuring a three-dimensional construct of career indecision among college students: A revision of the Vocational Decision Scale: The Career Decision Profile. *Journal of Counseling Psychology*, *36*(4), 477–486. doi:10.1037/0022-0167.36.4.477

Jungbluth, C., MacFarlane, I. M., Veach, P. M., & LeRoy, B. S. (2011). Why is Everyone So Anxious?: An Exploration of Stress and Anxiety in Genetic Counseling Graduate Students. *Journal of Genetic Counseling*, *20*(3), 270–286. doi:10.1007/s10897-010-9348-3 PMID:21264500

Jung, Y., & Love, A. R. (2017). *Systems thinking in museums: theory and practice*. Rowman & Littlefield.

Kahn, P., & Anderson, L. (2019). *Developing Your Teaching Towards Excellence*. Routledge. doi:10.4324/9780429490583

Kaminstein, D. S., Stevens, A., & Forst, M. (2022). Experiential Work in a Virtual World: Impactful and Socially Relevant Experiential Learning. *The Journal of Educators Online*, *19*(2), n2. doi:10.9743/JEO.2022.19.2.6

Kandlbinder, P. (2014). CA in university teaching. *HERDSA News*, *36*(3), 5–6.

Kang, X., & Wu, Y. (2022). Academic enjoyment, behavioral engagement, self-concept, organizational strategy and achievement in EFL setting: A multiple mediation analysis. *PLoS One*, *17*(4), e0267405. doi:10.1371/journal.pone.0267405 PMID:35486654

Keiler, L. S. (2018). Teachers' roles and identities in student-centered classrooms. *International Journal of STEM Education*, *5*(1), 34. doi:10.1186/s40594-018-0131-6 PMID:30631724

Kim, J., Hagedorn, L. S., Williamson, J. H., & Aquino, J. (2020). The effects of cooperative education participation on student employment and starting salary: A propensity score matching analysis. *Journal of College Student Retention*, *22*(1), 61–77.

Kim, N. R., & Lee, K. H. (2018). The Effect of Internal locus of Control on Career Adaptability: The Mediating Role of Career Decision-making Self-efficacy and Occupational Engagement. *Journal of Employment Counseling*, *55*(1), 2–15. doi:10.1002/joec.12069

Kim, N., & Kim, M. K. (2022). Teachers' perceptions of using an artificial intelligence-based educational tool for scientific writing. *Frontiers in Education*, *7*, 755914. Advance online publication. doi:10.3389/feduc.2022.755914

Kings College. (2023). UK Now Among Most Socially Liberal of Countries. *Kings College London*. https://www.kcl.ac.uk/news/uk-now-among-most-socially-liberal-of-countries#:~:text=The%20UK%20now%20ranks%20among,divorce%2C%20according%20to%20new%20data

Kirtchuk, D., Wells, G., Levett, T., Castledine, C., & de Visser, R. (2022). Understanding the impact of academic difficulties among medical students: A scoping review. *Medical Education*, *56*(3), 262–269. doi:10.1111/medu.14624 PMID:34449921

Knouse, S. B., Tanner, J. R., & Harris, E. W. (2016). Behavioral outcomes of the interview: An examination of college internship programs and student selections. *The Psychologist Manager Journal*, *19*(4), 196–220.

Köhler, T., Smith, A., & Bhakoo, V. (2022). Templates in qualitative research methods: Origins, limitations, and new directions. *Organizational Research Methods*, *25*(2), 183–210. doi:10.1177/10944281211060710

Kolb, A. Y., & Kolb, D. A. (2005). Learning styles and learning spaces: Enhancing experiential learning in higher education. *Academy of Management Learning & Education*, *4*(2), 193–212. doi:10.5465/amle.2005.17268566

Kolb, D. A. (2015). *Experiential learning: Experience as the source of learning and development*. FT Press.

Kortmann, B. (2019). *Language Policies at the LERU Member Institutions*, LERU Briefing Paper (4). https://www.leru.org/files/Publications/Language-Policies-at-LERU-member-institutions-Full-Paper.pdf

Kost, D., Fieseler, C., & Wong, S. (2020). Boundaryless Careers in a Gig Economy: An Oxymoron? *Human Resource Management Journal*, *30*(1), 100–113. doi:10.1111/1748-8583.12265

Kowalski, G., & Ślebarska, K. (2022). Remote Working and Work Effectiveness: A Leader Perspective. *International Journal of Environmental Research and Public Health*, *19*(15326), 15326. doi:10.3390/ijerph192215326 PMID:36430045

Koyuncuoğlu, Ö. (2021). An Investigation of Academic Motivation and Career Decidedness among University Students. *International Journal of Research in Education and Science*, *7*(1), 125. doi:10.46328/ijres.1694

Krathwohl, D. R. (2002). A Revision of Bloom's Taxonomy: An Overview. *Theory into Practice*, *41*(4), 212–218. doi:10.1207/s15430421tip4104_2

Kris Metz, A. J. (2009). Career aspirations and expectations of college students: Demographic and labor. *Journal of Career Assessment*, *17*(2), 155–171. doi:10.1177/1069072708328862

Krishnamurthy, S. (2020). The future of business education: A commentary in the shadow of the Covid-19 pandemic. *Journal of Business Research*, *117*, 1–5. doi:10.1016/j.jbusres.2020.05.034 PMID:32501309

Krumboltz, J. D., Mitchell, A. M., & Jones, G. B. (1976). A social learning theory of career selection. *The Counseling Psychologist*, *6*(1), 71–81. doi:10.1177/001100007600600117

Kubicek, B., & Korunka, C. (2017). *Job Demands in a Changing World of Work: Impact on Workers' Health and Performance and Implications for Research and Practice*. Springer International Publishing.

Kuh, G. D. (2008). *High-impact educational practices: What they are, who has access to them, and why they matter*. Association of American Colleges and Universities. https://www.aacu.org/publication/high-impact-educational-practices-what-they-are-who-has-access-to-them-and-why-they-matter

Kulcsár, V., Dobrean, A., & Gati, I. (2020). Challenges and Difficulties in Career Decision Making: Their Causes, and Their Effects on the Process and the Decision. *Journal of Vocational Behavior*, *116*, 103346. doi:10.1016/j.jvb.2019.103346

Kumar, R. (2010). *Human Resource Management: Strategic Analysis Text and Cases*. I.K. International Publishing House Pvt. Limited.

Kumar, S., & Bhandarker, A. (2020). Experiential learning and its efficacy in management education. PURUSHARTHA- A journal of Management. *Ethics and Spirituality*, *13*(1), 35–55. doi:10.21844/16201913103

Kunjufu, J. (2007). *Raising Black Boys*. Academic Press.

Kunjufu, J. (1997). *To Be Popular or Smart: The Black Peer Group*. African American Images.

LaPrade, A., Mertens, J., Moore, T., & Wright, A. (2019). *The enterprise guide to closing the skills gap. Strategies for building and maintaining a skilled workforce*, IBM Institute for Business Value. https://www.ibm.com/thought-leadership/institute-business-value/en-us/report/closing-skills-gap

Larkin, H., & Richardson, B. (2013). Creating high challenge/high support academic environments through CA: Student outcomes. *Teaching in Higher Education*, *18*(2), 192–204. doi:10.1080/13562517.2012.696541

Lastner, M. M., & Rast, R. (2016). Creating win-win collaborations for students: An immersive learning project for advanced sales courses. *Journal for Advancement of Marketing Education, 24*, 43–48.

Lauridsen, K. M. (2013). Higher education language policy- Report of European Language Council working group. *European Journal of Language Policy, 5*(1), 128. https://www.liverpooluniversitypress.co.uk/journals/id/73/

Lave, J., & Wenger, E. (1991). *Situated learning: Legitimate peripheral participation.* Cambridge University Press. doi:10.1017/CBO9780511815355

Laverick, D. M. (2016). *Mentoring Processes in Higher Education.* Springer International Publishing. doi:10.1007/978-3-319-39217-2

Lawson, R. A., Blocher, E. J., Brewer, P. C., Cokins, G., Sorensen, J. E., Stout, D. E., Sundem, G. L., Wolcott, S. K., & Wouters, M. J. (2014). Focusing accounting curricula on students' long-run careers: Recommendations for an integrated competency-based framework for accounting education. *Issues in Accounting Education, 29*(2), 295–317. doi:10.2308/iace-50673

Leber, J., Renkl, A., Nückles, M., & Wäschle, K. (2018). When the type of assessment counteracts teaching for understanding. *Learning: Research and Practice, 4*(2), 161–179. doi:10.1080/23735082.2017.1285422

Lee, J. C.-K. (2019). Teachers' work, change and learning: Roles, contexts and engagement. *Teachers and Teaching, 25*(4), 399–403. doi:10.1080/13540602.2019.1625616

Lee, M. C. Y., McMahon, M., & Watson, M. (2018). Career Decisions of International Chinese Doctoral Students: The Influence of the Self in the Environment. *Australian Journal of Career Development, 27*(1), 29–39. doi:10.1177/1038416217743023

Lent & Steven. (2012). Career Development and Counselling: Putting Theory and Research to Work. Wiley Publications.

Lent, R. W., & Brown, S. D. (2020). Career decision making, fast and slow: Toward an integrative model of intervention for sustainable career choice. *Journal of Vocational Behavior, 120*, 103448. doi:10.1016/j.jvb.2020.103448

Lent, R. W., Brown, S. D., & Hackett, G. (2000). Contextual supports and barriers to career choice: A social cognitive analysis. *Journal of Counseling Psychology, 47*(1), 36–49. doi:10.1037/0022-0167.47.1.36

Lent, R. W., Brown, S. D., & Hackett, G. (2002). Social cognitive career theory. In D. Brown (Ed.), *Career choice and development* (4th ed., pp. 255–311). Jossey-Bass.

Leonard, A. J., Akos, P., & Hutson, B. (2021). The impact of work-study participation on the career readiness of undergraduates. *Journal of Student Financial Aid, 52*(1). Advance online publication. doi:10.55504/0884-9153.1758

Lester, J., & Costley, C. (2010). Work-based learning at higher education level: Value, practice and critique. *Teaching in Higher Education, 15*(3), 291–302.

Lewis, K. (2020). Technology in the workplace: Redefining skills for the 21st century. *The Midwest Quarterly, 61*(3), 348–356.

Li, Y., Liu, Y., Nguyen, K., Shi, H., Vuorenmaa, E., Jarvela, S., & Zhao, G. (2022). Exploring Interactions and Regulations in Collaborative Learning: An Interdisciplinary Multimodal Dataset. *arXiv preprint arXiv:2210.05419.*

Li, C., & Xu, J. (2019). Trait emotional intelligence and classroom emotions: A positive psychology investigation and intervention among Chinese EFL learners. *Frontiers in Psychology, 10*, 2453. Advance online publication. doi:10.3389/fpsyg.2019.02453 PMID:31736840

*Compilation of References*

Lipka, O., Sarid, M., Aharoni Zorach, I., Bufman, A., Hagag, A. A., & Peretz, H. (2020). Adjustment to higher education: A comparison of students with and without disabilities. *Frontiers in Psychology*, *11*(923), 1–11. doi:10.3389/fpsyg.2020.00923 PMID:32670127

Liu, Z. Q., Dorozhkin, E. M., Davydova, N. N., & Sadovnikova, N. O. (2020). Co-Learning as a New Model of Learning in a Digital Environment: Learning Effectiveness and Collaboration. *International Journal of Emerging Technologies in Learning*, *15*(13), 34–48. doi:10.3991/ijet.v15i13.14667

Li, Y., Guan, Y., Wang, F., Zhou, X., Guo, K., Jiang, P., Mo, Z., Li, Y., & Fang, Z. (2015). Big-five personality and BIS/BAS traits as predictors of career exploration: The mediation role of career adaptability. *Journal of Vocational Behavior*, *89*, 39–45. doi:10.1016/j.jvb.2015.04.006

Lomer, S., & Mittelmeier, J. (2021). Mapping the Research on Pedagogies with International Students in the UK: A Systematic Literature Review. *Teaching in Higher Education*. https://www.tandfonline.com/doi/full/10.1080/13562517.2021.1872532

Long, B. T., & Kurlaender, M. (2009). Do community colleges provide a viable pathway to a baccalaureate degree? *Educational Evaluation and Policy Analysis*, *31*(1), 30–53. doi:10.3102/0162373708327756

Lopes, B., Silva, P., Melo, A. I., Brito, E., Paiva Dias, G., & Costa, M. (2019). The 'lunar side' of the story: Exploring the sustainability of curricular internships in higher education. *Sustainability (Basel)*, *11*(21), 5879. doi:10.3390/su11215879

Lorente, J. P. (2012). The development of museum studies in universities: From technical training to critical museology. *Museum Management and Curatorship*, *27*(3), 237–252. doi:10.1080/09647775.2012.701995

Lubicz-Nawrocka, T. (2018). Students as Partners in Learning and Teaching: The Benefits of Co-creation of the Curriculum. *International Journal for Students as Partners*, *2*(1). doi:.v2i1.3207 doi:10.15173/ijsap

Lubicz-Nawrocka, T., & Bovill, C. (2023). Do students experience transformation through co-creating curriculum in higher education? *Teaching in Higher Education*, *28*(7), 1744–1760. doi:10.1080/13562517.2021.1928060

Lucas, U., & Mladenovic, R. (2007). The potential of threshold concepts: An emerging framework for educational research and practice. *London Review of Education*, *5*(3). Advance online publication. doi:10.1080/14748460701661294

Luke, C. (2018). *Museum studies: An anthology of contexts*. John Wiley & Sons.

MacDonald, L., Thomas, E., Javernick-Will, A., Austin-Breneman, J., Aranda, I., Salvinelli, C., Klees, R., Walters, J., Parmentier, M. J., Schaad, D., Shahi, A., Bedell, E., Platais, G., Brown, J., Gershenson, J., Watkins, D., Obonyo, E., Oyanedel-Craver, V., Olson, M., ... Linden, K. (2022). Aligning learning objectives and approaches in global engineering graduate programs: Review and recommendations by an interdisciplinary working group. *Development Engineering*, *7*, 100095. doi:10.1016/j.deveng.2022.100095

Maggiori, C., Rossier, J., & Savickas, M. L. (2015). Career Adapt-Abilities Scale–Short Form (CAAS-SF). *Journal of Career Assessment*, *25*(2), 312–325. doi:10.1177/1069072714565856

Maher, C. (2023). *Understanding Stressors for International Students*. Sharing Pedagogic Research and Practice in Greenwich University Business School. https://blogs.gre.ac.uk/sebe/2023/10/19/understanding-stressors-for-international-students/

Maher, C. (2018). *Understanding Managerial Career Anchors and Career Path Preferences: A Case Study of Third Sector Social Enterprise Managers*. Scholar's Press.

Maher, C. (2020). *Career Needs and Career Values: The Mediating Role of Organisational Culture. In Recent Advances in the Roles of Cultural and Personal Values in Organizational Behaviour.* 240-260. IGI Global. doi:10.4018/978-1-7998-1013-1.ch012

Mahmud, M. I., Noah, S. M., Jaafar, W. M. W., Bakar, A. Y. A., & Amat, S. (2019). The career readiness construct between dysfunctional career thinking and career self-efficacy among undergraduate students. *Strategies (La Jolla, Calif.), 7*(1), 74–81.

Maican, M. A. (2019). European Language Policies and the Development of Language Competences in Higher Education. *Bulletin of the Transilvania University of Brasov. Series V: Economic Sciences, 12*(2), 127–132. doi:10.31926/but.es.2019.12.61.2.16

Maican, M. A., & Cocoradă, E. (2021). Online Foreign Language Learning in Higher Education and Its Correlates during the COVID-19 Pandemic. *Sustainability (Basel), 13*(2), 781. doi:10.3390/su13020781

Maican, M. A., & Cocoradă, E. (2023). University students' foreign language learning behaviours in the online environment. In T. D. Neimann, L. L. Hindman, E. Shliakhovchuk, M. Moore, & J. J. Felix (Eds.), *Multifaceted Analysis of Sustainable Strategies and Tactics in Education* (pp. 32–67). IGI Global. doi:10.4018/978-1-6684-6035-1.ch002

Mak, K. K. L., Kleitman, S., & Abbott, M. J. (2019). Impostor Phenomenon Measurement Scales: A Systematic Review. *Frontiers in Psychology, 10*, 671. doi:10.3389/fpsyg.2019.00671 PMID:31024375

Male, S. A., Bush, M. B., & Chapman, E. S. (2011). Understanding generic engineering competencies. *Australasian Journal of Engineering Education, 17*(3), 147–156. doi:10.1080/22054952.2011.11464064

Manpower, I. (2020). *The 2022 global talent shortage survey result*. Retrieved November, 9, 2022 from https://go.manpowergroup.com/talent-shortage

Marconi, G., Vergolini, L., & Borgonovi, F. (2023). *The demand for language skills in the European labour market: Evidence from online job vacancies*. OECD Social, Employment and Migration Working Papers, No. 294. doi:10.1787/1815199X

Mariasse, A. L. (1985). Vision and leadership: Paying attention to intention. *Peabody Journal of Education, 63*(1), 150–173. doi:10.1080/01619568509538505

Martin, A. J., Nejad, H. G., Colmar, S., & Liem, G. A. D. (2013). Adaptability: How students' responses to uncertainty and novelty predict their academic and non-academic outcomes. *Journal of Educational Psychology, 105*(3), 728–746. doi:10.1037/a0032794

McCrae, R. R., & Sutin, A. R. (2018). A Five-Factor Theory Perspective on Causal Analysis. *European Journal of Personality, 32*(3), 151–166. doi:10.1002/per.2134 PMID:30140117

McCune, V., & Entwistle, N. (2000, August). The deep approach to learning: analytic abstraction and idiosyncratic development. In *Innovations in Higher Education Conference* (Vol. 30). University of Helsinki.

McElwee, R. O., & Yurak, T. J. (2010). The Phenomenology of the Impostor Phenomenon. *Individual Differences Research, 8*(3), 184–197.

McGowan, B. L., Palmer, R. T., Wood, J. L., & Hibbler, D. F. (2016). *Black Men in the Academy: Narratives of Resiliency, Achievement, and Success*. Palgrave Macmillan. doi:10.1057/9781137567284

McHann, J. C. (2012). Changed learning needs: some radical reflections on B-School education. *Business Administration Education: Changes in Management and Leadership Strategies*, 105-128.

McHenry, R., & Krishnan, S. (2022). A conceptual professional practice framework for embedding employability skills development in engineering education programmes. *European Journal of Engineering Education, 47*(6), 1296–1314. doi:10.1080/03043797.2022.2164255

McNamara, J., Brown, C., Field, R., Kift, S., Butler, D., & Treloar, C. (2011). Capstones: Transitions and professional identity. In *Proceedings of the World Association for Cooperative Education (WACE) 17th World Conference on Cooperative & Work Integrated Education* (pp. 1-12). World Association for Cooperative Education, Inc.

McNeill, M., Gosper, M., & Xu, J. (2012). Assessment choices to target higher order learning outcomes: The power of academic empowerment. *Research in Learning Technology*, *20*, 20. doi:10.3402/rlt.v20i0.17595

Meglino, B. M., & Ravlin, E. C. (1998). Individual values in organizations: Concepts, controversies, and research. *Journal of Management*, *24*(3), 351–389. doi:10.1177/014920639802400304

Meißner, F., Weinmann, C., & Vowe, G. (2022). Understanding and Addressing Problems in Research Collaboration: A Qualitative interview study from a Self-Governance perspective. *Frontiers in Research Metrics and Analytics*, *6*, 778176. Advance online publication. doi:10.3389/frma.2021.778176 PMID:35224422

Mello, R., Suutari, V., & Dickmann, M. (2022). Taking Stock of Expatriates' Career Success After International Assignments: A Review and Future Research Agenda. *Human Resource Management Review*, 100913.

Melvin, B., Galles, J. A., & Lenz, J. G. (2012). Assessing career readiness in culturally and ethnically diverse populations. *Career Planning and Adult Development Journal*, *28*(1).

Meng, J., Kim, S., & Reber, B. H. (2022). Ethical challenges in an evolving digital communication era: Coping resources and ethics training in corporate communications. *Corporate Communications*, *27*(3), 581–594. doi:10.1108/CCIJ-11-2021-0128

Merino-Tejedor, E., Hontangas, P. M., & Petrides, K. V. (2018). Career adaptability mediates the effect of trait emotional intelligence on academic engagement. Revista de Psicodidáctica, *23*(2), 77–85. doi:10.1016/j.psicoe.2017.10.002

Merriam, S. B., & Tisdell, E. J. (2016). *Qualitative research: A guide to design and implementation*. Jossey-Bass.

Meshram, K., Paladino, A., & Cotronei-Baird, V. S. (2022). Don't Waste a Crisis: COVID-19 and Marketing Students' Self-Regulated Learning in the Online Environment. *Journal of Marketing Education*, *44*(2), 285–307. doi:10.1177/02734753211070561

Meyers, S. A. (2005). Part-time work and university students' success: A daily diary analysis. *Journal of Employment Counseling*, *42*(2), 74–83.

Middleton, D. (2020). The art museum as educator: A constructive study on African American youth. *Museum Management and Curatorship*, *35*(3), 220–234.

Midhat Ali, M., Qureshi, S. M., Memon, M. S., Mari, S. I., & Ramzan, M. B. (2021). Competency framework development for effective human resource management. *SAGE Open*, *11*(2), 21582440211006124. doi:10.1177/21582440211006124

Miller, A. (2004). *Mentoring Students and Young People: A Handbook of Effective Practice*. Taylor & Francis. doi:10.4324/9780203417188

Mirabela-Constanta, M., Maria-Madela, A., & Leonard-Calin, A. (2020). The Future of Work in the Post-Pandemic Era. Annals of the University of Oradea. *Economic Science Series*, *29*, 49–50.

Mooney, S. P., Sherman, M. F., & Lopresto, C. T. (1991). Academic locus of control, self-esteem, and perceived distance from home as predictors of college adjustment. *Journal of Counseling and Development*, *69*(5), 445–448. doi:10.1002/j.1556-6676.1991.tb01542.x

Morgan, C., Isaac, J. D., & Sansone, C. (2001). The role of interest in understanding the career choices of female and male college students. *Sex Roles*, *44*(5/6), 295–320. doi:10.1023/A:1010929600004

Morrison-Smith, S., & Ruiz, J. (2020). Challenges and barriers in virtual teams: A literature review. *SN Applied Sciences, 2*(6), 1096. Advance online publication. doi:10.1007/s42452-020-2801-5

Mostafa, B. A. (2021). *The effect of remote working on employees wellbeing and work-life integration during pandemic in Egypt.* Academic Press.

Murry, V. M., Bynum, M. S., Brody, G. H., Willert, A., & Stephens, D. (2001). African American single mothers and children in context: A review of studies on risk and resilience. *Clinical Child and Family Psychology Review, 4*(2), 133–155. doi:10.1023/A:1011381114782 PMID:11771793

Myers, M. D. (2020). *Qualitative Research in Business and Management.* SAGE.

Mykerezi, E., & Milis, B. F. (2008). The Wage Earnings Impact of Historically Black Colleges andUniversities. (cover story). *Southern Economic Journal, 75*(1), 173–187. doi:10.1002/j.2325-8012.2008.tb00897.x

Nägele, C., & Stalder, B. E. (2016b). Competence and the need for transferable skills. In Technical and vocational education and training (pp. 739–753). doi:10.1007/978-3-319-41713-4_34

Nair, C. S., Patil, A., & Mertova, P. (2009). Re-engineering graduate skills – a case study. *European Journal of Engineering Education, 34*(2), 131–139. doi:10.1080/03043790902829281

Nankervis, A., Baird, M., Coffey, J., & Shields, J. (2019). *Human resource management.* Cengage.

Nasri, N., Mohamad Nasri, N., & Abd Talib, M. A. (2023). Developing an inclusive curriculum: Understanding cocreation through cultural lens. *International Journal of Inclusive Education, 27*(9), 1072–1083. doi:10.1080/13603116.2021.1880652

National Center for Education Statistics. (2020). *Race/Ethnicity of College Faculty.* Author.

National Institute of Statistics. (2023). *Monthly average earning.* https://insse.ro/cms/ro/tags/comunicat-castig-salarial

Nayak, A. K., & Neill, J. T. (2016). The University Student Satisfaction and Time Management Questionnaire v.9. In *Time Management.* InTech. idl.isead.edu.es:8080/jspui/bitstream/10954/1767/1/9789535103356.pdf

Naylor, R., Bird, F. L., & Butler, N. E. (2021). Academic expectations among university students and staff: Addressing the role of psychological contracts and social norms. *Higher Education, 82*(5), 847–863. doi:10.1007/s10734-020-00668-2

Norman, M. V. (2008). Coping Strategies: A Case Study of an African-American Male. *Annals of the American Psychotherapy Association, 11*(3), 15–19.

Noveanu, E., & Potolea, D. (2016). *Education sciences. Encyclopedic Dictionary.* Sigma.

Núñez Pérez, J. C., Cerezo Menéndez, R., Bernardo Gutiérrez, A. B., Rosário, P. J. S. L. D. F., Valle Arias, A., Fernández Alba, M. E., & Suárez Fernández, N. (2011). Implementation of training programs in self-regulated learning strategies in Moodle format: Results of a experience in higher education. *Psicothema, 23,* 274–281. PMID:21504681

Nurius, P. S., & Kemp, S. P. (2019). Individual-Level Competencies for Team Collaboration with Cross-Disciplinary Researchers and Stakeholders. In Springer eBooks (pp. 171–187). doi:10.1007/978-3-030-20992-6_13

O'Connor, H., & Bodicoat, M. (2017). Exploitation or opportunity? Student perceptions of internships in enhancing employability skills. *British Journal of Sociology of Education, 38*(4), 435–449. doi:10.1080/01425692.2015.1113855

O'Connor, M. C., & Paunonen, S. V. (2007). Big Five personality predictors of post-secondary academic performance. *Personality and Individual Differences, 43*(5), 971–990. doi:10.1016/j.paid.2007.03.017

O'Neill, N. (2010). Internships as a high-impact practice: Some reflections on quality. *Peer Review : Emerging Trends and Key Debates in Undergraduate Education*, *12*(4), 4–9.

OCHA. (2021). *Year in Review 2021: Regional Office for Latin America and the Caribbean*. Regional Office for Latin America & the Caribbean.

OECD. (2015). *Skills for Social Progress: The Power of Social and Emotional Skills*. OECD. doi:10.1787/9789264226159-

Ogunlana, B. E. (2023). *The Career Success Formula: Proven Career Developmental Advice and Finding Rewarding Employment of Young Adults and College Graduates*. TCEC Publisher.

Olesen, K. B., Christensen, M. K., & O'Neill, L. D. (2020). What do we mean by "transferable skills"? A literature review of how the concept is conceptualized in undergraduate health sciences education. *Higher Education, Skills and Work-based Learning*, *11*(3), 616–634. doi:10.1108/HESWBL-01-2020-0012

Ordine, P., & Rose, G. (2015). Educational mismatch and unemployment scarring. *International Journal of Manpower*, *36*(5), 733–753. doi:10.1108/IJM-03-2013-0048

Organisation for Economic Co-operation and Development (OECD). (2019). *Talent Abroad: A Review of Romanian Emigrants*. OECD Publishing. doi:10.1787/bac53150-

Oruç, E., & Demirci, C. (2020). Foreign Language Anxiety and English Language Achievement in Higher Education: The Mediating Role of Student Engagement. *European Journal of Education Studies*, *7*(3), 199–212. https://zenodo.org/records/3756910

Osika, A., MacMahon, S., Lodge, J. M., & Carro, A. (2022). Emotions and learning: what role do emotions play in how and why students learn? *Times Higher Education*. https://www.timeshighereducation.com/campus/emotions-and-learning-what-role-do-emotions-play-how-and-why-students-learn

Osipow, S. H., & Fitzgerald, L. F. (1996). *Theories of Career Development*. Allyn and Bacon.

Owens, D., Lacey, K., Rawls, G., & Holbert-Quince, J. A. (2010). First-Generation African American Male College Students: Implications for Career Counselors. *The Career Development Quarterly*, *58*(4), 291–300. doi:10.1002/j.2161-0045.2010.tb00179.x

Palmer, R. T., Davis, R. J., & Maramba, D. C. (2010). Role of an HBCU in Supporting Academic Success for Underprepared Black Males. *Negro Educational Review*, *61*(1–4), 85–106.

Pandya, Patterson, & Ruhi. (2022). The readiness of workforce for the world of work in 2030: perceptions of university students. *International Journal of Business Performance Management*, *23*(1-2), 54-75.

Pan, Q., Zhou, J., Yang, D., Shi, D., Wang, D., Chen, X., & Liu, J. (2023). Mapping Knowledge Domain Analysis in Deep Learning Research of Global Education. *Sustainability (Basel)*, *15*(4), 3097. doi:10.3390/su15043097

Parker, S. K., & Grote, G. (2022). Automation, algorithms, and beyond: Why work design matters more than ever in a digital world. *Applied Psychology*, *71*(4), 1171–1204. doi:10.1111/apps.12241

Pascarella, E. T., Pierson, C. T., Wolniak, G. C., & Terenzini, P. T. (2004). First-generation college students: Additional evidence on college experiences and outcomes. *The Journal of Higher Education*, *75*(3), 249–284. doi:10.1080/00221546.2004.11772256

Patton, W., & McMahon, M. (2006). *Career development and system theory. Connecting theory and practice*. Sense Publishers. doi:10.1163/9789087903343

Patton, W., & McMahon, M. (2021). *Career Development and Systems Theory: Connecting Theory and Practice* (4th ed.). Brill. doi:10.1163/9789004466210

Peacock, M., Stewart, E. B., & Belcourt, M. (2020). *Understanding Human Resources Management: A Canadian Perspective*. Nelson Education Limited.

Pekrun, R., Frenzel, A. C., Goetz, T., & Perry, R. P. (2007). The control-value theory of achievement emotions: An integrative approach to emotions in education. In P. A. Schutz & R. Pekrun (Eds.), *Emotion in education* (pp. 13–36). Elsevier Academic Press., doi:10.1016/B978-012372545-5/50003-4

Pekrun, R., & Stephens, E. J. (2012). Academic emotions. In K. R. Harris, S. Graham, T. Urdan, S. Graham, J. M. Royer, & M. Zeidner (Eds.), APA educational psychology handbook: Vol. 2. *Individual differences and cultural and contextual factors* (pp. 3–31). American Psychological Association. doi:10.1037/13274-001

Peltier, J. W., Chennamaneni, P. R., & Barber, K. N. (2022). Student anxiety, preparation, and learning framework for responding to external crises: The moderating role of self-efficacy as a coping mechanism. *Journal of Marketing Education*, *44*(2), 149–165. doi:10.1177/02734753211036500

Peteet, B. J., Montgomery, L., & Weekes, J. C. (2015). Predictors of Imposter Phenomenon among Talented Ethnic Minority Undergraduate Students. *The Journal of Negro Education*, *84*(2), 175–186. doi:10.7709/jnegroeducation.84.2.0175

Ployhart, R. E., Ziegert, J. C., & McFarland, L. A. (2003). Understanding racial differences on cognitive ability tests in selection contexts: An integration of stereotype threat and applicant reactions research. *Human Performance*, *16*(3), 231–259. doi:10.1207/S15327043HUP1603_4

Poláková, M., Suleimanová, J. H., Madzík, P., Copuš, L., Molnárová, I., & Polednová, J. (2023). Soft skills and their importance in the labour market under the conditions of Industry 5.0. *Heliyon*, *9*(8), e18670. doi:10.1016/j.heliyon.2023.e18670 PMID:37593611

Popadiuk, N. E., & Arthur, N. M. (2014). Key relationships for international student university-to-work transitions. *Journal of Career Development*, *41*(2), 122–140. doi:10.1177/0894845313481851

Pordelan, N., Sadeghi, A., Abedi, M. R., & Kaedi, M. (2020). Promoting Student Career Decision-Making Self-Efficacy: An Online Intervention. *Education and Information Technologies*, *25*(2), 985–996. doi:10.1007/s10639-019-10003-7

Poropat, A. E. (2016). Beyond the shadow: The role of personality and temperament in learning. In L. Corno & E. M. Anderman (Eds.), Handbook of educational psychology (pp. 172–185). Routledge/Taylor & Francis Group.

Poropat, A. E. (2014). Other-rated personality and academic performance: Evidence and implications. *Learning and Individual Differences*, *34*, 24–32. doi:10.1016/j.lindif.2014.05.013

Pouyaud, J., Vignoli, E., Dosnon, O., & Lallemand, N. (2012). Career adapt-abilities scale-France form: Psychometric properties and relationships to anxiety and motivation. *Journal of Vocational Behavior*, *80*(3), 692–697. doi:10.1016/j.jvb.2012.01.021

Pretorius, L., Bailey, C., & Miles, M. (2013). CA and the Research Skills Development Framework: Using Theory to Practically Align Graduate Attributes, Learning Experiences, and Assessment Tasks in Undergraduate Midwifery. *International Journal on Teaching and Learning in Higher Education*, *25*(3), 378–387.

Pripoaie, R., Crețu, C., Turtureanu, A. G., Sîrbu, C., Marinescu, E. Ș., Talaghir, L., Chițu, F., & Robu, D. M. (2022). A Statistical analysis of the migration process: A Case study—Romania. *Sustainability (Basel)*, *14*(5), 2784. doi:10.3390/su14052784

Pryor, R., & Bright, J. (2011). *The Chaos Theory of Careers: A New Perspective on Working in the Twenty-First Century.* Taylor & Francis. doi:10.4324/9780203871461

Purohit, D., & Jayswal, R. (2022). Developing and Validating Protean and Boundaryless Career Scale for College Passing Out Students. *European Journal of Training and Development.* . doi:10.1108/EJTD-07-2021-0115

Quinlan, K. M., & Renninger, K. A. (2022). Rethinking Employability: How Students Build on Interest in a Subject to Plan a Career. *Higher Education, 84*(4), 863–883. doi:10.1007/s10734-021-00804-6

Ragins, B. R., & Cotton, J. L. (1999). Mentor functions and outcomes: A comparison of men and women in formal and informal mentoring relationships. *The Journal of Applied Psychology, 84*(4), 529–550. doi:10.1037/0021-9010.84.4.529 PMID:10504893

Raj, V., Hardik, P., Puranik, P. S., & Acharya, G. D. (2015). *Engineering Graduates Competence and Employability.* Academic Press.

Rakhmanova, M., & Meylieva, M. (2021). Socio-Psychological Features of the Formation of a System of Attitudes to Career Choice in Adolescents. *Indiana Journal of Humanities and Social Sciences, 2*(12), 4–7.

Ramsden, P. (2003). *Learning to teach in higher education.* Routledge. doi:10.4324/9780203507711

Ramsden, P., Beswick, D. G., & Bowden, J. A. (1986). Effects Of Learning-Skills Interventions On 1st Year University-Students Learning. *Human Learning, 5*(3), 151–164.

Reifman, A., Arnett, J. J., & Colwell, M. J. (2007). Emerging adulthood: Theory, assessment, and application. *Journal of Youth Development, 2*(1), Article 0701FA003. https://www.nae4ha.org/ directory/ jyd/index.html

Reshma, P. S., Aithal, P. S., & Acharya, S. (2015). An empirical study on Working from Home: A popular e-business model. *International Journal of Advance & Innovative Research, 2*(2).

Rhee, H., Han, J., Lee, M., & Choi, Y. W. (2020). Effects of interdisciplinary courses on future engineers' competency. Higher Education. *Skills and Work-Based Learning, 10*(3), 467–479. doi:10.1108/HESWBL-05-2019-0071

Richiteanu-Nastase, E. R. (2011). *Modalități de realizare a consilierii pentru carieră a studenților* [Doctoral dissertation]. Universitatea din Bucuresti. https://www.scribd.com/doc/138482571/Rezumat-Ramona-Stoiculescu-c-richiteanu-Nastase

Richiteanu-Nastase, E. R., Cace, C., & Staiculescu, C. (2012). E-learning about self-career. An analysis of Romanian e-counselling services. *The International Scientific Conference eLearning and Software for Education, Carol I" National Defence University, 1,* 282-288. https://www.ceeol.com/search/article-detail?id=41722

Richiteanu-Nastase, E.R. (2019*) Consiliere și orientare pentru carieră și viață Fundamente teoretice și metodologice.* Editura ASE.

Richiteanu-Nastase, E. R., & Staiculescu, C. (2015). The impact of career factors on students' professional insertion. What measures are to be taken by the university? *Procedia: Social and Behavioral Sciences, 180,* 1102–1108. doi:10.1016/j.sbspro.2015.02.216

Rivera, L. A. (2011). Ivies, extracurriculars, and exclusion: Elite employers' use of educational credentials. *Research in Social Stratification and Mobility, 29*(1), 71–90. doi:10.1016/j.rssm.2010.12.001

Roberts, B. W., Kuncel, N. R., Shiner, R. L., Caspi, A., & Goldberg, L. R. (2007). The Power of Personality: The comparative validity of personality traits, socioeconomic status, and cognitive ability for predicting important life outcomes. *Perspectives on Psychological Science, 2*(4), 313–345. doi:10.1111/j.1745-6916.2007.00047.x PMID:26151971

Roberts, L. (2016). Addressing the lack of diversity in museums: The role of museum studies programs. *American Studies (Lawrence, Kan.), 54*(4), 123–143.

Robertson, P. J., Hooley, T., & McCash, P. (2021). *The Oxford Handbook of Career Development*. Oxford University Press.

Rose, G. (1997). Situating knowledges: Positionality, reflexivities and other tactics. *Progress in Human Geography, 21*(3), 305–320. doi:10.1191/030913297673302122

Rosenberger, A. (2021). The Impostor Phenomenon. *ITA Journal, 49*(2), 24–26.

Rothwell, W. J., Benscoter, B., King, R., & King, S. (2008). *Beyond training: The rise of learning and performance support*. Human Resource Development Press.

Rottinghaus, P. J., Day, S. X., & Borgen, F. H. (2005). The Career Futures Inventory: A Measure of Career-Related Adaptability and Optimism. *Journal of Career Assessment, 13*(1), 3–24. doi:10.1177/1069072704270271

Rowley-Jolivet, E. (2002). Science in the making: Scientific conference presentations and the construction of facts. In E. Ventola, C. Shalom, & S. Thompson (Eds.), *The language of conferencing* (pp. 95–125). Peter Lang.

Rowley-Jolivet, E., & Carter-Thomas, S. (2005). The rhetoric of conference presentation introductions: Context, argument, and interaction. *International Journal of Applied Linguistics, 15*(1), 45–70. doi:10.1111/j.1473-4192.2005.00080.x

Rubio-Alcalá, F. D. (2017). The Links between Self-Esteem and Language Anxiety and Implications for the Classroom. In C. Gkonou, M. Daubney, & J.-M. Dewaele (Eds.), *New Insights into Language Anxiety: Theory, Research, and Educational Implications* (pp. 198–206). Multilingual Matters. doi:10.21832/9781783097722-012

Rudolph, C. W., Lavigne, K. N., & Zacher, N. (2017). Career adaptability: A meta-analysis of relationships with measures of adaptivity, adapting responses, and adaptation results. *Journal of Vocational Behavior, 98*, 17–34. doi:10.1016/j.jvb.2016.09.002

Rusu, S., Maricuțoiu, L. P., Macsinga, I., Vîrgă, D., & Sava, F. A. (2019). Evaluarea personalității din perspectiva modelului Big Five. Date privind adaptarea chestionarului IPIP-50 pe un eșantion de studenți români. *Psihologia Resurselor Umane, 10*(1), 39–56. https://www.hrp-journal.com/index.php/pru/article/view/148/152

Sáiz-Manzanares, M.-C., Casanova, J.-R., Lencastre, J.-A., Almeida, L., & Martín-Antón, L.-J. (2022). Satisfacción de los estudiantes con la docencia online en tiempos de COVID-19. *Comunicar., 30*(70), 35–45. doi:10.3916/C70-2022-03

Saldaña, J. (2014). *Ethnodrama: An anthology of reality theatre*. Rowman & Littlefield.

Salisbury, M. H., Pascarella, E. T., Padgett, R. D., & Blaich, C. (2012). The effects of work on leadership development among first-year college students. *Journal of College Student Development, 53*(2), 300–324. doi:10.1353/csd.2012.0021

Salleh, N. M., Prikshat, V., Nankervis, A., & Burgess, J. (2017). Undergraduate Career-Readiness Challenges in Malaysia. *World Applied Sciences Journal, 35*(12), 2659–2664.

Samis, P. S., & Michaelson, M. (2017). *Creating the visitor-centered museum*. Routledge.

Sanahuja Vélez, G., & Ribes Giner, G. (2015). Effects of business internships on students, employers, and higher education institutions: A systematic review. *Journal of Employment Counseling, 52*(3), 121–130. doi:10.1002/joec.12010

Sangster, C. (2017). *Planning and Organizing Personal and Professional Development*. Taylor & Francis. doi:10.4324/9781315246734

Satyam & Aithal, R. K. (2022). Reimagining an Experiential Learning Exercise in Times of Crisis: Lessons Learned and a Proposed Framework. *Journal of Marketing Education*.

Savickas, M. L. (2005). The theory and practice of career construction. In R.W. Lent & S.D. Brown (Eds.), Career development and counseling: Putting theory and research to work. (pp. 42–70). John Wiley & Sons, Inc.

Savickas, M. L. (1997). Career adaptability: An integrative construct for life-span, life-space theory. *The Career Development Quarterly*, *45*(3), 247–259. doi:10.1002/j.2161-0045.1997.tb00469.x

Savickas, M. L. (2013). Career construction theory and practice. In S. D. Brown & R. W. Lent (Eds.), *Career development and counseling: Putting theory and research to work*. John Wiley & Sons, Inc.

Savickas, M. L., & Porfeli, E. J. (2012). Career Adapt-Abilities Scale: Construction, reliability, and measurement equivalence across 13 countries. *Journal of Vocational Behavior*, *80*(3), 661–673. doi:10.1016/j.jvb.2012.01.011

Schein, E. H. (2010). Career Anchors for Leaders. In F. Bournois, J. Duval-Hamel, S. Roussillon, & J. L. Scaringella (Eds.), *Handbook of Top Management Teams* (pp. 126–133). Palgrave Macmillan. doi:10.1057/9780230305335_14

Schermerhorn, J. R., & Bachrach, D. G. (2017). *Exploring Management*. Wiley Publications.

Scully-Russ, E., & Torraco, R. (2020). The Changing Nature and Organization of Work: An Integrative Review of Literature. *Human Resource Development Review*, *19*(1), 66–93. doi:10.1177/1534484319886394

Shan, Y. (2020). Whether successful language learners require intrinsic motivation. *Open Journal of Modern Linguistics*, *10*(05), 549–559. doi:10.4236/ojml.2020.105031

Shapiro, D., Dundar, A., Wakhungu, P. K., Yuan, X., Nathan, A., & Hwang, Y. (2015). Deficit or advantage? The role of federal work-study participation in student outcomes. *ASHE Conference*, 40.

Shepard, L. (2015). Measuring the impact of work-study participation on post-college earnings. *The Annals of the American Academy of Political and Social Science*, *657*(1), 160–179.

Shepperd, L. (2021). *Foreign languages: skills in the workforce*. UK Parliament. House of Lords Library. https://lordslibrary.parliament.uk/foreign-languages-skills-in-the-workforce/

Sheu, H., & Bin, L. (2010). Testing the choice model of social cognitive career theory across Holland themes: A meta-analytic path analysis. *Journal of Vocational Behavior*, *76*(2), 252–264. doi:10.1016/j.jvb.2009.10.015

Shin, Y.-J., & Lee, J.-Y. (2019). Self-Focused Attention and Career Anxiety: The Mediating Role of Career Adaptability. *The Career Development Quarterly*, *67*(2), 110–125. doi:10.1002/cdq.12175

Shonk, K. (2023, March 24). *How to Handle Conflict in Teams: Lessons from Scientific Collaborations*. PON - Program on Negotiation at Harvard Law School. https://www.pon.harvard.edu/daily/conflict-resolution/how-to-handle-conflict-in-teams-lessons-from-scientific-collaborations/

Shorette, C. R. II, & Palmer, R. T. (2015). Historically Black Colleges and Universities (HBCUs): Critical Facilitators of Non-Cognitive Skills for Black Males. *The Western Journal of Black Studies*, *39*(1), 18–29.

Shriver, L. H. (2018). Work-study students and the labor market: Do they experience improved employment outcomes? *Journal of College Student Development*, *59*(4), 471–476.

Shumaker, R., & Wood, J. L. (2016). *Understanding First- Generation Community College*. Academic Press.

Siddiqui, S., & Ahamed, M. (2020). Teachers' Roles Beyond and Within the Context: An Ever-Changing Concept. *Arab World English Journal*, *11*(1), 282–296. doi:10.24093/awej/vol11no1.21

Sidiropoulou-Dimakakou, D., Mikedaki, K., Argyropoulou, K., & Kaliris, A. (2018). A Psychometric Analysis of the Greek Career Adapt-Abilities Scale in University Students. *International Journal of Psychological Studies, 10*(3), 95–108. doi:10.5539/ijps.v10n3p95

Silva, P., Lopes, B., Costa, M., Melo, A. I., Dias, G. P., Brito, E., & Seabra, D. (2018). The million-dollar question: Can internships boost employment? *Studies in Higher Education, 43*(1), 2–21. doi:10.1080/03075079.2016.1144181

Simon, M., & Atkins, J.R. (2011). *The participatory museum.* Museum 2.0.

Simon, N. (2016). *The art of relevance.* Museum 2.0.

Simpson, A. (2019). Why academic museums matter: Four frameworks for considering their value. *University Museums and Collections Journal, 11*(2), 196–202.

Sinche, M., Layton, R. L., Brandt, P. D., O'Connell, A. B., Hall, J. D., Freeman, A. M., Harrell, J. R., Cook, J. G., & Brennwald, P. (2017). An evidence-based evaluation of transferrable skills and job satisfaction for science PhDs. *PLoS One, 12*(9), e0185023. doi:10.1371/journal.pone.0185023 PMID:28931079

Sinnaiah, T., Adam, S., & Mahadi, B. (2023). A strategic management process: The role of decision-making style and organizational performance. *Journal of Work-Applied Management, 15*(1), 37–50. doi:10.1108/JWAM-10-2022-0074

Snow, K., Wardley, L., Carter, L., & Maher, P. (2019). Lived experiences of online and experiential learning in four undergraduate professional programs. *Collected Essays on Learning and Teaching, 12*, 79–93. doi:10.22329/celt.v12i0.5388

Soft vs. hard skills: Know the difference. (2022). *Administrative Professional Today, 48*(2), 4.

Spady, W. G. (1994). *Outcome-Based Education: Critical Issues and Answers.* American Association of School Administrators.

Spady, W. G. (1995, June 1). *Outcome-Based Education: Critical Issues and Answers.* https://doi.org/doi:10.1604/9780614251012

Stamov Roßnagel, C., Fitzallen, N., & Lo Baido, K. (2021). CA and the learning experience: Relationships with student motivation and perceived learning demands. *Higher Education Research & Development, 40*(4), 838–851. doi:10.1080/07294360.2020.1787956

Stamov Roßnagel, C., Lo Baido, K., & Fitzallen, N. (2021). Revisiting the relationship between CA and learning approaches: A perceived alignment perspective. *PLoS One, 16*(8), e0253949. doi:10.1371/journal.pone.0253949 PMID:34428210

Stebleton, M. J., & Kaler, L. S. (2020). Preparing college students for the end of work: The role of meaning. *Journal of College and Character, 21*(2), 132–139. doi:10.1080/2194587X.2020.1741396

Stebleton, M. J., Kaler, L. S., Diamond, K. K., & Lee, C. (2020). Examining career readiness in a liberal arts undergraduate career planning course. *Journal of Employment Counseling, 57*(1), 14–26. doi:10.1002/joec.12135

Steindórsdóttir, B. D., Sanders, K., Arnulf, J. K., & Dysvik, A. (2023). Career transitions and career success from a lifespan developmental perspective: A 15-year longitudinal study. *Journal of Vocational Behavior, 140*, 103809. doi:10.1016/j.jvb.2022.103809

Stepanova, O., Polk, M., & Saldert, H. (2019). Understanding mechanisms of conflict resolution beyond collaboration: An interdisciplinary typology of knowledge types and their integration in practice. *Sustainability Science, 15*(1), 263–279. doi:10.1007/s11625-019-00690-z

Steup, M., & Neta, R. (2020). Epistemology. *Stanford Encyclopedia of Philosophy.* https://plato.stanford.edu/entries/epistemology/

Stoner, G., & Milner, M. (2010). Embedding generic employability skills in an accounting degree: Development and impediments. *Accounting Education*, *19*(1-2), 123–138. doi:10.1080/09639280902888229

Storme, M., Çelik, P., & Myszkowski, N. (2020). A forgotten antecedent of career adaptability: A study on the predictive role of within-person variability in personality. *Personality and Individual Differences*, *160*(1), 109936. doi:10.1016/j.paid.2020.109936

Students: An Analysis of Covariance Examining Use of, Access to, and Efficacy Regarding Institutionally Offered Services. (n.d.). *Community College Enterprise, 22*(2), 9–17.

Suleiman, A., & Abahre, J. (2020). Essential competencies for engineers from the perspective of fresh graduates. *Engineering Management in Production and Services*, *12*(1), 70–79. doi:10.2478/emj-2020-0006

Sultana, R., & Malike, O. F. (2019). Is Protean Career Attitude Beneficial for Both Employees and Organizations? Investigating the Mediating Effects of Knowing Career Competencies. *Frontiers in Psychology*, *10*, 1284. doi:10.3389/fpsyg.2019.01284 PMID:31214088

Sung, S., Alon, L., Cho, J. Y., & Kizilcec, R. (2022). How to Assess Student Learning in Information Science: Exploratory Evidence from Large College Courses. *Proceedings of the Association for Information Science and Technology*, *59*(1), 500–504. doi:10.1002/pra2.659

Sun, R., & Shek, D. T. L. (2012). Student Classroom Misbehavior: An exploratory study based on teachers' perceptions. *TheScientificWorldJournal*, *2012*, 1–8. doi:10.1100/2012/208907 PMID:22919297

Super, D. E. (1980). A life-span, life-space approach to career development. *Journal of Vocational Behavior*, *16*(3), 282–298. doi:10.1016/0001-8791(80)90056-1

Swales, J. M. (2004). *Research genres: Exploration and applications*. Cambridge University Press. doi:10.1017/CBO9781139524827

Swanson, J. L., & Fouad, N. A. (1999). *Career theory and practice: learning through case studies*. Sense Publishers.

Swanson, J. L., & Fouad, N. A. (2009). *Career Theory and Practice: Learning Through Case Studies*. SAGE Publications.

Taber, B. J., & Blankemeyer, M. (2015). Future work self and career adaptability in the prediction of proactive career behaviors. *Journal of Vocational Behavior*, *86*, 20–27. doi:10.1016/j.jvb.2014.10.005

Takahashi, A. (2008). Learners' Self-perception of English Ability: Its relationships with English language anxiety and strength of motivation for learning the language. *Departemental Bulletin Paper,* (1), 57-69. https://niigata-u.repo.nii.ac.jp/records/27414

Takahashi, A. (2009). Self-perception of English Ability: Is it related to proficiency and/or class performance? *Psychology.* https://www.semanticscholar.org/paper/Self-perception-of-English-Ability%3A-Is-it-related-Takahashi-%E9%AB%98%E6%A9%8B/98ed59be9cf961fa46ca4846b2569044e2f1f396

Tan, L. M., Laswad, F., & Chua, F. (2022). Bridging the Employability Skills Gap: Going Beyond Classroom Walls. *Pacific Accounting Review*, *34*(2), 225–248. doi:10.1108/PAR-04-2021-0050

Taylor, Z. E., Larsen-Rife, D., Conger, R. D., Widaman, K. F., & Cutrona, C. E. (2010). Life stress, maternal optimism, and adolescent competence in single mother, African American families. *Journal of Family Psychology, 24*(4), 468–477.

Teichler, U. (2009). *Higher Education and the World of Work: Conceptual Frameworks, Comparative Perspectives, Empirical Findings*. Sense Publishers. doi:10.1163/9789087907563

The Adecco Group. (2022). *Guidebook for investors in Romania*. http://investromania.gov.ro/web/wp-content/uploads/2022/11/Guidebook-for-investors-nov.2022.compressed.pdf

Tipton, D. J. (2015). *Personal and Professional Growth for Health Care Professionals*. Jones & Bartlett Learning, LLC.

Toldson, I. A. (2014). Myths Versus Realities. *Crisis, 121*(4), 12–17.

Tolentino, L. R., Garcia, P. R. J. M., Lu, V. N., Restubog, S. L. D., Bordia, P., & Plewa, C. (2014). Career adaptation: The relation of adaptability to goal orientation, proactive personality, and career optimism. *Journal of Vocational Behavior, 84*(1), 39–48. doi:10.1016/j.jvb.2013.11.004

Toth, E. L. (2010). Federal Work-Study employment and college students' success. *Review of Higher Education, 33*(3), 399–425.

Tracey, T. J., & Sedlacek, W. E. (1984). Factor structure of the Career Factors Inventory. *Journal of Counseling Psychology, 31*(2), 209–212.

Trading Economics. (2023). *European Union - Employment rates of recent graduates - 2023 Data 2024 Forecast 2006-2022 Historical*. https://tradingeconomics.com/european-union/employment-rates-of-recent-graduates-eurostat-data.html

Transilvania University of Brasov. (2023). *Regulation on students' professional activity*. https://www.unitbv.ro/documente/despre-unitbv/regulamente-hotarari/regulamentele-universitatii/studenti/Regulament_activitate_profesionala_a_studentilor_2023-2024_22.05.2023.pdf

Treleaven, L., & Voola, R. (2008). Integrating the development of graduate attributes through CA. *Journal of Marketing Education, 30*(2), 160–173. doi:10.1177/0273475308319352

Trends, M. (2024). *World Youth Unemployment Rate 1991 – 2024*. Macro Trends. https://www.macrotrends.net/global-metrics/countries/WLD/world/youth-unemployment-rate

Tripathy, M. (2020). Relevance of soft skills in career success. *MIER Journal of Educational Studies Trends and Practices*, 91-102.

Tudor, I. (2009). Promoting language learning in European higher education: An overview of strategies. *European Journal of Language Policy, 1*(2), 188–205. link.gale.com/apps/doc/A243358479/AONE?u=anon~30fa6f62&sid=googleScholar&xid=7ca6bfb8

Turnea, E.-S. (2021). Organizational Rewards in the Online Work Environment. Is There Any Chance of Full Accomplishment? Ovidius University Annals. *Series Economic Sciences, 21*(1), 434–438.

Turner, J. E., & Waugh, R. M. (2007). A dynamical systems perspective regarding students' learning processes: Shame reactions and emergent self-organizations. In P. A. Schutz & R. Pekrun (Eds.), *Emotion in education* (pp. 125–145). Elsevier Academic Press. doi:10.1016/B978-012372545-5/50009-5

U.S. Census Bureau. (2006). *Current population survey: America's families and living arrangements*. Retrieved from www.census.gov/population/www/socdemo/hh-fam/cps2006.html

Uber Grosse, Ch. (2004). The Competitive Advantage of Foreign Languages and Cultural Knowledge. *Modern Language Journal, 88*(3), 351–373. doi:10.1111/j.0026-7902.2004.00234.x

UCL. (n.d.). What we Mean by Co-Creation. *UCL ChangeMakers*. https://www.ucl.ac.uk/changemakers/what-we-mean-co-creation

UNESCO. (2002). *Handbook on career counseling. A practical manual for developing, implementing, and assessing career counseling services in higher education settings*. UNESCO. https://unesdoc.unesco.org/images/0012/001257/125740e.pdf

*Compilation of References*

Üstünlüoğlu, E. (2013). Understanding misbehavior at university level: Lecturer perceptions from the US and Turkey. *Education in Science*, *38*(169), 224–235.

Valiente-Riedl, E., Anderson, L., & Banki, S. (2021). Practicing What We Teach: Experiential Learning in Higher Education That Cuts Both Ways. *Review of Education, Pedagogy & Cultural Studies*, *44*(3), 231–25. doi:10.1080/10714413.2021.1985372

Van Buren, H. J. III. (2003). Boundaryless Careers and Employability Obligations. *Business Ethics Quarterly*, *13*(2), 131–149. doi:10.5840/beq20031329

van Rooij, E. C. M., Jansen, E. P. W. A., & van de Grift, W. J. C. M. (2018). First-year university students' academic success: The importance of academic adjustment [Correction]. *European Journal of Psychology of Education*, *33*(4), 769. doi:10.1007/s10212-017-0364-7

Van Rossum, E. J., & Schenk, S. M. (1984). The relationship between learning conception, study strategy and learning outcome. *The British Journal of Educational Psychology*, *54*(1), 73–83. doi:10.1111/j.2044-8279.1984.tb00846.x

VanMaaren, R. L., & Hooley, T. (2018). 'He is always in my corner': Mentorship support for career development. *Journal of Vocational Behavior*, *105*, 1–11.

Varghese, M. E., Parker, L. C., Adedokun, O., Shively, M., Burgess, W., Childress, A., & Bessenbacher, A. (2012). Experiential internships: Understanding the process of student learning in small business internships. *Industry and Higher Education*, *26*(5), 357–367. doi:10.5367/ihe.2012.0114

Vecchione, M., Alessandri, G., & Marsicano, G. (2014). Academic motivation predicts educational attainment: Does gender make a difference? *Learning and Individual Differences*, *32*, 124–131. doi:10.1016/j.lindif.2014.01.003

Velez, W., & Gray, D. E. (2019). Collaborative social class transitioning: Navigating higher education with intersectionality. *Journal of College Student Development*, *60*(3), 375–394.

Ventola, E. (1999). Semiotic spanning at conferences: Cohesion and coherence in and across conference papers and their discussions. In W. Bublitz, U. Lenk, & E. Ventola (Eds.), *Coherence in spoken and written discourse* (pp. 101–123). John Benjamins. doi:10.1075/pbns.63.09ven

Ventola, E., Shalom, C., & Thompson, S. (2002). *The language of conferencing*. Peter Lang.

Vigoda-Gadot, E., Grimland, S., & Shoham, A. (2017). The effect of internships on students' career aspirations. *Journal of Education for Business*, *92*(5), 221–230.

Villarreal, A., Broido, E. M., & Moore, K. B. (2016). Student outcomes of co-curricular involvement: The role of gender, class level, and pre-college experiences. *Journal of College Student Development*, *57*(4), 411–427.

Villeneuve, P. (2008). *From periphery to center: Art museum education in the 21st century*. National Art Education Association.

Villeneuve, P., & Love, A. R. (2017). *Visitor-centered exhibitions and edu-curation in art museums*. Rowman and Littlefield.

Virolainen, M. H., Stenström, M. L., & Kantola, M. (2011). The views of employers on internships as a means of learning from work experience in higher education. *Journal of Vocational Education and Training*, *63*(3), 465–484. doi:10.1080/13636820.2011.580360

Vogel, A. L., Knebel, A. R., Faupel-Badger, J. M., Portilla, L., & Simeonov, A. (2021). A systems approach to enable effective team science from the internal research program of the National Center for Advancing Translational Sciences. *Journal of Clinical and Translational Science*, *5*(1), e163. Advance online publication. doi:10.1017/cts.2021.811 PMID:34527302

Vulperhorst, J. P., van de Rijst, R. M., & Akkerman, S. F. (2020). Dynamics in Higher Education Choice: Weighing One's Interests in Light of Available Programmes. *Higher Education*, *79*(6), 1001–1021. doi:10.1007/s10734-019-00452-x

Wagner, L., & Ruch, W. (2015). Good character at school: Positive classroom behavior mediates the link between character strengths and school achievement. *Frontiers in Psychology*, *6*. Advance online publication. doi:10.3389/fpsyg.2015.00610 PMID:26029144

Walker, A., & Leary, H. (2009). A problem based learning meta analysis: Differences across problem types, implementation types, disciplines, and assessment levels. *The Interdisciplinary Journal of Problem-Based Learning*, *3*(1), 6. doi:10.7771/1541-5015.1061

Walker, B., Bair, A. R., & Macdonald, R. H. (2022). Supporting students' career development: A call to action. *New Directions for Community Colleges*, *2022*(199), 93–106. doi:10.1002/cc.20526

Wang, H., Xu, L., & Li, J. (2023). Connecting foreign language enjoyment and English proficiency levels: The mediating role of L2 motivation. *Frontiers in Psychology*, *14*, 1054657. Advance online publication. doi:10.3389/fpsyg.2023.1054657 PMID:36844295

Wang, Q., & Xue, M. C. (2022). The implications of expectancy-value theory of motivation in language education. *Frontiers in Psychology*, *13*, 992372. Advance online publication. doi:10.3389/fpsyg.2022.992372 PMID:36425822

Wang, X., & Zhang, W. (2021). Psychological anxiety of college students' foreign language learning in online course. *Frontiers in Psychology*, *12*, 598992. Advance online publication. doi:10.3389/fpsyg.2021.598992 PMID:34122211

Wang, Y., Niu, W., & Lent, R. W. (2022). Social cognitive career theory. In P. Robertson, T. Hooley, & P. McCash (Eds.), *The Oxford Handbook of Career Development* (pp. 51–66). Oxford University Press.

Wats, R. K., & Wats, M. (2009). Developing Soft Skills in Students. *International Journal of Learning*, *15*(12), 1–10. doi:10.18848/1447-9494/CGP/v15i12/46032

Weeden, K., Reed, D., & Espinoza, A. (2019). Internship participation, high-impact educational practices, and student learning. *The Journal of Higher Education*, *90*(3), 348–374.

Weil, S. E. (1999). From being about something to being for somebody: The ongoing transformation of the American museum. *Daedalus*, *128*(3), 229–258.

Weimer, M. (2013). *Learner-centered teaching: Five key changes to practice*. John Wiley & Sons.

Whitley, D. M., & Fuller-Thomson, E. (2017). African-American Solo Grandparents Raising Grandchildren: A Representative Profile of Their Health Status. *Journal of Community Health*, *42*(2), 312–323. doi:10.1007/s10900-016-0257-8 PMID:27651164

Wiernik, B. M., & Kostal, J. W. (2019). Protean and Boundaryless Career Orientations: A Critical Review and Meta-Analysis. *Journal of Counseling Psychology*, *66*(3), 280–307. doi:10.1037/cou0000324 PMID:30777774

Wigfield, A., & Eccles, J. S. (2020). 35 years of research on students' subjective task values and motivation: A look back and a look forward. *Advances in Motivation Science*. doi:10.1016/bs.adms.2019.05.002

Wilczewski, M., & Alon, I. (2022). Language and communication in international students' adaptation: A bibliometric and content analysis review. *Higher Education*, *85*(6), 1235–1256. doi:10.1007/s10734-022-00888-8 PMID:35855684

Williams, M. K. (2017). John Dewey in the 21st Century. *Journal of Inquiry and Action in Education*, *9*(1), 91–101.

Wood, J. L., Harrison, J. D., & Jones, T. K. (2016). Black Males' Perceptions of the Work–College Balance. *Journal of Men's Studies*, *24*(3), 326–343. doi:10.1177/1060826515624378

Wood, L., & Louw, I. (2018). Reconsidering Postgraduate "Supervision" from a Participatory Action Learning and Action Research Approach. *South African Journal of Higher Education*, *32*(4), 284–297. doi:10.20853/32-4-2562

World Economic Forum. (2020). *The future of jobs report 2020*. Author.

World Economic Forum. (2022). *Centre for the New Economy and Society Accenture (Firm). Jobs of tomorrow: the triple returns of social jobs in the economic recovery*. World Economic Forum.

World Economic Forum. (2022, Jan 18). *5 forces driving the new world of work*. https://www.weforum.org/agenda/2022/01/the-5-forces-driving-the-new-world-of-work/

Wulff, S., Swales, J. M., & Keller, K. (2009). "We have about seven minutes for questions": The discussion section from a specialized conference. *English for Specific Purposes*, *28*(2), 79–92. doi:10.1016/j.esp.2008.11.002

Xing, S. (2022). Ethical Conflict and Knowledge Hiding in Teams: The moderating role of workplace friendship in the Education sector. Frontiers in Psychology, 13. doi:10.3389/fpsyg.2022.824485

Xu, M., David, J. M., & Kim, S. H. (2018). The fourth industrial revolution: Opportunities and challenges. *International Journal of Financial Research, 9*(2), 90-95.

Xu, S., Van Hoof, H., & Nyheim, P. (2018). The effect of online scheduling on employees' quality of life. *Journal of Foodservice Business Research*, *21*(2), 172–186. doi:10.1080/15378020.2017.1364592

Yates, M. S. (2017). *Internships: Theory and practice*. Routledge.

Yavuz, O. (2019). A Quantitative Exploration of Students' Mindsets and Behaviors: A Whole Child Academic, Emotional, and Career Development. *International Journal of Educational Reform*, *28*(4), 319–347. doi:10.1177/1056787919856735

Young, M. R. (2002). Experiential learning= hands-on+ minds-on. *Marketing Education Review*, *12*(1), 43–51. doi:10.1080/10528008.2002.11488770

Younus, A. M. (2021). Technological Advancement and Economic Growth for The Business Sector. *Academic Journal of Digital Economics and Stability*, *10*, 56–62.

Yu, C. (2022). An autoethnography of an international English language teaching assistant's identity paradoxes in an EFL context. *International Journal of Qualitative Studies in Education*. doi:10.1080/09518398.2022.2061624

Yuen, M., Zhang, J., Man, P. K. W., Mak, J., Chung, Y. B., Lee, Q. A. Y., Chan, A. K. C., So, A., & Chan, R. T. H. (2022). A strengths-based longitudinal career intervention for junior secondary school students with special educational needs: A mixed-method evaluation. *Applied Research in Quality of Life*, *17*(4), 2229–2250. doi:10.1007/s11482-021-10028-6 PMID:35035601

Yu, H., Mckinney, L., & Carales, V. D. (2020). Do community college students benefit from Federal Work-study participation? *Teachers College Record*, *122*(1), 1–36. doi:10.1177/016146812012200111

Zacher, H. (2014). Career adaptability predicts subjective career success above and beyond personality traits and core self-evaluations. *Journal of Vocational Behavior*, *84*(1), 21–30. doi:10.1016/j.jvb.2013.10.002

Zafar, B. (2013). College major choice and the gender earnings gap. *The Journal of Human Resources*, *48*(3), 545–595. doi:10.3368/jhr.48.3.545

Zhang, H., Dai, Y., & Wang, Y. (2020). Motivation and second foreign language proficiency: The mediating role of foreign language enjoyment. *Sustainability (Basel)*, *12*(4), 1302. doi:10.3390/su12041302

Zhang, J. (2021, September). Research on the interdisciplinary competence and its influencing factors of engineering college students under the emerging engineering education. In *Proceedings of the 5th International Conference on Digital Technology in Education* (pp. 163-169). 10.1145/3488466.3488486

Zhang, Z. M., Yu, X., & Liu, X. H. (2022). Do I decide my career? Linking career stress, career exploration, and future work self to career planning or indecision. *Frontiers in Psychology*, *13*, 997984. doi:10.3389/fpsyg.2022.997984 PMID:36081730

Zlate, M. (2000). *Fundamentele psihologiei*. Editura Pro Humanitate.

# About the Contributors

**Cassandra Sligh Conway** (Ph.D., LPC-A, CRC, GCDF, SAS, aPHR) is a Full Tenured Professor at South Carolina State University. Sligh Conway has authored books, book chapters, and refereed articles on many topics in higher education. Her research focus is on persons with disabilties, adult learners, mentoring, higher education and professional development, disaster preparedness and prevention, substance abuse and early recovery services, and pastoral counseling. Sligh Conway grants toal about 2 million over the last 12 years. Grant and projects include areas such as disaster preparedness/prevention, mentoring, rehabilitation counseling, transportation/food and nutrition services throughout the state of South Carolina, student mentoring, women empowerment, Hope 6 grant project, case management services, and foster care and adoption advocacy services.

**Andy Jiahao Liu** is currently a Global Professor of English at University of Arizona, where he delivers international foundations writing courses to multilingual writers. His research interests lie in second language writing, English for research publication purposes, and language testing and assessment. His research has been published in the Journal of Second Language Writing, Innovations in Education and Teaching International, and many others. Besides, Andy is an active and enthusiastic participant in his professional communities. Founding co-chair of the Language Tester Mentoring Program at the International Language Testing Association (ILTA), Andy now serves as the co-chair of the Test-taker Insights in Language Assessment SIG at ILTA. In the TESOL International Association, Andy is the current co-editor of the Applied Linguistics Forum, the newsletter of the Applied Linguistics Interest Section; he was also elected as the incoming Chair of the Second Language Writing Interest section in March 2024.

*\*\*\**

**Catherine Bedwei-Majdoub** is a Senior Lecturer and Course Leader in Business Management at a London University. Catherine has extensive experience within Higher Education, teaching in marketing, business ethics, employability, and philosophy. Dr Bedwei-Majdoub is particularly interested in interdisciplinary studies.

**Elena Cocoradă** Ph.D., is a Professor at Transilvania University of Braşov, Romania, where she teaches Academic Integrity and Ethics within the Doctoral School. She is also the President of the Scientific Research Ethics Committee of the university. She has authored seven books and co-authored 60 chapters in collective volumes, over 80 scientific articles, and coordinated five collective volumes. Her research focuses on the psychology of learning in the case of teenagers and adults, school climate and violence in school, and gender studies. She is a member in the scientific committees of journals in the field and an ad-hoc reviewer. Until the year 2000, she worked in secondary education, and, as of 2001, she has been working in higher education and as a trainer for adults.

**Felicia Constantin**, Ph.D. in Language Sciences from the University of Reims, with master's studies in Literature and Economics, currently teaches business French at the University of Oradea in Romania. Her main research areas include intercomprehension, French for specific purposes, foreign language didactics, and the impact of plurilingualism and multilingualism on the business environment.

**Shivnath Ghosh** is working as a Professor at Computer Science & Engineering Department at Brainware University, India.

**Swati Gupta** is an accomplished academician, mentor for change, and a beacon of inspiration in the world of education. With over a decade of experience, she has made significant contributions to the academic landscape. As an Associate Professor at Universal AI University, her passion for teaching and commitment to academic excellence have been instrumental in shaping the minds of aspiring leaders. She has taught courses in entrepreneurial finance, entrepreneurial leadership, excel, and corporate finance, instilling not only subject knowledge but also ethical values in her students. Beyond the hallowed halls of Universal AI University, Dr. Gupta's influence extends internationally, as she has been associated with prestigious institutions such as Grant Thornton Bharat LLP, where she imparts her expertise in analytics. Additionally, she has organized workshops on entrepreneurship, design thinking, and finance for renowned institutes, including DST, Niti Ayog, YESBUD University, and South Africa. Dr. Gupta's mentoring prowess shines as she nurtures budding entrepreneurs, providing unwavering support to bring their innovative ideas to life. Her dedication to fostering positive change has earned her immense respect among her peers and students alike. In summary, Dr. Swati Gupta's journey in academia and mentorship exemplifies a tireless pursuit of knowledge, an unwavering commitment to education, and a passion for empowering the next generation of leaders. Her impact in both teaching and mentoring is a testament to her valuable contributions to the academic and entrepreneurial ecosystem.

**Elizabeth Jasmine**, Ph.D., is Professor of Psychology at Indian Institute of Psychology and Research (IIPR), Bangalore. Orchid ID: 0009-0006-4084-2773

**Ruby Jindal** has been a part of K.R. Mangalam University, where she presently serves as an Associate Professor in the Physics Department of School of Basic and Applied Sciences. Her academic journey spans over a decade, encompassing both teaching and research across esteemed educational institutions. Her primary focus lies within the realm of crystallography and lattice dynamics. Having obtained her Doctorate from Sant Longowal Institute of Engineering and Technology in 2014, Dr. Jindal's doctoral pursuits delved into the exploration of phonon properties in multiferroic materials. Her research, conducted at IIT Delhi, has been recognized for its significance. Her dedication to the pursuit of knowledge is highlighted by her extensive record of publications, encompassing over 20 research papers featured in reputable journals and conference proceedings indexed in SCI/SCOPUS with good impact factors. Dr. Jindal's scholarly engagement extends beyond her written

**About the Contributors**

contributions. She has been an active participant in over 15 national and international conferences. Furthermore, she plays a vital role in the academic growth of aspiring researchers, currently overseeing the guidance of three Ph.D. scholars. In addition to this, she has lent her expertise to the supervision of numerous graduate and postgraduate students, steering them through their own research undertakings.

**Chi Maher** is an Associate Professor and has developed teaching partnerships and collaborative engagements with several sectors to facilitate greater student exposure to business management skills and career development. Winner of the West focus Enterprising Business Award; an industry award for outstanding enterprise development in industry. Henry Walpole Teaching Award winner for contributions to innovative learning and teaching.

**Maria-Anca Maican**, PH.D., is a Lecturer at the Faculty of Letters, Transilvania University of Brașov, Romania, where she teaches General English and English for Specific Purposes, particularly Business English. Mirroring her teaching activity, her scientific research mainly focuses on the teaching and learning of foreign languages at higher education level and on the cognitive, linguistic and emotional factors that influence this process. She has authored or co-authored 38 articles published in Romanian and international scientific journals.

**Kathryn Medill** (Ph.D.) is an Assistant Professor of Art History in the Liberal Arts Department for Rocky Mountain College of Art and Design (RMCAD). In the past, she has worked for art galleries and museum education departments in Spain, England, and the United States. Her work has been published in museum and interdisciplinary journals and she has presented her research on museums as informal learning spaces for undergraduate students both nationally and internationally. Most recently Kat's work appeared as a chapter in "Engaging Communities Through Civic Engagement in Art Museum Education" (2021) edited by Bryna Bobick and Carissa DiCindio. As well as, a chapter in "Narratives on Becoming: Identity and Lifelong Learning" (2021), edited by Emilie Clucas Leaderman and Jennifer S. Jefferson.

**Subrata Paul** is working as an Assistant Professor at Computer Science & Engineering Department at Brainware University, India.

**Randika Perera** is an academic member of Gampaha Wickramarachchi University of Indigenous Medicine, bringing a unique perspective to career and professional development. With a background in psychology. He specializes in counseling, psychotherapy, career guidance, positive psychology, and personality development. His dedication lies in empowering adolescents and undergraduates to confidently navigate the exciting world of work. Through innovative research, he is developing effective strategies to equip students with the skills and knowledge they need to thrive in their chosen careers in the work world. Future research studies will directed towards introducing an evidence-based approach to career preparation. This approach will not only prepare them for immediate success but also cultivate them into well-rounded professionals across diverse fields. Orchid ID: 0000-0002-4398-624x

**Amitava Podder** is working as an Assistant Professor at Computer Science & Engineering Department at Brainware University, India.

**Elena-Ramona Richiteanu-Nastase** is a university lecturer at the Bucharest University of Economic Studies, Teachers Training Department, has a PhD in Educational Sciences, over 15 years of experience in education / training / research/ counseling: national and international educational projects and programs or collaborations within NGOs (Romanian Center for Economic Education, Education 2000+), individual counseling and group counseling (students and their families, teachers, unemployed), 15 years of teaching experience at the Teachers Training Department (course holder for subjects such as Counseling and Guidance, Curriculum Theory and Methodology, Training Theory and Methodology, Evaluation Theory and Methodology,) and 6 years as a trainer of the National Institute of Magistracy (Personal Development and Communication, head of department). She has a rich publishing activity: book as sole author (Counselling and guidance for career and life Theoretical and methodological foundations) or in collaboration (over 10), articles and studies (over 30). ORCID ID: 0000-0003-0105-1697(. f8b70d1c-a33a-4e30-b82a-6854b5d26c31)

**Piyal Roy** is working as an Assistant Professor at Computer Science & Engineering Department at Brainware University, India.

**Saptarshi Kumar Sarkar** is working as an Assistant Professor at Computer Science & Engineering Department at Brainware University, India.

**Ranjit Singha** is a Doctorate Research Fellow at Christ (Deemed to be University) and a distinguished American Psychological Association (APA) member. His expertise lies in research and development across various domains, including Mindfulness, Addiction Psychology, Women Empowerment, UN Sustainable Development Goals, and Data Science. He has earned certifications from renowned institutions, including IBM and The University of Oxford Mindfulness Centre, UK, in Mindfulness. Additionally, he holds certifications as a Microsoft Innovative Educator, Licensed Yoga Professional, Certified Mindfulness Teacher, and CBCT Teachers Training from Emory University, USA. Mr Ranjit's educational qualifications include PGDBA (GM), MBA (IB), MSc in Counseling Psychology, and completion of a Senior Diploma in Tabla (Musical Instrumentation). His dedication to continuous learning is evident through his involvement in the SEE Learning® (Social, Emotional, and Ethical) Learning program. As a committed researcher and educator, Mr Ranjit focuses on mindfulness and compassion-based interventions. He has an impressive publication record, having authored twenty-three research papers, ten chapters, four books, and five edited books. His research interests encompass various aspects of mindfulness, such as assessment, benefits of mindfulness-based programs, change mechanisms, professional training, mindfulness ethics, cognitive and neuropsychology, and studies related to high-risk behaviours. Apart from his research endeavours, Mr Ranjit has extensive teaching experience, instructing courses in diverse subjects like Forensic Psychology, Positive Psychology, Organizational Planning, Strategic Management, Psycho Metric Tests, Counseling Skills, Disaster Management, Basic Computer Science, Business Planning, Business Law, and Auditing. He has mentored numerous Postgraduate and undergraduate research projects, demonstrating his commitment to nurturing young minds in psychology. Ad Hoc Reviewer at International Journal of Cyber Behavior, Psychology and Learning (IJCBPL), Reviewer and author at IGI Global, and Editor and Reviewer at TNT Publication. Furthermore, Mr Ranjit actively provides personal counselling services, showcasing his genuine concern for his students' well-being and academic success. His unwavering dedication to research and education has solidified his position as a valuable contributor to psychology. ORCID iD: 0000-0002-3541-8752

*About the Contributors*

**Surjit Singha** is an academician with a broad spectrum of interests, including UN Sustainable Development Goals, Organizational Climate, Workforce Diversity, Organizational Culture, HRM, Marketing, Finance, IB, Global Business, Business, AI, K12 & Higher Education, Gender and Cultural Studies. Currently a faculty member at Kristu Jayanti College, Dr. Surjit also serves as an Editor, reviewer, and author for prominent global publications and journals, including being on the Editorial review board of Information Resources Management Journal and contributor to various publications. With over 13 years of experience in Administration, Teaching, and Research, Dr. Surjit is dedicated to imparting knowledge and guiding students in their research pursuits. As a research mentor, Dr. Surjit has nurtured young minds and fostered academic growth. Dr. Surjit has an impressive track record of over 75 publications, including articles, book chapters, and textbooks, holds two US Copyrights, and has successfully completed and published two fully funded minor research projects from Kristu Jayanti College. ORCID ID: 0000-0002-5730-8677

**Patrick L. Stearns** (Ph.D., Bowling Green State University) is an associate professor in the Mass Communications Department, Claflin University. His teaching interests are electronic media announcing and digital audio production. His research interests include ethnic images and audience reception in film, and audio and visual media's portrayal of people of color, and educational challenges and solutions affecting the Black Diaspora.

# Index

## A

Academic Adjustment 186-189, 194, 197, 199-200
Academic and Career Integration 246, 265
Academic Success 4, 6, 11, 142, 199-200, 233, 258
Academic-Student Co-Creation 29, 31
Adaptability 47, 54-57, 59, 86-89, 92-95, 97-99, 102-113, 115-116, 118, 121-122, 132, 137, 165, 178, 197, 199, 227, 232-236, 239, 243, 246-252, 258, 262-263, 265, 267, 273-274, 277, 280, 283, 286, 291
African American Males 1-2, 5, 7-8
Assessment 10, 33, 38, 43, 46, 57-59, 61-65, 68-71, 73, 75-78, 82, 105, 107, 111-112, 119, 136, 139, 141-142, 165-166, 171-172, 177, 197-198, 211, 219, 226, 244, 257, 266, 288, 290-291
Autoethnography 14-15, 25-26, 119

## B

Behaviors in Foreign Language Learning 116
Bloom Taxonomy 53, 74

## C

Career 1-2, 5-9, 11-14, 16, 24-25, 29-38, 40-49, 51-55, 59-60, 63, 67-68, 78, 86-90, 92-95, 97-99, 102-105, 107-113, 115-121, 123, 126-127, 131-135, 139-148, 161, 163-165, 170-171, 176-179, 181-182, 186-211, 213-233, 235-243, 245-251, 254-263, 265-273, 275-288, 290-292
Career Adaptability 47, 86-89, 92-94, 97-99, 102-105, 107-113, 115-116, 178, 197, 199, 227, 263, 291
Career Counselling Strategy 186
Career Counselling Theories 186, 200
Career Counsellors 267-268, 286-287
Career Development 9, 11, 45, 47, 63, 86, 88, 110, 113, 119-120, 126-127, 132, 134-135, 140-142, 144-146, 170-171, 177, 181-182, 189, 192-193, 198-200, 204, 206-210, 212-213, 215, 217, 220, 222-231, 238, 242, 245, 248-249, 254, 257-259, 261, 275, 278, 280, 286, 291
Career Exploration 110, 140, 192, 199, 230, 256, 261-262, 266
Career Factors 144, 186-190, 194, 198, 200
Career Maturity 223, 231
Career Planning 171, 199, 206, 219, 225, 227, 230-231, 243, 282, 291
Career Preparation 1, 7, 9, 31, 120, 123, 140, 194, 217, 259, 261-262, 265, 267-269, 272-273, 276, 279-280, 283, 286, 292
Career Readiness 29, 53, 118, 142-143, 206, 209, 217-218, 226, 228, 230-231, 238-240, 246, 248-251, 256, 259-263, 265, 290-291
Collaborative Learning 76, 266
Community of Practice 12, 14, 18, 21-22, 24
Competences 88, 93-94, 97-98, 103, 105, 111, 116, 171, 176, 182
Conference Presentation 12-14, 19, 25-27
Consistent Behaviors 267
Constructive Alignment 53, 57-58, 61
Counseling strategy 187, 189, 194, 196, 200
COVID-19 10, 30, 42, 74, 87-88, 106, 111, 163-166, 169-170, 172, 174, 180-183, 214, 243
Critical Thinking 30, 32, 44, 53-57, 59, 66-67, 69, 71, 89, 116, 146, 165, 215, 233-235, 242, 245-247, 250-254, 256-257, 262-263, 266, 285-286
Curriculum Design 29, 37-38, 42-43, 46, 49, 60-61, 64, 72, 74, 260
Curriculum Development 29, 43, 45, 61-62, 215

## E

Emerging Market 163, 165, 172
Employability 30, 36, 41-42, 48-49, 54-55, 60, 66, 69, 71, 75-77, 86-88, 93-94, 96, 99, 102, 104, 115-116, 121, 141, 170-171, 178-180, 182, 195, 227-228, 236, 244, 248-249, 256, 263, 265

*Index*

Employment 35-36, 40, 45, 47, 70, 72, 87-88, 93-94, 96-98, 104-105, 108, 111, 114, 116, 118, 140, 142-145, 147, 171, 179, 181, 193, 195, 200, 218, 227, 229-230, 237, 249, 260, 262, 268, 273, 280-281, 285-287

Engagement 14, 23-24, 29-30, 33, 47, 49, 52, 63, 75, 89-90, 92, 96, 110-111, 116-117, 120-121, 123-124, 130, 137-138, 145, 148, 161, 191, 212, 217, 236, 244, 252, 259, 262-263, 282

Experiential Education 169

Experiential Learning 49, 54, 63, 73-74, 117-122, 124, 142, 145, 163, 165, 168-170, 172, 174-175, 177-182, 257-258, 261

## F

Federal Work Study (FWS) 117, 122, 145
First-Year Students 1, 3, 7, 188, 194, 196
FL Anxiety 90-92, 94, 97-98, 102-103, 105, 116
FL Language Proficiency 89, 116
Foreign Language Achievement 86, 110, 115
Foreign Language Learning 86, 96, 106, 109, 111, 114-116
Foreign Language Outcomes 116

## G

Graduate Students 12-14, 16-24, 27, 49, 122, 145, 198
Guidance and Mentoring 283, 291

## H

HBCUs 1-3, 6, 8, 10-11
Higher Education 2, 9, 29-37, 39, 41-43, 45-49, 52-53, 57, 74-77, 87, 103, 105-106, 108, 110-111, 114-115, 118-119, 121, 123, 132, 140-141, 143-145, 163, 178-182, 198-199, 206-208, 212, 214-218, 222, 225-228, 230, 257, 263-265
Holistic Approach 72, 232-233, 243, 245, 250
Home Office 163, 168, 174, 176, 178, 182

## I

Importance of FL Skills for Employability 116
Importance of FL Skills for Professional Tasks 116
Inclusive Learning 29, 52
Information Exchange 282, 291
Intended Learning Outcome 53, 61, 72
Interdisciplinary Curriculum 53-57, 59-60
Internship 8, 121-123, 141-142, 145, 163-168, 170-177, 182-183, 196, 206-207, 217, 222, 237, 244, 259-260, 284-285, 287-288

Internship Program 166-167, 170, 182

## K

Keynote 15, 18, 27
Kolb´s Model 163, 170

## L

Labor Market 35-36, 86-88, 92, 97, 99, 102, 104-105, 115-116, 144, 163-165, 167, 169, 171-172, 176-178, 187, 189-190, 193-196, 203, 267
Learning Behaviors 90, 92
Legitimate Peripheral Participation 14, 26
Long-Term Success 188, 254, 262, 281, 291

## M

Mentorship 2-4, 7, 9, 118, 120-123, 125-126, 144-145, 150-151, 161, 196, 232-233, 237-238, 240, 243-244, 253, 255, 257-258, 260, 283-284, 287
Motivation 30-31, 36, 52, 61, 77, 89-92, 94, 96-98, 102-105, 108-110, 112-115, 179, 188, 190-191, 195, 197, 208-209, 221, 240, 254, 276-278, 283, 288, 292

## N

Narrative Inquiry 119, 125, 145
Networking 18-19, 24, 27, 31, 52, 118, 123, 165, 177, 208, 221-222, 226-227, 231, 233, 237-238, 240-241, 249, 251, 255-257, 259, 268, 276, 282-290, 292
Networking Event 27
New Normal 14, 168, 176-177, 182

## O

Objective-Oriented Focus 280, 292
Online Learning 81, 163, 169, 178, 182, 245, 289

## P

Pandemic COVID-19 164-166, 169-170, 172, 182-183
Paper Presentation 27, 45
Parallel 15, 27
Personal Career Map 186-187, 189-195, 200-201, 204
Personal Development 41, 188, 224, 231, 241, 244, 279, 287
Personality Traits 91-92, 94, 97, 99, 102-103, 107,

109-110, 112, 115, 209-210, 221
Poster Presentation 27
Pre-Conference Workshop 27
Predatory Conference 18, 28
Prioritization 280, 292
Problem-Solving 53-54, 63, 66-67, 71, 73, 118, 121-122, 133, 146, 165-166, 191, 215, 232-236, 242, 244-247, 249-250, 252-254, 256, 262, 266, 270, 272-273
Procrastination 279-282, 284, 292
Productivity and Efficiency 281, 292
Professional Development 8, 25, 27, 120-121, 133, 135, 138, 195, 206, 211, 213, 215, 218, 223-225, 229, 231, 236-237, 239-240, 242, 250, 253, 255, 258-259, 272, 288, 291
Professional Insertion 186-187, 189-190, 193-198, 200
Professional Tasks 86-88, 94, 96, 104, 116, 281
Professionalism 8, 132-134, 138-139, 191, 206-209, 212, 215, 217-218, 220, 222, 224-226, 231, 238, 252-253

# R

Real-World Professional Settings 267
Research Productivity 12

# S

Self-Efficacy 46-48, 61, 88, 115, 119-121, 125-128, 131-133, 135-136, 140, 145-146, 150-151, 181, 192-193, 215, 218, 221, 227-228, 240-241, 243, 245, 248, 263, 275-278, 291
Self-Perceived FL Proficiency 86, 89, 91-92, 94, 96, 102-104, 116
Skill Development 65-67, 133, 142, 171, 215, 227, 232-235, 238, 245, 257, 267, 269-271, 279, 285-286

Skill Improvement 267, 270
Social Cognitive Career Theory (SCCT) 117, 119, 135, 145
Socialization and Development 12
Soloist Imposter Syndrome 1-3
Stress Reduction 276, 281, 292
Student Preparedness 232-233, 235, 238-239, 242-243, 245
Student Success 2, 4, 7, 46, 246, 266
Student Voice 29, 46, 52
Symposium 28, 259

# T

Task Completion 281, 292
Technology and Tools 288, 292
Time Management 4, 71, 87, 122, 131-132, 164, 169, 198, 224, 252-253, 267-268, 276, 279-282, 288, 290, 292
Transferable Skill 132, 146-147
Transition to Career 232, 245

# U

Undergraduate 2, 5, 11, 77-78, 95, 104, 119, 122, 142, 145, 166, 171, 179, 181, 206-209, 215-218, 221-222, 224-226, 228-230, 244, 264
University Students 31, 109-111, 113, 115, 143, 199-200, 229, 264

# W

Work-Life Balance 7, 169, 224, 231, 281, 288, 292
World of Work 29-32, 36-37, 40-42, 44, 92-93, 110, 164, 170-171, 206-210, 213-218, 220-222, 225, 228-231, 267, 285

## Publishing Tomorrow's Research Today

### Uncover Current Insights and Future Trends in Education
with IGI Global's Cutting-Edge Recommended Books

Print Only, E-Book Only, or Print + E-Book.
Order direct through IGI Global's Online Bookstore at **www.igi-global.com** or through your preferred provider.

ISBN: 9781668493007
© 2023; 234 pp.
List Price: US$ **215**

ISBN: 9798369300749
© 2024; 383 pp.
List Price: US$ **230**

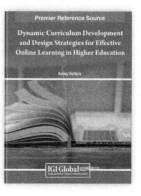

ISBN: 9781668486467
© 2023; 471 pp.
List Price: US$ **215**

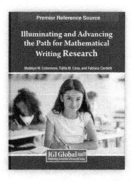

ISBN: 9781668465387
© 2024; 389 pp.
List Price: US$ **215**

ISBN: 9781668475836
© 2024; 359 pp.
List Price: US$ **215**

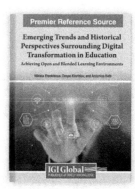

ISBN: 9781668444238
© 2023; 334 pp.
List Price: US$ **240**

**Do you want to stay current on the latest research trends, product announcements, news, and special offers?**
Join IGI Global's mailing list to receive customized recommendations, exclusive discounts, and more.
Sign up at: **www.igi-global.com/newsletters**.

Scan the QR Code here to view more related titles in Education.

www.igi-global.com   Sign up at www.igi-global.com/newsletters   facebook.com/igiglobal   twitter.com/igiglobal   linkedin.com/igiglobal

# Ensure Quality Research is Introduced to the Academic Community

## Become a Reviewer for IGI Global Authored Book Projects

 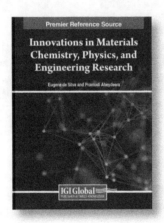 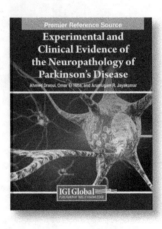 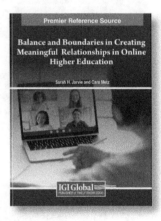

The overall success of an authored book project is dependent on quality and timely manuscript evaluations.

### Applications and Inquiries may be sent to:
development@igi-global.com

Applicants must have a doctorate (or equivalent degree) as well as publishing, research, and reviewing experience. Authored Book Evaluators are appointed for one-year terms and are expected to complete at least three evaluations per term. Upon successful completion of this term, evaluators can be considered for an additional term.

If you have a colleague that may be interested in this opportunity, we encourage you to share this information with them.

www.igi-global.com

## Publishing Tomorrow's Research Today
# IGI Global's Open Access Journal Program

Including Nearly 200 Peer-Reviewed, Gold (Full) Open Access Journals across IGI Global's Three Academic Subject Areas: Business & Management; Scientific, Technical, and Medical (STM); and Education

**Consider Submitting Your Manuscript to One of These Nearly 200 Open Access Journals for to Increase Their Discoverability & Citation Impact**

Web of Science Impact Factor **6.5**

Web of Science Impact Factor **4.7**

Web of Science Impact Factor **3.2**

Web of Science Impact Factor **2.6**

Journal of Organizational and End User Computing

Journal of Global Information Management

International Journal on Semantic Web and Information Systems

Journal of Database Management

## Choosing IGI Global's Open Access Journal Program Can Greatly Increase the Reach of Your Research

**Higher Usage**
Open access papers are 2-3 times more likely to be read than non-open access papers.

**Higher Download Rates**
Open access papers benefit from 89% higher download rates than non-open access papers.

**Higher Citation Rates**
Open access papers are 47% more likely to be cited than non-open access papers.

Submitting an article to a journal offers an invaluable opportunity for you to share your work with the broader academic community, fostering knowledge dissemination and constructive feedback.

## Submit an Article and Browse the IGI Global Call for Papers Pages

We can work with you to find the journal most well-suited for your next research manuscript. For open access publishing support, contact: journaleditor@igi-global.com

# Are You Ready to Publish Your Research?

IGI Global offers book authorship and editorship opportunities across three major subject areas, including Business, STM, and Education.

## Benefits of Publishing with IGI Global:

- Free one-on-one editorial and promotional support.
- Expedited publishing timelines that can take your book from start to finish in less than one (1) year.
- Choose from a variety of formats, including Edited and Authored References, Handbooks of Research, Encyclopedias, and Research Insights.
- Utilize IGI Global's eEditorial Discovery® submission system in support of conducting the submission and double-blind peer review process.
- IGI Global maintains a strict adherence to ethical practices due in part to our full membership with the Committee on Publication Ethics (COPE).
- Indexing potential in prestigious indices such as Scopus®, Web of Science™, PsycINFO®, and ERIC – Education Resources Information Center.
- Ability to connect your ORCID iD to your IGI Global publications.
- Earn honorariums and royalties on your full book publications as well as complimentary content and exclusive discounts.

**Join Your Colleagues from Prestigious Institutions, Including:**

- Australian National University
- Massachusetts Institute of Technology
- Johns Hopkins University
- Tsinghua University
- Harvard University
- Columbia University in the City of New York

**Learn More at:** www.igi-global.com/publish
or Contact IGI Global's Aquisitions Team at: acquisition@igi-global.com

www.ingramcontent.com/pod-product-compliance
Lightning Source LLC
LaVergne TN
LVHW081907200925

821343LV00066BB/594